MOON HA S®

GEORGIA

FIFTH EDITION

KAP STANN

AVALON TRAVEL

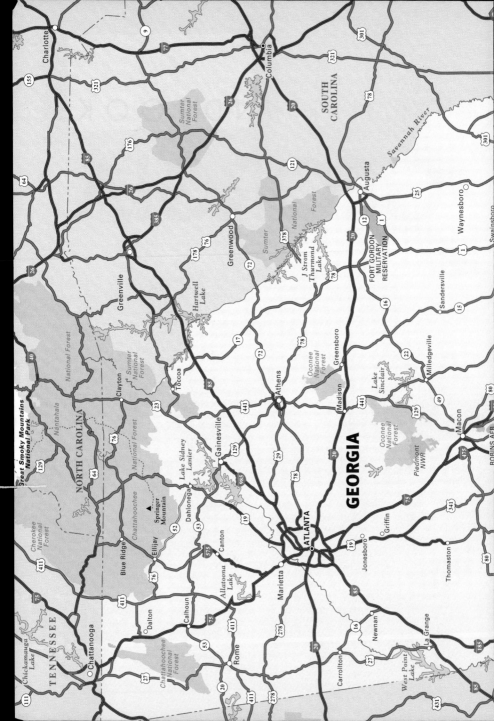

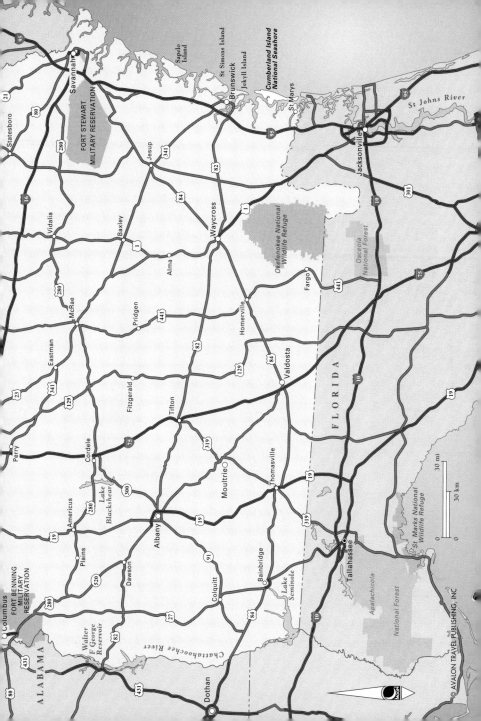

CONTENTS

Discover Georgia

Explore Georgia

MAPS

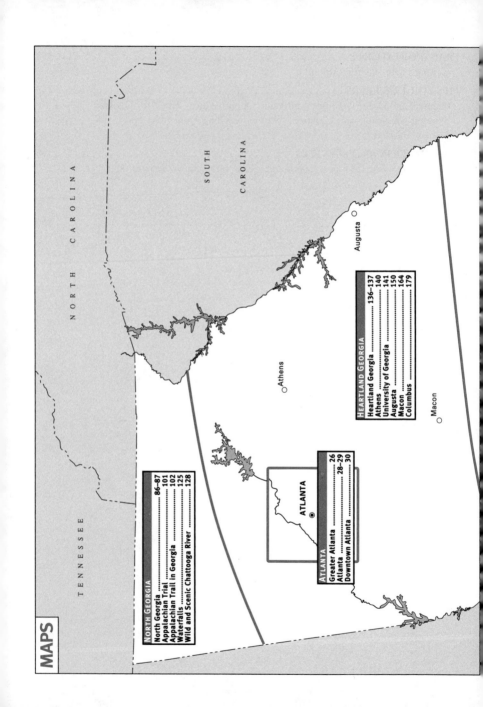

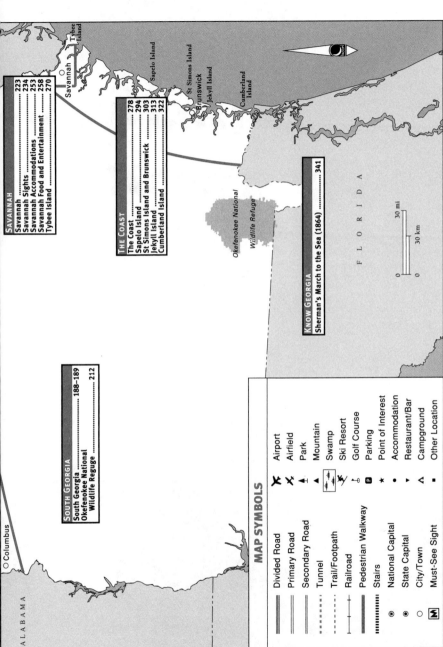

ALABAMA

○ Columbus

Tybee
Island

○ Savannah

Sapelo Island

St Simons Island

Brunswick

Jekyll Island

Cumberland
Island

Okefenokee National
Wildlife Refuge

F L O R I D A

0   30 mi
0   30 km

MAP SYMBOLS

▬▬	Divided Road	✈	Airport
▬▬	Primary Road	✈	Airfield
▬▬	Secondary Road	⚐	Park
-----	Tunnel	▲	Mountain
---	Trail/Footpath	🌲	Swamp
┼┼┼	Railroad	⛷	Ski Resort
▬▬	Pedestrian Walkway	⛳	Golf Course
▪▪▪▪	Stairs	P	Parking
⊛	National Capital	★	Point of Interest
◉	State Capital	•	Accommodation
○	City/Town	▶	Restaurant/Bar
⬛	Must-See Sight	▲	Campground
		▪	Other Location

© AVALON TRAVEL PUBLISHING, INC.

Discover
Georgia

I grew up in New York and had family in California, and I've driven cross-country more times than I can remember. I came to think I knew the U.S. pretty well. It wasn't until I was in my twenties that I first visited the South, and what struck me was how different it was. People talk about how, with fast food and television and chain stores, things are the same all over, but that's not what I think.

What I discovered was a region with an astonishing history, with its own culture, language, cuisine, religion, and collective memory. Traveling end to end, from the barrier islands to the Blue Ridge Mountains, I could also see how much of that history is shaped by the land. I was fascinated, and I ended up researching and writing about it for the next 10 years, eventually covering every state south of the Mason–Dixon line from Maryland to Louisiana. I saw Georgia first, and I know Georgia best.

What I like best about Georgia—well okay, barbecue and blues; I might as well get that on out there. But in between the rib shacks and roadhouses, I like the exotic landscapes and wildlife, and the fact that everywhere you go, you stumble across the footprints of a complex human history.

On a blue-blazed detour off the Appalachian Trail, a half-day out from North Georgia's Springer Mountain, through thickets of rhododendron and mountain laurel, across streams, and through towering stands of oak and hickory, you come upon a cemetery. Not so remarkable; such coves were sprinkled with small farming communities throughout the Highlands, but what was remarkable was meeting their descendants. It was the weekend of the annual homecoming, as it turned out, and through the dust on the license plates, you could see they'd come from Texas and Oklahoma and the Carolinas, carrying covered dishes and gardening tools, and making their way in pickups and LeSabres up double-rutted Forest Service roads to come back here, reunite, tend to the graves, and honor their ancestors before making their way back home.

On the coast, the barrier islands are lined with wide beaches, high dunes, and a thick forest canopy of oaks to protect the palmetto and wild horses, boars, and bobcats within. Cedar stands point the way to shell middens, and back rivers lead to the tabby ruins of French, Spanish, and English islanders (they say the islands have fewer residents now than at any time of their human history). Birds head to the wild rice now filling the square ponds of the abandoned industry that shaped the distinctive Gullah heritage. Descendants of the people who worked the fields sing songs in West African dialect and continue to protest for the return of land deeded to their enslaved ancestors.

In the South Georgia interior of piney woods, red dirt, and flowering vines, geometrical mounds with hundreds of lifetimes stacked in basketfuls of earth rise up stories high where temples once stood. Jimmy Carter writes about growing up not far away, in Plains, and remarks how the farming methods they used when he was a boy hadn't changed much over the past thousand years. The deep swamp of the Okefenokee—which is plenty wild, with its hammocks, black bears, and alligators—marked the base of operations for Seminole resistance to U.S. expansionism. It gets to where the courthouse squares, boxwood borders, and Confederate monuments appear as much as relics of an ancient civilization as mounds and middens.

I suppose this is what they mean when they talk about "a sense of place." It's the same thing that has had such a distinguishing influence on the work of Southern writers such as Flannery O'Connor, whose Middle Georgia farm of magnolia and dogwood is down the street from where Sherman's troops staged a mock session of the legislature...and also near a military academy and mental institution... and also about 30 miles north of the capital of the Creek Confederacy. (And you wonder where she got her raw material.)

Anyway, it gives you a lot to think about while you're waiting for your order of short tips, or floating down a stream, or cycling down a mountain, or watching dolphins chasing the ferryboat. I hope this book will point you in the direction of great adventures, wild places, and memorable stories.

It's easy to visit Georgia. As the joke goes, even going to heaven requires changing planes in Atlanta. Hartsfield International is an airline hub for Delta and Song, and a light-rail train runs from the airport terminal right downtown. For short trips to downtown Atlanta destinations, you could get by without renting a car, but for extended stays or statewide travel, a car is most practical. Beyond the congested metro region, it's a pretty smooth-sailing road trip. Back roads get you closer to the ground and out to exotic natural adventures; to get you started, see the itineraries that follow.

One of the most common rail trips from the capital is the short jaunt to Gainesville, where hikers shuttle up to the southern terminus of the Appalachian Trail, otherwise, traveling from Atlanta by rail isn't particularly practical, though not impossible. Savannah is much better connected by rail, with easy access to the entire Eastern Seaboard—it's one of Amtrak's package destinations.

Savannah's modern airport is ideally convenient for city visitors, but if your trip also includes the Georgia coast (which is highly recommended), you'll find cheaper and more frequent flights out of Jacksonville, Florida—a little more than an hour's drive south. The car trip from Atlanta to Savannah is a monotonous six-hour drive; taking a flight or even a bus trip (premium service is available) are good options to consider (you can easily do without a car in downtown Savannah), and the bus goes directly to the historic district downtown.

WHEN TO GO

Georgia experiences the full four travel seasons. Spring and fall are the most temperate and lovely throughout the state, and many festivals, house-and-garden tours, and other special events are scheduled during this time to take best advantage of the weather and foliage. Summers can be insufferably hot and humid during the day but appealingly balmy at night, when the residents come out to play. You can find hotel discounts for most areas of the state in summer, except for at the beaches and in the mountains, where summer is high season. Winters are relatively mild—snow is a rare occurrence in Atlanta or further south—but you can count on snow in the North Georgia mountains each winter (the furthest-south ski jump in North America is in the northeastern corner of the state).

WHAT TO TAKE

Outdoor recreation is very popular in Georgia, so pack for the sport; cycling, tennis, golf, and swimming gear; an old pair of sneakers for paddling trips; clothes that cover limbs for hiking (also pack insect repellant—locals swear by Avon's Skin So Soft and Deep Woods Off with deet—and bite cream.)

Dress tends to be more modest and formal in the South than in other parts of the country, and even in the dog days of summer, men wear sport coats to dinner. A conservative dressy outfit will also come in handy if you're invited to attend church services (when in Rome...). Of course in Atlanta's bohemian neighborhoods, almost anything goes. Dressing in layers is always practical, and even in summer you should carry a cover-up; interiors are air-conditioned to an overcompensating degree. Denim is way too thick for summer. For spring or fall, a light jacket is all you need; a slightly heavier one works for winter (not too heavy—this isn't Chicago).

ATLANTA

Sitting up on the Piedmont region, bordered to the northeast by the Chattahoochee River, the metro region sprawls across two counties surrounding downtown Atlanta. As recently as 10 years ago, downtown was a forlorn district largely abandoned after dark, but today, "intown" is one of the city's most interesting areas, along with robust Midtown, Buckhead, and Atlanta's homier outlying neighborhoods.

The capital boasts the most sophisticated cultural arts scene and entertaining nightlife in the state, if not in the entire South. You could easily spend a fun urban weekend in town (or find diversions from a weeklong business conference) and use the city as a jumping-off point to small towns and surprisingly rural places nearby (some folks drive the hour to Athens for an evening's entertainment).

NORTH GEORGIA

The southernmost stretch of the fabled Blue Ridge Mountains occupies northeast Georgia, where the Wild and Scenic Chattooga River attracts white-water rafters, and hikes lead to waterfalls, mountaintop balds, and panoramic views of three states. The Appalachian Trail starts on North Georgia's Springer Mountain, outside the charming gold-rush town of Dahlonega. Cabins and campsites typically rent by the week for families to settle in for a summer vacation of hiking, paddling, and fishing in and around the region's wonderful state parks, including Amicalola, Unicoi, Vogel, Black Rock, and Tallulah Gorge.

Northwest Georgia is marked by the long ridges and sheer bluffs of the Cumberland Plateau, with Civil War battlefields, old-timey Rock City, and Howard Finster's folk art environment, Paradise Gardens, among the attractions. TAG corner (named for the initials of the three states that meet here) was so remote that until the early 20th century, the northwest corner of the state was more readily accessible from Tennessee or Alabama than from Georgia. Though I-75 provides easy access today, the region remains a quiet refuge, particularly at Cloudland Canyon State Park.

THE HEARTLAND

Central Georgia stretches across the wide middle of the state from the Chattahoochee River, at the state's western boundary with Alabama, to the Savannah River, at the northwestern border with South Carolina. The cities of Columbus, Macon, and Augusta were founded at the "fall line" along this belt, where mountain rivers drop into the southern plain, the furthest navigable point inland. While the cities are nice enough (centrally located Macon offers the most of the three), rural areas near each of these major cities are truly unique: FDR's Warm Springs retreat outside Columbus, the fox-hunting region around Augusta, and the backwoods route to Macon tracing the footsteps of Flannery O'Connor, Alice Walker, and Br'er Rabbit.

SOUTH GEORGIA

The vast piney woods of South Georgia reward trekkers willing to cover long distances with such disparate charms as the Little Grand Canyon, Paw Paw Capital of the World, ancient burial mounds, catfish shacks, and living-history pioneer homesteads. Among the most appealing and accessible portions of this region is Jimmy Carter Country (southeast of Columbus, southwest of Macon). The most appealing and remote portion is the Okefenokee Swamp, a place of haunting and primordial beauty and stillness, with three different "entrances" offering three different experiences. This is raw road-trip material, and as is true throughout Georgia, the state parks make a great base of operations, offering historic interest and the best of the local environment (often with lodging, dining, and recreation as well)—Stephen C. Foster, Kolomoki Mounds, and Providence Canyon are among South Georgia's highlights.

SAVANNAH

Sitting on a high bluff of the Savannah River, the uncommonly beautiful city of Savannah was founded in 1733. It was Georgia's first city as well as the southernmost British outpost in the American colonies. Today Savannah is a wonderful place to visit and wander around, with its landscaped squares surrounded by architecturally rich historic houses, many now reborn as luxurious inns or fine restaurants serving delicious low country cuisine. Nearby marshland wilderness and beach resorts offer plenty of recreation. It's a wonderful destination for a long weekend of indulgence (or more time, as your budget allows). It's also a great place to kick off a week of more remote coastal adventures.

THE COAST

Vast tidal marshlands, live oak draped with Spanish moss, canopies gnarled by salt spray, and long wide beaches are the treasures found along Georgia's Atlantic coast, which is wilder and less developed than neighbors to the north or south. Of 13 major barrier islands, only three are bridged to the mainland—the resort islands of Tybee, St. Simons, and Jekyll. The rest of the islands offer remote adventures, deserted beaches, exotic wildlife, and a fascinating history, from middens and presidios to plantations and the promised land of "40 acres and a mule."

The mainland offers colonial outposts, small fish camps, rice fields overtaken by wildlife, and the midcentury ruins of the old Atlantic Coast Highway. You could easily spend a week here if you were on the go; longer if you tune into "Island Time," slowing your pace down and bobbing with the tide.

In 1863, Union General William T. Sherman rightly theorized that a crushing blow to Atlanta's railroad hub would cripple the Confederacy. From here, his campaign "to make Georgia howl" torched plantations and sacked towns in a 60-mile-wide swath across the state—an unprecedented assault on non-military targets. Sherman's March remains seared in the collective memory of generations of Georgians. Tens of thousands of African Americans followed the wake of Sherman's troops toward the promised land of "Sherman's Reservation."

The path of war through Georgia is a clear sweep south from Chattanooga to Atlanta and east to Savannah; it's easily accessed via I-75 and I-16. Many of the sights and towns along the way stage reenactments and other special events commemorating Civil War history.

General William Tecumseh Sherman

COURTESY NATIONAL ARCHIVES

DAY 1

Start in northwest Georgia near Fort Oglethorpe, where the Chickamauga and Chattanooga National Military Park provides an overview of the campaign at the scene of the battle that took 4,000 lives. Detour to Point Park, atop Lookout Mountain, where an outpost of the military park opens Confederate headquarters at Craven House and offers a stark view of waging war "above the clouds," 1,716 feet straight up from the narrow river canyon encircling Chattanooga.

Stay in Chickamauga's Gordon Lee Mansion, which served as Union headquarters and as a troop hospital in 1863; it now operates as a historic inn (but is also open to group tours).

DAY 2

With 100,000 troops, Sherman chewed up the path of the railroad to Atlanta, leaving a path still

© KAP STANN

Margaret Mitchell House

strewn today with old breastworks, depots, cemeteries, and other landmarks cataloged in a driving-tour map available at military parks and visitor centers.

Outside Marietta, at Kennesaw Mountain National Military Park, a mountaintop trail provides a panoramic overlook of the battle scene. The Southern Museum of Civil War and Locomotive History relates how Union raiders hijacked a local train—an event memorialized as *The Great Locomotive Chase* in Disney's film version.

In Marietta's 19th-century downtown square, Sherman alighted in Kennesaw House, which is now a museum. The welcome center in the 1898 railroad depot directs visitors to Civil War cemeteries nearby. Eat around the square and stay at the historic inn, Sixty Polk Street, a block away.

DAYS 3–4

After four more battles, Atlanta surrendered on September 2, 1864, and the "Great Lamplighter" set fire to the city, leaving only the smoldering chimneys, nicknamed "Sherman's sentinels." The Battle for Atlanta is related at the modern Atlanta History Center and also at the old-time Cyclorama, where the audience revolves around a story-high mural created in 1884.

A more popular history is told at the Margaret Mitchell House, home to the Pulitzer prize–winning *Gone With the Wind* author. Movie fans might stay at the Georgian Terrace, where the premiere reception was held in 1939. The historic Fox Theatre is across Peachtree Street. Down the block, Mary Mac's will acquaint you with Southern cuisine.

DAY 5

People seeking GWTW Atlanta are often directed to historic-house tours south in Jonesboro or east to Madison, conveniently off I-20. Madison, which was spared Sherman's torch, has an attractive town square with several restaurants. A drive south from Madison on Highway 441 leads to Milledgeville, Georgia's Civil War capital.

At the imposing Confederate state capitol now on the Georgia Military College campus, Sherman's officers paused to stage a mock session of the legislature and set boxes of Confederate currency aflame. Further south, in Macon, the 1853 Cannonball House displays the mark of Union artillery, and nearby Rosehill Cemetery holds Confederate graves. Stay in the historic 1842 House down the block.

Detour 60 miles southwest of Macon to the haunting National Prisoner of War Museum, in Andersonville, or follow Sherman's route by taking I-16 east to Savannah.

DAYS 6–7

Reaching Savannah on December 22, 1864, Sherman commandeered the Green-Meldrim House and sent a telegram to Abraham Lincoln, offering the city as a Christmas gift. Union troops bivouacked in Colonial Cemetery, and their vandalism remains evident on headstones today. At the Second African Baptist Church, Field Order No. 15, allotting the Sea Islands for freed slaves, was issued. The historic district is full of inns, restaurants, and more sights.

East of Savannah, Fort Pulaski National Monument preserves the brick fortress that succumbed to experimental rifled cannons. In Richmond Hill, Fort McAllister State Historic Park maintains the best-preserved earthwork fortifications of the Confederacy and tells the story of the fort's 1864 capture.

© KAP STANN

National Prisoner of War Museum

From Savannah, you can hop on I-95 south and blast clear over the Florida border in little more than an hour. Venturing off on the old Atlantic Coast Highway (Highway 17), you're drawn into the storied, wild Georgia coast—a Southern landscape of strangely silent marshlands, remote islands, distinctive language, low country cuisine, and midcentury ruins from the days of the first transcontinental highways.

in America; left turns lead to tidal marshlands and fish camps. Detour around **Eulonia** onto Route 99 for a deeper backwoods route, also the jumping-off point for overnight trips to remote **Sapelo Island** (by advance reservation only).

DAY 4

By bike or guided tour, explore Sapelo's offbeat mix of attractions—the marine institute, Big House, tabby ruins, **Hog Hammock**, and shell-strewn beaches—before the return ferry departs. Back on the mainland, discover a colonial fort, the Altamaha River canoe trail, the Howfyl-Boardfield rice plantation, and a compelling literary history in the town of **Darien**. Stay in town or continue south to find many more lodging choices in the Golden Isles if you're restless for civilization.

DAYS 1–2

Begin your trip in **Savannah**, Georgia's first city, founded in 1733. Spend two days exploring the museums, cuisine, inns, and nightlife of the historic district, with a side trip east to the beach at **Tybee Island**. Campers, paddlers, and families might choose to flip this, instead staying on Tybee, with a side trip to town.

DAY 3

Catch up with Highway 17 about 10 miles southwest of Savannah's historic district. Landmarks include a bamboo farm, a giant weekend flea market, and all-you-can-eat catfish before the traffic thins out on the far side of **Richmond Hill**. The highway drops to two lanes and passes Ida Mae and Joe's truck stop, colonial cemeteries, and the Smallest Church

DAY 5

At **St. Simons,** find the haunting ruins of a colonial outpost, or opt for sporting fun at beaches, golf courses, and action-packed marinas, as well as at crab shacks and margaritaville saloons. It's a favorite stop of Intracoastal Waterway yachters. Stay in the village or at the beachfront King and Prince Resort for the whole golf/tennis/five-swimming-pools package.

DAY 6

Once the exclusive preserve of America's early industrialists, **Jekyll Island** is now open to anyone who wants to visit the elegant old clubhouse—which is now the island's premier hotel—and tour the "cottages"(huge villas) built by the likes of

Georgia's tidal marshlands are the most extensive on the East Coast.

the Rockefellers, Duponts, and Pulitzers. The rest of the island is a giant playground of beaches, golf courses, tennis courts, bike paths, fishing piers, a water park, many affordable motels, and a great campground.

DAY 7

Take a day trip out to **Cumberland Island** to get a glimpse of wild horses running along the wide beach and to see the ruins of the homes of Nathanael Greene and the Carnegies, and take a walk along the trails of the lush, wild, subtropical island. Backpackers could venture farther into the wild northern end. If cost is no object, a stay at Greyfield Inn is one of the most aristocratic adventures on the East Coast.

Classic Savannah Weekend

Savannah's beautiful historic district (the largest in the country) offers a compact set of attractions, and strolling from one to the other—pausing to eat, drink, and shop along the way—is a great way to spend a relaxing weekend while covering a lot of ground. The surrounding natural environment provides a wonderful contrast to the city's urbane pleasures, best seen on the water or at the beach. It's a popular weekend destination, so make hotel reservations early.

FRIDAY NIGHT

Arriving at the riverfront in the early evening, you'll find plenty of underground lairs to choose from along the cobblestone lane of River Street, but in decent weather, Huey's offers an unbeatable second-story patio overlooking the busy channel. (Tondee's Tavern, in the River Street Inn, is an air-conditioned or rainy-day alternative.)

For a cheap thrill, take a two-minute water-taxi ride across the river and back for a beautiful view of the waterfront, particularly around sunset. A 50-minute carriage ride orients newcomers to the city.

Make reservations at Elizabeth on 37th, in the Victorian district, a five-minute cab ride from downtown, to feast on nouveau Southern cuisine in a turn-of-the-century mansion. Wrap up there with a glass of port, or choose a nightcap from among complimentary carafes at your inn.

SATURDAY MORNING

Enjoy breakfast in bed or on the veranda at your hotel, and get out for a walk along Factor's Row before the Bay Street traffic or heat builds up. Among the magnolias, statuary, and monuments, see the Cotton Exchange that dictated cotton prices for more than a century and was responsible for the wealth behind the city's architectural distinction.

At City Hall, head down Bull Street with map in hand to begin exploring the city's historic squares in whatever direction your whim takes you, taking in one of the city's acclaimed historic house tours—say, either the Owens-Thomas House, Davenport House, or Mercer House of *Midnight in the Garden of Good and Evil* fame.

Aim for City Market at lunchtime, where you'll find more than a dozen choices of eateries, from the inexpensive Express Bakery, on Barnard Street, to the more upscale Belford's, at Franklin Square. If you've wandered in the opposite direction, find Wall's Bar-B-Que in an alley south of York Street at Price.

SATURDAY AFTERNOON

The stunningly modern expansion of the Telfair Academy of Art, designed by Moshe Safdie, represents a bold new look for the museum, which is actually the oldest in the South and is renowned for its collection of Impressionist paintings. Across Telfair Square, the museum displays opulent period rooms in the 1818 Regency-style mansion of Alexander Telfair, complete with Telfair family furnishings.

© KAP STANN

River Street

After the museum, take a break at **Madison Square** for afternoon tea and sweets at the Gryphon Tea Room, set in an old Victorian pharmacy overlooking the square. The **Savannah College of Art and Design** is set in the red-brick Guards Armory across the street; check out their gallery here or the SCAD Shop on the corner for jewelry, prints, textiles, and other artwork designed by students of the Savannah College of Art and Design. Don't miss E. Shaver Books, also on the square, with a wonderful selection of glamorous art books on the city's architecture and gardens.

SATURDAY NIGHT

After a siesta and cocktails with appetizers at your inn, head to **Reynolds Square** for dinner at the Olde Pink House—call for reservations in the refined upstairs dining rooms of the 1789 Colonial mansion, or descend the narrow staircase to its Planters Tavern below, where you can choose from the same menu while sitting at dimly lit tables and couches around the fireplace (you'll hear piano music most nights).

City Market's entertainment district offers music for a wide range of tastes within a few blocks (blues, jazz, alternative), and many outdoor concerts are also held here. The notorious Club One offers three floors of merrymaking, including a huge dance floor with caged dancers and top-floor drag shows occasionally featuring Lady Chablis (call for the Lady's schedule).

SUNDAY MORNING

Head back to River Street in its sleepy calm for New Orleans–style beignets and café au lait. You might want to attend services at one of the city's historic churches. Head east for sightseeing at **Bonaventure Cemetery** and **Fort Pulaski**, both dramatically set along the marsh. Better yet, get out onto the water on a kayak trip through the low country's rising and falling maze of tidal marshlands.

SUNDAY AFTERNOON

After boating or sunbathing at the beach on **Tybee Island**, the North Beach Grill, on Tybee's north shore, makes a wonderful sandy stop for fresh seafood. The best place to be at sunset is at a deck-side table under the oaks at the Crab Shack, on Chimney Creek.

Most trips to Georgia start rightly in Atlanta, and even if you're eager to explore the backcountry, take the opportunity to discover the capital's own wild side. Then, depending on your time and inclinations, take one or both loop trips north and south, or extend your stay with more-remote South Georgia adventures. If you want to include the coast in a one- to two-week trip starting in Atlanta, the best use of time is to head east on I-16 to Savannah.

ATLANTA

Start downtown at the Centennial Olympic Park fountains, see the High Museum's folk-art and photography galleries, and head to the King Memorial, in Sweet Auburn. Head up Peachtree Street to see the expanded High Museum in Midtown and the Atlanta History Center in Buckhead, then relax and enjoy Southern food and hospitality in the city's homier neighborhoods, such as Virginia Highland, Little Five Points, and Inman Park. The edgier areas are the industrial frontier of downtown and West Atlanta. Go native and shoot the "Hootch"—that is, take a lazy float trip down the Chattahoochee River—and cheer on the Braves at Turner Field.

NORTHERN LOOP

An easy week's worth of adventures can be found in a loop trip from Atlanta east through Athens and north to Clayton; west across North Georgia via Highway 76 to the Cumberland Plateau before returning southeast to Atlanta. Start in the fun college town of Athens, with its great music scene, then head north to the Chattahoochee National Forest.

In the lush Blue Ridge Mountains around Clayton, see Tallulah Gorge, raft Chattooga whitewater, hike to waterfalls, and settle in at Black Rock State Park to enjoy the view. The highland route west along Highway 76 to Blue Ridge takes you out of the fray, or you could drop down to Amicalola Falls State Park, home to one of only a handful of hike-in lodges in the U.S. and located near the southern terminus of the Appalachian Trail. Moun-

tain biking trails are found further west along Highway 52 around Ellijay.

West of Ellijay, highways skirt the rugged Cohutta Wilderness and land in Chatsworth. For Civil War history, head west to Chickamauga. For Native American history, drop south to New Echota. For bike touring, head to McLemore Cove, near Cedar Grove. For one of the most acclaimed folk-art environments in the country, head to Howard Finster's Paradise Gardens, in Summerville. From any one of these adventures, return to Atlanta via prehistoric Etowah Mounds, off I-75.

Chattooga whitewater

© GEORGIA DEPARTMENT OF INDUSTRY, TRADE & TOURISM

© KAP STANN

cemetery near Athens

SOUTHERN LOOP

Another week's adventures await in the Heartland and South Georgia. Head south on I-75 to barbecue landmarks around Jackson, then east on Highway 16 to literary landmarks in Eatonton and Milledgeville. Wind down to Macon to see the Georgia Music Hall of Fame, the Sports Hall of Fame, and Ocmulgee Mounds.

From Macon, head southwest to Americus for many fascinating attractions, including Habitat for Humanity's world village, Jimmy Carter's birthplace, and Providence Canyon. Head back north through Alabama to bypass Fort Benning toward Columbus (home of Carson McCullers and Ma Rainey), then north on I-185 to Pine Mountain.

Around Warm Springs, FDR's Little White House, Callaway Gardens, and backpacking and horse trails offer another compact set of attractions. Return to Atlanta by heading north to Moreland to see Erskine Caldwell's cabin, and then hooking up with I-85 east.

FARTHER AFIELD

With more time to spare, extend a trip from Providence Canyon by taking lonely Highway 39 south, past Kolomoki Mounds, a peanut monument in Blakely, over to the Mayhaw Capital of the World in Colquitt, and clear down to Lake Seminole. Boat across or drive all the way around to get to fish shacks on the southern side. This is the land of the bizarre festival: try to plan a trip around Rattlesnake Roundup in Whigham, Mule Day in Calvary, or Swine Time in Climax. More refined retreats are found in Thomasville.

It's a long, hot drive from most anywhere to the Okefenokee Swamp. The entrance at Fargo is the most remote, where Stephen C. Foster State Park offers cabins and camping on a peninsula out into the park. If you've made it this far, after your swamp adventure, take the old Atlantic Coast Highway north to Savannah and return to Atlanta via I-16 west. For a back-road alternative, Highway 341 is a through route from the Golden Isles to Atlanta.

A local art form, Southern barbecue has subtleties that natives devote lifetimes to capturing, but visitors can get started with a few basics. First, pork is the meat of choice. (Georgia humorist Ludlow Porch wrote "If someone comes in and wants barbecue beef, the waitresses will all laugh and the cook will holler things about his mama till he leaves.") Sauces are made from tomatoes, vinegar, mustard, or some combination thereof; they are typically sweeter in North Georgia, more vinegary in the Heartland, and mustard-laced on the coast. The choice may be hot, mild, or "mix." Meat is served with Wonder bread or cornbread and two side orders, such as coleslaw, baked beans, or potato salad—but ordering the Brunswick stew, a local beef-and-chicken gumbo, shows you're serious.

The best places to participate in this revered culinary tradition are roadside shacks with concrete floors covered with sawdust and cords of hickory logs stacked a story high out against the smokehouse. Preferably, it'll be a place you get lost trying to find, and you get bonus points if it's near a prison. But barbecue joints come in all shapes and sizes, from fern bars with websites to white-tablecloth restaurants that accept American Express (don't count on shacks accepting credit cards, however).

A particularly festive, cheap, and delicious way to sample favorite recipes is at local festivals. The official state barbecue championship cook-off is the Big Pig Jig. It's held in Vienna, south of Macon, each October—worth wrapping a trip around; visit the website at www.bigpigjig.com. More barbecue spots are listed in the destination chapters, but here are some highlights.

© KAP STANN

Daddy D'z Bar-B-Que

ATLANTA
Grant Park: Daddy D'z, Factory's BBQ (page 64)
Buckhead: Fatt Matt's Rib Shack (page 67)
Southeast Atlanta: Harold's BBQ (page 70)
Emory Area: Dusty's BBQ (page 70)

METRO REGION
Smyrna: Low Country Barbecue, Old South Bar-B-Q (page 75)
Roswell: Swallow at the Hollow (page 77)
Jonesboro: Dean's Barbecue (page 80)
Lilburn: Spiced Right (page 138)
Duluth: Corky's Ribs and BBQ (page 138)

NORTH GEORGIA
Ball Ground: Two Brothers Barbeque (page 97)
Ellijay: Colonel Poole's Bar-B-Q (page 98)

Don't forget the Brunswick stew.

HEARTLAND

Danielsville: Zeb Dean's Hickory Smoked BBQ (page 146)
Augusta: Sconyer's Barbecue (page 152)
Clinton: Old Clinton Barbecue (page 160)
Flovilla: Fresh-Air BBQ (page 161)
Macon: Fincher's, Satterfield's (page 172)
Newnan: Sprayberry's (page 174)

SOUTH GEORGIA

Thomasville: J. B's Bar-B-Que & Grill (page 202)

Vienna: Mamie Bryant's BBQ Pit (page 204)
Valdosta: Old South BBQ House (page 206)
Statesboro: Vandy's (page 207)
Waycross: The Pig (page 215)

SAVANNAH

Historic District: Wall's Bar-B-Que (page 259)
East of downtown: Johnny Harris (page 262)

COAST

Brunswick: Georgia Pig (page 301)

Explore
Georgia

Atlanta

Atlanta is a lively, sprawling city of 430,000 and is surrounded by rather ungainly suburban development, particularly to the north, which boosts the 10-county metro Atlanta population to 3.3 million. Much of that rise has been in the last few decades, as Atlanta has successfully positioned itself as a corporate boomtown. Coca-Cola, CNN, Delta Air Lines, Home Depot, InterContinental Hotels, and UPS are a few corporate giants that have their worldwide headquarters here, attracting a largely white-collar work force from all over the country. So while the influx means you can now find world-class art exhibits, opera, and ethnic cuisine, you'll also find gridlock, $4 caffe lattes, and more Northerners than any Southern town should be expected to absorb.

The city can best be appreciated as an urban oasis—the cultural arts center of the South—with exciting nightlife, art, and music scenes. In the last decade Atlanta has established itself as an urban-music capital, with recording studios, producers, and local celebrities the likes of Andre 3000, Ludacris, Usher, and Jermaine Dupri. The reputation of nearby Athens as an alternative-music capital is near mythic, and many indie-rock fans make the hour's drive east for an evening's entertainment. Around town there's also no shortage of down-home blues, roots rock, folk, and jazz—such annual festivals as Music Midtown, the National Black Arts Festival, and Athens' Athfest are great ways to sample the mix.

Must-Sees

M Atlanta History Center: Within a beautiful wooded part of Buckhead, the history center's museum, historic houses, and special events present a graceful introduction to the history of Atlanta and of the South (page 38).

M High Museum of Art: The best art museum in the South presents lively, engaging exhibits accompanied by an exciting slate of films, lectures, and special events—and don't miss the folk art gallery downtown (page 44).

M Fox Theatre: The over-the-top Art Deco Arabian-inspired Fox Theatre is a fun place to see a wide variety of events, from Broadway hits and

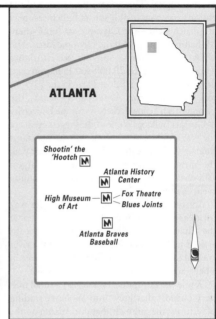

ATLANTA

Shootin' the
'Hootch **M**

Atlanta History
M   Center

High Museum— **M** ╱ Fox Theatre
of Art   ╲ Blues Joints

M

Atlanta Braves
Baseball

Fox Theatre

© KAP STANN

ballet to indie rock bands and movie matinees (page 51).

M Blues Joints: Wind down in one of several great spots to hear down-home blues music, from neighborhood nightclubs and roadhouses to rib shacks (page 53).

M Altanta Braves Baseball: Go native and cheer on the beloved home team in the glamorous stadium where Muhammad Ali lit the Olympic flame in 1996 (page 59).

M Shootin' the 'Hootch: Take a lazy half-day rafting trip through the Piedmont woodlands of the Chattahoochee River National Recreation Area—there are plenty of great hikes here too (page 74).

Since the Summer Olympic Games were held here in 1996, Atlanta has also established itself as a sports capital. The Atlanta Braves, one of the nation's most successful sports franchises, play at Turner Field—the Olympic stadium where Muhammad Ali ignited the Olympic torch. The NBA Atlanta Hawks and the NHL Atlanta Thrashers play in the 20,000-seat Phillips Arena, downtown; the NFL Falcons play in the 71,500-seat Georgia Dome. As for college teams, the Georgia Tech Yellow Jackets versus the University of Georgia Bulldogs is one of the biggest events of the year. And it's not known only for spectator sports—with more than 55,000 runners last year, the annual Peachtree Road Race is the largest 10K race in the world and is a major community event each July 4.

Apparently this sporting tradition goes way back. Standing Peachtree (the Creek settlement at the Chattahoochee River when the Europeans arrived in 1814) and the land south of the river are said to have been won from the Cherokee in a ball game played with land rights at stake.

While the Europeans established a small military outpost that grew into an active trading post, it was the railroads that put Atlanta on the map in 1837. Trying to link up Chattanooga with rail lines in Augusta, the natural contours of the land led them to choose a site eight miles southeast of the Chattahoochee River as their midway point. The white stone marker identifying the precise meeting point of the rail lines, the Zero Mile Post, was planted near where Underground Atlanta is today.

The town got off to a quick start, and by the time the Civil War broke out, Atlanta was an important rail center and a vital supply line for Confederate troops. In 1863, Union General William T. Sherman rightly theorized that a crushing blow to Atlanta's railroad hub would cripple the Confederacy, and his army followed the rail line south from Chattanooga, fighting a series of battles before the city surrendered in 1864. Although the fire set by Sherman's troops largely leveled the town—a scene recalled most romantically by native author Margaret Mitchell's *Gone with the Wind*—the town and railroads were rebuilt into a thriving city.

Today Hartsfield-Jackson International Airport continues the city's historical role as a transportation hub, with more than 78 million passengers passing through its gates every year. The airport has been recently renamed to honor two former mayors: William Hartsfield, who served 1938–1961, and Maynard Jackson, the city's first African American mayor and also its longest-serving one. This joint honor succinctly symbolizes the coalition that led the city through the most tumultuous times of the civil-rights movement.

Atlanta's racially progressive reputation was firmly established in the early days by such city leaders as Ivan Allen Jr.—the only Southern mayor to support federal civil-rights legislation in 1963—and William Hartsfield, who in 1959 proclaimed Atlanta "the city too busy to hate."

Georgia's governor during this time, Carl Sanders, remembers it this way: "When the whole South was in turmoil and chaos over the questions of civil rights and matters of that kind, Atlanta took a responsible position and elevated itself above the demagoguery of the day. It took a giant step forward. Because of that, people from other parts of the country were attracted to Atlanta, and today we have a cosmopolitan city with people from all parts of the world and all walks of life."

Above all, it was the leadership of Dr. Martin Luther King Jr. that firmly established the city's reputation for progressive racial politics. Dr. King was born here, preached here, and founded the Southern Christian Leadership Coalition here—all in the Sweet Auburn district, less than a mile from the state capitol. Today King's tomb is a pilgrimage site for generations moved by his message of interracial equality and nonviolence.

As home of the nation's largest consortium of African American colleges, the city is considered to be a mecca for the black intelligentsia, from Andy Young to Spike Lee. But the last decade has seen many different groups flourish here, including sizable Latino and Asian populations centered on the city's northeastern side. A vibrant gay and lesbian community most visible in Midtown also contributes to Atlanta's dimension and increasingly has become a vocal political force in the city, as well as the state and region.

PLANNING YOUR TIME

Mild weather most of the year and the scenic changes of the full four seasons make Atlanta pleasant to visit and suitable for outdoor recreation most of the year. In July and August, the heat and humidity are oppressive, and locals avoid venturing out of air-conditioned enclaves until dark. Fall is warm and dry; each winter, a trace of snow appears; and in spring, temperatures may fluctuate from frosty or rainy one day to a sunny mid-80s the next.

With the busiest airport in the country, Atlanta is very easy to visit. A convenient light-rail train ride from the terminal to the city center takes just a short 20 minutes. It's a huge convention town (2.9 million conventioneers in 2003) with plenty of hotels to choose from—more than 92,000 rooms at last count. If you're downtown for a short stay, you don't need a car, but to get beyond the city center, a car is most practical—if you're willing to tackle urban driving and congestion. (Inquire about overnight parking charges at downtown hotels; they can easily bump an inexpensive room into the mid-range budget.)

A good map is vital for getting around; narrow surface streets curve with a scenic disregard for typical urban grids, and many streets have similar-sounding names. Also, the lack of natural boundaries like mountains or large bodies of water makes Atlanta hard to spot on the horizon.

Business people dress conservatively; even in the summer heat, men wear serious suits (seersucker is jocular) and women wear stockings, though they're acclimated to the weather, and conventioneers and vacationers would be expected to appear more casual. Prepare for chilly air-conditioned interiors. People dress up for a night on the town in Buckhead; jeans are fine for Virginia Highland; and dreads and tattoos work for Little Five Points.

HISTORY

"Terminus" was the first name for the city established where two rail lines would meet. The name changed to Marthasville to honor the then-governor's daughter. Finally, in 1845 the town that grew around the railroad depot was renamed Atlanta—for the Western & Atlantic Railroad. By the time Georgia seceded from the Union in 1861, Atlanta was already a major transportation hub and had a population of 8,000.

"Atlanta was too important a place in the hands of the enemy to be left undisturbed," said Union General William T. Sherman, "with its magazines, stores, arsenals, workshops, foundries, and more especially its railroads, which converged there from the four great cardinal points."

Following the rail lines south from Chattanooga with 100,000 Federal troops, Sherman engaged Confederate General Joseph Johnston's smaller army several times in northwest Georgia before entering four more engagements for possession of the city. Atlanta surrendered on September 2. Although the terms of surrender were to leave citizens and property unscathed, Sherman ordered the city evacuated, then burnt it down, tore up the rail lines, and continued to burn a 60-mile-wide swath across Georgia out to the Atlantic Ocean.

When Sherman left Atlanta, every business was leveled, as were most homes. Only 400 of the city's 4,500 buildings were left standing, inspiring a 1960s politician to call Sherman "Atlanta's first urban-renewal director." Today, disgruntled locals display bumper stickers asking "Where's Sherman When You Need Him?"

Rebuilding quickly enabled the city to regain its position as a regional center, and Atlanta was named capital of Georgia in 1867. In the 1880s, when tiny Southern Bell opened the city's first switchboard and a local drugstore began selling a new headache-and-hangover tonic called Coca-Cola, the start of Atlanta's solid business base took hold.

After the Civil War the population grew to 50–50 white and black. While segregation was the official policy for more than 60 years, for the most part, it gave way quietly in the early 1960s under the influence of Atlanta's then-emerging coalition of the progressive (and pragmatic) elite of both races, the politicians, and the industrialists, as well as the strong influence of Dr. King and his Southern Christian Leadership Conference.

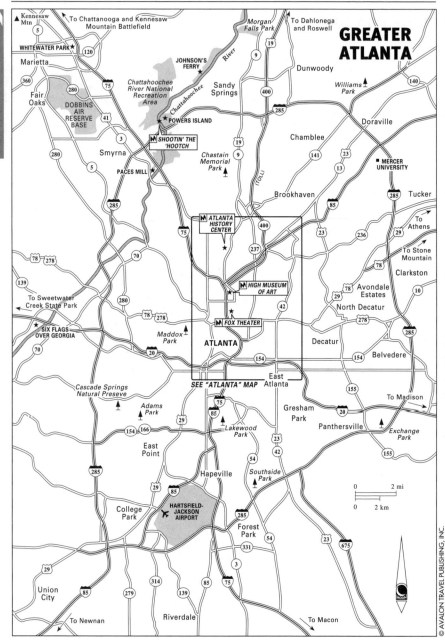

GREATER
ATLANTA

In 1973, Atlanta elected the first African American mayor of a major Southern city, the formidable Maynard Jackson. After serving term limits, Jackson was relieved for a term by the distinguished Andrew Young, who had been the U.N. ambassador during the Carter Administration. Jackson resumed the post in 1987 and served until 1993, when Bill Campbell inherited the mantle of Atlanta's African American leadership and served to term limits. The next contest pitted three African American candidates against one another, with the victorious Shirley Franklin becoming the city's first woman mayor in 2001. Such leadership has ensured the strong participation of African American firms in the city's economic base and has helped Atlanta gain a reputation for economic opportunity across the board.

ORIENTATION

To orient yourself to sprawling metropolitan Atlanta, it helps to visualize the city divided up by its north-south and east-west highways, which are in turn bounded by the city's perimeter highway. With that scheme in mind, you'll find the city's central corridor along its north-south axis, from Buckhead (at the northern perimeter) to downtown (at the central crosshairs), with the airport at the southern perimeter.

The following geographical guide characterizes the city's major districts, tells you how to get about, and introduces some of the landmark sights, hotels, and restaurants to be found within each area.

Downtown

Named for Standing Peachtree, the original Creek settlement at the banks of the Chattahoochee River, **Peachtree Street** runs for miles north from downtown. Not to be confused with West Peachtree Street, Peachtree Center Avenue, Peachtree Road, or Peachtree Place, Atlanta's historic central artery is one of 100 streets with the word "Peachtree" in its name. Early prestige associated with having a Peachtree address prompted businesses to use the word liberally (also note that it's often written in an abbreviated form: "P'tree").

The heart of downtown can be found within roughly a five-block radius of Five Points, nestled into the curve formed at the intersection of interstate freeways. The following guide starts at Five Points MARTA (Metropolitan Atlanta Rapid Transit Authority) station, moves north, and then rotates clockwise around the hub before moving on up to the Civic Center and on to points farther north.

Five Points Station to Woodruff Park: The **Zero Mile Post** planted near Five Points in 1850 marked the spot around which the city of Atlanta would grow. The spot still signifies the intersection of major rail lines. Today the Five Points MARTA station serves as the city's Grand Central, where passengers transfer between the north-south and east-west metro rail lines. Five Points gets its name from the star-shaped intersection linking Peachtree, Marietta, and Decatur Streets with Edgewood Avenue.

Across from the Five Points MARTA station, Underground Atlanta, on Alabama Street between Peachtree and Central, is a set of subterranean "streets" that in the past became encased under the bridges that were built over the original rail lines. After many decades of slumber, the hidden ghost town was richly renovated in the 1970s into a 12-acre pedestrian mall with more than 130 underground shops, restaurants, and cafés in a complex that retains the uneven cobblestone walks and some of the historic ornamental facades. It's appealing to walk around, particularly in summer, when it makes a cool refuge. Among the special events at the complex, each December 31, revelers crowd around to watch the "giant peach" drop down to signal the New Year.

Above ground, a friendly **visitors center** distributes free maps, event calendars, and city and state information, and displays free exhibits on the city's cultural and arts heritage (restrooms are here too). Next door, **AtlanTix**, offers half-price tickets to local performances and attractions. There's also a **Gray Line** tour booth. The **World of Coca-Cola** occupies a modern building not far from Underground; there are plans to move to new quarters in Centennial Olympic

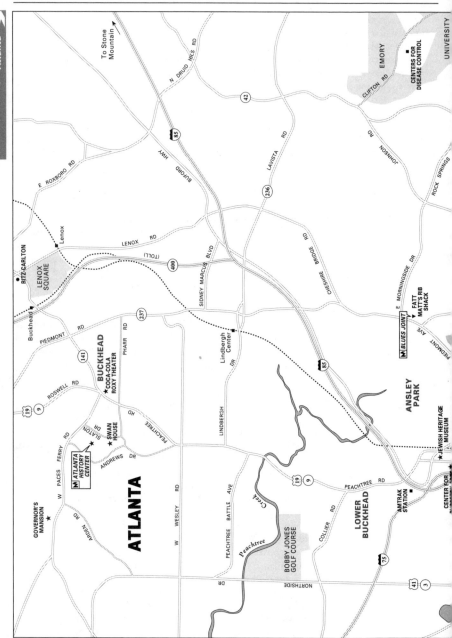

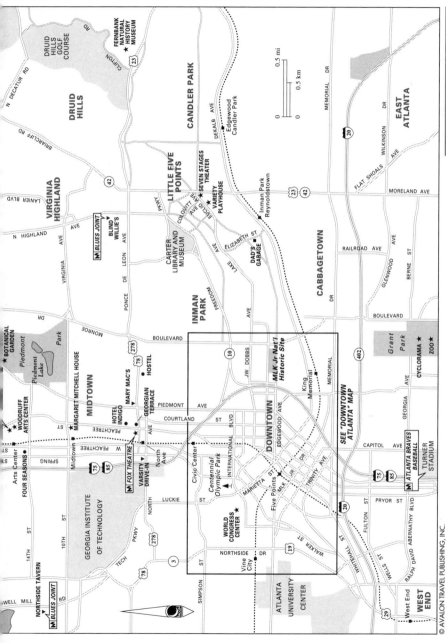

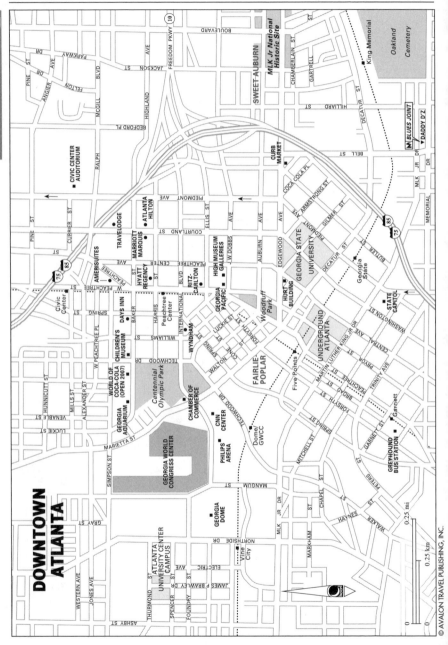

© AVALON TRAVEL PUBLISHING, INC.

Park in 2007. (For all sights, drivers can park at Underground Atlanta—it's not cheap, but it's convenient to the freeway.)

Among the many eateries in Underground Atlanta, **Café du Monde** is a good place for coffee and New Orleans style beignets, or try the dependable burger joint **Mick's.** Among places to stay, **Howard Johnson's Plaza Suites** offers historic touches right at Underground.

Woodruff Park, a block north of the MARTA station, up Peachtree, makes a shady retreat for brown-bagging office workers, with a roaring story-high water wall and occasional lunchtime concerts. A block east of the park, on Edgewood Avenue, the Corinthian-columned 1912 Hurt Building is a rare historic construction, with the acclaimed **City Grill** within (or find **Luxe,** on Park Place). From the park, Auburn Avenue leads east one mile to the Martin Luther King Jr. National Historic District.

A block up Peachtree Street from Woodruff Park, the free **High Museum Folk Art and Photography Galleries** can be found a half-block down John Wesley Dobbs Avenue in the Georgia-Pacific Building (find barbecue at the food court within; enter at Peachtree Street).

Fairlie-Poplar District: Between Woodruff Park and Centennial Olympic Park, directly north of Five Points station, is Fairlie-Poplar, Atlanta's oldest commercial district. Buildings constructed between 1890 and 1920 trace the city's evolution from a pioneer railroad town to a modern city, with styles from Victorian to midcentury modern. It's the one place in town that looks most like a regular city—buildings old and new, redeemed or not, small storefronts, people living in lofts above—all on a human-scale street grid shaded by mature trees.

Architectural highlights include early skyscrapers such as the 17-story 1906 Asa Candler Building and the 1897 Flatiron Building. The Central Library of the Atlanta-Fulton County Library is at 1 Margaret Mitchell Square, right off Peachtree Street.

The district could still stand for a bit more restoration, but for the moment, it's one of the city's most interesting frontiers, anchored by the

nicely restored 1950s **Rialto Center for the Performing Arts** and the funky **Tabernacle** (a former sanctuary that's now one of the city's best entertainment venues). **The Mark** is a swank n club downstairs from the casual **Sidebar. Ted's Montanta Grill** brings bison downtown to Spring and Luckie Streets.

Centennial Olympic Park: Centennial Olympic Park successfully knits together the Peachtree Center hotel zone to the east with the **Georgia World Congress Center** convention gulch to the west. Since it was built for the Olympic Games in 1996, the 21-acre park has become the focus of the city's new downtown. The **Atlanta Children's Museum** opened here in 2003, and the new **Georgia Aquarium** and **World of Coca-Cola** are under construction. CNN, the Omni Hotel, and Embassy Suites also surround the park.

The centerpiece of the attractive park is the **Fountain of Rings,** a walk-through fountain in the shape of Olympic rings (it's very popular

© GEORGIA IT&T

World of Coca-Cola

with children; bring towels). A memorial honors the two people killed in the bombing here during the 1996 Summer Games.

The trees have grown to give the park some heft, and it's a popular spot for concerts and festivals, including a big Independence Day celebration with fireworks. In winter, a small ice rink is set up and the trees are decorated with lights.

A **visitors center** near the fountain distributes maps and houses a convenient café. The **Atlanta Chamber of Commerce,** across the street, provides more information.

Marietta Street leads north from here into a warehouse district that is being reclaimed with lofts and what's left of the city's Internet businesses. A short drive up Marietta leads to **Thelma's Kitchen,** a soul-food restaurant transplanted up to these nondescript quarters by park construction.

The convention center and CNN, along with nearby Phillips Arena and the Georgia Dome to the west, are best approached via the Omni Dome–World Congress Center MARTA station. For the park's newest attractions, Peachtree Center would be the best station to use.

Peachtree Center: This area is the main hotel zone, supporting downtown Atlanta's huge convention business. Visitors should note right off the bat that the name "Peachtree Center" refers to the general area, the MARTA subway station by that name (with the longest escalator in the Southeast), the twin Peachtree Center office towers, the adjacent underground mall, and the city street behind it—so if you need to meet someone "at Peachtree Center," be sure to get precise directions.

It's all part of a vast, interconnected pedestrian maze of gleaming glass-and-steel skyscrapers, skywalks, tunnels, steep escalators, elevators, and interior plazas. And considering that much is built underground and on a slope, also note that "ground level" is a relative term.

More than a dozen major hotels sit in a compact area about 10 blocks square, anchored by the **Ritz-Carlton,** at Ellis Street to the south, and the **Hyatt Regency,** at Baker Street to the north. Among the majors are the **Hilton, Sheraton,** **Marriott Marquis, Wyndham,** and the 72-story **Westin,** tallest hotel in the world.

As an alternative to lavish, expensive, revolving hotel restaurants, try the Irish pub **Dailey's,** on International, a half-block down from Peachtree Street, or the Indian restaurant **Haveli's,** within the Gift Mart on Spring Street at Harris Street. A notable exception: the **Atlanta Grill** at the Ritz-Carlton offers an inviting 2nd-story patio to survey the Peachtree scene. The **Corner Bakery** is a good breakfast spot across from the Hyatt. In a pinch, the deli at the Hyatt and the coffee shop at the **Days Inn** on Baker Street are open 24 hours.

The **Hard Rock Cafe** and its Velvet Underground nightclub below are decorated to celebrate Southern music and musicians. Rich-Macy's heads up a shopping district of several brand-name stores. The small Peachtree Center shopping mall includes **the Spa at Peachtree Center**.

At the freeway overpass at Courtland Street and Ralph McGill Boulevard, see whimsical folk art sculptures that honor self-taught Georgia artists Howard Finster and St. EOM.

Capitol Hill to Castleberry Hill: The 25.5-acre campus of **Georgia State University** (GSU) dominates the district east of Five Points station, from Edgewood Avenue to the GSU station. Above the station, twin office towers are named for former politician James H. Floyd—affectionately nicknamed "Sloppy" (find an inexpensive cafeteria on street level).

Georgia's **state capitol** sits atop the knoll of Capitol Hill. Topped with a gleaming dome of authentic Georgia gold, the white-columned 1889 building—home to the state legislature from January to June—welcomes visitors with several Georgia-boosting exhibits inside and modern sculpture and statuary outside. Stately government buildings, many made with Georgia marble, surround the capitol. **Capitol Avenue** runs south from here, past the stark 17-story windowless **Georgia Archives** to **Turner Field** in under a mile.

The foot of Peachtree Street around the Garnett MARTA station occupies a Bowery-like district whose predominant public feature is the Greyhound bus terminal (conveniently adjacent to MARTA). It was somewhat cleaned up for the Olympics, and several of the district's long-abandoned industrial structures have undergone condo-conversion. Many pioneering businesses and galleries have opened as well, largely to the west, in old railroad buildings on Castleberry Hill—the urban fringe.

Civic Center: Back up to Peachtree Street, north of Ralph McGill Boulevard, Civic Center is the quiet district between the Peachtree Center hotel zone and Midtown. The **Civic Center Auditorium,** along Piedmont Avenue and three blocks east of Peachtree, is the new home of the Atlanta Opera. The area is served by the Civic Center MARTA station.

Midtown

Midtown is a vast district stretching along Peachtree Street from North Avenue to where Peachtree heads across the freeway this side of Brookwood Drive. The district has been growing increasingly popular, not only with the pioneering gay community that first rehabilitated the area's aging bungalows, but also among the straight crowd, including singles, couples, and young families. The neighborhood has spread east to the borders of Virginia Highland and west across the freeway, at the periphery of the **Georgia Tech** campus, home of the Yellow Jackets, Bobby Dodd Stadium, the Olympic natatorium, and the Ferst Center for the Performing Arts. The area served by three MARTA stations: North Avenue, Midtown, and Arts Center.

North Avenue: Two of Atlanta's most popular local institutions are on North Avenue, surrounded by several other sights in a compact, walkable area that is easily accessed by the North Avenue MARTA station. The **Varsity Drive-In** is a favorite greasy spoon right above the freeway and serves chili dogs and onion rings. The landmark, Art Deco **Fox Theatre,** on Peachtree Street, was built in 1929 as the Yaarab Temple of the Ancient Order of the Nobles of the Mystic Shrine; then it turned into a movie theater, was threatened with demolition in the 1970s, and became a cause célèbrè of the local preservation

movement. Today the Egyptian-motif palace hosts a wide variety of performing arts, from Broadway musicals to nationally known bands, and is the home of the Atlanta Ballet.

The glamorous **Georgian Terrace Hotel,** across from the Fox Theatre, is where the *Gone with the Wind* premiere reception was held in 1939; it's now a beautifully restored hotel. **Hotel Indigo,** Atlanta's first boutique hotel, is next door. The city hostel is a few blocks east, on Ponce de Leon Avenue.

For classic Southern plates, lunch at **Mary Mac's,** down Ponce de Leon; for great Jamaican food, try **Bridgetown Grill,** on Peachtree Street; for an artsy café, there's **Churchill Grounds,** next to the Fox. For entertainment, the **Apache Cafe** and **Masquerade** dance club are nearby.

Drivers might note that Ponce de Leon (PONTS-de-LEE-on) Avenue heads east from Peachtree Street to access the Freedom Parkway and such popular eastside neighborhoods as Virginia Highland and Little Five Points.

Around 10th Street: Near the Midtown MARTA station, the **Margaret Mitchell House and Museum,** at Peachtree and 10th Streets, is now enshrined as a monument to the author of *Gone with the Wind.* Mitchell wrote the famous novel here and was killed three blocks away when she was struck by a taxi while crossing Peachtree Street.

The commercial center of the Midtown neighborhood is two blocks east, at 10th Street and Piedmont Avenue. Here the neighborhood bar **Blake's** and **Outwrite Bookstore** form the cornerstones for the city's gay community. For great alfresco dining, the nicely renovated **Einstein's** offers shady decks on Juniper and 10th Street. Some of the city's most popular clubs are in this district, including the gay dance club **Backstreet,** the swank R&B **Velvet Room,** and the ultra-swank **Vision** nightclub. The **Wyndham Midtown** hotel tower and **Shellmont Inn** B&B provide lodging. The Virginia Highland district is a mile and a half east via 10th Street.

Piedmont Park is the city's Central Park, where lush acres of woods give way to paved walkways, bike paths, and wide meadows—the scene of spring festivals and summer concerts.

Bicycle and skate rentals are at the park's southwestern perimeter. At the park's northern tip are the grand conservatory and gardens of the **Atlanta Botanical Gardens.**

Lining the park up here between Piedmont Avenue and Peachtree Street are the wide winding lanes of **Ansley Park,** a historic residential district of 600 homes built between 1904 and 1930. The **Ansley Park Inn** here occupies one of the old homes and offers a gracious alternative to skyscraper hotels.

Arts Center: The city's cultural arts nucleus, the **Robert Woodruff Arts Center**—established to honor a hundred members of Atlanta's arts community killed in a plane crash en route to Paris in the 1960s—is home to the Atlanta Symphony Orchestra, the Alliance Theatre, the 14th Street Playhouse, and the Atlanta College of Art, on a campus undergoing vast expansion. The **High Museum of Art** occupies a strikingly modern four-story building next door, also undergoing expansion.

At Spring and 18th Streets, the **Center for Puppetry Arts** hosts performances and maintains a puppetry museum. The **William Breman Jewish Heritage Museum,** across the street, contains the most extensive Jewish-heritage exhibits south of Washington, D.C. The studios of the **Atlanta Ballet,** the city's 60-year-old company, are on Spring Street, nearby. One of the few survivors of Victorian Peachtree Street is **Rhodes Hall,** with its stained-glass windows depicting scenes of the Confederacy; it's currently occupied by the Georgia Trust for Historic Preservation. Atop the hill across the street, **the Temple** is home to Atlanta's oldest Jewish congregation, rebuilt after a bomb destroyed the former sanctuary in 1958.

For a great selection of places to eat, browse along **Restaurant Row,** on Crescent Avenue, a block west of Peachtree. Here, in a two block-stretch between 12th and 14th Streets, there's the **Front Page News** (its Press Room bar is a local journalists' watering hole), casual **Vickery's,** and the acclaimed nouveau Southern **South City Kitchen.** The **Four Seasons Hotel,** on 14th Street at Peachtree, provides deluxe accommodations and dining.

The 140-acre Atlantic Station redevelopment project on the former Atlantic Steel Mill property where the freeways split apart will add a flank of new hotels, offices, and housing to the district in 2005.

Use the Arts Center MARTA station for all the sights in this section.

West Midtown: Starting a decade or so back, Midtown refugees homesteaded a new district among the warehouses and rail yards west of Midtown. Since the King Plow artist's center, at 887 West Marietta, first established a beachhead a decade or so back, the district has grown from a dangerously seedy industrial area to one of the city's trendiest neighborhoods, complete with chain supermarkets and in-town subdivisions.

Bacchanalia is an outstanding restaurant in this area, along with **Food Studio,** in King Plow. The **Nuevo Laredo Cantina** is also worth seeking out for authentic Mexican food, and the **Northside Tavern** is great for roadhouse blues music.

Buckhead

Three miles north of downtown, Buckhead is large and independent enough to be a city in itself—only four or five cities within the state are larger. The city's most posh district, Buckhead is home to Southern mansions on manicured lawns, deluxe megahotels, haute cuisine, swank nightclubs, and upmarket galleries, boutiques, and shopping malls.

But for all its exclusivity, Buckhead is hardly staid and polished at night. In fact, the bar scene had grown so rowdy in recent years that after violence erupted in 2003, the city imposed a 3 A.M. closing time, to the outrage of the hardcore partying citizenry. You can find pockets of cool amid the feverish nightlife.

Lower Buckhead: Heading north up Peachtree Road across the interstate, you enter lower Buckhead. Historical markers up around Peachtree Creek recount day-by-day troop movements during the Battle for Atlanta, fought here under command of Union General William T. Sherman and Confederate General John Bell Hood. The battle led to a 75-day siege that ended with the city's surrender, followed by the fire set by Sherman that destroyed all but 400 of the city's 4,000 buildings.

Miles of cafés and bistros further along this route make this Atlanta's version of the Via Veneto—starting with **Wolfgang Puck Express,** in the shopping center across from the **Amtrak Station,** on Peachtree Street at Brookwood.

A more remote stretch of lower Buckhead can be found by following Piedmont Road north as it morphs into Cheshire Bridge Road. Along a largely desolate strip with some seedy establishments, you can find **Fatt Matt's Rib Shack** and the Southern comfort-food institution called the **Collonade Restaurant,** adjacent to the cheap **Cheshire Motor Inn.**

Buckhead Village to Lenox Square: Considered "the Beverly Hills of the East," Buckhead proper is centered at the intersection of Peachtree Road, Roswell Road, and West Paces Ferry Road. Here the Buckhead Triangle offers a compact district to stroll and explore shops, galleries, and cafés. The village is also the epicenter for Buckhead nightlife: **Eleven50** is among the newest see-and-be-seen hotspots; **Tongue-and-Groove** is a more established but still trendy club. Or find the second-story **Havana Club** sitting above the fray of frat bars below. The **Roxy Theater** is a good, reliable concert venue. **Dante's Down the Hatch,** further up Peachtree Road, is a venerable jazz club with a pirate ship, a moat, and crocodiles.

The city's premier historical homes and museums are west and north of here, and like Beverly Hills, you need a car to get around. A scenic drive west along West Paces Ferry Road leads to the **Atlanta History Center** and its elegant **Swan House** museum (drop south on Andrews Drive a quarter mile for a beautiful exterior view). The Greek Revival–style **Governor's Mansion,** slightly west at 391 West Paces Ferry Road Northwest, is open to the public.

A mile north of the village up Peachtree Road, the **Lenox Square** and **Phipps Plaza** anchor Buckhead's premier shopping district (there is valet parking), while the **Ritz-Carlton Buckhead** the **Grand Hyatt Hotel,** and the new **In-**terContinental Hotel** head up its luxurious hotel district.

Buckhead is known for its many top-end restaurants. Among the most acclaimed in the region are **Seeger's, Bluepointe,** and the **Ritz-Carlton Dining Room.** More accessible upmarket choices include **Emeril's** for high-style Cajun, **Bone's** steakhouse, **Atlanta Fish Company,** and **Buckhead Diner.**

Despite its haute reputation, with towering hotels, modern office buildings, and conventional shopping malls ringed by moats of asphalt, the district lacks charm and more closely resembles a suburban corporate business park than the lap of luxury. Drivers should note that traffic is often hopelessly snarled through here, particularly along Peachtree Road, Lenox Road, and toward any freeway access. While the Lenox Square and Buckhead MARTA stations provide public-transit alternatives, the district is designed for cars, not pedestrians. The Buckhead Uptown Connection (BUC) provides free shuttles from MARTA stations to shopping centers and several other stops within a five-mile loop.

Neighborhoods

West End: Dominating the West End district, **Atlanta University Center** (AUC) encompasses the campuses of Morehouse College, Spelman College, Morris Brown College, and Clark-Atlanta University, and is linked by the central collegiate drag of James P. Brawley Drive. The sprawling campuses hold some handsome buildings dating back as far as 1869, but much of the district is run down. The AUC campuses are surrounded by a residential neighborhood of bungalows and shady lanes that historically housed the city's African American elite, and the neighborhood remains home to many local academicians.

Three house museums show the West End at its best. The **Herndon Home** displays upper-class urban life in the 1910 mansion of Alonzo Herndon, a former slave who rose to become a millionaire as founder of the Atlanta Life Insurance Company. The 1857 Victorian **Hammonds House** exhibits African American artwork and also serves as a community center. **Wren's Nest,** the 1870 Victorian home of Joel Chandler Harris, holds a fanciful shrine to Br'er Rabbit, Br'er Fox, and all the other Uncle Remus characters recorded by the Atlanta journalist. For eats, **Busy Bee Cafe,** on Martin Luther King Jr. Drive Southwest, has been a soul-food landmark since 1947.

To visit Atlanta University Center, use the West End MARTA station, but Vine City MARTA is more convenient for Herndon Home visitors.

Sweet Auburn and Vicinity: A thriving African American commercial center from the 1890s, Sweet Auburn was known at the turn of the 20th century as "the richest Negro street in the world." While its heyday began to ebb in the 1940s, it was the center of civil-rights movement leadership in the 1960s, as it was home to Ebenezer Baptist Church, the Southern Christian Leadership Coalition, and Martin Luther King Jr. This legacy has become enshrined in the **Martin Luther King Jr. National Historic District,** which encompasses not only sights directly related to Dr. King but also the surrounding neighborhood, revitalizing Sweet Auburn and endowing it with visitors and pilgrims from around the world.

The annual King Festival brings arts, music, and performers to the neighborhood around MLK's birthday, on January 15. Both the National Park Service and the Atlanta Historical Preservation Society lead guided tours of the district.

It's less than a mile-long walk, along Auburn Avenue from Woodruff Park on Peachtree Street east to the King Center, past such sights as the **APEX Museum** and **Wheat Street Baptist Church.** Your nose will lead you naturally to **Rolling Bones Barbecue,** or you can venture a block up to the **Sweet Auburn Curb Market.** Established in 1923, the market fell into disrepair and was threatened with closure in 1974 until the community raised funds for its repair and revival. Today among the produce, seafood and flower stands, you can find eateries patronized by students, businesspeople, and hospital workers from nearby Grady Memorial Hospital.

The King Memorial MARTA station is several blocks away from the King Center through a rundown residential neighborhood; the more-traveled route down Auburn Avenue from the Five Points MARTA station downtown is recommended.

Oakland Cemetery, adjacent to the King Memorial station, holds historic gravesites and monuments on several acres of rolling hills. To the south, **Grant Park** holds two of the city's most popular attractions: **Zoo Atlanta** and the historic **Atlanta Cyclorama.** Find **Daddy D'z,** on Memorial Drive, for blues and barbecue.

Virginia Highland: The sophisticated little village of Virginia Highland has a European charm—scones, cafés, Chianti—with comfortable neighborhood pubs, arty boutiques, and used-book stores. The bouncy street life starts at dawn, when the first joggers hit the streets, and continues until the last joint closes its doors at 4 A.M.

The village is centered at the intersection of Virginia and North Highland Avenues. Here, a row of storefront cafés, taverns, and restaurants converge into one collective 2nd-story patio out back, overlooking not much more than a shady parking lot, but with great back-alley style.

Across the street, **Murphy's Deli** is a smart restaurant as well as a deli, and **Moe & Joe's** bar serves as the unofficial neighborhood welcome center.

A short walk south on Highland from this central village is the nightlife strip anchored by **Blind Willie's** blues club and the long-established saloon **Atkins Park.**

A few blocks away, south of Ponce de Leon Avenue on Highland, the outpost **Manuel's Tavern** has the smoke-filled ambience of a local politico's hangout, which it is—a great place to watch election returns or bring up such subjects as the state flag or the 11th congressional district. The 24-hour greasy spoon **Majestic Diner,** on Ponce de Leon Avenue at Highland, is where crowds go when the bars close.

The **Highland Inn** B&B offers a neighborly alternative to staying downtown.

Emory/Druid Hills: In the exclusive Druid Hills neighborhood, large homes such as those featured in the movie *Driving Miss Daisy* (which was filmed here) are set back on expansive landscaped lawns; among these, the **Callanwolde** mansion serves as an arts center for performances and galleries. The district's premier attraction is the **Fernbank Natural History Museum,** with three floors of interactive science exhibits, an IMAX theater, and miles of trails in the surrounding Fernbank Forest.

Emory University, the Ivy League of the South, occupies a huge campus with many impressive neoclassical buildings built in the early 20th century. Its **Michael C. Carlos Museum** exhibits archaeological treasures. Within the expansive Emory campus is the federal enclave of the **Centers for Disease Control,** which is constructing a visitors center due to open in 2005.

Across from campus, a small village centered on Decatur Road at Oxford Street holds popular student watering holes and such inexpensive eateries as **Burrito Art.** Also in the neighborhood is **Dusty's Barbecue,** on Briarcliff Drive.

Little Five Points and Inman Park: Atlanta's Bohemians hang out at Little Five Points (L5P), sitting around with kerchief-collared dogs in the triangle park at Euclid and Moreland Avenues, kicking up a game of Hacky Sack, or drumming up a spontaneous jam session. Dreadlocked artists hawk beadwork from carts, street poets read from self-published tracts, runaways meet suburban punks. The vegetarian, ecological, egalitarian L5P community offers cheap eats, live entertainment, and roosts to sit with a coffee mug or bottle and watch the nose-ring and crystals crowd.

Among the funky shops are **Urban Tribe** for body piercing and tattoos, **Junkman's Daughter** for used clothing by the box, and **Stefan's** for pristine vintage fashion. **A Capella Books** sells used books, and **Charis Books** is the local feminist bookstore. **Mountain Ventures** has outfitting equipment. **Sevananda Market,** the neighborhood grocery collective, has a deli case as well as organic produce and health foods—its community bulletin board has postings for roommates wanted, bodywork, and used bongo drums for trade.

The neighborhood offers many inexpensive restaurants, including **Bridgetown Grill, L5P Pizza,** the **Vortex** burger joint (enter through the giant skull), and ethnic eateries. The **Euclid**

Avenue Yacht Club tavern serves as the local community center, and the **Star Community Bar** features live roots rock. The **Variety Playhouse** is a great venue for concerts and performances, one of the city's best. **Seven Stages Theater** hosts theatrical performances.

Adjacent **Inman Park** down Euclid Avenue is Atlanta's first planned suburb. Here old Victorian and "Bungaloid" homes are set around large trees and gracefully overgrown vines and greenery. At the top of the hill, the **Carter Center** occupies a large landscaped campus at the end of Freedom Parkway (a bike path runs parallel to the parkway). At the bottom of the hill, **Dad's Garage** holds performances from music to comedy, and **Sotto Sotto** offers evocative Italian food on Highland at Elizabeth Street.

The Inman Park/Reynoldstown MARTA station is a quiet 15-minute walk through the comfortable neighborhood to L5P. Across from the station, there's **Son's Place,** a landmark Southern restaurant that inherited the mantle (and the cast-iron skillets) from the beloved Deacon Burton, who ran a restaurant at this somewhat isolated outpost for many decades.

A two-mile drive south on Moreland from L5P lands you in East Atlanta.

East Atlanta: Centered at Flat Shoals and McPherson Avenues, just south of I-20, East Atlanta is largely a shady residential district inhabited by old-timers and more recent refugees from high-priced Midtown and other closer-in neighborhoods. New restaurants, bars, cafés, and arty shops have sprung up in the small commercial district alongside storefronts housing the Body of Christ Christian Fellowship Church and Soul Zodiac Hair Salon. While many are pleased with the increase in business, some worry that gentrification will drive up rents and push older tenants out—a subject that can be debated at any neighborhood counter.

The acclaimed new restaurant **Iris** is here, along with neighborhood favorites like **Heaping Bowl and Brew** and **Burrito Art.** The sleek Ayn Rand–inspired **Fountainhead** serves cocktails and a selection of California wines. **Echo Landing** is the place to hear local bands.

There's no practical mass transit here, and the neighborhood can be tricky to find. It's a half mile south of the I-20 Moreland Avenue exit (*not* the Flat Shoals exit). Turn in at the "East Atlanta" sign on McPherson Avenue, then turn right toward the library. Note too that the long expanse of Flat Shoals Avenue is disjunctive; from surface streets, you're better off approaching via Moreland Avenue.

Within the Beltway

East side towns within the I-285 bypass are an easy reach for Atlanta visitors. For destinations outside the bypass ring—including Stone Mountain and northern suburbs—see the Vicinity of Atlanta section.

Decatur: Founded in 1823, Decatur let history pass it by when early town residents, fearing noise and pollution, refused to let the railroad stop there. So the railroad went on to Terminus instead, the depot town that evolved into Atlanta. They're still thanking city founders for that foresight. Today Decatur is the home of **Agnes Scott College** and is a comfortable small-city alternative to bustling downtown Atlanta. Situated between Atlanta and Stone Mountain, Decatur is a quick 10 minutes from downtown by rail.

Decatur's compact downtown square is directly above the Decatur MARTA station. The 1889 **County Courthouse** has a small museum of local history and artifacts, including Union and Confederate memorabilia.

Eddie's Attic, above the square, features largely acoustic music; a half-mile walk away is the **Freight Depot,** for bluegrass music. The **Watershed** restaurant draws city folk; **Our Way Cafe** is a homey spot for Southern plates; and **Twains** is a popular billiards bar. The **DeKalb Farmer's Market,** out on East Ponce de Leon Avenue, offers much more than fresh produce—the hangar-size building attracts foodies from around the city to its wonderful selection of ethnic and gourmet specialties (there's a cafeteria and bakery on site).

Sights

HISTORY AND HERITAGE

M Atlanta History Center

Georgia's premier history exhibits are found at the Atlanta History Center, 130 W. Paces Ferry Rd. N.W., 404/814-4000, atlantahistorycenter.com, operated by the Atlanta Historical Society. The 33-acre campus features several historic homes, guided and self-guided tours, a farmyard, and interpretive centers. It's open Mon.–Sat. 10 A.M.–5:30 P.M. and Sun. noon–5:30 P.M.

The centerpiece is the grand **Atlanta History Museum,** which occupies a 83,000-square-foot building designed to evoke the city's railroad heritage. Exhibits explore the city's historical and cultural milestones, "from Civil War to Civil Rights." Special mixed-media displays highlight Atlanta's early African American elite society and regional folk arts; the most provocative exhibit critically examines whether commonly held perceptions of Southern history are "Fact or Myth." A new wing will cover the Centennial Olympics in Atlanta. The museum's 1950-style café serves lunch and snacks.

The center's two historic-home tours present contrasting views of mid-19th-century rural Georgia and 1920s Atlanta high society. The **Tullie Smith Farm,** a restored 1840s plantation, exemplifies the kind of simple two-story clapboard house Margaret Mitchell had in mind for Tara (as opposed to the white-columned vision of the filmmaker). The working farm, with live animals, includes demonstrations of sheep-shearing, weaving, open-hearth cooking, and other traditional skills and crafts. Visitors are free to explore the house and grounds; check at the center's admission desk for tour and demonstration schedules.

The majestic 1928 **Swan House** sits regally among acres of landscaped gardens (the exterior view is particularly impressive from Andrews

Drive). Period furnishings, sculpted in exquisite detail (a swan motif appears throughout in furniture, stained glass, and even dishware) and the grand spiral staircase are most memorable. Visitors are allowed only on guided tours, which are offered every half hour.

A modern interpretive center houses additional exhibits, a casual café, a gift shop, and archives. Give yourself at least half a day to explore all the offerings, and try to catch one of many special events scheduled at the center.

An annual **storytelling festival** takes place in February, and lectures by nationally known historians and authors are held throughout the year. For a weekend each July, the center hosts a **Civil War Encampment,** with costumed living-history interpreters acting out Civil War scenes.

Admission is $12 for adults, $10 for students and seniors, $7 for youth ages 4–12, and free for children under age four. The fee includes visits at most sites; guided tours and some special events are extra.

Georgia State Capitol Museum

Georgia's 1889 capitol, 214 Capitol Ave., 404/656-2844, can be easily identified atop Capitol Hill by its gleaming dome of North Georgia gold. The stately white-columned building (home to the state legislature January to June) displays flags-of-state, flora and fauna collections, historic artifacts, and a Hall of Fame honoring native sons and daughters in its impressive interior. There is a short film, and tours are offered. It's open weekdays during business hours.

Outside, statuary dot its landscaped lawns, including a metal sculpture honoring the 33 African American legislators expelled during Reconstruction. Use the Georgia State MARTA station.

Underground Atlanta

More of a contemporary mall than a historic site, Underground Atlanta, 50 Upper Alabama St., 404/523-2311, underground-atlanta.com, was reconstructed in 1986. Originally, it was a ghost town that had been enclosed by overhead bridges in the early part of the 20th century.

Today, shoppers promenade on original rail-inlaid cobblestone lanes, brick walls bear fading Coca-Cola ads, and historical facades of stone and terracotta evoke design. A particularly cool refuge in summer, the 12-acre complex supports more than a hundred shops, restaurants, and clubs. It's open Mon.–Sat. 10 A.M.–9 P.M. and Sun. noon–6 P.M. Admission is free.

The center connects directly with the Five Points MARTA station. Drivers may want to use Underground's easily accessible public parking lot to explore the downtown area.

Atlanta Cyclorama

In Grant Park, Cyclorama, 800 Cherokee Ave. S.E., 404/658-7625, tells the story of the 1864 fight for Atlanta, using battle sound effects as the studio audience revolves around a story-high, 9,000-pound painting that was completed in 1885. Despite the modern studio, the Cyclorama retains the slightly campy appeal of an attraction from another era, like an old talkie or giant camera obscura. Expect overstimulated modern children to find it incredibly dull.

It's open daily 9:30 A.M.–4:30 P.M., till 5:30 P.M. in summer. Admission is $7 for adults, $6 for seniors, $5 for youth under 13, and free for children under the age of six. Find the entrance in Grant Park right next to the zoo.

Jimmy Carter Library and Museum

The National Archives operates the Carter Library and Museum, 441 Freedom Parkway, 404/331-3942, jimmycarterlibrary.org. The museum displays artifacts from Carter's presidency, including a replica of the Oval Office, the First Lady's inaugural gowns, gifts from world leaders, and the notorious brown cardigan Carter wore during his famous fireside chats.

There's a 30-minute biographical film, and scheduled events have included a reenactment of the Camp David accords. The gift shop sells all of Carter's books and fine china in the Carter White House pattern. It's open Mon.–Sat. 9 A.M.–4:45 P.M. and Sun. noon–4:45 P.M. Admission is $7 for adults and $5 for students.

Atlanta

KING'S LEGACY

"I Have a Dream. . .

. . . that one day on the red hills of Georgia, sons of former slaves and sons of former slave owners will be able to sit down together at the table of brotherhood. I have a dream that my four little children will one day live in a nation where they will not be judged by the color of their skin but by the content of their character. I have a dream!"

Dr. Martin Luther King Jr.,
1963, Washington, D.C.

Martin Luther King Jr. was born in Sweet Auburn on January 15, 1929, a block away from Ebenezer Baptist Church, where, 39 years later, the city and the nation mourned the death of the man who founded the American civil-rights movement. The tomb of the Nobel Peace Prize winner now rests next to the church where he, his father, and his grandfather had preached; its simple inscription reads "Free at last, free at last, thank God Almighty I'm free at last."

Also, the **Carter Center** (cartercenter.org) here houses private public-policy organizations devoted to global issues, conflict resolution, and human rights projects around the world. One highlight, the **Atlanta Project,** is devoted to the idea that "somewhere on earth, there is one place where poverty and the social ills associated with it can be overcome," according to President Carter. The center occupies a 35-acre hilltop landscaped with a rose garden, cherry orchard, wildflower meadow, ponds, and waterfalls within a formal Japa-

King's birth home, church, and gravesite—all national historic landmarks—make a stirring tribute to the American hero who moved the world with his passion for equal justice. But what truly memorializes Dr. King are the millions of visitors (around a half million each year) who pause before his grave, read his printed remarks, view his last effects, and explain to their children what the man and the time meant to them. How times have changed for minorities in America, how they haven't—it's the old people remembering, and the young people imagining, who create the most powerful memorial.

The King Center
The crypt of Dr. Martin Luther King Jr. stands in the center of a long reflecting pool near an eternal flame at the King Center for Nonviolent Social Change, 449 Auburn Ave., 404/524-1956. Founded by King's widow, Coretta Scott King, and now administered by Martin King III, the center continues Dr. King's work toward economic and social equality. Within their Freedom Hall offices, an exhibit hall houses a collection of

crypt of Dr. Martin Luther King Jr.

© KEVIN C. ROSE, ATLANTA CVB

nese garden. A dignified cafeteria serves inexpensive Southern lunches and snacks with a patio overlooking the gardens. There's no charge to wander the grounds, and diners can patronize the restaurant without paying admission.

William Breman Jewish Heritage Museum
Opened in 1996, the Selig Center, 1440 Spring St. N.W., 678/222-3700, thebremen.org, houses the largest Jewish heritage museum south of

King's personal effects and mementos, including exhibits on Mahatma Gandhi, who inspired King's dedication to nonviolence. Exhibits are on view daily 9 A.M.–5 P.M. for no charge. The gravesite outside can be visited around the clock.

NPS Visitor Center
The National Park Service Visitor Center, 450 Auburn Ave., 404/331-5190, nps.gov/malu, holds powerful exhibits on the history of American apartheid and the evolution of the civil-rights movement. An impressive 30-minute film contains historical footage of civil-rights marches and clashes. The visitor center is open daily 9 A.M.–6 P.M. in summer, till 5 P.M. the rest of the year.

Birth Home
Martin Luther King Jr. was born in an upstairs bedroom in a two-story Victorian house at 501 Auburn Ave. His father, Reverend Martin Luther King Sr., and mother, the former Alberta Williams, had been married in the house three years earlier, and all three of their children were born here. The nine-room Queen Anne–style house has been restored and furnished to reflect the time when "M. L." (as he was known) was growing up. Ranger-guided tours of the house begin at the NPS visitor center.

Ebenezer Baptist Church
Three generations of King-family preachers presided over the historic sanctuary of Ebenezer Baptist Church, 407 Auburn Ave. In 1957, Martin Luther King Jr. organized the Southern Christian Leadership Conference in the church's basement. In 1968, crowds of mourners paid last respects at Dr. King's funeral here after his assassination in Memphis. Another family tragedy occurred here in 1974, when Dr. King's mother was killed by an assassin's bullet while seated at the church organ.

The historic 750-person-capacity church became so popular as a civil-rights shrine that an expanded modern sanctuary was built across the street for worship services, preserving the original 1922 church for tours and special services.

MLK Jr. National Historic District
The King memorial sites are all part of a national historic preservation district within the surrounding Sweet Auburn neighborhood. The NPS oversees this district and distributes maps to all historic sites from its visitor center.

The King Center is a mile from the Five Points MARTA station, a pedestrian route past many community landmarks; the No. 3 bus also rides this route. It's less than half that distance from the King Memorial MARTA station, but through a less-traveled, hard-luck residential district. Drivers will find ample signs pointing the way from major freeways to the parking lot behind the NPS Visitor Center.

Washington, D.C. Its Holocaust gallery chronicles the systematic murder of more than half of Europe's 11 million Jews and the failure of the world to react to the massacre—the exhibit winds up with a contemporary group photo of local survivors and their families. The heritage gallery relates the stories of Atlanta's Jewish community from the first German immigrants in 1845—including the temple bombing in 1958.

It's open Mon.–Thurs. 10 A.M.–5 P.M., Fri. 10 A.M.–3 P.M., and Sun. 1–3 P.M. Admission is $10 for adults, $6 for seniors, $4 for students, $2 for children ages three to six, and free for children under the age of three. It's next to the Center for Puppetry Arts.

Margaret Mitchell House and Museum
The Margaret Mitchell House, 990 Peachtree St., 404/249-7012, gwtw.org, is the historic home of the famous Atlanta native. Mitchell wrote *Gone with the Wind* here in a cramped basement apartment she called "the Dump"— not exactly Tara. The **museum** displays the typewriter on which the manuscript was written, Mitchell's Pulitzer, and a great collection of movie posters. Hour-long guided tours of the house and apartment emphasize "Peggy's" unconventional life and the pains of restoring the house, which nearly rival the author's written drama.

© KAP STANN

Margaret Mitchell House

The three-story Tudor Revival house had been carved up into apartments and was occupied until 1978, when it was abandoned and boarded up. It remained urban blight for nearly two decades. Early faltering restoration attempts went up in flames after arsonists struck in 1994. A German industrial group contributed $5 million for restoration, but 40 days before its scheduled opening in 1996, the house was again torched by arson. After repairs, the house opened to the public in May 1997.

Tours are given daily 9:30 A.M.–5 P.M. Admission is $12 for adults, $9 for seniors and students with I.D., $5 for youth under 17, and free for children under the age of six. Purchase tickets at the **visitors center,** which displays photographs of the house fire and screens a 17-minute film on the author and the restoration; there's also a gift shop. The house is easily found next to the Midtown MARTA station.

Other Historic House Museums and Buildings

The **Governor's Mansion,** 391 W. Paces Ferry Rd. N.W., 404/261-1776, is a Greek Revival house elegantly appointed with Federal-period antiques, furnishings, and paintings. It's open Tues.–Thurs. 10–11:30 A.M., and admission is free.

One of the few survivors of Victorian Peachtree Street, **Rhodes Hall,** 1516 Peachtree St., 404/885-7800, rhodeshall.org, is home to the Georgia Trust for Historic Preservation. The castlelike mansion was built in 1904 and features stained-glass windows depicting scenes of the Confederacy. The price of admission includes a tour. It's open Mon.–Fri. 11 A.M.–4 P.M. and Sun. noon–3 P.M. Admission is $5 for adults and $4 for seniors and students.

The **Herndon Home,** 587 University Place N.W., 404/581-9813, herdonhome.org, showcases the 1910 mansion of Alonzo Herndon—a Georgian born into slavery who later established the first black-owned life insurance company. It's in West End, near the Vine City MARTA station. It's open Tues.–Sat. 10 A.M.–4 P.M. Admission is $5 for adults and $3 for students.

The **Fox Theatre,** 660 Peachtree St. N.E., 404/881-2100, foxtheatre.org, is the city's most potent symbol of historic preservation, as well as its quirkiest architectural landmark. Rescued from Atlanta's rampant urban-renewal binge in

THE *GONE WITH THE WIND* CITY TOUR

The Pulitzer prize–winning novel that's sold more copies than any book besides the Bible, *Gone with the Wind*, was written by Georgia native Margaret Mitchell in her Atlanta home in 1936. Selling more than one million copies in the first six months of its issue, the novel has been translated into 70 languages. In 1939, MGM released the film based on Mitchell's book—starring Clark Gable and the then-unknown Vivien Leigh—which went on to become one of the most popular movies in film history.

Mitchell's compelling account of antebellum plantation life and the Civil War gained an international reputation for the author, and also for Atlanta, where the story was largely based.

Yet today, visitors coming to Atlanta expecting to find scenes out of the movie are bound for disappointment. Whatever antebellum homes and buildings Sherman didn't burn eventually succumbed to fast-moving Atlanta's urban renewal binges, so that now most of the "Capital of the New South" looks just about as classically Southern as Toronto (Taraseekers should head to plantation house tours in Roswell, Jonesboro, and Madison). Yet those on a dedicated Margaret Mitchell tour of metropolitan Atlanta can hunt down traces of GWTW glory.

999 Peachtree St. The late 19th-century Tudor revival **Margaret Mitchell House and Museum,** in midtown Atlanta, affectionately called "the Dump" by its most famous tenant, was where Mitchell composed the opus during a 10-year period. After being abandoned for years, boarded-up, and twice set ablaze, the three-story house has now been meticulously restored with special attention to the tiny Mitchell apartment downstairs. The museum houses memorabilia from the author, the book, and the film, including Scarlett's bonnet and corset; the gift shop stocks GWTW souvenirs. Daily tours start at the visitor center next door. (Mitchell's girlhood home, at 1401 Peachtree St., was torn down at her request.)

Forsyth Street at Carnegie Way. In the downtown **Atlanta Public Library,** "Peggy" consumed so many books, her husband complained in frustration that he couldn't find any she hadn't read, so he bought her a typewriter and challenged her to write her own. Today the library maintains a small collection of mementos (mostly documents) at its central library downtown, at (where else?) 1 Margaret Mitchell Square, 1st floor.

130 W. Paces Ferry Rd. The Atlanta History Center's **Tullie Smith House,** an 1840s farmhouse, was closer to what Mitchell had in mind for the fictional Tara than the opulent mansion pictured in the movie (which is more like the plantation houses found in Mississippi). Mitchell felt her story was a tale of survival, and disapproved of the way the movie romanticized the Old South. (Catch a behind-the-scenes view of the movie at the center's exhibit of candid photographs taken on the GWTW set.)

659 Peachtree St. The glamorous **Georgian Terrace Hotel** was where the movie's white cast members stayed for the film's premiere at Loews Theater. Segregation laws kept African American cast members from attending the opening or staying at the hotel.

1296 Piedmont Ave. The **Della Manta Apartments,** at the corner of South Prado (exterior views only), was where Mitchell moved after leaving "the Dump." A plaque at the door commemorates the author, who was named "Georgia's most famous person" by an act of the state legislature in 1985.

Peachtree and 12th Streets. At this intersection three blocks north of Mitchell's home in midtown Atlanta, a drunken off-duty taxi driver struck Margaret Mitchell on August 11, 1949 (the driver was charged with involuntary manslaughter). Mitchell died at Grady Memorial Hospital downtown five days later; her funeral service was held at Patterson's Funeral Home.

248 Oakland Ave. Oakland Cemetery is the eternal resting place of Margaret Mitchell and her husband John Marsh. Her grave is a pilgrimage site for diehard fans, such as members of the Gone with the Wind Fan Club, based in South Carolina.

the 1970s and '80s by a strong civic campaign to "Save the Fox," the Moorish/Art Deco fantasia is now the most unusual venue in town. Tours are offered for a fee, but availability depends on performance schedules; call 404/688-3353 for the latest information. To get there, use the North Avenue MARTA station.

Oakland Cemetery

Atlanta's most historic cemetery, 248 Oakland Avenue S.E., 404/688-2107, oaklandcemetery.com, serves as the eternal home of 70,000 of the city's residents, including Margaret Mitchell, Confederate Vice President Alexander Stephens, and golfer Bobby Jones, along with mayors and governors and the nameless Unknown Confederate Dead. Gravestones, statuary, and memorials clutter the scenic cemetery on its slight rise in Atlanta's Cabbagetown district, and the ambience is lively enough to attract lunchtime picnickers and joggers. It's open daily dawn to dusk; admission is free. A $2 brochure, available at the cemetery office, identifies major sites; also inquire about the guided tours that are offered for a fee. It can be easily found uphill from the King Memorial MARTA station or by car right along Memorial Drive.

VISUAL ARTS

High Museum of Art

From 18th-century Oriental ceramics to soulful contemporary street expressions, the High Museum, 1280 Peachtree St. N.E., 404/733-45750, high.org, opened in 1989 and houses four artful stories in a modern building so striking, the *New York Times* called it "among the best any city has built in at least a generation." Upon completion in 2005, the major overhaul and expansion of the entire Woodruff Arts Center here will double gallery space.

The High features works of artists with Georgia roots (such as the visionary Reverend Howard Finster and the self-taught painter Mattie Lou O'Kelley) alongside an extensive sub-Saharan African art collection, 19th-century American paintings, and an inviting interactive children's gallery. Recent blockbuster traveling exhibitions (special rates and extended hours may apply) have included the largest Impressionist exhibit in the Southeast and a colorful selection of Pop Art. Past film series have included a Latin American film festival, animation shorts, and a Johnny Depp retrospective; call the film hotline at 404/733-4570 for current screenings. Wafting scents from the

© E. ALAN MCGEE

High Museum of Art

atrium coffee bar and a well-stocked museum store (regional-flavor art books and crafts, wearable art, etc.) enhance the museum's welcoming come-as-you-are, see-art ambience.

It's open Tues.–Sat. 10 A.M.–5 P.M. and Sun. noon–5 P.M. Admission is $8 for adults, $6 for students and seniors, $4 for youth under 18, and free for children under six. On the first Thursday of every month, the museum stays open till 9 P.M. and features live music, grown-up art activities, and cocktails. There's a jazz series every third Friday. The café below the entrance opens earlier. The museum is a block from the Arts Center MARTA station.

The High's satellite **Folk Art and Photography Galleries,** 30 John Wesley Dobbs Ave., 404/577-6940, at Georgia-Pacific Center, brings an edgy selection of choice exhibits within free-and-easy reach, right downtown. It's open Mon.–Sat. 10 A.M.–5 P.M.; admission is free. To get there, use the Peachtree Center MARTA station.

Michael C. Carlos Museum

Northeast of downtown, in the historic quadrangle of the attractive Emory University campus, this art and archaeology museum, 571 S. Kilgo St., 404/727-0519, carlos.emory.edu, displays ancient artifacts from around the world and artwork dating anywhere from the Middle Ages to the 20th century. Exhibits include an Egyptian mummy, pre-Columbian pottery, and Greek statues. Located in a civilized and academic corner of the city, the refined museum is a worthwhile diversion from the bustle of downtown. Adjacent to the museum is a bookstore and café. It's open Tues.–Sat. 10 A.M.–5 P.M., till 9 P.M. Thurs., and Sun. noon–5 P.M. Admission is $5. Follow signs to the museum from the university's main entrance, on Decatur Road at Oxford Street.

Other Galleries and Exhibits

The **Museum of Contemporary Art of Georgia,** 1447 Peachtree St., 404/881-1109, mocaga.org, collects contemporary works by native Georgia artists. It's open Tues.–Sat. 10 A.M.–5 P.M. Admission is free.

Three art schools maintain galleries that exhibit the work of students, faculty, and alumni,

as well as of nationally known artists: The **Atlanta College of Art Gallery,** 1280 Peachtree St. N.E., 404/733-5001, in the Woodruff Arts Center; **savannah,** 3096 Roswell Rd., 404/816-0247, the Savannah College of Art and Design's gallery in Buckhead; and Georgia State University's **School of Art and Design Galleries,** 10 Peachtree Center Ave., 404/621-2257. GSU's gallery is one of a dozen downtown featured in **Turner's First Thursdays,** a self-guided gallery tour held the first Thursday of each month; for more information, visit atlantadowntown.com.

NATURAL HISTORY AND SCIENCE

A grand addition to the city's natural-history attractions is the Georgia Aquarium, under construction at the head of Centennial Olympic Park and due to open in 2005.

Fernbank Museum of Natural History

The natural-history museum at Fernbank, 767 Clifton Rd. N.E., 404/929-6300, fernbank.edu/museum, holds three floors of engaging interactive exhibits on a range of subjects from plate tectonics to indigenous

© KAP STANN

Fernbank Museum of Natural History

cultures to bubble science. It's housed in a grand showcase that opened before the 1996 Olympics, and there are entrance pools and a spiral stone staircase in a three-story circular atrium, castle-style. It's open Mon.–Sat. 10 A.M.–5 P.M. and Sun. noon–5 P.M.

The state-history exhibit traces the evolution of humans in Georgia's varied habitats and serves as a good introduction to the woodlands, marshlands, and coastal plain. One favorite is the Okefenokee Swamp exhibit, where owls hoot, cicadas chirp, and alligators bellow as night falls at the push of a button. There's also a popular IMAX theater (Friday evenings, the museum is open longer for movie viewers) and "discovery room" play areas, one exclusively for preschoolers.

Admission to the museum is $12 for adults, $11 for students and seniors, and $10 for children ages 3–12. There is a separate charge for the IMAX movies, and combo tickets are available. The museum also has a nice café with many fresh selections.

Fernbank's **Science Center,** in a low-key space nearby that originally housed the museum, now features a NASA Aeronautics Education Lab with spacecraft exhibits; admission is free. Call 404/874-7102 for a schedule and fees for shows in the center's 70-foot-diameter **planetarium,** one of the world's largest. The center's **Observatory** houses a 36-inch reflecting telescope and holds evening hours in clear weather.

Nearly two miles of trails within the 65-acre **Fernbank Forest** lead hikers through undisturbed stands of large tulip trees, oak, beech, and hickory—a surprisingly wild pocket just five minutes from downtown. Gates to the forest may be open afternoons only Sunday to Friday, and all day Saturday; there is no fee. The **greenhouse** there is presently open Sunday afternoons only.

Find the Fernbank complex and forest off Ponce de Leon Avenue in the Druid Hills district east of downtown. A bus runs along Ponce de Leon from the North Avenue MARTA station.

Zoo Atlanta

With 700 animals representing 200 species from around the world, Zoo Atlanta, 800 Cherokee Ave. S.E., 404/624-5600, zooatlanta.org, is par-

ticularly renowned for its primates, who have become affectionately known as local heroes and mascots. The zoo displays representative species from Georgia's coastal and swamp regions in natural habitat settings that give a nice taste of the state's diversity. They also have an aviary and feature wildlife shows. It's a well-maintained facility right next door to the Cyclorama in scenic Grant Park and is a popular attraction for all ages. It's open Mon.–Fri. 9:30 A.M.–5:30 P.M. and Sat.–Sun. 9:30 A.M.–6:30 P.M. Admission is $17 for adults, $13 for seniors, and $12 for children ages 3–11. Parking is free, but the lot may fill on weekends.

Atlanta Botanical Garden

The lush displays in the strikingly modern and massive **Fuqua Conservatory** and the surrounding hardwood forest make Piedmont Park's 30-acre botanical garden,1345 Piedmont Ave., 404/876-5859, atlantabotanicalgarden.org, a tranquil urban retreat. Tropical, desert, and endangered plants complement the naturally profuse and flowering native varieties. There are also fragrance gardens and a playful children's garden. The gardens are open Oct.–Mar. Tues.–Sun. 9 A.M.–5 P.M., Apr.–Sept. 9 A.M.–7 P.M. Admission is $10 for adults, $7 for seniors, and $5 for children 6–12. It's under a mile from the Arts Center MARTA station, a nice walk.

KIDS' FAVORITES

The zoo and upcoming aquarium will hold high rank among children's favorites, along with the children's museum downtown. For pure fun, families often head to the Six Flags amusement park in Austell, west of Atlanta, and to the White Water Park in Marietta, northwest of Atlanta (for information on these, see *Vicinity of Atlanta*, later in this chapter).

Imagine It! The Children's Museum of Atlanta

Downtown's children's museum, 275 Centennial Olympic Park Dr. N.W., 404/659-5437, imagineit-cma.org, opened in 2003 across from the northeast corner of the park. Touching on history, science, and world cultures, the chil-

The South's storytelling tradition is carried on at the Wren's Nest in Atlanta.

© KAP STANN

dren's museum presents a colorful, stimulating, child-sized environment full of play space, performing space, and a Town Square. One exhibit features where food comes from, with a barnyard and delivery truck; another features tools. There are also art stations and a gift shop with many wonderful toys and books to take home.

Hours are Sept.–May Tues.–Fri. and on Federal holidays 10 A.M. to 4 P.M., Sat. till 5 P.M., Sun. noon–5 P.M.; June–Aug. Mon.–Sat. 10 A.M.–5 P.M. and Sun. noon–5 P.M. Admission is $11 for everyone three years and up (children two and under are free).

Center for Puppetry Arts

In Midtown, the Center for Puppetry Arts, 1404 Spring St., 404/873-3391, puppet.org, claims to be the largest performing-arts company in the U.S. that's dedicated to the art of puppetry. Its well-produced performances are entertaining for adults as well as children (note that not all shows are G-rated). In addition to hosting wonderful shows in an intimate theater, they maintain a small museum with puppets, Muppets, and *Pigs in Space* on display (also a self-serve puppet theater). Call or visit the website for prices and schedules.

The Wren's Nest

One of Atlanta's hidden treasures is the Wren's Nest, 1050 Ralph D. Abernathy Blvd. S.W., 404/753-7735, the enchanting Victorian home of Georgia writer Joel Chandler Harris, chronicler of the Uncle Remus stories. The house is a low-key yet somehow magical shrine to Br'er Rabbit and all his br'erly shenanigans. Guided tours are of the historic home are offered, but it's the quarterly storytelling programs featured here that would appeal to children. Wonderful raconteurs bring the old African tales to life. It's open Tues.–Sat. 10 A.M.–2:30 P.M. Admission is $7 for adults, $6 for seniors and teens, $4 for children, and free for children under age four. It's a half-mile from the West End MARTA station through a run-down district.

FACTORY TOURS

Only New York and Houston have more Fortune 500 companies than Atlanta, and the city is proud of its status as a corporate capital. No surprise then that two of its most popular attractions are monuments to hometown corporate titans. Raising the factory tour to dazzling new heights are the Cable News Network (CNN) Studio Tour and the World of Coca-Cola.

CNN Studio Tour

On guided tours through CNN Studios, visitors are introduced to the history of Ted Turner's media empire—not only the Cable News Network (CNN), but also Turner Broadcasting Systems (TBS) and Turner Network Television (TNT). Turner also owns the rights to many classic films, including the hometown saga *Gone with the Wind.* CNN's program *TalkBack* is filmed live in the central plaza weekdays at 3 P.M.; tickets are free.

A 45-minute guided studio tour culminates with a look at the kinetic central newsroom from a gallery overhead. Tours begin every 20 minutes 9 A.M.–5 P.M. daily. Adults pay $8, seniors pay $6, children ages 6–12 are charged $5. Advance reservations are required; call 404/827-2300 or visit cnn.com/studiotour. Visitors must pass through a metal detector, and bags are subject to search.

The 14-story **CNN Center,** on Marietta Street at Techwood Drive, encloses offices and the **Omni Hotel** around a central atrium, all above a ground-level mall of restaurants, snack bars, shops, and a cinema (an unlikely place to find the international headquarters of a broadcasting network).

For souvenirs, the **Turner Store** sells videotapes of war news coverage, CNN/TBS/TNT logo–emblazoned golf balls, and paraphernalia from the Turner-owned Atlanta Braves baseball team. CNN Center is above the Omni /WCC/CNN MARTA station.

The World of Coca-Cola

Designed "to entertain and enlighten soft-drink consumers from around the world," the Coca-Cola museum, 55 Martin Luther King Jr. Dr. S.W., 404/676-5151, wocatlanta.com, pays tribute to the wildly successful marketing of Coke in 185 countries. The $15-million, three-story, carbonated and caffeinated fantasyland features continuously running Coke commercials, soda fountains ranging from vintage to high-tech, and a store selling hundreds of products with the familiar red-and-white logo. Can't beat the feeling. Hours are Mon.–Sat. 9 A.M.–5 P.M. and Sun. noon–6 P.M. Admission is $6 for adults, $4 for seniors and students, $3 for children, and free for children under age five.

A new World of Coca-Cola is under construction at the head of Centennial Olympic Park and is due to open in 2007. In the meantime, it's located across from Underground Atlanta. Prices include all the Coke you can drink.

SCHOOLS AND LIBRARIES

Metropolitan Atlanta's 38 colleges and universities stimulate the city's intellectual community and enroll nearly 100,000 students. Many maintain galleries of interest to the public and host public events such as lectures, performances, concerts, and festivals. University centers and cafeterias can be a networking resource for visiting students—check out bulletin boards and campus newspapers for notices and information. The following describes major campuses only.

Georgia State University (GSU)

Second largest in the state university system, Georgia State, 30 Courtland St., 404/651-3900, gsu.edu, occupies a 25.5-acre urban campus in the heart of downtown (a block from Underground Atlanta and above the Georgia State MARTA station). GSU's six colleges enroll more than 32,000 students.

Visitors can find the Welcome Center in **Alumni Hall** and a tribute to native son Johnny Mercer in **Library South** (where a jukebox plays Mercer classics such as *Jeepers Creepers* and *Blues in the Night*). An art gallery is at the corner of Peachtree Center Avenue and Gilmer Street.

GSU's **Cinefest Theater,** in University Center, screens foreign and art films that are booked nowhere else (for program information, call 404/651-2463); performing arts take place in the restored **Rialto Theater,** across Peachtree Street.

Georgia Institute of Technology

Grown from its establishment in 1885 to the South's largest center for technological education and research, Georgia Tech, 225 North

Ave. N.W., 404/894-2000, gatech.edu, which is part of the state university system, enrolls 12,000 students and ranks as one of the top tech schools in the nation. In 1996 it was the home of the Olympic Village, and its new bio-engineering and bioscience building establishes the school as a major player in the biotechnology field. Tech's **Bobby Dodd Stadium** is the home of the beloved Georgia Tech Yellow Jackets football team. The school recently opened the Ferst Center for the Arts on campus.

Atlanta University Center

The largest African American academic center in the country can be found at Atlanta University Center, 404/522-8980. Now a six-school consortium enrolling a total of 8,000 students, the institution has roots going back to the late 1860s, when a school for the formerly enslaved was founded here. The historic campuses—which include Clark Atlanta University, the all-male Morehouse College and the Morehouse School of Medicine, the all-female Spelman College (richly endowed early on by the Rockefellers and more recently by a $20 million gift from the Cosby family), Morris Brown College, and the Interdenominational Theological Center—establish Atlanta as a hub for young black intelligentsia.

The schools host many public events, film showings (which may include the work of alumnus Spike Lee), and African American art exhibits.

Emory University

Ranked by college presidents as one of the top 25 universities in the nation, Emory University, 1380 S. Oxford Rd., 404/727-6036, emory.edu, enrolls nearly 10,000 students and occupies a large scenic campus in Druid Hills. Known for its large medical center and for its extensive endowment from the Coca-Cola founders—a $1 million gift in 1915 was enough to turn the college into a full-fledged university—Emory has nine major academic divisions and numerous centers and affiliated institutes. On campus, the Michael C. Carlos Museum (see *Visual Arts,* in the *Sights* section

of this chapter) exhibits archaeological treasures and other artwork. The main gate is off North Decatur Road at Oxford Road.

The **Centers for Disease Control and Prevention** occupy a federal enclave within the Emory Campus and are building a visitors center that focuses on global health; it's due to open in 2005.

Libraries

The central branch of the **Atlanta-Fulton County Library,** 1 Margaret Mitchell Square, 404/730-1700, maintains special collections on Georgia history and a small *Gone with the Wind* exhibit, as well as plenty of local periodicals, community resource boards, and bulletin boards. The modern Auburn Avenue branch houses special African American collections. There's also a cozy midtown branch that's conveniently located along a busy stretch of Peachtree Street, near the Arts Center, as well as a branch near East Atlanta Village.

The **Georgia Department of Archives and History,** 404/521-8764, next to the capitol, houses state records from 1733 to the present. The **Atlanta Historical Society's** archives are housed in its library at the Atlanta History Center. The **Jimmy Carter Library,** at the Carter Center, is open only by appointment for students and scholars.

TOURING THE CITY
Guided Tours

Expert volunteer docents at the nonprofit **Atlanta Preservation Center,** 156 7th St., 404/876-2041, preserveatlanta.com, lead guided walking tours through 10 historic districts—including the Fox Theatre area, downtown, Sweet Auburn, and West End—between March and November. The tours cost $10 for adults and $5 for seniors and students (children under age four are free); call for reservations, or for more information, call their tour hotline, 404/876-2040.

Gray Line, 65 Alabama St., 404/767-0594 or 800/965-6665, offers the widest selection of non–English language bus tours in town and around. Call or find its booth next to the visitors center at Underground Atlanta for more information.

For a list of other private tour companies, call the **Atlanta Convention and Visitors Bureau,** 404/521-6600.

Scenic Drives

To see classic Southern mansions, ride along **Habersham Road,** one of the nicest drives through scenic residential Buckhead. From Peachtree Road in lower Buckhead, turn west onto Battle Avenue, then turn right onto Habersham Road.

Several other city neighborhoods also make particularly pleasant drives or bike rides, among them, Midtown's **Ansley Park** (east of Peachtree Street at 15th, around the western perimeter of Piedmont Park) and **Druid Hills,** where the house featured in the locally shot film *Driving Miss Daisy* is typical (turn left off Ponce de Leon Avenue onto Springdale Road).

Entertainment

Atlanta offers a range of entertainment to suit many tastes and styles, including outstanding classical music and experimental theater, but what it's best known for is its great nightlife, which feature a wide variety of live music in many concert halls that are attractions themselves—including several classic movie palaces, a former Baptist tabernacle, and an 1890 stone mill.

Entertainment Listings

Atlanta's indispensable entertainment guide is *Creative Loafing,* creativeloafing.com, a free weekly tabloid distributed in kiosks and cafés throughout the city. *Rolling Out,* another free weekly tabloid distributed around town, covers the urban music scene. *Southern Voice,* a widely distributed free monthly tabloid, covers news and events of particular interest to Atlanta's gay community.

The daily *Atlanta Journal/Constitution* lists events, with a weekend roundup in Friday's edition and in the Saturday edition's *Weekend* tabloid.

On the Internet, see atlantamusicguide.com for descriptions of and links to local venues and bands.

Discount Tickets and Full-Fare

At Underground Atlanta, **AtlanTix,** 50 Alabama St., 770/772-5572, operates a half-price day-of-performance discount-ticket booth next to the visitors center. There's only walk-up service. It's open Tues. 11 A.M.–3 P.M., Wed.–Sat. 11 A.M.–6 P.M., and Sun. noon–3 P.M.

Tickets to major events are often available through **TicketMaster,** 404/249-6400 or 800/326-4000, ticketmaster.com.

BEST ALL-AROUND VENUES

The city's best venues host a variety of choice acts, from rock stars one night to edgy theater or laid-back comedy the next. They're spread out throughout town, enabling you to stick close to your hotel or explore new neighborhoods to suit your mood. They each have restaurants and bars nearby for a full evening of pre- and postshow festivities without having to get back in the car. Check listings and pick any one; you'll have a fine time.

The Tabernacle

Downtown, the Tabernacle, 152 Luckie St., 404/659-9022, tabernacle.com, occupies the former Luckie Street Church, a monolithic clapboard cathedral a block from Centennial Olympic Park in the Fairlie-Poplar district. During the 1996 Olympics, it was the House of Blues.

The Tabernacle holds 2,500 people in its central sanctuary and hosts such national acts as Big Bad Voodoo Daddy, Burning Spear, Elvis Costello, Al Green, and RuPaul, along with musical happenings, such as the Ethiopian Music Festival. The Cotton Club, a separate venue, is below.

While it may appear isolated, a few sleek restaurants, bars, and the Mark nightclub are within a few blocks, and it's within walking distance or a quick cab ride from more than a dozen of the city's major hotels.

The Roxy heads up the central village of the city's busiest entertainment district, surrounded by plenty of restaurants, bars, and clubs. Anticipate traffic congestion, and arrive early to park. Also, note that "Coca-Cola" is a relatively recent part of its title, and in many listings, it's still just "the Roxy."

Variety Playhouse

In Little Five Points, the Variety Playhouse, 1099 Euclid Ave., 404/521-1786, variety-playhouse.com, is an intimate venue carved out of an old movie theater. It's got some of the best sound and lighting of any club in the city—it has been judged Best Concert Venue by *Creative Loafing* for seven years running—and is a favorite among performers.

The Variety holds 1,500 people for roots rock, indie music, jazz, folk, and even Celtic music, featuring artists from Junior Brown to the Drive-by Truckers. It's at the residential fringe of Little Five Points, with plenty of restaurants, bars, and clubs a block away—a great excuse to get out and explore Atlanta's bohemian neighborhood.

Dad's Garage

In Inman Park, Dad's Garage, 280 Elizabeth St., 404/523-3141, dadsgarage.com, hosts an eclectic selection of bands, comedy, theater, and happenings on the underground or experimental side. *Punk Rock Will Never Die*, a play on the Big Bang theory, and improv were recently on the bill. It's in big metal storage shed at the bottom of a largely residential neighborhood, with a couple of excellent Italian restaurants a half block away. Depending on what's showing, it could make for a great mellow night out without fighting traffic or crowds, as it's a quick cab ride from downtown. It's also a short drive to Little Five Points if you wanted to start or extend your evening there.

Outdoor Venues

On balmy summer nights, Atlantans come out to celebrate the break in the heat, and outdoor venues are another great choice for an evening's entertainment in Atlanta.

North of Buckhead, the 5,800-seat **Chastain Park Amphitheater,** 135 W. Wieuca

© KAP STANN

Fox Theatre

N Fox Theatre

In Midtown, the landmark Fox Theatre, 660 Peachtree St. N.E., 404/881-2100, foxtheatre.org, is a fabulously over-the-top Art Deco palace with an Arabian Nights motif. The Fox hosts a wide variety of performing arts, from the Atlanta Ballet and Broadway musicals to film festivals and bands like Wilco, the Pixies, and Jane's Addiction. It's also a great place to see a movie. Several restaurants are nearby, and it's easily accessible from the North Avenue MARTA station.

Coca-Cola Roxy Theatre

In Buckhead, the Roxy, 3110 Roswell Rd., 404/233-7699, is an old movie palace that's been turned into a popular concert hall, where nationally known artists playing rock 'n' roll, alternative, jazz, and R&B are featured. It holds 1,000 people on its sloping floor with good sightlines.

Atlanta

ATLANTA FESTIVALS AND EVENTS

Some of the South's most entertaining spectacles can be experienced through local festivals, which are usually multifaceted affairs with plenty of local music, arts and crafts, parades, and local food and drink that bring out local character and community spirit. Spring and fall weekends are particularly packed with events.

January

Martin Luther King Jr. Celebration, the second week of the month, features 10 days of cultural arts, entertainment, and action centering around the national holiday named for Martin Luther King Jr.'s birthday, on January 15. Speeches and interfaith services by Coretta Scott King and local religious leaders kick off the event.

February

The **Atlanta Storytelling Festival,** at the Atlanta History Center, brings folk tales, myths, and legends from around the world to life in this multicultural event, which also features jugglers, balladeers, and an evening concert.

The **Atlanta Flower Show,** a four-day event in February or March, previews the Southeast's spectacular spring blooming season through displayed gardens, landscapes, and an elegant opening gala benefiting the Atlanta Botanical Garden; call 404/220-2209.

March

The **St. Patrick's Day Parade,** with century-old roots reaching back to early Irish Catholic settlers, courses down Peachtree Street to Underground Atlanta with the usual revelry of bagpipes, politicians in convertibles, floats, and high school bands; spectators number 150,000.

April

The **Atlanta Dogwood Festival,** a weeklong rite of spring, brings art and music to various city venues before culminating in weekend festivities at Piedmont Park. The midmonth event features art shows, local bands, food booths, house tours, children's activities, hot-air balloons, and more.

Music Midtown Festival brings jazz, folk, rock, R&B, hip-hop, and more to the lively Midtown district.

May

The **Atlanta Jazz Festival,** reportedly the largest free jazz festival in the country, features a week of outdoor concerts around town, including Chastain, Piedmont, and Woodruff Parks.

Springfest, at Stone Mountain Park, where barbecue chefs compete in a massive "grill-off," celebrates the season in early May with live entertainment, arts and crafts, and plenty of pork.

June

Sweet Auburn Heritage Festival celebrates the revival of this African American historical neighborhood with heritage tours, parades, ethnic foods, lively jazz, rhythm and blues, and gospel music.

Rd., hosts a summer series featuring a range of performing arts, from the Atlanta Symphony Orchestra to a B.B. King Music Festival. It's at the northwest corner of Chastain Memorial Park, within a residential district less than two miles from Buckhead's top hotel and restaurant zone.

South of downtown, **HiFi Buys Amphitheatre,** off the Langford Freeway exit of I-75/85, has reserved seating for 7,000 and lawn space for 12,000 more; it hosts some of the biggest acts in town, the likes of the Lillith Fair or an All-Star Rap show, with headliners 50 Cent and Jay-Z.

LIVE MUSIC

Atlanta not only attracts national musical acts, it *creates* many of them. In recent years the city's recording studios have catapulted local artists to the national stage. Jermaine Dupri of So So Def and Southside Records (actually located on the north side) has produced the work of TLC, Kris Kross, and Usher, as well as his own hit *Welcome to Atlanta.* Then there's Outkast, Ludacris, and Jagged Edge. Amy Ray of the Indigo Girls has launched her own studio, Daemon Records.

The **Georgia Shakespeare Festival,** at Oglethorpe University, stages three different Shakespearean classics under a giant open-air tent (June to August).

The three-day **Pride Parade and Festival,** timed to coincide with the anniversary of the Stonewall riots, draws tens of thousands of participants for a parade, music, and festivities at Piedmont Park.

Athfest, in Athens, draws many city folk an hour east to hear more than 100 bands perform at the annual celebration of Athens' alternative music scene.

July
On **July 4th,** 50,000 runners race down Peachtree Street from Lenox Square to Piedmont Park in the annual 10K **Peachtree Road Race;** a **parade** through downtown is reportedly the largest regularly scheduled Fourth of July parade in the country, with 250,000 spectators; fireworks explode above Lenox Square, Centennial Olympic Park (with Atlanta Symphony accompaniment), and over Stone Mountain (with a laser light show).

The **National Black Arts Festival,** the country's premier African American cultural arts program, showcases dance, theater, various types of music (sacred steel drums, Mississippi blues, and gospel, to name a few), folklore, visual arts, and Afrocentric heritage programs in various venues for 10 days.

August
The **BBQ, Blues, and Bluegrass Festival** is held at the historic depot at the tracks in Decatur, east of Atlanta.

September
The **Atlanta Montreaux Music Festival** brings a weekend of free hip-hop, R&B, soul, gospel, rock, and blues performances to Piedmont Park in August or September.

October
Little Five Points **Halloween Parade and Festival** takes place in Atlanta's bohemian neighborhood.

November
The **Veterans Day Parade** on November 11 or thereabouts runs south along the downtown strip of Peachtree.

The **Lighting of the Holiday Tree** takes place at Lenox Square, as well as at Underground Atlanta.

December
Christmas at Callanwolde transforms the Gothic Tudor mansion to a yuletide fantasyland for the first two weeks of the month, accompanied by choral groups, bell ringers, and storytellers.

The **Candlelight Tour of Historic Homes,** at the Atlanta History Center, displays period decorations at the Swan House and a country Christmas at the Tullie Smith Farm in early December.

New Year's Eve at Underground Atlanta brings thousands of revelers out to watch the "giant peach" drop at midnight.

Live music can be found seven nights a week. Atlanta's music scene includes many trendy hotspots that come and go; the following selection emphasizes well-established clubs likely to still be around when you read this.

Another great way to sample the city's music mix is at a local festival. **Music Midtown Festival,** in April, and July's **Black Arts Festival,** nbaf.org, are two of the best, along with Athfest, athfest.org, in Athens in June.

Blues Joints
In Virginia Highland, **Blind Willie's,** 848 N. Highland Ave., 404/873-BLUE (404/873-2583), Atlanta's most venerable blues club, heads up the neighborhood's entertainment district. Even weekday nights, a wonderfully mixed crowd—from bikers and barflies to students and suburbanites—pack the club to hear rocking Chicago-style blues. On weekends the congestion and parking are tough.

West of Midtown, **Northside Tavern,** 1058 Howell Mill Rd., 404/874-8745, northsidetavern.com, is a classic roadhouse in an abandoned industrial zone. It packs people shoulder-to-shoulder to hear folk blues. It's about a mile and a half west of Midtown; take 10th Street west to Howell Mill Road and turn right.

Out toward Grant Park, **Daddy D'z,** 264 Memorial Dr., 404/222-0206, is a favorite barbecue joint where hipsters mingle with hardcore regulars for live blues out on the patio on weekend nights. Parking is easy, and it's a quick cab ride from downtown.

In a remote corner of Buckhead, **Fat Matt's Rib Shack,** 1811 Piedmont Rd. N.E., 404/607-1622, features crowd-pleasing blues, roots music, and finger-lickin' barbecue in a converted doughnut shop. Parking is easy.

Rock and Rockabilly

Downtown and below the Hard Rock Cafe, the **Velvet Underground,** 215 Peachtree St., 404/688-7625, deserves recognition if only for its decor—a shrine to Southern music and artists from throughout the Southeast, with photos and memorabilia.

In Midtown, **Masquerade,** 695 North Ave. N.E., 404/577-2007, masq.com, Atlanta's biggest dance club, hosts hardcore, head-banging rock the likes of Twiztid, Sevendust, and Lamb of God in its three-story club (the stories are named Heaven, Hell, and Purgatory). The place was carved from an 1890 mill that retains its old stone walls and rusty industrial equipment. Special DJ'd nights have featured '80s retro, techno, Sunday swing, and Dance-in-Foam Night ($2 off with scuba gear). It's popular with Georgia Tech students. Parking is easy.

In Little Five Points, **Star Community Bar,** 437 Moreland Ave., 404/681-9018, features roots rock and rockabilly the likes of Eugene Swank and the Atomic Honky Tonk, and Slim Chance and the Convicts, in a down-home bar with an Elvis shrine (watch for special tributes around the King's birthday in January and his deathday in August). It's in the busy L5P entertainment district; the parking lot behind fills quickly on weekends.

In East Atlanta, **Echo Lounge,** 551 Flat Shoals Ave., 404/681-3600, echostatic.com, features a great mix of indie rock and local acts and events

in a 500-person venue, including a recent El Vez for Prez show and a Daemon Records showcase from the roster of Indigo Girl Amy Ray's recording studio. It's a great excuse to visit this funky neighborhood.

Hip-Hop and R&B

In Midtown, **Velvet Room,** 1021 Peachtree St., 404/876-6275, is a palacial nightclub covered with red velvet with live and DJ'd hip-hop and urban music for serious drinking and dancing. It's in a very popular strip with several clubs; parking can be tough.

Nearby in Midtown, the **Apache Club,** 64 3rd St. N.W., 404/876-5436, apachecafe.info, was where India.Arie and Erykah Badu got their start. They feature MC battles on Tuesdays; Sunday is open mic night. Parking's OK.

Folk and Bluegrass

The heart of the folk scene is several miles east, in the city of Decatur. A couple of clubs and surrounding bars and cafés attract a low-key suburban crowd along with students from Agnes Scott College, an all-women's school with a thriving lesbian community. Decatur is a 10-minute MARTA ride from downtown; the station is right at the central town square. Parking is generally no problem.

Right on the square, **Eddie's Attic,** 515 N. McDonough St., 404/377-4976, serves as metro Atlanta's acoustic central, featuring local and regional artists in its spacious 2nd-story club.

The **Freight Room,** on East Trinity Place at the tracks, 404/378-5365, colorfully occupies an old railroad depot, an ideal venue for such local bluegrass favorites as Undergrass Blueground. The BBQ, Blues, and Bluegrass Festival is held here in August. It's about a half-mile south of the square.

Dance Clubs

In Midtown, **Vision,** 1068 Peachtree St., 404/876-6275, visionatlanta.com, is a glamorous nightclub with room for 1,000 (one of the city's largest) members of the see-and-be-seen celebrity-sighting crowd. Dress is high-fashion designer label only.

In Midtown, **Backstreet Atlanta,** 845 Peachtree St., 404/873-1986, backstreetatlanta.com, is Atlanta's most popular gay dance club. DJs and disco music draw lively mixed party crowds. Charlie Brown's Cabaret drag shows are featured Thurs.–Sun.

In Buckhead, **Havana Club,** 247 Buckhead Ave., 404/869-8484, features lively salsa music in a 2nd-story club above the village's frat-boy fray. It draws a demonstrably authentic Latin crowd on weekends but is welcoming for all comers, including beginners. Dress is casual; it's all about the dancing. Lessons are given Thurs. night at 9:30 P.M. Enter on Pharr Road.

BARS AND NIGHTCLUBS

Atlanta has hundreds of bars satisfying every possible niche; the following small selection highlights established taverns that anchor their neighborhoods, along with a few of the newer nightspots that have shot up around town in the last few years.

Downtown

In Fairlie-Poplar, **Sidebar,** 79 Poplar St., 404/588-1850, sidebaratlanta.com, fashions itself a neighborhood bar, but considering how relatively recently this area became a neighborhood, it's a trendy spot with a long black bar, satellite radio, and six flat-screen TVs—a sports bar for the loft set.

Underneath Sidebar, **The Mark,** 79 Poplar St., 678/904-0050, themarkatlanta.com, is a cool ultramodern basement lounge with a slick '60s design, including pod chairs, tiny TV monitors, and a waterfall wall (with great make-out corners at each side). There's valet parking.

Midtown

Blake's, 227 10th St. N.E., 404/892-5786, across from Piedmont Park, heads up the neighborhood at the heart of Atlanta's gay community.

Eleven50, 1150 Peachtree St., 404/874-0428, eleven50.com, is a swank, stylized club with the appearance of a boutique hotel—sleek couches and a great outdoor space with pools, fountains, and private cabana-like booths, as well as dancing to DJ music.

Virginia Highland

Moe and Joe's, 1033 N. Highland Ave., 404/873-6090, is a friendly sports bar for the Pabst Blue Ribbon crowd in the center of the village. Further south in the busy strip around Blind Willie's, **Atkins Park,** 794 N. Highland Ave., 404/876-7249, established in 1927; it attracts largely a clean college crowd and has a nice alleyway patio. **Manuel's Tavern,** 602 N. Highland Ave., 404/525-3447, is a politico's hangout and a staunchly Democrat stronghold that occupies a big well-worn wood-paneled cabin at the southern fringe of Virginia Highland (the *New York Times* has named Manuel's one of its 10 Favorite Places in the World).

Little Five Points

Euclid Avenue Yacht Club, 1136 Euclid Ave., 404/688-2582, is a friendly spot that predates the neighborhood's tattooed days; all are welcome. Down the street, **The Five Spot,** 1123 Euclid Ave., 404/223-1100, hosts a mix of events including poetry, jam sessions, short films, and Reggae Sundaze.

PERFORMING ARTS
The Woodruff Arts Center

In Midtown, the Woodruff Arts Center, 1280 Peachtree St., 404/733-4200, woodruffcenter.org, is the city's premier cultural arts institution. It was established to honor a hundred members of Atlanta's arts community who were killed in a plane crash en route to Paris in the 1960s. The center encompasses the Atlanta Symphony Orchestra, the Alliance Theater, and the 14th Street Playhouse, the Atlanta College of Art, and the High Museum. The center is easily accessible from the MARTA Arts Center station.

Atlanta Symphony Orchestra

The Grammy award–winning Atlanta Symphony Orchestra, 404/733-5000, atlantasymphony.org, led by music director Robert Spano, performs in the Woodruff Center Symphony

Hall during its master season. It also holds a popular summertime concert series outdoors at Chastain Amphitheater.

Atlanta Opera

The Atlanta Opera, 404/881-8801, atlanta-opera.org, presents 12 performances a year at the newly renovated, 4,600-seat **Civic Center Auditorium,** 395 Piedmont Ave., 404/523-6275.

Atlanta Ballet

The 60-year-old Atlanta Ballet 404/892-3303, atlantaballet.com, which they say is the nation's oldest continuously performing regional ballet company, operates from studios on Spring Street near the arts center. They perform at the Fox Theatre and at the Ferst Center for the Arts at Georgia Tech; their season runs from October through April.

Theater

Part of the Woodruff Arts Center, the **Alliance Theater Company,** 404/733-5000, offers pre-Broadway previews and regional premieres of New York hits the likes of Top Dog/Underdog, as well as Southern plays, such as a new adaptation of *The Color Purple* and Carson McCullers's *The Heart Is a Lonely Hunter.* They also sponsor a children's theater. The Woodruff also operates the **14th Street Playhouse.**

Also in Midtown, theatrical productions that are smaller scale, experimental, political, original, and local can be found at the three-stage **Academy Theater,** 501 Means St., 404/525-4111. In West Midtown, **Actors Express,** 887 W. Marietta St. N.W., 404/875-1606, actorsexpress.com, among the most avant-garde companies, performs in the cool King Plow Arts Center.

In Little Five Points, **Seven Stages Theater,** 1105 Euclid Ave., 404/522-0911, has maintained a reputation as one the most innovative theaters in town for more than 25 years. They premiere several plays each season, including political and international works, such as the recent *Maria Kizito,* about the Rwanda massacre.

In Midtown, the Center for Puppetry Arts, (see *Kids' Favorites,* earlier in this chapter) entertains adults as well as children (not all shows are

G-rated) with well-produced performances in its intimate theater.

CINEMA

Georgia State University's **Cinefest Theater,** in University Center, 66 Courtland St., 404/651-2463, screens art films and old classics. The film series at the **High Museum** (see *Sights*) shows more unusual selections, often scheduled to coincide with exhibits or lectures by directors. Easily accessible multiscreen cinemas include the sixplexes at **CNN Center,** 404/827-4000, and **Lenox Square,** 404/233-0338. The Atlanta Film and Video Festival, 404/872-3492, is held in June at various venues around town.

Starlight Drive-In

Open since 1949, the landmark Starlight Drive-In, 2000 Moreland Ave. S.E., 404/627-5786, starlightdrivein.com, shows drive-in movies seven nights a week, 364 days a year. You need a car radio to hear the movie. Admission is $6 per person, and only cash is accepted. They have a flea market on Sundays.

SHOPPING

Atlanta is the Hong Kong of the Southeastern U.S.—where people come to shop at exclusive department stores found nowhere else in the region. According to the local tourist bureau, Atlanta has more shopping-center space per capita than any other city besides Chicago. But metro Atlanta's malls are more than shopping emporiums: as clean, secure, climate-controlled environments, they have nearly replaced town centers, and nowadays people meet at the mall to stroll (walking clubs meet in early mornings), eat, and see films and performances, as well as shop.

What follows is a summary of the larger centers; see *Districts and Neighborhoods,* earlier in this chapter, for boutiques and funkier shopping districts.

Major Shopping Centers

Downtown, **Underground Atlanta** offers some local craft stalls but mostly national brand-name stores (such as Victoria's Secret and Walden-

Books) within a historical setting. More ambitious shoppers go a few blocks further north up Peachtree Street to a retail strip headed up by a **Rich-Macy's** department store, at Ellis Street.

Buckhead is the most exclusive shopping district, with everything from unusual boutiques and galleries in its village to huge malls at its

© KAP STANN

The Pink Pig, the holiday toy train ride

perimeter. **Lenox Square** is anchored by Rich-Macy's, Bloomingdale's, and Neiman-Marcus, and has boutiques such as Kate Spade. There are also cinemas and restaurants (including a French brasserie), a MARTA station, and valet parking. Last year Rich-Macy's reintroduced its popular Priscilla the Pink Pig minitrain ride at Christmas. Across Peachtree Road from Lenox, the elite **Phipps Plaza** has the Saks Fifth Avenue department store and designer shops, including Gianni Versace, Gucci, and A/X Armani Exchange, as well as cinemas.

Bookstores

In Buckhead, national chain bookstores include **Barnes & Noble,** 2900 Peachtree Rd., 404/261-7747, and **Borders Books and Music,** 3637 Peachtree Rd. N.E., 404/237-0707.

In Midtown, **Outwrite Bookstore,** 991 Piedmont Ave., 404/607-0082, declares itself Atlanta's Gay and Lesbian Bookstore and Coffeehouse.

In Little Five Points, **A Capella Books,** 1133 Euclid Ave. N.E., 404/681-5128, offers a great selection of inexpensive used books (particularly pertaining to counterculture), as well as rare editions. **Charis Books and More,** 1189 Euclid Ave. N.E., 404/524-0304, is Atlanta's feminist bookstore and also serves as a local resource for women; the store has a thoughtful children's book selection too.

Sports and Recreation

URBAN RECREATION

Favorite Parks
Centennial Olympic Park, 285 International Blvd., in the heart of downtown, offers a romp through the sprinklers, climbable boulders, shady benches, a playground, and a café and visitors center within 21 acres. Many concerts and special events are held at its amphitheater and Great Lawn, and there is often impromptu street music in its plazas.

Midtown's **Piedmont Park,** with its dogwood-rimmed lake, rolling lawns, shady coves, and

wooded walkways and paths, is a great place to run, bike, or skate; it also has a swimming pool, tennis courts, playgrounds, and ball fields. Rent skates or bikes (cruisers or 10-speeds) across from the main gate at **Skate Escape,** 1086 Piedmont Ave. N.E., 404/892-1292.

The 60-acre **Atlanta Botanical Garden,** adjacent to Piedmont Park (see *Sights*) offers 15 more acres of nature walks through fragrant gardens and surrounding woods.

Grant Park holds two of Atlanta's most popular attractions, the Cyclorama, exhibited here since 1885, and Zoo Atlanta (see *Sights*), as well

© CALVIN BURGAMY

an arts festival at Piedmont Park

N.E., 404/875-7284. Or ask at local bike shops, such as **Skate Escape,** 1086 Piedmont Ave. N.E., 404/892-1292.

Running and Walking

The monolithic **Peachtree Road Race**—considered "the Wimbledon of 10K"—inspires more than 55,000 runners to brave the summer heat every July 4th to run the course up Peachtree Street. It's sponsored by the Atlanta Track Club. If you'd rather just watch, cheering spectators congregate principally at lower Buckhead's streetside patio restaurants—many of which set up elaborate pit stops for the athletes. The race ends up at Piedmont Park, where runners are cooled in huge sprays of water. Souvenir T-shirts for the runners are prized items. Plenty of other 5K and 10K races are held throughout the year; check local papers.

Joggers favor Piedmont Park, and, perhaps strangely, the cobblestone lanes of historic Oakland Cemetery, off Memorial Drive (see *Sights*).

Hiking

For short in-city hikes, head to the 65-acre **Fernbank Forest,** adjacent to the Fernbank Science Center, near Druid Hills out east toward Decatur. Two miles of paved trails through thick tulip trees, oaks, beeches, and hickory are representative of the local terrain, flora, and fauna. Gates are generally open afternoons and all day Saturday.

Among other choices, Midtown's 15-acre forest at the Atlanta Botanical Garden, in Piedmont Park, makes for a nice stroll; so does Piedmont Park itself. Also, a 1.5-mile trail connects the Martin Luther King Jr. National Historic District with the Carter Library.

Surprising perhaps to cool-climate folks, a popular activity in summer is mall-walking, which enables residents to get their exercise within such climate-controlled environments as Lenox Square, either individually or in organized groups, and usually when the doors open.

For wonderful hiking trails right outside town, see Chattahoochee National Recreation Area and Sweetwater Creek State Park, in the *Vicinity of Atlanta* section.

as the old Confederate battery site of **Fort Walker.** The rest of the wooded, shaded acreage is devoted to lawns, recreation, and picnic areas.

The *Vicinity of Atlanta* section offers more information on recreational parks beyond the beltway, including the major recreational center at **Stone Mountain Park,** 17 miles east of downtown, as well as less-developed areas in the Chattahoochee River Recreation Area, north of downtown, and at Sweetwater Creek State Park, west of town.

Bicycling

A 15-mile city loop bicycle route east of downtown runs north from Irwin Street along Jackson, through Piedmont Park and Virginia Highland. Midtown's Piedmont Park has miles of paved bike paths, and the wide streets of the adjacent Ansley Park neighborhood are ideal for bicycling. A bike path runs along the length of Freedom Parkway to eastside neighborhoods.

Request bike-route information from the **Southern Bicycle League,** P.O. Box 870387, Stone Mountain, GA 30087, 770/594-8350, or the **Path Foundation,** 1601 W. Peachtree St.

Swimming

The indoor **Martin Luther King Jr.** Natatorium, next to the King Center, 70 Boulevard, 404/658-7330, is open to the public year-round; admission is $3 for adults and $1 for children. Seasonal outdoor pools are available at Piedmont Park, 404/892-0117, and Chastain Park, 404/255-0863. Pools are at most hotels and motels (they're almost a necessity in summer), except for some historic hotels, hostels, and bed and breakfasts.

Golf

In Atlanta Memorial Park, the city's public **Bobby Jones Golf Club,** 384 Woodward Way, 404/355-1009, t-off-now.com, is named for the native Atlantan who rose to golf greatness and is buried in Oakland Cemetery, downtown. The 18-hole championship course occupies part of the site of the Battle of Peachtree Creek. You'll find many more deluxe courses in the northern suburbs, such as the **City Club,** in Marietta, 510 Powder Springs St., 770/749-5611, or out at **Stone Mountain Golf Club,** 770/498-5715. Free putting practice is offered downtown inside the **Healey Building,** 57 Forsyth St., 404/521-1451.

Recreational Resources

Outdoor-adventure groups, environmental-advocacy organizations, commercial outfitters, and outfitting stores are all great resources for finding out about area recreation. The **Sierra Club,** 1447 Peachtree St. N.E., Ste. 305, Atlanta, GA 30309, 404/607-1262, sponsors a busy calendar of day and overnight adventures in addition to its legislative activism and environmental advocacy. Outings—often in North Georgia—include hiking, backpacking, rafting, fossil hunts, you name it. The preeminent statewide conservation organization, the **Georgia Conservancy,** 1776 Peachtree St. N.W., Ste. 400 S., Atlanta, GA 30309, 404/876-2900, produces detailed reference works on Georgia's natural areas and sponsors field trips.

REI, 1800 N.E. Expressway Access Rd., 404/633-6508, stocks the largest selection of outfitting gear in the city, rents camping equipment, and maintains a posting board of local events. Take I-85 exit 32, northeast of downtown.

PROFESSIONAL SPORTS

Tickets to major sporting events are available through **TicketMaster,** 404/249-6400 or 800/326-4000 outside Georgia, ticketmaster.com; local TicketMaster ticket centers include Blockbuster Music, Publix supermarkets, and Tower Records.

Atlanta Braves Baseball

The Braves are as much of a local legend as Scarlett O'Hara. Owned by CNN's Ted Turner, the Braves baseball team rose from obscurity to World Series champions in 1995. T-shirts proclaiming the banner headline "From Worst to First" are still proudly worn by loyal fans.

The Braves play at **Turner Field,** 755 Hank Aaron Dr., 404/522-7630, atlanta.braves.mlb.com, the state-of-the-art Olympic stadium with seating for 50,000. The stadium is off Capital Avenue, three-quarters of a mile south of the capitol.

Inside, the **Ivan Allen Jr. Braves Museum,** 404/614-2311, dedicates 4,000-square feet of the complex to a Hall of Fame and a collection of baseball memorabilia, including the ball and bat from Hank Aaron's 715th home run. Admission is $8 adults, $4 children. Hours are generally Mon.–Sat. 9 A.M.–3 P.M., Sun. 1–4 P.M. (it closes during home games).

Bus shuttles run between the Five Points MARTA station (Forsyth Street exit) and Turner Field for all stadium events, from 90 minutes before game time until the stadium is empty. It's free with a MARTA transfer or $1.50 each way without.

Atlanta Falcons Football

Atlanta's professional football team plays in the **Georgia Dome,** 404/249-6400, atlantafalcons.com. The massive 71,500-seat stadium is as tall as a 27-story building and covers 8.6 acres. The team's quarterback, Michael Vick, is one of the most talented and exciting players in the game.

Two MARTA rail stations, Omni and Vine City, serve both ends of the Georgia Dome (buy tokens in advance to avoid long lines). MARTA shuttles are available to outlying parking lots.

Atlanta Hawks Basketball

The NBA's **Atlanta Hawks,** 404/827-3800 roost in Philips Arena next to CNN Center.

Atlanta Thrashers Hockey

The NHL's **Atlanta Thrashers,** 404/249-6400, atlantathrashers.com, play hockey at the Philips Arena.

COLLEGE SPORTS

In the Atlanta area, and in most of the South, college football is king, and attendance and en-thusiasm at these games is often higher than for pro games. For 75 years, the 46,000-seat **Bobby Dodd Stadium,** at North Ave. and Techwood Dr., 404/894-5447, has been home to Georgia Tech's **Yellow Jackets** football team. Many football fans drive an hour east to Athens to watch the statewide mascots, the **Georgia Bulldogs,** play at the University of Georgia. The biggest competition in the state is when these two teams face off.

The Georgia and Georgia Tech basketball teams compete, respectively, in the SEC and ACC, two of the most competitive and talented college basketball conferences in the country.

Accommodations

As a big convention town, Atlanta is also a big hotel town: There were more than 740 properties and 92,000 rooms at last count. Every national hotel chain is represented at least once; many are represented several times in deluxe and budget versions. Most are modern high-rise hotels; only a handful of small inns offer an alternative or a historic ambience. Atlanta opened its first boutique hotel in 2004. A Midtown hostel serves low-budget travelers.

The main hotel district downtown, Midtown hotels, and Buckhead hotels are accessible to MARTA light-rail, which connects directly to the airport. The selections below emphasize centrally located properties in walkable areas near sights, restaurants, and MARTA. Major hotels offer shuttles to the airport or to the local MARTA station (or both).

DOWNTOWN

Atlanta's primary hotel zone is around Peachtree Center, within walking distance of major convention and event facilities at the World Congress Center and the Americasmart complex. More than a dozen major hotels sit in a compact area about 10 blocks square between Centennial Olympic Park and the interstate, from around Ellis Street north to around Baker Street

Prices are relative to availability: The rack rate can double when fully booked conventions are in town, or they can be sliced in half on a summer weekend. Use the prices in this section as a rough guide only, and book early to get the choicest locations. On the flip side, you can't go too far wrong within this district; all properties are well maintained, and a last-minute room may just mean a longer walk. Only individual websites are included in this section; see chain websites for all others.

Pools and parking are make-or-break issues: you could really use a pool in summer, and the cost of overnight parking and valet tips add up quickly. You don't need a car for a short stay, and there's an Enterprise rental place in the zone if you decide you want one.

The short list: stay at the Ritz-Carlton if your company's paying, though the Wyndham is livelier; the Hyatt Regency is most centrally located. The radical choice: stay at the Georgian Terrace in Midtown and take MARTA or a cab downtown.

Under $100

AmeriSuites, 330 Peachtree St. N.E., 404/577-1980 or 800/362-1980, a newer low-end hotel, is a bit of a misnomer: the "suite" we were shown is one large room with a kitchenette with two barstools, a couch, and a desk area within, all overlooking the bed. There are nice common areas but no pool; rates start at $69. It's two blocks to MARTA.

Best Western Inn at the Peachtrees, 330 W. Peachtree St., 404/577-6970 or 800/242-4642, overhauled to appear more modern than its 40-plus years, has rooms and exterior corridors overlooking a central courtyard with patio tables, fountain, and mature shade trees. Afternoons, they'll serve complimentary cocktails out here—pretty civilized for motel living. There's no pool. Rates start at $79 and include a hot breakfast; parking is extra. It's two blocks to MARTA.

Hampton Inn, 161 Spring St., 404/589-1111 or 800-HAMPTON (800/426-7866), an appealing peach-brick, eight-story hotel that was recently reconstructed from a former office building, has airy and spacious common areas, standard rooms, and no pool (rates start at $89 and include continental breakfast). The Wyndham, Ritz-Carlton, and Rich-Macy's are neighbors; it's a couple of blocks to the park and MARTA.

Days Inn Downtown, 300 Spring St.; 404/523-1144 or 800/325-2525, an older, 10-story hotel, is very standard, but north-facing rooms have a view of the Midtown skyline and tiny balconies too (rates starts $90). A 24-hour coffee shop is downstairs. The children's museum and park are a block away.

Atlanta Downtown TraveLodge, 311 Courtland St. N.E., 404/659-4545 or 800/578-7878, an older three-story motel with interior corridors and a pool, is on the fringe of the district. It has recently renovated rooms; rates start at $90 and include a continental breakfast and free parking. It's adjacent to the freeway, which means easy driving access, but noise may travel. Enterprise car rental is next door.

Howard Johnson Plaza Suites, 54 Peachtree St., 404/223-5555 or 877/477-5549, occupies an appealing old building directly above Underground Atlanta, across the street from the Five Points MARTA transfer station. The renovated small suites are spruced up with new linens, with perhaps new carpets on the way (rates start at $99); the front overlooks the plaza, but the back is quieter. It's out of the convention-hotel zone, which is a plus or minus depending on your viewpoint.

(Note that budget travelers in smaller motels can get to their room and car without waiting for elevators or valets—a bonus for the impatient.)

$100–150

Hyatt Regency Hotel, 265 Peachtree St. N.E., 404/577-1234 or 800/233-1234, the first to introduce the cavernous towering atrium concept that revolutionized luxury hotel design in the 1970s, remains the granddaddy today. The 1,224-room Hyatt anchors Peachtree Center with all the standard megahotel amenities—pool, fitness center, and restaurants (theirs revolves; they also have a 24-hour café). Rooms have been recently renovated (rates start at $114). Similar hotels nearby include the **Hilton, Marriott, Sheraton,** and **Westin Peachtree** (at 72 stories, the tallest hotel in the U.S.; an outside elevator to the restaurant at the top is another distinguishing feature).

Wyndham, 160 Spring St., 404/688-8600 or 800/WYNDHAM (800/996-3426), a great new addition downtown, has an inviting, spacious lobby, as well as a lively Latin tapas restaurant, high-quality decor with marble and warm woods, well-appointed rooms, a pool, and a friendly ambience that's welcoming to business and leisure travelers alike. You wouldn't think they could make so much of a location behind the Macy's parking lot. Rates start at $149 midweek and drop to $79 on weekends.

Embassy Suites Hotel, 267 Marietta St., 404/223-2300 or 800/EMBASSY (800/362-2779), was newly constructed adjacent to Centennial Olympic Park as the park was developed for the 1996 Olympics. The hotel is across from the World Congress Center, the Omni, and CNN, and it is due to come into its own as major attractions are completed next door in the next few years. Rates start at $115.

Over $150

In 2003, **Omni Hotel,** 100 CNN Ctr., 404/659-0000 or 800/843-6664, omnicnn.com, adjacent to CNN Center and across from Centennial Olympic Park and the World Congress Center, added a new 28-story tower in addition to the original 15-story hotel, making for a total of 1,067 deluxe rooms (rates start at $160). It's a block or two from the Philips Arena and Georgia Dome.

The 27-story **Ritz-Carlton Atlanta,** 131 Peachtree St. N.E., 404/659-0400 or 800/241-3333, is one of Atlanta's premier hotels, offering high-style luxurious amenities, impeccable service, and deluxe dining—but no pool (access to Peachtree Center Athletic Club facilities is available for $20 a day). Feather beds and goose-down pillows are standard features, along with an accommodating concierge and business services (rates start at $195). The Ritz straddles the boundary between the downtown business district to the south and the convention district to the north.

MIDTOWN

With its shady lanes and parks, neighborly restaurants, clubs, and shops, and easy access by car or by transit through three MARTA stations, Midtown is a great place to stay when visiting Atlanta. The district also offers some of the city's most outstanding and unique accommodations.

Hostel

Hostels of America's Atlanta, 229 Ponce de Leon Ave., 404/875-9449, hostel-atlanta.com, occupies a sagging but comfortable three-story Victorian house in a great location convenient to the Fox Theatre, several restaurants, clubs, and the North Ave. MARTA station. It is open only to travelers carrying a foreign passport or valid student I.D. They offer 75 dormitory beds (rates start at $17) and private rooms (starting at $43); reservations are advised. It closes noon–5 P.M.

$100–150

N Hotel Indigo, 683 Peachtree St. N.E., 404/874-9200 or 800/873-4245, which opened in late 2004 as Atlanta's first boutique hotel (an InterContinental brand), occupies a wonderful location within a historic facade across from the Fox Theatre. The crisp look and feel of white-washed Adirondack chairs, bold prints, over-stuffed linens, and spa showers are designed to attract the hot-spot set. There is no pool. Opening prices are around $100; parking costs extra.

The **Ansley Inn,** 253 15th St., 404/872-9000, ansleyinn.com, set in a 1907 Tudor house surrounded by landscaped lawns on a quiet side street near the Atlanta Botanical Garden, offers 22 rooms that would appeal to business or leisure

travelers (rates start at $100). They also rent a two-bedroom cottage down a gravel path. There is no pool.

Shellmont, 821 Piedmont Ave. N.E., 404/872-9290, shellmont.com, offers bed-and-breakfast lodging in eight antique-furnished rooms in an 1891 house on a main street several blocks from the commercial center of Midtown (rates start at $115). There is no pool.

N Georgian Terrace, 659 Peachtree St. N.E., 404/897-1991 or 888/285-3887, thegeorgianterrace.com, presiding regally at the gates to Midtown at the corner of Peachtree and Ponce de Leon, offers 318 rooms and suites in a glamorously restored 1911 landmark (rates start at $139). Some units have kitchens from its condo incarnation; there's also a small pool. To hear tell, Margaret Mitchell handed her manuscript to a literary scout downstairs in 1934; five years later, the premiere reception for *Gone with the Wind* was held in the hotel's grand ballroom. It's across from the Fox Theatre.

Over $200

Four Seasons Hotel, 75 14th St., 404/881-9898, one of the city's highest-ranked hotels (AAA five diamond, Mobil five star), offers a grand lobby, fine service, and 244 lushly appointed rooms and suites—even marble tubs with a view (rates start at $240; parking costs extra). The 19-story hotel also features a lap pool, sauna, and steam bath, as well as the acclaimed Park 75 restaurant. (The Four Seasons has also earned a top Four Paw rating for pet-friendly accommodations; dog walking is available for $15.) The city's Restaurant Row is around the corner. The Arts Center is two long blocks away; the 14th Street Playhouse is down the block.

BUCKHEAD

Atlanta's luxury hotel, restaurant, and shopping district, Buckhead is home to two flagship properties of the world's foremost hotels, Ritz-Carlton and InterContinental. The Grand Hyatt is another premium hotel in the district, and a W Hotel is on its way.

Under $100
Cheshire Motor Inn, 1865 Cheshire Bridge Rd. N.E., 404/872-9628 or 800/827-9628, is a bottom-end option at the southeastern fringe of what might be considered Buckhead. The 1950s road motel is 1.3 miles south of I-85 in a neglected stretch of strip bars and thrift shores. Doubles start at $65 in the older nine-unit building with tiny rooms; the more modern annexes run higher (there's no pool). It's adjacent to the Colonnade Restaurant, a local institution for Southern food.

$100–150
Beverly Hills Inn, 65 Sheridan Dr. N.E., 404/233-8520 or 800/331-8520, carved from a three-story apartment building built in the 1920s, offers 18 rooms with period furnishings in a quiet residential area a few minutes' drive from Buckhead village and attractions (rates start at $110; there is no pool).

$150–200
Grand Hyatt Atlanta, 3300 Peachtree Rd. N.E., 404/365-8100 or 800/233-1234, consisting of twin towers standing on an island of 40 acres of manicured lawns in the busiest part of Buckhead, features 25 stories of art and antiques, all corporate amenities, and a restaurant overlooking Japanese gardens (rooms start at $150).

InterContinental Hotel, 3315 Peachtree Rd. N.E., 770/604-5083 or 888/303-1758, with worldwide headquarters based in Atlanta, recently opened a flagship hotel in Buckhead, their first in town. The 22-story hotel is constructed around a central courtyard of gardens. Rooms start at $199.

Over $200
Ritz-Carlton Buckhead, 3434 Peachtree Rd. N.E., 404/237-2700, the flagship hotel of the international luxury hotel chain, offers gracious service, Old World interior design, and what's been called the finest restaurant in Atlanta. Rooms and suites offer a classic design, fine linens, and all business amenities (rates start at $205). The 22-story hotel is across from Lenox Square and Phipps Plaza shopping malls; Emeril's restaurant is down the street.

VIRGINIA HIGHLAND
Highland Inn, 644 N. Highland Ave. N.E., 404/874-5756, thehighlandinn.com, offers bed-and-breakfast lodging in Atlanta's attractive Virginia Highland neighborhood (rooms start at $60). It's walking distance to restaurants, clubs, shops, and parks, and it's 2.5 miles from downtown.

Food and Drink

Atlanta has many wonderful restaurants offering a wide variety of cosmopolitan choices, from exotic ethnic specialties to haute continental. In terms of cuisine, it's got the greatest variety in the state (arguably in the region), in settings ranging from down-home to swank. Because of the number of vegetarians in town, many restaurants offer at least a couple of meatless entrées (and a "vegetable plate" remains a Southern standard).

The following selection emphasizes dependable local places travelers might be less likely to stumble upon independently (we're presuming you can find your way to revolving restaurants, Benihana, or dinner at the Ritz without our help).

Also included are several impressive new contenders on Atlanta's culinary scene.

Farmers Markets
Atlanta's old-time farmers markets offer more than just groceries. In addition to produce, meats, and seafood, you can often find fresh flowers, specialty food products, and inexpensive eateries as well. They're guaranteed to offer a slice of local life.

Sweet Auburn Curb Market, 209 Edgewood St., within walking distance of downtown, on the way east toward the MLK district, has several eateries offering a variety of specialties, including oyster po-boys, jerk chicken, and some of the best Italian sandwiches in town.

DeKalb Farmer's Market, 3000 E. Ponce de Leon Ave., 404/377-6400, dekalbfarmersmarket.com, east of Atlanta in Decatur, is an enormous food emporium with a cafeteria, bakery, and wide selection of exotic fruits, vegetables, and wines.

Down by the airport, the **State Farmer's Market,** 16 Forest Pkwy., 404/366-6910, packs plenty of produce, poultry, pickles, plants, and Georgia specialty items onto 146 acres; a cafeteria serves fresh inexpensive food 24 hours a day.

DOWNTOWN AND VICINITY

(Including Sweet Auburn, West End, and Grant Park.)

Starts, Snacks, and Low-End

Around Five Points, **Café du Monde,** in Underground Atlanta, a branch of the famous New Orleans landmark, offers signature Crescent City beignets and café au lait. At Woodruff Park, **Starbucks,** 240 Peachtree St., 404/589-4522, is a reliable place to get the *New York Times* with your latte.

Around Peachtree Center, the **Corner Bakery,** on Peachtree Street at Baker, across from the Hyatt, offers a hot alternative to a motel breakfast and nice sandwiches as well. Note that the Hyatt has a 24-hour café, and the Days Inn coffee shop on Baker Street is also open around the clock.

Mick's is a lively modern diner chain for inexpensive burgers, salads, pasta plates, and friendly service. It's atop Underground Atlanta, 404/525-2825, and also on the corner of Peachtree Center Boulevard and International, 404/688-6425. It's open daily for lunch and dinner.

Southern

Two local landmarks downtown for old-style Southern food are **Thelma's Kitchen,** 768 Marietta St., 404/688-5855, for full Southern breakfasts and plate lunch specials (it's closed Sunday). **Busy Bee Cafe,** 810 Martin Luther King Jr. Blvd. S.W., 404/525-9212, busybeecafe.com,

has been a soul-food landmark for over 50 years. It's open daily for lunch and dinner.

For glamorous contemporary Southern plates, the Ritz-Carlton's **Atlanta Grill,** 131 Peachtree St. N.E., 404/221-6550, serves classic regional cuisine in an elegant but cozy grill with big leather booths and a second-story New Orleans-style ironwork veranda overlooking Peachtree St. It's open for lunch and dinner daily. (The formal dining room of the Ritz-Carlton downtown is a renowned continental restaurant.)

Barbecue

East toward Grant Park, **N Daddy D'z Bar-B-Que Joynt,** 264 Memorial Dr., 404/222-0206, daddydz.com, serves "ba-a-d-to-the-bone" smoked spare ribs, red beans and rice, and their very own 'Que Wraps (like a deep-fried pork bun). At night they host blues bands, so they serve till late. A short drive south, **Factory's BBQ,** 428 Boulevard S.E., 404/627-8448, sometimes offers salmon barbecue in addition to its usual pork menu.

Daddy D'z Bar-B-Que Joynt

Around Sweet Auburn, **Rolling Bones,** 377 Edgewood Ave., 404/222-2324, a newcomer operating out of a restyled Art Deco gas station with patio tables, specializes in Texas-style barbecue—try the beef brisket or whole pit-grilled chicken (around $10). They're open daily for lunch and dinner.

For a quick fix right downtown, the barbecue at the mezzanine cafeteria within the **Georgia Pacific Building,** on Peachtree Street at John Wesley Dobbs Boulevard, ain't half bad. It's open weekdays only.

American
A few blocks from worldwide CNN headquarters is **Ted's Montana Grill,** 133 Luckie St., 404/521-9796. It's mogul Ted Turner's Longhorn-style restaurant (one of five in Atlanta), and it serves bison burgers from Turner's own herd. Another celebrity restaurant, **Gladys Knight and Ron Winan's Chicken and Waffles,** 529 Peachtree St., 404/874-9393, continues a Harlem tradition from the 1930s. When late-night partying crowds couldn't decide between eating dinner or breakfast, they combined the two. It stays open till 4 A.M. (Georgia-born R&B artist Gladys Knight is best known for the hit *When the Lights Went Out in Georgia.*)

Around Peachtree Center, **Dailey's,** 17 International Blvd., 404/681-3303, serves up such favorites as pepper-crusted swordfish in a mustard cognac sauce, along with great desserts—it's a favorite for business lunch meetings (there is live jazz or karaoke downstairs most nights).

City Grill, 50 Hurt Plaza, Ste. 200, 404/524-2489, citygrillatlanta.com, a clubby gathering place for city power brokers, serves traditional American and regional cuisine from the upper floor of one of the city's rare preserved historic buildings.

Off Woodruff Park at **M Luxe,** 89 Park Place, 404/389-0800, inventive dishes like lamb shank with Tanzanian chocolate and lavender glaze come delicately flavored and beautifully presented along with thoughtful suggestions for accompanying wine. A bright long bar up front leads to a medieval dark dining hall with a roaring walk-in fireplace in back. It's open for

lunch and dinner, but the dramatic setting makes it more of a dinner place—a particularly excellent way to precede any performance at the nearby Rialto Theater. Entrées start at $18; it's closed Sunday.

Indian
Off Centennial Olympic Park, **Haveli,** 225 Spring St., 404/522-4545, serves North Indian lamb, goat, and vegetarian specialties beneath the Gift Mart. It's open for lunch Mon.–Sat. and dinner daily.

MIDTOWN AND WEST MIDTOWN
The city's most inventive cuisine can be found at Midtown restaurants, especially in the recently settled West Midtown area. Here there are also a few landmark spots and plenty of neighborhood favorites.

Starts, Snacks, and Low-End
Two old-style diners at either side of Midtown attract loyal crowds for breakfast and lunch: the **Silver Skillet,** 200 14th St. N.W., 404/874-1388, a classic Formica place west of Peachtree; and **Silver Grill,** 900 Monroe Dr. N.E., 404/876-8145, in a small cabin off the southeast corner of Piedmont Park.

M Varsity Drive-In, 61 North Ave., 404/881-1706, is an Atlanta institution for cheap onion rings and hot dogs, drive-through or sit-down (for the full cultural experience). It's above the I-75/85 North Avenue exit, down from the North Avenue MARTA station.

Southern
M Mary Mac's Tea Room, 228 Ponce de Leon Ave. N.E., 404/876-1800, marymacs.com, is a busy, cheery place for classic Southern catfish, fried chicken, hush puppies, collard greens, apple brown betty, and banana pudding—there's a new menu every day. This Atlanta institution, set off in a clapboard storefront a shady stretch from Peachtree Street, serves a varied clientele, including suited professionals, camera-swingin' tourists, white-gloved matrons, grunge hostelers,

and anyone else with an appetite. They hand you a blank bill and a pencil to write out your own order. They're open daily for breakfast, lunch, and dinner.

M South City Kitchen, 1144 Crescent Ave., 404/873-7358, in a sleek glass and blonde-wood interior carved from the shell of a traditional clapboard house, specializes in contemporary twists on traditional Southern dishes—searing, encrusting, and flash-frying shrimp, flounder, and pork and then serving it on beds of wilted collards and such. It's open for lunch and dinner.

South City Kitchen is one of a string of restaurants and bars on a compact block of Crescent Avenue south of 14th Street known as **Restaurant Row.** Here you'll also find **Vickery's** for good brunches and **Front Page News** (its Press Room bar draws local journalists); both have nice patios out front. At the head of the street, the acclaimed **75 Park Place** restaurant is within the Four Seasons Hotel.

Experimental American

Right off Peachtree Street, **Einstein's,** 1077 Juniper St., 404/876-7925, a busy neighborhood favorite with wide shady decks, offers an uncategorizable compendium of "quantum entrées" and "coefficients," e.g., pita pizza with grilled chicken and basil, or the generous vegetable stir. It's open for lunch and dinner and as a late-night spot on weekends.

In West Midtown, **Food Studio,** 887 W. Marietta St., 404/815-6677, is a trendy dinner spot for such "Bold American Cooking" as acorn squash risotto served in its shell. The restaurant is housed within the King Plow Arts Center and has a dramatic industrial setting. It serves dinner daily.

Also in the warehouse district, **M Bacchanalia,** 1198 Howell Mill Rd., 404/365-0410, won a James Beard award as best restaurant in the Southeast. Their inventive dishes are a fusion of California and French cuisine—the chef studied with Berkeley food guru Alice Waters—and their prix fixe dinner is considered among the best in the city. Its setting, in a renovated meatpacking plant, is also a winner.

Italian

Veni Vidi Vici, 41 14th St., 404/875-VICI (875-8424), is one of Atlanta's many upscale Italian restaurants in an elegant setting; these are popular with a professional clientele. As one of the best of the breed, Veni Vidi Vici also throws in alfresco seating and a bocce ball court to boot. Traditional Tuscan entrées for lunch and dinner start at around $18.

Jamaican

Bridgetown Grill, 689 Peachtree Ave. N.E., 404/873-5361, a casual place for such spicy island specialties as jerk chicken with black beans and rice, draws relaxed crowds to its colorful restaurant, which is centrally located down from the Fox Theatre. It's open for lunch and dinner; later on weekend nights.

Mexican

M Nuevo Loredo Cantina, 1495 Chattahoochee Ave. N.W., 404/352-9009, with its bloody crosses, plaintive saints, and candlelit shrines, might well be the most authentic Mexican restaurant east of the Mississippi. A bilingual menu is packed with *chorizo, flautas,* and *mole pollo* plates, including vegetarian options. Try the Guadalajara-style barbecued shrimp with a chilled Bohemia (around $15). It's open for lunch and dinner Mon.–Sat. (closed Sun.) and is set off in a white cabin in a wooded glen next to nowhere, off Howell Mill Road.

BUCKHEAD

Atlanta's luxury district is home to its top restaurants, including the preeminent French cuisine at The Dining Room of the Ritz-Carlton Hotel, and the see-and-be-seen mogul meeting grounds of Seeger's and Bluepointe. If you have a limitless expense account, go for it, or see plenty of varied alternatives below.

Starts, Snacks, and Low-End

In lower Buckhead, **Wolfgang Puck Express,** 1745 Peachtree St., 404/815-1500, offers excellent upscale fast food for under $10, like the smoked salmon and dill pizza that renowned chef Wolfgang Puck made famous in his California restaurant Spago. The four-cheese ravioli with golden squash sauce is delicious at any price. It's easily found at the interstate border between Midtown and Buckhead, across from the Amtrak station. It's open for lunch and dinner.

Uphill, on a stretch of lower Buckhead lined with many eateries, **R. Thomas Deluxe Grill,** 1812 Peachtree Rd., 404/872-2942, stands out with its Statue of Liberty and other weird art surrounding the patio café. They have a juice bar and serve healthy salads, sandwiches, veggie tacos, and the like 24-hours a day.

Southern

In Buckhead's neglected southeast corner, the local institution **Colonnade,** 1879 Cheshire Bridge Rd., 404/874-5642, dishes up such Southern classics as mountain trout, baked ham, and its famous yeast rolls, as it has since the 1940s—and it's patronized largely by the original clientele. It's open daily for lunch and dinner and is a popular midday Sunday dinner spot. (Find it 1.3 miles south of I-85.)

Celebrity owner Sean "P. Diddy" Combs has opened **Justin's,** 404/603-5353, where they serve nouveau soul food with a Caribbean influence.

Glamorous New Orleans-style cuisine at **Emeril's,** 3500 Lenox Rd., 404/564-5600, named for famous chef Emeril Lagasse, is served in the gleaming glass storefront of a corporate office tower downhill from the Ritz. Emeril's signature dishes include Cajun barbecue shrimp and banana cream pie; entrées start at $21. Lunch is served Mon.–Sat., dinner nightly.

Barbecue

In the same corner of town as Colonnade, **Fat Matt's Rib Shack,** 1811 Piedmont, 404/607-1622, barbecues pork ribs and chicken with traditional sides of slaw and beans, and roasts peanuts to snack on while blues bands heat the joint up at night. It's open from 11:30 A.M.–11:30 P.M. most days.

American

Buckhead has some of the best high-end American steakhouses in the country: the old-school

Bone's, 3130 Piedmont Rd., 404/237-2663, and opulent **Chops,** 70 W. Paces Ferry Rd., 404/262-2675 (with a lobster bar at its lower level). They're power-lunch affairs, serving whole sides of meat to robust executives with silk ties slung over their shoulders. Steaks start at around $30.

The deluxe **Buckhead Diner,** 3073 Piedmont Rd., 404/262-3336, may serve such familiar standards as meatloaf and handmade potato chips, but the day's special is as likely to be calamari or fettuccine—it's a diner with a wine list. Its blinding polished chrome and neon script re-creates the 1950s-diner look, high style.

Atlanta Fish Market, 265 Pharr Rd., 404/262-3165, can't be beat for the great variety of seafood offered in this Buckhead-casual restaurant; entrées start at $16.

Seeger's, 111 W. Paces Ferry Rd., 404/846-9779, housed in the shell of a bungalow and re-made into a cavernous expanse of white marble and dark hardwood, serves the likes of beef tenderloin poached in red wine and braised John Dory as fixed-price dinner fare (around $70 before wine and tip).

Italian

For high-end Italian in Buckhead, **Pricci's** (say pree-CHEESE), 500 Pharr Rd., 404/237-2941, serves northern Italian classics such as homemade saffron pasta and polenta with veal sausage, along with legendary bread and Italian wines. The decor is cozy booths and tables in a sleek setting. It's open Mon.–Sat. for lunch and dinner; on Sunday, dinners are served family-style 5–10 P.M.

French

The Dining Room of the Ritz-Carlton Hotel Buckhead, 3434 Peachtree Rd. N.E., 404/237-2700, is the flagship restaurant of the flagship hotel of the world's ritziest hotel chain. Chef Michael McNeill, who is, according to the *New York Times,* the only master sommelier in the Southeast, presents the finest in French cuisine in luxurious surroundings filled with antiques. Dinners run $300 with wine and tip; their famously elegant Sunday brunch costs around $60 per person (not including alcohol but including several trips to the caviar station).

VIRGINIA HIGHLAND

Heading out to Atlanta's homier neighborhoods to eat will enable visitors to see another side of Atlanta. Only two miles from downtown and a short jaunt from Midtown, Virginia Highland is a natural destination.

Start, Snacks, and Low-End

For 24-hour, really low-end American, head to **Majestic Food,** 1031 Ponce de Leon Ave. N.E., 404/875-0276. With its red Formica counter, white-apron waitresses, and vinyl booths patched with duct tape, the place comes to life after the bars close at 3 A.M. A couple of blocks south, **Manuel's Tavern,** 602 N. Highland Ave., 404/525-3447, serves breakfast and pub-style lunch and dinner.

American

In the center of the village,  **Murphy's,** 997 Virginia Ave., 404/872-0904, is a bright and crisp casual bistro for brunch, lunch, and dinner. An Appalachian breakfast features mountain trout and eggs; or you can choose from frittatas, salmon BLTs, roasted portobello sandwiches, or smoked pork chops for lunch or dinner. They also offer a full bar and retail wine shop. It's generally open 11 A.M.–10 P.M., but it opens earlier on Sundays.

Italian

La Tavola Trattoria, 922 Virginia Ave., 404/876-5655, one of the best neighborhood bistros in the city, dishes up hearty and inexpensive Italian standards in an intimate dark wood–paneled dining room or at café tables out on the back-alley veranda. This Va-Hi tradition is open for dinner Tues.–Sun.

Around the corner, **Everybody's,** 1040 N. Highland Ave., 404/873-4545, offers cheap and gooey pizza in high wooden booths or on the patio.

Cafés and restaurants merge into a collective patio in the Virginia Highland neighborhood.

© KAP STANN

LITTLE FIVE POINTS AND INMAN PARK

American

In the center of Little Five Points, walk through the story-high red-eyed skull to **Vortex,** 438 Moreland Ave., 404/688-1828, for more than a dozen specialty burgers, beef and beef alt, omelets, and bar food, like chicken quesadillas and nacho-tots.

Jamaican

Bridgetown Grill, 1156 Euclid Ave., 404/653-0110, is a colorful, casual place for spicy island specialties such as jerk chicken with black beans and rice, or just tapas and drinks. It's open for lunch and dinner, later on weekend nights.

Southern

In Inman Park,  **Son's Place,** 100 Hurt St., 404/581-0530, inherited the mantle (and the cast-iron skillets) from the beloved Deacon Burton, who ran a restaurant at this isolated outpost for many decades. Find skillet-fried chicken, hoe cakes, greens, and cobbler on the menu—it's the real deal. It's across from the Inman Park/Reynoldstown MARTA station.

Italian

Also in Inman Park is **Sotto Sotto,** 313 N. Highland Ave., 404/523-6678, a sleekly modern bistro at the bottom of a residential district. Here you'll find Tuscan favorites, homemade pasta, shellfish risotto, and entrées inspired by Michelangelo's letters (entrées start at $14). It's open for dinner Tues.–Sun. It's sister restaurant, **Fritti,** is next door in a converted garage and serves wood-oven gourmet pizza.

Pair either one of these up with a performance at Dad's Garage, down the street, for a great night out.

EAST ATLANTA

A bright newcomer on the city's restaurant scene, **Iris,** provides a great excuse to visit this emerging neighborhood. Team it up with a visit to **Echo Landing** to hear local bands.

© KAP STANN

You'll find ethnic eateries in Little Five Points, Atlanta's foremost bohemian neighborhood, as well as throughout the city.

Starts, Snacks, and Low-end

Heaping Bowl and Brew, 469 Flat Shoals Ave., 404/523-8030, specializes in innovative one-dish meals like their seafood bowl of swordfish, tuna, and calamari over linguini—or try the Italian sausage and sage-seared apples over pirogi. It's open for lunch and dinner daily and weekend brunch.

A few doors down, **Edible Art,** 481A Flat Shoals Ave. S.E., 404/587-0707, is an eight-table place with twisted takes on Southern themes—take the hoppin' John–stuffed pepper or Cajun-grilled chicken-red-bean-ravioli combo (entrées start at $9; closed Mon.).

Burrito Art, 1259 Glenwood Ave., 404/627-4433, concocts "Americanized" burritos, including a Southern barbecued chicken burrito or Asian meatloaf burrito (prices start at $5). It's open daily.

Gourmet American

Iris, 1314 Glenwood Ave., 404/221-1300, irisatlanta.com, is a great new bistro that toys with duck leg confit and whole flash-fried flounder, but according to one reviewer, it "maintains enough street cred to stock the bar with PBR tall boys." The place seats 28. It's open for dinner only Tues.–Sun.

OUTLYING DISTRICTS

Outlying Barbecue Landmarks

Near Emory University, find **Dusty's BBQ,** 1815 Briarcliff Rd. N.E., 404/320-6264, dustys.com. In Southeast Atlanta, find **Harold's BBQ,** 171 McDonough Blvd. S.E., 404/627-9268, near the prison. It's open for lunch and dinner Mon.–Sat. and accepts cash only.

Decatur

Another celebrity restaurant, **Watershed,** 406 W. Ponce de Leon Ave., 404/378-4900, was founded by Indigo Girl Emily Saliers. In a renovated garage, they serve inspired Southern fare—including legendary Tuesday-night fried chicken and a great Sunday brunch—to a sophisticated crowd.

By Agnes Scott College, **Our Way Cafe,** 303 E. College Ave., 404/373-6665, a favorite for Southern meat-and-three plates, is particularly known for its fresh vegetables and casseroles. It's open for lunch and dinner.

Transportation

GETTING THERE

By Air

Hartsfield-Jackson International Airport, 404/530-6834, atlanta-airport.com, the largest passenger terminal complex in the world, serves 79 million passengers a year. Twenty-six passenger airlines—including Atlanta-based Delta Air Lines—provide service to every major U.S. city and many international cities.

Ten miles south of downtown, near the junction of I-75, I-85, and perimeter highway I-285, the airport is a city in itself. At the main terminal, visitors pass through security and board trams to five outlying concourses, where gates are located according to airline. If you need help, go to the Traveler's Aid desk near baggage claim in the main terminal; here, volunteers offer wide-ranging assistance, from lodging information and language service to finding where you left your car. At baggage claim, you'll find courtesy phones to dozens of hotels and motels that run shuttle-van service to and from the airport.

From an in-terminal station near baggage claim, clean and efficient MARTA trains whisk passengers downtown in 10 minutes for $1.75. **Atlanta Link,** 245 University Ave. S.W., 404/524-3400, theatlantalink.com, provides van service from the airport downtown, to Midtown, Buckhead, and the Emory University for $24–32 round-trip, roughly half the cost of taking a cab one way from the airport.

By Car

Two major north-south interstate highways merge in northern Atlanta; the combined I-75/85 then splits again down by the airport. This combined interstate intersects with the major east-west route of I-20 at downtown Atlanta. All three interstates cross I-285, the perimeter route that encircles Atlanta, which can easily be the most confusing to newcomers. As directions in a circle are relative, "east" and "west" signs quickly turn to "north" or "south," and directional signs to Augusta or Birmingham don't help you find your way through town (Atlanta Braves pitcher José Peres legendarily missed the beginning of a game because he was stuck in perpetual motion on the perimeter). To avoid this common pitfall, plan your approach carefully and avoid rush hours. Atlanta's prolonged rush hours run 6–10 A.M. and 3–7 P.M. Travel time then may be doubled or tripled, particularly along routes north.

By Train

Amtrak, 800/USA-RAIL (800/872-7245), amtrak.com, provides daily service from Atlanta to New York, Washington, D.C., Philadelphia, and other northern cities, and to Mobile, Birmingham, New Orleans, and other points south. The Amtrak station, 1688 Peachtree Rd. (at the I-85 overpass), is in a quiet stretch of the Peachtree corridor, north of downtown and midtown. There's taxi and bus service at the station and a shopping center across the street with restaurants and a pharmacy.

By Bus
Greyhound-Trailways, 800/231-2222, provides bus service connecting Atlanta with the many major cities. The downtown bus terminal, 232 Forsyth St. S.W., 404/584-1731, is south of Five Points and conveniently adjacent to the Garnett MARTA station, making for easy access to the airport and destinations within reach of the MARTA line.

GETTING AROUND
Rental Cars
At Hartsfield-Jackson Airport (near baggage claim) and also at branch locations throughout metro Atlanta, major car rental agencies include **Dollar Rent-A-Car,** 800/800-4000; **Alamo,** 800/327-9633; **Budget,** 800/527-0700; **Hertz,** 800/654-3131; **Avis,** 800/331-1212; and **National,** 800/CAR-RENT (800/227-7368). All offer weekly discounts, weekend packages, unlimited-mileage rates, and even such perks as cellular-phone rentals. Frequent-renter clubs offer additional advantages, including discounts and express service. Summer travelers should select cars with air-conditioning and light-colored interiors.

Enterprise Rent-A-Car, 303 Courtland St., 404/659-6050, maintains an outpost in downtown Atlanta, right in the central convention zone.

Taxis
Taxis downtown charge a flat rate of $6 for a single passenger ($1 extra each for more than two passengers) traveling within the official downtown taxi zone. Bounded by Boulevard on the east, 14th Street (north of Georgia Tech) on the north, Northside Drive on the west, and Turner Field on the south, "the zone" encompasses the major business district north to Midtown. Metered rates for all other destinations are $1.50 for the first one-sixth mile, 20 cents each additional sixth of a mile, and $1 per person for each additional passenger. Some special-event flat rates apply. For a cab, call **Atlanta Taxicab Association,** 770/269-7553, or **Checker Cab Company,** 404/351-1111. A 10 percent tip is customary; more for bags or special services.

MARTA Public Transit
The Metropolitan Area Rapid Transit Authority (MARTA), 404/848-4711, itsmarta.com, operates the buses and Atlanta's impressive light-rail

© KAP STANN

MARTA provides fast and comfortable public transportation around town and to the airport, with 240 cars on more than 40 miles of tracks.

system, a convenient alternative to driving around town. Clean, safe, and frequent MARTA trains run along two lines (east-west and north-south) that intersect downtown at the central Five Points subway station.

Here passengers can pick up maps, schedules, tokens, and weekly passes. Riders can buy tokens for $1.50 each for a trip of any length (includes a free transfer to bus lines) from self-service machines. While the machines accept bills up to $10, they dispense only tokens (no change), so it's smart to carry crisp 1-, 5-, or 10-dollar bills; small change; and a handful of tokens. Parking at some MARTA stations also requires exact change. Both locally and in this text, the term MARTA is used to refer to the light-rail system exclusively.

MARTA's bus lines traverse the city for $1.75 a ride (or a token). Less convenient to visitors than the light-rail trains (long rides and exposed bus stops without benches are pet peeves), the buses are most useful for short jaunts from train stations to city attractions.

For information on MARTA's services for the disabled, call 404/848-5389.

Driving Maps and Tips

Though the MARTA line offers a relaxed alternative, most people get around Atlanta by car. This is straightforward enough in downtown areas, presuming you're familiar with urban driving patterns (one-way streets, traffic, and the like), but the wider metro region can be something else. Traffic congestion is a major regional problem.

With a city that sprawls like Los Angeles—yet without mountains on the horizon to help chart a course—metro Atlanta can be tricky to navigate without a good map. Get a comprehensive street map from auto clubs, gas stations, tourist outlets, or select newsstands. Hotels and tourist outlets distribute free city maps; these typically show only the main arteries, which is of limited help if you wander off them.

To park downtown and skirt the worst of the traffic, aim for Underground Atlanta's public parking lot, off Martin Luther King Jr. Dr. Around Peachtree Center, shoot for the public lot on Courtland Street at Harris. Private parking downtown is relatively expensive (around $8 an hour).

INFORMATION AND SERVICES

Telephones

Four overlapping area codes serve the Atlanta area—404 and 678 in the central city region, and 770 and 678 in the surrounding metro region. With three area code changes within eight years, expect to run across literature with phone numbers that may no longer apply.

Important Telephone Numbers

Dial 911 for emergency assistance—police, ambulance, or fire. In nonemergency situations, call the police at 404/658-6600, the fire department at 404/659-2121, or ambulance service at 404/521-4141. For local time and weather, call 404/455-7141. Traveler's Aid can be reached at 404/527-7400.

Tourist Offices

The **Atlanta Convention and Visitors Bureau,** 233 Peachtree St. N.E., atlanta.net, 404/521-6688 or 800/ATLANTA (800/285-2682), staffs information booths and distributes free information (including maps and events listings) at Underground Atlanta, the World Congress Center, Peachtree Center Mall, Lenox Square, and the airport. Send inquiries by mail to 233 Peachtree St., Ste. 100, Atlanta, GA 30303.

The State of Georgia **Department of Industry, Trade, and Tourism,** 285 Peachtree Center Ave., Atlanta, GA 30303, 404/656-3590, distributes a statewide guide. The **Atlanta Chamber of Commerce,** 235 International Blvd. N.W., 404/880-9000, is headquartered across from Centennial Olympic Park.

Publications

"Covering Dixie Like the Dew" since 1868, the *Atlanta Constitution,* 404/526-5151, produces a daily morning paper and expanded Sunday edition.

The free weekly alternative newspaper *Creative Loafing* is an indispensable guide to what's happening in the city—for the latest in local politics and activism, as well as entertainment and humor. Find it in street corner bins all over town.

For the upscale beat, find the four-color monthly *Atlanta Magazine* at newsstands. The *Atlanta Daily World* carries news of particular interest to the African American population, as it has since 1928. *Atlanta Asian News* (in English), *Georgia Magazine* (in Japanese), and *Mundo Hispánico* (bilingual Spanish–English) are just a few of a dozen or more international publications produced in metro Atlanta that cater to Atlanta's diverse ethnic populations.

Online Access

Most hotels now offer high-speed Internet connections if not wi-fi. **Kinko's** offers Internet access at several locations: downtown, 100 Peachtree St. No. 101, 404/221-0000; Midtown, 1371 Peachtree St., 404/262-9393; Buckhead, 3637 Peachtree Rd. N.E., 404/233-1329; and near Emory University, 1385 Oxford Rd. N.E., 404/377-4639.

Security

Crime is a major concern in any city, and Atlanta is no exception, though areas that attract visitors are among the best patrolled. An urban "ambassador" patrol, instituted for the Olympics and still in place, covers downtown Atlanta to help visitors find their way and to act as a deterrent to crime.

For added precaution, hide money and credit cards securely in a money belt or under clothing, and leave valuable jewelry at home. Some seasoned urban travelers recommend carrying a spare money clip with a $10 or $20 bill wrapped around a wad of ones, so if ever accosted, one can throw this mad money out and run in the opposite direction.

Vicinity of Atlanta

Sprawling metropolitan Atlanta encompasses 18 counties and 5,147 square miles. While the encircling perimeter highway (I-285) once encapsulated urban development, expanding suburbs now spread far beyond it, sparking calls for a second beltway farther out. Like Los Angeles, the car-dominated metro area consists of miles and miles of low-rise development, pockets of industry, and suburban-style strip malls. Yet unlike L.A., Atlanta's routes often roll and wind through thick deciduous woods under clear skies. Some of the metro area's best recreation and historical touring sites lie at its perimeter, just outside the I-285 beltway.

Clockwise from the west, **Six Flags Over Georgia** lies near a tranquil state park off I-20. West, the **Chattahoochee River National Recreation Area** sits at Atlanta's northwestern corner, near the city's most established suburb, Marietta. Directly north is the city of Roswell, which manages to retain a small-town central core. To the east, **Stone Mountain** is a major recreational center for city dwellers. (Off I-20 east, the small towns of Middle Georgia are covered in the *Heartland* chapter.)

WEST OF ATLANTA

Six Flags Over Georgia

Six Flags, 275 Riverside Pkwy., Austell, 770/948-9290, sixflags.com, west of Atlanta off I-20, is one of a national chain of amusement parks; this one has a Southern theme. Names of rides such as the Georgia Cyclone, the Great American Scream Machine, and Mind Bender let you know that daring roller coasters are the specialty of the park—guaranteed to bring that cotton-candy taste to the back of your throat. This gigantic amusement park features artificial whitewater rapids and live country music and performances.

Admission is $40 for adults, $25 for kids 48 inches and under, and free for children two and under. Hours change seasonally; summer hours run approximately Sun.–Thurs. 10 A.M.–10 P.M. and Fri.–Sat. till midnight. Call to confirm seasonal schedule and prices.

Sweetwater Creek State Conservation Park

A slice of wilderness only minutes outside metro Atlanta (I-20 exit 44), Sweetwater Creek State

Park, Mount Vernon Rd., Lithia Springs, 770/732-5871, gastateparks.org, features a placid creek, five miles of trails, fishing and boating on a reservoir (there are canoe and fishing-boat rentals and a bait shop available), and Civil War–era textile-mill ruins.

The **Factory Ruins Trail** follows Sweetwater Creek a half-mile through Piedmont hardwoods to the remnants of the New Manchester Manufacturing Company. Here, cloth was made for Confederate troops until Sherman ordered the factory burned on July 9, 1864. The blue-blazed trail continues a half-mile downstream to a platform overlooking waterfalls and the huge granite outcroppings at the water's edge. From here, you can retrace your steps back or follow an inland trail through moist coves and glens to the original trailhead. Pick up trail maps and interpretive guides at the park office. The conservation park is for day-use only; the fee to park is $2 per car. From I-20 exit 44, go south on Thorton Road a quarter-mile, and turn right onto Blairs Bridge Road, then turn left onto Mount Vernon Road, to the park.

CHATTAHOOCHEE RIVER NATIONAL RECREATION AREA

The Chattahoochee River National Recreation Area, 1978 Island Ford Pkwy., 770/399-8070, nps.gov/chat, a federally designated parkland along 48 miles of river corridor, offers the scenic natural beauty of the Piedmont region; recreational activities such as boating, fishing, and hiking; and ruins of old water-powered mills. Deciduous forests of oak, beech, and hickory line the river, along with huge rocks and cliffs that make for varied hiking challenges and scenic overlooks.

The river parkland stretches from Lake Lanier in the north to the outskirts of metropolitan Atlanta, not contiguous but cut up into distinct unconnected parcels called "units." The southernmost unit borders metropolitan Atlanta, 9.5 miles from downtown. The day use–only park system is great for hiking, jogging, biking, and rafting (no camping).

Park headquarters are on the Island Ford unit, a mile east of Hwy. 400 just south of Roswell. Request a brochure or trail maps from the superintendent's office, 1978 Island Ford Pkwy., Atlanta, GA 30350 (enclose a stamped, self-addressed, business envelope), 678/538-1200.

M "Shootin' the 'Hooch"

One of the most popular activities along the Chattahoochee is river rafting (locally called "Shootin' the 'Hooch"), a leisurely half-day or daylong float down calm currents and across wide shoals (a Class I and II waterway). Summer, from Memorial Day to Labor Day, is high season. The National Park Service enforcement against excessive rowdiness has enhanced the river's appeal to families and groups of all sizes, ages, and abilities, though it's still a tremendous hit with the sunbathing/beer-chest crowd (alcohol is permitted, but glass containers of any kind are prohibited). This lazy, sunny float feels much farther away from the busyness of downtown than a mere 10 miles.

High Country Outfitters, 3906B Roswell Rd., Buckhead, 404/814-0999, highcountry-outfitters.com, rents rafts for $100–125 per day for a 4- or 6-person raft. They'll meet you at the river with the raft and meet you where you come out, or you can go to their Buckhead shop and pick it up yourself for a 24-hour rental. They're open Mon.–Fri. 10 A.M. –8 P.M., Sat. 10 A.M.–6 P.M., Sun. noon–6 P.M. Call for reservations; credit cards are accepted. Unfortunately, shuttles are not available, but the *Victory Metropolitan Taxi,* 770/428-2626, knows the drill and can pick you up and get you back to your car for prices starting around $10.

Rafting trips range from two to six hours, depending on where you put in and take out. Count on floating about one mile an hour. It's six miles from Johnson's Ferry to Paces Mill, four miles from Johnson's Ferry to Powers Island, and two miles from Powers Island to Paces Mill.

Being prepared for a day on the river will make your experience more enjoyable. Bring a dry sack for car keys and your cell phone; wear swimsuits and river shoes (or old sneakers) or other light clothing and footwear. Pack a picnic, a litter bag, and cool drinks. Two real dangers are heatstroke, from hours in the direct sun (bring hats and sunblock), and hypothermia, from the cold water (it's 55°F year-round). Each craft is required to carry one life vest for each passenger; they are provided free with rental.

Spectators gather at **Ray's on the River,** 6700 Powers Ferry Rd., 770/955-1187, for an elegant Sunday brunch overlooking the streaming flotilla. The sunburned postrafting crowd heads to the patio cafés along lower Roswell Road.

Hiking, Biking, and Fishing

Hiking trails wind along the river and through the upland woods of the varied southern Piedmont, known for its beautiful seasonal colors in spring and fall, long-flowering trees and shrubs, and varied deciduous and coniferous trees. Giant rock outcroppings were once used by the Creek and Cherokee for temporary shelter. Several still-standing stone foundations of old water-powered mills (grist, textile, or paper) have crumbled back into the natural landscape, as many such recent "ruins" in the South have done. Bird-watchers: Look for great blue herons, green herons, kingfishers, and ospreys. Look for tracks of raccoons, muskrats, mink, beavers, and otters along the river—look also for beaver dams, turtles, toads, and the river's 22 varieties of fish. From south to north, the following are highlights of hiking trails, unit by unit. Contact park headquarters for trail maps and information.

Palisades Unit: Park at the rafting outpost parking lot off Cobb Parkway to reach the **West Palisades Trail.** After crossing under the freeway, the easy trail follows Rottenwood Creek up to the ruins of Akers Mill, a 19th-century gristmill about 1.5 miles from the start. Here a sandy beach and large boulders invite leisurely picnicking and sunbathing. East of the river, five miles of easy-to-difficult trails wind through wooded floodplains, ridges, and ravines to a panoramic view of the river gorge at Devil's Race Shoals (so called because they were a devil to navigate, according to local legend). One of the park's largest rock shelters, once a Native American fish camp, can be reached a half mile north of Long Island Creek. You get to all eastern riverbank trails from the north: take I-285 to Northside Drive, and drive southeast to parking lots and

trailheads, either at the foot of Indian Trail Road or Whitewater Road, farther south.

Cochran Shoals Unit: The fully accessible three-mile **Cochran Fitness Trail**—open to cyclists as well as hikers—parallels a stretch of river wetlands, with stops at observation decks, picnic areas, and exercise stations. The moderately steep **Sope Creek Trail** leads to the ruins of the Marietta Paper Mill, where paper products—including Confederate currency—were produced from 1855 to 1902.

Rangers and volunteers host free guided hikes of natural-history and cultural-history sites; call 678/538-1200 for a schedule.

Fishing is permitted in the Chattahoochee River. A valid Georgia fishing license is required, and a trout stamp is required to fish for trout; no live minnows are permitted as bait.

SMYRNA

This Atlanta suburb is most notable as the home to two landmarks on the Barbecue Trail. Find **Low Country Barbecue,** 2000 S. Pioneer Dr. S.E., 404/799-8049, lowcountrybarbecue.com, and **Old South Bar-B-Q,** 601 Burbank Circle, 770/435-4215.

MARIETTA

Northwest of Atlanta, along the historic railroad route demolished by Sherman's March, the 1824 town of Marietta has exploded into Atlanta's grandest suburb. This busy, affluent city mixes its historic town square with modern corporate towers; Civil War cemeteries border spanking-new housing developments.

The aerospace industry drives the prosperous local economy; Lockheed builds fighter jets here, and the county receives more federal money than any other suburb outside of the D.C. area and the Kennedy Space Center.

Marietta is the county seat of the notoriously conservative Cobb County—home of Newt Gingrich and the object of many progressive-led protests from its liberal neighbor of Atlanta, from the civil-rights era to 1996, when organizers considered rerouting the arrival of the Olympic Torch to bypass Cobb. Cobb's reactionary stances can reach comic extremes: the city of Kennesaw responded to national gun-control trends by *requiring* each household to own a gun, and in 2003, the council passed a resolution "to publicly recognize God as the foundation of our national heritage." Yet, as always, politicians don't necessarily represent all residents, and many progressive folks from all over are drawn to the county's good jobs and good schools, and as a relief from urban congestion.

Visitors will also find many attractions in the area: historical touring downtown and at nearby Kennesaw Mountain battlefield, antebellum house tours, and the popular summertime White Water Park with its adjacent amusement park. The most notorious local landmark is the Big Chicken, a 56-foot-tall sheet-metal rooster that towers over the corner of Hwy. 41 and Roswell Road. It's so large that pilots use it for navigational purposes—so do locals; you'll hear directions such as "turn left at the Big Chicken."

Marietta Square

Even though Sherman's troops ravaged the town in 1864 en route to Atlanta, more than a hundred antebellum homes remain, and many more 19th-century structures are evidence of Marietta's quick recovery. The heart of the historic downtown is Marietta Square.

In the center of the square, scenic **Glover Park** dates from 1852. The park hosts summertime brown-bag concerts, art shows, and seasonal festivals. The lively square is lined with browse-worthy antique shops, practical stores, cafés, restaurants, and the Theatre in the Square.

The **welcome center**, 4 Depot St., 770/429-1115 or 800/835-0445, in the 1898 railroad depot behind the square, distributes self-guided walking- and driving-tour maps and event calendars. Hours are Mon.–Fri. 9 A.M.–5 P.M., Sat. 11 A.M.–4 P.M., Sun. 1–4 P.M. Also inquire about local historic house tours.

Marietta Museum of History

Across the street from the depot, the local history museum, 1 Depot St., 770/528-0430, illuminates the city's Civil War history within the

historic **Kennesaw House,** where Sherman shacked up while devising his Atlanta Campaign ($3 for adult admission). It's open Mon.–Sat. 10 A.M.–4 P.M., Sun. 1–4 P.M.

Marietta-Cobb Museum of Art

A block south of the square, the old 1909 post office has been converted into the Marietta-Cobb Museum of Art, 30 Atlanta St., 770/528-1444. The museum features 19th- and 20th-century American art. It's open Tues.–Sat. 11 A.M.–5 P.M. Admission is $5 for adults and $3 for students and seniors.

Scarlett on the Square

At 18 Whitlock Ave., 770/794-5576, this museum displays a collection of *Gone with the Wind* memorabilia, including Vivien Leigh's Oscar for Best Actress. It's open Mon.–Sat. 10 A.M.–5 P.M.

Civil War Cemeteries

Northeast of the square, the 1866 **Marietta National Cemetery,** 500 Washington Ave., contains 10,000 graves shaded by towering magnolias and oaks—24 acres speckled with monuments from many states honoring slain native sons. South of the square, the 1863 **Confederate Cemetery,** 381 Powder Springs St., holds the graves of 3,000 soldiers, a thousand of which are marked "unknown." To get there, take North Marietta Parkway south.

White Water Park

At White Water, 250 Cobb Pkwy., 770/424-9283, four million gallons of water create waves, pools, waterfalls, and plenty of daring slides in the shaded 35-acre park north of Atlanta. It is open seasonally: weekends only in spring, and daily from Memorial Day to Labor Day. An all-day pass to White Water for adults costs $20; for children three to four feet tall, the cost is around $12. Once you dry off, adjacent **American Adventures** offers the 40,000 sq. ft. Foam Factory, bumper cars, train rides, and an arcade. Take I-75 exit 113.

Accommodations and Food

Sixty Polk Street, 60 Polk St., 770/419-1688 or 800/845-7266, sixtypolkstreet.com, a bed-and-breakfast inn housed in a regal 1872 Victorian two blocks from the square, offers four guest rooms, each with private bath ($95–150). In the morning, your hosts, Joe and Glenda Mertes, serve a deluxe breakfast in the formal dining room.

National chain motels are clustered around I-75 exit 111, including the low-end **Motel 6,** 770/952-8161 and **Howard Johnson,** 770/951-1144.

Shillings on the Square, 19 N. Park Sq., 770/428-9520, serves American and continental dinners starting at $16. **Williamson Bros. BBQ,** 1425 Roswell Rd., 770/971-3201, serves Alabama-style barbecue—pork sandwiches and ribs. Salads and rotisserie chicken are also available. It's open for lunch and dinner.

Entertainment

The award-winning nonprofit **Theatre in the Square,** 11 Whitlock Ave., 770/422-8369, theatreinthesquare.com, hosts year-round entertainment in its 170-seat theater. Productions in the past have included the likes of *Always Patsy Cline.*

KENNESAW

Kennesaw Mountain National Battlefield Park

Established in 1917, this national historic park, 900 Kennesaw Mountain Dr., 770/427-4686, nps.gov/kemo, commemorates the Battle of Kennesaw (KEN-a-saw) Mountain, in which the Confederates under General James Johnston forestalled the Union advance of Sherman's troops in defense of Atlanta. In June of 1864, Sherman's attack on Confederate entrenchments here (still visible today) was repelled by rifle fire, by rocks that were rolled down the hillsides, and by hand-to-hand combat. The mountains "couldn't have been more suited for defense than if they'd been designed for that purpose," as one surviving Union soldier explained. Though Sherman returned to his previously successful flanking maneuvers to eventually capture Atlanta, Kennesaw Mountain was a proud Confederate victory. (And, as these things go, Confederate victory battlefields are often less well known and therefore more enlightening than their Union counterparts.)

The visitors center presents a slide show on the battle and distributes maps detailing memo-

rials, entrenchments, and trails. The quarter-mile **summit trail** is an easy walk. On weekdays you can drive to the top, but on weekends, you must park at the center and either walk or take a shuttle bus to the top. The center is open daily 8:30 A.M.–5 P.M. (till 6 P.M. on weekends). Take I-75 exit 116 and follow signs.

Sixteen miles of **hiking trails** crisscross the 2,884-acre park, through Piedmont forests of oak and dogwood, and along hillsides overlooking fields, farmland, and stately homes (the park's historic scenic corridor is threatened by development at its boundaries). Grounds are open dawn to dusk.

Southern Museum of Civil War and Locomotive History

This Smithsonian-affiliated museum, 2829 Cherokee St., 770/427-2117, southernmuseum.org, showcases how the locomotive has shaped history, in particular, local Civil War history. It's the home of the famous locomotive named *General,* which was stolen during the Civil War by Andrews' Raiders (a story told in the Disney movie *The Great Locomotive Chase*). Housed in an extensively remodeled old cotton gin, the Civil War memorabilia museum is open Mon.–Sat. 9:30 A.M.–5 P.M. and Sun. noon–5 P.M. (reduced winter hours). Admission to the museum is $8 for adults and $6 children (kids five and under are free).

ROSWELL

Directly north of Atlanta and east of Marietta, the growing suburb of Roswell retains at its core a small walkable village with a historic feel. Only 30 minutes out of town (if there's no traffic), it's popular with city visitors looking for a nice place to drive to, where they can walk around and do a little shopping at a few quaint shops and antique stores. The **welcome center,** 617 Atlanta St., 770/640-3253 or 800/776-7935, directs visitors to historic walking tours, performing arts, and area lodging (open daily).

On the Barbecue Landmark Trail, find the **Swallow at the Hollow,** 1072 Green St., 678/352-1975, swallowatthehollow.com, for contemporary barbecue and other dishes that even non-'cue fanatics will enjoy. They're open for lunch and dinner.

Historic House Museums

Bulloch Hall, 180 Bulloch Ave., 770/992-1731, opens the 1840 Greek Revival home of President Theodore Roosevelt's mother, Mittie Bulloch. Exhibits relate family history and Civil War history, and period gardens are also on display. Hours are Mon.–Sat. 10 A.M.–3 P.M. and Sun. 1–3 P.M. Admission is $6 for adults and $4 for children.

The **Archibald Smith Plantation Home,** 935 Alpharetta St., 770/641-3978, offers tours through the 1845 home of the city's founder. Plantation outbuildings include an original slave cabin. Admission is $6 for adults and $4 for children over age six. Tours are held hourly Mon.–Fri., 11:30 A.M.–2:30 P.M., and Sat. at 10:30 A.M.–1:30 P.M.

Chattahoochee Nature Center

Outside town, the **Chattahoochee Nature Center,** 9135 Willeo Rd., 770/992-2055, chatnaturecenter.com, is a private, nonprofit environmental-education and animal-rehabilitation center that maintains a 128-acre riverside preserve, with walking trails out to the marshlands or up through the woodlands. Admission to the interpretive center (adults $3, children and seniors $2) includes guided walks at 1 P.M. and 3 P.M. on weekends. Of the center's many scheduled programs (most are designed for children), the most popular is the two-hour canoe float down the Chattahoochee River, which takes place Tues. evenings Apr.–Sept. Access is from Azalea Road off Roswell Road (there are few signs; you might want to call for directions). Hours are Mon.–Sat. 9 A.M.–5 P.M. and Sun. noon–5 P.M.

STONE MOUNTAIN

Stone Mountain Park

East of Atlanta, a huge granite bubble surfaces out of the rolling Piedmont landscape. The 825-foot-high natural landmark has been a meeting place since the time of the Creeks and early set-

tlers. Now the unusual formation is the centerpiece of Stone Mountain Park, Hwy. 78, 770/498-5690, stonemountainpark.com, which attracts six million visitors annually. The 3,200-acre park ranks third in attendance nationally after both Disney parks, and it's Georgia's number-one attraction. Transformed into Olympic Park for the 1996 Summer Games, Stone Mountain Park and its 383-acre lake was the site of many Olympic competitions. (The park is overseen by state authorities but is not within the state park system.)

The geologically unusual rock outcropping is further distinguished by the fact that it displays the largest bas relief sculpture in the world. The landmark carving depicts three Confederate heroes on horseback: Confederate President Jefferson Davis, and Generals Robert E. Lee and Thomas ("Stonewall") Jackson. Originally begun in 1923 by Gutzon Borglum (who also carved Mount Rushmore), the three-acre design was not completed until 1970.

Park gates are open 6 A.M.–midnight, year-round. The entrance fee is $7 per car. Attraction hours and fees vary. Alcohol is prohibited in most public places except for designated picnic areas.

Natural History

A century ago, in its undeveloped state, Stone Mountain was crawling with naturalists and scientists observing and recording the dome's distinctive natural history. As the largest of only a dozen or so major granite outcroppings in the eastern United States, Stone Mountain was highly valued for its unique geology, botany, and animal life.

Such "monadnocks" were formed during the volcanic collision of the African and North American continental plates half a billion years ago. The huge molten bubbles cooled, gradually rose toward the surface, and with erosion became exposed. Scientists theorize the rocks cooled in onionlike layers, and that's why the rock sloughs off in exfoliated slabs. Visible at the base of the mountain, some of these granite slabs are as big as houses.

Because the dense rock holds only thin soil, retains little water, generates heat, and exposes plants to much sun and wind, these outcroppings support plant life more commonly associated with the desert than with the lush Southeast. The rare botanical enclaves are made rarer still by the disjunctive occurrence of these outcroppings, scattered as they are through the Atlantic Coast Piedmont region. Because of this, you can be assured that any one you visit forms its own unique habitat.

Of the score of rare plants found here, the most celebrated is the Confederate yellow daisy (*Viguiera porteri*). In early fall, bright yellow flowers spring from rock crevices and fill shallow soil pockets on the barren gray rock with vibrant color. The park's Yellow Daisy Festival marks the event. Eroded depressions in the rock form small freshwater pools that support tiny crustaceans.

Today heavy recreational use has blurred Stone Mountain's natural history, yet this granddaddy of granite domes remains a geological and botanical treasure. Smaller outcroppings in the region exhibit similar features but are less developed and hence more "natural."

Sights

From the wide **Memorial Lawn,** site of the park's many festivals, you can look up at the massive rock and its defining sculpture. Or take a Swiss-made **sky lift** to the summit for a bird's-eye view of the scene. From the top you'll see the panoramic view over the Piedmont, with city skyscrapers in the distance. The 1.3-mile **summit trail** leads from the mountain's base to the top along the rock slabs, where you can get a closer look at the mountain's rare botany.

Crossroads displays an 1870s town with homesteading crafts demonstrations. **Memorial Hall Museum** contains an excellent collection of Civil War weapons, uniforms, flags, and other memorabilia. The **Stone Mountain Railroad,** featuring replicas of 19th-century locomotives, takes passengers on a five-mile loop around the mountain's base—from the reproduction of Atlanta's 1853 railway depot through surrounding forest and past old granite quarries. Or get the view from the triple-decker **Paddlewheel Riverboat.**

On **wildlife trails** through natural woodlands, you may spot cougars, elk, bison, and other species once indigenous to Georgia; the petting zoo is home to domesticated species. The **Antique Auto and Music Museum** exhibits collectors' cars and nickelodeons.

Sports and Recreation

A lushly landscaped 27-hole **golf course** has golf cartways resembling a miniature autobahn; for tee-time reservations, call 770/498-5717. For **swimming and sunbathing,** the lake features an imported white-sand beach, a lifeguard-staffed swimming area, and canoe, rowboat, pontoon boat, or paddleboat rentals. Other recreation includes an ice rink, tennis courts, batting cages, miniature golf, hiking, and fishing in the stocked lake "behind" the mountain (a valid Georgia fishing license is required and sold, in season).

Accommodations, Camping, and Food

The classic white-columned **Stone Mountain Park Inn,** 770/469-3311, across from the central Memorial Lawn, is the traditional place to stay and eat—or just rest your feet in the front-porch rocking chairs. The inn's rates change seasonally, with the highest summer rates starting at $140. Its **Dining Room** serves Southern buffets—it's an Easter-brunch, Mother's Day–dinner kind of place.

The lavish 250-room **Evergreen Conference Center and Resort,** 770/879-9900, occupies a quieter corner of the park. Its modern hotel includes a dining room that features continental cuisine. Rooms start at $130.

The park's nicely situated 441-site **campground,** 770/498-5600, has wooded and shady sites along the lakeshore, with a disposal station, grocery store, and full or partial hookups.

Food service can also be found dispersed within the park. **Memorial Depot Chicken Restaurant** fries bird; the **Whistlestop Barbecue,** at the base of the trail, serves traditional barbecue and sides; and the **Memorial Plaza Deli,** atop Memorial Lawn, is mostly convenient. Picnic tables are sprinkled throughout. For restaurants outside the park, see City of Stone Mountain.

Special Events

A **laser show** on the natural one-million-square-foot "screen" of the mountain's face is put on nightly from early May to September 1 (then weekends only through October). The **Fourth of July** celebration brings major musical acts along with all-American food and fireworks. Hear bagpipe music performed by kilted marchers at the **Scottish Festival and Highland Games,** in September or October.

City of Stone Mountain

Adjacent to the park's south side sits the city of Stone Mountain, which is actually a quaint village of restored Victorian storefronts set across from an old-time railroad depot. A peanut stand, ice cream parlor, craft shops, and folk antiques complete the scene. It makes a small manageable stop—usually away from the crowds—for a snack, a short walk, or a quick bag of roasted goobers.

Drivers with time on their hands may note that Memorial Drive runs a straight shot to downtown Atlanta from here—it's not a particularly scenic route, but it's a decent alternative to crowded freeways.

SOUTHEAST OF ATLANTA
Panola Mountain State Conservation Park

Panola Mountain, 18 miles southeast of Atlanta, is a huge granite outcropping resembling Stone Mountain. Yet unlike Atlanta's familiar landmark, Panola Mountain remains undeveloped, so that visitors here may better see the unique botanical and geological features of these mammoth rock mountains. A 617-acre state conservation park off Hwy. 155 (south of I-20 exit 36), 770/389-7801, gastateparks.org, preserves the natural day-use area. Admission is $2 per car.

Hikers enjoy six miles of trails. Access to the 3.5-mile **summit trail** that leads to the top is restricted to protect the fragile habitat of the 940-foot dome. The trail is open for public use only on guided ranger walks on Saturday and Sunday. The 1.25-mile **micro-watershed trail** and .75-mile **rock outcrop trail** both start out behind the interpretive center and loop through the base hardwood forest; both trails are suitable for family outings. The park is open daily 7 A.M.–dark.

JONESBORO AND VICINITY

From its start in southeast Atlanta, Jonesboro Road winds its way down through one of the city's most neglected districts into Clayton County, where it follows the railroad line into Jonesboro and becomes Main Street. In 1864, Yankees and Confederates fought along the route after Atlanta was burned. At the corner of Johnson and McDonough Streets, the Battle of Jonesboro is remembered in the **Confederate Cemetery,** where the graves of nearly 1,000 unidentified Confederate soldiers lie. Their headstones are arranged to form the shape of the Confederate battle flag.

This Confederate history probably caught the imagination of young Margaret Mitchell, who traveled to Jonesboro often from her Atlanta home to visit relatives nearby. Mitchell wove scenes and stories from the battle into her famous novel, and today *Gone with the Wind* fans retrace her steps through the town's historic sites.

Among the landmarks are the **1898 Jonesboro courthouse,** in the center of town was where Margaret Mitchell researched her novel. **Fayetteville Academy,** built in 1855, was where the fictional Scarlett O'Hara went to school, 15 miles south of town.

The local barbecue landmark is **Dean's,** 770/471-0138, which has been in business since 1947 in a shack on Main Street. There's only chopped pork (ask for outside meat) with a Carolina-style sauce, only sweeter.

Jonesboro Depot Welcome Center and Road to Tara Museum

The 1867 depot now houses the local welcome center, 104 N. Main St., 770/478-4800 or 800/662-7829, where they have driving-tour maps and audiocassette rentals, along with lodging and dining information.

Also here is the **Road to Tara Museum,** visitscarlett.com, which displays autographed first editions of GWTW, movie posters and costumes, and a hundred GWTW dolls among its exhibits. Admission is $5 for adults and $4 for students and seniors. ("Road to Tara" was Mitchell's working title.)

Both the welcome center and the museum are open Mon.–Fri. 8:30 A.M.–5:30 P.M. and Sat. 10 A.M.–4 P.M.

Stately Oaks Plantation Historic House Museum

Visitors in search of the fictional Tara are directed to the 1839 Greek Revival Stately Oaks Plantation, 100 Carriage Lane, 770/473-0197, where guides in period costume lead tours through the house that could have served as a model for the movie version of Tara. Mon.–Fri. 10 A.M.–4 P.M. Call for fees and Saturday hours.

North Georgia

North Georgia is a richly varied mountainous region, from the linear mesas of the northwest Cumberland Plateau to the legendarily lush Blue Ridge Mountains in the northeast. The region offers exceptional recreational opportunities—with white-water rafting, hiking, fishing, and mountain biking among the most popular-and a history encompassing petroglyphs, the Cherokee Nation, the first gold rush, and Civil War.

Three states meet in Georgia's **TAG Corner—Tennessee, Alabama, and Georgia.** The far corner of Georgia is so remote that for the longest time it was more easily accessible from Alabama or Tennessee than from Georgia itself. It's hard to imagine the battles of Lookout Mountain and Chickamauga being waged in this impossible terrain. The area is also known for limestone caves—two of the deepest in the country are in this TAG region—and as the premier hang gliding site on the East Coast.

The high plateau gives way to a series of lesser ridges and valleys forming the high-basin watershed that shelters a unit of the Chattahoochee National Forest. Further east, the Great Valley, through which both the railroad and General Sherman entered Georgia, is today traversed by I-75. While the entire Blue Ridge region was once the dominion of the Cherokee, it was here in North Georgia that they formed the Cherokee Nation before they were banished on the Trail of Tears.

Must-Sees

Look for **M** to find the sights and activities you can't miss and **N** for the best dining and lodging.

M Rock City Gardens: An old-time attraction promoted by iconic "See Rock City" signs throughout the Southeast, Rock City offers panoramic Lookout Mountain views bespeckled with gnomes, fairies, and the bobble-headed Rocky the Elf (page 91).

M Cloudland Canyon State Park: A hidden gem, this state park offers trails and cottages set out at the rim, and waterfalls below, in a remote corner of the state (page 92).

M Paradise Gardens: The folk-art environment of artist Reverend Howard Finster conveys his life's philosophy through carved angels, an ornate temple, bicycle-spoke sculptures, and other ornamentation constructed with found objets d'art (page 93).

M Dahlonega Gold Museum: Find out about the nation's first gold rush—preceding California's 49ers—in this charming nugget-filled museum, housed in the old courthouse, in the center of the lively mountain town square (page 105).

M Len Foote Hike Inn: At Amicalola Falls State Park, a 4.6-mile hike leads to one of only a handful of walk-in lodges in the U.S; it's secluded, ecofriendly, and a great way to start off or wind up a trip on Georgia's Appalachian Trail (page 108).

© KAP STANN

a trademark Howard Finster icon

M Chattahoochee River Float Trips: The best way to see Georgia's popular ersatz Alpine village of Helen is from the center of an inner tube floating down the cool, kid-friendly stretch of the Chattahoochee through town (page 116).

M Tallulah Gorge State Park: A suspension bridge crosses the scenic chasm in this corner of the Blue Ridge Mountains for the best view of daring rock-climbers, hang-gliders, and paddlers battling the whitewater below (page 125).

M Chattooga River Whitewater Rafting: One of the greatest adventures in the Southeast is riding the whitewater of the Chattooga River—Section 4 for daredevils, Section 3 if you have dependents (page 128).

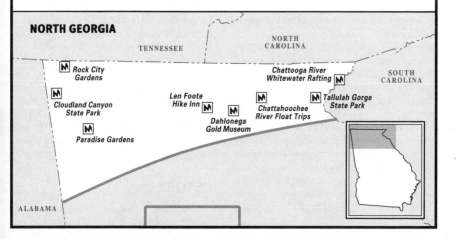

NORTH GEORGIA

TENNESSEE

NORTH CAROLINA

SOUTH CAROLINA

M Rock City Gardens

M Cloudland Canyon State Park

M Paradise Gardens

Len Foote Hike Inn **M**

M Dahlonega Gold Museum

Chattooga River Whitewater Rafting **M**

M Chattahoochee River Float Trips

M Tallulah Gorge State Park

ALABAMA

The flat, industrialized valley of carpet mills (Dalton bills itself as the Carpet Capital of the World) ends abruptly at the western flank of the Cohutta Mountains (co-HUT-a), in the center of North Georgia, where the rugged, 34,100-acre Cohutta Wilderness challenges hikers and backpackers and attracts anglers to some of the finest trout streams in the state.

From here, the **Blue Ridge Mountains** rise up to form the eastern front range of the southern Appalachians. Renowned for their beauty, the Blue Ridge is covered with a lush landscape of 1,500 blooming plant types and 130 tree varieties (compared with only 85 in all of Europe). The natural beauty and bounty attracted America's first pioneers, peopling the wilderness with Appalachian folk traditions still practiced in North Georgia today. You could cross this fabled landscape through Georgia in less than two hours, yet its attractions are so densely packed you could easily spend a week exploring a single river, wood, or trail.

Most of Georgia's Blue Ridge lies within the 750,000-acre Chattahoochee National Forest, filled with remote campgrounds and hundreds of miles of trails for hiking, horseback riding, and mountain biking. State parks are sprinkled throughout the region and are an excellent base of operations for a mountain vacation. The **Appalachian Trail** starts at Springer Mountain and extends north 2,144 miles to Maine.

Two hours north of Atlanta, **Dahlonega and vicinity** is a good place to begin exploring the Blue Ridge region. The town was the site of the nation's first gold rush in 1828 and has a gold museum, an attractive town square, and several inns. Heading **north to Blairsville** over the ridgeline brings you to the deeper forest beyond most crowds.

The most crowd-pleasing mountain town of all is Helen, a recreated Alpine village right down to the edelweiss and Tyrolean pipes (and family-friendly float trips down the Chattahoochee through town). The region from **Helen to Hiawassee** leads from the tourist town of Helen through Unicoi Gap to Georgia's bluegrass capital of Hiawassee.

Set off in the northeast corner, **Rabun County** attracts river runners from around the country to Chattooga River's white water. Sightseers head to Tallulah Gorge, where there is a dramatic suspension bridge over the chasm, and city weekenders flock to placid high-country lakes.

PLANNING YOUR TIME

The Blue Ridge Mountain region in northeast Georgia is the most popular with visitors. Their season starts in spring, when folks come up to see wildflowers, despite occasional cool and wet weather through April. Summer is the busiest season, when beautiful dry days in the mid- to high 70s draw flatlanders from all points south, escaping higher temperatures below. Fall continues warm, dry summer weather into October, and folks descend on North Georgia to see fall foliage. The winter is the quietest season—many places close up—and only hardy Southern drivers venture up to where they may encounter snow and ice. Prices vary accordingly: prime October lodging may cost up to twice as much as the same room come winter.

Start at select country inns or state parks for accommodations in lodge rooms, cabins (some families mark calendars to make reservations for coveted cabins up to 11 months in advance), or at the unique Len Foote Hike Inn, at Amicalola Falls State Park. Then call outfitters to work in a river run or mountain bike rentals, though these can often be booked spontaneously for all but large groups. Pick up a detailed national forest map at a Forest Service office for backcountry and off-road adventures.

Bring hiking boots (the lighter kind are more suitable for the weather), water shoes, river gear (dry bags, eyeglass straps), hiking and camping gear, and insect repellent and bite cream, though you can find most provisions locally.

HISTORY

While previously only the coast was known to support ancient societies, excavations of the

Nacoochee Mound, near Helen, earlier this century revealed skeletons and relics that may date back 1,000 years. Nearby petroglyph carvings may date back 3,500 years, and in the north-central mountains, a stone wall of mysterious origins at Fort Mountain is ascribed to aboriginal tribes.

Inheritors of this ancient past, the Cherokee inhabited North Georgia when the first Europeans arrived. In 1539, the Spanish explorer Hernando de Soto led a 600-man expedition from Florida to North Georgia in search of gold. His journey and those of other European explorers decimated the Cherokee by introducing diseases against which the Native Americans had no natural immunity.

British pioneers from coastal Charleston—as well as Scotch, Irish, and German emigrants from Pennsylvania—began settling on the Appalachian frontier in the mid-18th century. In their wilderness isolation, many pioneers maintained independent ways; they remained loyal to the Crown during the American Revolution and later refused to fight for the Confederacy during the Civil War.

White settlers fought with the Cherokee over territory, yet surprisingly, the two radically different groups managed to coexist peacefully much of the time, learning from one another's culture. From the Cherokee, the pioneers learned how to make the best use of natural resources, and in turn, the Cherokee adopted many European ways. They established the Cherokee Nation, with a representative system of government based on that of the United States. Yet their sovereignty and homeland nonetheless fell victim to U.S. expansionism, triggered by the discovery of gold on Cherokee territory.

Gold Rush

In 1828, a hunter named Benjamin Parks kicked up what resembled "the yellow of an egg," and what turned out to be a large gold nugget propelled the first major gold rush in American history (predating California's "'49ers"). Centered in the boomtown of Dahlonega (Cherokee for "yellow metal"), the rush brought thousands of miners to the area. The federal government founded a branch of the U.S. mint in Dahlonega, which produced more than six mil-

lion dollars in gold coins before it closed at the onset of the Civil War. The town's Gold Museum recounts gold-rush days.

Civil War

The critical Civil War battles for Chattanooga and Atlanta were staged in the stark terrain of northwest Georgia. Here, a single glance at the unforgiving landscape delivers a finer appreciation for the hard-fought victories and defeats than a lifetime of imagining the scene.

Union infantry, heading south, came up against Lookout Mountain—a daunting, hundred-mile linear barrier that rises like a sheer wall from the level valleys below. Narrow breaks channeled weary armies through, only to face equally formidable mesas beyond.

In the Chickamauga Valley in September 1863, Confederate troops led by Generals Braxton Bragg and James Longstreet repelled the advance of the Union armies under Generals William Rosecrans and George Thomas, yet at high cost. Remembered as the two bloodiest days of the Civil War, the Battle of Chickamauga Creek took 4,000 lives and caused 35,000 casualties. In November, the Battle Above the Clouds, atop Lookout Mountain, and fighting on Missionary Ridge led to Union General Ulysses S. Grant's eventual control of Chattanooga.

The following spring, Union General William Tecumseh Sherman resumed the advance south into Georgia. With 100,000 troops he chewed up the path of the railroad, engaging the vastly outnumbered troops of Confederate General James Johnston in Dalton, Resaca, Cassville, and New Hope Church before assaulting Atlanta. His path is today strewn with monuments, old breastworks, cemeteries, old depots, and other landmarks.

1865–1930s

After the Civil War, the economic and environmental destruction wrought by overfarming, hydraulic mining, overlogging, the chestnut blight, and the boll weevil added up to decades of hard times for mountain communities. Forced to rely more than ever on what could be drawn from the land, the mountaineers heightened their reliance on folkways—customs and crafts now regarded as

North Georgia

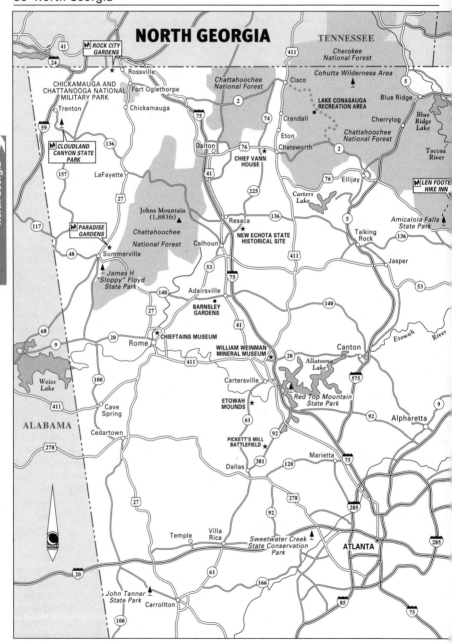

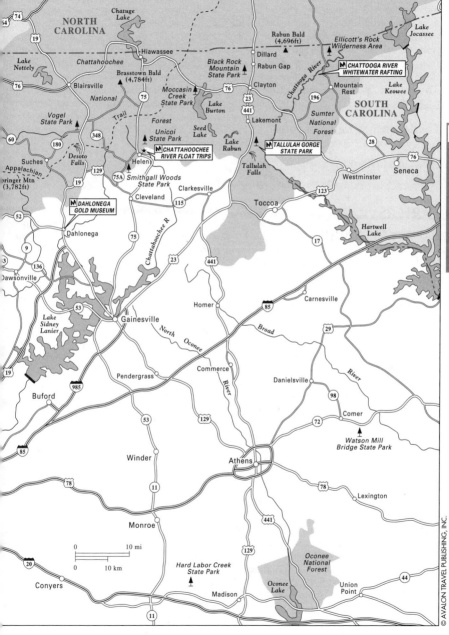

some of America's most creative pioneer expressions. Their extreme isolation began to diminish with the first rural postal delivery, highway construction, and later with radio and television, yet many mountaineers continued to practice traditional folkways in earnest for several more decades. The aging population of "old-timers" in the mountains today represents the last of a hardy breed.

Chattahoochee National Forest

In the 1920s and 1930s, the federal government bought most of North Georgia's land to establish the national forest. Land "reclamation" projects, designed to restore flora in areas of environmental devastation, were accomplished by the Depression-era Civilian Conservation Corps (CCC). Many CCC-built state parks, stone cabins, and lodges remain in active use today. The Wilderness Act of 1964 set aside the Cohutta and Ellicott Rock Wilderness Areas, and in December 1991, 56,000 more acres were designated as wilderness.

The Western Uplands

CARTERSVILLE

Pickett's Mill Battlefield

Off Hwy. 92 south of I-75 between Marietta and Cartersville, Pickett's Mill Battlefield, on Hwy. 381, 770/443-7850, remains one of the best-preserved Civil War battlefields in the nation. The state historic site recalls the 1864 battle, in which Federal troops attempting an end run around the Confederate line were decisively repelled. Admission is $1.25–2.50.

Etowah Mounds

Five miles southwest of Cartersville, at Etowah Mounds, on Hwy. 61, 770/387-3747, an aboriginal earthwork center offers a glimpse of the ancient civilization that thrived here about 400 years ago—the most intact Mississippian Culture site in the Southeast. The hallowed mounds, up to 63 feet high, served as platforms and temples for the priest-chief and as burial sites for nobility.

Artifacts at the site date back much further and provide evidence of an early continental trade network. The human statuettes and decorated mica sheets found at Etowah—the site's most acclaimed relics—clearly illustrate a style influenced by Mesoamerican designs (surmised to have been brought by traders).

The state-operated historic site and museum is open Tues.–Sat. 9 A.M.–5 P.M., Sun. 2–5:30 P.M. (closed Mon. except for legal holidays). Admission is $2–3.

Red Top Mountain State Park

At Allatoona Lake, a 1,428-acre peninsula out into 12,000-acre Lake Allatoona, holds this state park, 770/975-4226 or 800/864-PARK (864-7275), gastateparks.org, parking $2, which features a swimming beach, trails, fishing, tennis courts, and a restaurant overlooking the lake that serves three meals a day. Lodging options include a 33-room lodge ($69–89), a 95-site campground ($18–22), 18 rental cottages ($89–119), and a yurt ($35). The park is popular with boaters who bring their own; rentals are available from nearby marinas. The park is two miles east of I-75 exit 285, less than an hour from the Atlanta perimeter.

William Weinman Mineral Museum

Rock hounds will find gemstones, fossils, crystals, arrowheads, geodes, mastodon molars, petrified wood, and a simulated limestone cave in this mineral center on the southwest side of the intersection of Hwy. 411 and I-75 exit 126, 770/386-0576, weinmanmuseum.org. Hours are Mon.–Sat. 10 A.M.–5 P.M. Admission is $4 for adults and $3 for children.

ROME AND VICINITY

Founded during the 1830s on the site of a former Cherokee Indian settlement at the head of the Coosa River Valley, the city of Rome sheltered an important cannon foundry for the Confederacy. Evading earlier threats by Union troops

Aboriginal relics are displayed at Etowah Mounds.

in 1863, Rome succumbed to the routing forces that Sherman led through Georgia in 1864. But neither Sherman's destruction of the town's industry nor subsequent floods have kept Rome from maintaining its status as northwest Georgia's industrial center.

Downtown Rome is centered along several busy blocks of Broad Street, down from the river. A prominent landmark downtown is the **1871 Old Town Clock,** which is atop a 104-foot water tower. A more notorious one is the **statue of Romulus and Remus** in front of city hall; it was a gift from Benito Mussolini in 1929. The state of the naked infants suckling from a mother wolf caused such a stir that the twins were diapered when public events brought crowds to city hall. In 1933 one of the twins disappeared, but a replacement was sent from Italy. When Italy declared war on the Allies in 1940, the statue was put away for safekeeping until it was returned to display in 1952.

The **Rome Visitors Center,** 402 Civic Center Dr., 706/295-5576 or 800/444-1834, is housed in a turn-of-the-20th-century train depot off Highways 20 and 27; it's open daily.

Chieftains Museum
The Chieftains Museum, 501 Riverside Pkwy., 706/291-9494, is housed in the white clapboard home of the man who signed the treaty that led to the removal of the Cherokee from the area. Chief Ridge went west with his fellow Cherokee, only to be executed there for selling off tribal lands. The small museum examines southeastern Indian history from the 1st to the 19th centuries. The museum is open Tues.–Fri. 9 A.M.–3 P.M. and Sat. 10 A.M.–4 P.M. Admission is $3 for adults and $1.50 for children.

Berry College and Berry Home
In 1902, Martha Berry founded the Berry School to educate Appalachian youths. The school evolved into Berry College, which today occupies 28,000 acres of handsome buildings set amid forests, fields, lakes, and streams north of Rome. The campus waterwheel makes a picturesque stop, and the Weaving Room displays hand-woven items and other student crafts, all of which are available for sale. Pick up a map at the main entrance, off Hwy. 27.

Across the highway, **Oak Hill,** 706/291-1883, opens the Berry family's antebellum mansion and five acres of formal gardens. It's open Mon.–Sat. 10 A.M.–5 P.M. Admission is $5 for adults and $3 for students; children under six are free.

Cave Spring

Cave Spring is a charming little outpost at the Alabama border. The cool (56ºF) limestone cave for which the town is named is behind a miniature stone castle in the heart of town at **Rolater Park,** 706/777-3382, open for $1 tours regularly in the summer and the rest of the year by appointment.

Outside, the zealous spring streams forth from the cave, at the rate of three to four million gallons a day, into the park's huge public **swimming pool,** which is whimsically constructed in the shape of the state of Georgia (open summers only).

Beside the pool, find the two-story 1839 **Hearn Academy** schoolhouse, which is now operated by the city as a bed-and-breakfast. It has five guest rooms (rates start at $50 and include a full breakfast). The park is a short quarter-mile walk to the town square, where a row of shops includes a nursery, cafés, antique shops, and gift shops. **Todd's Country Kitchen,** 706/777-8327, features a lunch buffet and steak, chicken, and fish among the dinner entrées. The surround-

ing neighborhood has more than 90 structures on the Historic Register.

East of Cave Spring is **Chubbtown.** In pre–Civil War Georgia, one of the few communities of free blacks lived here. Descendants of the founding family still live here.

Atlanta drivers can reach Cave Spring by way of Route 278 to Cedartown, then Route 100 to Cave Spring.

ADAIRSVILLE

Barnsley Gardens, 597 Barnsley Gardens Rd., 770/773-1779 or 877/773-2447, barnsleyresort.com, a resort on 1,300 beautifully landscaped acres set around the ruins of an antebellum villa, originated as the vision of a English merchant. English emigrant Godfrey Barnsley bought the property in the 1840s and halted construction when his wife died—until her spirit appeared to him in the fountain and instructed him to complete the house. He built a grand Italian villa by her ghostly design, but it was largely destroyed by a hurricane in 1906. Descendants auctioned the house in 1942, and it fell into disrepair. German prince Hubertus Fugger bought the estate in the 1980s and began transforming it into a deluxe resort. The ruins of the villa remain standing on a knoll above the telltale fountain, and a small museum in the still-standing kitchen wing relates the family's saga.

Today the resort features 33 luxury cottages built in 19th-century English village style, with 70 individually decorated suites featuring woodburning fireplaces, Egyptian linens, ball-in-claw tubs, porches, and gardens (rates start at $275 for a double and include a full breakfast). The grounds also have a golf course (greens fees start at $75), tennis, and a spa with steam baths, saunas, and hot tubs (in gender-specific ones, clothing is optional; coed, clothing required). A 7-mile trail takes hikers within eyesight of the small buffalo herd on the property.

Two restaurants, the **Rice House,** for fine dining (open Fri–Sat. only), and the more casual **Woodland Grill** are rare outposts in northwest Georgia for such exotic fare as risotto and truffles. There's also a beer garden.

© KAP STANN

the entrance to Cave Spring, where it's a cool 56°F year-round

TAG Corner

The TAG corner—where Tennessee, Alabama, and Georgia meet—presents an unexpected landscape of mesas, canyons, limestone caves, boulder fields, and rock formations rising up from terrain covered with Appalachian forests. The land is scarred with Civil War battle sites, remnants of the fights for Chattanooga and Atlanta. Howard Finster's otherworldly Paradise Gardens, outside Summerville, presents a hallucinogenic flip side to the enchanted gnomes and fairies at the oldtimey Rock City attraction, at the Tennessee line.

The **Georgia Welcome Center** at Ringgold, 706/937-4211, inside the Georgia state line off I-75, can orient visitors to the region. For further information on the area, visit the Northwest Georgia Mountains tourist bureau's website at georgiahighcountry.org.

LOOKOUT MOUNTAIN

Lookout Mountain stretches more than a hundred miles through all three TAG states. Its northern tip overlooks the city of Chattanooga at the Tennessee–Georgia border, and on each side of the border lies one of two towns named Lookout Mountain. So when folks direct you to Lookout Mountain, they might mean the mountain's northern tip, one of the two towns, or the entire corner of the state. For dramatic overlooks and a sense of regional topography, cruise the **Lookout Mountain Scenic Parkway** (note that local route numbers change along the way).

Rock City Gardens

From Knoxville, Tennessee, to the Carolinas, "See Rock City" signs were painted on barns, birdhouses, and billboards to promote Lookout Mountain's fanciful rock gardens; some remain today and are relics as treasured as the old-time mountain landmark itself.

Rock City Gardens, 1400 Patten Rd., 706/820-2531, seerockcity.com, was created in the late 1920s as a private walk-through garden. It displays arresting rock formations of the Cumberland Plateau in entertaining ways designed to enchant youngsters in particular. You can cross a swinging suspension footbridge over rock canyons, walk through a narrow crevice called Fat Man's Squeeze, and see Balancing Rock and Lover's Leap.

Rocky the Bobble-Headed Elf greets all guests. Throughout the park, small concrete gnomes peek from behind rocks and trees, and sugarplum fairies (winged Barbie dolls) inhabit enchanted grottoes lined with glass crystals. At the visitors center, colored transparent sheets drape the windows with captions reading, "This is what Chattanooga would look like if everything were orange," or red, or green, whatever.

Admission is $13 for adults and $7 for children. Rock City is open every day except Christmas, 8:30 A.M.–6 P.M. Follow signs to Rock City from I-24; it's on Hwy. 157 off Hwy. 189.

CHICKAMAUGA
Chickamauga Battlefield

The oldest and largest military park in the country, **Chickamauga and Chattanooga National Military Park** is headquartered at Chickamauga Battlefield, on Hwy. 27 south of Fort Oglethorpe, 706/866-9241, nps.gov/chch. Established 25 years after the war upon the urging of veterans from both sides, the park commemorates the 4,000 dead and 35,000 casualties in two days of fighting—the two most costly days of the Civil War—over control of Chattanooga and Atlanta. The troop movements of Confederate Generals Braxton Bragg and James Longstreet, and Union Generals William Rosecrans and George Thomas (the "Rock of Chickamauga") are recounted with 1,500 historical markers and monuments, self-guided audiotape tours, summertime living-history reenactments, and ranger interpretive programs. Start at the **visitors center** for a slide show that details the battle nearly hour-by-hour. The center is open 8 A.M.–4:45 P.M. From I-75, take exit 141 (Hwy. 2) west to Fort Oglethorpe, then turn south on Hwy. 27 to the park.

Because most visitors come to hear the human history and rarely stray from their cars, more

North Georgia

than 80 miles of **hiking trails** through the Chickamauga Valley are generally quiet and untrampled. The rolling terrain is in a wide valley between two long ridges—a blend of thick forest, open meadows, and farm fields. Seven trails with interpretive signs explain the natural and human history of the region; a five-mile nature trail is the shortest, and the 20-mile perimeter trail is the longest.

Accommodations

In the town of Chickamauga, the **N Gordon Lee Mansion**, 217 Cove Rd., 706/375-4728 or 800/487-4728, gordonleemansion.com, served as headquarters to General Rosecrans for a few fateful days in September 1863. Today it operates as a historic inn. Four nicely appointed bed-and-breakfast rooms have private baths. Rates are $75–125 (double) and include a full breakfast.

CLOUDLAND CANYON

Tucked away in Georgia's northwest corner, Cloudland Canyon remained virtually unknown and inaccessible until roads were built into the area in the 1930s. Adventurers returned with tales of a breathtaking canyon with extraordinary scenery and waterfalls, and naturalists came to study the striped layers of exposed sandstone underlying Lookout Mountain. Now, a state park at the rim lets drivers ride straight up to the panoramic vista to witness an unexpected topography.

N Cloudland Canyon State Park

Cloudland Canyon State Park, off Hwy. 136 between Trenton and LaFayette, 706/657-4050 or 800/864-PARK (864-7275), gastateparks.org, parking $2, remains an isolated retreat today. The park straddles a deep gorge cut into the mountain by Sitton Gulch Creek, and the elevation varies from 800 to 1,980 feet.

Hikers can find beautiful views along two rim trails. The five-mile **West Rim Trail** crosses Daniel Creek and loops into a mixed hardwood forest (which is spectacular in autumn). **Falls Trails** lead down hundreds of steps and switchbacks into the canyon to two dramatic waterfalls—the trip back up can be agonizing, but it's worth it. Backpackers

must obtain permits to take the seven-mile **East Rim Trail** to primitive campsites.

Stay in one of 16 fully equipped and spacious cottages at the rim for $85–115. Or camp at one of 48 sites near rim trails ($19–22, hookups available) or one of 30 walk-in sites ($10). Overnight visitors need to carry all necessary food to avoid a lengthy descent into Trenton for supplies.

THE LOWER PLATEAU

McLemore Cove

Between Cloudland Canyon and LaFayette, two mesas meet. Pigeon Mountain extends from Lookout Mountain in the shape of a thumb—the sheltered nook between them is McLemore Cove. You can overlook the pastoral valley from the Lookout Mountain Scenic Highway (Hwy. 157) or get a close-up look by descending into the cove on Hwy. 193 (about 15 miles east of Cloudland Canyon and eight miles west of LaFayette).

The isolated valley of dairy farms, croplands, farmhouses, and tall cedar stands, wedged between the sandstone cliffs, starts where Hwy. 193 meets Hog Jowl Road (Hwy. 341) and fans out to Hwy. 136. Bicyclists will find this a pleasant, quiet touring route and can take loop trips of various lengths via either Hwy. 193 or Hwy. 136.

Once in the cove, hikers can find the steep six-mile **Pocket Trail,** which climbs Pigeon Mountain for a view of the valley and an upclose look at the mountain's unusual rock formations. To reach the trailhead, take Hog Jowl Road 2.7 miles south from Davis Crossroads (the junction of Highway 193 and Hog Jowl Road) to the fork in the road, then veer left. Continue past the Baptist church to the top of the hill and turn left onto a paved road. The pavement ends after a half-mile, then turns rugged and continues another 1.6 miles to a field where you can park. A wooden sign next to the stream marks the trailhead.

LaFayette

The town of LaFayette marks the western border of the Chattahoochee National Forest. Most of the forest's recreation areas are accessible via Hwy. 136 east. Travelers can pick up directions and trail guides at the Forest Service office, 806 E. Villanow St., 706/397-2265, fs.fed.us/conf.

Summerville

About 18 miles south of LaFayette on Hwy. 27, the little town of Summerville has become known to admirers of self-taught art as the home of Paradise Gardens. Also here, a quiet state park draws locals for fishing and boating.

In town, Finster pilgrims (see below), anglers, campers, and locals commune at **Armstrong's,** 216 N. Commerce St., 706/857-9900, a breakfast and barbecue joint. It's open Wed.–Sat. 11 A.M.–8:45 P.M.

Paradise Gardens

At Paradise Gardens outside Summerville, twisted shards of aluminum foil dangle from tree branches, bicycle-part sculptures and folk Madonnas grace the grounds, and signs quote scripture and proclaim the mystery of folk philosophy on mosaic paths leading to the World's Folk Art Church.

Visionary self-taught artist Reverend Howard Finster (1917–2001) started constructing this eccentric personal wonderland in the 1940s. In 1975, Finster came to national attention when his art was featured in *Esquire,* after which his work was exhibited around the country. He worked with Michael Stipe on cover art for R.E.M.'s album "Reckoning," and his painting on the Talking Heads' "Little Creatures" album was honored in 1985 by *Rolling Stone* as best cover of the year. Finster can be seen playing banjo in traditional call-and-response style in the art-house film *Athens, Ga.: Inside/Out.* One of the best-known purveyors of outsider or self-taught art, Finster was called "the Andy Warhol of the South" by one Smithsonian collector. Finster's iconographic portraits and angels can be found among the collections of museums throughout the country; the High Museum in Atlanta has the largest collection.

Finster's family opens his 2.5-acre visionary folk-art environment of Paradise Gardens, on Rena St. off Hwy. 27, 706/857-5791, finster.com, on Sat. 10 A.M.–5 P.M. for $5 admission, or by appointment with a $20 nonrefundable confirmation fee. A gallery and small store are open to visitors for no charge. Inquire about overnight stays and Finster festivals.

Paradise Gardens is in the community of Pennville, three miles north of Summerville, about a hundred yards off Hwy. 27. Turn east on Rena Street between Jim's Auto Supply and Penn Auto Parts.

James H. "Sloppy" Floyd State Park

Named for a revered state legislator who was affectionately nicknamed "Sloppy," J. H. Floyd State Park, 706/857-0826 or 800/864-PARK (864-7275), gastateparks.org, parking $2, is off Hwy. 100 south of town at the western edge of the national forest. The quiet park is surrounded by rural countryside and has two small lakes for fishing and boating; a long boardwalk leads out into the water, and boat rentals are available. Four cottages ($95–105) and a 25-site campground ($19–21, hookups available) are nestled on a thickly forested hillside alongside.

DALTON

As the Carpet Capital of the World, Dalton (I-75 exit 136) presides over the region's economic mainstay—the carpet-producing mills of the central valley. More than 60 percent of the world's carpet is made here, and more than 100 carpet outlets—many along the interstate—offer discount carpet samples.

Twice a year, a major regional fair is held 10 miles north of the city. The **Prater's Mill County Fair,** in May and October (on Mother's Day and Columbus Day weekends), is staged at the site of a historic gristmill (off Hwy. 2, a mile east of Hwy. 71). The historic mill, built by enslaved labor in 1855, is one of several historic structures to be seen at this celebration of rural folklife. The festival features mountain music, square dances, storytellers, and the original arts and crafts of 150 artisans—including the colonial art of hand-tufted bedspread-making that gave the town industry its start. The rest of the year, the historic grounds are open to the public from dawn to dusk, at no charge.

The **Dalton Welcome Center,** in the northwest Georgia Trade and Convention Center off I-75 exit 136, 706/272-7676, organizes carpet-mill tours and distributes downtown walking-tour guides, among other city information. It's open weekdays only.

CALHOUN AND VICINITY

Beyond the Last Chance carpet outlets, Wal-Mart, budget motels, and other national chains found at its freeway exits, Calhoun hides a rich history. It was once the home of the 1828 Cherokee Nation, and the Atlanta Campaign's battle at Resaca occurred six miles outside town in 1864—the battle is reenacted annually in mid-May.

New Echota State Historic Site

The Cherokee Nation was organized in 1828, with a representative democracy and a constitution similar to that of the United States. New Echota was named as its capital. Though the U.S. Supreme Court originally recognized the nation as a sovereign power, President Andrew Jackson sent Federal troops to remove the Cherokee from their ancestral homelands. In 1838, troops forcibly expelled and imprisoned the Cherokee before exiling them along the Trail of Tears to Oklahoma.

A museum and several restored buildings here display what little remains of the historic capital. Visitors can tour the Supreme Court house, the printing shop that produced the bilingual *Cherokee Phoenix* (printed in both English and Cherokee), Vann's Tavern, and the original home of missionary Samuel Worcester, an advocate for Cherokee rights. The visitors center tells the story and displays artifacts.

The state-operated site, on Hwy. 225 one mile east of I-75, 706/624-1321, gastateparks.org, is open Tues.–Sat. 9 A.M.–5 P.M. and Sun. 2–5:30 P.M. (closed Mon. except for legal holidays). Admission is $3–4.

Johns Mountain

Six miles west of Calhoun, the Armuchee Ranger District of the **Chattahoochee National Forest** shelters the wooded ridges and valleys that stand between the central valley around Calhoun and the western Cumberland Plateau.

Johns Mountain overlooks Georgia's ridge-and-valley region. The 3.5-mile **Johns Mountain Trail** loops around the mesa-topped mountain; here, vistas of pastoral farms and fields have not much

CHEROKEE ALPHABET

Joseph Sequoyah, a visionary among the Cherokee, recognized that the written language of the European Americans offered a tremendous advantage over the Native Americans, who at that time had no written language. So Sequoyah set to work developing a syllabary that expressed the sounds of the Cherokee language (essentially, an alphabet). Within a few years after the adoption of his 85-unit syllabary in 1819, thousands of Cherokee became literate. Considering how rarely in the course of human history language-writing systems have been developed, Sequoyah's written language stands as a remarkable achievement.

changed since Sherman's troops marched through in 1864. Find the trailhead from Hwy. 136, about 18 miles northwest of Calhoun and I-75. Turn left (south) onto Forest Service Road 203 (Pocket Road) just before you reach Villanow; continue south on this route five miles to the two-mile rugged gravel road to the mountaintop.

About halfway around the Johns Mountain loop, hikers arrive at the top of Keown Falls. A spur trail descends to the base and connects with the 1.8-mile **Keown Falls Trail.** This trail runs from the wispy waterfalls, along a stream, to a scenic area near the 27-site Forest Service **Pocket Campground.** The campground features a 2.5-mile loop through the surrounding wooded glen. To reach the campground and waterfalls trailhead, follow the directions to Johns Mountain above, and continue south on Pocket Road past the turnoff to the overlook trail.

The Cohutta Mountains

North Georgia's Cohutta Mountains are centered between the linear mesas of the Cumberland Plateau to the west and the knobbly Blue Ridge Mountains to the east. As part of the Blue Ridge geological province, the Cohuttas resemble the eastern Blue Ridge range, with similarly rolling elevations laced with rivers and creeks. Yet with a less "enclosed" canopy and a drier climate, the Cohuttas feel more ruggedly western than the moist and sheltered Blue Ridge.

The small towns surrounding the remote range can be characterized in much the same way. While more rugged and Western in style than the boutiquey towns farther east, the communities of north-central Georgia share the same Appalachian heritage; many of the traditions of the Blue Ridge Mountains can also be found here.

Highways run along three sides of the range— Hwy. 411 to the west, Hwy. 5/76 to the east, and Highways 52 and 76 to the south.

COHUTTA WILDERNESS

Some of the wildest and most rugged country left in the eastern United States, the Cohutta Wilderness Area contains 35,000 acres of primitive backcountry bordered by a 95,000-acre wildlife management area. Anglers claim the Cohuttas hold the best trout streams in the state— Jacks and Conasauga Rivers are favorites of anglers and hikers. The area was extensively logged in the 1920s, and now the old logging roads and beds of narrow-gauge railroads serve as hiking trails, with names such as Tearbritches Trail, Rough Ridge, and Penitentiary Branch. Bears, wild hogs, and white-tailed deer are a few of the larger species found here in isolated mountain coves and on forested ridge tops.

Forest Service roads skirt the perimeter of the wilderness; many have rough, narrow climbs not suitable for delicate cars, drivers, or passengers. From the west, adventurers can gain access from three entrances off Hwy. 411 north of Chatsworth—via the towns of Eton, Crandall, and Cisco. From the south, follow signs from Hwy. 52. From the east, take Hwy. 5 northwest of the town of Blue Ridge to Rte. 271.

Hiking and Backpacking

The 16.7-mile **Jacks River Trail** nearly crosses the wilderness from northwest to southeast. The trail runs largely along what was once the bed of a narrow-gauge railroad. It's a wet and demanding route with 30-some river crossings. Yet the rewards are great, with many scenic waterfalls and beautiful spots to camp (try around Horseshoe Bend). Bring a walking stick to help cross rivers, wear shoes that can get wet, and watch the weather to avoid raging waters after rains or flash floods during thunderstorms.

The 78-mile **Benton MacKaye Trail,** named for the founder of the Appalachian Trail, starts farther east at Springer Mountain. The trail winds its way west, skirting the eastern boundary of the Cohutta Wilderness up to the Tennessee line. Road crossings at Hwy. 60 and Hwy. 5/76 permit easy access. Contact the **Forest Service office,** 706/632-3031, on East Main

Street in Blue Ridge, for trail maps and Cohutta Wilderness maps.

For a 12-mile overnight backpacking loop within the Cohutta Wilderness, take the 3.4-mile **Tearbritches Trail** to the **Conasauga River Trail;** follow the river southeast for about five miles, then drop down south on the 1.8-mile **Chestnut Lead Trail.** The Tearbritches trailhead lies east of the Lake Conasauga recreation area; take Forest Service Road 68 a half-mile north till the road forks, veer right and continue another half-mile east (still Forest Service Road 68) to the trailhead on the north side of the road. The Chestnut Lead trail ends 1.5 miles down the road from the Tearbritches trailhead.

CHATSWORTH AND VICINITY

At the western foot of the Cohuttas, at the end of a long, dry drive from every direction, the remote town of Chatsworth vaguely resembles an old stage stop—isolated clapboard buildings are scattered off wide dusty streets, stacked road signs point to faraway destinations, and the mountains loom large in the background.

It's fitting that the town's major annual event is the **Appalachian Wagon Train** in July—up to 200 wagon trains and 2,000 horseback riders create a spectacular parade, and half-day wagon-train trips take passengers through local wilds.

In town, a **Forest Service office,** 401 Old Ellijay Rd., 706/695-6736, sells and distributes trail maps to the Cohutta Wilderness and other forest areas.

At lunchtime, find your way to **Edna's,** on Hwy. 411, 706/695-4951, for inexpensive, home-style Southern lunch and early dinner, topped off with peanut-butter pie.

Chief Vann House

The town's main attraction is the Chief Vann House, at the junction of Hwy. 52A and Hwy. 225, 706/695-2598, gastateparks.org. Called the Showplace of the Cherokee Nation, it was built in 1804 by James Vann, a contentious character who was killed at a local tavern in 1809. His son Joseph became a Cherokee statesman and lived in the two-story Federal-style brick mansion until

the Cherokee were banished to Oklahoma. The house has been restored and furnished with period antiques and is open Tues.–Sat. 9 A.M.–5 P.M. and Sun. 2–5:30 P.M. (closed Mon. except legal holidays). Admission is $2–3.

Fort Mountain State Park

Fort Mountain State Park, on Hwy. 52 about five miles east of Chatsworth, 706/695-2621 or 800/864-PARK (864-7275), gastateparks.org, parking $2, occupies a mountain summit named for a mysterious stone wall. Because the 855-foot wall is aligned to the position of the sun at equinox, some speculate it was a religious center for the Woodland people who inhabited the area around A.D. 500. More romantic theorists assert instead that it was made by a nomadic Welsh prince who predated de Soto; the least romantic claim it to be the natural weathering of hard caprock.

Whatever the origin, the **Old Fort Trail** leads to the wall through an inviting forest of scarlet oak, gnarled white oak, and Virginia pine. The wall itself (about a quarter-mile out) is anticlimactic compared to the dramatic legends (how could it not be?); it resembles a typical New England property line. Beyond the wall, summit

canoeing in Fort Mountain State Park

trails loop a mile or so to an observation tower and several overlook platforms. Backpackers hike the 8.2-mile **Gahuti Trail** across old logging roads, passing scenic vistas of the interior wilderness and three primitive campsites. Three short nature trails take hikers to a view of the falls and around the lakeshore.

The park has 30 miles of **mountain biking** trails and 37 miles of **horse trails,** as well as horse rentals nearby (call 706/517-4906). Pick up maps to all trails at the park office.

Among the park's other outstanding features are a 17-acre lake—with a swimming beach, dock, seasonal boat rentals, and a 400-foot waterfall.

Fifteen fully equipped cottages rent for $80–120. A 70-site campground at the lake's north shore charges $20–22, including water and electric hookups.

Lake Conasauga and Vicinity

At the end of backwoods drives south of the Cohutta Wilderness Area, the Forest Service **Lake Conasauga Recreation Area** lies along the shores of a 19-acre lake. Here folks can swim, sunbathe on a grassy ledge, launch boats, and fish for bass, rainbow trout, bream, and crappie. The two-mile **Songbird Trail** leads to a habitat of warblers, cuckoos, and chickadees; other trails lead around the lake and up to an old fire tower.

The 35-site campground ($5 per night) has tent pads, restrooms, and water. On summer weekends, it's often full, so there's an overflow camping area with portable toilets but no water. To reach the lake from Chatsworth, travel north on Hwy. 411 to Eton, turn right at the traffic light, and go east along this road until the pavement ends. Here it becomes Forest Service Road 18; turn left on Forest Service Road 68 and proceed northeast for 10 miles.

The five-mile **Windy Gap Cycle Trail,** southwest of Lake Conasauga, is designed for experienced mountain bikers. The trailhead is off Hwy. 411 north of Chatsworth. Turn right at the traffic light in Eton and go east around five miles. Turn left on Forest Service Road 218 (Muskrat Road) and continue three miles to the trailhead. For other off-road-vehicle trails in the vicinity, contact the Forest Service office in Chatsworth.

TATE AND JASPER

Highway 5, which merges with Hwy. 76 north of Ellijay for a stretch, traces the valley that divides the Cohuttas to the west from the Blue Ridge Mountains to the east. In the foothills, only an hour and a half from Atlanta, two country inns stand within five miles of one another in the marble-quarry region around Tate and Jasper. Jasper hosts the **Georgia Marble Festival** each October.

In Tate, two miles east of Hwy. 5, find the landmark pink-marble mansion of the **Tate House,** on Hwy. 53, 770/735-3122, tate-house.com. Five luxury suites within are decorated with antiques, and private baths are lined with local marble. Out back, nine modern log cabins are equipped with fireplaces, lofts, and hot tubs (doubles start at $120 and include breakfast). They also have a pool, tennis courts, horse stables, and a restaurant.

In Jasper, two miles east of Hwy. 5, the **Woodbridge Inn,** 411 Chambers St., 706/692-6293, offers dining in a rustic antebellum setting with a panoramic mountain view. The inn specializes in steak and fish. They also let rooms from around $60 (without breakfast). From downtown Jasper, go north on Main Street and cross the small wooden bridge on the right to the inn.

On approach via I-575, find **Ⱦ Two Brothers Barbecue,** on Old Federal Rd. in Ball Ground, 770/735-2900, on the Barbecue Landmark Trail.

ELLIJAY AND VICINITY

The Apple Capital town of Ellijay centers around a homey old square set on a wooded rise above a stream. Around the square, a streamside café and other dusty wooden storefronts selling country wares give the town a fine funky flavor. Here, kayakers and mountain bikers meet apple farmers over grits and coffee.

The town's trademark event, the **Apple Festival,** is held the second weekend in October and features plenty of home-style apple treats, a pet parade, mountain music, and local crafts. A rodeo highlights local **Fourth of July** festivities; and you can check out the livestock at the **Gilmer County Fair** the second week in August.

In East Ellijay, **Colonel Poole's Bar-B-Q,** on Hwy. 515, 706/635-4100 or 888/632-8778, poolesbarbq.com, is on the Barbecue Landmark Trail and needs no map to find. Look for the Pig Hill of Fame, the Taj-Ma-Hog, and Pig-Moby-il off the side of the road. It may be cheesy, but it's decent 'cue.

Coosawatee River Running

The Coosawatee River was once a long stretch of dramatic wilderness white water—some say it inspired novelist James Dickey's white-water adventures in *Deliverance*—but its biggest rapids, highest cliffs, and scenic gorge were obscured by the dam (the highest east of the Mississippi) that created Carters Lake. White-water enthusiasts still enjoy the upper part of the wild river, which drops more than 500 feet in 22 miles. Yet these rapids do not exceed Class III, and their spacing allows paddlers time to enjoy spectacular scenery.

Gilmer County Park, south of the intersection of Hwys. 5 and 282, provides a put-in point; the take-out is at the **Ridgeway Park** boat ramp administered by Carters Lake.

CITY OF BLUE RIDGE AND VICINITY

The city of Blue Ridge sits near the junction of three states and three mountain ranges. The long narrow valley from Ellijay to Blue Ridge (traced by Highway 76) divides the Blue Ridge Mountains on the east from the Cohutta Mountains on the west. North of Blue Ridge—where Georgia, Tennessee, and North Carolina come together—the Cohuttas become the Great Smoky Mountains. Across the border, Georgia's Toccoa River changes its name too, becoming the Ocoee River so familiar to white-water rafters.

Blue Ridge, the western gateway to the Blue Ridge Mountains, more resembles a town from the Old West than the hillside-hugging towns deeper in the mountains farther east. Downtown, flanks of brick storefronts surround a working depot with a steam train that offers scenic excursion rides, and folks can browse through antiques, folk art, and books while they wait. Mountain-music fans know Blue Ridge best for

the bluegrass, country, and gospel festivals and concerts held west of town, while serious recreationers find great hiking, fishing, and boating in and around Blue Ridge Lake and in the many natural areas in the vicinity.

Modern development—supermarket shopping malls and familiar franchise outlets—lines Hwy. 76 on each side of the Hwy. 5 intersection. Find downtown tucked southeast of this intersection. Blue Ridge is 90 miles north of Atlanta.

Blue Ridge Scenic Railway

Operating out of the old depot in the center of town, the Blue Ridge Scenic Railway, 241 Depot St., 706/632-9833 or 800/934-1898, brscenic.com, offers excursion rides along the Toccoa River in vintage passenger cars drawn by a massive whistle-blowing steam locomotive.

BLUE RIDGE LEXICON

From Georgia through eight states to Pennsylvania, the lush landscape of the Blue Ridge Mountains has inspired a lexicon all its own to describe its unique topographical features: visitors enter a land of coves, balds, gaps, knobs, licks, and cataracts.

"Knobs" are thickly forested low rises spread throughout the mountains that create small fertile valleys in between called "coves." These secreted niches supported most agriculture of the early settlers, while hunting revolved around naturally occurring salt deposits called "licks," which attracted wild animals. "Gaps" may be either water gaps in river valleys or wind gaps in mountain passes.

Inexplicably bare summits are called "balds." Botanists can only guess why the forest stops abruptly below these grassy knolls. Tree line doesn't explain it; the elevation is not that high. Are they lightning-set fire scars? Or ancient Indian sacred grounds? No one explanation suffices. Georgia's highest elevation—4,784-foot Mt. Enotah, better known as **Brasstown Bald**—belongs to this mysterious group.

The well-watered Blue Ridge is also known for many rivers, creeks, and waterfalls—locally called "cataracts."

The 13.5-mile trip to the Tennessee border takes an hour and a half, and there's an hour or so layover in the humbly scenic riverside border towns of McCaysville and Copperhill, where you can stand in two states at once. The train has a commissary car; you can also find small cafés and an ice cream parlor in the twin river towns. Sometimes local musicians perform old-time mountain music on the train.

Trains run year-round, daily in late June, July, and October and clustered Fri.–Mon. Apr.–Dec., with premium fall-foliage trips in October and Santa trips in December. Tickets cost $22–28 for adults and $11–15 for children ages 2–12 (children under age two are free if sitting on a parent's lap). Inquire about combo train/rafting trips.

Concerts and Events

Mountain-music concerts take place at **Sugar Creek Music Park,** west of town off Hwy. 5 north. Regularly scheduled concerts include the two **Sugar Creek Bluegrass Festivals,** in the second weeks of May and October (featuring cloggers, square dancers, fiddlers, and plenty of country cookin'), and July's **Bluegrass Weekend,** which includes free on-site camping with the price of admission.

Country-and-western concerts usually follow bluegrass festivals by one week; and in December, the park hosts a Christmas Music Show. Downtown's city park hosts an **Appalachian crafts festival** on the Saturday before Memorial Day, as well as the annual **Labor Day Barbecue.**

Information and Supplies

The Blue Ridge Scenic Railway depot, in the center of town, serves as the local visitors center, or you can call the local chamber of commerce at 706/632-5680 for more information or a schedule of events. The **Forest Service office,** Hwy. 515 E, 706/632-3031, provides guides and directories to trails and Forest Service campgrounds nearby.

For groceries and supplies, two supermarkets are north of downtown: Ingles Market, visible from Hwy. 76 E, and the Piggly Wiggly, on East 1st Street.

Blue Ridge Lake

Blue Ridge Lake, a 3,290-acre impoundment of the Toccoa River maintained by the Tennessee Valley Authority (TVA), features 100 miles of shoreline with beaches, a full-service marina, public boat ramps, campgrounds, and of course, favorite fishing holes. Walleye, smallmouth bass, white bass, and bluegill are the most common catches. Waterskiing and motorboats are permitted on the lake.

At the north shore near the dam, the **Blue Ridge Lake Marina,** 706/632-2618, is the only commercial outlet on the lake for gas, food, and supplies. It also rents fishing boats. At **Morganton Point,** a Forest Service recreation area offers swimming, boat launching, fishing, rock-hounding trails, and a 37-site campground ($5 a night). Take Hwy. 76 southeast from Blue Ridge for six miles, turn right at Morganton on paved County Road 616 and proceed for one mile to the campground.

At the south shore, the **Lake Blue Ridge** Forest Service recreation area offers swimming, boating (launching ramps available), fishing, a short loop shoreline trail, and a 48-site campground ($5 a night). From Blue Ridge, go 1.5 miles down *old* Hwy. 76, turn right on Dry Branch and go three miles to the entrance.

The 8.8-mile **Rich Mountain Trail** leads from the south shore east of the Forest Service campground up to the Rich Mountain Wilderness Area south of Blue Ridge Lake. The trail deadends near the middle of the 78-mile **Benton MacKaye Trail.** To find the lakeshore trailhead, take old Hwy. 76 to Aska; follow this road for three miles, then turn left on Campbell Camp Road and continue for two miles. For closer access to the MacKaye Trail, find the Hwy. 60 road crossing, 15 miles south of Morganton.

Ocoee River

The Ocoee River, site of the 1996 Olympic white-water rafting competition, races through Polk County, Tennessee, between two dams built by the Tennessee Valley Authority (TVA). The river ran dry for 63 years until a broken flume reflooded the riverbed and brought in white-water enthusiasts. The monolithic TVA eventually agreed to let the waters run for recreation at certain times and divert it at other times for hydro-electric power.

The river's continuous series of Class III and IV rapids—with names such as Broken Nose, Diamond Splitter, Tablesaw, and Hell Hole—makes it one of the Southeast's greatest whitewater runs. Because of its nonstop action, the overall rating is Class IV. Surrounded by the Cherokee National Forest, the Ocoee offers beautiful scenery as well as an outstanding white-water challenge. Tennessee Hwy. 64 parallels the river, easing access for rafters and spectators.

From river outposts centered around Ocoee, Tennessee, a consortium of two dozen outfitters leads guided rafting expeditions downriver for half-day or full-day excursions ($45 and up). Some offer canoe and kayak rental, classes, overnight trips, wetsuit rentals, and package deals with overnight lodging.

Try **Ocoee Rafting, Inc.,** 800/251-4800; **Southeastern Expeditions,** 800/868-7238; or **Nantahala Outdoor Center,** 800/232-7238.

Copper Basin

The Copper Basin, at the Georgia–Tennessee border, so named for the copper mines that created its stark, desertlike environment, now stands out as an arresting scene of smooth red- and copper-hued hills against the surrounding lush green forested mountains. The mid-19th-century mining industry generated enough copper-sulfide fumes to devastate the area's vegetation (that is, whatever was left over once the forest was cut to fuel the smelters). After the industry collapsed early this century, the Civilian Conservation Corps began a reclamation project to reseed the rolling hills.

By now the environmental nightmare has been transformed into a historic legacy, and today the principal industry is tourism from Ocoee River white-water enthusiasts. Visitors can tour the old mines and visit historic districts in the neighboring border towns of **McCaysville, Georgia,** and **Copperhill, Tennessee.** Self-guided walking- and driving-tour maps, available at the visitors center in downtown Copperhill, 615/496-1012, incorporate sites in both towns.

Appalachian Trail

Every spring, thousands of eager and over-packed hikers flock to North Georgia to undertake the demanding 2,144-mile Appalachian Trail in hopes of reaching trail's end in Maine before winter. Beginning at Springer Mountain northeast of Dahlonega, the trail follows the front ridge of the Appalachian range through 14 states and seven national parks. The oldest continuously marked footpath in the world (according to the Appalachian Trail Conference), the Appalachian Trail is known to trekkers as simply the A.T.

Georgia's 78-mile stretch of the A.T. crosses terrain more rugged than in neighboring states, allowing hikers to test their mettle. Clearly marked and well maintained, the trail passes through thick deciduous woods, scales panoramic overlooks, and skirts the many beautiful waterfalls for which Georgia's Blue Ridge is famous. March through May is the season for thru-hikers

Each year only 150 hikers complete the entire Appalachian Trail, which runs 2,144 miles, from Georgia to Maine.

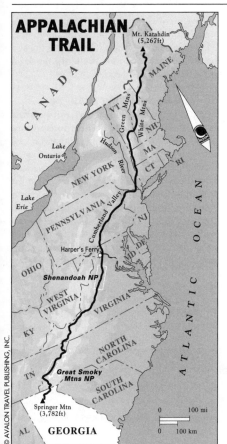

APPALACHIAN TRAIL

Mt. Katahdin
(5,267ft)

CANADA

MAINE

Lake
Ontario

VT

Green Mtns

White Mtns

NH

MA

Hudson River

NEW YORK

CT

RI

Lake
Erie

PENNSYLVANIA

Cumberland Valley

NJ

DE

MD

Harper's Ferry

OHIO

Shenandoah NP

WEST
VIRGINIA

VIRGINIA

ATLANTIC OCEAN

KY

NORTH
CAROLINA

TN

Great Smoky
Mtns NP

SOUTH
CAROLINA

Springer Mtn
(3,782ft)

AL

GEORGIA

0   100 mi

0   100 km

© AVALON TRAVEL PUBLISHING, INC.

The Appalachian Trail Conference (ATC), a private nonprofit entity that works in cooperation with the National Park Service, administers the trail. Scores of small volunteer organizations—such as Georgia's local A.T. club—raise shelters and repair and maintain the trail. The National Park Service holds overall responsibility for the A.T., so you could call it the narrowest park in the nation.

Georgia's A.T.

The A.T.'s 78-mile starting stretch (for hikers who started in Maine, it's the final heat) lies entirely within the Chattahoochee National Forest. Although rising to elevations over 4,400 feet, the ridgeline trail hovers for the most part around elevations of about 3,000 feet. Occasional steep ascents are rewarded by scenic vistas.

White blazes (eye-level tree cuts painted white) mark the length of the A.T.; blue blazes indicate side trails and trails to water. Double blazes signal caution—expect a turn in the trail. Eleven three-sided trail shelters are spaced an approximate day's hike apart. On Blood Mountain, a CCC-built stone cabin shelters hikers. Four road crossings lead to nearby communities and allow day hikers easy access to the trail.

At the **Springer Mountain** summit, you'll find a whimsically incongruous mailbox—one of many that line the trail—with a notebook register of hikers' comments and conversation. A brass plaque bears the classic A.T. hiker symbol, and a huge road sign proclaims the way to Maine.

To reach the trailhead, take the 8.27-mile **A.T. Approach Trail** from **Amicalola Falls State Park,** considered a good test for the rugged Georgia section to come. You can also start or end your trip by detouring over to the **Len Foote Hike Inn,** one of only a handful of walk-in lodges in the U.S. The day hikes listed below include some of the highlights of Georgia's Appalachian Trail.

(trekkers attempting the journey to Maine), but anyone can enjoy the trail anytime from one of several access points and road crossings.

History and Development

The A.T. is largely a product of the vision of one man, Benton MacKaye (rhymes with "pie"), who originally conceived of the idea of a continuous trail along the backbone of the Appalachians in 1921. The idea developed into a crusade, and the following year, the first section opened to the public in New York. By 1937 the original 1,200-mile route was completed. Since then, urban growth has pushed the route farther into the mountain wilderness, adding 800 miles to its length.

Suggested Day Hikes

Road crossings and access trails are easily reached from several spots along Georgia's 78-mile stretch of the Appalachian Trail. From the first road crossing at **Woody Gap** (Hwy. 60), a hike north takes you to the rocky overlook of Big Cedar Mountain—it's two miles roundtrip, and parking is available.

From the next road crossing, at **Neels Gap** (Hwy. 19/129), hikers go west to the panoramic overlook at Blood Mountain, the highest point on the Georgia A.T. (4.2 miles roundtrip).

A 5.5-mile trip east from Neels Gap crosses under the stone arch at **Walasi-Yi Center**—the only place along its entire length that the A.T. passes through a manmade structure—and leads along a scenic ridge to **Tesnatee Gap** (Hwy. 348). Note that only limited parking is available at Neels Gap; drive north a bit to the Byron Reese parking area.

For a 5.3-mile loop trip, start from the **Lake Winfield Scott** recreation area (and campground), off Hwy. 180. Here two trails connect with the A.T. to create a triangular loop. Starting from the lake, hike south to **Jarrard Gap,** then north on the A.T. to **Slaughter Gap,** then back west to the lake. Or detour one mile north on the A.T. at Slaughter Gap for the view from Blood Mountain before descending back down to the lake.

At **Unicoi Gap** (Hwy. 17/75), a 10.4-mile roundtrip hike leads north to views from Tray Mountain's rocky summit. The summit can also be reached by a one-mile roundtrip north on the A.T. from Forest Service Road 79.

50-Mile Backpacking Loop

Three long-distance trails converge in a triangle in North Georgia's remote Blue Ridge wilds, enabling backpackers to sample all three on a localized backpacking adventure. Depending on individual pace, the trip might take a week or two; you could also tack on an overnight at the Amicalola Falls State Park trailhead. Starting at **Springer Mountain,** the A.T. heads north and connects with the **Duncan Ridge Trail,** which leads west to the **Benton MacKaye Trail,** which heads back south to Springer Mountain. Consult topographical maps, Chattahoochee National Forest trail maps, or park rangers to plan the details.

Precautions

A.T. elevations invite colder and rainier weather

APPALACHIAN TRAIL MYSTIQUE

Why hike on a path as traveled as the Appalachian Trail when other trails offer more seclusion? The first answer is factual: the well-marked, well-maintained A.T. crosses some of the most spectacular country in North America. It's a narrow ribbon of wilderness from Maine to Georgia that passes through as many eons of natural history as it does miles.

But the second answer is less tangible. There's something about the A.T. that *draws* people. Much more than a hike, the A.T. has come to mean a quest by thousands of dedicated thru-hikers who "went the distance," and by the thousands more who arrive in North Georgia every spring with high hopes and a heavy pack.

Aspirants anticipating the 2,144-mile walk create an infectious optimism and energy—comments alongside hikers' names and pack weights at the A.T. register at Amicalola Falls State Park run from "Go for it!" and "Just DO it!" to "I've promised myself this for 20 years." The average backpack weighs out at about 50 pounds, though the frequently scrawled "Too Much" is the most common measure (and perhaps also the most accurate).

By the first road crossing (20 miles north), reality hits. The postmaster at Suches stays busy mailing back home every extraneous ounce that weary neophytes are eager to shed. By Neels Gap, hikers have usually adopted trail names, the Native American likes of Lightfoot or Eagle Feather.

Thru-hikers are a hearty breed. Not simply a walk in the woods, thru-hikes require painstaking research, planning, and preparedness; hikers clear their calendars for six months or more for the journey, and supplies and expenses can add up to more than $5,000. Of the thousands who start out at Springer Mountain each year, only about 150 make it all the way to Mount Katahdin in Maine. Those tenacious souls share a lifetime solidarity, retelling "war stories" of Pennsylvania's boulder fields, soaked river crossings, and blistered feet, as well as tales of generous fellow hikers and favorite all-you-can-eat buffets along the way.

The A.T. is much more than a trail—to many, it is a *path*.

---

than in mountain towns; hikers who start out early in the spring should prepare for freezing temperatures and rain. Water is available right off the trail, but it should be treated or boiled. Watch for snakes sunning themselves on rock ledges. November and December are deer-hunting months in North Georgia, and cautious hikers wear orange vests and pack covers.

Transportation and Parking

To reach Amicalola Falls State Park from Atlanta, take Hwy. 400 north to Hwy. 53 west past Dawsonville, then take Hwy. 183 north to Hwy. 52 east. From Dahlonega, take Hwy. 52 west. Free long-term parking is easily arranged at the visitors center—$2 per vehicle is charged to enter the park. Forest Service roads could take you closer to the trailhead, but they aren't recommended for drivers unfamiliar with the area. Unsecured short-term parking is also available at road crossings.

Public transportation from Atlanta reaches only as far north as Gainesville; from there hikers can take a taxi or meet a prearranged shuttle. **Appalachian Outfitters,** 706/864-7117, can help arrange shuttles from the Gainesville Amtrak station to Amicalola Falls State Park.

Resources and Information

Walasi-Yi Center (wal-a-SEE-a), the CCC-built stone lodge at Neels Gap (where the A.T. crosses Hwy. 19) houses the **Mountain Crossings** outfitting store, 706/745-6095, a resource for maps, freeze-dried foods, and other supplies. They're open every day but Christmas.

Contact the **Appalachian Trail Conference,** P.O. Box 807, Harpers Ferry, WV 25425-0807, 304/535-6331, for a brochure and list of publications. You can buy the ATC *Guide to the Appalachian Trail in North Carolina and Georgia* at local outdoor stores (or order it from the ATC; it's item No. 110 and costs $15.95). Contact the all-volunteer **Georgia Appalachian Trail Club,** P.O. Box 654, Atlanta, GA 30301. (If requesting information, enclose a business-sized self-addressed, stamped envelope and a small donation to defray costs.)

For more information about Amicalola Falls State Park, see the *Dahlonega and Vicinity* section in this chapter or gastateparks.org.

The **Northeast Georgia Mountains Travel Association,** P.O. Box 464, Gainesville, GA 30503, 770/535-5757, visitnortheastgeorgia.com, distributes free publications to the region.

TRAIL ETHICS

Built and maintained by volunteers, the Appalachian Trail demands that hikers share responsibility for keeping the trail in good shape.

Don't shortcut switchbacks (correcting erosion damage is the most difficult part of trail maintenance), carry out all trash, avoid camping in heavy-use areas (camp beyond sight of the trail when possible), and carry a small cooking stove to avoid campfires or use only downed wood in an established fire ring to minimize the impact on the environment. Respect the flora and fauna, and keep water sources clean (always wash away from water sources, especially if you're using soap). Where no privy is available, dig a "cat hole" at least six inches deep and at least 75 feet from water sources, and bury all waste and paper.

Of course, this leave-no-trace ethic applies to all outdoor areas, not just the A.T.

Dahlonega and Vicinity

In 1828, the discovery of gold near Dahlonega propelled thousands of fortune-seekers to descend on the region, heralding the nation's first major gold rush and producing more than six million dollars coined at a local branch of the U.S. Mint. Gold mines, panning operations, and hydraulic mining changed the face of the hills and added a new element to traditionally conservative Appalachian communities, a discernibly freer spirit still felt today.

Gold-country pleasures are centered in Dahlonega (dah-LON-ah-ga), a bustling country town that makes the most of its unique heritage. In the surrounding woods and rivers of the Chattahoochee National Forest, visitors can hike, run rivers, ride horses, and try their hand at gold-panning. Amicalola Falls State Park, west of Dahlonega, named for its dramatic 729-foot waterfall, offers lots more recreation, along with a campground, lodge, and new hike-in lodge. The park is the traditional starting point for Appalachian Trail thru-hikers.

Less than an hour and a half from Atlanta, Dahlonega can be reached by taking Hwy. 400 north to Hwy. 60/19 north. To reach the state park from Dahlonega, take Hwy. 52 west (a 40-minute drive from town). To go directly to the state park from Atlanta, you can bypass Dahlonega by taking Hwy. 136 west off Hwy.

400 just past Dawsonville, to Hwy. 183 west and then to Hwy. 52 east.

History

Named from the Cherokee term *talonega,* meaning "yellow metal," Dahlonega was chosen as county seat of the new gold-rush region in 1835, displacing Auraria. In 1838, the federal government built a branch of the U.S. Mint in Dahlonega, stamping the town's name on six million dollars' worth of gold coins before the operation was shut down at the onset of the Civil War in 1861. Today Price Memorial Hall, of Dahlonega's **North Georgia College and State University,** stands on the foundation of the old mint, with a gleaming crown crafted of 13-ounce gold leaf.

When California's 1849 gold rush threatened to lure miners away, miners were implored to stay in Dahlonega with the call Mark Twain paraphrased as "There's gold in them thar hills!" Gold mining and panning operations continued in earnest until the early 1920s, when legislation that fixed the price of gold at $35 an ounce was enacted, and mining suddenly became unprofitable.

Though panners still try their luck in nearby streams, the region is now richest in its gilded history, attracting visitors to its historic gold museum, spelunky gold-mine tours, and festivals that celebrate Appalachian mining traditions. Dahlonega's mother lode today is tourism, bringing in more than $20 million annually.

SIGHTS

Set against a backdrop of the pristine Appalachian forests, Dahlonega's historic **town square** makes the most inviting sight of all. Revolving around the 1838 Greek Revival courthouse that now houses the gold museum, the busy square is lined on all sides with colorful two-story Victorian storefronts.

The windows of the square's antique stores, bookshops, jewelers, and general store display the town's heritage—you can find antique scales used for weighing gold, audiocassettes of mountain music, and even pans and glass vials to help you try your luck. Strollers saunter down brick walkways lined with flower barrels, past monuments, park benches, and the old town well. At night the old-fashioned streetlights let off a hazy glow.

A few minutes from town, the ghost town of **Auraria** had a population of 10,000 in its heyday, in the booming 1830s. The town declined once Dahlonega was named county seat, and today Auraria contains only a handful of residents and a historical marker to attest to its bustling past (from Dahlonega, take Hwy. 52 to Auraria Road, then drive south two to three miles).

Dahlonega Gold Museum

The Gold Museum, 706/864-2257, gastateparks.org, occupies the oldest building in North Georgia, in the center of the Dahlonega town square. The former courthouse was constructed in 1836 with locally cast bricks; look carefully and you may see gold flecks. The state-operated museum exhibits gold nuggets, gold coins, and tools of the mining trade on the ground floor. Upstairs, a small theater presents an enlightening 20-minute film that introduces gold-rush history and Appalachian culture through interviews with local old-timers.

The museum is open year-round Mon.–Sat. 9 A.M.–5 P.M. and Sun. 10 A.M.–5 P.M. The ad-

mission fee is $3 for adults and $1.50 for youth (ages five and under are free).

Gold Panning and Mine Tours

State-of-the-art at the turn of the 20th century, the **Consolidated Gold Mine,** 185 Consolidated Rd., 706/864-8473, featured electrical wiring and a railcar system that pulled as much as 50 pounds of gold per day out of its renowned "glory hole." After extensive reexcavation, the mine is now open to the public for guided tours.

Visitors enter the mine through a dramatic stone passageway and descend stairs and cuts to 125 feet below the water table. The 40-minute tour covers mining history, geology, and technique, including displays of equipment such as the "widowmaker"—a drill named for the lung disease–causing dust it generated. Back above ground, costumed "prospectors" show visitors how to pan for gold in rows of wooden sluice boxes behind the gift shop.

Tours run throughout the day 10 A.M.–4 P.M. (till 5 P.M. summers). Adult admission is $11 and $7 for children 4–14. It's north of town, at the intersection of Hwys. 60, 52, 9 and 19, down a small paved road that snakes below the Wal-Mart.

Crisson Gold Mine, Hwy. 19, 706/864-7998, dates from 1847, and is owned and still operated by fourth-generation miners. It's open to the public for gold panning daily 10 A.M.–6 P.M. Admission is free, but you pay for an ore run (a "find" is guaranteed). It's on Hwy. 52W, two miles down the road from the Consolidated Gold Mine.

Festivals

Held every October since 1954, **Gold Rush Days** is Dahlonega's major festival. Hundreds of thousands of visitors descend on the small town to witness and enjoy such rural pastimes as a greased-pig chase, tobacco-spitting and hog-calling contests, Wild West shoot-outs, clogging dances, gold panning, and plenty of local foods and crafts. In recent years, the event has drawn more than 250,000 visitors, so if you *don't* plan to attend, steer wide—approach roads get snarled.

Among other highlights, May's **Wildflower Festival of the Arts** celebrates traditional Appalachian arts and crafts, such as wood carving, quilting, and pottery. The third week in June, the **Bluegrass Festival** brings out fiddlers and down-home mountain music. The **Family Day Fourth of July** celebrates with traditional American fare, music, and fireworks. Fall brings September's **Autumn Fest** and October's **Auraria Gold Festival.** Each December, the town dresses up for an **Old Fashioned Christmas,** stringing miniature white lights and decorations—a picturesque scene accompanied by mountain holiday festivities and caroling.

ACCOMMODATIONS AND FOOD

Accommodations

Dahlonega makes a good base of operations for a visit to the Blue Ridge. *See also* Amicalola Falls State Park for lodge accommodations just 40 minutes west.

The **Smith House,** 84 S. Chestatee St., 706/867-7000 or 800/852-9577, a revered Blue Ridge inn for more than 70 years, offers overnight lodging in a turn-of-the-20th-century Victorian house a half block from the town square. The sunny, yellow, three-story farmhouse, reportedly built above a gold mine, blooms with flowering vines wound around its porches, trellises, and a pool. Sixteen guest rooms upstairs and a modern suite annex are comfortably furnished in keeping with the country-inn spirit—practical, nothing too precious. Their doubles rates are illustrative of seasonal demand, starting at $69 in winter, $80 spring, $89 summer, and $98 fall, including a continental breakfast.

The 1845 **Worley Homestead,** 410 W. Main St., 706/864-7002, is a well-established resident-operated bed and breakfast with eight guest rooms (all private baths) in a nice location just a short walk west of the square. Rates average $80 and include a full country breakfast.

Of several motel chains not far from the square, **EconoLodge,** Hwy. 19 N, 706/864-6191 or 800/55-ECONO (800/553-2666), is among the oldest and least expensive; newer chains are clustered on Hwy. 60 at the bypass (less practical for pedestrians), including **Days Inn,** 706/864-2338.

Camping

Three basic Forest Service campgrounds with water and chemical flush toilets only are within a half hour's drive north of Dahlonega: **Waters Creek** sits beside a beautiful mountain stream 12 miles north of town on Hwy. 19, then left on paved Forest Service Road 34 for one mile; **Dockery Lake** has sites near a popular three-acre trout lake off a gravel road from Hwy. 60; and the campground at **DeSoto Falls** (easily approached from Hwy. 60) is near the namesake waterfalls. Fees are $5–12 per night. See *Amicalola Falls State Park* for additional camping 40 minutes west.

Food and Drink

Folks come from all over to go to the **Smith House,** 84 S. Chestatee St., 706/864-2348, for all-you-can-eat, family-style Southern meals—up to 2,000 meals are served on popular Sundays. The prices are high for boardinghouse fare, particularly for families, unless you want to factor in the entertainment value of dining with strangers. Fixed-price dinners are $15 adults, $10 ages 10–12, $7.50 ages 4–9 (under 4 free), paid in advance. They're closed Monday, except on major holidays and during October.

Other choices around the square include the casual Italian fare at the friendly **Caruso's,** 706/864-4664, with pasta, pizza, and a kids menu. They open for lunch and dinner.

Rick's, 47 S. Park St., 706/864-9422, draws an Atlanta crowd for goat-cheese appetizers, steak salad, and stuffed trout, along with such kid-friendly options as burgers and a triple grilled-cheese sandwich. It's invitingly set in an old house just up from the square. They're open daily 11:30 A.M.–9 P.M. (till later Fri.–Sat.).

Locals eat at the **Wagon Wheel,** on Hwy. 19 one mile north of the square, 706/864-6677, for standard Southern plates (fried chicken and all-you-can-eat catfish on Fri.–Sat.) served cafeteria style. It's open 6 A.M.–8 P.M. Wed.–Mon.

See *Amicalola Falls State Park* for its lodge restaurant listing.

North Georgia

OTHER PRACTICALITIES
Shopping
Downtown's 19th-century courthouse square offers some scenic shopping. Antiques, mining memorabilia, old-time penny candy, locally mined and made gold jewelry, and mountain crafts and music are among the distinctive souvenirs to be found. The biggest bargain is a five-cent cup of coffee at the **General Store** that you can sip while you browse through the store's tinny treasures.

At the **Hometown Bookstore,** off the square, 706/864-7225, Deborah and Bill Kinsland sell regional guidebooks and other books, mountain-music cassettes, and topographical maps. They also serve as an unofficial visitor information center, gathering comprehensive information on climate, autumn colors, and the like and distributing it free of charge.

Information and Services
On the square, the **Dahlonega Welcome Center,** 13 Park St. S., 706/864-3711 or 800/231-5543, dahlonega.org, is open daily 9 A.M.–5:30 P.M. to distribute local maps and information (there are free restrooms here too). A little gold-panning station is right next door.

A **Forest Service visitors center,** in a strip shopping center within the Wal-Mart parking lot off Hwy. 52, 706/745-6928, distributes information on local recreation in the Chattahoochee National Forest. It's open Tues.–Sat. 8 A.M.–4:30 P.M.

For medical emergencies, contact **Chestatee Regional Hospital,** two miles south of town off Hwy. 60, 706/864-6136.

RECREATION
Water Sports
The Chestatee River, popular with paddlers for canoeing or kayaking, crosses Highways 60 and 52 south and east of Dahlonega. First-timers and families usually choose its Class I lower section; experienced paddlers may prefer its more challenging Class II–III upper section.

Appalachian Outfitters, 706/864-7117, rents canoes and organizes guided paddling excursions

from its river outpost on Hwy. 60 at the river (southeast of town). They also help arrange shuttles for paddlers and hikers.

The Amicalola Creek southwest of Dahlonega on Hwy. 53 offers a chance to swim, canoe, kayak, raft, tube, or hike in the protected corridor of this scenic Appalachian river. Under the Hwy. 53 bridge six miles west of Dawsonville, you'll find a put-in point with a river marker and a trail down the eastern bank. This trail leads south to the swimming hole, with natural slides for inner-tube riders and a refreshing cold-water "natural Jacuzzi."

AMICALOLA FALLS STATE PARK
At Amicalola Falls State Park, 18 miles west of Dahlonega via Hwy. 52, visitors enjoy scenic overlooks of the centerpiece waterfalls and wooded trails through the park's 1,210 acres. The most famous of these hikes is the 2,144-mile **Appalachian Trail,** which draws

© KAP STANN

Amicalola Creek

thousands of ambitious backpackers to the park each spring to begin the long trek north. Like many mountain state parks, the park has so much to offer that a solace-seeker could stay weeks without venturing off the mountain except to hike.

Pick up a park guide, trail maps, and interpretive information at the visitors center near the base of the falls. Contact Amicalola Falls State Park at P.O. Box 215, Dawsonville, GA 30534, 706/265-4703, gastateparks.org. For lodging and camping reservations, call 800/864-7275. The park is open year-round. A $2 per vehicle fee is charged.

Sights and Trails

Amicalola Falls' dramatic 729-foot cascade—three times taller than Niagara, though a fraction as wide—can be seen from scenic overlooks a short walk from parking lots at the lower Reflection Pool or at the summit (where you'll find the classic Blue Ridge panorama that's so often photographed). Or you can hike to scenic overlooks off 3.5 miles of falls trails.

The **Appalachian Trail** (A.T.) officially begins at Springer Mountain, out in the Blue Ridge wilds just beyond the park boundary. The classic route to get there is the **A.T. Approach Trail,** which starts behind the park's visitors center near the base of the falls (or you can pick up the trail near the summit lodge). Considered a good test for thru-hiker hopefuls, the approach trail offers a taste of the rugged backcountry to come along Georgia's 78-mile A.T.

A moderate 4.6-mile trail leads to the **Len Foote Hike Inn;** it's another 2.5 miles from here to Springer Mountain.

Amicalola Falls Lodge and Restaurant

The modern four-story Amicalola Falls Lodge, 706/265-8888, sits majestically atop a steep summit. The three-story glass lobby, restaurant, and all 57 guest rooms have a panoramic view of the surrounding Blue Ridge wilderness—a beautiful scene anytime, though most dramatic in the fall. Many of the modern, tasteful lodge rooms have porches and lofts, and several are

especially equipped for disabled guests. Standard rooms start at $59 for doubles.

The glass-walled 200-seat **Maple Restaurant** at the lodge serves generous buffets, enough to make your mouth water after a strenuous hike. Roast turkey, baked ham, or fried catfish may be among the dinner entrées; the spread includes four types of vegetables, soup, salad, and desserts. The hot breakfast buffet includes eggs, grits, sausage, bacon, and biscuits and gravy. Three reasonably priced meals are served daily, along with beer and wine.

Cottage Accommodations and Camping

Fourteen fully equipped cottages, some with fireplaces, are nestled in the woods a short drive from the lodge (except for Nos. 1–5, which are more exposed, near the base of the falls). Rates start at $69 but depend on size (1–3 bedrooms).

Each of the park's 17 wooded **campsites** hooks up to water and 110-volt power; nearby bathhouses have hot showers, flush toilets, coin-laundry facilities, and soda machines. Because of the entrance road's 25 percent grade, trailers must be under 16 feet. Sites cost $17–19 per night.

⋈ Len Foote Hike Inn

One of only a handful of hike-in lodges in the United States, the Len Foote Hike Inn offers hikers an exceptional opportunity to enjoy a three-hour hike 4.6 miles through Appalachian backcountry and arrive at a remote mountain lodge right in time for dinner. Opened a few years back, the lodge is operated by an affiliate of the Georgia Appalachian Trail Club and is named for a Georgia author and conservationist.

The 20-room wooden lodge, surrounded by decks and wide verandas outfitted with Adirondack chairs, features a living room built around a wood-burning stove and stocked with board games, cards, and puzzles. The "bunkrooms" are simple, dormlike rooms with bunk beds and reading lights. Sheets and blankets are provided.

The ecofriendly lodge has been designed to be low impact, with an environmentally sensitive bathhouse and laundry facilities. Yet by rustic standards, it's glamorous—clean com-

© KAP STANN

Len Foote Hike Inn

fortable bunks, thick towels, hot showers, family-style dinners, and a hot breakfast (sack lunches are available by request and for an additional fee).

The cost is $70 per adult for double occupancy and $97 per adult for single occupancy, with discounts for children. Families and children are welcome (adjoining rooms available); there's even a room accessible to the disabled (reserve transportation in advance). Call 800/573-9656 or visit the website hike-inn.com for more information about the inn.

Services, Facilities, and Programs

The **visitors center** at the park entrance displays natural-history exhibits, distributes trail maps, and sells books, gifts, and firewood. This is where you check in for the Len Foote Hike Inn and head off under the stone arch for the A.T. Also inquire about a full slate of interpretive programs and special events, including backpacking expeditions, wilderness survival overnights, hayrides, and hoedowns. Seasonal trout fishing within the state park, as elsewhere in Georgia, requires a Georgia fishing license and trout stamp.

More maps, guides, and scenery books can be found at the lodge gift shop.

Dawsonville

South of Amicalola Falls State Park via Hwy. 183, the center of Dawsonville can be found on Hwy. 53. Downtown, the 1858 Greek Revival Dawson County Courthouse anchors the central square. Just off the square, the historic jail now serves as the local **welcome center.**

The town, which is the home of racing champion Bill Elliott, pays tribute to its native son at **Thunder Road USA,** the Georgia Racing Hall of Fame, 706/216-RACE, thunderroadusa.com.

Off the square, the **Dawsonville Pool Room,** 101 E. 1st St., 706/265-2792, has short-order meals—burgers and steak sandwiches—and tributes to Bill Elliott adorn the walls.

North to Blairsville

North of Dahlonega, the country highway climbs through wind gaps and water gaps up to the ridgeline traced by the Appalachian Trail. The primary route through Georgia's central Blue Ridge is through Neels Gap (Hwy. 19/129), largely carved by the Nottely River.

To every side, trailheads lead into Blue Ridge wilds—here hikers find the tallest peaks, the panoramic ridge, towering stands of cathedral pines, and sparkling waterfalls framed by flowering thickets of mountain laurel and rhododendron. Its human history is retained by ancient petroglyphs, the grave of a Cherokee princess, and local legends of Spanish explorers and arklike canoes of mythological proportions.

Over the ridge, the no-nonsense mountain town of Blairsville leaves the trim latticework and lace curtains of valley towns far behind. Cafés open before sunrise to fry eggs and fling hotcakes for farmers wearing well-worn overalls, and most shopping to be done is at the local feed-and-grain. But visitors find all they need to outfit themselves for weeks backpacking in the wilderness, fishing and boating at high-country lakes, or relaxing in cozy pond-side cabins tucked into Blue Ridge coves.

Follow Hwy. 60/19 north from Dahlonega nine miles to its split. From here, Hwy. 60 leads northwest to Woody Gap and Forest Service camps and creeks; Hwy. 19 continues north, merging with Hwy. 129 five miles up and heading to Blairsville through Neels Gap—the route that de Soto marched through in the mid-16th century, in search of gold.

HIGHWAY 60 WEST

The 35-mile stretch of highway between the Hwy. 19 split and Morganton bisects the thick of the national forest. To either side of Hwy. 60, rugged Forest Service roads wind up the mountains to remote camps, cool creeks, and prime fishing holes. The split is marked by a shoulder-high rock pile in the center of the road. This is said to be the grave of Cherokee Princess Trahlyta—the Native American custom was to heap stones on a grave to show you've been there to pay your respects.

Five miles northwest of the grave marker, a mile-long gravelly turnoff east leads to **Dockery Lake,** where an 11-site Forest Service campground ($5 per night), trailhead parking lot, and popular three-acre trout lake are set in a large cove accented in May by white dogwood blossoms and purple rhododendron. A half-mile barrier-free trail leads around the lake, and a 3.4-mile trail north provides access to the Appalachian Trail. The **Chestatee Overlook,** on Hwy. 60 just north of this turnoff, provides a scenic roadside vista of Blood Mountain cove.

A mile farther north, the road meets the A.T. at **Woody Gap.** Park here for easy access to the 2,144-mile trail; a two-mile roundtrip hike north takes you to the rocky overlook of Big Cedar Mountain. Picnic tables at the turnout provide a nice view too.

The beautiful little town of **Suches** (on Hwy. 60 a mile north of Woody Gap) is set in a picturesque valley of pasturelands, red barns, and sparkling lakes. Its post office is a landmark for

hikers—when overloaded thru-hikers hit this first road crossing after 20 rugged miles on the A.T., they detour to the Suches post office to mail home every extraneous ounce. Highway 180 leads northeast from here to **Lake Winfield Scott,** another bucolic little find nestled away in the high country.

About 10 miles northwest of Suches on Hwy. 60, Forest Service roads lead off to remote recreation areas and campgrounds north and south of the highway. Drivers should note that Forest Service roads, though scenic, may be narrow and steep and offer few places to turn around—they're not recommended for delicate cars, drivers, or passengers. The cautious driver who is planning on extensive back-road travel should carry emergency supplies. Forest Service roads make great trail-biking routes; just watch out for those trailers coming around the bend.

Beyond the Forest Service areas described below, Hwy. 60 continues northwest 14 miles to Morganton and sights around Blue Ridge Lake.

Forest Service Areas North

About 10 miles northwest of Suches, Forest Service Road 4 leads from Hwy. 60 six miles east through rugged backcountry to the 1,240-acre **Cooper Creek Scenic Area.** Besides a few faint traces of human habitation or fire, the area represents largely untouched original forest. In stands of large hemlock and white pine (this is just about the southern geographic limit of both varieties), many trees measure three to four feet in diameter. To see these giants, follow the southern riverbank from the bridge over trout-stocked Cooper Creek (about a half-mile south of Forest Service Road 4 on Cavender Creek Road, also labeled Forest Service Road 236). From here a rough angler's path passes through a white pine grove, rhododendron thickets, and hemlock stands a quarter-mile in.

The 20-site **Cooper Creek** campground, adjacent to the scenic area (at the Forest Service Road 4 junction with Forest Service Road 236), and the 10-site **Mulky Creek** campground (slightly west off Forest Service Road 4), both provide drinking water, picnic tables, grills, and vault toilets. Most sites are $5; premium creek-side sites may be more, and farther-flung primitive sites are free.

Forest Service Areas South

Slightly west of the Cooper Creek turnoff, the Forest Service **Deep Hole** campground on the south side of Hwy. 60 provides eight sites along the trout-stocked Toccoa River. Take the next turnoff south (Forest Service Road 69) to reach the trout-rearing "raceways" (outdoor tanks) of the **Chattahoochee National Fish Hatchery** (open daily 7:30 A.M.–4 P.M.) and the 11-site **Frank Gross** Forest Service campground and picnic area, five miles south of Hwy. 60 along Rock Creek.

HIGHWAY 19 TO NEELS GAP

From a round wooden table in the café at **Turner's Corner,** you can look out to the crossroads of two country highways. Coming in from the direction of the cash register is Hwy. 19. Out behind the swinging saloon door that leads to the kitchen is Highway 129, up from Cleveland. As the last low-level stop before committing to crossing the mountain, a meal at Turner's Corner almost invariably marks the brink of an adventure.

Step outside to where the ancient gas-pump totems stand, and you'll see the bridge over Waters Creek. If you follow the creek up a half-mile or so (paved Forest Service Road 34 leads around from Hwy. 19), you come upon the prettiest lit-

tle (eight-site) campground right off the side of the road. It's set right against a bend in the creek, and there's not a spot where you can sit and not hear the rushing waters.

Seven miles farther up the narrowing Hwy. 19, you'll find **Blood Mountain Falls,** where a mountain stream flows about 20 feet through a rock cut, creating a churning sluice of water. A trail on the right leads .8 mile from the road to the falls.

DeSoto Falls Scenic Area

The highlights of the 650-acre DeSoto Falls Scenic Area (west of Hwy. 19/129) are the spectacular waterfalls. Legend has it that a piece of armor found near these falls belonged to the 1540s expedition of Hernando de Soto, thus the name. A 24-site campground ($5 per night), near clear streams for fishing and wading, provides water, grills, flush toilets, and cold showers.

Drivers can pull over to view the falls from the highway, but for a closer look, hike the three-mile **DeSoto Falls Trail.** The trail leads easily to the lower falls, which cascade 20 feet, then continues more steeply up to the most scenic 80-foot middle falls, and finally to the upper falls, which surge 200 feet down a granite incline.

Neels Gap

At Neels Gap, the ridgeline A.T. meets the historic route now carved by Hwy. 19/129 (eight miles north of the junction of those two highways; 10 miles south of Blairsville). This is the hiking epicenter of Georgia's Blue Ridge Mountain range. Within several miles of here, many of the most adventurous Blue Ridge trails converge into a vast trail network—the wilderness equivalent of a major freeway cloverleaf.

The gap is marked by the **Walasi-Yi Center** (wal-a-SEE-a), a sturdy stone lodge with a terraced overlook constructed by the CCC in 1934. Approximately 1,000 thru-hiker hopefuls annually pass through its breezeway—the only place on the 2,144-mile route that the A.T. cuts through a manmade structure. The state-owned historic lodge now houses an outfitting store that's open every day except Christmas—a great local resource.

SASSAFRAS

With three differently shaped leaves on the same tree, sassafras *(Sassafras albidum)* inspired a Cherokee folktale. As legend has it, a young brave enters the forest alone on a vision quest. Facing the bracing cold, the resourceful man is warmed with a hat made from the oval-shaped leaves of the sassafras tree, mittens made from its mitten-shaped leaves, and socks from its three-lobed foot-shaped leaves.

The tree bark was also used by the Cherokee and Appalachian mountaineers—a tea infusion served as an all-around tonic.

Day hikers can head west for the scenic views from atop 4,458-foot **Blood Mountain,** the highest point on Georgia's A.T. (4.2 miles roundtrip). A 5.5-mile A.T. trip east leads along the scenic ridge to **Tesnatee Gap** (Hwy. 348). Note that only limited parking is available at Neels Gap, and hiker parking displaces shoppers and short-term sightseers; drive north a bit to the Byron Reese parking area and take the short A.T. access trail up the hill.

VOGEL STATE PARK

Vogel State Park, off Hwy. 19/129 south of Blairsville, 706/745-2628 or 800/864-PARK (864-7275), gastateparks.org, parking $2, is among the oldest and prettiest of Georgia's state parks and is nestled around a shaded lake in a large cove. This full-service park offers water sports, lodging, camping, prime hiking and backpacking trails, and a full slate of entertaining and interpretive programs and events.

Lake Trahlyta, named for a Cherokee princess, is stocked with trout and ringed by a swimming beach, a boathouse with boat rentals, and a lakeside trail. At the park office you can find a small, well-stocked camp store, trail maps, and a coin laundry; outside you can play miniature golf and volleyball, or join the kids on the playgrounds. The compact facilities and dramatic scenery make it one of the most desirable mountain parks for camping and cottage rental.

This jewel of a resort park is so popular, however, that it's nearly loved to death by its admirers. "Yard for yard, we see as many people as Yosemite," says one ranger. In high seasons (summer and October), the park comes to resemble an outdoor metropolis, with crowds of spatula-wielding barbecue chefs, kids riding Big Wheels, and "camp potatoes" watching TV inside massive trailers, running the generator to keep the air-conditioner on at full blast. It's a scene. If you're looking for rustic, seek out the walk-in campsites, get out on the rugged backpacking trail, or come back in the off-season.

Many special events and interpretive programs—including such kid-friendly diversions as a foot-powered wheel race, Wiffle ball tournaments, and a ranger-supervised planetarium field trip—are listed on a weekly schedule available at the office. The annual highlight is rousing **Old Timers Day,** in August; it's a celebration of mountain music performed by old-time Appalachian fiddlers and is accompanied by handicrafts booths and traditional foods.

Hiking and Backpacking

Besides the park's own 17 miles of trails, Vogel connects with a wider trail network, offering impressive opportunities for many different hiking adventures. Backpackers can arrange overnight secured parking at the park office. Short walks include a mile-long trail that loops around the lake and spurs off to a rushing waterfall (also visible from the highway), and a half-mile-loop nature trail that features interpretive signs.

The orange-blazed **Bear Hair Trail** is a moderate-to-strenuous four-mile loop over rocks and logs, across a footbridge, through a hardwood forest, and up a steep rhododendron thicket. It's best to hike the loop in a counterclockwise direction (though you can hike it either way). About a third of the way in, a green-blazed spur trail climbs to the 3,260-foot summit overlook (a mile roundtrip). Beyond the midpoint, the trail merges with the backpacking trail (see below); a sign at the junction marks the way south to the A.T. or north back to the park, both about two miles one-way.

The demanding 12.7-mile-loop **Coosa Backcountry Trail,** which is also best hiked counterclockwise, is recommended for experienced hikers only. Obtain the required permit and a trail map for no charge at the park office. The yellow-blazed trail climbs one rounded summit after another, fords streams, crosses Hwy. 180 twice, and merges with the Duncan Ridge Trail for two miles. At Slaughter Gap, the backcountry trail's southernmost point, hikers can either continue to follow yellow blazes back to the park or take a short spur trail over to the A.T.—from here you can hike a mile one-way south to the beautiful views of 4,461-foot Blood Mountain, the highest point on Georgia's Appalachian Trail. Hardy day-hikers wishing to see Blood Mountain can follow the Coosa trail clockwise from the trailhead (turn left—south—at the end of the access trail) to the A.T. and continue south on the A.T. to the summit (3.6 miles one-way).

Cottages and Camping

The park's 35 fully equipped cottages range in size from compact studios to spacious three-bedroom cabins; all have fireplaces. The nicest ones are the CCC-built stone-and-wood cottages by the lake (Nos. 31–36) and the cabins nestled up the hill (Nos. 21–30); the remaining central cabins are exposed near roads in the thick of the action and traffic—not the place to get away from crowds and activity. Prices range $65–125, depending on size.

The 85-site campground charges $20–22 a night, with water and electric hookups at most sites. Eighteen walk-in sites ($12) are secluded from the glare of the trailer encampments. The campground is packed in high seasons, but if you like lots of "activity," you'd be lucky to get a site here.

Vicinity

A rugged Forest Service road off Hwy. 19/129 south of the park leads to **Helton Creek Falls,** a set of three majestic waterfalls that drop a total of 100 feet. A short trail leads to both ends of the lower falls, but be careful—the rocks are deceptively slippery. From the park, go south on Hwy. 19/129 one mile; turn left onto an unpaved road that leads east (Helton Creek Road/Forest Service Road 118). Take this narrow rocky route for 2.1 miles and watch for the orange paint on a pine tree to your right; park at the wide spot in the road and follow the 300-yard trail to the falls. You can turn your car around three-tenths of a mile farther down the road. The route is not recommended for cars with low suspension; four-wheel drive or mountain bikes would be best.

Several scenic recreational sights lie west off Hwy. 180, within seven miles of its junction with Hwy. 19/129, a mile north of the park. The **Sosebee Cove Scenic Area** shelters 175 acres of prized hardwood timber, a forest floor lined with ferns and wildflowers, a boulder field, and babbling

creeks. A half-mile trail encircles the area, starting from the trailhead in the parking pullout.

At **Lake Winfield Scott,** a Forest Service recreation area provides a 32-site campground ($5 a night), picnic areas, trails, boating, fishing, and swimming around the 18-acre lake. From here, two trails lead to the A.T., enabling hikers to take a triangular 5.3-mile loop trip.

BLAIRSVILLE

Tucked in the national forest, the mountain town of Blairsville is centered on its 1898 courthouse. The town's **Sorghum Festival,** on the second through fourth weekends in October, features sorghum-crushing demonstrations and "Biskit Eatin' and Syrup Soppin'" contests.

North of town, **Lake Nottely,** a 4,180-acre TVA impoundment of the Nottely River off Hwy. 19/129, attracts fisherfolk to its high-country shores in pursuit of largemouth bass, crappie, and striped bass. South of town, the **Nottely River Campground,** on Hwy. 19, 706/745-6711, rents inner tubes for leisurely floats downriver and will shuttle you back up.

The **visitors center,** on the rise above Hwy. 76 west of town, distributes maps and lists of local lodging with prices. Or contact the local **chamber of commerce,** P.O. Box 727, Blairsville, GA 30512, 706/745-5789. The **Forest Service office,** 1881 Hwy. 515 west of town, 706/745-6928, distributes and sells maps and directories to national forest recreation areas, campgrounds, and hiking and trails for off-road vehicles.

East to Hiawassee

Highway 76, the major east-west route through the upper Blue Ridge, cuts a smooth path through the high valleys and rolling knobs to each side. To the east, between Blairsville and Young-Harris, a turn south on Trackrock Road takes you 2.2 miles to the **Trackrock Archaeological Area,** where ancient petroglyphs are etched in sandstone boulders above the road. The petroglyphs are speculated to date back as long as 3,500 years and depict images of animal tracks. They are unfortunately surrounded by metal frames for protection. Park at the turnout south of the historical marker and back-track up the short trail. The 5.5 mile Arkaquah Trail ascends to the Brasstown Bald Summit from the petroglyphs.

In Young-Harris, nine miles east of Blairsville, the campus of **Young-Harris College,** 706/379-3111, holds a planetarium (open to the public for occasional programs).

On campus, a trail leads from behind the women's dormitory to Brasstown Bald, Georgia's highest peak.

Brasstown Valley Resort, 6321 Hwy. 76, 706/379-9900 or 800/201-3205, offers deluxe accommodations (lodge rooms start at $169), along with golf, tennis, horseback riding, hiking, and other recreation on 503 private acres.

Highway 75 to Helen and Hiawassee

The Bavarian-style town of Helen, Georgia's most popular Blue Ridge destination, flanks the Chattahoochee River at the head of a large pastoral valley studded with gristmills and country inns. Behind it to the north, the mountains rise up dramatically, cresting at Brasstown Bald—the highest point in the state. Highway 75 winds its way north over these mountains and down to Hiawassee on the other side, passing one of Georgia's most beautiful state parks along the way.

The central location of the region around Helen makes it a convenient base of operations for visitors, if you're up for the scene. It's less than an hour away from any Blue Ridge destination in Georgia—except during festivals, when it takes nearly that long to clear downtown Helen; choose other routes at busy times if you don't plan to attend.

Cleveland

Cleveland is the largest foothill town between the tourist centers of Helen, to the north, and Dahlonega, to the west. Situated on Hwy. 129, Cleveland is also a gateway to the deeper Blue Ridge around Neels Gap.

All roads lead to the town square, where a few country antique shops and cafés make Cleveland a welcoming stop. In the center of the square, the **Old White County Courthouse,** constructed around 1857 by slaves and paid for in Confederate dollars, stands as a small-scale imitation of Philadelphia's Independence Hall. The **White County Chamber of Commerce,** on Hwy. 129, 706/865-5356, housed in a renovated jail built in 1901, provides information about local attractions and businesses.

Once prominent as a gold-mining town, Cleveland is now best known as the birthplace of the Cabbage Patch doll craze that swept the country years back. **Babyland General Hospital,** 19 Underwood St., 706/865-5164, has produced more than 100,000 Cabbage Patch Kids since 1978. In the "hospital," which is actually housed in a 1919 clinic building, the yarn-haired babies sprout from fantasyland cabbage fields strung with twinkling lights—a sight bound to astound (and confuse) curious children. Uniformed nurses deliver the babies to consumers after completing the adoption papers. The doll hospital is open Mon.–Sat. 9 A.M.–5 P.M. and Sun. 10 A.M.–5 P.M.; admission is free.

East of town, you'll find one of the Blue Ridge's most unusual craft shops off Hwy. 17. **Gourdcraft Originals,** Duncan Bridge Rd. (Hwy. 384), 706/865-4048, creates household items and whimsical decorations from hollow bottle gourds (an ancient Native American practice handed down to Appalachian settlers) and displays gourdcraft from around the world.

West Family Restaurant, on Hwy. 75 north of town, 706/865-0525, offers reasonably priced Southern buffets in a convenient location (4.5 miles south of Helen). They serve from the buffet or menu for three meals daily, 7 A.M.–9 P.M.

Smithgall Woods-Dukes Creek State Park

This new 5,664-acre state park, 61 Tsalaki Trail, 706/878-3087, set along North Georgia's premier trout stream, offers a catch-and-release fishing program that includes shuttles (call for reservations), 22 miles of trails, and lodging at a refined mountain retreat (rates start at $189 with meals); for reservations, call 800/864-7275 or visit the website gastateparks.org. It's on Hwy. 75A, three miles west of Helen.

Sautee-Nacoochee Valley

The gazebo-crowned **Nacoochee Mound,** whose excavated artifacts date back 10,000 years, marks your arrival to the magical intersections of Tyrol and Appalachia in Georgia's central Blue Ridge. From here, follow Hwy. 75 north to Helen or Hwy. 17 east to Sautee. With its sight-studded, smooth country highways made for slow-paced rambling, the Sautee-Nacoochee Valley is ideal for leisurely drives or bicycle touring, if it's not too congested.

The **Old Sautee Store,** 706/878-2281 or 888/463-9853, at the crossroads in Sautee, hasn't changed much since it opened for business 115 years ago, unless you count the toll-free number. Farmers still find the basics here.

A mile or so north, **Stovall House,** 1526 Hwy. 255N, 706/878-3355, stovallhouse.com provides five guest rooms in a Victorian farmhouse on 26 acres (rates start at $92 for doubles; breakfast is included). Dinner features mountain trout three ways, along with lamb, stuffed chicken, and pasta (entrées start at $10); it's served Thurs.–Sat. 5:30–8:30 P.M., or come for the midday Sunday brunch.

Farther north off Hwy. 255, see the smallest **covered bridge** in Georgia (36.8 feet long) and order a soda at the old-fashioned counter of the **Skylake Country Store,** Skylake Rd., 706/878-2940.

HELEN

Helen started out in 1913 as just another lumber town. Named for a local official's daughter, Helen floundered after the logging bust until several native sons put their heads together to drum up a scheme to save the town. With fond memories of travels to Germany, one entrepreneur suggested redesigning the town to resemble a Bavarian village, and in 1969, the tiny town of 300 was transformed into Alpine Helen. Never ones to quibble about geography, the local concept is

elastic enough to include things Belgian, Dutch, Scandinavian, and Danish, as well as strictly Swiss or German.

By coincidence, a trace of German ancestry exists in Southern Appalachia (from 18th-century Pennsylvania emigrants), though Anglo-Saxon stock predominates by far (so why not a Scottish Highland wonderland with bagpipes and plaid?). Yet success like this— 1.5 million vacationers every year; 300,000 for Oktoberfest alone—is bound to turn plain folks into *volks.*

Coming into Helen on the Hwy. 75 corridor, you're introduced to the local Tyrolean flavor by gabled roofs on modern motels, billboards written in Renaissance script, and an unusually high number of German bakeries per capita for a rural Georgia town.

At the entrance to the village, a scenic bend of the Chattahoochee River crosses under the narrow bridge of Main Street. Shade trees, patio cafés, hotel balconies, and the FestHalle line the river. Cobblestone byways skirt a small plaza adorned with park benches, flower boxes, and fountains. Browsing among the dozens of shops, you'll see products found nowhere else in Georgia—hand-painted cowbells, cuckoo clocks, Hummel figurines, and the like.

Throughout town, shopkeepers parade in felt caps, and horse-drawn carriages carry sightseers to the next strudel-laden meal or pint of beer. Sure it's kitsch, yet no matter how you feel about accordion music or grown men wearing lederhosen, to find Wiener schnitzel, schwartzwaldtorte, and draft Heineken in rural Georgia is definitely a foreign experience.

Sights

Charlesmagne's Kingdom, 706/878-2000, presents Germany to scale, with 400 feet of miniature railroad and a 22-foot-high Matterhorn. Admission is $5 for adults and $2.50 for children. It's open 11 A.M.–6 P.M. daily, till later Sat.

Back down on Hwy. 75 south of Helen, the **Nora Mill Granary,** 706/878-2375, features an old gristmill powered by the Chattahoochee River; the granary still produces and sells stoneground grains.

Oktòberfest

The biggest annual event in the region, Okto-berfest draws 300,000 revelers to six weeks' worth of fall festivities. The German holiday of Oktoberfest originated in 1810, when King Leopold declared his son's rousing engagement bash to thereafter be an annual holiday. For years, Helen has likewise celebrated the holi-day, with Bavarian dances and costumes, oom-pah-pah sing-alongs, polkas, waltzes, and plenty of German food and beer.

While the whole town works itself into a cel-ebratory frenzy, the main event takes place in the **FestHalle**, an open-air pavilion set out over a bend in the river two blocks east of the Main Street bridge. The fest begins on the weekends in mid-September, then daily through October—world's longest Oktoberfest, they say.

Other Seasonal Events

In winter, the Old World **Altstadt Christmas Market** brings out citywide decorations in December. Outdoor booths under red-and-white striped tents sell crafts and plenty of hand-warming beverages and holiday treats. The town's official tree-lighting ceremony takes place in the central Marketplatz the Friday after Thanksgiving; a 60-foot tree is illumi-nated, and Santa arrives in a horse-drawn car-riage. In January or February, **Fashing Karnival** re-creates a costumed German Mardi Gras for four merrymaking weekends (Friday and Saturday nights).

In spring, a Bavarian **Volksmarch** has *volks* heading through the forest on 3K, 10K, and 20K hikes on the third weekend in April. On the first weekend in May, the **MayFest** celebrates a mini-Oktoberfest in the FestHalle.

In summer, the annual **Hot Air Balloon Race** to the Atlantic takes off the first Thursday in June; later in the month, there's the **Sum-mer Festival,** in the FestHalle. The **Fourth of July** sends tubing parades down the Chatta-hoochee River and brings out all-American fare and fireworks.

Nearby Unicoi State Park hosts many addi-tional festivals, most of which celebrate tradi-tional Appalachian arts and music.

Chattahoochee River Float Trips

The scenic stretch of the Chattahoochee River through Helen is fun for summertime swimming or wading, but the best cheap thrill is taking float trips down the calm waters through town. Start at the bottom of the strip near the grid of modern motels. Here several riverfront companies rent out oversize inner tubes or small rafts and offer shuttle service upriver for a leisurely float trip through the cool, shallow waters (at some spots, so shallow that adults embarrassingly scrape bot-tom as children glide through). The bottom stretch is deep enough for swimming, and the current kicks in a bit more. At the bridge, the flotilla is cheered by crowds lining both sides of the river. It's a mellow, fun ride that kids love, and some stay on the river all day. The take-out point is staffed all day (it's also a popular hangout for bikini-clad teenagers). Charges start at $5 (de-pending on length of trip) and include shuttles, which leave frequently throughout the day. The outpost has restrooms, snack food, and plenty of parking; cafés are within easy walking distance. Try **Cool River Tubing,** 706/878-2665, or **Flea Mar-ket Tubing,** 706/878-1082.

Downriver, an outpost at the Hwy. 117 cross-ing arranges canoe and raft trips down the Class II and III waterway. For canoe rentals and guided river trips, call **Wildwood Outfitters,** 7272 S. Main St., 706/878-1700.

Other Recreation

For mountain bike rentals, find **Woody's,** 706/878-3715, next to Fred's Famous Peanuts, on the way to Unicoi. They'll brief you on local trails and conditions.

A steep 18-hole golf course and tennis club at the **Innsbruck Resort,** up off Hwy. 75 south, 706/878-2400, are part of a complex with condo rentals and a restaurant. An 18-hole public course, **Skitt Mountain Golf Course,** 706/865-2277, is in nearby Cleveland.

Accommodations and Camping

Because of its popular attractions, the Helen area's 1,233 guest rooms cost more than com-parable accommodations elsewhere in the mountains. Standard price fluctuations apply: higher in October and during festivals and holidays, lower for weekdays and winter. Naturally, hotels along the Chattahoochee are most scenic, and premiums may be charged for riverfront rooms. (Unfortunately, some local proprietors put more stock in the exterior appearance of their property than they do the interior; check out the room before you accept it.)

Festival-goers note: A hotel beyond your walking distance from town means competing with day-trippers for parking spots downtown—unless the hotel provides shuttles, as many do.

Unicoi State Park, four miles north of Helen, offers lodge rooms ($69–129 for doubles) and lakeside cottages ($79–149).

Five properties are scenically set on the river right downtown. This list runs from north to south. The 1960s-era **Chattahoochee Riverfront Motel,** 8949 N. Main St./Hwy. 76, 706/878-2184 or 800/830-3977, is in the center of the action and has a pool, restaurant, river floats (rooms start at $70). Newer freestanding cabins on stilts at the quiet **River Bend Chalets,** 152 Dye St., 706/878-3000 or 800/247-7761, are outfitted like condos. A

Hampton Inn, 706/878-3313 or 800/426-7866, in a quiet residential area, is the best bet for a chain motel. **Chalet Kristy,** 134 River St., 706/878-2155, is nicely set at the river and is only a long block from the town center, but room interiors could use renovating. The **Helendorf River Inn,** 706/878-2271 or 800/445-2271, an older motel, is adjacent to the busy Hwy. 75 bridge (prices start at $60) overlooking the river.

Modern chain motels are clustered in a flat, less interesting area south of the Main Street bridge, including Holiday Inn Express, Ramada Inn, Comfort Inn, EconoLodge, Best Western, and Super 8. Prices might start at $40 in the off season; in October, they may start at $125.

For campers, **Unicoi State Park,** four miles north of town, offers a 99-site campground with many amenities. Campsites are also nestled alongside a mountain stream in **Andrews Cove,** a Forest Service recreation area five miles north of Helen off Hwy. 75/17; an Appalachian Trail access route leaves from the campground.

Food and Drink

Not many rural Georgia towns serve the variety of

AUTUMN COLORS

People familiar with the deciduous forests of eastern North America are sometimes surprised to realize how rare such forests are around the world. The familiar annual cycle of broadleaf trees turning spectacular colors and shedding their leaves in fall, and renewing their growth each spring, happens elsewhere in Europe, central China, and a few other places 30 to 60 degrees of latitude from the equator, but that's it. The most extensive of these forests is in North America, on the slopes of the Appalachians.

The Cherokee tell a legend of how the trees came to lose their leaves: the Great One told all the plants and animals to stay awake for seven days, yet as the nights wore on, all but a few succumbed to sleep. The ones who remained awake— the cedar, pine, spruce, holly, and laurel—were rewarded by remaining evergreen, while the rest lose their leaves each fall.

This list of autumnal shades may help to identify a few dominant tree types in the fall forest:

American beech—yellow and orange
Black cherry—yellowish orange
Dogwood—scarlet
Hickory—yellow and orange
Red maple—from yellow to red to orange
Sassafras—orange
Scarlet oak—scarlet
Sourwood—dark red
Sugar maple—reddish yellow
Sumac—brilliant red
Sweet gum—scarlet, purple, and gold (sometimes all three shades on the same tree)
Yellow poplar—brilliant yellow

The timing and brilliance of the fall display depend on several factors, such as temperature and seasonal rainfall, but you'll most likely see colors from mid-September to mid-November, peaking the third week in October. Plan early for popular October accommodations.

Swiss-German-Dutch-Scandinavian cuisine you can find in Helen. The area's 35 restaurants may not be Munich, but it's a change of pace from fried chicken (although there's that too). Helen is also one of the few places in the conservative mountains where you can get a mixed drink.

Budget travelers have their pick of *wurst* (knockwurst, bratwurst, and Polish sausage are common choices) in a bun, heaped with sauerkraut (as it happens, pickled sauerkraut is an authentic Appalachian tradition) and served with a side of German potato salad and a cold draft beer—available at low cost from many cafés and stands. Plenty of gingerbread cottage bakeries present a delicious assortment of morning Danishes, as well as strudel, cookies, and *torten* (including Black Forest cake). Belgian waffles are a local breakfast specialty, and you can even find strong, European-style coffee—all right, maybe not *that* strong, but richer than usual.

In places like the **Hofbrauhaus Inn Wurst Haus,** on Main St., 706/878-2247, you might just want to lift a stein on the deck of the open-air beer garden while strolling minstrels play Rhineland favorites, unless you want the full-scale stroganoff, fondue, and schnitzel with noodles.

At **Paul's,** on Main St., 706/878-2468, the oldest restaurant in town, prime rib accompanied by country-and-western music and riverside views are the specialties of the house (closed Sun.).

Mountain Valley Kitchen, on Chattahoochee St., 706/878-2508, serves country cooking, including stone-ground grains from nearby Nora Mill.

For farm-fresh produce, barbecue meats, prepared deli specialties, penny candy, and other provisions artfully arranged in a nouveau old country store, go to **Betty's Country Store,** on Hwy. 75 north of town, 706/878-2943.

Toward Unicoi State Park, three or so miles north of Helen, **Fred's Peanuts** sells boiled peanuts—a mountain specialty—along with other local food items. One of the best-value buffets in the region is served at the lodge in **Unicoi State Park.**

Information and Services
Alpine Helen–White County Convention and

Visitors Bureau, P.O. Box 730, Helen, GA 30545, 706/878-3842 or 800/858-8027, helenga.org, operates the welcome center at 726 Bracken Strasse at Edelweiss Street, south of the Main Street bridge, in the chain-motel gulch. They're open Mon.–Sat. 9 A.M.–5 P.M. and Sat. 10 A.M.–4 P.M.

You might want to park south of town by the river to avoid the bridge bottleneck that slows all north-south traffic through town.

UNICOI STATE PARK

Five miles northeast of Helen, Unicoi State Park, P.O. Box 849, Helen, GA 30545, 706/878-3983 or 800/864-PARK (864-7275), gastateparks.org, parking $2, is the granddaddy of Georgia's mountain parks. With a jewel-like lake for boating, access trails to cascading Anna Ruby Falls, beautifully set lodging in cabins or lodge rooms, and an impressive schedule of festivals, Unicoi is a popular mountain destination.

Anna Ruby Falls
Though technically within the national forest, access to Anna Ruby Falls is through Unicoi State Park, so it is most appropriately covered in this section of the book. Follow the winding road off Hwy. 356 to the interpretive-center parking lot ($2 parking fee). From here, a paved path of just less than half a mile climbs moderately through a lush glen to two observation decks overlooking the spectacular waterfalls. Anna Ruby's unique double waterfall, the most popular stop on the Blue Ridge "cataract" itinerary, is formed from two separate creeks originating from underground springs at Tray Mountain to the north.

Recreation and Facilities
At **Lake Unicoi,** the 53-acre park centerpiece, you can swim, boat, or fish. The boathouse rents canoes and paddleboats. Four lighted **tennis courts** are also available. A 2.5-mile **hiking trail** leads around the lake, and another trail follows Smith Creek five miles up to Anna Ruby Falls.

The four-mile, moderately difficult **Helen Trail** leads into town—a rustic approach to the town's enchantments—also accessible to mountain bikes. Find trail maps at the lodge,

SOUTHERN HIGHLANDERS

The southern Appalachians are united not only geologically, botanically, and historically, but also culturally. In many ways, North Georgians hold more in common with mountain folk three states removed than with flatlanders in their own state.

Historically, the forest provided the means to their self-sufficiency. From log cabins to the smallest peg, virtually everything on an Appalachian farm was made from wood. Nut trees provided an important source of protein and attracted small game animals, which were easily hunted. Wild fruits ripe for the pickin' grew profusely, including red mulberries, wild plums, wild cherries, black haws, persimmons, crabapples, wild strawberries, and pawpaws (described as 'somewhere between a banana and a persimmon'). Plenty of 'pick-your-own' fields still dot the region today.

Like the Cherokee, the mountaineers crafted many useful items from the bottle gourd plant, including dippers, water jugs, cups, bowls, and even banjos. But today, you'll most commonly see the gourds used as birdhouses to attract the purple martins that keep the local insect population down.

Folk Beliefs

Traditional Appalachian farmers subscribed to a strong belief in astrology. The signs of the zodiac and phases of the moon determined auspicious times to plant and harvest, and even influenced when to get a haircut, paint a house, or wean a child. Each sign was identified with a different part of the body, so, by example, folk logic would hold that the best time to plant beans was with the moon in Gemini ('the arms'). Root crops were best gathered with the moon in Capricorn or Aquarius (the knees or ankles), and all crops that yield below the ground were best planted in a waning moon—those that yield above were best planted in a waxing phase.

With few trained health-care practitioners, farm families relied on folk medicine. This ranged from sound herbal remedies (whose physiological properties have been long ignored by modern science) to superstition. Common ailments were treated with herbal teas and poultices, kerosene oil, and healthy doses of homemade whiskey. More ingenious treatments included: carrying buckeye seeds to combat rheumatism, turning shoes upside down overnight to relieve cramped feet, and burying hair under a rock to cure headaches (it's said old-timers would never allow their cut hair to be thrown away, because it was too valuable). Faith healing also carried weight; to test faith, some Primitive Baptists handled venomous snakes and drank poison.

Arts and Crafts

Appalachian baskets, pottery, quilts, weavings, and all manner of woodworking are prized Appalachian crafts. Skilled artists demonstrate these crafts today at mountain fairs and festivals, and sell their wares at local craft shops. Look for baskets woven from honeysuckle vines and oak splits; clay pottery shaped into 'face jugs' (believed to derive from African traditions and English Toby mugs); and whittled carvings, wooden toys, and hardwood furniture (either rustic or refined). Natural expressions of folk art decorate gravestones, road signs, and side yards throughout the mountains; similar 'primitives' are sold in craft and antique shops.

Music, Dance, and Entertainment

Bluegrass music emanates from the mountains, where it's performed at all local festivals and on front porches throughout the region. Folk and traditional music, accompanied by homemade dulcimers, fiddles, and banjos, date back generations to Old English ballads. Today's 'mountain music' also includes gospel and country and western.

Clogging is a distinctively Appalachian dance form, which originated from the flat-footin' African American style introduced earlier this century. Most festivals feature clogging performances. Square dancing is also a popular mountain pastime.

Storytelling reaches a pinnacle in the mountains. A strong oral-history tradition, a flair for grandiose hyperbole, and local idioms and accents combine to make mountain storytelling an entertaining art form. Tales of local 'haints' (haunts) are particularly popular, especially around mountain campfires.

the camp store, and the information center at the lake.

Accommodations and Camping

Unicoi Lodge, 706/878-2201, houses a restaurant, meeting rooms, shops, and the lodge desk in the central building; outlying two-story lodge buildings contain guest rooms with interior corridors. Guest rooms have been recently renovated (rates start at $69).

Thirty fully equipped **cottages** are sprinkled at lakeshore and farther up Smith Creek. One-bedroom cabins rent for $79–149.

The 84-site **campground** creates a camp city in the woods, with a playground, amphitheater, nightly summertime campfire programs, and "trading post" camp store; sites cost $18–24. Secluded wooded sites are available, including 32 walk-in tent sites ($14) and "squirrel's nest" platform shelters ($10).

Lodge Restaurant

The Unicoi Lodge restaurant serves hearty reasonably priced buffets in a beautiful setting. The dining hall occupies a spacious room with high ceilings and a massive stone fireplace; a glass-walled patio overlooks the woods. Georgia mountain trout is the house specialty, but catfish, barbecued chicken, and glazed ham are also often served.

The dining room serves a generous breakfast buffet 7–10 A.M. (until 10:30 A.M. on weekends); lunch is served noon–2 P.M. daily (though on Sunday that means the all-out midday dinner, and higher prices); dinner is served daily starting at 5 P.M. Prices are $6–10. Restaurant patrons aren't required to buy the $2 parking pass.

Programs and Events

Highlighting the park's full schedule of special events are its Appalachian arts festivals, such as the **Spring Bluegrass Concert and Dance,** on the third week in March; April's **Whittle Inn** (woodcarvers display their skills and sell their wares); June's **Mountain Living** festival (blacksmithing, weaving, and quilting demonstrations); and the **Appalachian Music Festival,** in July, an old tradition that brings fiddlers from all over for folk and traditional music, as well as bluegrass.

NORTH OF HELEN

Ravens Cliff and Vicinity

The Brasstown-Russell Scenic Hwy. (Hwy. 348) traverses a high leisurely route from Helen to Vogel State Park. (From downtown Helen, take Hwy. 75 north to Hwy. 75A and turn left. Highway 348 is a short distance down on the right.) On a clear day, drivers can overlook a Blue Ridge skyline of Slaughter Mountain, Turkey Pen Flats, Lordamercy Cove, Saddle Gap, Stoney Knob, and the Blue Ridge escarpment. As it forms the northern boundary of the Ravens Cliff Wilderness Area, the route provides easy roadside access to pristine waterfalls and adventurous trails—including the Appalachian Trail.

At 2.3 miles in from Hwy. 75A, a mile-long trail leads to **Dukes Creek Falls,** which drop 150 feet down a sheer granite canyon. An observation deck at the parking lot overlooks the falls. At 2.8 miles in, you'll find the trail to **Raven Cliff Falls** on the southern road bank. Follow a 2.5-mile blue-blazed trail to these unusual falls, which emanate from a split in the face of a solid rock outcropping and drop 100 feet to Dodd Creek.

Unicoi Gap

Highway 75 leads from Helen through Unicoi Gap and the Hiawassee River valley to the town of Hiawassee, at the North Carolina line. At **Andrews Cove,** off Hwy. 75 five miles north of Helen, a secluded, 11-site Forest Service campground lies along a beautiful mountain stream. From here, an old logging road heads two miles north up the ridge to connect with the Appalachian Trail. Farther north up Hwy. 75, the A.T. crosses Unicoi Gap. Park here to take a 10.4-mile round-trip hike north to Tray Mountain. The rocky summit overlook, with remarkable panoramic views and a challenging boulder field on its north face, can also be reached by a one-mile round-trip hike north on the A.T. from Forest Service Road 79.

You'll find the road to **Horse Trough Falls** on Hwy. 75, eight miles north of Helen; turn left on Forest Service Road 44 (Wilkes Creek Road) and continue 5.4 miles to an open camping area. Take the dirt road on the right for .2

mountain cabin, Hiawassee

mile to an iron gate and park; then, on foot, take the left fork of the old road and follow the winding, blue-blazed trail through a serene forest to these 70-foot falls.

High Shoals Falls grace a 170-acre scenic area off Hwy. 75. Eleven miles north of Helen, turn right (east) onto the rugged dirt-and-gravel Indian Grave Gap Road (Forest Service Road 283); ford a small stream, and continue up the hill. A parking area is about 1.3 miles in from the highway. From here a moderately steep 1.2-mile trail winds its way to the succession of five falls (there's a total vertical drop of 500 feet) framed by rhododendron and mountain laurel. An abandoned access road parallels the falls for inspiring views from two observation platforms.

Brasstown Bald

In the Cherokee version of Noah's Ark, the canoe that holds the surviving People comes to rest here, on the top of Brasstown Bald. As with other bald summits throughout the southern Appalachians, the exact cause for the missing forest is unknown.

The 360-degree view from Georgia's highest mountain encompasses four states: South Carolina, North Carolina, Tennessee, and Georgia. The steep half-mile paved **Brasstown Bald Trail** leads to the 4,784-foot summit (officially dubbed

Mount Enotah); shuttles are available for a small fee. At the top, the visitors center presents a short film on the region's cultural and geological heritage, and observation-deck placards identify sights in the distance. At the parking lot trailhead, a small concession sells local products and some refreshments.

Three trails connect at the approach to the summit (off-road parking is available). **Arkaquah Trail** descends 5.5 miles along the ridgeline to the petroglyphs at Trackrock. **Jacks Knob Trail** runs 4.5 miles south until it intersects with the Appalachian Trail. The original double-rutted **Wagon Train Trail** spurs off the paved summit trail and heads northwest six miles through the surrounding Brasstown Wilderness, ending behind the women's dormitory at the Young-Harris College campus (unmarked at both its beginning and end).

HIAWASSEE

Straddling the North Carolina border on the southern shore of Lake Chatuge, Hiawassee is best known for the popular mega-events staged at its 2,000-seat lakeside pavilion and fairgrounds. Plenty of local recreation areas, motels, restaurants, and bait-and-tackle shops cater to concertgoers and fisherfolk.

Entertainment and Events

In August, the **Georgia Mountain Fair** brings two weeks of mountain merrymaking to North Georgia. Ferris wheels, arcade games, pig races, and other amusements fill the fairgrounds, while the music hall hosts one lively mountain music act after another. Old-timers hold forth from wooden shacks, demonstrating the revered Appalachian arts of pot-throwing, whittlin', and moonshine-making. Admission is $5 (fair-goers in overalls are admitted free on "pioneer day"), and you may want to go back several times for different musical acts, such as bluegrass, country and western, gospel, and traditional.

The play ***The Reach of Song*** tells the story of Appalachian history and heritage with a traditional music score. Fiddle-pickin', two-steppin', and storytelling—it's all here. Call 800/262-SONG (262-7664) for more information. More homegrown mountain music can be heard at **Music Festivals,** in mid-May and mid-October, and at a **Fiddlers Convention,** in late October.

Recreation

The Forest Service's Lake Chatuge recreation area, on Hwy. 288 a mile south of Hwy. 76 west, provides access to the 7,050-acre **Lake Chatuge,** an angler's favorite for spotted and largemouth bass. Here a 32-site Forest Service campground ($5 a night) is set on a pine-covered peninsula jutting into the reservoir. The nearby **chamber of commerce,** on Hwy. 288 right off Hwy. 76, 706/896-4966, can direct you to commercial marinas, launches, and other services around the lake and throughout Hiawassee.

Eleven miles east of town, Hwy. 76 meets the Appalachian Trail, the fourth and final road crossing in Georgia from the Springer Mountain trailhead. The A.T. heads north from here five miles or so into the **Southern Nantahala Wilderness Area** before crossing over into North Carolina.

Accommodations and Food

The **Fieldstone Inn and Restaurant,** on Hwy. 76 at the western shore of Lake Chatuge, 706/896-2262 or 800/545-3408, offers a full-service hotel complex. A sleek stone-and-glass lobby leads to 66 modern guest rooms, all with balconies overlooking the lake (doubles start at $100) Boat rentals are available at the hotel's boathouse, and a swimming pool, tennis court, and restaurant are also on the premises.

At the low end, **Mull's Motel,** 213 N. Main St., 706/896-4195, offers basic rooms for about $50 and can arrange shuttles to the A.T.

The **Georgia Mountain Restaurant,** on Hwy. 76, 706/896-3430, serves popular country cooking for three meals in the thick of the action. It's open daily 6 A.M.–9 P.M.

At the **Deer Lodge,** on Hwy. 75 south, 706/896-2726, crowds gather before the doors open—scratch your name on the notepad tacked outside, take your ticket, and wait for your number to be called. It's worth the wait for its meaty steaks, delicious mountain trout, and other hearty entrées served in cozy, wood-paneled rooms. Dinners are served Wed.–Sun. 5–9 P.M.

Cornelia to Clarkesville

The oldest resort in North Georgia, Clarkesville sits at the lower slope of the river valley that stretches southeast from Helen. The surrounding countryside is perfect for a leisurely drive or bike tour past an old mill here, a covered bridge there, and past renowned Glen-Ella Springs, an elegant country resort. North of Clarkesville, Hwy. 441 leads to high-country lakes and the deeper wilds of Rabun County.

To the east, between Clarkesville and the foothill city of Toccoa, the southernmost branch of the national forest offers natural areas within easy access to urban travelers. At the intersection of the Blue Ridge and Piedmont provinces, the forest here exhibits species from both physiographic areas. Most of the region's recreation areas are easily reached from Cornelia.

CORNELIA AND VICINITY

Cornelia, the southernmost Blue Ridge town, borders the most readily accessible branch of the national forest. Besides that, the town is known for its Giant Apple Monument, a tribute to the local industry, on Rte. 23 downtown at the train depot. Visitors to town and forest areas east follow Hwy. 441 business; a modern bypass skirts the town for through-travelers.

About 20 minutes south of Cornelia, the **Habersham Winery,** off Hwy. 365 in Baldwin, 706/778-WINE (778-9463), allows visitors to sample its local favorite white muscadine wine, as well as other varieties. A gift shop sells Georgia food items along with the winery's products. It's open Mon.–Sat. 10 A.M.–6 P.M. and Sun. 1–6 P.M.

Trails and Recreation

At **Lake Russell,** 3.5 miles southeast of Cornelia, the Forest Service operates a recreation area for swimming, fishing, boating, camping,

Cornelia is Georgia's apple capital.

and hiking. The recreation area is set around a 100-acre lake with a grassy beach. The beach parking lot charges $2 per vehicle in season. From Cornelia, take Hwy. 441 to Hwy. 197; turn right on old Hwy. 197; turn right onto Dicks Hill Hwy., go .8 mile, and turn off on Forest Service Road 59, Lake Russell Road.

The 4.6-mile **Lake Russell Trail** follows the southern shore of the lake from dam to dam; the entrance road along the northern shore provides an alternate loop trip back. The other two trails start in the group camp area around Nancytown Lake. The 6.2-mile **Ladyslipper Trail,** a horse and foot trail, leads one mile up to a loop around Red Root Mountain, with its panoramic views and a few steep climbs. The 2.7-mile-loop **Sourwood Trail,** ideal for families and less ambitious hikers, reaches Nancytown Falls a mile in, passes a beaver pond, and follows a creek through the woods back along Red Root Road to the trailhead.

The 42-site Lake Russell campground is one of the few Forest Service camps with a trailer dump station. Campsites start at $10.

CLARKESVILLE

More than 150 years ago, coastal families seeking refuge from the oppressive summer heat at the shore established Clarkesville as a cool summer home resort. Today this little mountain town tucks urbane delights into its rustic country setting.

Downtown Clarkesville's three-block row of wooden storefronts is centered on a shaded plaza where many town festivals take place. Colorful quilts in centuries-old Appalachian patterns flutter outside corner flea markets and antique boutiques, and a bank, drugstore, book cellar, bakery, and sandwich shop round out the stores. Forty buildings around town, mostly former summer homes, are listed on the National Historic Registry.

Several major country crossroads come together in Clarkesville. Visitors from the south probably arrive via Hwy. 441, which continues northeast to Rabun County. Highway 17 leads west, through the Sautee-Nacoochee Valley to Helen. Highway 197 follows the scenic Soque River—across a ford in a stream affectionately called "the upside-down bridge"—north to Batesville and Lake Burton.

North Georgia

Take this last route to the **Mark of the Potter,** an old mill perched at the waterfalls of the Soque River. At this Blue Ridge landmark you can feed trout from the 2nd-story balcony, see millwork underpinnings, and shop for handcrafted pottery.

Where Highways 197 and 255 meet, the **Batesville General Store,** 706/947-3434, sells groceries, gas, and bait, and a café out back specializes in cinnamon rolls.

A **Forest Service office,** on Burton Rd. (Hwy. 197), 706/754-6221, sells and distributes maps and guides to local Forest Service trails and recreation areas.

Accommodations

Hundred-year-old **⚑ Glen-Ella Springs Inn,** on Bear Gap Road off Hwy. 441 north, 706/754-7295 or 800/552-3479, glenella.com, North Georgia's premier country inn, is set on 17 acres tucked away down miles of country roads. The two-story lodge, built in 1875, overlooks both a meadow and herb and perennial gardens that lead to woods and nature trails along Panther Creek. Sixteen guest rooms are lined in heart-of-pine and furnished with antiques and rocking chairs out on the porch (rates start at $100 for weekdays, including a full breakfast in the dining room). There is also a pool.

The **dining room** serves an elegant dinner daily. Pecan-encrusted trout was on a recent menu, along with apple-bread pudding. Call for reservations; overnight guests should be sure to reserve a table along with their room if they want dinner. Habersham is a dry county, so if you want wine, you'll need to bring it with you.

Rabun County

Bordering both Carolinas in Georgia's northeast tip, Rabun County packs natural wonders, outdoor adventures, and down-home Appalachian spirit into one small isolated corner made famous by *Foxfire* and infamous by *Deliverance.* Chattooga River white water (rated among the top 10 river runs in the United States) is the biggest draw, and sightseers take in the spectacular 600-foot drop of sheer-walled Tallulah Gorge.

Christmas-tree farms, dairies, and car graveyards dot the old-time mountain towns, and country dogs run free. Rooted residents in homey cabins and old trailers grow corn in side yards, hang hollow bottle gourds for nesting purple martins, and advertise "Mountain Honey for Sale" on hand-painted wooden signs.

Such rugged communities contrast sharply with the posh, picture-postcard resorts bordering the county's high-country lakes. Generations of Atlanta's elite have summered in stately "cottages" around Lake Rabun, whose boathouses alone are more elaborate than most county residences.

Towns are laid out linearly through the valley along Hwy. 441. Modern stretches of the "new" highway bypass the more serendipitous "old" highway.

TALLULAH FALLS

The town of Tallulah Falls, balanced precariously over the precipitous gorge and thundering cascades of the Tallulah River, has an illustrious history—the dramatic sheer-walled gorge has both haunted and attracted people for centuries. The wary Cherokee heeded legends that warriors who ventured in never returned, and many a curious settler had a waterfall or pool named in his honor—posthumously, after an untimely slip. Yet word of the natural wonder spread, and crowds were drawn to the breathtaking sight.

By the turn of the century, Tallulah Falls was a fashionable resort, with several elite hotels and boardinghouses catering to lowland sightseers. A railroad transported visitors to the rim. But fortunes changed once the power company set sights on harnessing water power for hydroelectricity. Despite public objections, the dam was completed and slowed the water—and the crowds—to a trickle. Despite the impressive sight of the dry gorge, the once-famous resort of Tallulah Falls likewise faded and reverted to an earthy Blue Ridge mountain community.

After decades of talk about restoring the

gorge's former glory, in 1993 the power company sent the Tallulah River spilling 600 feet down the gorge once again. After that, an impressive new state park was built on the north rim. Hang gliders enjoy the dramatic float over the gorge; gliders congregate around the southeast rim at the cabins of **Hang Glider Heaven,** 706/782-6218.

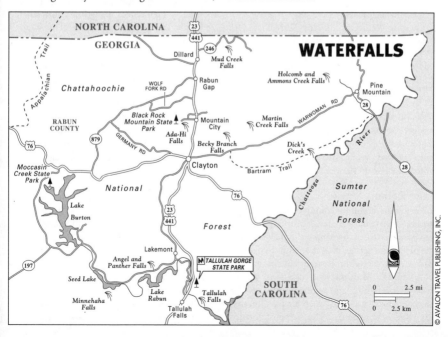 Tallulah Gorge State Park

In 1886, an acrobat by the name of Professor Leon crossed the gorge on a tightrope suspended across its breadth. In 1970, the flying Karl Wallenda replicated the historic feat before a crowd of 35,000 onlookers. Today all daring visitors can cross the gorge on a **suspension bridge** that opened in 2004; it's now the centerpiece of this dramatic state park.

Tallulah Gorge State Park, at the north rim off Hwy. 441, 706/754-7970, gastateparks.org, parking $4, also features an impressive interpretive center set on the north rim of the gorge. Inside, an exciting film shows close-up, live-action footage of kayakers braving the white water;

outside, rim trails lead to scenic views. Permits are required to kayak and to hike into the gorge (no charge); inquire about schedules. A six-mile mountain biking trail leads to Tugaloo Lake; the trailhead is near the gatehouse.

At Tallulah Lake, the 63-acre impoundment of the Tallulah River, there's a small swimming beach and tennis courts. A 50-site **campground,** 706/754-7979, is nicely set among woods; rates are $14–16.

WEEKENDER LAKES

In the 1920s, Georgia Power constructed several more dams to impound the once-raging Tallulah River. The resulting placid lakes—Rabun, Seed, and Burton—now offer beautiful mountain scenery and recreation easily glimpsed from a smooth, slow-moving drive or an ideal bicycle tour. For a scenic flatwater canoeing adventure, cross the three lakes west-to-east, with short portages past two dams. Contact **Appalachian Outfitters,** 706/864-7117, for canoe rentals and shuttle information.

North Georgia

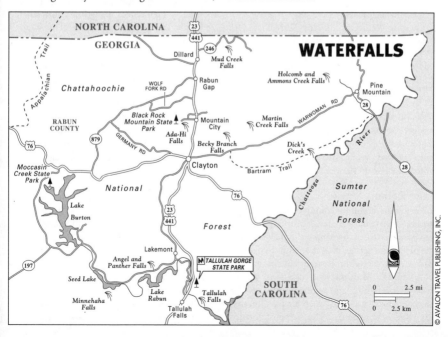

WATERFALLS

© AVALON TRAVEL PUBLISHING, INC.

WATERFALLS

Something about a waterfall is compelling—the beauty, the roar, the spray—and the Blue Ridge is full of these graceful primal attractions. Nearly every stream has one at some point, and each scene is guaranteed to be framed by thick lush growth and blooms, or sparkling with winter ice. You'll find the grand, well-known Amicalola Falls and Anna Ruby Falls (along with many other scenic waterfalls) farther west, and Toccoa Falls farther south, yet Rabun County's many waterfalls have a distinctive quality—tranquil and removed, yet easily accessible to the casual hiker.

Mountaineers use such terms as misty, cascading, or thundering to describe their favorite local "cataracts" (from Middle English for "floodgate"). Waters may spill down in double falls, stair-step falls, free falls, or shoals.

Rangers warn against climbing near any falls. The prime local hazard is slipping off slick rocks, and getting stuck endangers rescuers. Blazes are eye-level, rectangular gashes in trees, created to indicate a trail.

Becky Branch Falls

A steep walk through the dense Warwoman Dell leads to the tranquil waterfalls of Becky Branch ("branch" is an Appalachian synonym for "stream"). The Bartram Trail—named for 18th-century Quaker naturalist William Bartram—begins a hundred feet below the falls. Nearby, old stone steps lead to an abandoned railroad bed.

From Clayton, drive east on Warwoman Road (County Road 5) to the junction with Pool Creek Road. Go 2.8 miles and park on the left. Walk 200 yards up the steep trail at the right side of the falls to the bridge.

Dick's Creek

Here water spills 60 feet into the federally designated "Wild and Scenic" Chattooga River, and an observation platform overlooks the sheer drop.

Take Warwoman Road east six miles out of Clayton to Pool Creek Road. Follow it for .6 mile and turn right on Dick's Creek Road (also called Sandy Ford Road). Follow this road 3.5 miles past the second ford to where it crosses the Bartram Trail. Park and walk north along the trail for 600 yards.

Martin Creek Falls

Naturalist William Bartram wrote admiringly of these falls—then called Falling Branch Falls—in *Travels*, the late 18th-century account of his Southeastern expeditions. To get to this series of three falls on Martin Creek, follow Warwoman Road east from Clayton 2.5 miles. Drive up Martin

To reach the lakes from Hwy. 441, drive two miles north of Tallulah Falls, crossing the gorge bridge, a second bridge, and turning left immediately before the third bridge. Continue 2.5 miles (crossing yet another bridge), and turn left onto Lake Rabun Road.

Lake Rabun

Lake Rabun, a clubby colony of 400 lakeshore homes for Atlanta's elite (each property is identified on the lake map by name), also shelters one of the best Forest Service recreation areas in the Blue Ridge, off Lake Rabun Road in Lakemont.

At **Hall's Marina,** you can find a boat launch and fishing and boating supplies. The adjacent Boat House, an open-air pavilion over the lake, is treasured as the scene of rousing weekend concerts and parties in its past heyday. Today the only gatherings religiously held are the Sunday morning services called forth to a floating congregation. But you might get lucky—check at the marina for bluegrass concerts or other events that might be taking place during your stay.

At the Forest Service **Rabun Beach** recreation area, a small strip of sandy beach brings sunbathers and families to the lifeguard-supervised swimming area. A boat launch is available, and a trail to waterfalls begins across the road. The attractive 50-site Forest Service **campground,** across the way, offers many secluded sites on a gently sloping hillside—it's one of the nicest places to camp in the region (rates are $15 a night; it's first-come, first-served).

Creek Road a half mile and park, then hike up the west side of the creek.

Holcomb and Ammons Creek Falls

These picturesque waterfalls on the Holcomb Creek Trail drop and shoal for 150 feet—first at Holcomb Creek, then at Ammons Creek, a third of a mile up.

Take Warwoman Road east of Clayton 10 miles. At Hale Ridge Road, turn left and go nine miles; the 1.5-mile trail starts at the intersection of Overflow Road.

Mud Creek Falls

The falls cascade for 350 feet with a spouting flume down the middle.

Take Hwy. 441 north from Clayton, then north on Hwy. 246 to Sky Valley. Go through the main gate down Sky Valley Way, turn right on Tahoe Road, proceed three-quarters of a mile to the three-forks intersection and park. Walk 500 yards down on left (grills and picnic tables are available).

Angel and Panther Falls

Along the trail you'll first find 50-foot Angel Falls; half a mile upstream along the climbing trail lies Panther Falls.

Head south from Clayton on Old Hwy. 441 to Lake Rabun Road, then turn in to the Rabun Beach recreation area, which is divided into two sections. Look for trail signs in Area Two.

Minnehaha Falls

One hundred feet high, this beautiful waterfall drops and shoals from the top of a secluded path that gently climbs through rhododendron and mountain-laurel thickets.

Go south from Clayton on Old Hwy. 441 and follow Lake Rabun Road to the west, which takes you around the north side of the lake. One mile past the Rabun Beach recreation area, you'll see the dam. Cross the bridge, bear left onto Bear Gap Road, and continue straight after the full stop for 1.6 miles. Trail markers disappear mysteriously; watch for the bend with a widened left shoulder to park, and follow the narrow footpath across the way to the half-mile trail.

Tallulah Falls

After being bottled up for half a century, the magnificent falls at Tallulah Gorge once again roar through the dramatic 1,000-foot gorge—now the centerpiece of a state park; overlook trails and a suspension bridge have a panoramic view.

Follow signs off Hwy. 441 north of the gorge bridge (parking $4).

There are also a couple of good restaurants nearby: **Louie's on the Lake,** 1 Lake Rabun Rd., 706/782-3276, for pizza; and **Inger's Fine Foods,** 88 Lofty Branch Lane, 706/782-3159, for fine dining.

Lake Burton and Lake Seed

Lake Burton, the biggest and most remote of the three Weekender Lakes, takes its name from the former town of Burton, submerged under its namesake lake since 1925. A mile or so west of the dam at the lake's southern end, signs off Hwy. 197 lead drivers down dirt roads to **Cherokee Landing.** Here you'll find a marina, boat launch, bait store, burger joint, and a scattered collection of cabins. The lake's public swimming area, **Timpson Cove Beach,** lies at the northeastern shore, off Hwy. 76 west of Clayton.

On Lake Seed, the power company maintains primitive campsites without water; follow signs off Lake Burton Road. The same turnoff leads to Minnehaha Falls.

Moccasin Creek State Park

This postage stamp–sized park—Georgia's smallest state park—is nestled invitingly on the shores of Lake Burton off Hwy. 197, 706/947-3194 or 800/864-PARK (864-7275), gastateparks.org, parking $2. The 54 campground site ($14–24) are close parking spots with only a few trees to shade you from your neighbor, but it nevertheless makes a good base of operations if you don't covet your privacy.

Naturally, it attracts mostly trailer-camper fishing families.

A fully accessible fishing pier is open "only to physically challenged visitors, senior citizens, and children." From a trailhead at the trout hatchery intake across the road, the 6.2-mile **Moccasin Creek Trail** follows a scenic trout stream to high falls, about an hour's hike away.

THE CHATTOOGA RIVER

Slicing through the Appalachian wilderness at the junction of three states, the "Wild and Scenic" Chattooga River rates among the nation's top 10 white-water river adventures. The world-class river attracts 100,000 visitors a year to Rabun County for rafting, canoeing, kayaking, tubing, swimming, fishing, and bank-side hiking, but you wouldn't know it from the desolate feel of the wilderness.

Rated Class IV overall, the river is divided into four sections of increasing difficulty. **Section One,** mainly the west fork above the Hwy. 28 bridge, is a shallow preserve of fly fishers and frolicking inner tubers. **Section Two** picks up the pace; families and beginners enjoy light paddling with some rough-water rapids. **Section Three** is where the action starts—a dozen miles of fast water with as many Class III and IV rapids, plus the kicker, Class V Bull Sluice (the name Decapitation Rock gives you an idea of this rapid's thrills). **Section Four** follows, with hardcore white water such as the Screaming Left Turn, Deliverance Rock, and an eye-of-the-needle run through Crack in the Rock. Some of these rapids rate up to Class VI and are more hazardous in higher water. *There are no atheists on Section Four.*

While professionally guided rafting excursions have reliable safety records, independent paddlers be forewarned: the river is extremely dangerous, and only experienced paddlers should attempt it.

Chattooga River Whitewater Rafting

To minimize traffic and wear-and-tear on the river, only three companies are licensed to operate on the Chattooga: **Southeastern Expeditions,**

800/868-7238; **Nantahala Outdoor Center,** 800/232-7238; and **Wild Water Ltd.,** 800/451-9972. All three run daily trips from around March to October; most trips take about six hours and cost around $80 per person (weekday rates are lower, Section Four is higher). All offer overnight or weeklong excursion trips—some combined with biking, hiking, or horseback riding—and package deals combine rafting prices with overnight accommodations at local lodges.

All outfitters provide personal flotation devices, helmets, rafts, paddles, food, shuttle service from outposts, and car-key containers. Stow your valuables safely out of sight in your car or hotel. Bring a towel and change of clothes, and leave them in the car. In summer, wear shorts or a bathing suit, and old sneakers or river shoes. In cold weather, wear wool socks and a wool cap or synthetic equivalents.

Hiking and Backpacking

The 20-mile **Chattooga River Trail** follows the river upstream from the Hwy. 76 bridge, crossing

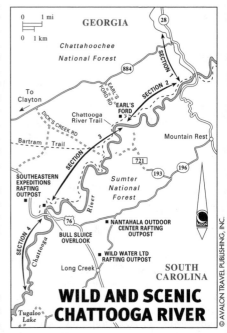

WILD AND SCENIC CHATTOOGA RIVER

Chattooga whitewater rafting

in the late 18th century, stretches from the North Carolina line through Georgia's tip downhill to South Carolina. Hikers can pick up the trail midway by parking at **Warwoman Dell,** a Forest Service area east of Clayton off Warwoman Road. A half-mile **nature walk** here identifies native plants. From this point, the Bartram Trail heads east to the river and merges with the Chattooga River Trail.

Accommodations and Food

Beechwood Inn, 220 Beechwood Dr., 706/782-5485, beechwoodinn.ws, perched on the side of a thickly forested rise about a quarter mile from downtown, occupies a two-story clapboard lodge overlooking the woods. David and Gayle Darugh have six guest rooms, some with working fireplaces and copper tubs, and each with private bath (starting at $119 with breakfast) from March to November. Inquire about monthly gourmet dinners and their private wine label.

Out Hwy. 76 a half-mile east of town, **A Small Motel,** 706/782-6488 or 800/786-0624, asmallmotel.com, caters to river runners with a neat and friendly set of rooms (starting at around $50) seven miles from the Chattooga River (about the closest lodging to the river from the Georgia side).

For diner fare, the **Clayton Cafe,** on Main St., slings down-home breakfasts, burgers, and other basics from a syrup-stained menu; it's open Mon.–Sat. 6:30 A.M.–2:30 P.M. Among celebrity restaurants, the **Cookie Jar Cafe,** US Hwy. 441, 706/745-3600, is co-owned by Billy Redden, the Banjo Boy of *Deliverance* who recently returned to film as the Banjo Man in Tim Burton's *Big Fish.*

Green Shutters, on S. Main St., 706/782-3342, serves three family-style Southern meals a day, accompanied by cinnamon rolls, sweet-potato bread, buttermilk biscuits, and corn muffins. It's open Thurs.–Sat.

Information and Services

The enthusiastic folks at the Rabun County Chamber of Commerce run the resourceful **welcome center** on Hwy. 441 north of Warwoman Rd., 706/782-5113.

Hwy. 28, and continuing north another 15 miles into South Carolina. The route is blazed with both a metal diamond marker and yellow paint to indicate that the river trail and **Bartram Trail** merge here. With notably scenic exceptions, the trail passes through the thick mixed-hardwood forest largely out of sight of the river, though you can hear the roaring rapids. The Forest Service office in Clayton sells detailed river maps.

CLAYTON AND VICINITY

The down-home mountain town of Clayton, the largest city in Rabun County, is a good base of operations for excursions into the wild forest and river areas to the east. Main Street, a three-block length of wooden storefronts on a sunny rise, still looks like a place you might hitch a horse outside to do your trading and salooning.

Recreation

The 57-mile **Bartram Trail,** named for the naturalist William Bartram, who mapped this route

The **Forest Service office,** on Hwy. 441, 706/782-3320, sells comprehensive Chattooga River maps and distributes guides to recreation areas in the surrounding national forest.

For provisions, look for the supermarket shopping centers off Hwy. 441. The coin-operated laundry on Hwy. 76 one block east of Main Street offers drop-off laundry service.

For medical emergencies, call **Rabun County Hospital,** 706/782-4233.

MOUNTAIN CITY

Coming into Mountain City from the south at the end of the day, drivers watch the monolith of Black Rock Mountain impose an early twilight on the broad valley to its east. Behind scruffy roadside cabins with their lean-to signs, the granite mountain's shadow slowly reaches past grazing black-and-white cows and tractors parked between haystacks. Turn left, and a winding route climbs to the summit, where it's still bright with daylight.

Continue north another mile on the highway to South Wolf Fork Road. If you turn in toward the mountain, you'll pass an old garage overtaken with flowering vines and a red storybook barn before coming to **Sylvan Mill,** sitting next to a waterfall pouring over gleaming granite. A red waterwheel standing two stories high churns through the silver water, still grinding hominy into speckled grits. The miller now operates the mill as a **bed and breakfast,** 706/746-7138, syl-

BLUE RIDGE MOUNTAIN STATE PARKS

One of the best places to start exploring North Georgia is a state park. Some of the best land, views, and trails, and hideaway cabins and lodges (at excellent values) lie within the seven Blue Ridge state parks. Many offer recreation such as swimming (pools or beaches), fishing, boat rentals, hiking, and backpacking. Festivals, mountain-music concerts, guided backpacking trips, Appalachian and Cherokee crafts demonstrations, and guided nature walks and workshops for low or no cost add to the attractions. All vehicles require a $2 park pass, except at Tallulah Gorge, where the parking fee is $4.

Lodging rates for cottages vary by season, location, weekday or weekend, and size (one to three bedrooms), and start at $65. Lodge rooms start at $69. Camping rates are around $15; more for hookups, less for walk-in. For all reservations, call 800/864-PARK (800/864-7275) or visit gastateparks.org.

Amicalola Falls: 240 Amicalola Falls State Park Rd., Dawsonville, GA 30534, 706/265-4703—a modern lodge and restaurant with a panoramic view, remote Len Foote Hike Inn, cottages, campground, Appalachian Trail terminus.

Black Rock Mountain: Mountain City, GA 30562, 706/746-2141—panoramic views of three states, backpacking, remote campground and mountaintop cottages near the "Wild and Scenic" Chattooga River for whitewater rafting.

Moccasin Creek: 3655 Hwy. 197, Clarkesville, GA 30523, 706/947-3194—a modest fish camp on beautiful Lake Burton; camping only.

Smithgall Woods-Dukes Creek State Park: 61 Tsalaki Trail, 706/878-3087, catch-and-release fishing on premier trout stream, 22 miles of trails, and lodging at a refined mountain retreat.

Tallulah Gorge: Hwy. 441, Tallulah Falls, GA 30573, 706/754-8257—a suspension bridge, panoramic views of dramatic gorge and waterfalls, modern interpretive center, rock-climbing, whitewater paddling, mountain biking trail, lakeside beach, campground.

Unicoi: P.O. Box 849, Helen, GA 30545, 706/878-3366—the granddaddy of Blue Ridge Parks, central location, modern lodge and restaurant, cottages, campground, rental boats, waterfall trails.

Vogel: Rte. 1, P.O. Box 1230, Blairsville, GA 30512, 706/745-2628—popular cottages and campground set around a small lake, rental boats, beach, center of large hiking-trail network.

vanfallsmill.com. There are four rooms, each with private bath (starting at $95).

On York House Road east of the highway, beyond the cows and hay and over the gully bridge, the trim white **York House,** 706/746-2068, banks up against the forest wall. This historic inn has been open for business since 1896, and not much has changed since then, except the addition of indoor plumbing in every room. The antiques weren't antique then, just furniture, and the fireplaces still work. The 2nd-story veranda catches the last stretch of valley sun before the light goes out (starting at $80 with continental breakfast).

The **Foxfire Information Center,** 2837 Hwy. 441N, 706/746-5828, distributes maps and guided-tour information on their model village, set in a high cove not far from the highway. Foxfire, an educational movement begun in the 1960s that caught fire with the back-to-the-land movement, is dedicated to preserving traditional Appalachian folkways. Tours are held weekdays only, for $5 for adults.

BLACK ROCK MOUNTAIN

The temperature drops as you climb 2,700 feet up the steep grade to the top of Black Rock Mountain. At the wind-worn 3,640-foot summit, a visitors center and flagstone terrace look out over a grand, south-facing Blue Ridge panorama. If there's no fog, you can see clear to the South Carolina Piedmont, 80 miles away. The rocky crest also marks the eastern continental divide—from here, waters part to follow a path to either the Atlantic Ocean or the Gulf of Mexico.

A local legend tells the story of a Cherokee chief's son who asked a neighboring Catawba chief for his daughter's hand in marriage. The girl's reluctant father told the prospective bridegroom he would grant consent only if the boy found "where the waters part"—which was probably a Native American version of "when hell freezes over." Well, it happened that the boy stumbled upon this mountaintop divide, and though he reported back to the chief with joy that his hopes would be fulfilled, the Catawba still refused him. So the young lovers ran off together to Hiawassee.

Black Rock Mountain State Park

The highest state park in Georgia, Black Rock Mountain State Park, 706/746-2141 or 800/864-PARK (864-7275), gastateparks.org, parking $2, offers panoramic views from several observation platforms. The north-facing, campground overlook spans a view across the Blue Ridge to the southern Nantahala and the Great Smoky Mountains. At sunset, look for the Tennessee Rock overlook, just beyond the visitors center and a short jaunt up from the sign on the right.

The 1,718-acre park also features 10 miles of trails, hideaway cabins, and a 17-acre lake stocked with trout. In winter, at least a light dusting of snow covers the higher elevations, and rangers can show you photos of the blizzard that dropped a foot of snow at the year-round park several winters back.

Park Hiking and Backpacking Trails

Though the trail to **Ada-Hi Falls** is only a fifth of a mile, in that distance, it drops 220 feet. Naturally, the trip up feels a whole lot longer. The sloping trail and steps dead-end at a wooden platform that overlooks the small waterfall (but it's worth the climb).

The two-mile, yellow-blazed **Tennessee Rock Trail** largely follows the contour of the eastern continental divide, climbing 440 feet across the forested ridge crest.

The 7.2-mile, orange-blazed **James E. Edmonds Backcountry Trail** covers similar territory, but drops lower, climbs higher, crosses two creeks, and passes under stands of white pine, a hemlock forest, and thickets of fragrant mountain laurel. Midway in, the trail spurs off to a primitive campsite and vista point on 3,162-foot **Lookoff Mountain.**

Ask for trail maps and interpretive nature trail guides at the visitors center. Inquire about guided overnight **backpacking trips,** led by staff naturalists.

Park Cottages and Camping

Ten spacious cottages are set off in a ring at the top of the mountain. The lucky campers in cottage Nos. 1–6 get the panoramic view, but all cabins are exquisitely removed from lowland

North Georgia

civilization—no phones and no TVs, just fireplaces and porch rockers. The cottages sleep up to 10 people and are rented year-round—a nice snowy winter retreat for brave drivers. The cost is $75–115 for a two-bedroom.

A 48-site wooded **campground** sits high atop the eastern continental divide (sites cost $19–21; hookups are available). Twelve walk-in tent sites offer additional seclusion ($10). The red wooden Trading Post at the entrance to the campground sells a bare-bones assortment of batteries, charcoal, ice, and firewood. Sometimes when it rains, rangers open up the camp store's dusty attic for video shows to entertain the kids. If you sit on the porch, you can watch the waters part on the pavement out front.

DILLARD AND VICINITY

The Dillard name dates from the 18th century in these parts. For generations, the Dillard family has run a local hospitality empire. In addition to the rambling landmark inn, the family oligarchy operates a row of roadside businesses off Hwy. 441, selling "collectibles," "keepsakes," and even supplies.

Dillard House

A sprawling set of bungalows, lodges, and halls all go by the name Dillard House, off Hwy. 441, 706/746-5348. Heading them up is the restaurant, famous for its all-you-can-eat country cooking. From its glass-walled patio, diners can look out over the broad green valley to see horses in the pasture. Brisk waiters deliver plates of country ham, fried chicken, pan-fried trout, vegetables, cornbread, and assorted relishes and desserts. Having grown to meet the mushrooming demands of flocks of tourists, the legendary institution may today impress you more as an institution than as a legend—nevertheless, you never leave hungry. Guest rooms are around back—in low-slung lodges scattered near a swimming pool and tennis courts—and nearby at the

original inn (rates start at around $80). Inquire about horseback riding trips.

Betty's Creek Road

From Dillard, a left turn onto Betty Creek Road leads west through one of North Georgia's most beautiful valleys. The gently rolling, winding route is perfect for bicycle touring.

Five miles up at **Andy's Trout Farm,** 706/746-2550, you don't need a license to fish for rainbow trout, and Andy's lends you a pole and line. They also rent wooden cabins around the ponds for around $60—that way you can stay over for the nightly square dances.

The **Hambidge Center,** six miles west of Dillard, 706/746-5718, was founded by Mary Hambidge—a cultural artist, iconoclast, and environmentalist—to preserve traditional Appalachian crafts. The center houses a gallery, studio, cabins, and administrative buildings on 600 picturesque acres. It sponsors an on-site artists-in-residence program and hosts occasional programs devoted to Appalachian heritage. An old gristmill on the premises is still in operation. Visitors are welcome to roam about the grounds, providing that they first check in at the office.

Sky Valley

Sky Valley, 706/746-5302 or 800/437-2416, east of Dillard via Hwy. 246, is home to the southernmost ski resort in the eastern United States. Here, in an isolated niche within Georgia's northeasternmost wilderness, an exclusive year-round gated resort occupies a small valley at the base of the 3,320-foot runs. The length of the winter-sports season varies with the weather, though the resort "blows snow" if it's cold enough. Besides the winter sports, the deluxe resort is open year-round for guests to enjoy the remote setting, an 18-hole golf course and pro shop, a swimming pool, tennis courts, a restaurant, and a bar. Chalet and condominium rentals start at $135 a night for a place that sleeps six.

Heartland Georgia

Georgia's heartland stretches across the wide middle of the state from the Chattahoochee River at the state's western boundary with Alabama to the Savannah River at the northwestern border with South Carolina, on the high plateau of thickly forested rolling hills between North Georgia's Appalachian mountains and South Georgia's coastal plain. The plateau—called the Piedmont—is separated from the plain by the "fall line," the drop in elevation that creates a line of rapids on inland waterways from Georgia on up the Eastern Seaboard. Because these rapids marked the extent of inland navigation, cities formed along the rivers at the fall line. Augusta was established on the Savannah River in 1735, followed by Milledgeville on the Oconee, Macon on the Ocmulgee, and Columbus on the Chattahoochee; all at the fall line.

Augusta became the capital in 1784; later, the capital moved to other fall-line cities—first Louisville, then Milledgeville. Before the Europeans arrived, Macon was the capital—of the Creek Confederacy.

During the Civil War, this region was most hard-hit by Sherman's March to the Sea in 1864. Ruins from this time are still evident, and spared towns and structures provide a glimpse of antebellum architecture.

Must-Sees

M Athens Nightlife: Considered one of the best music towns in the country by *Rolling Stone,* Athens has a great nightlife, with dozens of bars and clubs—also try to catch the annual Athfest in June. The University of Georgia here spawned the art scene, and it's also the state's intellectual and literary center (page 144).

M Uncle Remus Museum: Three tiny cabins in Eatonton, a Middle Georgia landmark, are a tribute to the trickster Br'er Rabbit stories published by Joel Chandler Harris (page 157).

M Andalusia: Flannery O'Connor's rural estate in Milledgeville opens the home of the queen of Southern letters for an evocative look at the wellspring of her Gothic tales (page 159).

M Piedmont National Wildlife Refuge: Getting out into the trails of the refuge offers a sense of the rural region's history, with its overtaken fields, farming ruins, and songbirds (page 162).

M Georgia Music Hall of Fame: Macon's music museum enshrines the music of the state's native artists, including Ma Rainey, Johnny Mercer, Ray Charles, Otis Redding, James Brown, Allman Brothers, REM, OutKast, and more (page 165).

© KAP STANN

Eatonton

M Ocmulgee National Monument: The capital of the Creek Confederacy, Ocmulgee preserves a mound city, sweat lodge, trails, and an interpretive center that tells the story of early inhabitants (page 168).

M Little White House: This small cabin in the woods is a moving memorial to Franklin Delano Roosevelt, who frequented the therapeutic waters of Warm Springs—the town seems to be set in amber from that time (page 177).

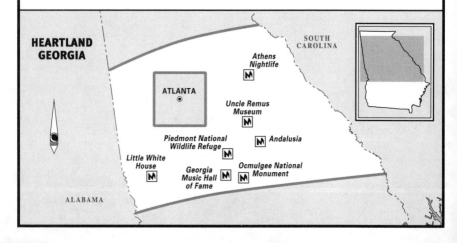

Erosion from the land-depleting industries of cotton production and lumbering, combined with the boll weevil blight and finally the Great Depression, drove many farmers to abandon their lands. The advent of hydroelectric power brought renewed development to fall-line cities, and modern water power ran the textile mills that were established at the waterfalls. Old mills and mill towns—company-built rows of identical small cottages—still dot riverbanks.

The Piedmont National Wildlife Refuge, north of Macon, was established as a reclamation project in 1939; the refuge and adjacent Oconee National Forest represent model restorations of natural environments. The central forests have now grown back with a profusion of grasses, shrubs, vines, and trees, including pines and hardwoods such as oak and hickory. A walk through a Piedmont forest exhibits this verdant regrowth and might also reveal an occasional abandoned farmhouse under thick vines, a rusting moonshine still, or an old barbed-wire fence running through forests that were once pasture.

This is the true Georgia heartland. While the cities are nice enough—Athens is the most entertaining of the lot—it's the surrounding small towns and rural areas that are most compelling, such as FDR's Warm Springs retreat, outside Columbus, and the backwoods route to Macon, tracing the footsteps of Flannery O'Connor, Alice Walker, and Br'er Rabbit.

PLANNING YOUR TIME

This is leisurely road-trip material, and you can capture a full sweep of the region in easy loop trips from Atlanta. For a compact trip, start northeast of Atlanta in Athens, then take Hwy. 441 south through arty Watkinsville and Madison to literary landmarks in Eatonton and Milledgeville and down to Macon. After sightseeing and staying in Macon (top pick: the 1842 House), work your way back north up the scenic Hwy. 23 back road past the Piedmont National Wildlife Refuge through Juliette and Jackson (BBQ!) before meeting up with I-75 to Atlanta.

Another easy loop to the southwest of Atlanta is the largely two-lane Hwy. 85 south through Senoia toward the compact set of attractions around FDR's historic retreat in Warm Springs. After sightseeing, hiking, and staying around Pine Mountain, head north up Hwy. 27 to pick up I-85 east to Atlanta.

Start with reservations at distinct inns, and consider aiming for a local festival. Around Athens, avoid home football weekends in fall—every room in the vicinity fills up. Otherwise, you can easily be spontaneous if you don't mind staying in one of the many motels in the area.

Travelers with more time can easily extend a trip from Macon east to the coast or can continue south to Plains from either Macon or Pine Mountain.

North of Atlanta

The closest Atlanta has to a coastal resort, Lake Sidney Lanier (named for a poet from Macon) is casually considered Atlanta's beach. An hour north, the lake draws party crowds of boaters, water-skiers, swimmers, and anglers to cabins, camps, and hotels around its shores. On some summer weekends, the water gets so wild with speedboats and personal watercraft that local patrols began a crackdown to reduce the number of accidents attributable to drivers who were underage or BUI (boating under the influence).

The 38,000-acre lake was created in 1957, when the Army Corps of Engineers (COE) built Buford Dam to impound the Chattahoochee River. Much to the engineers' surprise, when the new lake filled up, a string of hilltops at its southern end remained above water level. Turning miscalculation into opportunity, the islands were transformed into resort parklands, today managed by a consortium of federal, state, and private authorities. Its proximity to the 3.5 million people of metro Atlanta makes Lake Lanier the most visited COE reservoir in the United States.

Along 540 miles of shoreline, you'll find 20 public swimming beaches, 10 marinas, 54 boat launches, and 10 COE campgrounds. For a map

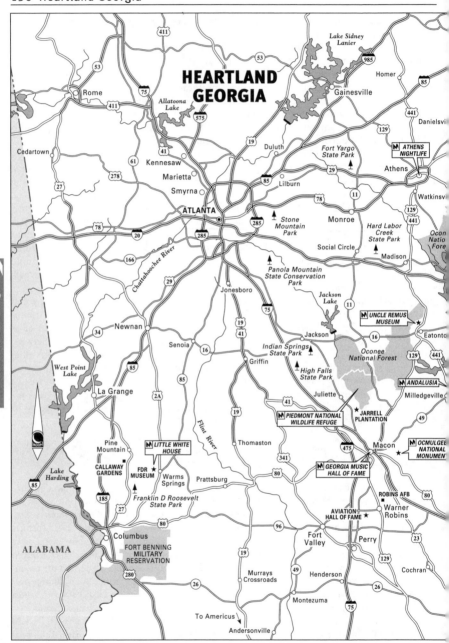

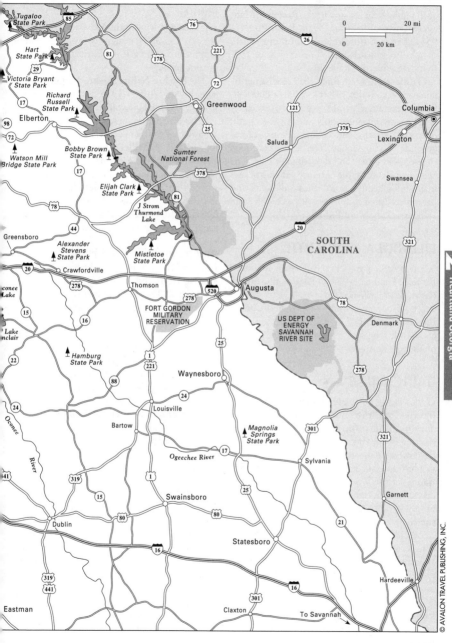

of all public facilities, stop by the **Resource Manager's Office,** off Buford Dam Rd., 770/945-9531, between Buford and Cumming, where there's also a boat launch. The impressive 192-foot dam is worth a look.

On the southeastern shore, the **Lake Lanier Islands** resort complex, 770/932-7200 or 800/840-5253, lakelanierislands.com, features sandy beaches, swimming pools and a water park, deluxe golf courses, and lodging in hotels, campgrounds, and houseboats. The facilities are open to overnight guests and day-trippers alike. The Welcome Center at the entrance gate distributes maps, full schedules of activities and events, and pamphlets listing current fees. It's accessible from I-985 exit 2, north of Buford.

LILBURN AND DULUTH

North of Atlanta, you'll find two restaurants on the Barbecue Landmark Trail. In Lilburn, find **Spiced Right,** 5364 Lawrenceville Hwy. N.W., 770/564-0355, spicedright.com. In Duluth, find **Corky's Ribs and BBQ,** 1605 Pleasant Hill Rd., 770/564-8666, corkysbbq.com. They both make great stops on the way to Athens or North Georgia.

GAINESVILLE

Gainesville sits at the eastern shore of Lake Lanier. Incorporated in 1821, the town retains an active downtown square on Main Street. The rooster statue in Poultry Park at West Academy St., west of the downtown square, celebrates the local industry that has earned Gainesville the nickname "Poultry Capital of the World." An attractive residential district of 19th-century Victorian and neoclassical homes is most readily seen along a mile-long stretch of Green Street north of downtown.

As a gateway to Georgia's Blue Ridge Mountains, Gainesville's local **Convention and Visitors Bureau,** 830 Green St. N.E., 770/536-5209, distributes mountain region maps and brochures, as well as city information.

Forest Service headquarters, 1755 Cleveland Hwy. (Hwy. 129), 770/536-0541, distributes recreation directories to national forest areas (open weekdays only).

Sights

The **Georgia Mountain Museum,** 311 Green St., 770/536-0889, relates city history, including exhibits on its Appalachian heritage, for a $2 admission fee.

The **Elachee Nature Science Center,** Old Atlanta Hwy., 770/535-1976, is a woodland museum devoted to local wildlife and ecology within a 1,200-acre nature preserve.

In Rabbitown, at Gainesville's northern fringe, folk artist **R. A. Miller** (famous in primitive-art circles for his "Blow, Oscar" tin paintings imploring a neighbor to honk) can often be found working outside his cottage less than a mile east of I-985 exit 7; if you see the whirligigs atop the hillside south of the road, then you've just passed the small dirt drive that leads to Miller's cottage.

Accommodations and Food

In a restored 1910 house in the historic district, **Dunlap House,** 635 Green St., 770/536-0200 or 800/276-2935, offers sophisticated bed-and-breakfast lodging with all the modern conveniences to make either business or leisure travelers comfortable. Ten guest rooms furnished with period reproductions and private baths start at $85 and include a full breakfast that's served in the lobby. It's on a shady stretch of the main Hwy. 129 drag, near galleries and across from the city's premier restaurant.

Rudolph's, 700 Green St., 770/534-2226, in the English Tudor mansion across from Dunlap House, serves prime rib and fresh Georgia trout, among other continental selections, in an upscale setting.

Getting There

Gainesville offers the closest Amtrak station to North Georgia's mountains, so it's the first stop for many Appalachian Trail hikers; call 800/USA RAIL (800/872-7245) for fares and schedules. The station is at the foot of Main St., a mile south of the downtown square in a so-so warehouse district that a couple of businesses (including a new café) are struggling to gentrify. **Appalachian Outfitters,** 706/864-7117, in Dahlonega, can help arrange shuttles to trailheads by reservation.

The Greyhound bus depot and Western Union desk is off Hwy. 129 on Myrtle Street, around a half-mile from the train station. Call 800/231-2222 for fares and schedules.

OFF I-85 EAST

Braselton

What resembles an 18th-century French château above the interstate in Braselton is the **Château Élan** winery and resort, I-85 exit 48, 770/932-0900 or 800/233-9463. Guests sample local wines and wander through grand interior plazas adorned with murals of French landscapes, past shops, restaurants, cafés, and even an Irish pub with live Irish music. Five stories of deluxe hotel accommodations start over $200 in peak season. Four golf courses, an equestrian center, a health spa, pools, and tennis courts are among the amenities on the 2,400-acre grounds (open daily).

Chestnut Mountain Winery, I-85 exit 48, 770/867-6914, offers free tastings and a wine-cellar tour on its 30 acres of wooded grounds (closed Mon.).

Athens and Vicinity

The University of Georgia (UGA), home of the Georgia Bulldogs and Georgia's intelligentsia, dominates the stately town of Athens and nearly doubles the town's residential population with a student enrollment of 30,000. As the home of the University of Georgia Press and *Georgia Review,* Athens is also the seat of the state's literary community.

But nationally, Athens is best recognized for its alternative music scene, which was proclaimed the number one college-music scene in the country by *Rolling Stone* in 2003. It grew out of UGA's art-school crowd in the late 1970s and rocketed to the national stage with the success of homegrown bands REM and the B-52s in the 1980s, followed by Widespread Panic and popular "jangle rock" bands in the '90s. Today, with dozens of clubs and music halls, music promotion and record companies, and two local radio stations in town supporting the scene, Athens has a well-earned reputation as an incubator for hundreds of local bands. Athfest, the city's premier music festival in June, is a great way to sample 120 of the city's best bands for free. Live music can also be heard year-round at great local venues (though the college town slows down in summer), and pilgrims can find musical landmarks throughout town.

The center of the action is the compact, walkable downtown across from the UGA campus. Within 20 square blocks or so of early 20th-century buildings from the intersection of Broad Street and College Avenue, you'll find bookstores, restaurants, cafés, bars and clubs, music halls and theaters, and stores and galleries selling vintage clothes, beads, crystals, handicrafts, recordings, and musical instruments.

For hanging out, for wandering through gardens or museums, for attending a ball game, and particularly for its nightlife, Georgia's number one art town makes a great destination and is within easy access of metro Atlanta.

SIGHTS

University of Georgia–North Campus

The University of Georgia, America's oldest chartered state university, was founded in 1785 at the banks of the Oconee River, at a frontier settlement near an old Cherokee trail crossing. Today the esteemed university has grown to 13 colleges and professional schools, and it serves as headquarters for the statewide university system.

The UGA campus occupies 40,000 acres in the heart of downtown Athens. North Campus is the historic and geographic head of campus, adjacent to downtown; a stroll downhill leads to newer South Campus. Because of its biologically diverse collection of trees, shrubs, and plants, the campus has been designated an arboretum.

Start at **University Arch,** the 1857 cast-iron gate at the foot of College Street (by tradition, freshmen are forbidden to pass under it). Here

Heartland Georgia

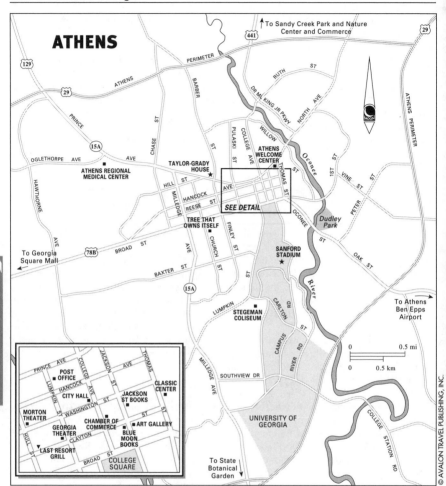

ATHENS

you enter College Square, a lush greensward shaded by thick oaks and surrounded by UGA's oldest buildings.

Two centuries ago, the view from the hill where the classic **University Chapel** now stands reminded school founders of the Greek Acropolis in Athens—and the city was renamed. South of College Square, at **Founders Memorial Garden,** 325 S. Lumpkin St., 706/227-5369, 2.5 acres of formal garden rooms, fountains, and arbor surrounding an 1857 home are open for a tranquil stroll (no

charge). A walk south leads to the campus bookstore and **Tate Student Center,** (open till midnight) in the center of the campus near **Sanford Stadium.**

The Hargrett Rare Book and Manuscript Library at **UGA Archive,** Jackson St., 706/542-7123, houses the original Confederate Constitution, displayed once yearly on Confederate Memorial Day, April 26.

University of Georgia–South Campus

Crossing Cedar Street to South Campus, the

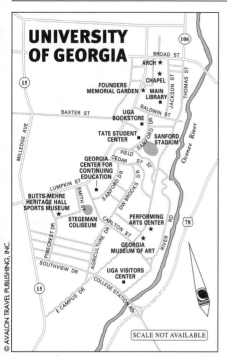

UNIVERSITY OF GEORGIA

SCALE NOT AVAILABLE

© AVALON TRAVEL PUBLISHING, INC.

Georgia Museum of Art

On South Campus, the official state art museum, 90 Carlton St., 706/542-4662, displays 8,000 paintings, drawings, and sculptures of 19th- and 20th-century American artists in spare, elegant galleries in a quiet modernist building backed up against the woods. Recent shows have included photography and textile exhibits, interpreted with artist lectures and family activities.

The gift shop carries locally made arts, and the café has a nice view of the museum's hilltop perch. Gallery hours are Tues.–Sat. 10 A.M.–5 P.M. (Wed. till 9 P.M.) and Sun. 1–5 P.M. (closed Mon. and most state and federal holidays). It's well worth a visit. The suggested donation is $2.

State Botanical Garden of Georgia

This peaceful 313-acre enclave, 2450 S. Milledge Ave., 706/542-1244, alongside the Middle Oconee River, is full of sculpted gardens inside and out. An impressive, three-story, tropical **Conservatory** overlooking the International Garden serves as the visitors center and also holds galleries, a gift shop, and a café. The conservatory is open Tues.–Sat. 9 A.M.–4:30 P.M. and Sun. 11:30 A.M.–4:30 P.M. The **Garden Room Café** serves lunch daily.

Outside, the **Heritage Garden** highlights plants that helped shaped the state. Five miles of **nature trails** lead through rhododendron dells, rose gardens, and shady woodland coves populated by deer, raccoons, squirrels, and many different bird species. The grounds are open daily 8 A.M.–sunset. It's a beautiful spot, and admission is free.

Historic Houses

The **Athens Welcome Center,** 280 E. Dougherty St., 706/353-1820, visitathensga .com, housed in the Federal-style Church-Waddel-Brumby House (built in 1820), serves as an apt introduction to the city's many distinguished historic houses. Inquire about events, van tours, and self-guided tour maps, including a detailed music tour that's also online. They're open daily 10 A.M.–5 P.M.; there is no charge for admission.

Taylor-Grady House, 634 Prince Ave., 706/549-8688, the mid-1840s Greek Revival

Georgia Center for Continuing Education, 706/542-2056 or 800/488-7827, holds short-term residential educational programs, along with a café, restaurant, and hotel.

Stegeman Coliseum holds basketball games and gymnastics events. The **Butts-Mehre Heritage Hall Sports Museum,** 1 Selig Circle, 706/542-9036, houses UGA athletic memorabilia, including Athens Olympics exhibits. Adjacent to the tennis stadium is the **Tennis Hall of Fame,** 706/542-8064, open weekdays.

On a hilltop to the east, the **Georgia Museum of Art** and **UGA Performing Arts Center** are the university's most impressive visitor attractions and are near the **Ramsey Center for Student Activities** sports complex.

The **UGA Visitor Center,** in the Four Towers Bldg. on College Station Rd. at River Rd., 706/542-0842, uga.edu, conducts campus tours and distributes walking-tour maps and campus tree guides. It's open daily except holidays.

mansion home of *Atlanta Constitution* editor and "New South" promoter Henry Grady, occupies an entire city block and is furnished with period antiques. It's open Mon.–Thurs. 9 A.M.–5 P.M. (closed during lunchtime). Admission is $3.

The **Lyndon House Arts Center,** 293 Hoyt St., 706/613-3623, opens an Italianate antebellum house as a historic house museum, as well as a modern annex as a municipal arts center. Hours are Tues. and Thurs. noon–9 P.M. and 9 A.M.–5 P.M. on Wed., Sat., and Sun. (no charge).

Yet the **T. R. R. Cobb House,** an 1840s Greek Revival mansion presently under restoration, generates the most historic debate. Thomas Reade Rootes Cobb, the founder of UGA's law school who died at the Battle of Fredericksburg, was a militant segregationist who helped frame the Confederate Constitution. The expensive restoration of his home in the attractive Cobbham residential district has been a hot controversy in this liberal college town. Inquire at the welcome center about the status of the project.

Ecological Wonders

The **ENSAT Center,** at Sandy Creek Park on Hwy. 441, 706/613-3615, opened in 1998 as a revolutionary facility dedicated to Environment, Natural Science, and Appropriate Technology (ENSAT). The 11,400-square building, a model of sustainable green construction, houses ecological exhibits on wetlands and woodlands, a 2,000-gallon aquarium, and a crawl-through beaver lodge. The exhibits are open Tues.–Sat. 8:30 A.M.–5:30 P.M. Trails leads through 225 acres.

One of the city's most unusual landmarks is the **Tree That Owns Itself,** a white oak in a small square at Dearing and Finley Streets (near Broad). It was deeded its small plot of land by its owner, a former UGA professor who enjoyed its shade for many years. The original tree was destroyed in a 1942 storm but was sentimentally replaced by a seedling from one of its own acorns, which has now grown into a quite respectable tree.

SPORTS AND RECREATION

UGA Spectator Sports and Recreation

The English bulldog is the school's mascot, whose image adorns T-shirts, caps, and license plates across Georgia. And not just any bulldog, but a particular individual, Uga V, who is descended from earlier Ugas and presently lives in Savannah. The princely mascot can often be seen in the VIP section at home games. Three dozen larger-than-life bulldogs painted by local artists are on permanent display around town.

Home of UGA football, **Sanford Stadium,** the fifth-largest on-campus college stadium in the country, sits in the center of campus. Each fall, more than 86,000 Bulldog fans fill the stadium, the most gung-ho wearing red-and-white, shouting "Go Dawgs!" and barking. Tickets are hard to come by. The stadium was also the site of Olympic soccer in the 1996 Summer Games.

Stegeman Coliseum, on Carlton St., is the 11,000-seat arena where the Georgia Bulldog basketball team and the nationally ranked women's gymnastics team compete. **University Tennis Center,** 706/542-4584, hosts annual NCAA tennis championship matches, and visitors can sign up to use the indoor courts. The 18-hole **University of Georgia Golf Course,** 706/369-5739, offers a par-72 course.

Tickets to most UGA athletic events can be purchased at the ticket office (open weekdays only) in the **Butts-Mehre Heritage Hall,** 1 Selig Circle, 706/542-9036, georgiadogs.com. The hall was named for famed Georgia coaches Wally Butts and Harry Mehre—if only they'd switched the order of the names, it wouldn't sound like the campus joke it has regrettably become. It's on South Campus near Pinecrest Drive and Rutherford Street.

Outdoor Recreation

For swimming at a lakeside beach, fishing, canoeing (rentals available), hiking and camping, head north up Hwy. 441 to **Sandy Creek Park and Nature Center,** 706/613-3631, sandycreekpark.com. While the beach is open only Apr.–Sept., the park's ENSAT nature center and

Morton Theater

the rest of the scenic 782-acre park are open year-round.

The **North Oconee River Greenway and Heritage Trail** is a linear park that stretches 13 miles to provide an alternate transportation corridor from the country's northern boundary to town along Old Commerce Road/Hwy. 441.

Broad River Outpost, 706/795-3243, broadriver.com, is a well-established local outfitter that runs paddling adventures down the Broad River north of Athens.

ENTERTAINMENT

Athens has a tremendously varied arts and entertainment scene for a city its size, thanks to its nationally renowned music scene, with hundreds of local bands—and to its proximity to sophisticated populations at UGA and nearby Atlanta. The "colorbearer" for the local arts scene is *Flagpole,* a weekly alternative news and entertainment weekly distributed widely around town and online at flagpole.com. Atlanta's *Creative Loafing* also lists Athens events.

Georgia Theater

The Georgia Theater, 215 N. Lumpkin, 706/549-9918, an old movie theater, has hosted all the town's top acts, as well as the likes of Tom Waits, Wynton Marsalis, and the Reverend Horton Heat—it's one of the best venues in town.

Morton Theater

The Morton Theater, 195 W. Washington St., 706/613-3770, built in 1910 and restored in 1993, brings one of the first African American vaudeville theaters in the U.S. back to life as a 544-seat community performing arts center downtown (it's featured in an REM music video).

Classic Center

The Classic Center, 300 N. Thomas St., 706/357-4555, is downtown behind the Athena statue, at a modern complex built in 1995 to match the 1912 brick fire house next door. It features varied performances in its season (from October to April), such as Broadway shows, Holiday on Ice, Celtic dance, and children's theater.

UGA's Performing Arts Center

On South Campus, UGA's modern art center, 230 River Rd., 706/542-4400, uga.edu/pac, showcases world-class performances primarily in music and dance, such as the Stuttgart Philharmonic, Jean-Pierre Rampal, the Atlanta Ballet and Atlanta Symphony (local chauvinists say the acoustics are better than at the symphony's home, in Atlanta).

 Athens Nightlife

Athens has dozens of bars and clubs that feature (and employ) local musicians. To get you started, the following are among the most historic and well established, with a few newcomers thrown in too. See *Flagpole,* in print or at flagpole.com, and tune into the student-run WUOG 90.5 FM for who's playing where. Watch for performances by local favorites Vic Chestnutt, Jack Logan, Five-Eight, and Elf Power.

Bars and Clubs

40 Watt Club, 285 W. Washington St., 706/549-7871, 40watt.com, legendarily named for the lone bulb that lighted its first location, is the granddaddy of the dozens of nightclubs that fade in and out on the Athens scene. The cavernous 40 Watt attracts national and international acts, as well as an underground audience that's just as wide.

40 Watt Club

© KAP STANN

Heartland Georgia

Georgia Bar, 159 W. Clayton St., an anchor of Athens' "Bar-muda Triangle," is a rugged spot for a wide range of blues, rock, and folk rock.

Caledonia Lounge, 256 W. Clayton St., is an intimate late-night spot that books some of the best local bands, and **Manhattan Cafe,** 337 N. Hull St., is a favorite of artists and musicians.

Flicker Theater and Bar, 263 W. Washington St., is an art-house theater that features acoustic music and frequent film and video screenings, with a separate, candlelit bar with well-worn couches and local artwork on display.

Boneshakers, 433 E. Hancock Ave., 706/543-1555, started out as a gay dance club but now draws a mixed audience for dancing to DJ'd music; they also host cabaret drag shows.

For the best jukebox in town, look for the **No Where Bar,** 240 N. Lumpkin St., where the volume is kept low enough for conversation.

Special Events

For a full calendar of special events, contact the visitors center, 800/653-0603.

Athfest, in late June, draws tens of thousands of Athens music fans to hear up to 120 bands performing all over town. The city's signature music event features a KidsFest, art market, and *Flagpole* music awards. All outdoor stages are free, and all-venue weekend wristbands are available for sale; see athfest.com. CDs have been issued from previous Athfests by the local label Ghostmeat Records.

In April, spring house and garden tours are popular.

The **Dawgfest,** UGA's annual homecoming, is held in mid-October.

ACCOMMODATIONS
Downtown

The most desirable accommodations are right downtown near campus. Note that on fall football weekends, prices rise dramatically (as much as double) and rooms sell out early.

On campus, UGA's **Georgia Center for Continuing Education,** 1197 S. Lumpkin St., 706/542-2056 or 800/488-7827, a residential conference center with a café and restaurant, has

THE ATHENS SOUND

Athens is a modern-day Memphis, with aspiring musicians clamoring to its streets and recording studios for some of the magic dust that has sent local bands to the national stage. But while Memphis takes pride in the recognizable sound of its steadfast session artists, the Athens sound is a little harder to characterize. One critic's assessment of "chime-filled janglerock, earthy hippie music, and/or quirky, campy retro dancerock" comes close.

The venerable REM has been considered alternative pop, but 20 years on the national charts should more than qualify the band as roots rock by now. Widespread Panic could be Southern grunge, proudly inspired by bluesy Allman Brothers–rock, punk, and the anti-elitist sentiments of Lynryd Skynyrd. More recently, the scene has been dominated by psychedelic pop experimentalists.

By tradition, Athens musicians reject any notion of orthodoxy and prefer to be known for innovation. Today, music in town ventures all over the map—from blues and bluegrass to funk and hip-hop, with a whole lot of garage bands and earnest young singer-songwriters in the mix.

For more on the historic Athens music scene, see the 1986 documentary "Athens, Ga: Inside/Out," or Rodger Lyle Brown's recently rereleased book *Party out of Bounds,* an insider's guide to the Athens music scene of the 1970s and '80s. Online, visitathens.ga features a detailed musical-landmarks city tour, and flagpole.com lists the lowdown on local acts, venues, and performances.

200 guest rooms for people visiting campus (starting at $70); call the front desk, at 706/548-1311, for reservations.

Adjacent to campus, the 308-room **Holiday Inn,** 197 E. Broad St., 706/549-4433 or 800/465-4329, hi-athens.com, is the premier property downtown; rates start at $90 for double rooms in two towers or a motel annex. They also have an indoor pool and shuttle service to the Atlanta airport for $30 one way.

Best Western Colonial Inn, 170 N. Milledge

Ave., 706/546-7311 or 800/528-1234, charges around $60 for doubles; it's a half mile from campus across from the Varsity drive-in restaurant. For the low end downtown, the **TraveLodge,** 898 W. Broad St., 706/549-5400 or 800/578-7878, starts at $45; it's a half mile from campus.

For bed-and-breakfast lodging, **Magnolia Terrace,** 277 Hill St., 706/548-3860, offers guest rooms in a 1912 house in a historic residential district that's just a short walk from the Grit restaurant (there's no pool; doubles start at $90).

Beyond Downtown

For bargain motels beyond downtown, the **Downtowner Motor Inn,** 1198 S. Milledge Ave. (Hwy. 15), 706/549-2626, offers comparably priced accommodations in the fledgling Five Points neighborhood near South Campus, with a couple of cafés nearby. The **Bulldog Inn,** Hwy. 441 N, 706/543-3611, a mile north of downtown, has the lowest rates and ample truck parking.

Newer, cleaner, modern chain motels are found along the Atlanta Hwy. west of downtown. Among these are the higher-end **Hampton Inn,** 706/548-9600 or 800/426-7866, two miles west near the State Farmer's Market; and farther out, **Comfort Inn,** 706/227-9700 or 800/228-5150, and **Perimeter Inn,** 706/548-3000, which are both five miles west near Georgia Square Mall.

Camping

Year-round primitive camping is available at secluded wooded sites in Athens' **Sandy Creek Park,** 706/613-3631, with access to the park's lake and varied amenities. More campgrounds are available at Watson Mill Bridge State Park, within 20 miles of Athens.

FOOD AND DRINK

You'll find a wide selection of cheap eats downtown at sidewalk cafés, food stalls, smoothie stands, and mobile espresso bars across from College Square. There are lots of vegetarians in town, so most all places have vegetarian selections. Most places are very casual.

The **Grill,** 171 College Ave., 706/543-4770, serves neon-lit burgers (including Gardenburgers), squiggly fries, and milkshakes around-the-clock. Breakfasts range from traditional ham-and-cheese omelets to granola or lox and bagels. (The space above is the site of the original 40 Watt Club.)

A half-mile from downtown, near the fire station at Barber Street, **M The Grit,** 199 Prince Ave., 706/543-6592, is a vegetarian restaurant started up by REM musician Michael Stipe (his film company's upstairs, and his residence is nearby). Spinach lasagne, stir-fry, and falafel are on the menu, along with a decent wines, prompting one customer to say, "I wish we had a place like this in Berkeley!"

Weaver D's Fine Foods, 1016 E. Broad., 706/353-7797, is a musical and soul-food landmark: Its automated, cafeteria-service motto, "Automatic for the People," inspired REM's 1992 album title. They serve such Southern staples as fried chicken, collards, and mac-and-cheese (lunch served Mon.–Sat.).

The **Last Resort Grill,** 174 W. Clayton St., 706/549-0810, takes its name from a legendary local nightclub and offers inventive California cuisine in an arty, airy storefront that opens onto the street. Exotic quesadillas (veggie, shrimp, or salmon and black bean); roasted eggplant or fried green tomato sandwiches; and pasta topped with grilled shiitake mushrooms, herbs, and feta are some of the house specialties (many entrées are under $10). They have a full bar and espresso drinks too. It's open daily for lunch and dinner.

The toast of Atlantan foodies, **M Five and Ten,** 1653 S. Lumpkin St., 706/546-7300, in Athens' Five Points district, draws locals and city folks alike for the fresh American cuisine of chef Hugh Acheson, who was recently voted among the 10 best chefs in the country by *Food & Wine* magazine. Such entrées as shrimp and grits with andouille sausage start at $15; an excellent brunch is served Sundays only.

North of Athens in Danielsville, find **Zeb Dean's Hickory Smoked BBQ,** 5742 Hwy. 29 N, 706/795-2701, on the Barbecue Landmark Trail as a local favorite for lean pork with peppery, vinegar-based sauce. It's open Tues.–Sat. 9 A.M.–9 P.M.; credit cards are accepted.

OTHER PRACTICALITIES

Getting There and Around

Athens is 60 miles northeast of Atlanta; from Atlanta, take I-85 north to Hwy. 316 east; exit onto Hwy. 78 east. Hwy. 78 west of Athens is called "the Atlanta Highway" west of Athens, once you're in town, it's Broad Street.

Downtown streets are identified as either East or West of College Avenue. The most convenient parking lot downtown near the university is at the corner of College Avenue and Washington Street. On-campus visitor parking is available at the visitors center on College Station Road, at River Road, and in three other areas: behind the UGA bookstore, next to the Tate Student Center, and in the parking deck next to the Georgia Center for Continuing Education.

Shopping

Among fun boutiques and shops downtown are **Wuxtry Records,** 197 E. Clayton St., 706/369-9428 (where REM's Michael Stipe and Peter Buck first met; it's also a good resource for information on local bands and venues); **Junkman's Daughter's Brother,** 458 E. Clayton, for vintage clothes; and **Musician's Warehouse,** 447 E. Clayton St., 706/548-7233, for Athens music. The **Daily Groceries Co-Op,** 523 Prince Ave., 706/548-1732, offers natural and organic foods, deli meals to go, and community activism.

For a cultural adventure and all the trailer trash you can carry, the **J & J Flea Market** is held weekends four miles north of town on Jefferson Highway.

Information and Services

Athens Welcome Center, 280 E. Dougherty St., 706/353-1820, occupies one of the city's oldest houses and distributes maps and hosts van tours. It's open daily 9 A.M.–5 P.M.

For more city information, contact the **Athens Convention and Visitors Bureau,** 300 N. Thomas St., Athens, GA 30601, 706/357-4430 or 800/653-0603, visitathensga.com. Their website features a detailed musical-landmarks guide.

VICINITY OF ATHENS

Watson Mill Bridge State Park

One of Georgia's most picturesque parks, Watson Mill Bridge, 650 Watson Mill Rd., 706/783-5349, gastateparks.org, parking $2, named for the longest original-site covered bridge in the state (1 of only 20 covered bridges remaining in the state), has seven miles of hiking trails and five miles of bicycling trails—and you can swim in the natural slide of the river shoals just below the dam. The 1,018-acre park also has a five-acre mill pond for fishing and boating (rentals are available). Camp in one of 21 campsites for $15–19; call 800/864-PARK (800/864-7275) for reservations. From Athens, take Hwy. 72 northeast to Hwy. 22 and go south three miles.

Watkinsville

Eight miles south of Athens, Watkinsville—with its arty community, sophisticated bed and breakfast, and quality shops—is a nice small town that's a tranquil refuge for city dwellers who like their country *very* civilized.

The historic **Eagle Tavern,** on Main St., 706/769-5197, originally an 1801 stagecoach stop, is now a welcome center that also sells a few crafts. It distributes guides to local art studios, downtown walking-tour maps, road maps, and information on sights along Hwy. 441's Antebellum Trail. It's open Mon.–Sat. 10 A.M.–5 P.M. and Sun. 2–5 P.M.

Five miles south of town, the **Elder Mill Covered Bridge,** on Rose Creek, remains a picturesque sight after two centuries, and now a tiny garden at the entrance adds to its appeal. Find it off Hwy. 15 South; turn right onto Elder Mill Road.

Get away overnight downtown at **M Ashford Manor Bed-and-Breakfast Inn,** 5 Harden Hill Rd., 706/769-2633, ambedandbreakfast.com. Proprietors Jim and David Shearon and Mario Castro are Chicago transplants who bring big-city style and service to their rural four-acre retreat. ("We knew we were here to stay when we traded in our classic Thunderbird for a King Cab pickup," says Dave.) They offer seven "costumed" rooms (including one dog-friendly nook) in a

© KAP STANN

Central Georgia's lush vegetation envelops a cemetery near Athens.

lovely two-story Victorian for around $100, which includes a private bathroom and breakfast; cocktails can be served poolside on the landscaped terrace overlooking the woods beyond. Find them behind the stone wall on Main Street, next to the Methodist church.

Skull Shoals

From Watkinsville, Hwy. 15 bisects a parcel of the Piedmont's **Oconee National Forest** and runs through Greensboro on its way to I-20. Twelve miles north of Greensboro, off Hwy. 15 at the Oconee River, the Forest Service– maintained **Oconee River Recreation Area** provides river access and a six-site campground.

The ghost-town ruins of **Skull Shoals,** a 1784 trading post and frontier settlement, lie an easy one-mile trail upstream from the boat launch near the campground. In 1811, Georgia's first paper mill operated here, and the town's industry grew to include a gristmill, cotton gin, and sawmill. At its peak in 1850, the town had 500 residents. Erosion from unsound farming practices, a severe flood in 1887, and the decline of farming eventually caused the town's demise. The largely abandoned area was incorporated into the national forest in 1959. Today, the charred ruins of a brick boardinghouse still stand. From here, hikers can cross over unpaved roads a half-mile to the trailhead that leads to a set of aboriginal mounds—take the road a quarter-mile to the first junction; turn left and continue a quarter-mile.

Crawfordville

Downtown Crawfordville paints a poignant portrait of a Southern gothic landscape—dusty storefronts appear largely abandoned, a lone pickup sits at the curb, and you could practically imagine a hound dog sleeping in the middle of the street.

Downtown, **Alexander H. Stephens State Historic Park,** 706/456-2602 or 800/864-PARK (864-7275), gastateparks.org, parking $2, memorializes the former Georgia governor who served as the vice president of the Confederacy and later returned to Washington as a U.S. senator after the Civil War. Stephens' residence, the two-story Liberty Hall, has been restored to its 1875 style. The adjacent Confederate museum houses a collection of Civil War artifacts, including uniforms and weaponry. Admission is $3 adults. Guided gaslight house tours are held year-round Tues.–Sat. 9 A.M.–5 P.M. and Sun. 2–5 P.M. (closed Mon. except legal holidays).

In the woods beyond the tranquil home, the 1,177-acre park offers a fishing lake with boat rentals, three miles of trails, a pool, and a 25-site campground ($16–18). Four cottages are also available ($60–85). You'll find the park off I-20 exit 148; follow signs north on Hwy. 22 for two miles.

Washington

Washington, Georgia, was the first city chartered to honor the nation's first president, and George Washington acknowledged the tribute on his trip through the town in 1791. Its tree-shaded courthouse square, red-brick storefronts, and landscaped antebellum homes make Washington a nicely preserved Southern town.

The region was settled two centuries ago—here, references to past battles usually refer to the American Revolution—though the region's role in the Civil War is the source of more avid speculation. Washington was the last city to harbor the legendary Confederate treasury, a long-sought half-million dollars in gold, moved here from Richmond in April 1865 and never seen again.

Robert Toombs Avenue (Hwy. 78) leads directly to the courthouse square in the center of town. Inquire about self-guided tour maps and house tours at the local **chamber of commerce,** 104 E. Liberty St., 706/678-2013, housed in a Greek Revival building.

The **Washington Historical Museum,** 308 E. Robert Toombs Ave., 706/678-2105, tells city's history with Native American artifacts, antebellum furnishings, Civil War relics, and other memorabilia. The stately, red-brick, 1888 **Mary Willis Library,** 204 E. Liberty St., is ornamented with stained-glass windows designed by Louis Comfort Tiffany.

A couple of blocks from the square, the **Robert Toombs House,** 216 E. Robert Toombs Ave., 706/678-2226, opens to the public the historic home of the senator who led Georgia to secession. A successful planter and lawyer, Toombs served in the U.S. Congress and Senate before his alliances shifted to the Confederate States of America. Though he aspired to the presidency of the Confederacy, he served instead as its Secretary of State. After the Civil War, Toombs steadfastly refused to take the oath of allegiance to the United States and died an unreconstructed rebel. The state-operated historic site is open Tues.–Sat. 9 A.M.–5 P.M. and Sun. 2–5:30 P.M. Admission is $3 for adults.

Augusta

Around Augusta, a forgotten world of full-dress fox hunts, cutting-horses, and choral performances in gilt cathedrals lives on—a tranquil life steeped in history, tradition, and stability, where people are identified by congregation and their grandmother's maiden name. Then comes Masters Week, and the place fills with spectators who have come to see one of the world's premier golf tournaments, played at the Augusta National Golf Club.

Colonial Georgia's second city, Augusta was founded in 1736 on the banks of the Savannah River at an old Native American river crossing. Establishing itself as the capital of cotton production, Augusta soon became the state capital as well. Remaining untouched during the Civil War, Augusta was able to supply munitions to Confederate armies. Nature wrought a greater damage; the overflowing banks of the Savannah River flooded the town half a dozen times during the last 250 years. Today, dams and canals block the free-flowing Savannah into a series of placid lakes and gently streaming currents. (Every year, the community sends thousands of yellow duckies downstream for the annual Rubber Duck Race.)

The Medical College of Georgia (the health sciences campus of the state university system), Augusta State University, and Paine College are here, and students stir up a bit of activity. But for the most part, the city reposes in its august history. The boyhood home of Woodrow Wilson and James Brown, quiet Augusta is today more Wilson than Brown.

SIGHTS

Riverwalk Attractions

Augusta's Riverwalk is a compact promenade and is the city's central attraction. It creates an inviting plaza along the river atop the high levee. It's a nice stretch by foot, bike, or skates (rentals are available) between the art museum at one end and a lively science museum at the other. The Riverwalk entrance plaza is at 8th and Reynolds Streets (notice the high-water marks of past floods in the levee tunnel). Alongside the Riverwalk is a mix of modern and historic buildings that includes attractions, a hotel, shops, and several cafés.

St. Paul's Episcopal Church, 605 Reynolds St., at the Riverwalk, is the "mother church" of Augusta and dates back to 1750. It is built on the site of the city's original frontier fort.

Morris Museum of Art

On the west end of Riverwalk, the modern Morris Museum of Art, 1 10th St., 706/724-7501, themorris.org, maintains an extensive collection of traditional oil paintings by Southern artists grouped by such themes as antebellum portraiture, Civil War art, and Southern landscapes—though one small gallery is devoted to lively and colorful contemporary folk art. The museum is open Tues.–Sat. 10 A.M.–5 P.M. and Sun. noon–5 P.M. Admission is $3 for adults and $2 for students and seniors.

National Science Center's Fort Discovery

On the east end of the Riverwalk, Fort Discovery, 1 7th St., 706/821-0200 or 800/325-5445, offers 128,000 square feet of high-tech playground, with high-wire bike rides, an Air Chair, robotics, virtual sky-diving, Internet access, Lego sculptures, and water fountains that shoot up when you hit the target with lasers. Admission is $8 for adults, $6 for seniors and youth ages 4–17, and free for children three and under; sensory-theater admission is extra. Fort Discovery is open Mon.–Sat. 10 A.M.–5 P.M. and Sun. noon–5 P.M. There's fast food inside and pay parking below.

Augusta Museum of History

The city's modern history museum, 560 Reynolds St., 706/722-8454, augustamuseum.org, covers the Archaic period (some of the earliest pottery in North America was found on Stallings Island, in the Savannah River near here) through colonial and cotton eras to the present day, including Masters memorabilia and

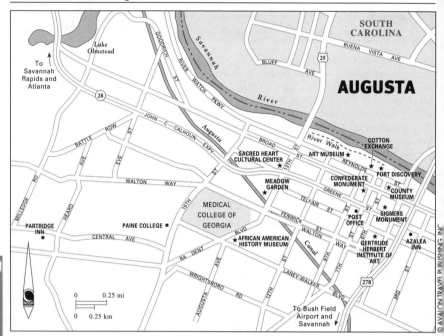

a James Brown costume. It's open Tues.–Sat. 10 A.M.–5 P.M. and Sun. 1–5 P.M. Admission is $4 for adults. The city's welcome center is within (no charge).

Augusta Golf and Gardens

Landscaped gardens, 1 11th St., 706/724-4443, surround larger-than-life bronze statues of such golf greats as Arnold Palmer, Jack Nicklaus, and Bobby Jones while fundraising continues for the Georgia Golf Hall of Fame, a work-in-progress. Call for seasonal hours and fees.

Other Downtown Sights

The main thoroughfare downtown is Broad Street. Grand in design, with a wide central plaza studded with fountains and monumental statues, the historic commercial district currently feels somewhere between its past heyday and its future renaissance. A few colorful murals, art studios, and boutiques in the 1000 block of Broad represent the new breed.

Two of the most venerable landmarks include the 1878 marble **Confederate Monument,** towering 72 feet above Broad Street between 7th and 8th Streets, and the 1848 **Signers Monument,** in the 500 block of Green Street, a 50-foot obelisk marking the graves of two of Georgia's three signers of the Declaration of Independence.

The **Gertrude Herbert Institute of Art,** 506 Telfair St., 706/722-5495, holds classes and galleries inside the distinctive Federal-style mansion, which by itself is an impressive display. The 1818 mansion features an elliptical interior spiral staircase among its extravagant architectural details. It's open Tues.–Fri.; admission is free.

Meadow Garden House Museum, 1320 Independence Dr., 706/724-4174, is the oldest documented house in the city. The pre-1791 farmhouse of George Walton, one of the state's signers of the Declaration of Independence and a two-time Georgia governor, is open for tours on weekdays only, 10 A.M.–4 P.M. Adult admission is $4.

Laney-Walker Sights

The Laney-Walker Historic District—bounded roughly by Laney-Walker Boulevard, Walton Way, Twiggs Street, and Dent Boulevard—honors educator Lucy Laney. Laney was born into slavery but later founded a school in 1883 that became the pride of Augusta's African American community. Laney's restored home now serves as the **Lucy Craft Laney Museum of Black History,** 1116 Phillip St., 706/724-3576. It's open daily; adult admission is $3.

The most soulful approach from downtown is down 9th Street, which becomes **James Brown Boulevard** as it nears the neighborhood. The Godfather of Soul owns WAAW 94.7 FM, a local radio station that features his granddaughter Tonya Brown on the air from studios downtown at the corner of 9th and Broad Streets. A mural depicting Brown appears on 10th Street between Jones and Reynolds.

RECREATION AND ENTERTAINMENT

Augusta Canal Headgates at Savannah Rapids

Outdoor recreation can be found northwest of town around the Savannah Rapids Pavilion, 3300 Evans-to-Lock Rd., 706/823-0440, augusta-canal.com, which also provides a scenic overlook of river rapids and the Augusta Canal, built in 1845. An interpretive center holds exhibits on the historic canal, hydroelectricity, and textile-mill manufacturing (admission is $5 for adults). A 9-mile hiking and biking trail follows the path worn by mules to tow barges up the canal from downtown to the dam. You can take boat tours on replicas of canal cargo boats, and paddlers can put in for a leisurely float down the canal or a wilder ride downriver.

The local outfitter **American Wilderness Outfitters Ltd.,** 2328 Washington Rd., 706/738-8500, (its acronymic motto is "Go AWOL") rents canoes and kayaks, runs shuttles, and can organize paddling trips.

Golf

"Like Mardi Gras without the costumes or floats" is how one bartender describes the city's *raison d'être,* the **Masters Golf Tournament,** held in April at **Augusta National Golf Course,** at 2604 Washington Rd., 706/667-6000. It's the country's most exclusive golf club and is composed of 300 of the nation's most powerful chief executives. Bill Gates was put on the waiting list, and the club admitted its first African American member in 1990. Women are still not admitted, which is the source of protests outside the tournament.

The first full week in April, hundreds of thousands of visitors descend on the sleepy city, packing roadways, restaurants, hotels, and houses, and pumping an estimated $100 million into the local economy annually. Schools close and many residents leave, renting their homes for as much as $25,000 for the week. Though the tournament is not open to the public, visitors can call 706/667-6000 to get an application for tickets to a practice round. The tickets are awarded by lottery. Tournament tickets are worth up to $5,000, but the pimento-cheese sandwiches famously served at the club are only $1.

Visiting golfers might try one of the city's two 18-hole public golf courses, **Augusta Golf Course,** 2023 Highland Ave., 706/796-5058, and **Forest Hills Golf Club,** 1500 Comfort Rd., 706/733-0001.

Music and Performing Arts

Home to several arts organizations, **Sacred Heart Cultural Center,** 706/826-4700, at the corner of 13th and Greene Streets, also holds performances in an impressive 1891 Romanesque Revival building that was once a Catholic cathedral (now deconsecrated). Major acts are often booked at the **Civic Center Auditorium,** which is also where the Augusta Lynx play ice hockey from October to March. Pick up the free **Spirit** weekly tabloid for entertainment listings of Riverwalk nightspots.

ACCOMMODATIONS AND FOOD

Accommodations

The best hotel in town is the 10-story **Radisson Riverfront Hotel,** 2 10th St., 706/722-8900, which offers several restaurants, a lounge, a pool, and 234 rooms right at the riverfront, some with river views (rates start at $130). A short walk from downtown and not far from the marina, **Azalea Inn,** 312 Greene St., 706/724-3454, theazaleainn.com, offers 16 bed-and-breakfast rooms in two restyled Victorian houses in a quiet residential district adjacent to downtown (rates start at $100).

Just west of downtown, the **Partridge Inn,** 2110 Walton Way, 706/737-8888 or 800/476-6888, heads up the city's historic Summerville residential district known locally as The Hill. The original 1890 inn has been subsequently expanded and now has 156 rooms and a pool. It's a comfortable place within a six-story clapboard structure, but interiors lack historic character (rooms start at $100). The hotel's bar-and-grill has an appealing wide veranda overlooking the street below.

Most motels are found out by the interstate and are familiar national chains catering to interstate travelers in need of a pit stop overnight— they are not very convenient or conducive to visiting downtown. Note that during Masters Week, room rates throughout the vicinity will likely double or even triple, and some establishments will take reservations only for a four- or seven-night minimum.

Food and Drink

Downtown, at the foot of 9th St. at the Riverwalk, **Boll Weevil Cafe,** 706/722-7772, has such bestsellers as the Curious George: turkey and provolone on toasted honey-wheat bread and slathered with warm spinach dip ($7) and tempting desserts. It's open daily 11 A.M.–10 P.M.

South of town, an Augusta Barbecue Landmark, **M Sconyer's Barbecue,** on Sconyers Way via I-520 exit 6, 706/790-5411, was rated among the nation's top 10 barbecue restaurants by *People* magazine. Here, hickory-smoked ribs and sandwiches are drenched with tangy sauce and served in a family-restaurant setting. Take I-520 exit 6 to Peach Orchard; turn left on Sconyers Way.

Hidden among generic chain restaurants in the interstate gulch at I-20 exit 65 is a rare local find: lively **Rhinehart's Oyster Bar,** 3051 Washington Rd., 706/860-2337, for you-shuck-'em

oysters, rock shrimp, crawfish, and chowder on big picnic tables inside or out. It's under a half mile west of I-20 and is open daily.

Across the river in North Augusta, South Carolina, **Sno-Cap** offers an original 1950s-style drive-in, where teenage servers bring 95-cent burgers and banana milkshakes out to your car. From downtown Augusta, cross the 13th Street bridge, pass the golf course and the Irish Traveler trailer community, and go uphill, then turn left on Jackson.

Information and Services

A **Georgia Visitor Center** off I-20 at the South Carolina border provides statewide as well as local information; it's open daily. Or contact the **Augusta Metropolitan Convention and Visitors Bureau,** 1450 Green St., Augusta, GA 30901, 706/823-6600 or 800/726-0243, augustaga.org.

NORTH OF AUGUSTA: THE BIG LAKES

On the eastern Piedmont north of Augusta, Big Lake parks line the border with South Carolina. Created by impounding the Savannah River, Strom Thurmond and Russell Lakes offer shoreline state parks that are popular with anglers and boaters, including Mistletoe, Elijah Clark, Bobby Brown, and Richard Russell; visit gastateparks.org.

For maps, inquire at the Resource Manager's Office, 706/722-3770, on Hwy. 221 at the dam (on the South Carolina side of the river, northeast of Pollard's Corner, Georgia). The **Georgia Visitor Center** at I-20 inside the border also distributes lake maps.

THOMSON AND VICINITY

Thirty-five miles west of Augusta off I-20, downtown Thomson centers on its 1870s courthouse square. The old train depot off Main Street now houses the local **tourist bureau,** 706/595-5584, and stands behind a monument dedicated to women who loyally supported the Confederate cause (depot open weekdays only). Inquire here

BLIND WILLIE MCTELL

Blind Willie McTell (1898–1959), one of the great blues musicians of the 1920s and '30s, was born in Thomson on May 5, 1898. Little is known about his early life, or whether he was blind from birth or from early childhood. He attended the Georgia State Academy for the Blind, in Macon, and learned to read and write music in Braille.

McTell became known for his extraordinary range on the 12-string guitar and recorded 120 songs that reflected influences from gospel, ragtime, hillbilly, and popular music, as well as Southern blues.

Thomson honors the memory of this great folk blues artist every year around his birthday with the Blind Willie McTell Blues Festival. For more information, call 706/597-1000 or visit blindwillie.com.

about Upcountry Plantation Tours of historic houses, including the Rock House, among the oldest dwellings still standing in Georgia. The fieldstone building dating from about 1785 was built by an ancestor of President Jimmy Carter.

Thomson hosts the **Belle Meade Fox Hunt** on select days from November to March. Spectators can join the scene and watch a traditional fox hunt from the seat of a "tally-ho" wagon; the season opens with a blessing of the hounds on the first Saturday in November. Thomson's other notable event is the **Blind Willie McTell Blues Festival,** honoring the memory of the native son who became a great folk blues artist; it's held around the May 5th anniversary of his birth.

Hamburg State Park

About 30 miles south of I-20, this 750-acre state park, 478/552-2393 or 800/864-PARK (864-7275), gastateparks.org, parking $2, features a 1921 water-powered gristmill that continues to grind corn into hominy and meal (sold at the country store). A pioneer museum displays old-time artifacts of rural life. Rent boats at a 225-acre stocked lake, or camp at one of 30 shaded sites along the edge of Hamburg Lake ($17–19, hookups available). In-

quire about park-sponsored **canoe trips** down the Little Ogeechee River.

SOUTH OF AUGUSTA

As a fall-line city, Augusta sits at the junction of the Piedmont Plateau and the coastal plain. South of town, the plain flattens into a wide expanse of piney woods and sandy soil where kaolin, Georgia's largest export product, is manufactured. This earthy substance is used in the manufacture of fine china, and China is the only other country to produce this raw material, which is essential to make luxurious brands such as Limoges and Wedgwood.

In this remote region of quarries, small towns, and quiet wooded rivers, drivers pass through the Kaolin Capital of the World, the Bird-Dog Capital of the World (in Waynesboro), yet another Old State Capital (in Louisville), and some hideaway state parks. As for famous sons, Elijah Muhammad, the leader of the Nation of Islam and once Malcolm X's mentor, hailed from Washington County.

Louisville

Louisville (LOO-is-ville), one of colonial Georgia's first inland settlements, was named after King Louis XVI. Strategically situated on the banks of the Ogeechee River, the town grew into an important port and even served as the state capital from 1795 to 1805. Most historic structures were destroyed by Sherman's troops on their way to Savannah.

Today the town's political might is limited to being the seat of Jefferson County. The county courthouse, built in 1904, sits on the site of the old capitol in downtown Louisville. The current population of 3,500 is half what it was when it was the state capital.

At the center of Broad Street downtown, the **Market House** has remained standing since its construction, in about 1758. Here, in addition to the auctioning of cotton, land tracts, and household goods, slaves were once sold in antebellum days. Inside the market hangs a bell cast in France in 1772. On Hwy. 24 east of town, a small cemetery contains graves from the colonial era.

Heartland Georgia

Magnolia Springs State Park

Among Georgia's prettiest state parks, Magnolia Springs, on Hwy. 25 five miles north of Millen, 478/982-1660 or 800/864-PARK (864-7275), gastateparks.org, parking $2, takes its name from the park's clear natural springs—seven million gallons a day are estimated to flow from the source. Today the springs attract an abundant variety of wildlife—ducks, herons, egrets, deer, tortoises, and alligators appear on its shores. The three-mile **Upper Loop Trail** follows the eastern shore of the lake and crosses over a wooded swamp of cypress, tupelo, and maple.

During the Civil War, this ample freshwater source led to the site's selection as a Confederate POW camp—Camp Lawton once imprisoned 10,000 Union soldiers, and the ruins of earthen breastworks can still be seen. Inquire about Confederate encampments and canoe trips down the Ogeechee River.

The lushly wooded 1,071-acre park also offers a swimming pool, freshwater aquarium, 10 miles of trails, and canoe and fishing-boat rentals. Five fully equipped two-bedroom cottages rent for $60–105, and the 26-site campground charges $17–19, including hookups; less for walk-in sites.

Middle Georgia

Middle Georgia is the name for an egg-shaped region that encompasses the mid-central Piedmont from Atlanta on past Macon, widening farther south and dipping into the coastal plain. This fertile region, fed by the Ocmulgee and Oconee Rivers, was soundly trounced by Sherman on his devastating march from Atlanta to Savannah. As a result, Middle Georgia shares a common history and culture distinct from other regions. Here in Middle Georgia, "the war" refers strictly to the one between the states. (The southernmost reach of Middle Georgia, south of Macon, is covered in the *South Georgia* chapter.)

For travelers, the area within the triangle created by Atlanta, Macon, and Athens is among the state's most interesting rural regions and is easily accessible from all three cities. Picturesque small towns cherish their remaining antebellum homes, and courthouse squares remain lively community centers.

Off I-20 east of Atlanta, sprawling suburbs have subsumed many of the region's northernmost towns, but a Middle Georgia heritage still lies beyond the freeway's neon corridor. Picturesque Madison, with its many antebellum homes spared from Sherman's torch, is both scenic and accessible— and within an hour from downtown Atlanta.

From Madison to Milledgeville along Hwy. 441, an intriguing set of historical attractions varies from a prophetic effigy mound and rivers named in native tongues to the state's antebellum capital and tributes to trickster Br'er Rabbit.

The I-75 route between Atlanta and Macon provides easy access to more Middle Georgia pleasures—you'll find a working plantation, historic mill ruins, and a wildlife refuge within the welcoming woods of the Oconee National Forest.

ATLANTA TO MADISON VIA I-20

Conyers

Eight miles from Olde Town Conyers, the **Monastery of Our Lady of Holy Spirit,** 2625 Hwy. 212 S.W., 770/483-8705, trappist.net, was founded in 1944 by Cistercian monks who practice self-sufficiency. Visitors may tour the church and 2,000-acre grounds—a scenic duck pond and bonsai greenhouse offer a tranquil urban refuge. Mass is offered daily. At the gift shop, the monks sell books, religious ornaments, and fresh breads baked on the premises. Overnight religious retreats are available for men only.

Social Circle

Social Circle takes its name from the well in the middle of the town where residents used to gather and swap stories; that remains a landmark today. More than 50 19th-century homes and buildings decorate its historic district downtown, four miles north of I-20. The Victorian storefront drugstore still sells penny candy.

But its most widely known landmark is the grand Greek Revival mansion that houses the **Blue Willow Inn,** 294 N. Cherokee Rd., 770/464-2131 or 800/552-8813, bluewillowinn.com. The inn raises Southern buffet to aristocratic heights and is open daily for lunch and dinner; inquire about the weekend seafood buffet.

The trout-inclined can find a **fish hatchery** on Hwy. 278, southeast of town (take I-20 exit 48). Next door, the state **Wildlife Management office,** 2123 Hwy. 278, distributes information on hunting and fishing and maintains an interpretive trout habitat along Little Amicalola Creek.

Rutledge

Downtown Rutledge is a charming little crossroads dating from 1871 that gets enough side-road traffic from Madison and the nearby state park to support several businesses and a nice restaurant.

Among the historic storefronts downtown, you'll find a 75-year-old hardware store that sells such interesting garden accessories as ceramic bird feeders and yard art. The red caboose sells homemade fudge and serves as an unofficial welcome center.

Housed in a 19th-century drugstore, the **Yesterday Cafe,** 120 Fairplay St., 706/557-9337, is plastered with local historical photographs, farm tools, and other rural tchotchkes. Its nouveau Southern menu delivers such comfortable staples as biscuits and gravy, buttermilk pancakes with sugarcane syrup, and pan-fried catfish alongside fresh vegetables, soups, salads, and pasta (entrées start at $10; beer and wine are available).

A giant bouquet of colorful metal flowers downtown is sculpted by local folk artist Blue Chilton, best known for his whimsical animal sculptures made with old car parts. See his creatures inhabiting the lane to his studio a couple miles from downtown. From the bouquet at the corner of Hwy. 278 and Newborn Road, take Newborn Road to Walter Shepard Road to Chilton Wood Road, and look for the dragon.

A few miles west of downtown, just inside the Morgan County line, **Cowboy's Feed Lot,** 7201 Hwy. 278, 706/557-9552, serves "steaks and stuff" and features country-and-western bands and dancing on the huge dance hall's sawdust-sprinkled floors. Beef-lovers order the house specialty—a 22-ounce T-bone named "the Stud"—baby-back ribs, or the euphemistically named "calf fries" (testicles). Call for dining, entertainment, and dance-lesson schedules. It's 2.25 miles east of I-20.

Hard Labor Creek State Park

Two miles north of Rutledge, this full-service, 5,804-acre park, 706/557-3001 or 800/864-PARK (864-7275), gastateparks.org, parking $2, is the busiest state park in Georgia. It draws plenty of city folk to its 5,805 acres, which are packed with recreational facilities.

Golfers know it best for its popular creekside 18-hole course, which offers cart rentals, a pro shop, and a café (starting at $37; call 706/557-3006 for tee times). Two shaded lakes provide swimming, fishing, and boating (rentals are available); 24 miles of trails accommodate hikers, cyclists, and horses (bring your own).

Twenty fully equipped two-bedroom cottages rent for $75–100. A 51-site campground charges $20–22; hookups are available.

MADISON

Established in 1807, early Madison prospered on the cotton economy. Wealthy planters built the town's many elegant houses in ornate period styles between 1830 and 1860; today the remaining 19th-century structures lend the town its charm. Many homes are still owned by descendants of the original residents.

The town was lucky to be spared the wrath of Sherman, who brought 50,000 troops within blazing range of town on his 1864 March to the Sea. The story goes that Madison resident Senator Joshua Hill rode out to ask Sherman that no harm come to Madison—and as Hill was a staunch Unionist who resigned his congressional seat rather than agree to secession, Sherman spared the town. A fire in 1869 was not so merciful, however. The construction wave that followed endowed the town center with its late-19th-century flavor.

Heartland Georgia

© KAP STANN

Spared destruction in the Civil War, Madison offers tours of its antebellum homes.

Today, Madison's town square remains as vibrant as many such downtowns were half a century ago, before modern malls and suburban sprawl. The 1905 Beaux Arts courthouse, with its cupola towering above massive oaks and magnolias, dominates the square, and city auctions are still held on its steps. Brick sidewalks are furnished with colorful flowerboxes and park benches, and Victorian storefronts hold shops selling antiques and local arts and crafts. Attractive residential neighborhoods surround the square.

Tourism is now Madison's second-largest industry, after agriculture. On the square, the **welcome center,** 115 E. Jefferson St., 706/342-4454 or 800/709-7406, madisonga.org, distributes maps of all sights. It's open daily.

Sights

Historic house tours highlight architectural details while shedding light on antebellum caste society. At **Heritage Hall,** 277 S. Main St., 706/342-9627, guides describe high-style life in a glamorously restored 1811 doctor's residence a block from the square. Admission is $5 for adults; hours are Mon.–Sat. 11 A.M.–4 P.M. and Sun. 1–4:30 P.M.

Two restorations beside the courthouse, 706/343-0190, are the 1809 **Rogers House,** an example of where an antebellum middle-class white family might have lived, and the 1890 **Rose Cottage,** across the gravel garden path; the latter was built by a former slave. Tours include both houses; admission is $3 for adults. Hours are Mon.–Sat. 10 A.M.–4:30 P.M. and Sun. 1:30–4:30 P.M.

The 1895 Romanesque Revival **Madison-Morgan Cultural Center,** 434 S. Main St., 706/342-4743, has been transformed from a schoolhouse into an impressive multipurpose regional arts center. Upstairs, one classroom has been restored to its Victorian origins and another serves as an art gallery. Downstairs, several rooms of exhibits tell the town's story, highlighting 19th-century decorative arts and interior design; a 395-seat theater hosts a **summer theater festival** in August and other performances throughout the year.

At the **Morgan County African American Museum,** 156 Academy St., 706/342-9191, former schoolteacher Reverend Thelma Lee leads visitors through three rooms of a small Victorian cottage describing the life of its former residents.

The house is open Tues.–Fri. 10 A.M.–4 P.M. and Sat. noon–4 P.M. Admission is $3 for adults.

Food and Drink

Ye Olde Colonial Restaurant, 108 W. Washington St., 706/342-2211, is a landmark for hungry visitors. The cafeteria-style restaurant is housed in an old bank building—sit in the vault if you like—and serves such classic Southern buffet choices as fried chicken, country-fried steak, sweet potatoes, butterbeans, corn bread, and cobbler, all with bottomless iced tea. It's open Mon.–Sat. 5:30 A.M.–8:30 P.M.

More modern fare is served around the square inside or out at **Amici's** Italian restaurant for lunch and dinner (and occasional live music) and the **Snapdragon Cafe,** for morning muffins and light lunches.

Just off the square on South Main Street, **Same Old Place** is the local hangout for home-style Southern food (fried pork chops are their specialty); it's open for breakfast and lunch from 5 A.M.–2 P.M.

Near the interstate, **Crowe's,** on Hwy. 441 1.4 miles north of I-20, 706/342-7002, serves good hickory-smoked 'cue for lunch only.

EATONTON AND VICINITY

The small country town of Eatonton is surrounded by the dairy farms that constitute the mainstay of the local economy—the town's **Dairy Festival,** in June, highlights the industry. It's the home of literary legends Alice Walker and Joel Chandler Harris, whose Uncle Remus tales are enshrined in the town's small museum. North of town, an aboriginal mound presents a moving memorial to ancient tribes.

Uncle Remus Museum

The folksy Uncle Remus Museum, 2414 Oak St., Hwy. 441 downtown, 706/485-6856, consists of three cabins that once housed enslaved families. First-edition books and little more than the aura of the tales of Br'er Rabbit, Br'er Fox, and the other famous stories published by Eatonton native Joel Chandler Harris are on display at this affecting little landmark set in a small park.

It's open Mon–Sat. 10 A.M.–5 P.M. and Sun. 2–5 P.M.; closed Tues. Sept.–May. Admission is 50 cents. A statue of the famous trickster rabbit adorns the courthouse square.

Rock Eagle Effigy Mound

As you look down from the observation tower, the thousand-year-old aboriginal Rock Eagle effigy mound (on Hwy. 441 five miles north of Eatonton) resembles a bird of prey standing upright with outstretched wings. The effigy, believed to be an eagle because of the eagle's high place in Native American mythology, measures 102 feet from wingtip to wingtip. The eagle takes its shape from thousands of rocks, which were laboriously transported here and heaped into a huge mound.

Rock Eagle is the only effigy site in Georgia, and it remains eerily pristine. Though now guarded by a tall wire fence, it looks as if no stone has been touched for centuries. Perhaps its earliest visitors heeded the parting words of a Creek chief, which are now inscribed on a marker at the site:

*Tread Softly Here White Man
For Long Ere You Came Strange Races
Lived, Fought, and Loved*

The site lies within a 1,452-acre 4-H center, 706/484-2800, rockeagle4h.org, that specializes in environmental education.

Recreation

Lake Oconee and Lake Sinclair, two power-company impoundments of the Oconee River, are Middle Georgia's playground for boating, fishing, and swimming. The reservoirs meet at the Hwy. 16 dam, 15 miles east of Eatonton, where Georgia Power's **Land Department Field Office,** 706/485-7701, distributes maps to all public facilities and campgrounds around the lakes.

The Oconee National Forest abuts the lakes. The **District Ranger Office,** on Hwy. 441 six miles north of Eatonton, 706/485-7110, provides recreation directories and trail maps.

Within the national forest, the seasonal **Lake Sinclair Recreation Area** offers a staffed swimming beach and campground ($7 a night; first-

TALES FROM THE HEARTLAND

"The writer operates at a peculiar cross-roads where time and place and eternity somehow meet. His problem is to find that location."

Flannery O'Connor

Three great fiction writers somehow found that elusive meeting place in this small rural patch of Georgia heartland.

Joel Chandler Harris, born in Eatonton in 1848, began chronicling the African American folktales of a fictional character named Uncle Remus in his *Atlanta Constitution* column in 1879. The tales originated in Africa but were transformed with Southern details when brought to America. They featured a wily trickster named Br'er Rabbit and his antagonist Br'er Fox (Br'er is short for Brother). *Br'er Rabbit and the Tar Baby* was the most famous of these Uncle Remus stories.

Harris recorded the tales in his version of black folk dialect of the period—barely intelligible for many contemporary readers (and frequently objectionable, with patronizing terms—such as "Uncle"—that were then in common use).

Eatonton's **Uncle Remus Museum,** on Hwy. 441, contains memorabilia from the life and times of Harris and his Remus and Rabbit characters.

The contemporary writer **Alice Walker** also hails from Eatonton. Her Pulitzer prize–winning

novel *The Color Purple* (which Steven Spielberg made into a film and which is now being made into a play) was set in this rural Georgia countryside in the 1930s. Now a California resident, Walker established the Color Purple Foundation in Eatonton, which sponsors local educational enrichment programs. The local chamber of commerce, at 105 W. Sumter St., distributes an *Alice Walker Trail* brochure with sites from the author's life and tales.

Flannery O'Connor, born in Savannah in 1925, wrote her famous novels, *Wise Blood* and *The Violent Bear It Away,* and such short stories as "A Good Man is Hard to Find" on the 1820 Milledgeville ranch called Andalusia; it's now open to the public for tours. She attended the local college—now Georgia College—which maintains a collection of her manuscripts and memorabilia in the **Flannery O'Connor Room** (upstairs in the main library). College scholars produce the O'Connor journal *The Peacock's Feet,* named for O'Connor's remark that "a peacock's pride in his stunning plumage is humbled by his awkward feet." O'Connor is buried in Memory Hill cemetery.

Middle Georgia writers are celebrated every year at the **Eatonton Literary Festival,** held the first weekend in August, with poetry readings, storytelling, historical tours, lectures, and a rare book fair. Descendants of the famous authors often make appearances. For more information, contact the Eatonton-Putnam County Chamber of Commerce, 706/485-7701.

come first-served; hookups available). It's open from Memorial Day to Labor Day. Parking costs $2. There's also a family-friendly hiking trail that winds two miles (one way) through a canebrake then follows the lakeshore (accessible year-round). To get there from Eatonton, go 10 miles south on Hwy. 129, then three miles east on Hwy. 212 to Forest Service Road 1062; turn left and follow signs for two miles.

The busy center of lake activity at the Hwy. 441 crossing between Eatonton and Milledgeville features a marina, a swimming beach, campground, and **Choby's Landing** seafood restaurant, 706/453-9744, all in the shadow of a monolithic coal-fired power plant on the far shore. The Sierra Club and other environmental advocacy groups have complained for years that heated discharges from the plant endanger local fish populations.

MILLEDGEVILLE

Founded at the fall line on the Oconee River in 1803, Milledgeville served as state capital for more than 60 years, until Atlanta was named capital during Reconstruction in 1868. Union General William Sherman bivouacked here on his March to the Sea. Union officers staged a mock session of the Georgia legislature in the state capitol, and troops tossed government documents out the windows and fueled fires with Confederate money. Into the midst of this frivolity straggled a couple of emaciated Union soldiers, who had escaped from the notorious Andersonville POW camp farther south. After Sherman heard their tales of conditions there, he continued his routing march with an increased vengeance.

Today the small city (population 14,000) is the home of three major state institutions: Georgia College and State University, Georgia State Military College, and Central State Hospital (founded in 1842 as the Georgia Lunatic Asylum).

Downtown is wrapped around the Georgia College campus. Neither the circa 1950s commercial district nor the jam-packed campus is particularly scenic, but the city is nevertheless appealing, with a certain hard-working, no-nonsense citizenry that loyally supports independent businesses and keeps downtown relatively free from franchise outlets. Attractive residential neighborhoods of old homes and tidy gardens line the south side of campus and downtown.

The **Milledgeville Convention and Visitors Bureau,** 200 W. Hancock St., 478/452-4687 or 800/653-1804, milledgevillecvb.com, operates a visitors center, arranges Andalusia tours, and hosts trolley tours of town sights. Also inquire about all local historic house museums. It's open Mon.–Fri. 10 A.M.–5 P.M. and Sat. 10 A.M.–4 P.M.

Old State Capitol and Antebellum Museum

Set on the original Statehouse Square, the old capitol is now found on the campus of **Georgia Military College,** 201 E. Greene St., 478/453-1803, gacmuseum.com. The turreted Gothic three-story structure, built in 1807, is considered the finest example of Gothic architecture in a public building in the U.S. The **Georgia Antebellum Capital Museum** within holds exhibits on local history and culture. The imposing entrance gates were constructed in the 1860s of bricks from the arsenal destroyed by Sherman's troops. It's open Mon.–Fri. 10 A.M.–3 P.M. (but closed at lunch) and Sat. 1–3 P.M. Call for fees.

M Andalusia

A touchstone for lovers of Southern literature, **Andalusia** opens the home of Flannery O'-Connor. O'Connor was at her most prolific while confined here with degenerative lupus, and it was here she remained until her death at age 39 in 1964. Two rooms of the house are on display: the writer's bedroom and her sitting room. In the bedroom, the desk stands close enough to the bed to imagine the arrangement was designed to suit someone whose disability made walking difficult.

Around the 21-acre property, old farm outbuildings hold settings from her stories: haylofts, hayfields, milking sheds. It's been compared with Rowan Oak, home of William Faulkner in Oxford, Mississippi, and for some it is more evocative.

For scheduled tours, contact the Milledgeville Convention and Visitors Bureau, 478/452-4687. Other O'Connor sights in town include

LINK GRAVE MARKERS

Tucked away in Milledgeville's Memory Hill cemetery, "slavery-time" graves are marked by small chains. Those with one link mark the grave of a person born into slavery; two links means the deceased was born and lived in slavery; and a three-link chain memorializes a person who was born, lived, and died a slave. The cemetery lies two blocks down the hill from the Governor's Mansion as you head away from town. Famous native daughter Flannery O'Connor is also buried at Memory Hill.

© KAP STANN

the Flannery O'Connor Room, at the Georgia College Library, and her grave, in Memory Hill Cemetery, at Liberty and Franklin Streets, downtown.

Georgia College and State University

The public liberal arts university of Georgia, Georgia College, 231 W. Hancock St., 478/445-5004, gcsu.edu, is home to the 1838 **Governor's Mansion,** 120 S. Clark St., 478/445-4545, an elegant, peach-colored building that over the years was home to 10 Georgia governors. It now houses the school's administration building. The mansion is generally open to the public for guided tours but was undergoing restoration at last visit; for updates, visit the website gcsu.edu/mansion.

Tucked away in the Ina Russell Library at Georgia College, 478/445-4047, the **Flannery**

O'Connor Room honors the Milledgeville native with a collection of manuscripts and memorabilia.

Central State Hospital Museum

Founded as the Georgia Lunatic Asylum, Central State Hospital, Swint Ave., 478/445-1757, centralstatehospital.org, maintains a museum chronicling the story of mental-health treatment in the U.S. and the hospital's 150-year-old history. It's open by appointment only.

Accommodations, Food, and Entertainment

Antebellum Inn, 200 N. Columbia St., 478/454-5400, housed downtown in a 19th-century Greek Revival house, offers five guest rooms and a pool (doubles start at $80) just south of the Hwy. 441 business route through town.

Downtown, **The Brick,** 136 W. Hancock St., 478/452-0089, serves pizza, calzones, sandwiches, and salads, at well-worn booths or seats at the bar. A couple miles north, **The Cornbread Cafe,** 168 Garrett St., 478/452-4812, serves Southern food including its signature cornbread muffins. It's open for breakfast, lunch, and dinner daily. Find it a few block west of N. Columbia St.

Even city folk from Macon drive up to **Cowboy Bill's,** on Hwy. 441 north of town, 478/453-3283, to stomp to country rock bands in their huge, warehouselike dance hall Wed.–Sat. nights.

Old Clinton

Georgia's fourth largest city in 1820, Clinton was devastated by Sherman's March and never recovered. Civil War battle reenactments each April replay 1864 scenes and are best watched from the vantage point of a covered-wagon ride. What's left of the town retains a New England appearance, with early 19th-century structures still standing.

Old Clinton Barbecue, on Hwy. 129 10 miles north of Macon, 478/986-3225, serves a mean barbecued pork daily in a classic no-frills setting—concrete block building, picnic tables, sawdust on the floor—in a near ghost town no less. They open around 7 A.M. and stay open until around 7 or 8 P.M. (closed Sun.).

ATLANTA TO MACON VIA I-75

The 80-mile freeway corridor between Atlanta and Macon cuts through thick Piedmont forests and offers ample services clustered at freeway exits. Beyond the freeway lie the lively parks, squares, and countryside of Middle Georgia bounded by the swells of the Ocmulgee River to the east and the Flint River to the west. Drivers considering parallel alternatives to the freeway might consider the largely four-lane Hwy. 19/41, which travels through several busy small towns; or the secluded Hwy. 23, a two-lane road through the Piedmont forest past several parks.

Flovilla

A mile and a half south of town in Flovilla, **Fresh-Air Barbecue,** on Hwy. 23, 770/775-3182, is considered the Mother Church of Georgia BBQ. Originally opened in 1929, in the woods out in the country, Fresh-Air hasn't changed much since then, from the sawdust on the floor to the long, family-style tables in the wooden cabin. It's pork only—they don't mess around—don't even bother with sides. It's open every day except Thanksgiving, Christmas, and Easter, from around 8 A.M. to 8 P.M.

Indian Springs State Park

Indian Springs, off Hwy. 42 (10 miles east of I-75 exit 188), 770/504-2277 or 800/864-PARK (864-7275), gastateparks.org, parking $2, draws its name from the Creek, who believed the spring had special healing powers and brought their sick and dying to drink of its waters—a practice adopted by some early Europeans. Here a Creek chief built a beautiful mansion, which variously was the scene of a notorious treaty signing (1825), a Yankee Civil War encampment (1864), exclusive spa resort (late 19th century), and finally a state park (1927). The park's impressive stone masonry and craftsman carpentry are the hallmark of the Civilian Conservation Corps; annual CCC reunions are held here.

The Indian Spring Hotel building was built in 1823 by Chief William McIntosh, leader of the lower Creek Nation. Here McIntosh, despite threat of death by fellow Creeks, signed over 4.7 million acres of Creek territory to whites in the Treaty of 1825. For his betrayal, the upper Creeks executed McIntosh, scalped him, and publicly displayed the scalp on a pole. Though the treaty was soon declared illegal by the federal government, state authorities disagreed and pressed for the eventual removal of all the Creek from their ancestral homelands. Today the house is the only Creek building that remains standing in the Southeast. Call 770/775-2493 about tours of the building.

The 528-acre park also features a 105-acre lake, with seasonal swimming and boat rentals. Ten fully equipped two-bedroom cottages rent for $80–90. An 88-site campground charges $18–20, including water and electric hookups.

High Falls State Park

High Falls, 1.8 miles east of I-75 exit 198 at High Falls Rd., 478/993-3053 or 800/864-PARK (864-7275), gastateparks.org, parking $2, occupies the site of an early 19th-century town on the banks of the Towaliga River. The half-mile **Historic Ruins Trail** begins below the dam and leads past ruins of the ghost town, including its gristmill foundation. An observation platform overlooks 100-foot Towaliga River falls.

The 998-acre park has a lake, swimming pool, four miles of trails, and canoe rentals. The park's 142 wooded campsites offer water and electric hookups for $18–23. Inquire about canoe trips in spring.

Juliette

The revived town of Juliette, 18 miles east of Forsyth on Juliette Road, was originally established on the banks of the Ocmulgee River in the early 20th century. Today it is best known as the home of the Whistle Stop Cafe, which served as the movie set for the film version of Fannie Flagg's novel *Fried Green Tomatoes at the Whistle Stop Cafe*. Flagg's story is emblematic of hundreds of rural Southern towns—including Juliette—whose thriving, tight-knit communities of the early 20th century fell ruin to modern times and urban flight.

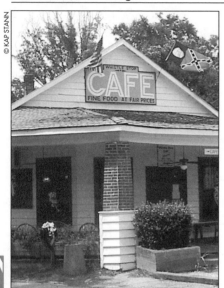

Order fried green tomatoes at Juliette's Whistle Stop Café.

Jarrell Plantation

Southeast of Juliette, Jarrell Plantation, 478/986-5172, gastateparks.org, opens an intact farm from the 1850s with 20 historic buildings. At the end of a long country drive through Middle Georgia, the living-history center makes a peaceful side trip at any time, yet it is best seen during special events, when traditional skill and craft demonstrations bring the place to life; otherwise, it's something of a ghost farm. The plain house is notable, typical of a 600-acre farm with 39 slaves as this once was, but far from the popular image of columned plantation homes. Jarrell hosts **A Folklike Celebration** in September; it features spinning, blacksmithing, and husbandry demonstrations.

It's open Tues.–Sat. 9 A.M.–5 P.M. and Sun. 2–5:30 P.M. Admission is $2–4. From Atlanta, take I-75 exit 185 in Forsyth east to Juliette, cross the river, and follow signs south. From Macon, take I-75 exit 171 north to Hwy. 18, heading east across the river, and follow signs north.

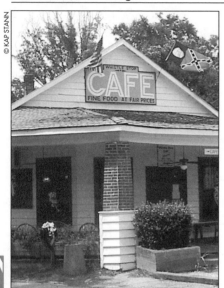 Piedmont National Wildlife Refuge

The Piedmont National Wildlife Refuge, 25 miles northeast of Macon, is restoring 35,000 acres of former cropland exhausted from 100 years of cotton farming. The second-growth preserve is still sprinkled with human history— a wisteria-laced stone chimney here, rock piles from cleared fields there, and old fences found deep within the pine-and-hardwood forest. The refuge shelters deer, opossums, raccoons, bobcats, and 200 species of birds.

The **visitors center,** 478/986-5441, off Juliette Road some 18 miles east of Forsyth, distributes bird lists, interpretive trail maps, tick precaution pamphlets, and hunting and fishing regulations, as well as information about the adjacent 109,000-acre Oconee National Forest. Also at the visitors center, a six-mile **nature drive** winds through the woodlands; the little-used gravel road is also suitable for hiking or mountain biking.

Two short hiking trails begin at the parking lot beyond the visitors center. The one-mile **Allison**

In its heyday, Juliette supported the world's largest water-powered gristmill, five stores, schools, churches, a courthouse, post office, an active railroad depot, and surrounding farms—a life punctuated by train whistles, the hiss of steam locomotives, the clanking of Model Ts on the wooden toll bridge, and the roar of the water over the dam. The industries began to decline in the 1950s, until in 1957 the cotton mill finally closed—leaving the six-story mill in ruins and turning Juliette into a ghost town until its modest revival since the movie was released.

Sample fried green tomatoes at the **Whistle Stop Café,** at the tracks, 478/992-8886, thewhistlestopcafe.com. The café serves Southern specialties such as catfish, barbecue, steaks, and ribs. It's generally open Wed.–Sun. 11 A.M.–4 P.M., sometimes earlier, sometimes later, but it's closed Mon.–Tues. A few shops recognizable in scenes from the movie operate around the café, tempting visitors with fudge, sweets, antiques, and wine-tasting.

Lake Trail loops out to a small scenic lake populated with wood ducks. The 2.5-mile loop **Woodpecker Trail** leads to a colony of red-cockaded woodpeckers a mile in. These endangered birds nest in mature loblolly pines, carving a cavity out of the heart of the tree about 15 feet above the ground. Pause at a bench in front of the white-ringed nesting trees for the chance to see the black-and-white birds with the red caps (recognizable also by their famed Woody Woodpecker cries).

Macon

From ancient Mississippian chiefdoms to contemporary American rock icons, a revered history bolsters the working city of Macon. Quintessentially Southern and Georgian (you almost cannot hear the name "Macon" without hearing "Macon, Georgia"), Macon historically competed with upstart Atlanta for the title of Georgia's number one metropolis. But that competition was settled more than a century ago, when Atlanta was named capital and soon eclipsed its former rival with its growing national stature. Macon (population 100,000), settling comfortably into its role as the heartland favorite, plays up its past like Atlanta plays the future.

The city is best seen in March, during the Cherry Blossom Festival, when the blossoming of 275,000 cherry trees signals not only the start of spring, but also a weeklong celebration of local arts and community spirit. No matter when you come through, climb the mounds at Ocmulgee National Monument, tour preserved antebellum homes, and visit the Georgia Music Hall of Fame.

The heart of the homespun Middle Georgia region, Macon is surrounded by classic Southern farmland, forests, small towns, shady lakes, and the state's renowned peach-growing region. The *South Georgia* chapter offers backcountry side trips south of Macon, including Jimmy Carter Country and the I-75 corridor.

History
The rich bottomlands of the Ocmulgee River attracted the Mississippians to establish a thriving village here thousands of years ago. Grand monuments to their complex civilization remain at Ocmulgee Mounds. A later combination of faded Mississippian culture and indigenous woodland culture created the Lamar civilization, which European explorer Hernando de Soto encountered in 1540. They say de Soto raised the first cross in North America here at a riverside religious ceremony.

In Georgia's colonial era, the regional government of the Creek Confederacy was centered here on the Ocmulgee. When early Americans settling in the interior recognized the water-power value of fall-line areas (*ocmulgee* is said to mean "bubbling waters"), they pushed the Native Americans out with a series of territory-stripping treaties.

The most notorious of these was the Treaty of Indian Springs, signed at what's now Indian Springs State Park by Creek Chief William McIntosh. When the Creeks discovered that McIntosh had betrayed them, he was sentenced to death and executed before the nation was exiled to Alabama.

The frontier Fort Hawkins, built on the Ocmulgee River in 1806, was Macon's first European American settlement. The city of Macon was established in 1823, laid out in a stately grid of broad avenues still preserved in the historic district today, and soon prospered on the cotton trade. Macon's architecture flourished during the early 19th-century Greek Revival period, and despite Civil War skirmishing by offshoots of Sherman's notorious march—one historic house marks the path of a cannonball that landed in its foyer—the city escaped the widespread destruction many other Georgia cities experienced.

GETTING ORIENTED

I-75 cuts through central Macon, but to visit the historic downtown areas where the city's major attractions are located, you'd need to veer off onto I-16 east, which parallels the Ocmulgee River through downtown and provides easy access to the

M
Heartland Georgia

Heartland Georgia

MACON

To Milledgeville

To Gray and Clinton

49

129

MILLERFIELD RD

OCMULGEE NATIONAL MONUMENT

SEE DETAIL

Ocmulgee River

16

Detail map:

CENTREPLEX COLISEUM

GEORGIA MUSIC HALL OF FAME

GEORGIA SPORTS HALL OF FAME

16

Ocmulgee River

CROWNE PLAZA

RIVERSIDE DR

1ST ST

2ND ST

TUBMAN MUSEUM

CHERRY ST

POPLAR ST

PLUM ST

PINE ST

DOUGLASS THEATER

TERMINAL STATION VISITORS CENTER

SPRING ST

ROSE HILL CEMETERY

WALNUT ST

CANNONBALL HOUSE

GRAND OPERA HOUSE

CITY AUDITORIUM

HAY HOUSE

BOND ST

GEORGIA AVE

WASHINGTON LIBRARY

SIDNEY LANIER COTTAGE

COLLEGE ST

1842 INN

BROADWAY

129

To Perry and Valdosta

75

HOUSTON AVE

PIO NONO AVE

ASH ST

FOREST AVE

MERCER UNIVERSITY

INGLESIDE AVE

PIERCE AVE

41

247

MERCER UNIVERSITY DR

ANTHONY RD

WILLIAMSON RD

River

Ocmulgee

HOWARD JOHNSON INN

BEST WESTERN

HOLIDAY INN EXPRESS

COMFORT INN NORTH

DAYS INN NORTH

RIVERSIDE DR

75

23

To Atlanta

VINEVILLE AVE

NAPIER AVE

MONTPELIER DR

UNIVERSITY DR

EISENHOWER PKWY

WESTGATE MALL

MACON MALL

BLOOMFIELD DR

BLOOMFIELD RD

MUSEUM OF ARTS AND SCIENCES

MUMFORD RD

AYERS

TUCKER RD

FORSYTH RD

WESLEYAN COLLEGE

41

LOG CABIN DR

MERCER

HAMPTON INN

COMFORT INN

DAYS INN

HOWARD JOHNSON INN

RED CARPET INN

CHAMBERS RD

MOTEL 6

TRAVELODGE

HOLIDAY INN

ECONOLODGE

EXIT 3

EXIT 2

EXIT 1

74

475

To Lake Tobesofkee

To Jameson Inn, Sleep Inn, and Fairfield Inn

FOSTER RD

COLUMBUS RD

22

80

To Columbus

0   0.5 mi

0   0.5 km

© AVALON TRAVEL PUBLISHING, INC.

city's primary attractions. I-475 bypasses the city entirely, with plenty of services for through-travelers at the southern junction of I-75 and I-475.

Downtown

Downtown Macon, like many cities, suffered near abandonment as development followed the interstate highways, but recent efforts to revitalize the city's historic commercial district has brought new attractions, entertainment venues, cafés, and restaurants downtown. The revived commercial district along Cherry Street features a broad, parklike promenade of cherry trees, benches, and statues in its central median. While the diagonal route of historic Cotton Avenue was cut to expedite the town's chief export to port, today the city's financial district centers along Mulberry Street.

The city's newest attractions can be found in a compact cluster on Martin Luther King Jr. Boulevard, between the Otis Redding Memorial Bridge (note the life-size statue in the riverfront park) and the massive Terminal Station. Located at the foot of Cherry Street, the Terminal Station is home to the Macon-Bibb County Convention and Visitors Bureau. Here the Georgia Music Hall of Fame, Georgia Sports Hall of Fame, and Douglass Theater are all within sight of one another, a quick quarter-mile south of I-16.

Historic Intown

The city's Historic Intown residential district can be found along Georgia Avenue (the westerly extension of Mulberry Street), anchored by the Hay House, the city's most impressive historic house museum. The 1842 House, one of the best historic inns in Georgia, is a block away on College Street. A popular walking-tour route of this historic residential neighborhood loops around from College Street back to Georgia Avenue along Bond Street, where there's a nice view of the city and the river from the crest of the hill. At night many homes in this district are dramatically lit to set off their architectural highlights to best advantage.

Pleasant Hill Historic District

North of downtown, Pleasant Hill is bordered by College, Vineville, Rogers, and Neal Streets. The

The Hay House in downtown Macon is one of Georgia's finest house museums.

district is the heart of Macon's historic African American neighborhood, which dates from the 1870s. Among the clapboard Victorian homes in the community is the birth home of "Little Richard" Penniman; also of note is the Otis Redding Memorial Library inside the Booker T. Washington Community Center, 391 Monroe St., and Linwood Cemetery, the final resting place of the city's most influential African American leaders.

SIGHTS

Ⅿ Georgia Music Hall of Fame

The Music Hall of Fame, 200 Martin Luther King Jr. Blvd., 478/750-8555 or 888/427-0257, gamusichall.com, opened in 1996 to commemorate the state's rich musical heritage with a series of "audio landscapes" in the exhibition hall of a 43,000-square-foot complex, which also houses musical archives.

BROTHERS AND SISTERS TOUR

The Allman Brothers Band (ABB), a trailblazing group that hit the music scene in the 1960s and came to define the era and its fans as the Southern equivalent of the West Coast's Grateful Dead, sprang to fame here at Capricorn Records in downtown Macon. Macon remains a pilgrimage site for fans ("brothers and sisters") rocked by such phenomenal ABB hits as *Whipping Post* and *In Memory of Elizabeth Reed.*

The **Georgia Music Hall of Fame** screens ABB music videos and tells the story of Macon native Phil Walden, a white boy ostracized by schoolmates during segregation for his attraction to "race music;" he established Capricorn and launched the careers of the Marshall Tucker Band and Elvin Bishop in addition to the famed ABB.

The former **Capricorn Records** studio, at 536 Broadway, now houses Phoenix Studios, which uses the original Capricorn mixing board and sound booth. Nearby, the **H & H Restaurant,** at 807 Forsyth St., served as a regular ABB hangout and displays ABB photographs and memorabilia.

ABB archivist Kirk West and his wife Kirsten maintain a small museum and store devoted to ABB paraphernalia at the "Big House"—ABB's home 1970–1972—at 2321 Vineville Ave., 478/742-5005.

Duane Allman died in a motorcycle accident October 29, 1971, at Hillcrest and Bartlett Streets, and band member Berry Oakley was killed in a motorcycle accident November 11, 1972, at Napier and Inverness Streets. The two are buried in **Rose Hill Cemetery** in side-by-side graves marked with the outline of electric guitars. ABB fans have made the site into an impromptu rock 'n' roll shrine, making pilgrimages, holding candlelight vigils, and leaving mementos, despite protests by some family members.

Rose Hill gravestones served as inspiration for ABB's songs *Little Martha* and *In Memory of Elizabeth Reed,* and the cemetery's Overlook Monument was pictured among other Macon scenes on the band's first album cover. (The cemetery office off Riverside Drive distributes maps to all sites.)

The Georgia Allman Brothers Band Association (GABBA), P.O. Box 6354, Macon, GA 31208, hosts a GABBA festival as part of the city's music festival in September. The Allman Brothers Band tour information hotline is 478/742-2888. The official ABB website can be found at allmanbrothersband.com.

From Johnny Mercer, Ma Rainey, Otis Redding, Ray Charles, and James Brown, to the Allman Brothers, REM, and OutKast, Georgia's musical stars are celebrated in a lively (but nevertheless scholarly) "Tune Town," recreating swing-era jazz street life, an R&B club, a country music café, a vintage vinyl rock 'n' roll record store, a 1950s soda fountain (complimentary soft drinks), and a gospel chapel. Outrageous costumes from the 1960s and 1970s, the anachronistic genre of album cover art, and a Wall of Fame are on display.

Minitheaters screen rare film footage and artist interviews, with lots of foot-stomping, heartpounding music (the gospel film is outstanding). Listening stations are posted throughout the museum, and you can record your own song in a soundproof booth. Short of annexing a smoky roadhouse serving iced bottles of Bud from a Coleman chest, the museum is the best introduction to the state's generous contribution to contemporary music. (Director of Visitor Services, tour guide, music scholar, and ardent fan Marty Willet can be counted among the state's natural musical resources himself.)

For children, a 2,400-square-foot Music Factory features a floor piano, a giant fiddle slide, hands-on instruments, and exhibits on world music, comparing musical genres, and even an exhibit on the anatomy of the human ear.

The museum sponsors music festivals, such as **Georgia Music Week,** in September, which features a Kidz Jam, Brown Bag Boogie concerts, and a free outdoor concert the night before the annual awards banquet, when inductees join the Hall of Fame. They also sponsor music-industry workshops on such topics as how to release your own CD and music publishing.

The gift shop has an excellent and uncommon selection of recordings by more than a hundred Georgia artists. No admission is required to visit the store, and if you're thinking of expanding your CD collection, you might want to first become a museum member to be eligible for discounts on admission and purchases—besides, it's all for a good cause.

At the foot of Mulberry Street (take I-16 exit 2 south), the museum is open Mon.–Sat. 9 A.M.–5 P.M. and Sun. 1–5 P.M. Admission is $8 for adults and $6 for seniors and students (children under age four are free).

Georgia Sports Hall of Fame

The state's massive Sports Hall of Fame, 301 Cherry St., 478/752-1585, georgiasportshalloffame.com, opened in 1999 in a $8.3 million redbrick building designed to evoke the look (and nearly the size) of a classic ballpark: the windows are shaped like baseballs, and columns are bats. The Hall of Fame honors more than 300 Georgia sports stars—the likes of Hank Aaron, Ty Cobb, Jackie Robinson, Bobby Jones, Herschel Walker, Fran Tarkenton, Bill Elliott, Evander Holyfield, Heisman trophy winners, Olympians, coaches, and sportswriters. A touch-screen computer lets you select athletes by sport or hometown.

The 14,000-square-foot exhibition hall tells the stories of the state's sports franchises—most notably, the bionic Braves, but also the Falcons and the historic Negro League—along with Georgia's most beloved college teams, UGA Bulldogs and Georgia Tech Yellow Jackets, with trophies, jerseys, and autographed balls. The Georgia Southern exhibit includes a homely gallon of brownish Eagle Creek water, which G.S.U's Eagles would pour on the opposing team's field for a hometown edge. There's also the referee's bow tie from the Holyfield–Tyson "bite fight."

The most fun are the NASCAR video race game in a racecar, a wheelchair sprint challenge, video golf, target football toss, and an indoor basketball court to release steam. Cool down watching a short film of sports highlights in the 205-seat theater.

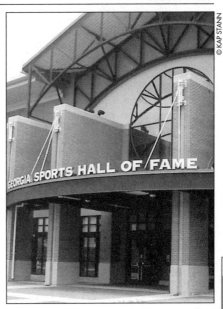

© KAP STANN

Heartland Georgia

Georgia Sports Hall of Fame

The Sports Hall of Fame is open Mon.–Sat. 9 A.M.–5 P.M. and Sun. 1–5 P.M. Admission is $6 for adults; $5 for seniors, students and military with I.D.; $3.50 for children ages 6–16; and free for children five and under. Inquire about family discounts. Souvenirs sporting mascots of Georgia teams in the gift store include pennants, pompoms, jerseys, bleacher seats, and more.

Historic House Museums

The Italian Renaissance **Hay House,** 934 Georgia Ave., 478/742-8155, georgiatrust.org, is the city's premier historic house museum and is among the finest in the region and the state. Built between 1855 and 1859, the ornate 24-room mansion showcases a ballroom, stained glass, an elevator, marble *trompe l'oeil* walls, and hidden passages (though docents discount the popular legend that the treasures of the Confederacy were once stored here). Restored and maintained by the Georgia Trust for Historic Preservation, which is also headquartered here, the Hay House is open Mon.–Sat. 10 A.M.–5 P.M. and Sun. 1–50 P.M. (closed on major holidays).

Admission is $8 for adults, $7 for seniors, $4 for students, and free for children under six.

The **Cannonball House,** 856 Mulberry St. (around the corner from the Hay House), 478/745-5982, cannonballhouse.org, earned its nickname during the Civil War, when it was struck by a cannonball during an 1864 federal attack. The ball itself is among the antique furnishings displayed at the 1853 Greek Revival home. A **Confederate museum** out back holds more Civil War memorabilia. The Cannonball House is open Mon.–Sat. 10 A.M.–5 P.M. Admission is $5 for adults, $4 for seniors, $1 for students, and free for children ages six and under.

The **Sidney Lanier Cottage,** 935 High St., 478/743-3851, is the delicate, sparsely furnished home of the celebrated poet, whose two famous poems set in Georgia—*The Marshes of Glynn* and *Song of the Chattahoochee*—are memorized by the state's schoolchildren. It's open Mon.–Fri. 9 A.M.–4 P.M. and Sat. 10 A.M.–4 P.M. Admission is $3 for adults and $2 for students.

Ocmulgee National Monument

Ocmulgee National Monument, 1207 Emery Hwy., 478/752-8257, nps.gov/ocmu, preserves the impressive earthworks of the late Mississippian culture that flourished here on the banks of the Ocmulgee River A.D. 900–1100, along with evidence of much earlier human habitation; projectile points found here date back 10,000 years.

For reasons that remain largely mysterious, the ancient Mississippians constructed massive earthen temples—the length of football fields and up to three stories high—a single basketful at a time. The mesa tops held chieftains' quarters, or religious rituals, and the remains of high-status individuals were interred below. A short walk from the visitors center, a restored earth lodge recreates a typical meeting place. Trails lead to the tops of mounds and also through the woodlands and along the riverside bottomland.

The visitors center houses ancient artworks, a theater showing a good interpretive film, hands-on exhibits, and a gift shop with a selection of Native American–made crafts, some made locally and others imported from Oklahoma, where the Creek nation is now based. The park sponsors storytelling programs relating Native American ghost stories, nature walks, and basket-making workshops. The park is open daily 9 A.M.–5 P.M. except on Christmas and New Year's Day (no admission fee).

Also administered by the National Park Service, the **Lamar Mound** site, a short drive away, features a rare conical mound with a spiral mount, preserved in its natural setting. Though the property is not improved for public access, curious visitors can make arrangements with rangers to see the remote site—inquire at the visitors center.

A long-debated fall-line freeway proposal threatens the sanctity of these ancient earthworks; you can voice your objections by writing to: State Legislature, Capitol Building, Atlanta, GA 30303.

Museum of Arts and Sciences

A 40-million-year-old whale fossil named Ziggy welcomes visitors to the city's Museum of Arts and Sciences, 4182 Forsyth Rd., 478/477-3232, masmacon.com. Ziggy is part of an "archaeological dig" that is one of the many interactive exhibits emphasizing creativity in the arts and sciences. An artist's studio features a weaving loom, and an inventor's laboratory offers hands-on computers. Walk across to the Tree House, which is an elevated wooden deck overlooking roaming animals. Live animal shows, science theater, and daily planetarium shows are all part of the package. The art galleries go beyond the visual and into the realms of aural, tactile, and fragrant.

The museum is open Mon.–Sat. 9 A.M.–5 P.M. and Sun. 1–5 P.M. Admission is $7 for adults, $5 for students, and $4 for children under 12.

The museum also oversees Brown's Mount and Bond Swamp, an archaeologically and ecologically rich wilderness downriver, and occasionally sponsors field trips there to examine the riparian ecosystem and unusual spiral mound (where, they say, the first cross was placed in North America, by de Soto in 1540).

Tubman African American Museum

The Tubman Museum, 340 Walnut St., 478/743-8544, tubmanmuseum.com, houses a collection of African art and colorful folk art, and exhibits on African American inventions (ask about "the real McKoy") and on African contributions to American cuisine. One historical display relates the story of the feisty light-skinned enslaved woman Ellen Craft, who escaped to freedom disguised as a white male slaveholder while her husband pretended to be her slave.

The museum is open Mon.–Sat. 9 A.M.–5 P.M. and Sun. 2–5 P.M. Admission is $5 for adults and $3 for children. It is due to move to a new location in 2005.

Colleges and Universities

Chartered in 1836 as the first college in the world for women, private liberal-arts **Wesleyan College,** 4760 Forsyth Rd., 478/477-1110, offers degrees in 28 subjects to undergraduates. The college's Midsummer Macon program hosts performances and instruction in the arts, and its fine-arts department sponsors events throughout the academic year.

Baptist-affiliated **Mercer University,** 1400 Coleman Ave., 478/752-2650, founded in 1833, offers undergraduate and graduate programs in seven schools, including liberal arts, law, medicine, engineering, and business. Its music department holds public performances.

Georgia State Academy for the Blind, 2895 Vineville Ave., 478/751-6083, the alma mater of blues musician Blind Willie McTell, has sensitized the community to the visually impaired; city festivals and museums frequently include touch and scent exhibits.

Macon State College, College Station Dr., 478/471-2700, is the newest college in the university system. Also within the state educational system, **Central Georgia Technical College,** 3300 Macon Tech Dr., 478/757-3504, offers more than 100 programs.

RECREATION
Spectator Sports

The **Macon Braves**—a minor league hometown baseball club and farm team for the Atlanta Braves—compete in the 1929 Luther Williams Stadium in Central City Park during their April-to-

August season (and some weekends in March and September). For ticket information, call 478/745-8943. The field is one mile from the junction of I-75 and I-16 via the I-16 Coliseum exit 2.

With perhaps the best name in competitive sports, the **Macon Whoopee** professional ice hockey team (Central Hockey League) competes in the Macon Coliseum from mid-October to mid-April. For ticket information, call 478/741-1000.

The **Macon Knights** play football in the Macon Centreplex. For tickets call 478/741-6700.

Municipal Parks and Recreation

The 250-acre **Central City Park** southeast of downtown, dating from the 1820s, consolidates much of the city's urban recreation, including sports fields and shaded picnic spots around a pond. An 1871 bandstand is the scene of many city festivals and summertime concerts most every weekend.

The public 18-hole **Bowden Golf Course,** 3111 Millerfield Rd., 478/742-1610, has a driving range, pro shop, and snack bar. Two city tennis centers maintain 36 lighted tennis courts at North Ingle Place and in Tattnall Square Park (Oglethorpe and College Streets); call 478/741-9196.

Around a 1,750-acre lake three miles west of I-475, the county-maintained **Tobesofkee Recreation Area,** 6600 Mosley Dixon Rd., 478/474-8770, offers swimming, fishing and boating with a full-service marina, as well as a campground. The day-use fee is $3. North shore parks are accessible from I-475 exit 5 (Hwy. 74 W).

ENTERTAINMENT

The highlights of Macon's performing arts are its richly restored historic theaters; even its modern coliseum, where large concerts are held, evokes an ancient design. The Macon Arts Alliance, a nonprofit community arts organization, announces local exhibits and performances at the Artsline, 478/743-ARTS, maconarts.org. Friday's *Macon Telegraph* features an "Out & About" tabloid with entertainment listings.

© GEORGIA DEPARTMENT OF INDUSTRY, TRADE & TOURISM

Cherry Blossom Festival

Grand Opera House

Grand Opera House, 651 Mulberry St., 478/752-5470, thegrand.mercer.edu, offers luxurious Old South elegance in the beautifully restored 1884 theater from the plush-and-gilt era, with one of the largest stages in the nation. The Grand hosts Broadway shows and other events; a recent bill featured *Porgy and Bess* and Native American flutist and storyteller Robert Mirabel.

Douglass Theatre

The 1921 Douglass Theatre, 355 Martin Luther King Jr. Blvd., 478/742-2000, douglasstheatre.org, hosted such black entertainers as Bessie Smith, Count Basie, and Dizzy Gillespie in its "Chittlin' Circuit" heyday, and launched the careers of James Brown, Little Richard, and Otis Redding in the 1960s before it was abandoned for two decades. Today the restored 312-seat theater is the city's liveliest venue for concerts, community events, and film series (including IMAX-format and a laser-light preview featuring *Georgia on My Mind,* by Ray Charles).

Macon Centreplex Coliseum

Centreplex, 200 Coliseum Dr., 478/751-9152, packs in the largest crowds for concerts, circuses, and big-time shows. Its design mimics the shape of the nearby aboriginal mounds. It's across the river from downtown, right off I-16 exit 2.

Nightlife

Downtown nightlife is pretty much a few bars on Cherry Street around 3rd. The **Rookery,** 543 Cherry St., 478/746-8658, features Southern rock, jazz and blues in a comfortable tavern that draws a nicely mixed crowd—from college kids to grandparents, singles, couples, and groups—to well-worn seats at the friendly bar or at intimate loft booths. **Trio,** 430 Cherry St., 478/738-8746, features jazz and blues. Or try **Dea Nightclub,** 420 Martin Luther King Jr. Blvd., 478/755-1620, a high-energy dance hall.

Country music fans head 40 miles north to Cowboy Bill's in Milledgeville (see that section). For traditional country, gospel, and bluegrass, **Swampland Opera House,** 30 miles east in Toomsboro on Hwy. 57 at Hwy. 112, 478/628-5314, hosts live performances Saturday nights.

Festivals

The city's largest annual event, the **Cherry Blossom Festival,** in late March, brings 10 days of activities that range from refined to wacky—bed races, hog-calling contests, storytelling, floats, parades, hot-air balloons, and many cultural arts performances—a major Southern-style block party that fills downtown. Rated (by those who rate festivals) as among the top 10 regional festivals in the Southeast, the Cherry Blossom Festival is also one of the most scenic, as more than 275,000 cherry trees bloom with the light pink blossoms that herald spring.

In mid-September, **Georgia Music Week** features an action-packed calendar of free concerts, from classic R&B and Athens music to mock-opera, with special events at all major attractions (heritage, food, Native American festivals, races) timed to coincide with the weeklong bash. Percy Sledge, the Swimming Pool Qs, and Women of Rock were recently featured. The event culminates with an annual awards banquet inducting new members to the Georgia Music Hall of Fame.

The **Georgia State Fair,** georgiastatefair.org, is held during Music Week at fairgrounds east of the city. Since 1851, it has brought traditional carnival games, livestock shows, and arts and crafts to Middle Georgia,

Each December, **Christmas in Macon** dresses up historic homes with period decorations and costumed docents. On New Year's Eve, **First Night Macon** is a family event, with performances and fireworks downtown.

ACCOMMODATIONS
1842 Inn

The place to stay in Macon is the 🏛 **1842 Inn,** 353 College St., 478/741-1842 or 800/336-1842, one of the nicest historic inns in the state, and reason alone to wrap a weekend around a trip to Macon. Housed in a stately Greek Revival mansion dating from (of course) 1842, the inn is set down a manicured lawn within a block of the Hay House and other antebellum restorations in the residential fringe of the Historic Intown neighborhood.

White columns, beveled glass, crystal chandeliers, oriental carpets, ceiling fans, and antique furnishings fill the two-story house; rooms in the inn's adjacent Victorian cottage across the garden courtyard are similarly outfitted in period furnishings but appear more modern; stay in the main house if you can. All 22 guest rooms have private baths and such modern amenities as TVs, phones, central heating, and air-conditioning. Guests have access to a nearby health club and a private golf club. Service is impeccable but gratefully not stiff. Rates start at $140 for doubles and include breakfast. Locals use the gracious salon as an intimate gathering spot for cocktails.

Accommodations Elsewhere

The major hotel downtown is the **Crowne Plaza,** 108 1st St., 478/746-1461, a 16-story building with standard rooms (rates start at $99).

Most of the city's 4,500 hotel rooms are designed for the convenience of drivers on the three interstate highways that intersect in Macon. Every national chain is represented. Closest to downtown is the stretch along Riverside Drive via I-75 exit 167, including such older motels as the Best Western Riverside Inn, Howard Johnson, and Days Inn. A newer gulch is off I-475 exit 3, where there are more than a dozen chain motels, including Motel 6, Hampton Inn, and Comfort Inn.

Camping

The county has two campgrounds with 120 first-come, first-served sites around a 1,750-acre lake at the **Tobesofkee Recreation Area,** three miles west of I-475, 478/474-8770. Nearby are swimming, boating, and tennis facilities. The north shore's Claystone Park campground can be reached via Hwy. 74 (I-475 exit 5); south shore's Arrowhead campground can be reached via Hwy. 80 (I-475 exit 3). Rates start at $12, and hookups are available.

FOOD AND DRINK
Downtown

The traditional Southern favorite is 🍴 **Len Berg's,** 478/742-9255, tucked away in Old Post Office Alley (follow the locals). A Macon institution since 1908, Len Berg's seats diners in well-worn wooden booths in small dark anterooms for daily specials such as fried chicken, baked turkey with dressing, pimento-cheese sandwiches, and salmon croquettes—also, fried green tomatoes and macaroon pie. They serve lunch Mon.–Sat. and dinner Fri.–Sat.

Another Macon tradition is **Nu-Way Wieners,** 430 Cotton Ave. at 1st St., a hot dog stand with a loyal following since 1918 (open weekdays only).

Soul food is on Mama Louise Hudson's menu at the **M H & H Restaurant,** 807 Forsyth St., 478/742-9810. Here you'll find full Southern breakfasts and meat-and-two plates for $6. A landmark haunt of the Allman Brothers, H & H has ABB photographs and memorabilia on the walls. It's open Mon.–Sat. 7 A.M.–7 P.M.

Good to Go, 194 Spring St. at the corner of Walnut, 478/743-4663, is a handy takeout eatery for generous daily specials for breakfast and lunch, weekdays only. It's the first block south of Riverside Drive, about a quarter-mile south of I-16 exit 1A.

Tic Toc Room, 408 Martin Luther King Jr. Blvd., 478/744-0123, serves modern food with a Cordon Bleu flair and a martini menu to Macon. The menu features items such as tilapia in a white-wine dill sauce over sautéed spinach (entrées start at $15).

Barbecue

Off I-75, **M Fincher's,** 3947 Houston Ave., 478/788-1900, claims distinction as the only barbecue ever shot into space—astronaut Sonny Carter (who trained at Robins Air Force Base south of town) took some Fincher's 'cue with him aboard the space shuttle. In operation since 1935 and largely untouched from that time, Fincher's is set in a drive-through diner with grill-covered windows and NASA memorabilia inside. Specialties include The Pig, a chopped pork sandwich with their pepper-and-tomato sauce. It's cheap and open daily. From I-75 exit 160B, go east and then take a left at the first traffic light to Fincher's, on the left.

Also off I-75, the sentimental favorite is **Fresh-Air Bar-B-Que,** 3076 Riverside Dr., 478/477-7229 (though loyalists drive an hour north to its original Flovilla branch, in Middle Georgia). Find **Satterfield's,** 120 New St. at Riverside Dr., downtown, about a quarter-mile south of I-16 exit 1A (weekdays only).

GETTING THERE AND AROUND

By Air

Most Macon-bound air travelers fly through Atlanta's Hartsfield-Jackson Airport and take **Groome Transportation,** 478/471-1616, groometrans.com, for the 1.25-hour drive to Macon; vans leave frequently throughout the day. The Middle Georgia Regional Airport, outside Macon, is served by Atlantic Southeast Airlines (ASA); there, taxis and car rentals are available.

By Bus

Greyhound bus service connects with major cities from its station at 65 Spring St., 478/743-5411 (where Macon native "Little Richard" Penniman wrote *Tutti Frutti* while washing dishes before he took the bus out to stardom). In temperate weather, you could walk the five long blocks to the Music Hall of Fame and other downtown sights from here.

Local bus service is provided by the **Macon-Bibb County Transit Authority,** 478/746-1318.

By Car

Three interstate freeways provide easy access to Macon: I-75 runs north-to-south through town, I-475 bypasses the city to the west, and I-16 shoots off east toward Savannah, providing the most direct access to downtown via I-16 exit 2 at Coliseum Drive. From here, cross the Otis Redding Bridge over the Ocmulgee River to reach the Halls of Fame, the Terminal Station visitors center, and other downtown sights. Parking is rarely any problem.

INFORMATION AND SERVICES

The **Macon-Bibb County Convention and Visitors Bureau,** 200 Cherry St., Macon, GA 31201, 478/743-3401 or 800/768-3401, maconga.org, is centrally located downtown in **Terminal Station,** at the foot of Cherry Street and off 5th Street. Here the center shows a short video on the city's history, distributes maps, and sponsors two-hour guided trolley tours. It's open Mon.– Sat. 9 A.M.–5 P.M.

Georgia State Welcome Center, off I-75 at mile marker 179 (9 miles south of Forsyth), 478/994-9191, is open daily 9 A.M.–5:30 P.M.

Shopping

Among the most distinctive shops downtown, **Karla's Shoe Boutique,** 603 Cherry St. at 2nd Street, 478/741-2066, is operated by Zelma and Karla Redding, the widow and daughter, respectively, of famed musical legend Otis Redding. **Golden Bough,** 371 Cotton Ave. at Cherry St., 478/744-2446, is a wonderful bookstore with used and rare books, Middle Georgia titles and authors, and meditative and New Age music in its reading room (closed Sun.–Mon.).

VICINITY OF MACON

Warner Robins

Fourteen miles south of Macon, the town of Warner Robins is dominated by the Robins Air Force Base. Occupying 43 acres on the base, the **Museum of Aviation,** Hwy. 247S at Russell Pkwy., 478/926-6870 or 800/807-3359, museumofaviation.org, displays more than 90 historic aircraft dating from World War I, including the world-speed-record-holder SR-71 *Blackbird,* U-2 *Dragon Lady,* a presidential helicopter, bombers, fighters, and reconnaissance planes. More than 200,000 square feet of indoor exhibits cover military memorabilia and the history of air power, including displays on the Flying Tigers and Tuskegee Airmen. It's also the home of the **Georgia Aviation Hall of Fame,** which honors more than 50 aviators, including the world's first African American military pilot, pioneer women aviators, and "Top Gun" Navy fighter pilot and astronaut Sonny Carter. It's open 9 A.M.–5 P.M. daily except Thanksgiving, Christmas, and New Year's Day. Admission is free. A 3rd-floor café affords an ideal view of the air base's runway. The museum can be reached seven miles east of I-75 exit 146.

Pine Mountain and Vicinity

Pine Mountain is the southernmost rise on the Piedmont Plateau and is a welcome landmark to altitude-seeking flatlanders. Northbound travelers will see Pine Mountain's wide ridge looming on the horizon like a huge temple mound.

Franklin Delano Roosevelt was the area's most famous part-time resident; he was drawn to the mineral waters on Pine Mountain's eastern slope. His Little White House and the charming town of Warm Springs still evoke his memory. Both Pine Mountain, at the western end of the ridge, and Callaway Gardens recall this era—the days before air-conditioning—when walking in a landscaped Southern garden or fishing in a quiet pond was all you could want out of a vacation. Despite modern conveniences and novel attractions, the appeal of Pine Mountain today remains in that simplicity.

Hikers and backpackers find the 23-mile Pine Mountain Trail the greatest highland hike this side of North Georgia, and a ridge-top state park squirrels away CCC-era cabins around a wooded lake.

ALONG STATE HIGHWAY 85

State Highway 85—not to be confused with I-85—meanders through a scenic stretch of the eastern Piedmont from Atlanta to Warm Springs, past gristmills, pasturelands, and cornfields. Outside Atlanta, the route is largely a seven-lane expanse of urban sprawl, but it thins to a two-lane country highway once you hit the old downtown in Fayetteville.

In the tiny town of **Senoia,** tucked a mile west of Hwy. 85, the **Culpepper House Bed and Breakfast,** 35 Broad St., 770/599-8182, culpepperhouse.com, offers an appealing getaway less than an hour from Atlanta. The attractively restored two-story yellow clapboard house features a wide veranda custom made for porch-rocking. Room rates start at $85 per couple and include breakfast.

Walk or bike to the local feed-and-tack, antique shops, and the **Senoia Coffee Co.,** 1 Main St., 770/599-8000, which roasts beans daily (ask to see the roaster in action) to serve along with breakfast pastries, desserts, and fancy chocolates. They also serve light lunches, sandwiches, tuna salad, egg salad, and the like.

ALONG I-85

The interstate route from Atlanta to Columbus is largely a monotonous corridor of four-lane blacktop and kudzu-lined forest straddling a region between the Flint and Chattahoochee Rivers.

A stop for barbecue at a local culinary landmark can break up a trip to Pine Mountain or Columbus. In operation since 1926, **Sprayberry's Restaurant** is well known for its hickory-smoked barbecue pork or beef, slathered with a vinegar-based sauce ("Double Aristocratic" plates run around $10). Giant onion rings and cobbler are also favorites. They have two locations: the newer drive-through restaurant on Hwy. 34E right off I-85 exit 9, 770/253-5080, and the more evocative original, north of town, at 229 Jackson St. (where Hwy. 70 and Hwy. 29 meet), 770/253-4421 (both are closed Sundays). The drive through town passes the attractive historic residential and commercial districts of downtown Newnan, and you may be drawn in by several inviting antique shops and flea markets along the way.

If you're headed to Pine Mountain, you can drop down Hwy. 27A at **Moreland,** the birthplace of two of Georgia's most celebrated writers. Readers captivated by such works as *God's Little Acre* and *Tobacco Road* may pay homage at the birthplace of author Erskine Caldwell (1903–1987), whose graphic tales of rural life scandalized the South in their time (they're *still* pretty racy!). His 1903 restored birth home, called The Little Manse, was moved to the center of Moreland, in the town square, E. Camp St., 770/251-4438, where it serves as a small museum; it's open Sat.–Sun. 1–4 P.M. or by appointment.

Another native son, Lewis Grizzard, was a beloved local humorist who gained national notoriety with his collections of essays, such as *Aim Low Boys, They're Riding Shetland Ponies.* (Unfortunately, his romantic career was less successful—inspiring the local bumper sticker "Honk If You've Been Married to Lewis Grizzard") A small

museum, 2769 US Hwy. 29S, 770/304-1490, commemorates his work with old typewriters, family photos, and mementos. It's open Thurs.–Sat. 10 A.M.–5 P.M. Admission is $1.

CITY OF PINE MOUNTAIN

The welcoming little city of Pine Mountain, nestled at the eastern slope of its namesake rise, centers around the old city hall downtown. A quaint collection of shops, galleries, and cafés make it a nice town to explore. Its most popular attractions are nearby Callaway Gardens and FDR State Park.

The downtown **Welcome Center,** 101 Broad St., 706/663-4000 or 800/441-3502, pinemountain.org, distributes local maps (closed Sun.).

Wild Animal Safari

At Wild Animal Safari, 1300 Oak Grove Rd., 706/663-8744 or 800/367-2751, animalsafari.com, a four-mile safari ride may reveal exotic animals from six continents, including zebras, ostriches, and rhinos. Visitors drive through the 500-acre park themselves or take a guided tour bus. An alligator pit, serpentorium, petting zoo, concession stand, and hayride are part of the package. It is open daily 10 A.M.–5 P.M. Find it off Hwy. 27, three miles north of town.

Accommodations and Camping

There are three modest, well-kept motels in town. The 13-room **White Columns Inn,** 19727 Hwy. 27, 706/663-2312, is invitingly tucked away in quiet woods but is still within a walk from some shops. The tidy, old-fashioned **Pine Mountain Motel,** Hwy. 27, 706/663-2306, is right downtown, closer to all the action. The **Fireside Inn,** 706/663-4141, is the least attractive of the three, standing between an auto parts store and a gas station, but it's decent, has a pool, and is also downtown. Rates start at around $45 for doubles during the winter and climb in summer.

More area lodging is available at the Callaway Gardens resort; cottage rental and camping is found at FDR State Park.

Pine Mountain Campground, Hwy. 27, 706/663-4329, is little more than a lot in a pasture right along the highway, but it is nevertheless convenient and welcoming and has a pool.

Food and Drink

Granny's, Hwy. 27, 706/663-2640, offers down-home Southern weekend buffets of roast beef, squash casserole, and fried okra, with tea and cobbler ($8). Friday features all-you-can-eat catfish dinners, and there are $6 blue-plate specials during the week. Hours change seasonally.

Across the street, **San Marcos,** 706/663-8075, serves good inexpensive Mexican plates—try the shrimp fajitas (closed Sun.).

CALLAWAY GARDENS

Callaway Gardens Resort and Preserve, Hwy. 27, 706/663-2281 or 800/CALLAWAY (225-5292), callawayonline.com, a unique private resort, encompasses 14,000 acres of blooming woodlands and natural attractions that make the most of lush Southern landscapes. Outdoor recreation is particularly compelling in this setting, and many visitors come for the day to hike or bike along flower-rimmed trails, golf at four manicured courses, play tennis, water ski, sunbathe, and swim at the mile-long lakefront beach. You can also stay overnight at lodges or cottages.

The standard day-use gate admission is $13 per adult and $6.50 per child ages 6–12 (five and under free). Sights are free with this gate fee; additional recreational and special-event fees may apply.

Sights

Virginia Hand Callaway Discovery Center, the base of operations for a Callaway tour, has historical and geographical exhibits, a theater, and restaurant overlooking Mountain Creek Lake. Check out the schedule of daily special events. From the center, tram tours lead around the grounds, or you can rent bikes.

Callaway's most outstanding attraction is the **Cecil B. Day Butterfly Center,** an 8,000-square-foot towering glass atrium filled with lush tropical plants and a thousand free-flying butterflies and hummingbirds. Fifty colorful va-

rieties from around the world, some as big as small birds, swoop overhead and frequently alight on visitors (the experience will likely dazzle but may overwhelm small children). Surrounding outside gardens are designed to attract native butterflies.

The 20,000-square-foot **John A. Sibley Horticultural Center** features a 22-foot indoor waterfall, a Mediterranean garden, an orchid grotto, and an English hedge maze. A streamside **Memorial Chapel** is patterned after 16th-century wayside chapels.

Daily programs include guided tours and walks, storytelling, and concerts. Major seasonal programs include a spring festival in March or April to coincide with the blooming peak, an acrobatic circus in summer, an autumn festival in October, and a "Fantasy in Lights" Christmas show in November and December. The map guides visitors to plants in bloom, month by month.

Recreation

The 65-acre Robin Lake is the center of much recreation. Here a mile-long lifeguard-staffed **beach** ("largest inland man-made white-sand beach in the world," so they say) attracts swimmers and sunbathers. Paddleboats and a minitrain ride through the woods are free with gate admission; fishing, canoe rental, and waterskiing are also available for additional fees.

A 10-mile **bike trail** winds through the beautiful woodlands. A ferry near the midpoint of the trail transports riders across Mountain Creek Lake. Miles of paved **hiking trails** weave through the gardens.

Four manicured **golf courses** carry green fees ranging from $33 (walking) at the Sky View course to $110 (including cart) at the Mountain View course. Tennis and racquetball fees start at $6 per person (doubles).

Lodging and Dining

Callaway provides lodging in its modern 349-room **Callaway Gardens Inn,** on Hwy. 27, 800/225-5292, in nearby townhouses or in detached cottages tucked away in the woods. Rates start at around $119 a night, with many

© KAP STANN

The train depot where FDR used to arrive is now the Warm Springs Welcome Center.

combination recreation and weekend package rates available.

Within the inn (no gate fee required), the **Georgia Room** offers the most deluxe and formal setting (dinner only, dress code, entrées start at $18). The **Plantation Room** here serves a generous, bottomless Southern buffet (breakfast $9, lunch $10, dinner $17, seafood Friday $20, Sunday brunch $17, kids 6–12 pay half price, no charge for children under six). The **Mountain Creek Café,** in the Discovery Center, offers a light cafeteria-style selection. Beachgoers watching their budgets and diet bring picnics to avoid high-priced fast food at the beach pavilion.

Most accessible and casual is Callaway's mountaintop **Country Kitchen,** on Hwy. 27 at Hwy. 190, which serves Southern breakfasts all day, meat-and-two platters for lunch and dinner, and a kid's menu, all with a panoramic view. It's open daily 7 A.M.–9 P.M. year-round.

The country store within sells custom foodstuffs (speckled grits, muscadine jams, pickled okra, relishes), distinctive garden ornaments, crafts, and toys.

WARM SPRINGS AND VICINITY

The 1930s set the tone for Warm Springs and Pine Mountain—thanks to the area's famous former part-time resident, Franklin Delano Roosevelt. The thermal waters of Warm Springs drew polio-stricken FDR for their therapeutic value (as they had drawn the Creeks for centuries), and his love for the area led him to establish a presidential hideaway in these woods. The Little White House now stands as a memorial as enchanting and powerful as the man himself. Today, to stay in a CCC-built log cabin at FDR State Park, to cruise Warm Springs' two-square-block downtown and nearby pools, to tour FDR's cottage, and to stroll among the traditional flowering gardens at neighboring Callaway Gardens is to be transported back to prewar days of fedoras, rumble seats, and an era of simple pleasures.

Today the Roosevelt Warm Springs Institute for Rehabilitation continues the therapeutic treatments that began with the outdoor mineral baths FDR frequented from 1924 until his death in 1945.

In the center of town, the old clapboard rail depot, where FDR would arrive, now serves as a **welcome center,** 706/655-3322 or 800/337-1927, warmspringsga.ws. A vintage passenger rail car is now a gift shop. Along Main Street, a dozen small shops and cafés invite visitors to poke around—particularly in the appealing alleyway courtyard that's hidden behind the storefronts (you'll find restrooms here too).

Little White House

A quarter mile from the depot, this state historic site, 401 Little White House Rd. on Hwy. 85W, 706/655-5870, fdr-littlewhitehouse.org, stands as a powerful memorial to Franklin Delano Roosevelt, who began traveling to Warm Springs in 1924 for treatment for the infantile paralysis (polio) that had struck him in 1921. The site serves as an intimate tribute to the complex man who led the United States through a rocky stretch of its history and to his courageous triumph over disability.

FDR had the house built in 1932, when he was governor of New York. After he was elected president, the house was inaugurated as the Little White House. The simple six-room house, where FDR died of a cerebral hemorrhage in 1945, can be appreciated for its clean symmetry and spare craftsman design. Admission is $5 for adults and $2 for children. It's open daily 9 A.M.–5 P.M.

The **FDR Memorial Museum** displays the incomplete portrait cut short upon FDR's death, along with recordings of his fireside chats and specially adapted 1938 roadsters—one with the license plate "FDR 1." Exhibits on FDR's life and legacy include buttons and banners bearing NRA, CCC, WPA, and other "alphabet soup" insignia, along with vintage antiques and a collection of gift canes from around the world. Opened in 2004, the new building features green design and universal access.

Special events commemorate FDR's birthday (January 30), Franklin and Eleanor's wedding anniversary (March 17), Fala Day in November (Fala was FDR's cherished lap dog), and Thanksgiving (which FDR had made into a treasured community tradition, with dinners with fellow polio patients).

The historic **therapeutic baths,** on Hwy 27A, frequented by FDR were restored and rededicated by President Clinton in 1995.

Accommodations and Food

In the center of town, the four-story 1907 **Hotel Warm Springs,** 47 Broad St., 706/655-2114 or 800/366-7616, hotelwarmspringsbb.org, captures the FDR era with handsome but modest rooms outfitted with cast-iron beds, chenille coverlets, ceiling fans, and tiny corner porcelain sinks (rates start at $65).

Feast on Southern buffet at the **Bulloch House,** Hwy. 27A, 706/655-9068, with an 1892 house on a hill around the corner from the downtown strip. Entrées include rib-eye steak and catfish, with peach cobbler and banana pudding to wrap up. They serve lunch daily 11 A.M.–2:30 P.M. and dinner Fri.–Sat. 5–8:30 P.M.

In the trailer behind the main drag, **Mac's Barbecue,** Hwy. 27A, 706/655-2472, serves quick barbecue plates and snacks daily 11 A.M.–8 P.M.

Recreation

Some of the nicest stretches of the Flint River are east of Warm Springs, accessible off Hwy. 36 between Woodland and Thomaston. To romp in the shoals and soak in a cool "natural Jacuzzi," follow signs from Hwy. 36 to **Big Lazer Creek** ("LIE-za") and head for the falls.

FRANKLIN D. ROOSEVELT STATE PARK

The 10,000-acre FDR State Park, 706/663-4858 or 800/864-PARK (864-7275), gastateparks.org, parking $2, sits atop Pine Mountain, offering fine views of the countryside. A stone CCC-built **visitors center and overlook** sits atop the scenic ridge route connecting downtown Pine Mountain to the west and Warm Springs to the east (Hwy. 190).

Hiking and Backpacking

The 23-mile **Pine Mountain Trail** starts at the Callaway Gardens Country Store, at the intersection of Hwy. 27 and Hwy. 190, and weaves east up and over the wooded ridge to trail's end,

Heartland Georgia

at a radio-tower parking area on Hwy. 85W. The trail gets better the farther east you go; buy trail maps at the FDR State Park visitors center.

Off the backpacking trail, the beautiful six-mile **Wolfden Loop** from the eastern terminus passes through a fern-lined forest of mountain laurel and provides views of scenic waterfalls and beaver dams along Wolfden Branch. The 4.3-mile **Dowdell's Knob Loop** takes hikers to FDR's favorite picnic spot and overlook—park at the Dowdell's Knob spur road off Hwy. 190 and follow the white-blazed trail.

Other Recreation

Roosevelt Riding Stables, 1063 Group Camp Rd., 706/628-7463 or 877/696-4613, roosevelt stables.com, a private concession within the park, takes riders out for short trips, longer cookout rides, or overnight adventures.

Other park facilities include a **swimming pool** (free for overnighters) and two small lakes for fishing and paddleboating.

Accommodations and Camping

Twenty-one fully equipped cottages, in scenic locations sheltered on lakeview hills or more exposed on the panoramic ridge, make great hideaways. Many are the original log cabins with stone chimneys constructed by FDR's New Deal CCC. The cottages rent for $65–135.

Spacious wooded sites at a 140-site **campground** go for $7–19; hookups are available.

Columbus

Columbus sits at the banks of the Chattahoochee River on Georgia's "West Coast" border with Alabama. Here the Chattahoochee drops 125 feet in the space of 2.5 miles. It has sculpted the region's history as an ancient Native American settlement, as the final city in the 13 original colonies, as a Civil War target, and as a Southern mill town. Columbus today makes the most of this riparian heritage with a renovated historic district behind an attractive Riverwalk promenade.

Columbus is home to Columbus State University and the largest infantry-training center in the world, at Fort Benning. It's also the birthplace of several Southern legends—Coca-Cola entrepreneur Robert F. Woodruff, the "Mother of the Blues" Ma Rainey, and author Carson McCullers, whose novels *The Heart Is a Lonely Hunter* and *Member of the Wedding* provide moving personal vignettes of small-town Southern life in towns much like Columbus once was.

Columbus lies at the end of I-185, which deadends at the military base. Several historical, cultural, and natural attractions can be found a short day trip from Columbus (see the *Pine Mountain and Vicinity* and *Jimmy Carter Country* sections).

History

Southeasterners had a long history along the navigable lengths of the Chattahoochee—excavations in the river valley have uncovered Archaic period habitation from 5000 B.C. The Creek dominated several Native American groups in the area around "Bull Creek" when the first Europeans appeared on the scene. Starting as a trading post, the town developed into the farthest-west frontier of colonial America, though the city wasn't chartered until 1828. Here industry flourished on fall-line water power, and when the Civil War broke out, the factories converted to weapons production.

Untouched by the war until 1865, Columbus was finally attacked by Union General James H. Wilson's troops (remembered locally as "Wilson's raiders") in the last land battle of the Civil War on April 16, 1865. Wilson had not yet heard of Lee's surrender at Appomattox a week earlier, and he left the city in ruins after setting fire to almost all its industry (a blessing in disguise, as the modernized rebuilt mills propelled economic recovery). Textile mills flourished, and traditional water power was later converted into hydroelectricity.

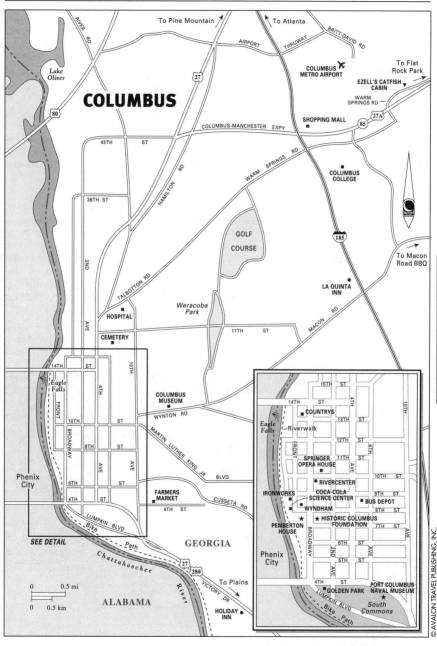

Heartland Georgia

SIGHTS

Riverwalk

The 12-mile Riverwalk offers a scenic waterfront park along the clay-stained Chattahoochee, from the falls at Fieldcrest Mills south to where the path winds inland, and ending up at the National Infantry Museum. Studded with fountains and monuments and with nice views of the falls, old brick mills, Ironworks, and arched bridges, the downtown Riverwalk makes a scenic place to stroll, bike, or skate.

Downtown

On a bluff at the water's edge, the city's 30-block commercial district features several renovated blocks of Broad Street on either side of a landscaped median. New businesses are gaining a foothold and drawing more people downtown to restaurants and cafés. The compact district is easily seen on foot or by bike.

Many old buildings have been recycled for modern uses, such as the **Wyndham Hotel,** 800 Front Ave., carved out of a former mill, and the old **Ironworks** across the street, now a convention center and performance venue.

The elegant 1871 **Springer Opera House,** 103 10th St., 706/327-3688, is the centerpiece of the historic district. Officially designated the "State Theater of Georgia," the intimate theater continues to hold performances and contains a small museum highlighting luminaries who have graced the Springer's stage, including Oscar Wilde, Ethel Barrymore, and John Philip Sousa. Guided tours are available by appointment.

The 245,000-square-foot **RiverCenter for the Performing Arts,** 13 E. 10th St., 706/653-7993, provides three performance halls for theater, dance, concerts, and is the home of the Columbus Symphony Orchestra.

Uptown

Adjacent to the commercial center is the Uptown historic residential district of tidy Victorian homes along several cobblestone blocks of lower Broadway. The district is bordered at the river by the Chattahoochee Promenade, which is an attractive park with a Liberty Bell replica, a Civil War cannon, and a Carson McCullers memorial.

The **Historic Columbus Foundation,** 700 Broadway, 706/323-7979, historiccolumbus.com, housed in an 1870 Italianate villa, offers guided

The 12-mile Chattahoochee Riverwalk in Columbus is a delightful stroll.

© KAP STANN

walking tours of its historic headquarters and nearby landmark homes. The foundation distributes walking-tour maps describing the architectural history of more than two dozen historic buildings in the area.

At the southern foot of the historic district, Bladau's Goetchius House is a nice restaurant for winding up a visit.

Coca-Cola Space Science Center

The city's splashy science center, 701 Front Ave., 706/649-1470, ccssc.org, features an Omnisphere theater (next-generation planetarium) for laser-light shows, science-fiction movies, films designed for young children, and changing space shows, along with an observatory (call for show schedule and fees). Lobby exhibits (no charge) include the snout of a space shuttle and an Apollo capsule, and the gift shop sells great glow-in-the-dark space stuff and freeze-dried astronaut food. It's open Tues.–Fri. 10 A.M.–4 P.M., Sat. 11:30A.M.–6 P.M. and Sun. 1:30–4 P.M.

Port Columbus Civil War Naval Center

By the South Commons ball fields, the mammoth Port Columbus Museum, 1002 Victory Dr., 706/327-9798, portcolumbus.org, is built around the 225-foot-long salvaged hull of a Confederate gunboat sunk in the Chattahoochee River. A catwalk guides you past the structure, and interactive displays explain Lincoln's Anaconda strategy and reveal the less-told stories of Civil War navies, beyond the ironclads and *Merrimac.* They schedule frequent talks on such subjects as Civil War medicine, music at sea, and the like.

It's open daily 9 A.M.–5 P.M. except Christmas. Admission is $4 for adults, $3 for students, and free for children age six and under.

Columbus Museum of Art

The pristine and spacious Columbus Museum, 1251 Wynnton Rd., 706/649-0713, columbus-museum.com, is the major arts center for the region, housing historical, cultural, and visual-arts exhibits. Catch the film *Chattahoochee Legacy,* shown throughout the day, and the historical exhibit surrounding the theater (particularly the

SCHOOL OF THE AMERICAS

Fort Benning is notorious as the home of the embattled School of the Americas (SOA). After a decade of protests by opponents charging that the school trains people to prop up military dictatorships in Central and South America, SOA was closed in December 2000. It was replaced by the Western Hemisphere Institute for Security Cooperation. Although the new school has added courses in human rights, due process, and the role of the military in a democratic society, critics charge that the institute is simply a 'repackaged SOA,' and protests continue.

Each November, thousands of protesters gather at the gates to Fort Benning to memorialize those who have died at the hands of soldiers trained at the school, marking the anniversary of the assassination of six Jesuit priests and two women supporters in El Salvador in 1989, for which Salvadoran army officers trained at SOA were found complicit.

Actors Martin Sheen and Susan Saradon have been among the high-profile protesters in years past, which also includes a wide coalition of such peace groups as Veterans for Peace, Witness for Peace, Pax Christi, Latin America Solidarity Coalition, and Catholic Worker, among others engaging in nonviolent civil disobedience. Some local hotels offer discounted protester rates.

Learn more through SOA Watch, soaw.org.

southeastern Native American exhibit). Its permanent collection is enhanced by traveling shows and special programs, and there's a hands-on children's room downstairs. The museum is open Tues.–Sat. 10 A.M.–5 P.M. and Sun. 1–5 P.M. Admission is free.

They have an Uptown branch, 1004 Broadway, featuring contemporary visual art, including folk art and nontraditional media. It's open Tues.–Sat. noon–8 P.M. There is no charge.

Oxbow Meadows Environmental Center

This environmental center, 3535 S. Lumpkin Rd., 706/687-4090, oxbow.colstate.edu, south of

Heartland Georgia

downtown, highlights the geographic feature of the oxbow, illustrative of how Southern rivers meander below the fall line. Situated on 1,600 acres of reclaimed land, the center is open Tues.–Sat. 10 A.M.–5 P.M. and Sun. noon–5 P.M. There is no charge.

National Infantry Museum at Fort Benning

The National Infantry Museum, on the Fort Benning military reservation, Baltzell Ave., 706/545-2958, traces American infantry history from the French and Indian War to Afghanistan with three floors of exhibits of weaponry, artillery, and military vehicles, along with uniforms, medals, and such artifacts as bugles, Civil War dominos, and a gas mask for a horse. It's open Mon.–Fri. 10 A.M.–4:30 P.M. and Sat.–Sun. 12:30–4:30 P.M. Admission is free. Note that the dress code forbids too casual wear, such as sleeveless shirts. A bike path leads from the Riverwalk to the museum.

RECREATION

Spectator Sports

The **Columbus Redstixx,** farm team for the Cleveland Indians, plays ball April to August at the 4,000-seat Golden Park, 100 4th St., on the Columbus South Commons, an attractive site of several ball fields and where the 1996 Olympic women's fast-pitch softball competition was held. Call 706/653-4482 for schedules and ticket information. **Georgia Pride,** a women's softball league, also plays at South Commons.

The **Columbus Cottonmouths** of the professional Central Hockey League play ice hockey at the Civic Center. Call 706/571-0086 for schedules and ticket information.

Outdoor Recreation

Out by the airport, a natural rock slide at **Flat Rock Park,** on Flat Rock Rd., offers a slippery down-home swimming hole.

Fishing folk and boat owners are drawn to large placid lakes formed by Chattahoochee River impounds directly north (Lake Oliver, Goat Rock Lake, and Lake Harding; the latter is the largest and has the most services), and south (Walter F. George Reservoir). The small marina at scenic Lake Oliver north of town is the closest launch site.

ENTERTAINMENT

Performing Arts

The beautiful **Springer Opera House,** 103 10th St., 706/327-3688, springeroperahouse.org, an intimate, red, plush-and-gilt jewel box of a theater, hosts musicals, dramatic performances, and children's shows (*Driving Miss Daisy* and the bluegrass gospel musical *Smoke on the Mountain* were on a recent bill).

The new 245,000-square-foot **RiverCenter for the Performing Arts,** 900 Broadway, 706/323-5059, provides three performance halls for theater, dance, and concerts and is the home of the Columbus Symphony Orchestra.

The **Liberty Theater,** 821 8th Ave., 706/653-7566, where Cab Calloway, Ma Rainey, and Lena Horne have performed, now serves as a cultural center that hosts performances and concerts.

The **Columbus Georgia Convention and Trade Center,** on Front St., 706/327-4522, recycled from the 19th-century Ironworks, is the scene of such large events as the city's annual Riverfest in April, which draws up to 100,000 participants over three days. Rooms spill out onto a riverfront plaza beside the Riverwalk and railroad bridge.

Nightlife

Downtown, **The Loft,** 1036 Broad St., 706/322-7410, features live jazz, folk, comedy, and an open mic night in a small, low-key café setting. The **Uptown Tap,** 1024 Broadway, 706/653-8277, features a weekly JaegerFest, martini nights, ladies nights, and SIN (Service Industry Night).

See Friday's *Columbus Ledger-Enquirer* for entertainment listings, or better yet, find the free weekly *Playgrounds.*

Cinema

Hollywood Connection, 1683 Whittlesey Rd. off Hwy. 80, 706/571-3456, offers a complex of family entertainments, including 10 movie theaters (four with stadium seating), a carousel, an arcade, laser tag, a restaurant, and roller-skating to contemporary Christian music in its 125,000-square-foot center north of town.

In the cinema complex west of I-185's airport exit, the **Screening Room** shows international films.

Festivals

The city's largest annual event is held the last weekend in April: the **Riverfest Weekend** city fair features a barbecue "Pig Jig," a children's carnival, outdoor arts and crafts, and plenty of folk food, music, and traditions on the riverbank.

Fort Benning's **Fourth of July** celebration presents an amazing military pageant of skydiving paratroopers, gleaming bands, single-step parades in full BDU (battle dress uniform), and fireworks from the folks who know how.

ACCOMMODATIONS AND FOOD

Lodging

The **Wyndham Columbus,** 800 Front Ave., 706/324-1800, is in the shell of a century-old gristmill at the boundary between the historic commercial district and historic residential district. It's the city's "Big House" and offers a pool, lounge, and restaurant (rooms start at $100).

The 1870 **Rothschild-Pound House,** 201 7th St., 706/322-4075 or 800/585-4075, features a wraparound porch, 14-foot ceilings, mahogany fireplace mantels, and antique beds. It offers 14 guest rooms starting at $125 for doubles in the main house and in surrounding cottages.

Many modern motel chains are represented out at interstate exits, including La Quinta Inn, Sheraton, Holiday Inn, Budgetel, and Days Inn.

Food and Drink

Downtown, the **Cannon Brewpub,** 1041 Broadway, 706/653-2337, offers a casual, comfortable place downtown for a nicely mixed crowd hungry for wood-fired pizza, burgers, and pasta plates, washed down with home brew (the amber Red Jacket Ale is one favorite). It's open daily for lunch and dinner.

Country's on Broad, 1329 Broadway, 706/563-7604, set in a 1930s bus depot, offers seating at booths, the counter, or in a vintage bus. It's a lively, brightly lit, inexpensive choice for barbecue plates, burgers, and salads.

Minnie's Uptown Restaurant, 100 8th St. at 1st Ave., 706/322-2766, offers cafeteria service for hearty meat-and-three plates for $5.25 in the Uptown neighborhood (call 706/322-1466 for a recording of daily specials). It's open for lunch weekdays only.

For dress up, go Uptown to **Bladau's Goetchius House** (GET-chez), 405 Broadway, 706/324-4863, for frog legs bourguignonne, châteaubriand, swordfish, or lobster in the 1839 mansion's formally appointed dining room, or just meet for a drink and oysters in the speakeasy downstairs; then surface for espresso at the patio overlooking the Chattahoochee River. It's open 5–10 P.M., until 11 P.M. Fri.–Sat., closed Sunday.

Beyond downtown there are a few local classics. The hardcore **Macon Road Barbecue,** on Avalon Rd. at Macon Rd., 706/563-0542, is set in a traditional smokehouse cabin in the woods a mile or so east of I-185's Macon Road exit (closed Sun.).

The lunch counter at the 75-year-old **Dinglewood Pharmacy,** 1939 Wynnton Rd., 706/322-0616, concocts the local specialty "scrambled dog"—a hot dog buried under chili, onions, and oyster crackers (an acquired taste). Their chili was served in the White House during the Carter administration and was served to Prince Charles in the Governor's Mansion in 1976.

Ezell's Catfish Cabin, 4001 Warm Springs Rd., 706/568-1149, is a comfortable family restaurant that fries up all-you-can-eat catfish, popcorn shrimp, and other seafood plates (it's a mile or so east of I-185). On Mon.–Thurs. they only serve dinner; Fri.–Sun., they serve lunch and dinner.

OTHER PRACTICALITIES

Getting There and Around

By car from Atlanta, take I-85 to I-185 south—keep to the speed limit along I-185; it's a notorious speed trap.

At the **Columbus Airport,** 706/324-2449, 10 minutes north of downtown, a handful of com-

M

Heartland Georgia

mercial carriers operate shuttle service to Atlanta and other destinations, but Atlanta travelers may find ground transportation more affordable and practical. **Groome Transportation,** 706/324-3939 or 800/584-6735, groometrans.com, runs shuttle van service between Atlanta's Hartsfield-Jackson Airport and Fort Benning.

Greyhound, 818 4th Ave. at 9th St., 706/323-5417, also serves the Atlanta-to-Columbus route from its downtown terminal.

Information and Services

The **Georgia Visitors Center,** on I-185 north of town, 706/649-7455, provides statewide information daily 8:30 A.M.–5:30 P.M.

Downtown across from the Riverwalk near the bridge, the **Columbus Convention and Visitors Bureau,** 900 Front Ave., Columbus, GA 31901, 706/322-1613 or 800/999-1613, visit-columbusga.com, is open Mon.–Sat. for maps, brochures, and other information.

South Georgia

The state's prime agricultural region, South Georgia remains overwhelmingly rural today. Only two cities of any size—Albany and Valdosta—bring urban development to this coastal plain region, which occupies half of Georgia's land. Within this broad expanse of peanut fields, peach orchards, and piney woods—where tractors, pickups, and logging trucks outnumber cars—visitors discover the remnants of Native American, antebellum, and folk traditions, and the most primordial wilderness in the nation.

The southwestern plain is particularly intriguing. Jimmy Carter's hometown of Plains sits around an unusual set of historical, artistic, and natural attractions, including the Andersonville Civil War POW camp and the worldwide headquarters of Habitat for Humanity. The Plantation Trace region, centered on Thomasville, is a pine-scented area of old homes and resorts that attest to its history as a cotton-producing area before the Civil War and an elite retreat at the turn of the century.

The region's clay-stained rivers course through fertile and swampy bottomlands in the flat terrain. To the west, the Chattahoochee River borders Alabama and joins with the Flint River at Lake Seminole. In the midsection, the Alapaha and Withlacoochee Rivers attract paddlers to their graceful Southern currents.

Farther east, I-75 cuts through the heart of wiregrass country. As part of the main route from the Midwest to the vacation mecca of Florida, this stretch of freeway is one of the nation's busiest. Under the corridor's iconographic spires advertising every franchise known to man lie a few pre-neon pleasures, such as Agrirama's living-history village.

Must-Sees

Look for **M** to find the sights and activities you can't miss and **N** for the best dining and lodging.

M **National Prisoner of War Museum:** On the site of the Civil War's most notorious POW camp, a powerful national museum now chronicles the plight of American POWs in all wars, up to the present day (page 191).

M **Habitat for Humanity:** This worldwide movement started here in Americus, and today, Habitat's world village displays houses constructed around the world, from local materials and to match local conditions and cultures (page 192).

M **Jimmy Carter National Historic District:** President Carter still lives in the town where he was born and raised; it's now preserved as a monument to the man and also to the American ideal of a world leader rising up from a small farming community (page 194).

M **Providence Canyon:** Georgia's "Little Grand Canyon" presents an unexpectedly Southwestern landscape to this remote borderland near Alabama, with stratified red rock seen close-up on trails at the rim or in the canyon (page 196).

M **Pasaquan:** The otherworldly vision of local eccentric Eddie Martin, known as St. EOM, is de-

© KAP STANN

Okefenokee Swamp boardwalk

picted across every surface of this compound in the Georgia woods (page 198).

M **Kolomoki Mounds:** Set off in a corner of the state, Kolomoki is a quiet place to reflect on these massive silent monuments and an excuse to wander the archaeological relics in the small museum, canoe on the still lake, and watch grass grow (page 199).

M **Stephen C. Foster State Park:** Perched out on the peninsula into the Okefenokee Swamp, this state park takes you to the deep swamp, and boat trips go further in to Billy's Island, a remote wilderness strewn with remnants of a 19th-century lumber town (page 217).

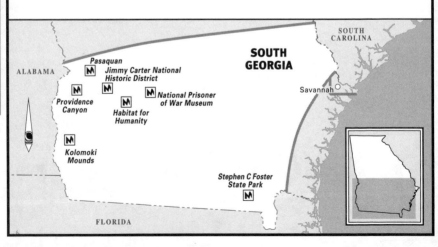

East of I-75, South Georgia's prime attraction is hidden among hundreds of square miles of pine barrens in the southeastern interior. The Okefenokee Swamp offers one of the Southeast's best wilderness adventures, with a natural history, botany, and resident wildlife all its own—the largest population of alligators in the state, turtles, frogs, bears, and birds enjoy the distinct habitats of the swamp's cypress stands, quivering islands, and open prairies. The swamp serves as headwaters to both the blackwater Suwannee and St. Marys Rivers.

Culturally, the southernmost third of the state is divided at an imaginary boundary called the "gnat line"; subtleties separate the folk traditions of South Georgia's Wiregrass region from those of the more urbanized Piedmont, directly north. This folk heritage can best be seen at the region's many homespun festivals, such as Gnat Days and mule parades, sugarcane-grinding parties and turkey-calling contests. But at any time, you can visit roadside stands, antebellum house museums, tobacco auctions, or peanut-packing factories to get a flavor for the region.

PLANNING YOUR TIME

The distances between attractions in the region and its high temperatures make for long road trips, but one exception is the compact and accessible set of diversions around Plains, easily reached from Macon. Aim for Americus, where the Windsor Hotel can serve as a good base of operations. Spring and fall are most temperate, and many of the region's events are scheduled at this time. It's not a highly populated or thickly traveled region, so reservations are not necessary and not hard to come by. Operating hours of some attractions and businesses may be seasonal, so it's a good idea to call and check before a long detour.

HISTORY

Georgia's oldest aboriginal mound center, Kolomoki Mounds, is evidence of a culture that thrived on the banks of the Chattahoochee 700 years ago. This ancient civilization spawned the modern-era Creek nation, named for its riverine culture. Later, some Creek left the tribe, becoming known as the Seminole (which means "runaway" in Creek). All indigenous groups were exiled by the U.S. government in the Indian Removal of 1836. Most headed on the Trail of Tears to Oklahoma; the Seminole managed to retreat farther south, into the swamps of Florida. Representatives of these and other Native American nations return to the area each May for the Chehaw National Indian Festival, a celebration of their traditional heritage on ancestral homelands.

Hernando de Soto was the first European to explore the area. He marched 6,000 troops through the area around the Flint River in 1540 on his search for gold throughout the Southeast. Yet South Georgia remained the last region of the state to be settled by Europeans; the Chattahoochee remained wild frontier until the mid-19th century. Then it developed with a flourish, particularly as planters recognized that cotton grew well in the rich, dark soils. Many plantations were built in the southwestern part of the state, while the pine barrens of the southeastern interior were logged.

To facilitate shipping out the agricultural products grown in the interior, settlements first developed at rivers, yet the earliest communities were made up mostly of subsistence farmers. The war destroyed the cotton plantations in the southwest, but that scenic region readily recovered as an elite retreat for wealthy Northerners. As the saying goes, they found that "a Yankee was worth two bales of cotton and was twice as easy to pick."

When the railroads arrived in the late 19th century, a traditional, near feudal way of life came to an abrupt end, bringing newcomers, modernization, and industry to isolated rural communities. Entrepreneurs saw a fortune in the virgin yellow-pine forests, which were clearcut for lumber and replaced by cropland. Farmers turned to raising cotton for cash instead of growing subsistence crops, and the resulting oversupply of cotton depressed prices and depleted lands, even before the boll weevil blight took its toll. But as agriculture faltered, industry boomed; towns developed around railroads and manufacturing centers, with the logging industry leading the way.

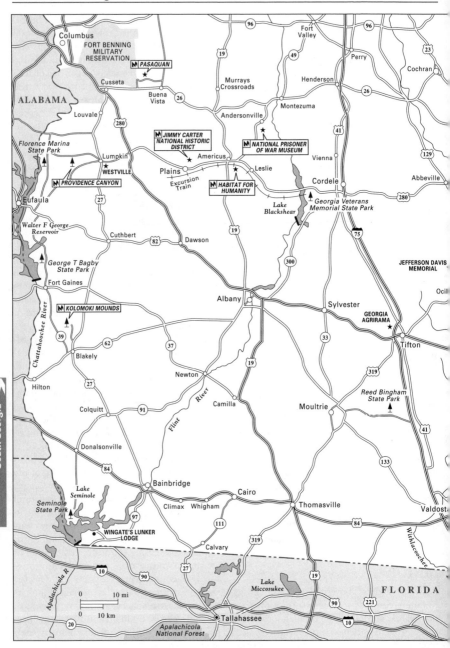

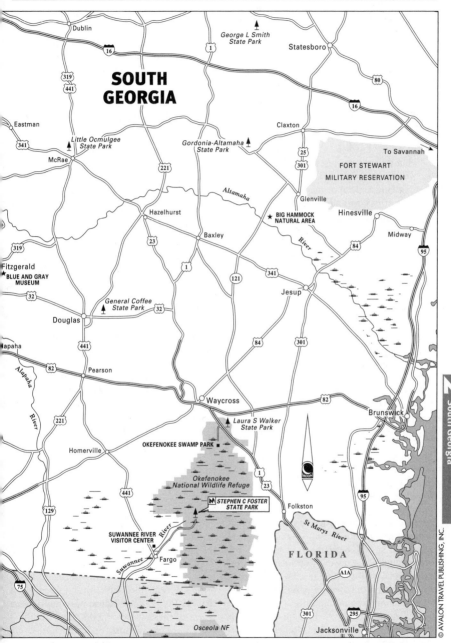

Logging remains a major industry today—for paper and pulpwood production as well as for lumber—but other crops grew in importance. Now South Georgia is the center of production for the state's number one cash crop—peanuts—as well as for pecans, peaches, and many other agricultural products. Tourism became a contributing factor to the southwestern region's economy as early as the 1870s. And since the opening of I-75—one of the busiest stretches of freeway in the nation—tourism has had an impact on the south-central region as well.

Jimmy Carter Country

Below the fall line between the Chattahoochee and Flint Rivers, where the scent of peanut fields overwhelms even the magnolias, a typical South Georgia landscape appears. Farmhouses with militarily trim lawns adjoin shacks with swept yards, mailboxes are crafted from plowshares, tractors slow traffic on country highways, and drivers lift a few fingers off the wheel to greet passing cars. At night, electric bug zappers glow iridescent blue and interrupt the nocturnal drone of the cicadas.

Within this ordinary backcountry, visitors see traces of an extraordinary heritage. Here a peanut farmer rose to international leadership, an idealistic commune gave birth to a worldwide movement to create liveable housing, and an eccentric folk artist constructed his otherworldly vision. Here too, Civil War ghosts haunt a notorious POW camp, and villages recreate 1850s Georgia in remote settings that are eerily convincing.

MONTEZUMA AND VICINITY

The sister cities of Montezuma and Oglethorpe were founded in the mid-19th century at facing banks of the Flint River. When the Flint overflowed its banks in 1994, downtown Montezuma was almost entirely under water. A few miles east of the river, mailboxes display distinctly German names, the likes of a Hershberger or Schwartzimmer, all Samuels or Nathans. Here 100 Mennonite families operate dairy farms and carry on a traditional way of life, as they have since 1954, when 11 families transplanted themselves here from Virginia (expanding military bases there propelled them to leave). Like the Amish, followers of the faith wear plain clothes—bonnets and long skirts for the women; men wear beards, caps, and suspenders. Yet unlike the Amish, Mennonites do not forsake modern machinery.

At **Yoder's Deitsch Haus,** 478/472-2024, members of the community serve a hearty cafeteria-style buffet in a large restaurant open to the public. Choose entrées such as roast beef, fried chicken, or Texas hash, each served with two vegetables, rice, and iced tea; pick up treats and fresh bread from the bakery around back. Three miles east of Montezuma on Hwy. 26, the restaurant is open for lunch Tues.–Sat. and dinner Thurs.–Tues.

A gift shop next door sells some of the best handmade country crafts this side of North Georgia: furniture that's either fine or rough-hewn, whirligigs, birdhouses, dolls in Mennonite garb, quilts, and homemade foods and candies.

(Visitors would show respect to dress conservatively here and in other rural areas; overexposed limbs and feet draw unwelcome attention, so keep a stash of cover-ups handy.)

ANDERSONVILLE
History
During the 19th century, Andersonville was a small Georgia village near the end of the Southwestern Railroad. In early 1864, Camp Sumter was established here to house Union prisoners who were moved south, away from the front lines in Richmond, Virginia. The POW camp grew to become the largest and most notorious of all Confederate military prisons. During the 14 months it existed, more than 45,000 Union soldiers were imprisoned here—of these, almost 13,000 died from disease, poor sanitation, malnutrition, overcrowding, or exposure to the elements. Once

On the site of a notorious Civil War POW camp, this powerful museum memorializes all American POWs.

its conditions became public knowledge after the war, public outrage was so great that the camp's commandant was hanged in Washington, D.C., in 1865—the only person to be convicted and executed for war crimes during the Civil War.

Also in 1865, the **Andersonville National Cemetery** was built here, adjacent to the old camp site to inter POWs and Civil War soldiers known and unknown. States from around the Union sent monuments to commemorate the loss of life. The veterans' cemetery remains in operation today.

ⓜ National Prisoner of War Museum

Opened in 1998, the National Prisoner of War Museum, on Hwy. 49 10 miles north of Americus, 496 Cemetery Rd., 229/924-0343, www.nps.gov/ande, is a hauntingly powerful memorial to American prisoners of war. Outside of the Holocaust Museum in Washington, D.C., it might well be the most powerful we've seen. (In fact, the quality of this museum resembles world-class museums in the nation's

capital.) Yet as strongly as anyone would recommend visiting, parents should be aware that it is designed to disturb; exercise caution with young children.

Some of its most raw exhibits are from the Vietnam War era, where bamboo "tiger cages" invite visitors to consider what life was like for prisoners trapped within. Next door a tiny dark cell has cast-iron leg shackles cemented in place. On the back wall, a bank of video monitors loops interviews with POW families to suggest the agony endured by those at home.

The exhibits lead visitors from the museum outside to the former **POW camp site,** where a reconstructed camp stockade leads the visitor to imagine tens of thousands of soldiers confined within its small frame.

In addition to the well-crafted exhibits, the museum maintains a POW database and research library (available by appointment), along with a bookshop that has an excellent, unsentimental selection of titles on military history. The museum is open daily 8:30 A.M.–5 P.M., closed on Christmas and New Year's Day (no charge for admission).

Andersonville Village

Off Hwy. 49 south of the cemetery, the Civil War village of Andersonville was where 45,000 captured Federal soldiers arrived by rail in 1864. A controversial monument erected by the United Daughters of the Confederacy memorializes Captain Henry Wirz, who was the keeper of the Andersonville prison; he was tried, convicted, and hanged by the U.S. government for war crimes.

The five-acre park has a few small shops and picnic areas around its historic depot, which now serves as a visitors center, 114 Church St., 229/924-2558. It's open daily 9 A.M.–5 P.M. (no charge).

AMERICUS

Founded in 1831, Americus (population 18,000) first gained statewide recognition as the home of the grand Windsor Hotel, built in 1892. With Jimmy Carter's campaign for president in 1976 from neighboring Plains, this county seat was brought to national attention. Today the town is best known as the global headquarters of Habitat for Humanity. An attractive, compact town with interesting people from all over, Americus makes a good base of operations to explore the region.

Downtown, the central square is dominated by the landmark Windsor Hotel, which is surrounded by shops and cafés. Down the street, the 1920s **Rylander Theater,** on W. Lamar St., 229/931-0001, www.rylander.org, has been renovated into an inviting 600-seat performing-arts venue with a full season of theatrical and musical performances. The town's historic residential neighborhood can be found behind the square around Lee, Taylor, and College Streets.

The **visitors center,** within the Windsor hotel at 123 W. Lamar St., 229/928-6059, directs visitors to the county's attractions and distributes county maps. It's open Mon.–Fri. 9 A.M.–5 P.M., Sat. 10 A.M.–2 P.M.

⋈ Habitat for Humanity

The global headquarters of Habitat for Humanity International (HFHI) are downtown, 121 Habitat St. at W. Lamar, Americus, GA 31709, 229/924-6935 or 800/HABITAT (800/422-4828), www.habitat.org. A nonprofit housing ministry, Habitat for Humanity developed out of the personal vision of Millard and Linda Fuller.

Millard Fuller had been a successful Alabama lawyer and entrepreneur before he and his wife decided to reevaluate their priorities—they sold everything they owned, donated most of the proceeds to charity, and joined the Koinonia farming commune, which inspired them to start their housing ministry.

Since the Fullers founded Habitat in 1976, the organization has overseen the construction of more than 100,000 houses in 79 countries around the world. The ecumenical organization depends on the work of thousands of volunteers who work alongside new owners to raise affordable housing. (HFHI maintains a simple RV park in town with hookups; it's for volunteers only.)

HFHI's **Global Village and Discovery Center** displays sample houses that Habitat has constructed in 15 countries around the world, including Kenya, Papua New Guinea, India, and Guatemala. It's an interesting six-acre house zoo that demonstrates the need to adapt to varying local materials, conditions, and customs. (Critics have suggested that the "before" displays may be more than is needed.) Free tours Mon.–Fri.; call for times.

Koinonia Farms

Sixty years ago, the racially integrated farming commune of Koinonia (koy-no-NEE-ah, a Greek term for fellowship) represented a radical departure from local cultural norms and was fiercely condemned by local segregationists. The ecumenical Christian community nevertheless managed to sustain itself with a mail-order candy making operation. After the Fullers joined the community and founded **Habitat for Humanity,** the first Habitat development was constructed at Koinonia, 1324 Dawson Rd., (Hwy. 49S), southwest of Americus toward Plains, 229/924-0391, www.koinonia-partners.org. Today, the small community continues to farm, make candy, and live by its utopian ideals. Stop by for a tin of bittersweet pecan bark or other organic goodies, and if it's

Jimmy and Rosalynn Carter put their hands where their hearts are, at work on a Habitat for Humanity project.

not too busy, someone will show you around. If you're interested in a longer stay, inquire about the volunteer program, which provides room-and-board and a small stipend to selected folks over 18 willing to help out around the farm for summers or longer. Inquire about RV camping by advance reservation or about joining community members at the noon meal for a small fee. The office is open Mon.–Fri. 8 A.M.–5 P.M.

Accommodations and Food

The grand **Ⓝ Windsor Hotel,** 125 W. Lamar St., 229/924-1555 or 888/297-9567, www.windsor-americus.com, occupies an entire city block in the center of town. An elegant 49-room brick hotel built in 1892, the sprawling Victorian hotel features an attractive three-story central atrium, with the original sloping wood floors, crystal chandeliers, and carved oak paneling. Rooms are modern relative to the lobby, with some period reproductions and ceiling fans along with color TVs, phones, central heat and air (from $99).

The fourth-floor honeymoon suite, in the round tower, is furnished with a tasseled canopy bed.

The **Windsor Dining Room** serves the most proper meal in town, with such entrées as roasted pork loin and Dijon rack of lamb at dinner (entrées from $15). They also serve breakfast, a luncheon buffet, and dinner (midday on Sunday).

With a 2nd-floor veranda overlooking the main street, the hotel's **Floyd's Pub,** offers casual meals and snacks, such as a nice chicken Caesar salad or quesadilla. **The Station,** 222 W. Lamar St., 229/931-5398, serves such railroad-themed entrées as Porter's Prime Rib and Conductor's Crepes (entrées from $12). It's open for dinner Tues.–Sat.

PLAINS

Founded in 1940 as the Plains of Dura, Plains is a small town even by South Georgia standards (population 716)—not much more than a strip of shops surrounded by peanut fields and country roads. Now it's known worldwide as the birthplace of the 39th president of the United States; the town was thrust into the national limelight when then-governor Jimmy Carter launched his presidential campaign from the old Plains depot.

The **Georgia Visitor Information Center,** east of town, 1763 Hwy. 280, 229/824-7477, operates a room-reservation service and distributes statewide information from a lakeside cabin. It's open daily 8:30 A.M.–5:30 P.M.

Jimmy Carter National Historic District

The **Jimmy Carter Museum,** 300 N. Bond St., 229/824-4104, www.nps.gov/jica, is housed in the old Plains High School where Carter went to school (his prescient principal, Julia Coleman, often told the students "someday one of you will grow up to be president of the United States"). There are several classrooms restored to the Carter boyhood era, as well as personal exhibits on the Carter family and on his political career. A biographical film screens in the auditorium, and

there's also a touching video of the Carters walking people through their home in Plains, pointing out the furniture Jimmy made and the treasured presents from family and world leaders. Hours are 9 A.M.–5 P.M. daily, except Thanksgiving, Christmas, and New Year's.

Self-guided driving-tour maps (with accompanying audiocassette rental) direct visitors to several sites around town. The gift shop sells books by and about Carter, as well as such souvenirs as Carter–Mondale campaign buttons. (And don't miss the 13-foot-high **Smiling Goober** up from the high school—an irresistible photo op.)

From the quaint 1888 **Plains Depot,** 229/824-3413, the oldest building in Plains, Carter ran his first presidential campaign in 1975. Today they show mementos from the campaign. The depot is across from a small park at the tracks downtown, across from brother Billy Carter's service station.

At **Maranatha Baptist Church,** on Buena Vista Rd., Jimmy Carter serves as a deacon and teaches the adult Sunday school class around 33

downtown Plains

© KAP STANN

out of 52 Sundays each year at 10 A.M. before worship services at 11 A.M. All are welcome to attend services and Sunday school at the 300-seat sanctuary; the church receives around 10,000 visitors a year.

The private, 4.5-acre **Carter Family Compound,** 209 Woodland Dr., off Hwy. 27, is off-limits and is presided over by the Secret Service. Built in 1961, the ranch house is the only home the Carters have ever owned. See the video tour at the Jimmy Carter Museum.

Jimmy Carter Boyhood Farm

The Jimmy Carter Boyhood Farm, 229/824-3413, restores to Depression-era appearance the single-story white clapboard house where the former president was raised. A walking tour around the 17-acre site leads past the swept yard, tennis court, store, barn, blacksmith shop, and gristmill. The restoration and exhibits seek to convey how growing up on a rural Southern farm in a predominantly African American community influenced Carter's character and values.

The farm is about 2.5 miles from the center of town, in the community of Archery. It's operated by the Park Service and is open daily 10 A.M.–4 P.M.

Southwest Georgia Excursion Train

SAM Shortline, based at Georgia Veterans State Park, in Cordele, 229/276-2715 or 800/864-7275, www.samshortline.com, runs vintage 1940s cars 40 miles between Archery and Cordele, with stops in Plains, Americus, and Leslie (home of the Georgia Rural Telephone Museum) before its eastern terminus, off I-75. The route passes through the bucolic countryside and stops within a mile's walk of local attractions, hotels, and restaurants. Call or visit the website for schedules and fees.

Accommodations and Food

A former Carter family home, the **Plains Bed and Breakfast Inn,** 100 W. Church St., 229/824-7252, offers B&B lodging in four rooms in a two-story, pink-and-ivory Victorian house on Hwy. 280, across from the depot. The house was once a boardinghouse where Jimmy Carter's mother, Miss Lillian, lived when she met Earl Carter. Rates start at $80 and include a full Southern breakfast.

Opened in 2003, the **Plains Historic Inn,** 106 Main St., 229/824-4529, offers seven guest rooms above a ramshackle antique flea-market shop downtown. The suites are each decorated to reflect a different era in President Carter's life, from the 1920s to the 1980s (the 1970s is the presidential suite), complete with magazines and knickknacks from the times. Rates start at $85 and include continental breakfast.

Mom's Kitchen, 203 Church St., 229/824-5458, is a local favorite for lunch and dinner buffets for around $6.

LESLIE

Georgia Rural Telephone Museum

Nine miles east of Americus via Hwy. 280, this quaint museum, 229/874-4786, claims to hold the world's largest collection of telephone memorabilia. Here in the renovated 1920s cotton warehouse it occupies, you can see such exhibits as the early liquid transmitter from 1876 and a model of Alexander Graham Bell's workshop. It's open Mon.–Fri. 9 A.M.–3:30 P.M. Adult admission is $3.

LUMPKIN AND VICINITY

Lumpkin's major attraction, Westville, re-creates an 1850s village, and anachronistic Lumpkin itself appears frozen in time. Among the historic buildings in town are three right that are located around the square: **Bedingfield Inn,** once a stop on the old stagecoach route, now a visitors center, 229/838-6419; **Dr. Hatchett's Drug Store Museum,** and **Singer Co.,** which bills itself as "the oldest hardware store in Georgia."

Follow Main St. one block east to an impressively folksy collection of **whirligigs** in front of the home of Mr. John Byrd. You'll likely see Mr. Byrd himself, clad in overalls, repairing his handiwork or tending his flowers outside.

Eat at **Michelle's,** 109 Main St., 229/838-9991, where they serve a generous buffet of catfish, rib-eye steak, fried chicken, assorted vegetables, cornbread, and breakfast all day in a homey little place (open 5:30 A.M.–9 P.M. daily).

Westville

One of the state's top three living-history centers, Westville is an authentically re-created 19th-century village on 57 acres outside Lumpkin (a mile and a half from the square; follow signs). Its 32 structures include a plantation house, schoolhouse, smithy, and bootery. Descendants of the original residents wear period dress, perform traditional crafts, and answer questions in character; just walking along the double-rutted red-clay roads recalls a bygone era.

The place comes to life during special folkways demonstrations in early April, early May, on July 4th, and in mid- to late December. But the biggest festival runs from mid-October to mid-November—the 17-day **Fair of 1850** brings homemade music, open-hearth cooking, sugarcane grinding, syrup making, basket making, weaving, woodworking, and demonstrations of the only animal-powered cotton gin in Georgia.

This private, nonprofit educational museum, 1 Martin Luther King Jr. Dr., 229/838-6310 or 888/733-1850, www.westville.org, is open Tues.–Sat. 10 A.M.–5 P.M., Sun. 1–5 P.M. Admission is $10 for adults, $8 for seniors, and $4 for children.

Providence Canyon

The two-lane blacktop of Hwy. 39C cuts through miles and miles of solid stick-straight pinewoods, which makes the first glimpse of Providence Canyon all the more unexpected. Called Georgia's Little Grand Canyon, it has pastel-shaded walls that bring Southwestern contours smack dab into South Georgia's forested plain. A stark departure from the surrounding environment, the erosion-worn canyon (actually 16 of them, some as deep as 150 feet) shel-

whirligigs in Westville

© KAP STANN

Providence Canyon

spurs off the loop trail deep down in the canyon and climbs back up to the ridge, where the trail continues through forested backcountry to five campsites along the next ridge. Then the trail drops down to a footbridge across the creek that flows from the canyons and loops back to the rim trail. Pick up free maps and permits at the interpretive center before backpacking.

Florence

What they now call Florence is largely **Florence Marina State Park,** 229/838-6870, www.gas-tateparks.org, reservations 800/864-PARK (864-7275), parking $2, built on the site of an abandoned 19th-century town. This small quiet refuge draws local anglers and boaters to the 150-acre park, which features a 66-slip marina with rental slips, a lighted fishing pier, a swimming pool, two tennis courts, and a "clubhouse" used for wedding receptions and other local get-togethers.

Ten fully equipped cottages rent year-round for $75–90; eight efficiency units rent for $50–60. A 43-site campground charges $18–20; full (water, electric, sewage) hookups are available.

The park's **Kirbo Interpretive Center** displays exhibits related to the submerged town, native flora and fauna, and the nearby **Rood Creek** archaeological site. At the site, eight ceremonial mounds date from A.D. 900–1540, when a village of 3,500 inhabited the area. The site is only accessible on a tour; inquire at the park office.

Eufaula National Wildlife Refuge

Abandoned farmland along the Chattahoochee River (off Hwy. 39 south of the state park) is now protected as a wildlife preserve. Here, the ruins of silos house bats and owls, armadillos frolic under strewn rusting tractors, alligator trails cross from pond to pond, and overhead you'll see anhingas, herons, and glossy ibis. The old roadbed and levees serve as trails; park at the sign where the road's blocked off.

Louvale

A favorite gathering place for anglers and hunters, the tiny town of Louvale is the only action on a long forested stretch of Hwy. 27 between Lumpkin and Cussetta, unless you count bait shops.

ters a rare botanical community, notably the rare plumleaf azalea, which blooms from July to September.

The canyon is protected as a 1,109-acre conservation area within the state park system. An **interpretive center,** 229/838-6202, www.gastateparks.org, parking $2, explains the unusual geology and can also arrange guided canyon tours. Park gates stay open 7 A.M.–9 P.M. Apr. 15–Sept. 14, and till 6 P.M. the rest of the year.

You'll see dramatic views at several overlooks close to parking. The three-mile **rim trail** loops largely around the perimeter, then dips down by wide switchbacks into the canyon at the interpretive center. Here hikers go from the dry, well-drained ridge to the moist and shaded canyon floor (it's slightly muddy during wet weather).

A seven-mile **backcountry trail** invites backpackers to explore further. The red-blazed trail

© KAP STANN

South Georgia

Louvale consists of an old-fashioned post office, a local barbecue, gas station, market, and above town, an unexpected collection of historic churches on display in an overgrown field. You'll find a free Army Corps of Engineers campground with water and pit toilets down Riverbend Road, on Walter F. George Lake.

BUENA VISTA

Buena Vista (BEW-na VIS-ta) has been placed on the map by a local eccentric who built his visionary art environment at the outskirts of town. Since the death of its creator, its discovery and exposure have brought art students and supporters of primitive expression to town.

⋈ Pasaquan

Four acres of an old South Georgia farmhouse and grounds have been transformed into a extraordinary folk-art environment by the late Eddie Owens Martin (1908–1986). Martin called himself "Saint EOM" (a derivative of his chantlike initials) and was a free spirit, fortuneteller, and bane of the local community for years until his death. He liked to consider himself the "Bodacious Mystic Badass of Buena Vista," and his biographer Tom Patterson (*St. EOM in the Land of Pasaquan*) called him "a cross between Walt Whitman, Sun Ra, Montezuma, Lord Buckley, and Boy George."

Over the years Martin designed and constructed walls and outbuildings from wood and poured concrete, which he molded, sculpted, and painted in hallucinogenic patterns and shades. The name Pasaquan appeared to him in a dream, which he explained as a combination of the Spanish word for "pass" and *quoyan*, purportedly an Asian term for integrating the past and present. His art reflects the influence of Asian, African, and Native American mythologies. Other beliefs were his alone—such as the unusual conelike hairdos on his painted figures, designed to draw energy upward.

Now operated by the county historical society (and maintained by volunteers—grab a brush at a painting party), Pasaquan is open by advance reservation only, catch as catch can, for a small fee; call 229/649-9444.

Buena Vista is 35 miles southeast of Columbus. Take Hwy. 280 south from Columbus to Hwy. 26; go east on Hwy. 26 for 2.7 miles to where it splits. Take the left fork (Hwy. 137; the sign says Camp Darby) and continue five miles or so. Watch for a small white sign in the woods and turn up a small paved road on the left.

Southwest Georgia

Among the live oaks draped with Spanish moss, Southern magnolias, poplar arcades, and orchards in the state's southwestern corner, visitors stumble upon sleepy courthouse squares, peanut-processing plants, sugarcane fields, aboriginal mounds, New Deal murals, frontier forts, and Native American totems. Country signs advertise "Goats for Sale—Barbecue Size," and pecan pie's the local specialty.

The Chattahoochee River flows along the region's western edge, forming the border with Alabama. Native American monuments sprinkled through the area attest to early human habitation along the river. But the wild and remote character of the lands here made for a sparsely settled frontier during colonial days. Much of the area remains wild today, although several dams along the Chattahoochee have tamed the river, creating placid lakes that draw anglers to their shores. The Flint River bisects the region, and evidence remains of the devastation caused when it overflowed its banks in the Great Flood of 1994.

The stately Plantation Trace region—renowned as an elite resort at the turn of the 20th century and noted for its aristocratic hunting resorts to this day—is centered in Thomasville.

BLAKELY AND VICINITY

Blakely's courthouse square, the crossroads of Highways 27, 39, and 62, features a concrete monument to the peanut; and the local post office, at Liberty and South Main Streets, has a classic New Deal mural titled *This Land Is Bought from the Indians.* Yet Blakely's most significant landmark predates the town by several thousand years—the Kolomoki Mounds site is considered one of the most significant archaeological sites east of the Mississippi.

A short drive southwest of Blakely, nine miles down Hwy. 62 to Hilton, you'll find the 96-foot **Coheelee Creek Covered Bridge,** on Old River Road. Built in 1891, it's the only remaining covered bridge south of Macon in Georgia.

Kolomoki Mounds

Six miles north of Blakely off Hwy. 27, seven pre-Columbian mounds preserve religious centers built by Swift Creek and Weeden Island Native Americans in the 12th and 13th centuries. Georgia's oldest temple mound rises here, along with two burial mounds and four ceremonial mounds. Here in the state's remote southwestern corner, visitors can view these ancient mounds with only a few interpretive signs to distract from their silent majesty, unlike the more heavily visited mounds on the Piedmont.

The mounds were painstakingly constructed, basketful by basketful. For the largest mound— 56 feet high, and 325 feet by 200 feet at its base—that translates to an estimated *two million* basketfuls. The mounds formed the center of village life for an estimated population of 1,500–2,000.

An **interpretive museum,** 229/724-2150, built directly into a partially excavated mound, retains skeletons and artifacts exactly as they were left by archaeologists. An audiovisual show and other exhibits further describe Kolomoki culture, and maps and guides to the site's **nature trails** identify the local plant life that sustained the native population through the centuries. The mound museum is open Tues.–Sat. 9 A.M.–5 P.M., Sun. 2–5:30 P.M. Admission is $2.50 for adults and $1.50 for children.

The mounds are just one part of 1,293-acre **Kolomoki Mounds State Park,** www.gastateparks.org, reservations 800/864-PARK (864-7275), parking $2, a major recreational center. Facilities include two small lakes for fishing and

© KAP STANN

Kolomoki Mounds State Park

boating (rentals are available), two swimming pools, miniature golf, and a calendar of special programs—such as October's Indian Artifact Day. Visitors can stay overnight for an after-dark look at the mysterious mounds; a 42-site campground provides water and electric hookups ($17–19).

Colquitt

On Hwy. 27 between Blakely and Bainbridge, Colquitt is the undisputed Mayhaw Capital of the World. This South Georgia fruit, which tastes faintly like guava, is hand-picked in the swamps and ponds of South Georgia for a relatively short harvest season each spring, an event marked by the town's **Mayhaw Festival,** held the third Saturday in April. The local chamber of commerce, 229/758-2400, promotes all events.

The town celebrates its folk life heritage with its acclaimed *Swamp Gravy* theater production, which is held several times a year in Cotton Hall, 229/758-5450, www.swampgravy.com, a 60-year-old warehouse. The play—the official Georgia state folk-life play—tells the story of such small farming communities around the turn of the 20th century. Within the warehouse, the

South Georgia

Museum of Southern Culture, 166 E. Main St., 229/758,6686, has exhibits on traditional Southern folkways, storytelling, and culture.

Joy Jinks operates the **Tarrer Inn,** on the square downtown, 229/758-2888. It's a restored 1861 boardinghouse that is now an historic inn in this remote corner of Georgia (rooms start at $90 and include breakfast).

BAINBRIDGE AND VICINITY

A 1903 brick courthouse clock tower presides over the square in downtown Bainbridge, a city of 27,000 on the banks of the Flint River. The one-time port hosts many events and concerts in the shady park green. The city's trademark festival, the **Riverside Artsfest,** puts a fresh spin on small town festivals—the first weekend each May, Bainbridge celebrates the cultures, arts, foods, and traditions of a state in the United States—a different one each year.

The chamber of commerce, 229/246-4774, operates a welcome center in an antebellum house off Basin Road in the riverside **Earl May Boat Basin Park.**

Many sporty travelers know Bainbridge best as the gateway to Lake Seminole, an impoundment of the Chattahoochee and Flint Rivers that covers 58 square miles. Get to the southern shore via Hwy. 97, or the northern shore via Hwy. 253. No bridge or ferry crosses the lake.

Lake Seminole

Ranking fifth among the best bass-fishing spots in the United States, Lake Seminole draws fisherfolk to 12,000 acres of stump-filled waters, 5,000 acres of grassy beds, a couple of thousand acres of lily pads, 250 islands, and natural lime sink ponds. Lake waters average only 15 feet deep—shallow for a lake of this size. Besides largemouth and white bass, you can also net stripers, bream, crappie—in fact, more fish varieties than in any other lake in the state.

M Wingate's Lunker Lodge, 229/246-0658, is the local fish camp mecca. Fishing sage and raconteur Jack Wingate presides over the south shore operation, which includes a marina, supply store, lodge, campground, and

an 18-bed men's dormitory called the Stag Hangout. And there's never any shortage of fishing or hunting advice. The 16 lodge rooms have heat, air-conditioning, and a color TV; the antler-adorned lodge restaurant serves seafood and catfish plates. Take Hwy. 97 south from Bainbridge to State Rd. 310 and turn right; it dead-ends at the lodge.

Farther down Hwy. 97 near the state line, see the Army Corps of Engineers (COE) **Resource Manager's Office,** 229/662-2001, for detailed maps listing every COE campground, swimming area, boat launch, and picnic site, as well as boating and fishing services around the lake.

Seminole State Park

Seminole State Park, 229/861-3137, www.gastateparks.org, reservations 800/864-PARK (864-7275), parking $2, occupies a remote peninsula jutting out into Lake Seminole at the northern shore. The 604-acre park squirrels away a swimming beach, boat and bicycle rentals, and miniature golf. The 2.2-mile Gopher Tortoise Nature Trail interprets the local wiregrass habitat.

Ten hideaway two-bedroom cottages rent for $75–100. A 50-site campground provides water and electric hookups; sites cost $17–21. The park is accessible from the north via Hwy. 39 (drive 16 miles south from Donalsonville), or from the east via Hwy. 253 (drive 23 miles west from Bainbridge).

ALBANY

At the head of navigation of the Flint River, Albany was founded in 1836 by Henry Harding Tift (for whom Tifton is named). He named the town after New York's capital, though here its pronunciation is a matter of some dispute (some say al-BENNY—according to one resident, "How country you say it depends on how far back in the sticks you were born"). Albany is the largest city in South Georgia (population 120,000) and is the center of the state's pecan-and peanut-producing area.

The **visitors center,** 225 W. Broad Ave., 229/434-8700, www.albanyga.com, distributes lodging and dining information.

Albany Museum of Art

The Albany Museum of Art, 311 Meadowlark Dr., 229/439-8400, is best known for its African art collection, begun by former African ambassador and Albany resident Stella Davis. The museum also displays 19th- and 20th-century American art. It's open Tues.–Sat. 10 A.M.–5 P.M., Sun. 1–4 P.M. Admission is $4 for adults and $2 for children.

The Parks at Chehaw

The city's major attraction, Chehaw Park, 229/430-5275, offers trails, a boat dock, picnic areas, camping, historical exhibits, and a wildlife preserve housing native Georgia species—all on 700 forested acres on the Flint River. The park is open daily 9 A.M.–7 P.M. in summer, until 5 P.M. in winter. Enter from Philema Rd. (Hwy. 91), off Hwy. 82/19 north of town (follow signs). Call for fees.

Mt. Zion Albany Civil Rights Movement Museum

Housed in the old Mt. Zion Church where Martin Luther King Jr. preached in 1961, this museum, 326 Whitney Ave., 229/432-1698, commemorates the role Albany played in the civil-rights movement. The museum is open Wed.–Sat. 10 A.M.–4 P.M., Sun. 2–5 P.M.; admission is $3 for adults, $2 for youth ages 6–17, seniors over 65.

Recreation

The **Flint River Outdoor Center,** 11151 Hwy. 3, 229/787-3004 or 888/572-6697, www.flintriveroutpost.com, organizes canoeing, rafting, and tubing adventures on the river's Class I–III rapids. Shuttle service, rentals, camping, and customized excursions are available.

THOMASVILLE

In its heyday at the turn of the past century, 10,000 Northerners descended on Thomasville each winter to unwind in the heart of Georgia's graceful Plantation Trace region. Dozens of posh hotels and guesthouses catered to the aristocratic likes of the Goodriches and Rockefellers, and

© GEORGIA DEPARTMENT OF INDUSTRY, TRADE & TOURISM

Pebble Hill Plantation

many of the country's elite built elegant estates in town and throughout the countryside.

They say it all started when a doctor published an article in 1870 asserting the therapeutic qualities of the region's pine-soaked air—and it sure is true: No one could help but feel healthier after inhaling the sultry scent. But even decades before that, Thomasville found itself an unlikely set of promoters—the Union prisoners who were temporarily moved down here from the POW camp at Andersonville returned north with tales of the region's "balsam breeze, long-blooming roses, and bobtail quails behind every hedgerow."

Today, Thomasville retains the old-timey appeal of a bygone resort, and its residents are grateful the crowds are gone but eager to host the curious few who make their way here. The **Welcome Center,** on the square, 114 E. Jackson St., 229/227-7099, www.thomasvillega.com, distributes information on local sights, B&Bs, events, and tours (closed Sunday).

For a fine introduction to the area, read Bailey White *(Mama Makes Up Her Mind, Sleeping at the Starlight Motel),* a former schoolteacher who has chronicled South Georgia life for National Public Radio from her Thomasville home.

Sights

Two historic house museums recall the town's hotel era. The Victorian **Lapham-Patterson House,** 626 N. Dawson St., 229/225-4004, www.gastateparks.org, offered state-of-the-art conveniences when it was built in 1884—gas lighting, hot and cold running water, and indoor plumbing—and today it's beautifully restored to period splendor. It's open Tues.–Sat. 9 A.M.–5 P.M. and Sun. 2–5:30 P.M. (open Mon. on major holidays only). Tours begin on the hour and last 45 minutes. The charge is $4 for adults and $2.50 for ages 18 or younger.

The **Pebble Hill Plantation,** 229/226-2344, www.pebblehill.com, off Hwy. 319 five miles south of town, opens to the public a 3,000-acre estate typical of winter hunting resorts built in the early 20th century. Guided tours take guests through the high-style mansion, from its dramatic black-and-white foyer with the French curved staircase through period-furnished rooms filled with artwork (much horse-and-hound imagery attests to the local leisure pursuit). One room is devoted to Native American artifacts from the region, and you can also see antique automobiles and carriages on display. It's open Tues.–Sat. 10 A.M.–5 P.M., Sun. 1–5 P.M.; closed Sept. and major holidays. Call for fees to enter the grounds or to tour the house (no children under 6 are allowed on the house tour).

At the **Thomas County Historical Museum,** 725 N. Dawson St., 229/226-7664, the local historical society displays a set of interesting exhibits, old hotel artifacts, and antique costumes recalling its past heyday. Outside there's a Victorian-era bowling alley, farmhouse, and vintage cars. It's open Mon.–Sat. 2–5 P.M.; admission is $5 for adults and $1 for students ages 6–18.

Accommodations

South of town, the **Melhana Plantation,** on Hwy. 319, 229/226-2290 or 888/920-3030, www.melhana.com, opened in 1997 with an aim to take a place among the most select luxurious historic inns in the South. The gracious 40-acre estate—with beautiful horse pastures, sunken gardens, a pool house, and even its own Showboat Theater, which hosted one of the first screenings of *Gone with the Wind* in 1939—holds guest rooms in a meticulously restored antebellum house, carriage house, cottage, barns, and stable (rooms start at $250).

Food and Drink

The **Billiard Academy,** at 121 S. Broad St., downtown, 229/226-9981, sells hundreds of chili dogs daily (85 cents each) through a streetside window, as it has since 1949 (when a dog cost a dime). It's open Mon.–Fri. 8 A.M.–9 P.M., Sat. 8 A.M.–6 P.M.

Barbecue aficionados drive 12 miles south of town to **J. B.'s Bar-B-Que & Grill,** on Hwy. 319 S, 229/377-9344, where J. B. cooks up meaty pork ribs (half slab $7.40) along with barbecued chicken, mullet, and shrimp with all the traditional sides in a family-style restaurant. Neighbor Jimmy Buffett is among the biggest fans of J. B.'s 'cue. It's open daily except Monday from noonish to 10ish.

You'll find acres of farm-fresh produce at the **state farmers market,** 502 Smith Ave., at Hansell St., 229/225-4072. Inside, the **Market Diner,** 229/225-1777, serves up market-fresh vegetables and fruits (open daily).

VICINITY OF THOMASVILLE

Out on Hwy. 84 W, **Cairo** (KAY-ro) is the home of Roddenbery's *Cane Patch Syrup.* The family-owned, 101-year-old firm distills syrup from South Georgia's native sugarcane. You'll find local agriculture celebrated in the New Deal mural *Products of Grady County,* which graces the post office at 203 N. Broad St. The town hosts an **Antique Car Rally** the second weekend in May that features a gaslight parade, street dance, and car displays.

Big-draw festivals at tiny towns can swell the local three-figure population to up over 50,000. In **Whigham** (on Hwy. 84 west of Cairo), a

Rattlesnake Roundup held on the last Saturday in January captivates onlookers with daring snake demonstrations and other entertainment. South of Whigham in **Calvary** (on Hwy. 11 near the Florida border), **Mule Day** is held the first Saturday in November (rainout date: the second Saturday). The festival features traditional country activities (cane grinding, syrup making), contests (tobacco spittin', greased-pig catchin'), 600 booths hawking crafts and country wares, and the crowning event: the hundreds-strong mule parade (prizes are awarded

for ugliest and most ornery). Barbecue, fish fry, gospel, bands, clogging, and a square dance round out the event.

Out Hwy. 84 west of Whigham, the town of **Climax** hosts **Swine Time** the Saturday after Thanksgiving. Locals celebrate the indispensable stock animal of subsistence farmers—a source of meat, lard, soap, and leather. Pigs parade in costume and are served in every dish imaginable—all this is accompanied by country music, bluegrass, and gospel. For more information call 229/246-0910 (sooo-EEE!).

Along I-75: Perry to Valdosta

From the I-75 corridor, which slices through the middle of wiregrass country, South Georgia looks like one great fluorescent strip of 24-hour gas stations, fast-food chains, and budget motels. Yet visitors looking beyond that find notable remnants of pre-neon history, such as Victorian mansions, gristmills, canoe trails down sandy Southern rivers, and boardwalks through moist coastal plain woodlands.

The central towns of Perry, Cordele, Tifton, and Valdosta—spread evenly along the 150-mile route from Macon to Florida—make logical pit stops for through-travelers on I-75. In fact, long stretches of empty highway in between the towns make them virtually necessary stops.

PERRY AND VICINITY

Once an old stagecoach stop, Perry continues to treat travelers with its small historic district and landmark New Perry Hotel. The small and scenic downtown, lined with antique and craft shops, lies two miles east of I-75 off the I-75 business loop.

The Georgia Agricenter, south of town at I-75, houses such major events as the nine-day **Georgia National Fair** in early October. Stop by the **Perry Welcome Center**, off I-75, 478/988-8000, www.perryga.com, for a schedule of local events.

New Perry Hotel and Restaurant

The New Perry Hotel, 800 Main St., 478/987-1000, is a light, airy, and spacious old-time hotel

built in 1925 to replace the "old" Perry Hotel built in 1870. The hotel retains its original thick Venetian blinds, white chenille bedspreads, and potted geraniums, but it also seems modern in its own retro-1940s way. The grandmotherly staff greets guests with such endearments as "sweetie" and "sugar."

The 39 rooms are split between the two-story 1925 building and an attractive motel, of more recent vintage, out back. An inviting patio between the two buildings surrounds a small pool (rooms start at $40).

Three classically Southern meals a day are served on white tablecloths in the dining room at reasonable rates. The mimeographed menu changes daily and may feature entrées such as ham with corn relish, grilled catfish, and fried chicken. Choose from among a half-dozen side dishes, such as squash Lorraine, fried eggplant, or congealed fruit salad. Of course, there's nearly always pecan and peach pie for dessert. Breakfast is served 7–10 A.M., lunch 11:30 A.M.–2:30 P.M., and dinner 5:30–9 P.M.

West of Perry

Eleven miles northwest via Hwy. 341, **Fort Valley** is the Peach Capital of the World. Georgia's prime peach-growing region encompasses much of the area between Fort Valley and Perry. See the orchards in full flower in early April, and find fresh fruit at roadside stands—or pick your own at do-it-yourself orchards—from late May through July.

South Georgia

West of Perry off Hwy. 341, the American Camellia Society opens to the public the colorful **Massee Lane Gardens,** 100 Massee Ln., 478/967-2358. The camellias bloom from November to March, and in springtime, visitors can see the flowering azaleas, dogwoods, irises, and many annuals and other perennials. The nine-acre site also shelters an art gallery, gift shop, and a tranquil Japanese garden, complete with koi pond. Hours are seasonal. Admission is $5; children under 12 are free.

South of Perry

Ten miles north of Cordele and a mile west of I-75, **Vienna** (VI-enna) is famous for its finger-lickin' **Big Pig Jig**—Georgia's official barbecue cooking competition—held the second weekend in October. Year-round, sample 'cue at **Mamie Bryant's BBQ Pit,** 310 8th St., 229/268-4179.

CORDELE AND VICINITY

With its miles-long strip of franchise restaurants, budget motels, and discount shopping centers along Hwy. 280, Cordele makes a handy pit stop for I-75 through-travelers. Others follow Hwy. 280 out nine miles to a major state park or another 20 miles or so to the intriguing area around Americus.

Lake Blackshear

Cordele's greatest recreational attraction is 8,700-acre Lake Blackshear, a Georgia Power impoundment of the Flint River. Around its 77-mile shoreline are municipal and utility-company public beaches, campgrounds, and boat launches. You'll find marinas at the Hwy. 280 bridge and off Hwy. 300 at the south side near the dam. Pick up maps at the **Resource Manager's Office,** by the dam, 229/273-3820.

Georgia Veterans Memorial State Park

Nine miles west of I-75 exit 101, Georgia Veterans Memorial State Park, 229/276-2371, www.gastateparks.org, reservations 800/864-PARK (864-7275), parking $2, is a major recre-

ational resource on Lake Blackshear. Designed as a memorial to veterans, the park's highlight is a **military museum,** which displays weaponry, uniforms, and other artifacts inside; and planes, cannons, and tanks outside. Museum hours are daily 8 A.M.–5 P.M., no charge.

The 1,308-acre park also offers a swimming pool and beach, boat rentals, a mile-long nature trail, fishing, and a lakeside 18-hole golf course. An 77-site campground charges $17–22, including water and electric hookups.

The privately owned **Retreat at Lake Blackshear,** 800/459-1230, provides 78 rooms at the water (from $100), along with 10 cottages and a restaurant.

Southwest Georgia Excursion Train

SAM Shortline, 229/276-2715 or 800/864-7275, www.samshortline.com, runs vintage 1940s cars 40 miles between the state park and Archery (Jimmy Carter's Birthplace), with stops in Plains, Americus, and Leslie. The route passes through the bucolic countryside and stops within a mile's walk of local attractions, hotels, and restaurants. Call or visit the website for schedules and fees.

TIFTON AND VICINITY

Originally Creek territory and under Spanish rule until 1763, this area was settled by marine engineer Henry Harding Tift in 1872, who set up a lumbering operation that grew into the city of Tifton. Today you'll see Tifton in the dateline of breaking agricultural news; its Agricultural Experiment Station is foremost in the field of agricultural research nationwide. The **Tifton Chamber of Commerce,** 100 S. Central Ave., 229/382-6200, is open weekdays.

Ashburn

North of Tifton, at the shoulder of southbound I-75, the **World's Largest Peanut** stands perched atop a 15-foot-tall brick pedestal. The 10-foot-tall goober rests in a golden crown, which boasts "Georgia: 1st in Peanuts." In town, the **Crime and Punishment Museum,** 241 E. College Ave., 229/567-9696, opens the 1906 Turner County jail to display original cells, a hanging hook, and the trap door where two men were hung for murder. They also operate the **Last Meal Cafe** on the premises, with desserts that are, of course, to die for.

Jefferson Davis Memorial

Northeast of Tifton near Irwinville, a park marks the site where Jefferson Davis, president of the Confederate States of America, was captured in 1865. On May 9 of that year, Davis and a few loyal members of his staff heading for the Western Theater camped in this pine forest, not knowing pursuit was close behind. At dawn, two groups of Union cavalry opened fire (actually, on each other—the museum tells the story), and Davis was taken prisoner and held in Virginia for two years until his release. Among the artifacts in the park's museum, on Hwy. 32, 229/831-2335, www.gastateparks.org, is part of the tree under which Davis was found. The site is open Tues.–Sat. 9 A.M.–5 P.M., Sun. 2–5:30 P.M.; adult admission is $2.50.

Fitzgerald

Northeast of Tifton, Fitzgerald was founded in 1895 and was named for an Indianapolis journalist who, together with a Georgia governor, conceived of resettling veterans of the Union army here. Townspeople say they had to build a hotel to accommodate all the people who wanted to come see a Yankee. The town's west-side streets are named for Confederate generals; Union generals are on the east. Other streets are named for Northern and Southern trees and flowers.

The newly renovated **Blue and Gray Museum,** in the old depot building in the center of town, 116 N. Johnston St., 229/426-5069, houses Civil War memorabilia from both sides and other local history exhibits. It's open Tues.–Sat. 10 A.M.–4 P.M. Adult admission is $3; children are admitted for $1.

Georgia Agrirama

In Tifton, Agrirama, 229/386-3344, www.agrirama.com, presents an impressive living-history village that takes visitors back in time to the late 19th century. More than 40 restored structures on 95 acres replicate farm and village life in South

Georgia, including a distinctive South Georgia "dogtrot" cabin, a gristmill, lumber mill, print shop, Masonic lodge, cotton gin, and two-story Victorian house. Agrirama is largely staffed by old-timers wearing period costumes; they speak from their personal experience as they shell peas, grind corn, distill syrup, and spin yarns—catch these living treasures while you can. Agrirama is generally open Mon.–Sat. 9 A.M.–5 P.M. but hours change seasonally (call for schedules and fees).

VALDOSTA AND VICINITY

Valdosta, home to Valdosta State University and Moody Air Force Base, is surrounded and supported by its agricultural industries—pine, peaches, pecans, and tobacco. In fact, tobacco is such a big player in the local economy that schools may delay opening if the harvest is behind schedule.

Downtown Valdosta's historic district centers on the 1905 courthouse square, on E. Central Ave. (off Hwy. 84, about a mile east of I-75), which is surrounded by attractive residential streets with many old homes. Around this agricultural county, you can attend tobacco auctions and tour pecan-processing plants, or you can visit pick-your-own cotton fields, peach orchards, and farms. The **Valdosta-Lowndes County Convention and Visitors Bureau,** 1 Meeting Place, 229/245-0513, within the county convention center, arranges agricultural tours and distributes driving tour maps. Or stop at the **Georgia State Visitors Center,** off I-75, open daily.

Accommodations and Food

At I-75 exits 2–6, through-travelers have the choice of many national motel and fast-food chains located a stone's throw from the freeway. Two local culinary landmarks are worth seeking out.

A local seafood shack overlooks a cypress swamp landscape at the family-operated 🝓 **Fish Net,** on Sportsmans Cove Rd., 229/559-5410, serving fresh fish dinners, including all-you-can-eat catfish and trout for around $10. Or, for the absolute freshest fish, catch one yourself at the adjacent public fishing ponds, and the chef will prepare it for you. They are open for dinner

Thurs.–Sat. Take I-75 exit 2 west along Hwy. 376 a half mile, turn right onto Loch Laurel Road and go two miles to Sportsmans Cove Road. (follow signs).

Along the Barbecue Landmark Trail, find the **Ⓜ Old South BBQ House** 1706 W. Hill Ave., 229/247-0505.

Recreation

The **Alapaha River,** one of the South's most beautiful swamp rivers, flows through central wiregrass country east of I-75. Meandering through timberlands of pine, live oak, and tupelo—at times narrow enough for trees to form an overhead canopy—the Class I river is lined with snow-white sand banks where you'll likely see beaver, otter, wild turkey, and deer. A designated **paddling trail** begins outside Willa-coochee (28 miles east of Tifton, where Hwy. 135 crosses the river) and runs south 83 miles to the Hwy. 94 crossing outside Statenville, six miles north of the Florida border.

For guided canoe trips or rental equipment, call **Suwannee Canoe Outpost,** an outfitter on Hwy. 129 at the Suwannee, across the border near Live Oak, Florida, 904/364-4991 or 800/428-4147. The Outpost also runs the Withlacoochee River west of Valdosta—Class III rapids here attract experienced paddlers at certain times in the year—and the Suwannee from Okefenokee Swamp headwaters.

An easy way to cool off is at **Splash Island Water Park,** 229/219-7080 or 800/808-0872, which is part of a Wild Adventures amusement park (seasonal hours; call for schedules and fees).

Southeastern Interior

Countless even rows of stick-straight Georgia pines line southeastern highways, interrupted by rust-red logging roads used to transport the state's signature product to mills. Deeper into the interior, the forests break into open farmland; roadside stands sell peaches, peanuts, pecans, and the regional agricultural oddity—the sweet Vidalia onion. While quiet country towns make diverting detours, most folks know this region best as the agonizing stretch of blacktop that's the necessary means to a beach vacation. The coast's distinct culture can be better understood and appreciated after crossing what seems even today like a daunting barrier.

Statesboro, the "big city" in these parts, is home to 10,000 Georgia Southern University students. Smaller towns hold other prized distinctions: Vidalia is the namesake of the sweet onion, McRae proudly displays a 32-foot wooden replica of the Statue of Liberty, Glennville boasts of having the world's largest cricket farm, and Claxton declares itself the Fruitcake Capital of the World. As is true throughout South Georgia, secreted parks—often at the shores of a lazy Southern river or fishing lake—display the coastal plain habitat at its best.

STATESBORO

Statesboro, 60 miles west of Savannah, is home to Georgia Southern University (GSU), whose 10,000 students dominate the city's population of 16,000. The original town was ravaged by Sherman during his 1864 march. Downtown's "new" Bulloch County Courthouse was built in 1894.

Along downtown's Main Street, find the town's **welcome center,** 332 S. Main St., 912/489-1869. Folks here distribute walking-tour maps of the 19th-century buildings and sell a small selection of gifts and crafts (open weekdays only).

On campus, the **Georgia Southern University Museum,** 912/681-5444, displays a 26-foot Mosasaur skeleton—a meat-eating sea serpent once native to the prehistoric seas that covered South Georgia during the Mesozoic era—as well as exhibits ranging from arts and folk life to coastal crustaceans and antique autos. Hours vary according to the academic calendar. There is no charge for admission. Ask the museum for an interpretive guide to the trail that runs through the adjacent **Herty Nature Preserve,** and also look for the 10-acre **Magnolia Garden** on campus.

Accommodations and Food

The **Statesboro Inn & Restaurant,** 106 S. Main St., 912/489-8628, set in a two-story 1904 Victorian house with a wraparound porch, offers 15 guest rooms starting at $95; the restaurant serves dinner only and is the local choice for fine dining.

Beaver House Restaurant, 121 S. Main St., 912/764-2821 (Hwy. 301 downtown), in a large, white-columned mansion built in 1911, serves classic Southern meals boardinghouse style. A typical spread includes fried chicken, rice and gravy, pole beans, fried okra, creamed corn, stewed tomatoes, black-eyed peas, macaroni and cheese, scratch biscuits, and cobbler. Lunch is served daily; Sunday, dinner is served midday.

On the Barbecue Landmark Trail, find **Ⓜ Vandy's,** 22 W. Vine St., 912/764-2444.

ALTAMAHA RIVER BASIN

The southeastern interior surrounding the Altamaha, a river formed by the conjunction of the Ocmulgee and Oconee Rivers near Lumber City, remains nearly as wild now as when it served as a critical source of food, trade, and transport for Native American groups many centuries back. In colonial days, the river formed the frontier between land claimed by the British to the north and by the Spanish to the south. In early Georgia statehood, European settlement spread out upriver to the navigational limits at Milledgeville and Macon, and the southeastern forests were cleared by simply floating logs downriver to the port at Darien.

Today the wide river basin is one of the most remote stretches in the state. Public boat launches at nearly every major road crossing draw fisherfolk and boaters to its shores, and the state opens wildlife management areas seasonally to hunters. Most river areas are accessible off Hwy. 341, which is also a popular route for city travelers headed for Golden Isles resorts.

Little Ocmulgee State Park

Little Ocmulgee State Park, 229/868-7474, www.gastateparks.org, reservations 800/864-PARK (864-7275), parking $2, two miles north of McRae on Hwy. 441, is a popular stopping point for drivers bound for Golden Isles resorts. The 1,277-acre lakeside park features boating, fishing, an 18-hole golf course, pool, and tennis courts.

Pete Phillips Lodge, 229/868-7474, offers 30 guest rooms from $60. The lodge restaurant overlooks the sixth tee and serves reasonably priced Southern buffets and menu selections; it's open for breakfast, lunch, and dinner.

Ten fully equipped rental **cottages** are set against the lake ($70–95). A 58-site **campground** with water and electric hookups is set among the pines and charges $17–19 per night.

Big Hammock Natural Area

Big Hammock Natural Area, on the northeast bank of the Altamaha River at the Hwy. 121/144/169 crossing (18 miles east of Baxley), presents the most expansive example of the strange sand ridges found in South Georgia's coastal plain. These sand dunes once belonged to an ancient sea that covered the plain a million years back, and the hundred-foot-high ridges now form the only contour in the otherwise flat terrain. Trails traverse the ridge, providing a close-up look at the distinct wildlife habitat that the sand hills support. Only a select group of hearty plant species tolerates the dry conditions, and even these appear stunted and wiry. Prickly pear cactus, Georgia plume, sand spikemoss, and twisted oaks and pine appear.

To find the trailhead, go two miles north of the bridge to the first paved road on the right; take this road 1.3 miles to the stone monument identifying the preserve. Park here and follow short fiberglass trail markers. The longest loop trail is six miles, and it traverses two parallel sand ridges. For a 1.5-mile loop hike, return on the cutoff between the ridges. Several short spur trails lead out to a cypress head, a lake, and the swamp and swamp forest around the sand hills.

Okefenokee Swamp

The Okefenokee Swamp is a place of mystery, but not the haunted foreboding kind most people associate with swamps. This pristine 680-square-mile wilderness is an ecological wonder, spiced with bizarre landscapes, exotic wildlife, and pioneer-spirited swamp folk.

As if passing through a looking glass, visitors step from the slatted South Georgia pine forest into a different environment altogether, where 80-foot cypresses rise out of black water, where ground that appears stable gives way, and where swampers who know the alligators by name pole shallow-draft skiffs through fern-lined channels. Even the climate changes: It's cooler, crisper, with a trace of echo under the canopy. Breezes stir draped Spanish moss, owls hoot in the middle of the day, and you know you're not in Waycross anymore.

The swamp's peculiar ecology of floating peat, which barely supports a person's weight, led the Seminoles to refer to the place as *ecunnau finocau*— "earth trembling"—and Okefenokee it became. From ancient mound- builders to turn-of-the-century canal-diggers, humans have left their mark on the swamp, but most traces of civilization have long since been reclaimed by nature.

As headwaters for two rivers, the swamp sends spring-fed Okefenokee blackwater to either the Atlantic or the Gulf of Mexico. St. Marys River, notorious as one of the crookedest rivers in the world, divides Georgia from Florida as it flows 175 miles from the swamp to the ocean—a distance of only 65 miles as the crow flies. The gulf-bound Suwannee earned its fame from the misspelled refrain in Stephen C. Foster's classic American folk song *The Old Folks at Home:*

> *Way down upon the Swanee River,*
> *far, far away,*
> *There's where my heart is turning ever*
> *There's where the old folks stay.*

Rivaling a tropical rainforest for the diversity of life within, the Okefenokee's delicate wetlands provide a critical habitat for abundant resident wildlife and migratory birds. Today a protected national wildlife refuge, the primitively beautiful Okefenokee Swamp remains a true great American wilderness.

Canoeing in the Okefenokee offers visitors an up-close and unforgettable experience of the swamp.

South Georgia

© KAP STANN

THE LAND

Technically, the Okefenokee is not a swamp but a vast peat bog. Rising to 130 feet above sea level, it's higher than some surrounding towns. Its waters are neither brackish, stagnant, nor muddy—but pure, drifting, and set on sand.

A million years ago, the Atlantic Ocean covered this part of Georgia. Over the eons, a sandbar took shape offshore, and when the ocean eventually receded, this rising ridge trapped the seawater inside. Salt gave way to fresh water, a clear lake gave way to plants, and vegetation decayed into peat. The oldest peat in the Okefenokee dates back only 8,000 years. So as primordial as the brooding vistas appear, on a geological scale the Okefenokee Swamp is practically a newborn.

Okefenokee blackwater, as dark as overly steeped tea, enhances dramatic swamp scenery with its silvery reflection. The color comes from the tannin produced by decaying vegetation. (Tannin is actually red, but the water appears black at depth.) Tannic acid acts as a natural preservative, purifying black water to higher standards than most city drinking water and surprising visitors who expect dirty water. (As one observer put it, in true Yogi Berra style, "If it wasn't so dark, it'd be clear!") In the 18th century, sailors valued Okefenokee blackwater because it stayed drinkable even on long voyages. Record has it that bog waters can effectively mummify a sunken corpse, though in the Okefenokee, alligators would get there first. Though it appears bottomless, the bog's depth averages four to five feet.

Three prominent physical features produce radically distinct swamp landscapes: islands, cypress stands, and prairies.

Battery-Hammock-Island Formation

In the Okefenokee, decaying vegetation produces peat, tannic acid, and methane gas. When the gas trapped between the peat layers on the swamp floor escapes, chunks of peat shoot to the water's surface, forming "blowups" (or "batteries"). Growing plants strengthen the floating peat beds; those strong enough to support human weight are called "hammocks." Eventually these root to the ground and create permanent islands. The Okefenokee has about 70 islands now, covering six percent of the swamp area. Cowhouse Island is the largest; it's nine miles long and two miles wide.

This battery-hammock-island succession continues today. You can see its various stages throughout the swamp, from sudden blowups in waterways (thus the necessity of shallow-draft skiffs) to mature hardwood islands at each swamp entrance. This process would eventually consume the swamp's open areas if wildfires didn't keep growth in check. Fires in 1954–1955 burnt much vegetation clear down to the surface of the water.

Cypress Stands

Dense cypress stands evoke the typical image of a swamp: a tall, dark forest planted underwater and draped with dangling Spanish moss. Eighty feet overhead, the cypress crowns into a thick canopy that cools the interior. Around each base, knobby cone-shaped "knees" protrude above the water like dark wooden stalagmites. Vegetation caught between bases forms a cypress "house" or "head," formations that were once favored by trappers as campsites. Cypress stands make up around 80 percent of the swamp and can be most readily seen on foot at the northern entrance and by boat at the western entrance.

Prairies

A third Okefenokee landscape offers a sharp contrast to the sheltered growth of islands and cypress stands. Large watery fields called prairies fill 60,000 swamp acres (15 percent of the total area) with such wispy vegetation as water lilies, grass, and aquatic sedge. Imagine an acres-wide expanse of pristine white water lilies on green pads. It's a placid scene until the wind kicks up their purple-veined undersides; set against rippling black water and a thunderous sky, the sight resembles nothing less than a moonscape.

Streams, lakes, and "gator holes" (small ponds clear of vegetation) dot the prairies, though all open-water areas combined make up only 1,000 of the swamp's 438,000 acres.

HISTORY

Early Inhabitants

Ancient "Mound-Builder" tribes, so named for the earthen constructions they raised on landscapes throughout the Southeast, left their mark on the Okefenokee as well. Sixty-five mounds dating back 4,000 years lace the swamp. Excavations of skeletons and relics have led archaeologists to conclude that these mounds served as sacred burial grounds for high-standing members of the community, and anthropologists speculate that tribes held religious rituals at these sites. Two of the most accessible mounds are on Chesser Island (east entrance) and Billy's Island (west entrance).

At the time of earliest European exploration, the Timucuan inhabited the swamp, then the Yuchi, then the Creek. Breaking off from the Creek, the Seminoles lived in the swamp when homesteaders began to settle, around 1800.

European Exploration

Two famous European expeditions, that of Spanish explorer Hernando de Soto in 1539 and Quaker naturalist William Bartram in 1773, passed by the swamp but never ventured inside. From skirting its periphery, both heard tales of the race of giant people said to live within (skeletal remains of Timucuan men confirm that they were uncommonly large) and of their beautiful, siren-like maidens.

Trappers and traders eager to exploit the fur-rich Okefenokee built a thriving business obtaining pelts and skins from the Native Americans, paving the way for future settlement.

As European settlers throughout colonial Georgia began encroaching on Native American territory, animosities naturally developed. An event well remembered to this day in the swamp is the Wilkes Family Massacre, in which a large homesteading family was wiped out (save a few children who escaped) by Seminoles in the 19th century. Their restored cabin, at Okefenokee Swamp Park, tells the story.

Expansionism reached a tragic climax in 1838, when Federal troops stormed through Georgia to expel all Native Americans from their ancestral homelands, sending most marching along the Trail of Tears to designated Indian territory in Oklahoma. The Seminoles, however, escaped this fate by fleeing southward.

When General Charles Floyd marched Federal troops into the Okefenokee, he met resistance from Seminole Chief Billy Bowlegs. Bowlegs managed to lead his people into Florida to safety, where they took refuge in the wilds of another swamp, the Everglades. (Their descendants live there to this day.) Two of the Okefenokee's largest islands, Billy's Island and Floyd's Island, commemorate these two historical characters.

Development

Homesteaders soon replaced the Seminoles, developing a self-sufficient swamper culture that lived off the natural bounty of the swamp. They hunted alligators for the valuable skins, lit their log cabins with pine-knot torches, and made stew from turtles and rattlesnakes. Their isolation in the unusual natural environment fostered unique folk customs whose threads can still be found around the swamp today.

Developers began looking for ways to cash in on the swamp's resources. In 1889, the Suwannee Canal Company bought much of the swamp from the state, intending to drain out the water and raise valuable cropland. From the sale price of $62,000 (less than 27 cents an acre), the company ended up spending a million dollars to build 12 miles of the still-standing canal before abandoning the effort. A far larger task than the canal-builders had imagined, the doomed effort, led by Atlanta lawyer Henry Jackson, was dubbed "Jackson's Folly."

At the turn of the century, the Charles Hebard Cypress Company of Waycross saw a lumber bonanza in the Okefenokee. During its 20 years of operation, the enterprise took nine million board feet of virgin cypress from the swamp. The central headquarters for the logging enterprise was on the same Billy's Island from which the Seminoles held off General Floyd.

Looking at the remote island wilderness now, it's hard to imagine Billy's Island was once a boomtown—complete with a hotel, school, store, and even a movie theater. At its heyday in the

SWAMP FOLK

When the Seminoles broke away from the powerful Creek Confederacy and moved to the swamp (Seminole means "runaway" in the Muskogean Creek language), they became the first of a long line of independents and renegades to inhabit the Okefenokee. The isolated blackwater swampland and bizarre "trembling earth" also attracted a reclusive lot, many escaping either injustice or justice.

Swamp island names reflect this colorful past. **Billy's Island** was named for Seminole chief Billy Bowlegs, who resisted ousting when the federal government sent in the army to evict all Native Americans from the Southeast in 1838 and banish them to Oklahoma. (The Seminoles escaped, fleeing to the sanctuary of Florida's Everglades.) **Floyd's Island** commemorates the ouster himself, General Charles Floyd, whose troops came against Bowlegs. Civil War times inspired **Soldier's Camp,** home to army deserters, and **Cowhouse Island,** where swampers hid cattle from marauding troops. Though **John's Negro Island** is named for a stolen slave, many runaway slaves fled to freedom in the swampland.

By rights, there ought to be an island honoring moonshiners, another outlaw swamp breed. (If there were, the name "Autumn Leaf" would immortalize the 190-proof swamp concoction said to make you change color and fall to the ground.)

Of course, the outlaw mystique tells only part of the story. Many God-fearing homesteaders settled the Okefenokee Swamp, too. Families such as the Chessers, who for several generations raised sugarcane on **Chesser Island.** The Wilkes' family cabin on Cowhouse Island is largely all that remains after most family members were killed in an Indian raid in the 19th century. The Lee family cemetery, on Billy's Island, dates from the 1850s, when Dan Lee and his bride settled there, to 1937, when the last of their descendants moved off the island to make way for the newly named refuge.

Yet the pioneer swamp spirit lives on around the periphery. Inside, the swamp offers living proof that nature can prevail over human intervention.

Cowhouse Island forms the northern entrance to the swamp, outside of Waycross. You can reach Chesser Island by a short trail from the nature drive at the eastern swamp entrance south of Folkston. Boat trails lead to Billy's Island (day-use only) and Floyd's Island (canoe campers, wilderness permit required). (Other islands mentioned are not accessible to the general public.) Guided swamp boat tours, available at each entrance, tell more of the Okefenokee's natural and human history.

---

early 20th century, 600 people lived here; workers earned $2.50 per day in company scrip redeemable only at the island store. A railroad, built 35 miles into the swamp, transported the lumber out.

Fire destroyed most of the remnants of that time, and jungle reclaimed the rest, so now it's hard to tell a rusted pipe from a dead branch. But you'll still stumble upon old steam-engine parts and chimneys, a cast-iron stove, and a washtub or two. (The old Hebard hunting cabin, on Floyd's Island, now shelters overnight campers.)

Okefenokee National Wildlife Refuge

In 1936, President Roosevelt established the 293,000-acre federal refuge as a result of an appeal by the wife of famed naturalist Francis Harper, a Cornell biologist fascinated by the swamp's natural history. In 1974, the most remote region of the swamp was designated a national wilderness area.

WHERE TO START

Three main entrances provide access to the swamp. The northern entrance, **Okefenokee Swamp Park,** lies 13 miles south of Waycross via U.S. 1/23 and Hwy. 177; the eastern entrance, **Suwannee Canal Recreation Area,** is 12 miles southwest of Folkston off Hwy. 23/121; and the western entrance, **Stephen C. Foster State Park,** is 18 miles northeast of Fargo on Hwy. 177.

Each entrance is managed by a different authority, is situated in distinct terrain, and holds its own natural and recreational attractions. At all three you can find guided boat trips, canoe

South Georgia

OKEFENOKEE NATIONAL WILDLIFE REFUGE

Waycross

To Valdosta

Laura S Walker State Park

OKEFENOKEE SWAMP PARK (NORTH ENTRANCE)

Cowhouse Island

MAUL HAMMOCK

KINGFISHER LANDING (LAUNCH)

Big Water Lake

Okefenokee National Wildlife Refuge

BIG WATER

Territory Prairie

Big Water Prairie

Floyd's Prairie

CRAVEN'S HAMMOCK

Minnie's Island

BLUFF LAKE

Pine Island

STEPHEN C FOSTER STATE PARK

Floyd's Island

FOLKSTON INN B&B

Folkston

SUWANNEE RIVER SILL

(WEST ENTRANCE)

CEDAR HAMMOCK

ROUND TOP

TRADER'S HILL RECREATION AREA

Billy's Island

CANAL RUN

Christie Prairie

Suwannee Canal

SUWANNEE CANAL RECREATION AREA (EAST ENTRANCE)

Buck Prairie

REFUGE OFFICE

To I-95

Suwannee River

Honey Island

Bugaboo Island

Okefenokee National Wildlife Refuge

Chesser Prairie

SUWANNEE RIVER VISITOR CENTER

Fargo

John's Negro Island

NATURE DRIVE

FLORIDA

Blackjack Island

Grand Prairie

St Marys River

Soldier's Camp Island

St George

Moniac

FLORIDA

To I-10

0   6 mi

0   6 km

© AVALON TRAVEL PUBLISHING, INC.

rentals, boardwalks above the swamp, and wonderful opportunities to see varied Okefenokee wildlife and swamp ecology.

Of two secondary swamp entrances, the **Suwannee River Sill** landing provides boat access but no other services; **Kingfisher Landing** provides boat access, and camping and canoe rentals are available at the **Kingfisher Wilderness Campground,** 912/496-7836.

For first-timers and experienced boaters alike, the best way to sense the secluded serenity and natural primitive beauty of the Okefenokee is to get out on the water. More than 120 miles of waterways course through the swamp, between islands, around lakes, and through the canal and prairies, offering panoramic scenery and glimpses of wildlife in action.

Getting There

Driving to Folkston (eastern entrance) from the nearest major airport (in Jacksonville, Florida) takes an hour and a half; from Savannah, less than two hours; from Atlanta, six hours. Distances around the swamp are considerable: to get from the eastern to the western entrance means a detour into Florida and a two-and-a-half-hour ride.

Because the Okefenokee Swamp is such an enclosed wilderness, no drive along its perimeter hints at the richness within. Highway 177 up from Fargo to the state park offers a chance to see swamp animals but not terrain, although its isolation makes this scenic drive impractical for drivers just passing through.

The 4.5-mile nature drive at the eastern entrance near Folkston provides the most convenient opportunity to see wildlife from the comfort of a car. The nature drive also provides access to short trails.

What to Bring

The Okefenokee inspires everyone to use binoculars and cameras; if you have them, bring them. In summer, carry insect repellent, sunscreen, and a hat; long pants and long sleeves offer the best protection. Boaters will want to carry drinking water and food, and remember dry bags (such as Ziploc freezer bags) for camera equipment.

Campers need to bring all necessary supplies; the few camp stores available carry minimal stock. For extensive outings, carry emergency supplies, including a compass, a flashlight, a first-aid kit, extra food and clothing, and a whistle (three toots sound a distress signal).

Safety

The greatest danger in the swamp is not from the wildlife, as one might fear, but instead from lightning. Electrical storms are common on summer afternoons, and rangers advise that boaters in exposed areas seek shelter under a thick growth of small trees when they see a storm approach. Adventurers should also know the signs and prevention of heatstroke (replenish fluids, carry salt tablets) and hypothermia (stay dry, warm, and sheltered).

Nevertheless, visitors must use caution and good sense to avoid the rare encounter with dangerous snakes or alligators: watch where you put hands and feet, turn canoes over cautiously, and check under seats. Never disturb animals or nests; no swimming, live bait, or pets (dogs are an alligator delicacy) are allowed.

Insects can be bothersome on humid summer days. Biting deerflies are present at swamp's edge but are less prevalent deeper in. Twilight brings the mosquitoes out; insect repellent is a must (other deterrents are campfire smoke, earth-toned clothing, citronella candles, and wax myrtle leaves). Long pants worn tucked into socks or boots are a good precaution against ticks and chiggers. A thorough body check after a wilderness day catches any ticks before they burrow too deeply to be easily removed. Small red chiggers are harder to spot—if an itchy red rash develops, it might be chiggers. Try suffocating them by covering the area with clear nail polish.

Refuge Regulations

The U.S. Fish and Wildlife Service operates the Okefenokee National Wildlife Refuge, and it means business. Uniformed rangers patrol roads and waterways to prevent poaching and ensure compliance with regulations.

Wilderness permits are required for overnight canoe camping in the swamp, deep swamp excursions, and trips beyond the Suwannee River sill. Motorboats up to 10 horsepower are permitted; some trails are reserved for canoes only. No swimming is allowed. Fishing is permitted; live minnows and trotlines are not.

The speed limit on roads within the refuge is 35 mph in the daytime and 10 mph after dark (watch carefully for animals). Call the refuge for information on wilderness permits or on the occasional managed hunting that is permitted by the Fish and Wildlife Service.

Entrance fees (excepting Okefenokee Swamp Park) are $5 per car per day; it's good for seven days at either the western or eastern entrance. Long-term parking requires a permit and is advisable only at secured primary entrances, not at unsecured secondary landings. For more information, call or write the Okefenokee National Wildlife Refuge, Rte. 2, Box 3330, Folkston, GA 31537, 912/496-7836, www.okefenokee.fws.gov.

WAYCROSS

Distinguishing itself as the Largest City in the Largest County in the Largest State east of the Mississippi, Waycross arose in 1872 at the intersection of stagecoach roads and pioneer trails. The town quickly built up sawmill, turpentine, and farming industries that were largely destroyed by boll weevils and careless logging earlier this century. As railroads and highways supplanted stage roads, modern industry helped the city grow to its present population of 16,000.

Its true heyday was the 1950s and '60s, when gas was cheap and travelers hadn't yet abandoned the state highways for newly completed interstate freeways. Florida-bound travelers pass-

GATORS

The Okefenokee was once so thick with alligators that a swamper could ford streams on their backs—so went the tales of early swamp settlers. But years of slaughter for valuable hides reduced this abundant species to endangered status. Though now protected, alligators continue to be threatened by illegal poaching. Gates around the Okefenokee's national wildlife refuge are locked up soon after dark to discourage the practice, and bumper stickers in the vicinity proclaim "Turn In Poachers!"

Current estimates place the Okefenokee's alligator population at about 10,000. (the alligator meat that's served in some local restaurants comes from alligator farms—not, of course, from the protected refuge.)

Easily seen basking on shore or in water, alligators are most active in spring, their mating season. First, "bulls" must fend off competing males in a show of strength: the two prehistoric giants lock jaws, splash, and roll about until the exhausted party gives up and slinks off. The victor then begins an equally tumultuous ordeal with the female. A bull alligator's bellow (often compared to a lion's roar) sounds a territorial warning throughout the year, but in spring, the cry has special meaning.

Females follow this sound to the love den, lured also by the musky odor of the bull's emission.

Females lay 40–60 eggs on a bank, covering them with decaying vegetation, which insulates the eggs. Sixty to ninety days later, "clucking" cries alert the mother to uncover her nine-inch hatchlings. Nest temperature decides gender: males hatch from warmer spots, females from cooler. The babies frolic around their mother for months in an unusually familial relationship for reptiles (though alligators have been known to eat their young in hard times).

Alligators live almost as long as humans, about 50 years, and grow to 18 feet. They eat anything in close range that moves; their appetite subsides in winter and they hibernate the coolest weeks of the year.

The American alligator, *Alligator mississippiensis,* got its name from Spanish sailors, who called it *el largota* ("the lizard"). They can be distinguished from their crocodile cousins by snout shape and overbite. Gators have rounded snouts, a crocodile's is pointed, and if a lower tooth juts outside the upper lip, it's a crocodile. (A moot point in the Okefenokee, which is without a crocodile to be seen.)

ing through Waycross brought hordes of visitors to the Okefenokee. Some attractions and businesses still evoke that family-station-wagon, road-motel feeling, creating an old-fashioned ambience that adds to the time-warp sense of the swamp itself.

Though locals boast about Waycross natives Burt Reynolds and writer Stanley Booth, the true patron saint of these parts is Ponce de Leon Montgomery County Alabama Georgia Beauregard Possum—better known as Pogo. This philosophizing critter, the cartoon creation of the late Walt Kelly, is honored at the town's annual **PogoFest** in March. (Wonderful cartoon collections are available year-round at the Okefenokee Swamp Park gift shop.)

Of a half-dozen motels clustered along Memorial Drive where Hwy. 82 and Hwy. 84 meet, the **Holiday Inn,** 912/283-4490, remains the most venerable hotel and meeting place in town. It's also where locals go for a nice reasonably priced Southern buffet, especially on Sunday.

On the Barbecue Landmark Trail, find **M The Pig,** 768 State St.,912/283-4875.

The **Waycross Tourism and Convention Bureau,** 315-A Plant Ave., 912/283-3744, www.okefenokeetourism.com, is within the historic rail depot.

Okefenokee Swamp Park

The northern entrance to the swamp, Okefenokee Swamp Park, 912/283-0583, www.okeswamp .com, is a private day-use attraction 12 miles southeast of Waycross. The old-timey swamp theme park features wildlife shows, swamp ecology exhibits, a serpentorium, and a restored pioneer homestead. Besides its natural kid appeal and retro charm, its greatest attraction is simply the swamp itself—rambling boardwalks above the blackwater lead out to a 90-foot observation tower overlooking the cypress-belt canopy; there are plenty of places to look and linger along the way. (Families with small children must be alert on unfenced walkways.)

Looping fern-lined waterways through the cypress weave past such Disney-worthy sights as an old moonshine still (built on a float to easily evade "revenooers"), a Seminole dugout canoe,

and a backward sign that reads correctly only in its black-water reflection.

The admission is $10, or better yet, purchase a combo admission ticket that includes a 30-minute boat trip for a mile and a half through the swamp. The boat trips are led by guides full of colorful anecdotes about swampland history and folklore, and are well worth the additional expense.

For an additional charge, take a 10-mile guided trip into the deep swamp (by reservation only). Or rent a canoe and wind your own way around. The park is open 9 A.M.–5:30 P.M. year-round every day but Christmas.

Laura S. Walker State Park

Set in the piney South Georgia woods 12 miles east of Waycross, Laura S. Walker State Park, 912/287-4900, www.gastateparks.org, reservations 800/864-PARK (864-7275), parking $2, features a 120-acre lake for boating and fishing and an 18-hole golf course, 912/285-6154. Waterskiing is a popular activity here (10 horsepower limit except midday); you can also rent canoes and swim in the pool (summers only). A 1.2-mile nature trail winds through the woods.

A small 44-site **campground** hasn't much privacy but is nonetheless invitingly set by the lake in a grassy area surrounded by pines ($17–21 per night; water/electrical hookups, dump station, and laundry facilities are available). The park is open 7 A.M.–10 P.M. (gates lock); office hours are until 5 P.M.

FOLKSTON

The sleepy town of Folkston (population 2,300) has traditionally catered to out-of-towners on weeklong fishing or hunting vacations. Lately a new breed of ecotourists have been frequenting the swamp, and you can see the changes it has brought to town: bed-and-breakfast lodging has sprung up, and folk artists have set up shop near the swamp. But some of the development remains along traditional lines—they've built a platform beside the railroad tracks, not for passengers (only freight lines come through), but for the folks who like to come downtown and watch the trains go by.

In the center of town, the **Train Museum,** 202 W. Main St., 912/496-2536, in the old 1903 train depot, displays old maps, lights, and logbooks. It's open Mon.–Fri. 8:30 A.M.–5 P.M. Across the way is an elaborate viewing platform shelter called the **Folkston Funnel,** set up for folks who like to watch trains pass.

Accommodations and Food

M The Inn at Folkston, 509 W. Main St., 912/496-6256 or 888/509-6246, is in a nice house in a residential neighborhood a few short blocks from downtown, which offers four rooms priced from $99, including a full breakfast.

The home-style **Okefenokee Restaurant,** 912/496-3263, on Main Street at U.S. 1 and Hwy. 301 (east of the tracks), serves three meals daily and specializes in a Southern buffet—look for the lines around lunchtime.

SUWANNEE CANAL RECREATION AREA

The eastern entrance to the swamp, the Suwannee Canal Recreation Area (SCRA) is 12 miles south of Folkston. The SCRA serves as the federal entrance to the Okefenokee National Wildlife Refuge; the **refuge office** is on Rte. 2 (outside the gates), 912/496-7836. This entrance provides access to the swamp's "prairies" and offers the most extensive services for boating excursions (including rental equipment).

The entrance fee is $5 per car, which is good for admission for seven days either here at SCRA or at Stephen C. Foster State Park (western entrance). The gates are open from a half-hour before sunrise until 5:30 P.M. in winter, 7:30 P.M. otherwise.

A nine-mile loop **nature drive** enables you to see local wildlife from the comfort of your car, or park and get out on the 4,000-foot **boardwalk,** which leads to a 50-foot observation tower overlooking Seagrove Lake and Chesser Prairie. Other short walking trails lead to a restored pioneer homestead and aboriginal mound on Chesser Island; the canal-digger's trail sheds light on the construction of the Suwannee Canal.

The SCRA **visitors center** is well worth a visit, particularly with children. There are climb-

aboard and under-the-swamp exhibits, a jukebox of animal sounds, and an impressive wildlife film. They also sell nature books and wildlife guides, along with books on Okefenokee history and folklore. It's open 9 A.M.–5 P.M. daily.

The boathouse at the swamp's edge is operated by Okefenokee Adventures, a private concessionaire. Inside there's a small snack bar and a store that sells insect repellant, sunscreen, hats, film, and bottled water (including the local vintage *Okefenokee Swamp Water,* which is great for souvenirs if you don't drink it first). They also rent bikes. For information about boating services and guided swamp tours, see the following, or call **Okefenokee Adventures,** 912/496-7156.

Typical of the eastern terrain are the "prairies"—large watery fields of wispy aquatic vegetation spotted with open ponds. Its dominant feature is the 12-mile canal, the remnant of an unsuccessful attempt to drain the swamp at the turn of the century.

Boating

Boating is the main event at the swamp, and this entrance has the most extensive boat services available at the swamp. For more information on guided tours or outfitting, contact **Okefenokee Adventures,** 912/496-7156 or 866-THE-SWAMP (843-7926), www.okefenokee adventures.com.

Guided tours on pontoon boats are a great introduction to the swamp, its natural history, and its folklore (if Omar is your guide, it's your lucky day). One-hour trips cost $10 and up; more for the longer tour. **Night tours** through the swamp are found here only, and the sounds and sights create a lasting impression (by reservation only).

Canoes (with paddles) rent for $22 per day; 14- to 20-foot boats start at $40 a day. Ask for a free water-trails map when you rent your boat.

The straight, wide, 12-mile **Suwannee Canal** creates a highway through the swamp that's most conducive to motorboating; this scenic arcade of cypress and slash pine ends at 6,000-acre Chase Prairie. Rest stops (at 2, 5.5, 7.5, and 12 miles in from the SCRA boat dock) provide shelter and chemical toilets.

At **Grand Prairie Lakes,** the clear pools within the thick growth of the prairies are prized fishing spots and are secluded areas from which to watch wildlife (travel in 2.2 miles from the dock to the lakes turnoff; follow the trail south four miles to the first set of lakes, or continue two miles to Gannett Lake, the southernmost accessible point in the swamp).

In addition to these all-access trails, two **canoe-only trails** leave the noise and wakes of motorboats behind. These trails lead off from the main canal two miles in from the SCRA boat dock, south to Cooter Lake or north across Mizell Prairie (named for Josiah Mizell, who designed the prototype swamp skiff). When water levels drop, these trails may be closed.

◪ STEPHEN C. FOSTER STATE PARK

The western entrance to the swamp, Stephen C. Foster State Park (SCF), 912/637-5274, www.gastateparks.org, reservations 800/864-PARK (864-7275), parking $2, is 18 miles northeast of the tiny town of Fargo (population 300). In the most remote corner of the swamp, this isolated 80-acre enclave has a lot to offer—the only overnight lodging at swamp's edge, access to the historically and ecologically rich Billy's Island, and 25 miles of waterways through some of the most spectacular scenery in the Okefenokee.

The park is on Jones Island at "the Pocket," a spit of land jutting out into the swamp, so it's the closest you can get to the heart of the swamp without getting your feet wet. Here the headwaters of the Suwannee River take shape and drain out of the swamp, aiming for the Gulf of Mexico.

Besides lodging, camping, and boating facilities, the park offers a 1.5-mile boardwalk trail, an interpretive center and programs, and bike rentals. A small store sells fishing licenses and stocks bare necessities (canned food, Kraft macaroni and cheese, matches, ice, and ersatz milk). The nearest supermarket or pharmacy lies a hundred miles away, so bring all you'll need.

The refuge entrance fee is $5 per car; admission is good for seven days here or at the eastern entrance near Folkston. Gates are open 6:30 A.M.–8:30 P.M. spring and summer, 7 A.M.–7 P.M. fall and winter.

Accommodations and Camping
In either a jungle hammock or a roomy air-conditioned cabin, ◪ **Stephen C. Foster State Park** is the place to stay if you like your adventure close to the land. Nine fully equipped two-bedroom cottages rent for $70–90.

Camp for $17–22 at 66 campsites, each with water/electric hookups, access to bathhouses and sanitary dump station. During the summer thundershower season, tent campers should bring thick ground cover (or spring for a cottage).

Boating
Park rangers lead **guided boat tours** of the western Okefenokee three times a day. **Boat rentals** include canoes, johnboats (skiffs), and motorboats. Ask for a free waterways map from the park office.

A free launch is available five miles south of the state park dock at the Suwannee River Sill, but there are no other services. Two water trails lead from the state park dock to the sill; one is all-access and the other is for canoes only.

Billy's Island
Exploring Billy's Island is one of the best boating and hiking adventures in the swamp. Imagine this 3,140-acre island wilderness as home to ancient tribes, the base of operations for Native American resistance to U.S. expansionism, a homestead, a logging boomtown turned bust, and now, once again, home only to swamp animals.

Within a half-mile of the dock lie many remnants from these times. The first you'll come across is the old Lee (no relation to Robert E.) family cemetery (descendants of this 1850s homesteading family still come out to the island to pay their respects). Up the trail from the cemetery, you'll come upon the old railroad bed from early 20th-century logging days; about 300 feet off this rise lies a 4,000-year old aboriginal burial mound. Back on the main trail, the path leads to the old "downtown." Watch for strewn steam boiler parts, chimney foundations, a rusty bed frame, and metal washtubs. As ruins go, these aren't the oldest or rarest, but as a contrast to the prevailing jungle wilderness, the rusty debris of Billy's Island is first-rate.

Stay on marked trails; watch where you reach and step; and pack out what you pack in (no trash containers are on the island). The day use–only island (4.25 miles long and 1.5 miles wide) is accessible to day-boaters only from the state park. Ask at the park office for an island trail map. From the state park boat dock, turn right out of the channel and go east through Billy's Lake 1.8 miles to Billy's Island (motor-boats are okay). Park boats at the dock or pull up on shore, and head up the trail.

Minnie's Lake/Big Water Lake

The middle fork of the Suwannee River branches off of Billy's Lake. Following the narrow winding channels of water lilies and cypress for five miles, boaters reach Minnie's Lake. From here the stream crosses Big Water Prairie to trail's end at Big Water Lake (12 miles from the SCF state park boat dock). Freestanding wooden platforms at both lakes offer rest stops for boaters; the one at Big Water has a chemical toilet.

Jimmy Walker, former director of the Oke-fenokee Swamp Park and great-grandson of early swamp pioneer Obediah Barber, considers Big Water "the most beautiful place in the swamp." Actually a wide expanse of the contracting-and-expanding Suwannee River, the six-mile-long, 100-foot-wide clearing is surrounded by forest so thick that animal sounds echo around the lake. As the dead center of the swamp, Big Water is the heart of the Okefenokee wilderness.

OVERNIGHT PADDLING TRIPS

Canoe and kayak campers can experience deep-swamp wilderness on overnight trips ranging in length from a 14-mile, two-day loop trip to a 43-mile, five-day trip crisscrossing the swamp. A permit is required from the Okefenokee National Wildlife Refuge authority in Folkston; reservations are accepted up to two months in advance by contacting the national wildlife refuge, Rte. 2, Box 338, Folkston, GA 31537, 912/496-7836, www.okefenokee.fws.gov.

Paddlers must make their own arrangements for equipment, supplies, and shuttles to and from put-in and take-out points, or they can make arrangements with a local outfitter, such as **Okefenokee Adventures,** 912/496-7156, www.okefenokeeadventures.com, which provides all equipment, transportation, and food for around $100 per person per day. The St. Simons–based **SouthEast Adventures Outfitters,** 912/638-6732, also organizes paddling excursions into the swamp.

Campers on the Canal Run or Craven's Hammock routes set up tents (freestanding only) on sheltered wooden sleeping platforms measuring 20 by 28 feet (except on Floyd's Island, where campers can stay in an early 20th-century wooden hunting cabin); a "jungle hammock" will suffice in place of a tent. Most rest stops provide chemical toilets; nevertheless the refuge requires canoes to carry portable toilets with disposable bags (both available from the refuge concessionaire).

Refuge regulations require canoeists to carry a life vest for each person, a compass, and a flashlight (remember extra batteries); outfitters include such supplies with their gear. Recommended supplies include drinking water, a first-aid kit, rain gear, litter bags, a whistle, insect repellent, rope (to pull your canoe across peat blowups or portage over Floyd's Island), mosquito netting, a sleeping bag or jungle hammock, camp stoves and fuel, sunscreen, and a hat.

Leave cars at secured entrances only; obtain necessary parking permits for the length of your trip from the gate kiosk or at the Suwannee Canal Recreation Area boathouse. Shuttles are available from Okefenokee Adventures for about a dollar a mile (calculated roundtrip from SCRA).

Three-Day Excursions

The **Green Trail,** a three-day 24-mile trip, runs from one remote corner of the swamp to the other, starting at Kingfisher Landing and ending at Stephen C. Foster State Park. Crossing all three varieties of swamp terrain, the Green Trail features an overnight stop on Floyd's Island. Campers may stay in a turn-of-the-century cypress cabin nestled among magnolias and oaks and explore the four-mile-long, mile-wide island (portage required over the island's narrow tip). For a fitting finale to roughing it in the swamp, reserve a furnished two-bedroom cabin at the trail's terminus, Stephen C. Foster State Park, and cook up some of that fresh-caught bass.

This trail demands the most shuttling around the swamp, which is both a logistical and financial consideration. Since cars are safest at secured entrances, many campers park at the Suwannee Canal Recreation Area when they check in at refuge headquarters and then take a prearranged shuttle to and from their put-in and take-out points. At a dollar a mile (calculated roundtrip from the refuge each way), shuttle fees for the Green Trail add more than $200 to the cost of your trip. (As the fee applies to 1–10 canoes, the price per person decreases with larger groups).

One-Night Excursions

Single-overnight loop trips, available from three starting points, offer short adventurous excursions into the swamp—ideal for weekenders.

From Kingfisher Landing in the northeast, two different roundtrips are available, to either Maul Hammock or Bluff Lake. Both routes explore remote areas of the swamp, including prized fishing lakes.

From Stephen C. Foster State Park's western entrance, one loop trip runs to Craven's Hammock; the other goes to Canal Run, passing Billy's Island. Trips to and from the state park offer the bonus of staying overnight at park cabins or campsites (reservations are required).

Of the three single-overnight loop trips starting at the Suwannee Canal Recreation Area's eastern entrance, the narrow winding canoe-only trail is more scenic than the all-access routes through the canal.

One trip crosses the swamp in a single overnight. East-to-west or west-to-east, this trail passes Billy's Island and includes paddling through the 12-mile canal. (Shuttling is required.)

Savannah

An 18th-century village that lives resolutely in the present, Savannah brings together an exotic history (all the Redcoats, silkworms, Indian chiefs, blockade runners, Crypto-Jews, and utopian ideals you could ask for) and a subtropical nature (tendrils of Spanish moss, wisteria, and wild grapevines drape like tinsel off majestic oaks), and wraps it up in one compact, charming package. As Taos is to the American Southwest, Savannah is to the Southeast—the city that best encapsulates the regional aesthetic. If you see one city in the American Southeast, make it Savannah.

Rows of European townhouses line a city grid punctuated by shady garden squares full of Grecian fountains, obelisks, and towering magnolias. Throughout the cobblestone and oyster-shell lanes you'll see gold domes and Corinthian columns, wrought-iron balustrades and sweeping staircases. But Savannah often adds a touch of whimsy—like dolphin-shaped drain spouts, flowerboxes gone wild, and water fountains for dogs—and residents live comfortably among the griffons, never too far from a favorite corner bar or student dive (after all, this isn't Charleston).

© KAP STANN

Must-Sees

M Carriage Tours: Even folks who wince at the idea of organized tours could find them evocative in Savannah, where a horse-and-buggy pace seems just about the right speed to survey the lushly landscaped squares and cobblestone lanes of the historic district (page 235).

M Owens-Thomas House: Among the city's preeminent house museums, the elegantly furnished 1816 Regency-style villa designed by William Jay also includes rarely preserved slave quarters, offering a look at antebellum life from all sides (page 240).

M Ralph Mark Gilbert Civil Rights Museum: The legacy of King Cotton is told through exhibits and a film that focuses primarily on the movement in the 1960s (page 242).

M Telfair Museum of Arts and Sciences: The oldest public museum in the South, now housed in a strikingly bold modern building, displays an impressive permanent collection of Impressionist paintings and the fine decorative arts for which the city is famous (page 242).

M SCAD Galleries: The Savannah College of Art and Design (SCAD) maintains 10 galleries around town exhibiting the work of faculty, students, and other artists. Openings, lectures, and other events bring nationally known filmmakers, photographers, and other artists to town (page 243).

M Bonaventure Cemetery: John Muir was among the first to popularize the attraction of a trip to Bonaventure, long before the cemetery played a starring role in Berendt's tale. The low canopy of oaks with drifting tendrils of moss creates an intimate, brooding landscape, where salt-swept monuments appear as so many strangely geometric stones rising from the sand (page 268).

M Fort Pulaski National Monument: This brick behemoth presents a dramatic horizon of brick and marsh, where the winds whip up waves in the medieval moat surrounding the famously doomed fortress (page 268).

M North Beach: The broad expanse of porcelain sand and the gradual incline of the central beach attracts sunbathers and families; better beachcombing and deeper swimming holes are found towards each tip, and you might even be accompanied by a dolphins or two (page 270).

M Guided Sea Kayaking Excursions: If your visit is confined to Savannah, get out into the eastern marshlands on a guided kayaking excursion (page 271).

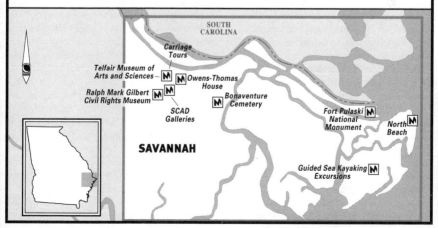

Savannah

Here the local Kress five-and-dime and sprawling '50s motels are as likely to be restored as gingerbread Victorians. As Savannahians know more than most, history is unruly.

The past decade is as illustrative as any. The once-sleepy tidewater city found its repose disturbed with the phenomenal success of John Berendt's 1994 bestseller, *Midnight in the Garden of Good and Evil*, which provocatively captured the city's mystique in the racy retelling of a local murder trial. More than a decade later, tourists still flock to town with "The Book" in hand. With that popularity has come the Radissons and Courtyards, an Outback Steakhouse on Bay Street, and bewildered out-of-state drivers trying to circumnavigate the squares. Locals are grateful for the prosperity and how it has improved downtown but are wistful for the days when they could visit favorite haunts without waiting in line.

The *Midnight* phenomenon vastly accelerated efforts that had been under way for a half-century. In the middle of the last century, the city was busy expanding into Southside and left the historic city center largely abandoned. An uptick in economic activity returned attention downtown when in 1955, the city's plans to replace the 1820 Davenport House with a parking lot galvanized local society women to organize against the demolition. The women founded the Historic Savannah Foundation and set about saving not only the Davenport House but also more than a thousand other buildings downtown in the next 30 years. In 1966 Savannah was named a national historic district, becoming one of the largest urban historic districts in the nation.

In 1978, the Savannah College of Art and Design (SCAD) was founded, adding historic preservation and architectural history to its list of avant-garde programs in the arts. Renovating the 1892 Volunteer Guard Armory at Madison Square for its headquarters, SCAD set in motion an ambitious program to preserve and adaptively reuse more than a thousand structures in the historic district and neighboring Victorian District, including the vernacular HoJo's, diners, movie theaters, and the local jail, among more acclaimed architectural landmarks. With 6,500 students from around the world, they also bring in boatloads of aspiring artists and creative energy, which adds a youthful vitality and cutting edge to the city.

As a result, Savannah is a city of architectural treasures and beautiful urban landscapes. Many historic structures have found second lives as bed-and-breakfast inns or restaurants, and one of the pleasures of visiting Savannah is to indulge in the city's luxurious hospitality, low country cuisine, and one-of-a-kind lodging. Travelers with recreation in mind enjoy just as grand a time exploring the lush natural environment—camping under the oaks, paddling through the marsh, and swimming with dolphins out at the barrier islands. With steamy mists rising off the water and Spanish moss swaying in the humid breeze, it's a romantic setting that can dramatize any adventure.

PLANNING YOUR TIME

A big part of Savannah's appeal is the exceptional selection and quality of historic inns and fine restaurants in the historic district—it's a great place for a splurge. Considering the costs, a weekend spent living it up downtown makes more sense than scrimping to extend your visit by staying in a nondescript motel in Southside. Tybee or Skidaway Islands both have wonderful campgrounds, and this is a practical alternative for budget travelers or people planning lots of outdoor recreation. (Camping in the summer will get buggy but is still worthwhile; and there's nothing like those warm summer nights.) Families may want to aim for franchise hotels; many historic inns have a minimum age requirement of around 12 and an atmosphere that is not conducive to small children.

Also be aware that spring and fall are high seasons in Savannah (along with Christmas, New Year's, and St. Patrick's Day), while summer is the high season 18 miles east on Tybee Island. So in the dog days of August, you may discover rooms in Savannah's most exclusive inns are going for nearly the same price as a standard chain motel double on the beach.

For a few days in the historic district you could easily do without a car. Let yourself fall under

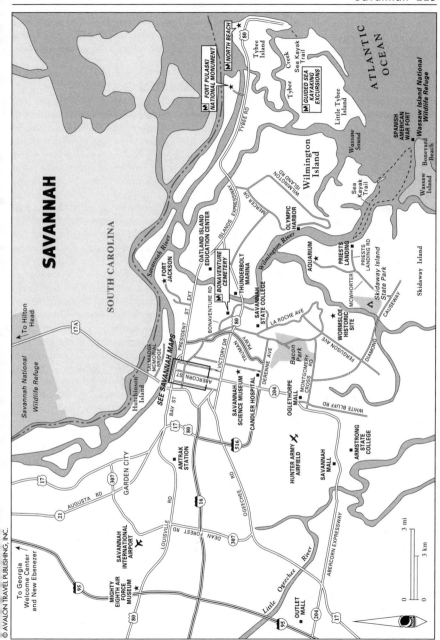

SAVANNAH

SOUTH CAROLINA

ATLANTIC OCEAN

© AVALON TRAVEL PUBLISHING, INC.

To Georgia Welcome Center and New Ebenezer

Savannah National Wildlife Refuge

To Hilton Head

Hutchinson Island

Savannah River

TALMADGE MEMORIAL BRIDGE

SEE SAVANNAH MAPS

FORT JACKSON

PRESIDENT ST EXT

★ MIGHTY EIGHTH AIR FORCE MUSEUM

■ SAVANNAH INTERNATIONAL AIRPORT

GARDEN CITY

AUGUSTA RD

DEAN FOREST RD

LOUISVILLE RD

OGEECHEE RD

■ AMTRAK STATION

BAY ST

CANDLER HOSPITAL

★ SAVANNAH SCIENCE MUSEUM

ABERCORN ST

VICTORY DR

DERENNE AVE

HUNTER ARMY AIRFIELD ✈

SAVANNAH MALL

ARMSTRONG STATE COLLEGE

OGLETHORPE MALL

Bacon Park

MONTGOMERY CROSS RD

WHITE BLUFF RD

FERGUSON AVE

DIAMOND

LA ROCHE AVE

★ WORMSLOE HISTORIC SITE

SAVANNAH STATE COLLEGE

BONAVENTURE RD

Ⓜ BONAVENTURE CEMETERY

■ OATLAND ISLAND EDUCATION CENTER

THUNDERBOLT MARINA

ISLANDS EXPRESSWAY

MERCER DR

OLYMPIC HARBOR

WILMINGTON ISLAND RD

Wilmington Island

TYBEE RD

★ FORT PULASKI NATIONAL MONUMENT Ⓜ

Ⓜ NORTH BEACH

Tybee Island

Tybee Creek

Sea Kayak Trail

Little Tybee Island

Ⓜ GUIDED SEA KAYAKING EXCURSIONS

Wassaw Sound

SPANISH AMERICAN WAR FORT

Wassaw Island National Wildlife Refuge

Boneyard Beach

Wassaw Island

Sea Kayak Trail

AQUARIUM

PRIESTS LANDING

PRIESTS LANDING RD

MCWHORTER

Skidaway Island State Park

CAUSEWAY

Skidaway Island

Wilmington River

Little Ogeechee River

Ogeechee River

ABERCORN EXPRESSWAY

OUTLET MALL

3 mi

3 km

Savannah

the spell of the city by spending your days walking around the waterfront and the squares; taking in the sights, sounds, and scents; working up to a fine meal; and enjoying the city's nightlife before returning to comfort and luxury at one of the city's historic inns. Pack comfortable walking shoes and fancy clothes if you're looking for an excuse to go all out (only a few restaurants require jackets for men, and native women favor loose, flowing dress).

More sightseeing and recreation are found out east to Tybee Island, including stops at Bonaventure Cemetery and Fort Pulaski. Kayaking trips, swimming, beachcombing, and paddling trips out to deserted islands are some of the highlights. The usual precautionary supplies apply—dry bags, water shoes or old sneakers, bug spray, bite cream or aloe vera (but don't let that stop you if you haven't come stocked). A favorite creek-side crab shack and beachfront café are good ways to wrap up a day exploring the marsh or beach.

See Savannah at its party finest by scheduling your trip around such events as St. Patrick's Day (Savannah's version of Mardi Gras; celebrated for three days, with a parade on March 17), the Savannah Tour of Homes and Gardens, in late March, and the Savannah Music Festival, spreading out over two weeks around early April. The Savannah Film and Video Festival is held in fall.

Savannah is 250 miles from Atlanta; 110 miles from Charleston, South Carolina; and 140 miles from Jacksonville, Florida. The Savannah airport is a short 15-minute drive from downtown, but if your trip includes the rest of the Georgia coast, you will find more frequent economical flights through Jacksonville.

HISTORY

When British General James Oglethorpe founded the southernmost outpost of England's American colonies, the bluff that is now Savannah was inhabited by the Yamacraw, a group broken off from the Creek Confederacy. Local mico (chief) Tomochichi welcomed the settlers and struck up a friendship with Oglethorpe, celebrated most notably by a trip to England for Tomochichi,

his wife, and nephew, where the Yamacraw were greeted by the royal court. Tomochichi is buried under a boulder of Stone Mountain granite in Wright Square.

13th and Final Colony

Named for King George II, Georgia was conceived as a socially philanthropic experiment in which Oglethorpe offered those jailed for excessive debt a chance for a new life if they would come and populate the new colony (and relieve England of the burdens of a cripplingly harsh social policy). European Protestants, Jews fleeing the Spanish Inquisition, and other persecuted religious refugees soon expanded the scope of this mission.

In February 1733 Oglethorpe arrived with 114 colonists and mapped out the new town of Savannah to exacting 18th-century British specifications still evident today. Around the squares and narrow lanes rose Oglethorpe's utopian enterprise—he and the original trustees of the new Georgia colony envisioned a place without slavery, alcohol, speculation, religious persecution, or oppressive class differences. Not all of those ideals held fast—most notably slavery, as the trustees succumbed to colonists' complaints about unfair competition from neighboring slaveholding states.

Oglethorpe tried to establish silk and wine-making industries in Trustees Garden, on the east side of the bluff, and though the city's mulberry trees and wild muscadine vines are all that remain of those dashed hopes, what did flourish were crops of cotton, peaches, rice, and tobacco.

American Revolution

As the newest colony and one begun by British philanthropy, Georgia remained largely Loyalist and was the only colony not represented in the first Continental Congress. Savannah's "Liberty Boys" first raised voices of protest, erecting a liberty pole outside Tondee's Tavern on Whitaker and Broughton Streets, and in 1776 they read the Declaration of Independence there when Georgia joined the rest of the colonies in opposition to the crown.

Two years later, British forces attacked the coast and captured Savannah. Among the bloodiest battles to ensue after that was the Siege of Savannah in 1779, when 700 troops, including Polish Count Casimir Pulaski, died in a battle lasting less than one hour. By the end of 1779, every important town in Georgia had fallen under British control.

Yet General Nathanael Greene, the commander of Southern troops, managed to strategically overturn every British victory, until the British evacuated Savannah in 1782 (taking with them steadfast Loyalists). Much acclaimed for his campaign, Greene was rewarded for his service by the people of Georgia with a gift of Mulberry Plantation two miles upriver, where he died of sunstroke in 1786. He is buried in Johnson Square.

Antebellum Period

On Mulberry Plantation in 1793, Eli Whitney and Greene's widow, Catherine, put the finishing touches on a new invention, the cotton gin. The cotton gin revolutionized cotton farming and made it far more profitable, heralding a wealthy era of lavish development in Savannah. The Cotton Exchange, which still heads up Factor's Row today, set cotton prices around the world for nearly a century. Slavery, a dying institution before the cotton gin, was revived in order to deal with increased production.

Yet not all blacks in the South before the Civil War were enslaved. From colonial times on, slaves who bought their freedom, escaped, or were manumitted (released from slavery) joined in free black communities with African immigrants, including former slaves who had emigrated with the French fleeing the Haitian revolution. In 1860, Savannah's free black population of 3,000 was the largest in the state.

That same year, after 18 years of construction, the federal government was nearing completion of a massive brick fort on Cockspur Island, 15 miles downriver from Savannah, as part of a coastal fortification system implemented by President James Madison in response to the War of 1812. Complete with a medieval moat and drawbridge, the fort was named for Revolutionary War hero Count Pulaski, and was considered invincible.

Civil War

Even before Georgia officially seceded in 1861, one of the governor's first moves was to seize Fort Pulaski, and one of the Union's first moves was to take the fort back. After the Confederate Army abandoned Tybee Island, the Union Army erected artillery batteries at its northwest shore. While in 1862 it was widely thought the fort could withstand attacks from that distance with standard ordnance, Union Captain Quincy Gillmore tested new rifled cannons that tore through the brick walls, forcing a Confederate surrender only 30 hours later and ending the era of masonry forts. Federal troops waited out the rest of the war here, monitoring blockades and playing baseball until the action caught up to them (reenactors team up for games at the fort to honor the ball-playing Yankee spirit).

When General William T. Sherman arrived at the end of his infamous March to the Sea in 1864, he set up headquarters in the Green-Meldrim House, on Madison Square (now open to public tours). From here he sent a telegram to President Lincoln: "I beg to present to you as a Christmas gift, the City of Savannah, with 140 heavy guns and plenty of ammunition and also about 25,000 bales of cotton."

After conferring with local black leaders, Sherman issued Field Order No. 15, which called for the Sea Islands south of Charleston and abandoned rice fields up to 30 miles upriver to be apportioned for newly freed slaves. The field order was announced at the Second African Baptist Church on Greene Square. During the following years of Reconstruction, federal legislation rescinded Sherman's decree and returned property to former landowners. The unmet promise of "40 acres and a mule" spurs the call for reparations to this day.

Civil Rights

The Jim Crow South enforced segregation between blacks and whites throughout the South, and Savannah was no exception. Yet due to the highly organized efforts of local African American leaders—notably NAACP President Ralph Mark Gilbert, for whom the city's civil rights museum is named—Savannah was able to make the

Savannah

transition to integration without the violence that marked that transition elsewhere. Local law enforcement was integrated as early as 1947.

As local historian W. W. Law took up the mantle after Gilbert's death, the African American community organized to pressure white businesses to desegregate through a systematic economic boycott in the 1960s. Otis Johnson, who later became mayor, was the first to integrate Armstrong College, a historically white state school in Savannah. The First African Baptist Church, on Franklin Square (with a congregation dating back to 1773), was the center of the local civil-rights movement.

20th-Century Renaissance

After downtown Savannah was named a national historic district in 1966, tourism became one of the town's major industries, particularly after the French magazine *Le Monde* dubbed Savannah "the most beautiful city in North America" in 1989. Savannah now receives an estimated 5.8 million visitors a year.

Other major industries in Savannah include port operations and manufacturing—principally pulpwood, paper, and aircraft production. Nearby Fort Stewart is the region's largest single employer. Much of the metropolitan area's population of 302,000 stays in the outlying districts and in the islands of Chatham County.

The Historic District

GETTING ORIENTED

The historic district measures a compact 2.5 square miles, and the original 1732 city grid is easily grasped. From Bull Street in the center, the district is divided neatly into symmetrical eastern and western sections, bounded by East Broad and Martin Luther King Jr. Boulevard (formerly West Broad), respectively. Bay Street runs along the waterfront. The historic district ends at Gaston Street (historic district chauvinists are proudly dubbed "NOGs," meaning they stay "North of Gaston").

South of Gaston, the Victorian district surrounds Forsyth Park. One of the city's most venerable inns, the Magnolia Inn, and the Mansion, its newest hotel, overlook the park. A few blocks away from the park, however, the district is in varying stages of rehabilitation and can become dodgy territory for visitors.

Victory Drive is the boundary between the Victorian district and the small residential Midtown district. Victory Drive runs out to Tybee Island (Hwy. 80), 18 miles east. The large Southside district runs south and east of DeRenne Avenue. Abercorn Avenue (Hwy 204) is the north-south thoroughfare that connects the historic district with Midtown and Southside and runs out to Hwy 17 and I-95, a distance of

around 10 miles (the Truman Hwy. provides a convenient bypass to much of this surface route).

Savannah Visitors Center and History Museum

The Savannah Visitors Center, 912/944-0455, 301 Martin Luther King Jr. Blvd., housed in the restored Central of Georgia railroad station, is a good first stop for visitors new to town. Pick up free maps and guides, rental audio tours, shuttle schedules, scores of brochures, and discount coupons for local lodging, dining, and attractions. There is no admission charge to enter the visitors center. They also run a gift shop and small snack concession. The center is open Mon.–Fri. 8:30 A.M.–5 P.M., Sat.–Sun. and holidays 9 A.M.–5 P.M. You can park at the visitors center free for the first hour; after that it costs $1 for the second hour and 50 cents for each additional hour.

The Savannah History Museum, 912/238-1779, within the train shed adjacent to the center, displays an 1890 locomotive, the famed park bench from the *Forrest Gump* movie filmed in Savannah, a cotton gin, and historical and industrial exhibits largely about rice and shipping. You may prefer to skip the museum and just get out into the real thing. A 15-minute film presents a promotional overview, seen to best advantage if you need a cool quiet place to sit; otherwise, the same advice applies. Admission to the museum annex is $4 for adults and $3 for children, including the film. The museum is open the same hours as the visitors center.

Chatham Area Transit, 912/233-5767, runs free trolleys called CAT Shuttles that loop from the visitors center around major sights and hotels downtown frequently throughout the day and year-round, and on into evenings from February to September. Catch these green, air-conditioned, wheelchair-accessible trolleys on Martin Luther King Jr. Boulevard a half block north of the visitors center (exiting from the front door, turn left). Privately operated, narrated trolley tours start in the parking lot behind the visitors center.

Nearby sights within walking distance of the visitors center include The Roundhouse Railroad Museum, a block south; the Ralph Mark Gilbert Civil Rights Museum, several blocks further south (under the freeway overpass); the Savannah College of Art and Design gallery, next door; and a great bookstore and café across the street. The Greyhound/Trailways bus depot is a couple of blocks north. Under construction to the west is a battlefield park commemorating the 1779 Siege of Savannah.

Satellite visitors centers can be found at the airport and on River Street behind city hall.

RIVERFRONT

Factors Row

Savannah is scenically set on a bluff above the Savannah River, 18 miles upriver from the Atlantic Ocean. At the top of the bluff is **Factors Row,** named for the cotton merchants, called "factors," who dominated the riverfront when the **Cotton Exchange** here set worldwide cotton prices in its heyday. A griffon serves as sentry for the venerable red-brick 1887 Romantic Revival building, which stands at the head of Drayton Street. Today the building is a Masons hall.

With its gleaming golden dome visible throughout the waterfront, **City Hall** presides over Factors Walk from its central position at the head of Bull Street. Step inside to see the impressive rotunda, with its stained-glass crown, seven stories up.

The 10-block flank of ballast-stone and brick buildings surrounding these two landmarks once served as cotton warehouses. Today they house inns, shops, taverns, and offices. A series of ironwork catwalks and ramps connects these five-story buildings to the bluff. The cobblestone alleyway below is **Factors Walk.**

At the western tip of the bluff, **Emmett Park** holds a collection of landmarks and monuments, including the 1852 harbor light, a Celtic cross, and the Vietnam Veterans Memorial.

The promenade along Bay Street, dotted with statuary and fountains and shaded by magnolias and oaks, makes a lovely stroll from end to end, and it's easily turned into a loop trip by dropping down to River Street at the foot of the bluff. A short detour east to Bay and East Broad Streets leads to the site of **Trustees Garden,** the first experimental agricultural garden in the U.S., established in 1733. Next door in the **Pirates House,** a 1794 sailor's tavern that's now a family restaurant, a robotic pirate tells swashbuckling tales.

River Street

Eye-level with the busy tugs and barges of the brimming ship channel, River Street is the city's prime entertainment district, lined with dozens of shops, restaurants, raw bars, and clubs, including Kevin Barry's Irish pub (on the western side of the Hyatt) and the down-home Bayou Café (to the east).

You can reach River Street through several steep cutaway alleys and staircases from Factors Walk, or look for the public elevator behind City Hall on the Hyatt Hotel side. The elevator leads down to a small branch visitors center with convenient public facilities. Riverboats, dolphin tours, and water taxis depart from the central dock behind City Hall.

The many city festivals held here turn River Street into one long block party, with live entertainment inside and out, fireworks, sidewalk margarita stands (plastic containers only), seafood-cocktail stalls, and dancing in the streets.

The *Waving Girl* statue, marking the eastern entrance to the channel, honors Florence Martus, a local woman who greeted ships from when she was 19 years old (in 1887) until her

Riverboat tours provide beautiful views of the historic Savannah skyline.

death, in 1931. Her iconic image, memorialized by the same sculptor who created the Iwo Jima monument in Arlington Cemetery, is Savannah's answer to Copenhagen's famous mermaid. The **Olympic Cauldron,** nearby, commemorates the yachting competition held in Savannah during the 1996 Olympic Games.

From the Marriott Hotel Dock, water taxis make another stop to ferry passengers across the channel to the convention center on Hutchinson Island.

Hutchinson Island

Throughout the city's history, Hutchinson Island was a swath of wilderness at the far side of the river, a sand spit between the shipping channel and the back river that constitutes the boundary between Georgia and South Carolina. In 2000 the city completed the four-acre **Savannah International Trade and Convention Center** here, with water taxi service to transport passengers back and forth to the historic district, a two-minute ride. Drivers cross the dramatic **Herman Talmadge Memorial Bridge** to reach the island, a 15-minute drive from the historic district.

CITY MARKET

Completed in the mid-1980s, the reconstructed City Market complex, along West St. Julian Avenue between Barnard and Montgomery, dates back to 1755, when the city's first public market was held at Ellis Square. The market building (constructed in 1872) was replaced with a parking lot in 1954, galvanizing the efforts of outraged local preservationists. After half a century, preservationists are finally getting their due: the parking lot is due to be razed in early 2005 and restored to its original purpose. A farmers market will sell produce, flowers, and wares around a central green.

Today, City Market anchors an arts and entertainment district rivaling River Street, with shops, bars, clubs, artist studios and galleries, and restaurants, including the popular **Lady & Sons, Garibaldi's, Bistro Savannah, Belford's,** and Lady Chablis' notorious **Club One.** Outdoor concerts and events are held in the plaza, and you can also catch carriage tours here. Many more restaurants, shops, and clubs line West Congress Street, some occupying 19th-century warehouses that served the original marketplace.

Savannah

BROUGHTON STREET

One of three broad avenues that serve as east-west thoroughfares through the historic district, Broughton Street, the city's most recently revitalized commercial district, recaptures not a colonial past but largely the mid-20th century of five-and-dimes, low box buildings, and classic movie palaces. The exposed strip of pavement is a sharp contrast from the shady cobblestone lanes around the squares, but not an unwelcome one. As more and more structures are rehabilitated, Broughton Street conveys a refreshing enthusiasm to embrace all of the city's history rather than to turn it into a colonial museum, and allows preservationists and designers to flex their muscles on modern style for a change.

One period exception is the **Marshall House,** a beautiful restoration of an 1851 hotel. With attractive ironwork balconies, French windows, and inviting public areas, the hotel's reopening five years ago ushered in the renaissance of the avenue. Now some of the city's most glamorous restaurants, avant-garde shops and galleries, and the **SCAD Trustee's Theater** can be found here, interspersed with The Gap, wig shops, and abandoned storefronts of its unreconstructed past.

HISTORIC SQUARES

Georgia's founder James Oglethorpe arrived at Yamacraw Bluff with map in hand, laying out the city's grid consistent with the neighborhoods of 17th-century London. The blueprint featured broad avenues, gardens, and symmetrical squares with public buildings to the east and west and residential buildings to the north and south of each pocket green. His grid remains largely intact today, preserving the city's original character.

Squares line up along six north-south arteries: Montgomery, Barnard, Bull, Abercorn, Habersham, and Houston Streets (though the Montgomery Street set has largely been lost to urban renewal). The greatest concentration of attractions are found along the central north-south axis of Bull Street and the east-west axis of President Street, intersecting in the shape of a cross across a map of the historic district.

From City Hall to Forsyth Park, Bull Street forms the heart of the city's commercial district, from Johnson's Square's financial center to Madison Square's refined shopping district. Along President Street you will find many of the city's best museums: Telfair Square's Academy of Art; the Juliette Gordon Low House museum, off Wright Square; Oglethorpe Square's Owens-Thomas House museum; and the Columbia Square's Davenport House museum. Further south of President Street and off to each side from Bull Street, the squares generally become quieter and more residential.

The following guide introduces Savannah's historic squares along their north-south axes, starting from the waterfront.

ALONG MONTGOMERY STREET
Franklin Square

At West St. Julian Street, Franklin is the only square that remains of the Montgomery Street original set. The others were lost in the name of progress as the Civic Center and county courthouse areas were developed and the freeway thoroughfare was constructed at the southwestern end of the historic district.

Franklin Square is the first square drivers encounter when approaching the waterfront from I-16. The **First African Baptist Church** and **First Bryan Baptist Church** here represent the oldest African American congregations in the U.S., reaching back to 1773. Named for Benjamin Franklin, the square marks the western end of the **City Market** complex. Several restaurants and cafés overlook the square. The **Ships of the Sea Maritime Museum** is one block west.

ALONG BARNARD STREET
Ellis Square

Currently overtaken by the City Market parking garage, Ellis Square at West St. Julian Street held the city marketplace from 1872 until it was

The Telfair Academy of Arts, housed in an 1819 Regency-style former governor's mansion, is notable for its exhibits of 18th-century decorative arts.

demolished in 1954. Local preservationists have succeeded in turning back the clock: in 2005 the parking lot will be razed and Ellis Square restored to its original purpose. The new market square will feature a new farmers market with produce and flower vendors around a central green. City Market is directly west, at the center of an entertainment district stretching along West Congress Street.

Telfair Square

At West President Street, Telfair Square is home to the South's oldest public museum, the **Telfair Academy of Arts,** which has now expanded into a striking modern building designed by renowned architect Moshe Safdie. The 1819 Regency mansion designed by William Jay that has housed the museum since the 1880s still presides over the aristocratic square. Nearby, the sanctuary of the Corinthian-columned **Trinity United Methodist Church** dates from 1848.

Orleans Square

At West McDonough Street, the large **Civic Center Auditorium** dominates the area around Orleans Square. Commemorating the Battle of New Orleans in the War of 1812, the square holds a fountain dedicated by Savannah's German Society to the city's early immigrants from Germany. The **Savannah Visitor Center** and future Siege of Savannah battlefield park are two blocks west on Martin Luther King Jr. Boulevard, along with a convenient café within the **Ex Libris** bookstore.

Pulaski Square

At West Macon Street, Pulaski Square was named for the highest-ranking foreign officer to die in the American Revolution: Polish Count Casimir Pulaski, who fell during the Siege of Savannah in 1779. But don't look for his statue here; it adorns Monterey Square.

Chatham Square

At West Wayne Street, Chatham Square is named for William Pitt, Earl of Chatham, from whom the county also gets its name. **Gordon Row** here consists of 15 four-story identical townhouses that are 20 feet wide, including the **Bed and Breakfast Inn.**

ALONG BULL STREET

Johnson Square

The first and foremost of the city's original 24 squares, Johnson Square remains its commercial hub. Presiding at the head of Bull Street a block from **City Hall,** the square is surrounded by financial institutions (nicknamed Banker's Square) and is further dignified by **Christ Church,** the Mother Church of Georgia, at the site of the colony's first church (built in 1733). The square is named for Robert Johnson, royal governor of South Carolina when Georgia was founded. The statue in its center marks the **grave of Nathanael Greene,** the Revolutionary War hero rewarded for his service with nearby Mulberry Plantation, where Greene's widow and Eli Whitney later developed the cotton gin.

Wright Square

Dominated by the **U.S. Court House,** Wright Square at President Street is named for Georgia's last colonial governor, Sir James Wright. The granite boulder in its southwest corner marks the **memorial to Tomochichi,** the Yamacraw Indian chief who welcomed Oglethorpe and the first colonists. The chief was buried in the square in 1739. The central monument honors early city mayor William Washington Gordon, founder of the Central of Georgia Railroad and father of Girl Scouts founder Juliette Gordon Low, whose home (two blocks south) is now a popular historic house museum. The congregation of the **Lutheran Church of the Ascension** here dates back to 1741; the present sanctuary was completed in 1879.

Chippewa Square

Guarded by a bronze statue of James Oglethorpe (facing south, on the lookout for Spanish advances), Chippewa Square, at McDonough Street, is a lively square with several historic and contemporary landmarks, including the 1833 **First Baptist Church** and the **Savannah Theater,** originally designed by William Jay in 1818. The bus stop scenes from the movie **Forrest Gump** were filmed here. The historic **Foley House** inn overlooks the square.

Madison Square

At Macon Street, stately Madison Square is home to **St. John's Episcopal Church** and its parish house, the 1853 **Green-Meldrim House.** Now a historic house museum, the house was General Sherman's headquarters during the Civil War. Named for the fourth U.S. president, the square bears the statue of Sergeant William Jasper, who died in the Siege of Savannah in 1779.

The 1893 Romanesque Revival–style Guards Armory here now houses the flagship building of the **Savannah College of Art and Design,** which operates the **Gryphon Tea Room** across the street (though it was once a Victorian pharmacy) and the **SCAD Shop** of student wares next door. Heading up this refined shopping stretch of Bull Street is **E. Shaver Books.**

Monterey Square

At Wayne Street, Monterey Square holds two of the city's most unusual landmarks. **Mercer House** opens to public tours one of the city's most beautiful houses, the home of the central character in John Berendt's book *Midnight in the Garden of Good and Evil.* One of the nation's oldest Jewish congregations in the U.S., the **Temple Mickve Israel,** founded in 1733, is further distinguished with the only Gothic Revival synagogue in the U.S., built in traditional cruciform style in 1876 (look for the Star of David on the arched entryway). The square is named to commemorate the city soldiers who fought in the 1846 Battle of Monterey during the Mexican-American War.

ALONG ABERCORN STREET

Reynolds Square

At East St. Julian Street, Reynolds Square is named for John Reynolds, Georgia's first Governor. The gowned statue at its center is John Wesley, the founder of Methodism, whose parsonage sat on the square in the site now occupied by the **Planters Inn** (they say that in the early 20th century, a notorious brothel occupied the same spot). The 1921 **Lucas Theatre** has been restored to its original Vaudevillian splendor. Another landmark is the **Olde Pink House,** a 1789 Georgian mansion that is now one of Savannah's

Savannah

best restaurants (there's a tavern below). Many walking tours meet in the regal square.

Oglethorpe Square

At East President Street, Oglethorpe Square is named for the founder of Savannah and its first urban planner (though his statue stands in Chippewa Square). In its center is a marker dedicated to the Moravians who immigrated to the city in 1735. The **Owens-Thomas House** here is one of the city's preeminent historic house museums, complete with intact slave quarters.

Lafayette Square

At East Macon Street, Lafayette Square, with its central fountain, honors the Marquis de Lafayette for his help during the Revolutionary War. The many attractions here include the **Andrew Low House** museum; the **Flannery O'Connor Childhood Home;** and the towering **Cathedral of St. John the Baptist,** a 1876 landmark. The 1873 **Hamilton Turner House** is best known to *Midnight* readers as the party house of Joe Odom. **Suites on Lafayette** rents apartments overlooking the square.

Calhoun Square

At East Wayne Street, Calhoun Square was named for South Carolinian and U.S. Vice President John C. Calhoun. It's the only square that retains all its original buildings, including the 1890 **Wesley Monumental United Methodist Church.** With a classic Greek Revival design, the **Massie Heritage Interpretation Center** opens the oldest school in continuous operation in Georgia, with historical and educational exhibits within.

ALONG HABERSHAM STREET
Warren Square

At East St. Julian Street, Warren Square is named for Revolutionary War General Joseph Warren, killed at the Battle of Bunker Hill. With no grand museums or churches at its borders to draw crowds or circling trolleys, the square is simply a quiet respite for the surrounding residential community.

Columbia Square

At East President Street, dignified Columbia Square holds the **Davenport House,** the 1820 Federal mansion threatened with demolition in the early 1960s, that spurred local society women to save the building and form the **Historic Savannah Foundation.** In the years since, the foundation has saved more than a thousand endangered buildings; their headquarters remain on the square. The central fountain is from the Wormsloe plantation, an early Savannah estate on the Isle of Hope that is now a historic site open to the public. The stately Queen Anne Victorian **Kehoe House** here is one of the city's premier historic inns.

Troup Square

An **armillary sphere** stands at the center of Troup Square at East Macon Street. This type of astronomical model of interlocking rings was developed in the 16th century to reveal relationships among celestial circles. The square is named for Senator and Georgia Governor George Michael Troup. The **Unitarian Universalist Church** and **McDonough row houses** are among its distinguishing landmarks.

Whitefield Square

At East Wayne Street, Whitefield Square honors George Whitefield, founder of the oldest orphanage in the U.S. Today the Bethesda Home for Boys remains in operation on an estate out by Skidaway Island. The **First Congregational Church** is a landmark on the square.

ALONG HOUSTON STREET
Washington Square

At East St. Julian Street, Washington Square is surrounded by some of the city's oldest homes, with such characteristic features as Savannah gray-brick and cast-iron balconies. The Port of Savannah maintains the **International Seaman's House** here providing a hall and chapel for visiting seamen, within a contemporary building designed to blend in with its historic surroundings. A short walk east leads to the **Mulberry Inn,** on Bay Street, and the **Pirates House,** on East Broad Street.

Greene Square

At East President Street, Greene Square honors Revolutionary War hero Nathanael Greene, though his grave lies in Johnson Square. At the **Second African Baptist Church** organized in 1802, Sherman's Field Order No. 15, setting aside the Sea Islands and abandoned rice fields 30 miles inland for freed slaves, was first announced. Original colonial-era street names can be found on houses around the square: President Street was once King Street, State was Price, and Congress was Duke Street.

Crawford Square

At East McDonough Street, Crawford Square is named for William Harrison Crawford, Minister of France. **Colonial Park Cemetery** is two blocks west.

FORSYTH PARK

This beautiful 20-acre park stretches from the southern boundary of the historic district through the heart of the Victorian district. Its central fountain, built in 1858, is a hallmark of the city, and its image adorns many postcards and souvenirs. Attractions surrounding the fountain include the **Fragrant Garden for the Blind,** statues of Confederate Generals McLaws and Bartow, a Spanish-American War memorial, and a World War I "dummy fort," soon to be transformed into a café. Across the street, **The Mansion** is Savannah's newest hotel, overlooking the park on the Drayton Street side. On the Whitaker Street side just south of Gaston, the **Magnolia Place Inn** is one of the city's best inns. **Elizabeth on 37th** is a deluxe restaurant also in the Victorian district.

Sights

GUIDED TOURS

Visitors can board buses, trolleys, paddlewheel boats, or horse-drawn carriages, or can stay on foot for a wide variety of guided tours that provide a good introduction and orientation to the city, even if you're not the guided tour type. There are historic house tours, ghost tours, garden tours, and tours of sights in *Midnight in the Garden of Good and Evil* (contact the visitors center for the full selection). Most last around an hour or so, and many leave from the visitors center or from the riverfront. Some will pick you up at your hotel. You might find open-air tours more engaging than being sheltered away from the city's sounds and scents in an air-conditioned bus, despite the summertime heat.

Walking Tours

Of plentiful walking-tour services available, **Savannah History Walks,** 912/232-4268, thoroughly covers literary and Civil War history sites. The fee is $12 for adults, $10 for seniors, $8 for students, and $7 for children.

On **Victorian Lady Tours,** 912/236-1886, your personal guide dresses the part, complete with parasol and colorful tales that mix in movie trivia, *Midnight* sights, and apparitions along with local history ($65 an hour; ask about group discounts).

Trolley Tours

Two companies operate trolley tours that depart from the Savannah Visitors Center and loop around downtown, providing a 90-minute overview of the city's sights and history. You may also choose to get on and off at any one or more than a dozen stops and catch a subsequent trolley; they loop around frequently during the day. The locally owned **Old Savannah Tours,** 912/234-8128 or 800/517-9007, operate white trolleys; the fare is $21 for adults and $9 for children. **Old Town Trolley Tours,** 912/233-0083, have orange trolleys; the fare is $21 for adults and $10 for children. The two companies offer all sorts of combination tickets and specialty tours, but you might just want to choose the cheapest, shortest, next available trolley if you go this route.

Savannah

SAVANNAH SIGHTS

Savannah   River

CONVENTION CENTER ■   ■ WATER TAXI

RIVERBOATS/ TOURS/WATER TAXI ■

RIVERFRONT   WATER TAXI ■   WAVING GIRL STATUE ■

VISITORS CENTER ■

W. FACTORS WALK

WILLIAMSON ST

BARNARD RAMP

CITY HALL ★

RIVER   ST

E FACTORS   WALK

OLD COTTON ★ EXCHANGE

Emmet Park

W BAY   ST   E BAY   ST

FIRST AFRICAN BAPTIST CHURCH

M *CARRIAGE TOURS*

W BRYAN   ST

Johnson Square

E BRYAN   ST

SHIPS OF THE SEA MARITIME MUSEUM ■ ★

★ *Franklin Square*   *City Market*   *Ellis Square*

CHRIST EPISCOPAL ■ CHURCH   *Reynolds Square*

P

Warren Square   *Washington Square*

W CONGRESS   ST

NATHANAEL GREENE GRAVE

P

E CONGRESS   ST

(W BROAD)

ST

W   BROUGHTON   ST

BULL   ST

DRAYTON   ST

ABERCORN   ST

★ LUCAS THEATRE

E BROUGHTON   ST

CHATHAM COUNTY COURTHOUSE

P

TELFAIR HOUSE

W STATE   ST

M ★ OWENS-THOMAS HOUSE

DAVENPORT HOUSE

E BROUGHTON   LN

Liberty Square

M *TELFAIR MUSEUM OF ARTS AND SCIENCES*

Telfair Square

Wright Square

E PRESIDENT ST

Oglethorpe Square

E STATE   ST

Columbia Square

Greene Square

BUS DEPOT

MARTIN LUTHER KING JR BLVD

MONTGOMERY ST

JEFFERSON   ST

BARNARD   ST

W YORK   ST

TOMO-CHI-CHI MEMORIAL

E YORK   ST

ST

OGLETHORPE AVE

JULIETTE GORDON LOW HOUSE ★

W OGLETHORPE AVE

E OGLETHORPE AVE

PRICE   ST

HOUSTON   ST

TURNER   ST

Elbert Square

W HULL   ST

E HULL   ST

VISITORS CENTER/ SAVANNAH HISTORY MUSEUM ★

CIVIC CENTER

Orleans Square

Chippewa Square

SAVANNAH ■ THEATRE

COLONIAL PARK CEMETERY

Crawford Square

W PERRY   ST

E PERRY   ST

SIEGE OF SAVANNAH BATTLEFIELD PARK ★

LOUISVILLE   RD

W LIBERTY   ST

P

CATHEDRAL OF ST JOHN THE BAPTIST

LINCOLN   ST

HABERSHAM   ST

E LIBERTY   ST

P

RAILROAD ROUNDHOUSE MUSEUM

W HARRIS   ST

GREEN-MELDRIM HOUSE

E SHAVER, ■ BOOKSELLER

E HARRIS   ST

Pulaski Square

★ *Madison Square*

Lafayette Square

Troup Square

E MACON   ST

W CHARLTON   ST

E CHARLTON   ST

SAVANNAH ★ COLLEGE OF ART AND DESIGN

★ FLANNERY O'CONNOR HOUSE

BEACH INSTITUTE ★

E CHARLTON   LN

W CHARLTON   ST

M *SCAD GALLERIES*

ANDREW LOW HOUSE

E JONES   ST

W JONES   ST

W TAYLOR   ST

Monterey Square

Calhoun Square

E TAYLOR   ST

M *RALPH MARK GILBERT CIVIL RIGHTS MUSEUM* ★

Chatham Square

MERCER ★ HOUSE ■

E WAYNE   ST

Whitefield Square

W GORDON   ST

MICKVE ISRAEL TEMPLE

WESLEY MONUMENTAL UNITED METHODIST CHURCH

E GORDON   ST

W ALICE   ST

E ALICE   ST

W GASTON   ST

E GASTON   ST

LANDMARK FOUNTAIN ★

KING-TISDELL COTTAGE ★

MONTGOMERY   ST

TATTNALL   ST

W HUNTINGDON   ST

E HUNTINGDON   ST

DRAYTON   ST

ABERCORN   ST

Forsyth

Park

W HALL   ST

E HALL   ST

DUMMY ■ FORT

0   200 yds

0   200 m

© AVALON TRAVEL PUBLISHING, INC.

Savannah

ⓜ Carriage Tours

One of the most evocative ways to see Savannah is aboard a horse-drawn carriage. **Carriage Tours of Savannah,** 912/236-6756 or 800/442-5933, provides 12-seat English carriages that ride at an ambling pace through the historic district past major sights and squares. The price for the 50-minute tour is $19 for adults and $9 for children under 12; major credit cards are accepted on-site. You could call for a schedule or drop by carriage stands at either City Market or the Hyatt Regency Riverfront to catch the next ride; times vary at each location. A twilight ride makes a particularly appealing tour through the shadowy streets, as guides tell tall tales and legends in drawling coastal accents. More intimate private tours on smaller carriages are also available (starting at $85).

Ghost Tours

Savannah has an illustrious supernatural history, from waving girls to pirates; tales told to best effect at night through the historic district by lantern, taking in such sights as Colonial Park Cemetery. Several tour operators meet at downtown squares for walking tours; try **Hauntings Tour,** 912/234-3571 or 800/574-9255; admission is $13 for adults and $5 for children 6–14. If after a full day of walking you'd prefer to ride, **Old Town Trolley,** 912/233-0083, runs a Ghosts and Gravestones tour that leaves from their depot, 234 Martin Luther King Jr. Blvd., across from the Savannah Visitor Center. The 90-minute tour costs $25 for adults and $10 for children ages 4–12 (though whether the ghoul-led Trolley of the Doomed tour would be appropriate for all young children is a parent's call). Reservations are required. Also notable among ghost options is a haunted pub tour ($14 for adults and $12 for seniors): **Savannah Spirits Pub Crawl,** 912/604-3007.

African American Heritage Tours

The **Freedom Trail Tour,** 912/232-7477, covers such sights as the 1865 Beach Institute school, First African Baptist Church, First Bryan Baptist Church, and the Ralph Mark Gilbert Civil Rights Museum while relating local African American history from the slave trade, free black communities, and Field Order No. 15, to Geechee culture and struggles for integration in the 1960s. Tours, which are aboard air-conditioned minibuses, cost $18 for adults, $12 for students, and $9 for children.

Multilingual Tours

Gray Line, 912/234-TOUR (912/234-8687) or 800/426-2318, features the widest selection of bilingual tours (French, German, Spanish, Dutch, and Japanese). Tours are aboard red trolleys, and prices start at $18 for adults.

Boat Tours

A wonderful way to see Savannah is from the water. For cheap thrills, Chatham Area Transit (CAT), 912/233-5767, operates the **Savannah Belles Ferry,** colorful miniature tugboats adorned with the names of famous Savannah women. The wheelchair-accessible ferries depart from two docks on River Street (at Bull Street and further east, at the Marriott) and cross the channel to the trade center. The fare is $1 for adults; up to two children under 41 inches ride free per accompanying adult.

The **River Street Riverboat Company,** 912/232-6404 or 800/786-6404, offers narrated daytime tours down the Savannah River on 400-passenger paddleboats; the charge is $16 for adults and $10 for children under age 12. They also offer specialty cruises, such as Sunday brunch cruises and gospel dinner cruises. Purchase tickets at their storefront window at 9 E. River St., behind City Hall.

Though not a city tour, another popular boat ride is a dolphin cruise, offered by **Dolphin Magic Tours,** 800/721-1240, departing from the Hyatt dock on River Street. The fare is $20 for adults and $10 for children over age three.

Offbeat Tours

Savannah Movie Tours, 912/877-444-FILM (444-3456), covers sights from films shot in the movie capital of the South—including *Forrest Gump, Glory, The Legend of Bagger Vance,* and of course, *Midnight in the Garden of Good and Evil*—on a walking tour that leaves from Clary's Café, at Jones at Abercorn Streets ($15 for adults and $8 for children 8–16).

MIDNIGHT TOURS

According to a local voodoo priestess, the difference between good and evil in the low country is a single half-hour either side of midnight. Yet in Savannah proper, the line is less clearly drawn, or that's what author John Berendt would have you believe in his 1994 book *Midnight in the Garden of Good and Evil.* Though it reads like fiction, the book tells a true story of decorum and decadence, murder and mayhem in Savannah society. After standing more than a solid year on the *New York Times* bestseller list, *Midnight* is credited with increasing tourism in Savannah by more than 50 percent, as book-in-arm readers flock to visit sights from the story. So welcome to Berendt's Savannah, a "semitropical terrarium, sealed off from a world that suddenly seemed a thousand miles away."

The first stop is **Mercer House,** on azalea-studded Monterey Square. Even without the intrigue associated with murder, the salmon-brick Italianate mansion (named for the great-grandfather of composer Johnny Mercer) is a stunning sight, with its formidable four-column entrance and intricate ironwork balconies woven with tendrils of wisteria. This is the scene of *Midnight's* crime. From its arched 2nd-story windows, its ornery resident (the book's protagonist) once draped a huge Nazi flag to disrupt a movie scene being shot in the square by less-than-considerate filmmakers.

On Lafayette Square, the imposing **Hamilton-Turner House** likewise stands on its own architectural merits—it has been called the "Charles Addams House" after the whimsically haunted cartoons of the famous *New Yorker* illustrator for its shipdeck crown and raised-eyebrow window-work—but lovers of Berendt's postmodern Southern gothic tale will know it as the residence of beloved local con man Joe Odom. The ivory-tickling opportunist outraged local sensibilities (and zoning regulations, to boot) by offering impromptu house tours and concerts. Today the notorious house operates as a bed-and-breakfast inn.

Overlooking Colonial Park Cemetery, the refined **Mary Marshall Row** townhouses on Oglethorpe Avenue were due to be dismantled in the 1960s for the price of the bricks alone until local patron Lee Adler (Mercer House neighbor and the book's antagonist) spared them and saw to their restoration.

Hearse Tours, 912/695-1578, takes sporting visitors around for evening tours in an customized hearse with a sunroof large enough for all eight passengers to peer out the top at once ($14 for adults). **Savannah Pedicab Tours and Bike Rentals,** 200 W. Congress St., 912/232-7900, takes couples on half-hour or hour-long tours of the historic district ($25–45), and also operates as a taxi service to transport people around downtown. Most rides run $5–10. You could also hail an empty one; they're often around City Market.

HISTORIC HOUSE MUSEUMS

Savannah is blessed with many exquisite historic house museums that lead visitors through period rooms of lush drapery, fine antique furniture, appointed table service, and other rich decorative arts. Impressive at any time, and always a wonderful step-back-in-time introduction to Savannah, historic homes are at their best when decorated for seasonal tours. The annual **Tour of Homes and Gardens** is the city's all-out three-day house-tour extravaganza and has been held annually in late March since its inception in the 1920s.

Davenport House

On Columbia Square, the Davenport House, 324 E. State St., 912/236-8097, was completed in 1820 and now ranks among the great Federal houses in America. Master builder Isaiah Davenport, of Rhode Island, built the house for his family and as an example of his work. Elegantly austere from the outside, a step into the interior re-

A short drive east through the palm arcade of Victory Drive is **Bonaventure Cemetery,** site of Johnny Mercer's grave, along with the grave of the 21-year-old hustler fatally shot at Mercer House. The book's beguiling cover photograph of the *Bird Girl* statue at the cemetery was taken by the late Jack Leigh (posters are available at his gallery, across from Colonial Park Cemetery at 132 E. Oglethorpe Ave., 912/234-6449). The original *Bird Girl* statue can now be seen at the Telfair Academy of Arts (and reproductions are available for sale all over town).

But the scene-stealer in the book—the audacious Lady Chablis—is still very much alive, shakin' it and raking it in with performances over at **Club One Jefferson.** The transvestite shows start around midnight, slowing down just long enough for stiff-shouldered Marines, limber lads, and sturdy young women to reach up and stuff dollar bills into the plunging bodices of the drag queens.

Footnote to Murder

The rowhouses spared by Lee Adler (see above) represent an earlier sordid local drama: the Pulitzer prize–winning poet Conrad Aiken was born in one of these rowhouses. When Aiken was 11, his father killed his mother in their 3rd-story bedroom before turning the gun on himself. The orphaned Aiken moved away, and then closed the circle of his life by retiring in the house next door, where he lived out his last 11 years.

At Bonaventure Cemetery, the double headstones of Aiken's parents sit across from a bench that serves as the grave marker for the poet. The bench bears the inscription *Cosmos Mariner, Destination Unknown,* and is littered with pennies left by visitors. (Aiken's memorial is one of two famous benches in town, the other one being the poster perch of Tom Hanks in the blockbuster movie *Forrest Gump,* filmed in Chippewa Square, now on display at the museum in the visitors center).

Bonaventure Cemetery

veals luxurious detailing, from Grecian columns and intricate woodwork in the asymmetrical entrance hall to such dignified appointments as Chippendale furnishings and Davenport china found throughout the house. "Before" photographs of the house are displayed in the unrestored attic. A local garden club created the courtyard garden in 1976.

The proposed demolition of the Davenport House in 1955 set off the preservationist movement in Savannah. Seven society women raised $22,500 to save the house and went on to found the Historic Savannah Foundation, which saved more than 1,100 buildings downtown over the next 30 years. The foundation's headquarters are across the square.

The Davenport House is open –Mon.–Sat. 10 A.M.–4 P.M. and Sun. 1–4 P.M. Tours start every 30 minutes. Admission to the house and garden is $7 for adults and $3.50 students. A museum shop, in the basement, displays items that evoke 19th-century Savannah; proceeds support Historic Savannah Foundation projects.

Savannah

SAVANNAH'S ARCHITECTURAL HERITAGE

Much of the visual charm of Savannah's historic district comes from impressive 18th- and 19th-century styles of architecture, artfully restored and preserved in mansions, cottages, churches, and public buildings. Even a novice can begin picking out certain details that define a particular style and era.

Early brick buildings were constructed from imported brick, often brought over on sailing ships as ballast (the now elegantly restored buildings that line Factors Walk are composed of cruder ballast stone). Later, local kilns produced "Savannah Gray" bricks, named for the distinctive color they derived from local sandy soils.

Georgian Style

Rows of three- to four-story brick townhouses date from this period. While resembling the older streets of London, these rowhouses also reflect a tropical sensibility. Because the upper floors were considered to be "above" the risk of malaria, the ground floors were devoted to offices, and the living spaces were reserved for the 2nd floor and higher, reached by curved staircases ornamented with wrought-iron handrails. Kitchens were typically the back room of the ground floor. The **Olde Pink House,** now a restaurant, typifies Georgian style.

Federal Style

Postrevolutionary architecture is best exemplified by the 1820 **Davenport House.** Considered more flexible and delicate than the more formal Georgian style, Federal style in the South often features red-brick construction, white porticos, and fan-shaped pediment windows.

Regency Style

Savannah's prosperity of the early 19th century coincided with the Regency period, and as a result, many fine old houses were built in this style. Grander flourishes were added to Georgian sensibilities—high ceilings, oval rooms, intricately carved moldings and great marble fireplaces were typical of that time. British architect William Jay designed many of Savannah's finest buildings in this style, most notably the **Owens-Thomas House** and **Telfair Academy of Arts.**

Greek Revival

The Greek Revival period brought the large colonnaded entrances and grand staircases associated most closely with Southern plantation architecture, thanks largely to director Selznick's vision of the fictional Tara in *Gone with the Wind.* Continuing prosperity meant that many homes, and particularly public buildings, conform to this style.

Victorian Era

The Victorian era (1827–1901) revived row houses of a different sort, many still constructed with brick but without the delicate ornamentation of the previous Georgian period. Wooden-frame houses with gingerbread accents and other elaborate Queen Anne–style homes make up the Victorian district, which lies outside the main historic district boundary. The **Green-Meldrim House** reveals a mixture of styles in this period, with its Gothic roofline and intricate French ironwork.

Borrowed Influences

As interesting as these classical architectural motifs are, changes were also brought about by different groups that settled in the city. Wrought-iron balcony rails, typically associated with New Orleans, were brought to Savannah by the French resettling there after fleeing slave rebellions in Haiti. From Barbados came the side-of-the-house gallery entrances associated with Charleston. Peaked roofs reflect the German Jews and Salzburg Protestants, who were among the city's original settlers.

Tabby Construction

Less prevalent in refined Savannah than elsewhere on the coast, but still readily found, are buildings constructed of tabby, a stucco-like mix of oyster shells, sand, lime from burned shells, and water. Used most often for outbuildings in Savannah, and for everything up to grand plantation homes down the coast, the material was also used by the natives. Origins of the term tabby are unclear; some theories say it comes from the Spanish *tapia,* others say the African *tabax.* Some say the method of tapping the mixture to settle it became the origins of "tappy," later Southernized to "tabby."

ARCHITECTURAL STYLES

FEDERAL

GREEK REVIVAL

ITALIANATE

QUEEN ANNE

VICTORIAN
RENAISSANCE

VICTORIAN
ROMANESQUE

VICTORIAN GOTHIC

VICTORIAN FUNCTIONAL

SECOND EMPIRE

Green-Meldrim House

On Madison Square, the 1850s Green-Meldrim House, 1 W. Macon St., 912/233-1251, was the home of a wealthy cotton merchant when General Sherman made it his headquarters, after the surrender of the city in December 1864. As his first act Sherman offered the city of Savannah to President Lincoln as a Christmas present, and it was here that he conferred with local African American leaders before drafting Field Order No. 15 in January 1865.

Today it's been restored to its original Gothic Revival style and serves as the parish house for St. John's Episcopal Church, next door. The covered porch, with its ornate ironwork surrounding three sides of the house, and the double parlor are two of the house's most distinguishing features.

The house is open Tues., Thurs., and Fri. 10 A.M.–3:30 P.M. and Sat. 10 A.M.–12:30 P.M. Tours are offered on the half hour. It's closed Sun. and Wed., and also Dec. 15–Jan. 15, and for two weeks prior to Easter. Admission is $5 for adults and $2 for students.

Ⓜ Owens-Thomas House

On Oglethorpe Square, the elegant 1816 Owens-Thomas House, 124 Abercorn St., 912/233-9743, was designed by William Jay. It is considered among the finest examples of English Regency architecture in the U.S. The Telfair Academy of Arts and Sciences maintains the villa, which features an entrance portico with Ionic columns, a winding double stairway, arched windows, inventive early plumbing, and an outstanding collection of period antiques and decorative arts.

House tours meet in the carriage house out back—one of the most intact urban slave quarters in the South, painted a characteristic shade of "haint blue" to protect against malevolent spirits. There is also a formal garden and a basement, housing the kitchen, laundry room, larder, and wine cellar.

The house is open daily except on major holidays. Guided tours leave every half hour Mon. noon–4:30 P.M., Tues.–Sat. 10 am–4:30 P.M. and Sun. 1–4:30 P.M. Admission is $8 for adults,

$7 for seniors, $4 for students and $2 for children ages 6–12. A combination ticket with the Telfair Academy costs $12. The gift shop sells handmade Gullah baskets from Sapelo Island, among many other distinctive crafts and 19th-century reproductions.

Juliette Gordon Low Birthplace

The Juliette Gordon Low Birthplace, 142 Bull St., 912/233-4501, was built 1818–1821 for city mayor James Moore Wayne, the great-uncle of Juliette Gordon Low. After she married, moved a few blocks south (to what is now the Andrew Low House museum), and was widowed, Juliette established the Girl Scouts of America. In the 1950s the organization bought the house and founded the museum to honor its founder.

The Birthplace, as it is affectionately known, was named Savannah's first national historic landmark in 1965. The grand four-story Regency-style mansion is furnished with Gordon family possessions, and the carriage house displays Girl Scouts memorabilia. Girl Scouts earn a pin by making a pilgrimage to the birthplace and receive discounts off the admission price. The Victorian garden is also on display.

It's open Mon.–Tues. and Thurs.–Sat. 10 A.M.–4 P.M. and Sun. 12:30–4:30 P.M. (closed Wed.). Admission is $7 for adults and $4 for children ages 6–17.

Andrew Low House

On Lafayette Square, this Italianate mansion, 329 Abercorn, 912/233-6854, was built for prominent British cotton merchant Andrew Low in 1848. The house features one of the city's most outstanding ironwork balconies and displays early American and English furnishings and decorative arts. Here Juliette Gordon Low founded the Girl Scouts of America and bequeathed the carriage house to the organization. The main house is owned and preserved by the National Society of the Colonial Dames of America, which has donated many fine furnishings and silver for display within.

The house is open for tours Mon.–Wed. and Fri.–Sat. 10 A.M.–4 P.M., and Sun. noon–4 P.M. (the last tour starts at 3:30 P.M.); it's closed Thurs.

Admission is $7 for adults and $4.50 for children (there's a Girl Scout discount).

Mercer Williams House

On Monterey Square at 429 Bull Street, 877/430-6352, the Mercer Williams House was built for General Hugh Mercer, the grandfather of composer Johnny Mercer, starting in 1860. Construction was interrupted by the Civil War, and afterward, the unfinished house was sold to John R. Wilder, who completed it in 1868. No Mercer ever lived in the house that bears their name.

The more notorious history of the house begins in 1969, when it was bought by James A. Williams, the character at the heart of the best-seller *Midnight in the Garden of Good and Evil*. In Berendt's retelling, the house may be a murder scene; the Williams family contends it was an accident that killed a young local gigolo here. The family opened the home for public tours in 2004; in part, the house seems to rewrite the legacy of Williams as a distinguished community leader devoted to historic preservation.

Tours cover the garden and 1st floor, which features such handsome architectural details as a spiral staircase leading to a stained-glass dome in the 60-foot entrance hall. Purchase tickets at the carriage house, 430 Whitaker St., once the antique shop of Jim Williams and now a gift shop selling books of Williams's essays and other souvenirs. The house is open year-round Mon.–Tues. and Thurs.–Sat. 10:30 A.M.–3:40 P.M., Sun. 12:30–3:40 P.M.; also, Wed. in season (spring to fall); closed major holidays. Admission is $12.50 for adults and $8 for students.

Flannery O'Connor Childhood Home

On Lafayette Square, 207 E. Charlton St., 912/233-6014, the 1856 row house of Georgia's most famous writer and pillar of Southern letters has been restored to its appearance when Flannery O'Connor lived there, in the 1930s. The restoration, furnished with select mementoes, is evocative but modest and tiny, and can perhaps be best enjoyed during readings and other literary events that are occasionally held here (the Savannah Writers Studio, 912/234-5494, holds classes here). There's a

lovely little garden out back surrounding a statue of St. Francis.

The house is open weekend afternoons only, Sat.–Sun. 1–4 P.M. A $2 donation is requested, or $1 for children.

King Tisdell Cottage

This 1896 gingerbread Victorian cottage, 514 E. Huntingdon St. at Price, 912/234-8000, displays period furnishings along with African art and exhibits on slave history and the unique Sea Island black culture. During research, it was closed for remodeling; check for reopening dates.

HISTORIC MUSEUMS

Ships of the Sea Maritime Museum

Ships of the Sea, 41 Martin Luther King Jr. Blvd., 912/232-1511, commemorates the art of sailing with ship models, maritime antiques, scrimshaw carvings, and ships-in-bottles. Of more than 100 models artfully displayed on several floors of the striking 1819 Regency-style mansion designed by William Jay, the *S. S. Titanic* is among the most popular, though the *S. S. Savannah*—the first steamship to cross the Atlantic Ocean—is the sentimental favorite. One of the principal owners of the city's namesake ship was William Scarbrough, the original resident of the villa that now houses the museum.

A 50-minute Discovery Channel video documentary airs downstairs. The garden out back is the largest in the historic district. Admission is $7 for adults and $5 for students. Hours are Tues.–Sun. 10 A.M.–5 P.M.

Roundhouse Railroad Museum

At 601 W. Harris St. at Martin Luther King Jr. Blvd., 912/651-6823, the railroad museum occupies the oldest and most complete antebellum railroad manufacturing and repair facility still in existence, a massive roundhouse featuring a working turntable and 125-foot smokestack. Exhibits include the oldest portable steam engine in the country among other machinery, locomotives, and railroad models. The Savannah Garden Exposition is held here in spring.

Savannah

The museum is open every day 9 A.M.–4 P.M. Admission is $4 for adults and $3.50 for children. It's a long block from the Savannah Visitor Center.

Mighty Eighth Air Force Museum

Near the Savannah International Airport, at 175 Bourne Ave., 912/748-8888, the Mighty Eighth is designed as a memorial to the million men and women who have served in the Eighth Air Force since its activation in 1942. The 90,000-square-foot interior contains historic aircraft and four theaters screening vintage and documentary footage.

The new Mission Experience gallery, due to open in 2005, offers the perspective of pilots on a bombing run over Nazi Germany, complete with a genuine WWII Quonset hut, control-tower replica, and life-size murals. There's also a restaurant, gift shop, art gallery, chapel, and garden. A public memorial to the colonel and crew of the famed B-17 *Memphis Belle* is an example of special events sponsored by the museum.

The museum is open daily 9 A.M.–5 P.M. Admission is $8 for adults and $6 for children; there are senior and military discounts. Find the Mighty Eighth at the intersection of I-95 and U.S. 80 in Pooler, off I-95 exit 102. It's around 15 miles west of downtown Savannah.

M Ralph Mark Gilbert Civil Rights Museum

Savannah's civil-rights museum, 460 Martin Luther King Jr. Blvd., 912/231-8900, traces the history of the era and movement with frank descriptions of local living conditions for blacks in the 1950s. A 15-minute film with vintage video footage and 1960s artifacts relate stories such as how the local African American community led an economic boycott that lasted 15 months before desegregation was achieved, a year prior to the passage of the Voting Rights Act. A lecture on the signing of the Civil Rights Act is an example of special events sponsored by the museum.

Named after the late local NAACP president and pastor of First African Baptist Church, the museum is housed in the 1914 Wage Earners Savings and Loan building, which was the largest African American bank in the country at the time. The museum adds an important dimension to a well-rounded perspective on city history and should be on the itinerary of at least every non-Southerner and young person visiting Savannah.

Admission is $4 for adults, $3 for seniors and $2 for students. It's open Mon.–Sat. 9 A.M.–5 P.M. It's at the southwestern corner of the historic district, several blocks south of the Savannah Visitor Center (under the freeway overpass) Parking is easy.

ART MUSEUMS AND GALLERIES

M Telfair Museum of Arts and Sciences

On Telfair Square, the Telfair Academy, 121 Barnard St., 912/232-1177, is the oldest art museum in the South. Savannah's preeminent arts institution since 1875, Telfair is to Savannah what the High Museum is to Atlanta—a must in any itinerary.

Since its founding, the museum has presided over Telfair Square, named for Edward Telfair, a three-time governor of Georgia and a patron of the arts. In 2005 the museum will open the boldly modern Jepson Center, designed by Moshe Safdie (architect of Montreal's Habitat '67 and the Skirball Cultural Center in Los Angeles) to house its expanding collection of Impressionist paintings and 18th- and 19th-century American and European furniture, silver, and decorative arts. (A more recent acquisition is Sylvia Shaw Judson's *Bird Girl* statue, popularized on the cover of *Midnight in the Garden of Good and Evil.*)

The museum's original building occupies a Regency-style mansion built on the site of the original British colonial governor's house. Completed in 1819, the regal house was designed by William Jay for Alexander Telfair, the governor's son. Several period rooms are on display, including the Octagon Room (considered among the finest period rooms in the country), drawing room, dining room, and plantation kitchen—much of it appointed with original Telfair family furniture.

The museum is open daily except on major holidays. Hours are Mon. noon–5 P.M., Tues.–Sat. 10 A.M.–5 P.M. and Sun. 1–5 P.M.Admission costs $8 for adults and $2 for students.

⋈ SCAD Galleries

The Savannah College of Art and Design (SCAD) maintains a dozen gallery spaces in Savannah, and beyond that, displays work by faculty, students, and nationally known artists. All exhibits are free and open to the public. At "gallery hops" held throughout the year, buses transport visitors between sites. For a schedule of current exhibits, openings, lectures, films, and other events, see scad.edu or call 912/525-4743.

Several galleries are conveniently located in the historic district. On Madison Square, at 342 Bull St., the college's flagship Poetter building holds the **May Poetter Gallery.** Among other major galleries: **Red Gallery, 201 E.** Broughton St. at Lincoln; **Pinnacle Gallery, 320 E.** Liberty St. at Habersham; and **Bergen Gallery, 101 Mar**tin Luther King Jr. Blvd. at Broughton. You might pop in wherever you see a SCAD building; many feature student work in the lobby and display postcards of current exhibits around town. Another gallery is located at Savannah International Airport.

Other Galleries and Exhibits

The **Jack Leigh Gallery,** 132 E. Oglethorpe Ave., 912/234-6449, across from Colonial Park Cemetery, offers prints and photographs by the Ansel Adams of Savannah (who passed in 2004). Leigh was most famous for the Bird Girl photo on the cover of *Midnight in the Garden of Good and Evil,* among other brooding, contemplative black-and-white images also on display. The shop is open Tues.–Sat. 10:30 A.M.–5:30 P.M. and Sun. 1–5 P.M.

The wooden sculptures of renowned folk artist Ulysees Davis, including a complete collection of carvings of American presidents, is among the exhibits at the **Beach Institute,** 502 E. Harris St., 912/234-8000. The building was originally a schoolhouse built in 1867 to educate newly freed slaves and now serves as an African American cultural center. It's open Tues.–Sat. noon–5 P.M.

RELIGIOUS CENTERS

Some of Savannah's most fascinating stories spring from the city's religious history, and today many of the city's most distinguished landmarks remain its churches, temples, and burial grounds. Most churches are open to the public during the week and hold services for members in the evenings and weekends (guests are often welcome). The following are some highlights to suggest the diversity of the city's religious communities.

Christ Church

On Johnson Square at 28 Bull St., 912/232-4131, Christ Episcopal Church is considered the Mother Church of Georgia. As Georgia was founded as a Church of England settlement, Christ Church, situated at this site since 1733, was the epicenter or religious life in the new colony. Then Anglican, now Episcopal, the present sanctuary is the third on the site, dating from 1838. It's open to the public Wed. and Fri. 10 A.M.–3 P.M.

Cathedral of St. John the Baptist

Wesley Monumental United Methodist Church

On Calhoun Square, on Abercorn at East Gordon Street, the 1876 Gothic Revival church commemorates Methodism's founders John and Charles Wesley with their likenesses in a window opposite the pulpit. The brothers, both ordained ministers who had been derisively called "methodists" at Oxford for their methodical devotion to study and religious duties, came to Georgia with James Oglethorpe, and founded the Methodist society in 1784 upon returning to England.

Temple Mickve Israel

On Monterey Square, at 20 E. Gordon St., 912/233-1547, Mickve Israel is the third-oldest Jewish congregation in the nation, and the oldest in the South. It was founded in 1733 by 42 Jewish settlers, largely Sephardic Jews fleeing the Spanish Inquisition and who had lived for years as Crypto-Jews, publicly practicing Roman Catholicism while secretly preserving their Jewish faith. The synagogue was constructed in 1878 in neo-Gothic cruciform style, the only such synagogue in the U.S. Mickve Israel retains its original Torah and historical artifacts related to the city's Jewish population. The temple is open for public tours by donation Mon.–Fri. 10 A.M.–noon and 2–4 P.M.

First African Baptist Church

On Franklin Square, at 23 Montgomery St., 912/233-6597, First African represents one of the oldest African American Baptist congregations in North America, dating from 1773 (church officially constituted in 1777). The church operated a station on the Underground Railroad, hiding people escaping from slavery under its floorboards. During the 1950s and 1960s, the church served as the center of the local civil-rights movement. The church is open to free public tours Mon.–Fri. at 11 A.M. and at 1 and 3 P.M.

First Bryan Baptist Church

On Franklin Square, at 559 W. Bryan St., 912/232-5526, First Bryan Baptist Church is also among the oldest African American congregations. It was founded in 1794 by Andrew Bryan, who was enslaved before he purchased his own freedom and became an ordained minister. The church is open to the public Mon. 9 A.M.–noon and Tues.–Thurs. 9 A.M.–3 P.M. Both First African and First Bryan Baptist Churches are across the square from City Market.

Cathedral of St. John the Baptist

On Lafayette Square, at 222 E. Harris St., 912/233-4709, the Cathedral of St. John the Baptist is the oldest Roman Catholic church in Georgia, with its congregation dating back to 1799. (The original strictures of the Georgia colony outlawed Papists, and Savannah turned away French Catholic Acadian refugees fleeing from le Grand Derangement in 1765.) The current Victorian Gothic sanctuary, graced with impressive Tyrolean stained-glass windows, an Italian marble altar, and Persian rugs, was constructed in 1898. The cathedral is open to the public Mon.–Fri. 9 A.M.–5 P.M.

Colonial Park Cemetery

Many famous city leaders permanently reside at Colonial Park Cemetery, on Abercorn Street and Oglethorpe Avenue. Among the notable Georgians buried here is Button Gwinnett, a signer of the Declaration of Independence. The cemetery opened around 1750; it filled quickly in the early 19th century as a result of the yellow fever epidemics that struck the city, and closed to burials in the mid-19th century. Although between 10,000 and 12,000 people were buried there, only about 600 headstones remain.

During the Civil War, Union soldiers occupying Savannah were quartered in Colonial Park grounds. Some mausoleums were emptied to provide shelter, and some graves were looted and desecrated. Headstones were knocked down, switched, and defaced. To this day, with a careful reading, you may find grave markers of people who appear to have died before they were born, children who were married and had grandchildren at the time of their young deaths, and other evidence of historic vandalism.

Visitors are welcome to explore the grounds and examine the old sandstone and marble tombstones and inscriptions; it's a popular stop on every ghost tour in town. The gates are open 8 A.M.–5 P.M. (no charge for admission).

SCHOOLS

Savannah College of Art and Design

The country's largest art school, SCAD, 342 Bull St., 912/525-5100 or 800/869-7223, enrolls 7,000 students from more than 80 countries into 22 programs—including art history, graphic design, photography, filmmaking, animation, illustration, painting, architecture, interior design, and historic preservation.

SCAD uses the city as its laboratory—acquiring and restoring more than 1000 structures (including train sheds, warehouses, mercantile and drug stores, motels, and a jail) for adaptive reuse as studios, classrooms, dormitories, galleries and cafés. In a little more than 25 years since their founding (in 1978), the college has had a profound impact on the city, not only by its preservation and reuse efforts, but also by transforming historic Savannah into a vibrant college town with many young, international residents downtown.

SCAD maintains a dozen gallery spaces featuring the works of faculty, students, alumni, and nationally known artists, including one at the airport. They also sponsor monthly gallery tours (called "hops"; buses provide transportation between sites), films, openings, lectures, and other events that bring big-name artists to town. The SCAD Trustees Theater, on Broughton Street, is the venue for the Savannah Film and Video Festival, which is held each fall, and for various performing arts and screenings throughout the year.

Check scad.edu for events and more information. Student work is sold in the SCAD Shop on Madison Square. The *District* is the student paper and is found free around town and at scad-district.com; hear student Internet radio programming at scadradio.org.

University of Georgia System

Two colleges outside the historic district are part of the state university system. As is common throughout the South, one was historically white—**Armstrong Atlantic State University,** in Southside—and one was historically African American—**Savannah State College,** east of town, in Thunderbolt. Founded in 1890 as Georgia State Industrial College for Colored Youths, Savannah State was the first publicly supported state college for African Americans in Georgia.

Parks and Recreation

Within the historic district, walking is the primary recreational activity. Given the historic architecture of most inns, the only pools to be found are at franchise hotels. The same largely goes for fitness centers, though some inns offer access to local gym and fitness facilities. Adjacent to the historic district, Forsyth Park offers tennis courts and is a popular place for jogging—ask for a jogging trail map at the Savannah Visitor Center.

Farther afield, many recreation opportunities can be found in Southside, on outlying islands, in the marsh, or at the beach. Golf and tennis are available at city parks and local resorts.

Water Sports

Fishing is a favorite activity of both locals and visitors. A one-day freshwater fishing license is available for $3.50, and a full-season freshwater fishing license costs $24 for nonresidents and $9 for residents; saltwater fishing does not require a license. Licenses and regulations are widely available at sporting goods stores and many local marinas. The visitors center distributes comprehensive guides to local marinas, charter-boat services, and water-sports equipment rental services.

The **Bull River Yacht Club Marina,** 8005 Old Tybee Rd., 912/897-7300 or 800/311-4779, is on U.S. 80 halfway between downtown and Tybee Island. From here you can sign up for offshore or inshore fishing trips, dolphin cruises, or a three-hour ecoexploration cruise of the barrier islands and tidal marshes. They're open year-round.

Paddlers head out to the many scenic creeks, rivers, and byways of the Savannah River delta region east of downtown. **Sea Kayak Georgia,** 1102 U.S. 80, in Tybee, 912/786-8732, organizes three-hour guided kayak excursion trips and instruction; check schedules at seakayakgeorgia.com. If you're going out on your own, be sure to note the tide tables—novices should start out when the tide is rising.

Golf

The 27-hole **Bacon Park Golf Course,** 1 Shorty Cooper Dr., 912/354-2625, complete with pro shop, carts, and a lighted driving range, is part of a 1,021-acre city park with many other recreational options, such as tennis courts, an archery range, and ball fields. Greens fees are $25–29. The 18-hole **Henderson Golf Course,** 1 Al Henderson Dr. off Hwy. 204, 912/920-4653, charges $33–44.

The most exclusive is the Westin resort's **The Club at Savannah Harbor,** 912/201-2007, on Hutchinson Island, across the river from the historic district; it's open to Westin guests only, for $95.

Tennis

You can find tennis courts downtown at **Forsyth Park,** 912/351-3852, at Gaston and Drayton Streets. In Southside, find courts at **Daffin Park,** 1001 E. Victory Dr., 912/351-3851.

Biking

In the historic district, rent bicycles at **Bicycle Link,** 22 W. Broughton St., 912/355-4771. You might note that the features that make the historic district so attractive to walk through, such as the small squares and cobblestone and shell lanes, can make it rough going for cyclists—be particularly cautious navigating bikes through squares (with trolleys, horses, Girl Scouts, and many bewildered drivers unaccustomed to roundabout right-of-way).

Birding

The **S & O Barge Canal Nature Center,** 681 Argyle Rd., 912/748-8068, reopens a corridor of a canal system built in 1831 between the Savannah and Ogeechee (S & O) Rivers that is a stop on the **Coastal Birding Trail** (brochure available at the museum). The multipurpose linear park offers a taste of the distinct tidal river swamp habitat environment that attracts songbirds, birds of prey, and wading birds in all seasons. Museum exhibits tell more about the area's history, flora, and fauna.

It's open daily 9 A.M.–5 P.M. Admission is $2 for adults and $1 for children. You can reach it from the intersection of I-95 and Hwy. 204 by following Hwy. 204 (Argyle Road) west for 2.3 miles. It's 15 miles southwest of downtown.

Spectator Sports

The **Savannah Sand Gnats,** 912/351-9150, play Class A baseball affiliated with the Texas Rangers in Grayson Stadium, in Daffin Park, 1500 E. Victory Dr., from April through August. General admission tickets are $5 for adults and $4 for seniors, military, and youth 4–14 (under 4 free). They have plenty of special-feature nights, like Feed Your Face Mondays, wedding nights, and two-for-one beer nights. Their bug-eyed mascot, Gnic the Gnat, helps move a lot of team T-shirts and merchandise. See sandgnats.com for more information.

Entertainment

A great variety of lively entertainment is available in Savannah, from cultural arts to drag shows, and music from alternative to down-home blues. For mainstream entertainment listings, Friday's *Savannah Morning News* features the entertainment tabloid ***Diversions.*** It's online at savannahnow.com: to find live music listings, navigate to Diversions (not Entertainment). Pick up the free entertainment weekly ***Connect*** in cafés around the downtown commercial district for more local listings. The city's underground entertainment scene is chronicled online at savannahunderground.com, with listings and commentary about local artists, poetry readings, political events, and who's playing where.

The Savannah College of Art and Design operates several venues and hosts some of the most interesting events, and SCAD students support the district's vibrant alternative scene. You can find listings of SCAD theaters, events, and gatherings through scad.edu, but note that the school's main event calendar is not comprehensive, and it's worth tooling around a bit through the site to find more obscure gallery openings, theatrical events, screenings, other happenings that interest you.

PERFORMING ARTS

In Savannah it's all about the buildings, so not surprisingly, some of the best seats in town are in lavishly restored historic theaters (best alternative: outdoor performances in the squares).

Lucas Theatre for the Arts

The 1,250-seat **Lucas Theatre for the Arts,** 32 Abercorn St. at Congress, 912/234-3200, a grand four-story movie palace built in 1921, has been opulently restored, making the most of the original Italian marble and 40-foot-diameter plaster dome with Wedgwood detailing. It also features the original Mighty Wurlitzer pipe organ. It reopened in 2000 as a performing arts and concert venue (the Preservation Hall Jazz

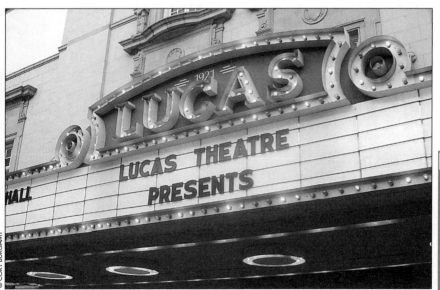

The Lucas Theatre reopens a grand movie palace built in 1921.

© CORY BURÇAMY

Savannah

SAVANNAH FESTIVALS AND EVENTS

Savannah's major events are St. Patrick's Day, Tour of Homes and Gardens, and Savannah Music Festival, all held in spring, the city's most lush time of year. The **First Saturday** of most months (February to December), River Street opens to a giant block party with food, drink, music, and outdoor stalls late into the evening. See the city's site, savannahvisit.com, for event listings; also check scad.edu for the many events hosted by the Savannah College of Art and Design or at SCAD venues, including several historic theaters downtown.

January
Martin Luther King Jr. Birthday, around Jan. 15. Observance celebrations include a parade and Freedom Ball.

February
Colonial Faire and Muster, Wormsloe Historic Site. In the anniversary month of Savannah's founding, the site of one of Georgia's first estates reenacts colonial life.

March
St. Patrick's Day Celebration and Parade, the week of March 17. The second-largest Irish celebration in the United States brings nearly 100,000 revelers to three days of festivities, which include live

jazz, rock, and blues—as well as traditional Irish music. This is Savannah's version of Mardi Gras.

Savannah Tour of Homes and Gardens, in late March. Beautifully restored, decorated, and landscaped historic homes and gardens are opened to public view. Four days of varied events that have been sponsored by the Historic Savannah Foundation for 70 years include walking tours, candlelight tours, a luncheon and cruise tours.

April
Savannah Music Festival, early April. A two-week celebration of zydeco, Mercer, Southern rock, gospel, opera, alternative, and more takes place at various venues downtown.

Siege and Reduction Weekend, at Fort Pulaski, on the weekend near April 11. Costumed performers stage military battles.

NOGs Tour of Hidden Gardens, a walking tour of gardens North of Gaston Street, culminates with a Southern tea at the Telfair Academy of Art.

Savannah Garden Exposition, Roundhouse Railroad Museum. Scents and flavors of Savannah are celebrated with gardening and cooking demonstrations.

Blues & BBQ Festival, Roundhouse Railroad Museum. Good music, food, and trains can be enjoyed by the whole family.

Band celebrated a Creole Christmas here one recent December) and also continues to screen films. The theatre is home to the **City Lights Theatre Company.**

Savannah Theater
The Savannah Theatre Company, 222 Bull St. at Macon St., 912/233-7764, presents 7–10 seasonal productions of contemporary drama, musicals, and comedy within what they say is the oldest continuously operating theater in the U.S. (Yet beyond the foundation and backstage bricks, little remains of the original William Jay–designed 1818 theater after several devastating fires). A children's theater troupe performs here as well.

SCAD Trustees Theater
The SCAD Trustees Theater, 216 E. Broughton St., 912/525-5100, a 1,100-seat Art Moderne theater built in 1946, anchors Savannah's most recently revived commercial district, with a giant SCAD marquee visible up and down the avenue. The theater was restored by the Savannah College for Art and Design and is now their most prestigious venue for lectures, live performances, film screenings, and other events, including the Savannah Film and Video Festival, held each fall.

Savannah Civic Center Arena
A modern auditorium within the historic district, Savannah Civic Center, 301 W. Oglethorpe, 912/651-6550, has little aesthetic attraction but

Sidewalk Arts Festival, Forsyth Park. SCAD students create chalk masterpieces on park squares; there's also an outdoor gallery of work by faculty, students, and alumni.

May

Savannah Seafood Festival, early May. Forget the costumes and drama, this event goes straight for the food, particularly the shrimp and shellfish specialties that make low country cuisine so delectable. It's held on River Street.

Beach Bum Parade, the Friday before Memorial Day, on Tybee Island. Islanders armed with water guns soak anyone within range of Butler Avenue; it's locally believed to be the world's biggest water fight.

July

Independence Day Celebration, July 4th. The classic American merriment here includes the largest fireworks display in the Southeast at the Savannah waterfront. Tybee Island also throws a party, with oceanside fireworks.

August

Seafood and Music Festival in late August, Tybee Island. It's a celebration of regional culinary specialties, accompanied by beach music.

September

Jazz Festival, midmonth or later. All stripes, all venues, all times are devoted to the city's annual celebration of the native southeastern art form, highlighted by a jazz parade.

October

Savannah Film and Video Festival, October or November. Independent and art films are included in this line-up at the SCAD Trustee's Theater.

November

Folklife Festival, second Saturday in November. Fifty southeastern artisans demonstrate (and sell) traditional crafts. There's also cane-grinding and folk music, all at the humble Oatland Island Education Center, on Oatland Island.

December

Christmas Celebrations, all month. Nineteenth-century decorations and festivities dress Savannah up for the holidays, with historic-home tours, the lighting of River Street, candlelight tours, and a decorated boat parade.

New Year's Eve Block Party, December 31. Live music, dancing, and food outdoors at City Market ring in the New Year.

---

is nevertheless the biggest venue in town, so it's the location of big-name performances and concerts that can fill 2,500 seats.

NIGHTLIFE

River Street and City Market are the city's main entertainment districts, with many bars and clubs that feature a wide variety of live music most nights. Check for the most recent developments along Broughton Street, which promises to be the next big thing.

River Street

On River Street, Savannah's answer to New Orleans' Bourbon Street, music pours from the doors of clubs, bars, and restaurants. Walk along the busy promenade until you find a beckoning sound, barker, or free table. Many festivals are also held here, with live music and dancing in the streets. The first Saturday of every month (from February to December) features a giant block party, with food and drink stalls set up along the sidewalk. It's a beautiful setting, with the lights of the boats and the bridge reflecting off the water and creating dramatic shadows on the klinker-brick walls of waterfront buildings.

Early on, the crowd includes young tourist families pushing strollers, and as it gets dark, the street becomes a dating and cruising scene—mainly young straight couples walking hand-in-hand and young men in groups, including

Savannah

uniformed soldiers on R&R and frat boys from Statesboro in shorts and baseball caps, looking for more elusive single women. Many bars feature music most nights. The music of Van Morrison, the Eagles, and the Allman Brothers is well represented in River Street clubs.

East of Bull Street: On the Abercorn Street ramp, the small **Bayou Café** attracts an authentic pack of regulars (despite its prime position in the tourist zone) with coveted spots on its tiny patio overlooking the channel. Beyond several underground lairs featuring crowd-pleasing karaoke and electrified rock, **Huey's,** 115 E. River St., features a large and inviting 2nd-story patio and outdoor bar, and gets our vote for the best seat (in decent weather) for whatever music's playing. Within the River Street Inn next door, **Tondee's Tavern** is named for the historic watering hole of Savannah's revolutionary Liberty Boys (which was not at this site, but the inn gets points for reviving the name). Here, a tony set enjoys air-conditioned views from 2nd-story picture windows. Fewer tourists venture to the eastern fringe of River Street, except for guests at the Marriott, and the regional chain **Spanky's** here has a largely local clientele.

West of Bull Street: On the far side of the Hyatt Hotel, the two-story **Kevin Barry's,** 117 W. River St., is a favorite landmark pub that features traditional Irish music, including popular electrified folk rock. The western fringe here gets dicey the farther west you go, with several raunchy clubs at the far end of the historic River Street strip across from the power station. A few blocks past the station, however, the **Conga Club,** 31 Martin Luther King Blvd. and River St., looks promising but was dark at a recent visit—in any case, go back up the bluff and approach from Bay Street to check it out.

Bay Street

On the top of the bluff you can hear live music at several clubs, including **Bay Street Blues,** which attracts a wide range of patrons for classic blues music. **Savannah Smiles** is a merciless tourist trap featuring "dueling" piano music, but nevertheless it occupies a great, old, speakeasy-like joint overlooking the waterfront and tucked behind the Quality Inn, at 314 Williamson St. (a spur off Bay Street, west of the Hyatt).

Around City Market

In the City Market's courtyard, many local bands can be heard for free outside **Malone's** bar and restaurant. Beer is sold at sidewalk stands, and you can help yourself to patio tables. Underneath the complex, **Savannah Blues** has a nice mixed clientele; the **Bar Bar** is set in a dramatically dungeonlike cellar and attracts young professionals and beautiful people.

Two of the city's most popular clubs are directly east of City Market. **The Jinx,** 127 W. Congress, the-jinx.com, attracts a young indie crowd for a wide range of music, from alternative and industrial to hip hop and stoner rock. Next door, at 125 W. Congress St., **Mercury Lounge** offers an equally varied line-up—including blues, rockabilly, and lounge music—to a slightly older hipster audience.

To the quiet western side of City Market, the **Rail,** 405 W. Congress St., is a comfortable neighborhood pub for chess and conversation. Next door, **B & B Billiards** is a friendly spacious pool hall.

Club One, 1 Jefferson St., 912/232-0200, a block north of City Market, is home to the notorious Lady Chablis (who performed in all her drag queen glory in the film *Midnight in the Garden of Good and Evil*). The huge three-story club features drag shows on its top-floor theater twice nightly Thurs.–Sat. Lady Chablis continues to perform a few times a month; call for her schedule. The 2nd floor is a dance floor with go-go cages; there's a quieter bar in the basement. The club draws a colorful, high-energy crowd of gays and straights, young and old, players, regulars and tourists. Cover charges vary around $10–15, with a premium of $25 for Lady Chablis shows.

Around the Historic District

Six Pence Pub, 245 Bull St. (across from the DeSoto Hilton), is a comfortable British-style pub complete with Toby mugs and bangers-and-mash; they also have inviting sidewalk tables (the fight scene between Julia Roberts and Dennis Quaid in *Something to Talk About* was filmed here). **Pinkie Masters,** at the corner of Drayton and East Harris Street, is a refuge from the tourist scene; it's a beer joint with a jukebox of 1980s hits, free popcorn, and an adamantly local clientele.

In the Victorian District at the foot of Forsyth Park, the bohemian **Sentient Bean,** 13 E. Park St., sentientbean.com, features live acoustic music, jam sessions, unusual films, poetry readings, community organizing, and other events.

SHOPPING

Walking through Savannah lends itself to leisurely browsing through shops, and the city makes it interesting with an eclectic assortment of antique, vintage, and contemporary-design boutiques set throughout the city but primaily in several commercial corridors. In addition, some unique items can be found in the gift shops of the city's house museums, as well as in art studios and galleries.

River Street

On River Street, the **Callaway Gardens Country Store,** 912/236-4055, sells Georgia food products, such as stone-ground grits, muscadine preserves, and pickled okra, along with cookbooks, gifts, and magnolia-anointed souvenirs. Other shops along the waterfront sell candy and maritime, pirate, marine-mammal, and seashell souvenirs. A candle shop demonstrates candle-dipping in back.

Broughton Street

A **Gap** store within a 1940s vintage Kress Five-and-Dime heads up the rags-to-riches story along Broughton Street. Still emerging from a long slumber in parts, the strip is fast becoming the city's newest entertainment and shopping district. A walk east from the Gap will take you past

a contemporary furnishings shop, African arts, Banana Republic, a florist, and a SCAD gallery, with well-appointed stops for food and drink.

Madison Square

The refined shopping district around Madison Square at Bull and Harris Streets is anchored by **E. Shaver Bookseller**, 326 Bull St., 912/234-7257, which offers an artful collection of local history, architecture, and design books, as well as audio books, children's books, smart toys, and Johnny Mercer recordings. It's open Mon.–Sat. 9 A.M.–6 P.M.

The Savannah College of Art and Design operates **Shop SCAD** here at 342 Bull St., 912/525-5180, selling student-designed prints, jewelry, textiles, and other wares.

Whitaker Street

They're fashioning a design district along a stretch of Whitaker Street, primarily between West Taylor and West Jones, with a dozen shops offering antiques, lighting, linens, garden shops, galleries, and other "chic du jour." **Folk Traditions,** 414 Whitaker, 912/341-8898, not only sells harps and flutes, and books on Savannah folk music, but also hosts jam sessions with traditional instruments. The **Mercer House Carriage Shop,** 430 Whitaker, once the antique shop of Jim Williams and now the box office for tours to the Mercer-Williams House museum, sells Mercer and *Midnight* memorabilia, as well as a small selection of arty gifts and housewares.

Around the Historic District

SCAD's **Ex Libris,** 228 Martin Luther King Jr. Blvd., 912/238-2427, offers a wonderful collection of gifts, crafts, and student and office supplies, in addition to a great selection of books and periodicals, in an inviting setting. There's also a coffee bar. It's across from the Savannah Visitors Center.

Savannah

Accommodations

Savannah has a wide variety of lodging, from a Victorian hostel to modern megahotels to unique historic inns. The luxurious inns are a big part of the city's attraction, and Savannah is a town worth a splurge. Try to stay in the historic district or adjacent Victorian district. In recent years several chain motels have sprung up downtown, offering nice options for families or budget travelers. Beyond the historic districts, standard chain motels can be found along Abercorn Street in the Southside district, yet the 10-mile drive is a full two centuries away from historic-district ambience.

High seasons are spring and fall; expect discounts in summer and winter (pretty much just January, excepting New Year's). Weekend rates are higher than weekday rates; prices may also vary considerably depending on availability. The rates listed here are for high-season weekend doubles, which is to say their highest rates. You might expect this to drop by a third for slack periods. Most historic-inn rates include a full Southern breakfast, and often an afternoon tea, aperitifs, pillow treats, and other perks as well; hotel rates generally do not.

For a complete list of properties, contact the **Savannah Convention and Visitors Bureau,** 912/944-0455 or 877/SAVANNAH (877/728-2662); also see savannahvisit.com. The nearest campgrounds to Savannah are at Skidaway Island and Tybee Island.

HOSTEL
Savannah Hostel
A turn-of-the-20th-century Victorian with 14-foot ceilings houses the Savannah Hostel, 304 E. Hall St., 912/236-7744. Fees run $21 for dormitory beds, including linens. Two private rooms with shared bath are available starting at $42 (great deal!). It closes 10 A.M.–5 P.M. They answer the phone only during office hours, which are 7–10 A.M. and 5–11 P.M. Note that on a recent visit, the owner was considering putting the place up for sale in 2005.

The surrounding Victorian district neighborhood is largely residential, with a supermarket and chain drug store a block away. It's a nice walk to the historic district through Forsyth Park during the day; at night, a cab back might be the best bet.

MODERN HOTELS
Riverfront
River Street is considered a prime location—it's in the center of the action at the waterfront, with premium river-view rooms. Of the three dominant modern hotels on the river, the Hyatt is at the center of the historic district, the Marriott is at its border, and Westin overlooks the historic district from the other side of the river, on Hutchinson Island.

The massive 347-room **Hyatt Regency Riverfront Hotel,** 2 W. Bay St., 912/238-1234 or 800/233-1234, presides over the waterfront just west of Bull Street with a massive boxy hotel that obviously preceded movements to keep construction within the historic district to scale; nevertheless, the Hyatt remains a luxury hotel in a prime location (rooms start at $150). The Hyatt was, for a long time, the city's primary full-service hotel, and it still serves as a central hub for much tourist activity, such as carriage tours from its entrance at the top of the bluff and boat rides from its dock below.

The 383-room **Savannah Marriott Riverfront,** 100 General McIntosh Blvd., 912/223-7722 or 800/228-9290, stands at the eastern fringe of the historic River Street strip, with a modern eight-story hotel alongside the channel, two pools (indoor and outdoor), and a waterfront restaurant (rooms start at $180). It's set against the marsh in what is largely a quiet residential area and is a short walk from Factors Row and the Pirates' House.

Across the river, on Hutchinson Island, the 16-story, 403-room **Westin Savannah Harbor Resort,** 912/201-2090, is the newest of the three—a luxurious, self-contained resort that opened in 2000 adjacent to the Savannah Trade

SAVANNAH ACCOMMODATIONS

© AVALON TRAVEL PUBLISHING, INC.

and Convention Center. The resort features restaurants, lounges, two pools, tennis courts, an exclusive golf course, a full-service spa, and a 400-foot floating dock (rooms start at $150). Hutchinson Island is a 15-minute drive from downtown Savannah or a two-minute water taxi ride from River Street. Note that the last water taxi ride on some nights is at 10:30 P.M.

Bay Street

Bay Street hotels are in the center of the action and convenient to the river, but they are on a popular thoroughfare with traffic throughout the day and into the evening. The river is visible from the uppermost floors of taller hotels; lower floors overlook urban streetscapes.

On Bay Street east of Bull Street, the 144-room **Hampton Inn,** 201 E. Bay St., 912/231-9700 or 800/426-7866, is a modern hotel attractively designed in red brick to blend in with the historic district (rooms start at $140 and include continental breakfast). They have a small pool and back up to a quiet residential area.

On Bay Street west of Bull Street, the five-story brick **Days Inn,** 201 W. Bay St., 912/236-4440 or 800/325-2525, is a larger-scale red-brick hotel centrally located a block from City Market (rooms start at $140). They have an outdoor pool and a handy 24-hour coffee shop.

At the northwest corner of the historic district, at Bay Street and Martin Luther King Boulevard, the district's newest hotel is the six-story Radisson, which was undergoing an affiliation change during research. Another hotel, next door on Bay Street, was under construction at that time. Across the street are two worn 1960s-style motels with a power station next door, aging rooms, and rates starting at $100 for the Quality Inn (no pool) and $140 for the Best Western (pool); these are not your best value.

A better bet is further west: The new **Comfort Suites,** 630 W. Bay St., 912/629-2001, is several blocks away from the historic district on a busy thoroughfare but offers 76 fresh suites (starting at $100) with room to stretch out and all modern conveniences and amenities, including a pool and ample parking out of the fray.

Around the Historic District

Many people prefer to find lodging away from the busy riverfront area and opt for quieter spots in the historic district, particularly around the squares.

On Reynolds Square, **Planters Inn,** 29 Abercorn St., 912/232-5678, offers 56 smallish rooms with historic period flourishes in a seven-story tower built in the 1980s. Room rates start at $150 and include continental breakfast and evening wine-and-cheese, served on an upper floor with a view of the city (including views of the the Lucas Theatre and the Olde Pink House). Big perk: Planters Inn guests can order dinner room service off the Olde Pink House menu. A block from Banker's Square, the hotel is popular with many business people (yet surprisingly doesn't offer desks in every room).

The 250-room **Hilton Savannah DeSoto,** 15 E. Liberty St. off Bull St., 912/232-9000 or 800/426-8483, is the central district's major hotel hub, a hulking, 15-story building constructed in the late 1960s, with a pool and restaurant (rooms start at $100). The refined Madison Square shopping district behind the hotel includes the city's best bookstore.

The 147-room **Courtyard by Marriott,** 415 W. Liberty St., 912/790-8287, opened its five-story hotel in 2001 (rooms start at $160). The attractively designed low-slung brick hotel has its own café, lounge, and heated outdoor pool. Across from the visitors center, history museum, and railroad museum, the hotel is also within several blocks of the civil-rights museum, the new battlefield park, and a SCAD bookstore/café, and it is convenient to the freeway and historic district shuttles—a nice family choice.

Victorian District

The Victorian district, south of the historic district, is a largely residential area that is now experiencing the same sort of restoration that swept through the downtown area years ago. Here the acclaimed restaurant Elizabeth on 37th, east of Forsyth Park, was one of the neighborhood's early pioneers; and the Magnolia Place Inn is a venerable destination.

Built around its namesake turreted red-brick Romanesque Victorian, **The Mansion on**

Forsyth Park, 700 Drayton St., 912/238-5158 or 888/711-5114, is designed with many period characteristics in mind but is the city's most ultramodern hotel. To open in 2005, the 126-room mansion offers fine dining, a cooking school, a ballroom, an art gallery, a courtyard pool, and a full-service spa with a 24-hour fitness center among its many amenities. Rooms are outfitted with oversized tubs and flat-screen TVs. Opening room rates for in-season doubles start at $275. The hotel borders the eastern side of Forsyth Park and will be operating the concession in the park's dummy fort once it is restored and reborn as a café.

HISTORIC INNS

Throughout Savannah's historic district, dozens of elegant century-old mansions provide overnight guests with a gracious ambience and romance that matches the city itself. Among the standard amenities you'll find porch swings or rockers on wide verandas, brandy served in front parlors, formal gardens, and of course, plenty of Southern hospitality.

Inside each luxuriously decorated inn, period furnishings are augmented by such modern conveniences as phones, TVs, central air-conditioning and heating, private baths, and sometimes indoor whirlpool tubs or outdoor hot tubs. Many offer passes to use local fitness clubs; but for a pool, you'd need a modern hotel. Business amenities are often available by request.

Most historic inns offer at least one barrier-free room; few have elevators. Several have honeymoon suites. Many inns request no children under 12 years old (families with young children may prefer more kid-proof lodging anyway). Inquire about parking availability and cost, and about breakfast options and times if you're a finicky eater or late sleeper, and ask about private entrances if you'd prefer not to greet the concierge at every trip through the door.

See photos of 15 of the city's most distinguished inns at historicinns-savannah.com.

Riverfront

The 86-room **⚏ River Street Inn,** 115 E. River St., 912/234-6400 or 800/253-4229, is a beautiful, spacious renovation of an 1853 cotton warehouse designed around a three-story, skylit atrium (elevator available). Small rooms (starting at $180) face either the stately Factors Walk promenade atop the bluff or the lively River Street scene below. Riverside balconies are coveted places to watch the fireworks displays that usually follow waterfront festivals. Breakfast is not included, but a New Orleans–style restaurant below the hotel offers beignets and chicory coffee, as well as breakfast entrées.

Around the Historic District

The 68-room **⚏ Marshall House,** 123 E. Broughton St., 912/644-7896 or 800/589-6304, reopens an 1851 hotel that was abandoned for four decades before its lavish restoration in 1999. It is, as they say, a nice combination of a full-service hotel (privacy and all amenities, including an on-site restaurant and lounge) and historic inn (elegant yet comfortable, colorfully decorated historic rooms with ironwork balconies accessible through windows, and other charming quirks). Rates start at $140 and include continental breakfast. It's on a broad exposed street that is quickly (thanks to the Marshall House) becoming the city's newest entertainment district.

On Columbia Square, the refined **⚏ Kehoe House,** 123 Habersham St., 912/232-1020 or 800/820-1020, offers European-style lodging in 13 guest rooms in a poshly restored 1892 Renaissance Revival red-brick mansion with an elevator and some private verandas. Breakfast-to-order, cocktail-hour appetizers, and pillow treats are among the amenities. Doubles start at $250. The Davenport House, the city's premier house museum, and the Historic Savannah Foundation are neighbors on the regal square.

The 1838 **⚏ Ballastone Inn,** 14 E. Oglethorpe Ave., 912/236-1484 or 800/822-4553, is one of Savannah's classic historic inns. Seventeen rooms in the main four-story house (with elevator) have been opulently furnished with an exacting eye for period authenticity. Cosmopolitan guests gather for cocktails in the front parlor or around a full-service bar that looks like a bar car out of the *Orient Express.* Doubles start

⚏ Savannah

The 1892 Kehoe House on stately Columbia Square is one of the city's finest historic inns.

at $250. It's on a divided street graced with tall oaks and magnolias in its parklike median.

Another classic choice, the **Gastonian,** 220 E. Gaston St., 912/232-2869 or 800/322-6603, offers two elegant 19th-century mansions joined by a winding raised ironwork walkway over a manicured garden, with a hot tub tucked under the trellis. Seventeen guest rooms are sparsely furnished with English antiques, gauzy canopy beds, fireplaces, and Persian rugs over hardwood floors; ceiling fans rotate from high ceilings. It's very romantic. Doubles start at $300.

On Chippewa Square, the smart **Foley House Inn,** 14 W. Hull St., 912/232-6622 or 800/647-3708, has 18 comfortable rooms (some are quirky) carved out of a three-story 1896 walk-up townhouse, with a slightly lighter touch and a nice central location off Bull Street. They offer a full breakfast in either the sophisticated parlor or out on the garden patio. Doubles start at $200. The square is a favorite for movie buffs; it's where the bus stop scenes in *Forrest Gump* were filmed. The Savannah Theatre is a neighbor on the square.

On Lafayette Square, **Suites on Lafayette,** 201 E. Charlton St., 912/233-7815 or 866/578-

4837, offers large two-bedroom Victorian flats that sleep up to 10 people—ideal for couples traveling together, families, or larger parties. It's also great for indulging fantasies of living in Savannah. The flats have high ceilings, fireplaces, complete modern kitchens, coffeemakers, washer-dryers, and all other comforts of home (starting at $200, breakfast not included).

Also on Lafayette Square, the **Hamilton-Turner House,** 330 Abercorn St., 912/233-1833, of *Midnight* fame, is now a bed-and-breakfast inn. *New Yorker* cartoonist Charles Addams could have drawn the house, with all its raised-eyebrow window arches and ironwork crown. The rooms are spacious and bright, and they are decorated with antiques and period reproductions (rooms start at $250). The inn is operated by a local family and is maintained by sprightly teenagers, a contrast to the largely professional hospitality industry in town. Lafayette Square is also home to the Flannery O'Connor Home and the Andrew Low House museum.

On Chatham Square, **Bed and Breakfast Inn,** 117 W. Gordon St., 912/238-0518 or 888/238-0518, is the largest of Savannah's guesthouses (small, resident-operated establishments that are less expensive than inns). There are 15 rooms that occupy two narrow 19th-century Federal rowhouses. Doubles start at $100 and include breakfast, and children are welcome; also inquire about suites. Mercer House is two blocks east; the civil-rights museum is two blocks west.

Victorian District

M Magnolia Place Inn, 503 Whitaker St., 912/236-7674 or 800/238-7674 (outside Georgia), is housed in a regal 1878 Queen Anne Victorian mansion. It has 13 spacious, antique-furnished guest rooms and wide verandas overlooking Forsyth Park from the far side of Gaston Street. In the elegant pale-yellow parlor, contemporary artwork blends right in with the brocade; this is where afternoon tea and evening aperitifs are served. Come morning, guests may elect to have their silver breakfast set delivered to the porch outside their rooms. Like Savannah, Magnolia Place is not precious, quaint, or stiff—but charming, comfortable, and gracious. (It's also a favorite haunt of author John Berendt, we hear.) Doubles start at $250.

Food and Drink

Call a restaurant to ask when it's open, and expect to hear the perfect Savannah response: "Why, we're open *now!*"

CASUAL

Farmers Markets and Groceries

In 2005, the city will reinaugurate Ellis Square at City Market as a farmers market, with fresh produce, flowers, and wares.

The 24-hour **Gregory M. Parker Market,** 222 Drayton St., 912/231-1001, is a handy round-the-clock resource for gourmet prepared meals (veggie and turkey wraps, salads, and the like) and has a good, reasonably priced wine and beer selection (you'll also find out-of-town newspapers and a gas station here).

At the south end of Forsyth Park, there's a natural-foods market: **Brighter Day,** 1102 Bull St., 912/236-4703, where you can purchase organic produce and packaged and bulk foods. It's open Mon.–Sat. 10 A.M.–6 P.M. and Sun. 12:30–5:30 P.M. The deli bar inside offers prepared foods; it's open midday but is closed Sundays.

The nearest supermarket to the historic district is in the Victorian district, at **Kroger's,** 311 E. Gwinnett St., 912/231-2260. It's good for a quick roasted chicken, impromptu sheet cake, or whatever. It's two blocks east of Forsyth Park, and there's a pharmacy here too.

Coffeehouses

Savannah's coffeehouses offer a place to start out, end up, or alight throughout the day for coffee drinks, pastries, and light meals for breakfast, lunch, and supper. They're some of your best bets for vegetarian food, and some also offer live entertainment. You can usually hang out and cool off for the price of a cup of joe.

Savannah Coffee Roasters, corner of Bull and Congress Sts., 912/352-2994, is a popular and often crowded spot for coffee, vegetarian entrées, and sandwiches (including PB&J); it has a few patio tables in the center of the action downtown. Further down the central Bull Street corridor, **Gallery Espresso,** 234 Bull at Perry St., 912/233-5348, is Savannah's original coffeehouse; it's pet-friendly and has high-speed Internet and art on display.

A new landmark on the café scene is the **Sentient Bean,** 13 E. Park St., 912/232-4447, at the foot of Forsyth Park at Bull Street (next door to the Brighter Day market). Not only a café with pastries, quiches, and veggie lasagne (starting at $6), "the Bean" is also the epicenter of bohemian Savannah, with poetry readings, songwriters nights, community meetings, offbeat films, and other diversions. It's open daily 7:30 A.M.–8 P.M. and stays open later on weekend nights.

Across from the Savannah Visitors Center, **Ex Libris,** 228 Martin Luther King Jr. Blvd., 912/238-2427, offers a wonderful coffee bar

SAVANNAH FOOD AND ENTERTAINMENT

Savannah *River*

■ WATER TAXI

■ WATER TAXI ■ WATER TAXI BAYOU CAFÉ

W FACTORS WALK

KEVIN BARRY'S ▼ VISITORS CENTER RIVER ST ▼ HUEY'S

WILLIAMSON ST

SAVANNAH ▼ SMILES BARNARD RAMP E FACTORS WALK

CITY HALL ★ Emmet Park

W BAY ST E BAY ST

CLUB ONE ▼ Ellis Square

VINNIE VAN-GO-GOS ▼ W BRYAN ST OLDE PINK HOUSE E BRYAN ST

Franklin Square City Market SAPPHIRE GRILL Johnson Square ▼ Warren ■ P Square Washington Square

▼ BELFORD'S LADY ▼ & SONS SAVANNAH COFFEE ROASTERS Reynolds Square

W CONGRESS ST E CONGRESS ST

GARIBALDI'S ▼ ▼ EXPRESS CAFÉ ▼ MERCURY LOUNGE 11 PASTICCIO ▼ P

BISTRO SAVANNAH ▼ SAIGON ▼ ▼ 45 BISTRO

A VÍDA ▼ W BROUGHTON ST E BROUGHTON ST

ALLIGATOR SOUL DEBI'S ▼ E BROUGHTON LN

W STATE ST E STATE ST

P Telfair Square Wright Square Oglethorpe Square Columbia Square Greene Square

Liberty Square W YORK ST E PRESIDENT ST E YORK ST

WALL'S BBQ ▼

OGLETHORPE AVE W OGLETHORPE AVE E OGLETHORPE AVE

To Siege of Savannah Battlefield Park ←

TURNER ST

EX LIBRIS ▼ Elbert Square Orleans Square W HULL ST Chippewa Square GREGORY M PARKER MARKET ▼ COLONIAL PARK CEMETERY E HULL ST Crawford Square

CIVIC W PERRY ST E PERRY ST

CENTER ▼ GALLERY ESPRESSO

FELICIA'S ▼ W LIBERTY ST E LIBERTY ST

LOUISVILLE RD P PINKIE MASTER'S ▼

W HARRIS ST E HARRIS ST

Pulaski Square Madison Square Lafayette Square Troup Square E MACON ST

W CHARLTON ST E CHARLTON ST

GRYPHON ▼ TEA ROOM W CHARLTON LN E CHARLTON LN

W JONES ST E JONES ST

MRS WILKES' BOARDING HOUSE ▼ CLARY'S

W TAYLOR ST E TAYLOR ST

Chatham Square Monterey Square Calhoun Square Whitefield Square

W GORDON ST E WAYNE ST E GORDON ST

W ALICE ST E ALICE ST

W GASTON ST E GASTON ST

Forsyth

Park

W HUNTINGDON ST E HUNTINGDON ST

0 200 yds

W HALL ST To Elizabeth on 37th, Sentient Bean, Brighter Day, and Kroger's ↓ E HALL ST 0 200 m

▼ 700 DRAYTON

© AVALON TRAVEL PUBLISHING, INC.

within a bookstore; both are operated by the Savannah College of Art and Design. **Starbucks** is at Bull and Broughton Streets.

Breakfast

At City Market, ⚡ **Express Cafe,** 39 Barnard St., 912/233-4683, has some of the best healthy breakfasts and lunches around: Belgian waffles, quiches, great soups, salads, and sandwiches with fresh, exotic ingredients (many choices are under $5). It's all served cafeteria-style in a bright airy storefront. It's open Tues.–Fri. 7 A.M.–3 P.M. and Sat.–Sun. 8 A.M.–3 P.M.

Huey's, 115 River St., 912/234-7385, is a full-service Cajun restaurant, but in the morning you can pop in for just New Orleans–style beignets and café au lait with a waterfront view.

Clary's Cafe, 404 Abercorn at E. Jones, 912/351-0302, of *Midnight* fame, is an okay spot for Southern breakfast, standard American lunches, and soda-fountain treats—it's very smoker-friendly, inside and out. Hours are Mon.–Fri. 6:30 A.M.–4 P.M., Sat. 8 A.M.–4 P.M., and Sun. 8 A.M.–2 P.M.

Lunch

On Madison Square, **Gryphon Tea Room,** 337 Bull St. at Charlton, 912/525-5880, starts with bakery treats in the morning and moves into salads (try a combo with their shrimp salad) and deli sandwiches (starting at $3.50 half). From 4–6 P.M. they serve a traditional British tea of cucumber sandwiches, scones, and pastries, or

LOW COUNTRY CUISINE

Coastal Georgia and South Carolina comprise a distinct geocultural region called the low country. Low country cuisine makes the most of local ingredients, particularly the abundant shellfish. The popular dish called low country boil consists of shellfish prepared with corn-on-the-cob and potatoes, and is similar to Cajun crawfish boils. She-crab soup and pan-fried softshell crabs are also delicious low country specialties. Many cooking traditions sprout from the Gullah culture and retain West African influences.

you can just drop by for a beautiful selection of desserts. Overlooking the lush square, the former apothecary (restored by SCAD) retains its old cabinets, mirrors, and mahogany paneling—an elegant setting worthy of Zurich's Banhofstrasse, particularly when the pianist is playing. Hours are Mon.–Fri. 8:30 A.M.–6 P.M. and Sat. 10 A.M.–6 P.M.

Find authentic back-alley barbecue at ⚡ **Wall's Bar-B-Que,** 912/232-9754. It's officially at 515 York St., yet it's actually tucked in a brick-red cabin in the dirt drive behind York off of Price Street, as it's been for more than 33 years. Their posted hours say Wed. 11 A.M.–6 P.M., Thurs.–Sat. 11 A.M.–9 P.M., but your best bet to catch them open is on Fridays and Saturdays, or to call first.

Southern Buffet

Tourists queue up for hours to eat classic Southern buffets at two Savannah institutions. Since the 1940s, generations of Wilkeses have dished out family-style meals at **Mrs. Wilkes' Boarding House,** from the basement of 107 W. Jones St., 912/232-5997. Sometime around the turn of the century, however, they elected to serve the food first and seat people second, and as a result the experience is more institutional than homey, and the food is less than piping hot. Tradition or not, sadly, it's not worth a wait.

At City Market, **The Lady and Sons,** 102 W. Congress St., 912/233-2600, a relative upstart on the comfort-food scene, offers a more spiffy version of boardinghouse fare, with self-serve stainless-steel buffet carts with heating lamps, two spacious dining floors in a glass-walled building, and a convivial atmosphere. Not bad for a heaping plate of chicken, mac-and-cheese, and collards, but an hour-long wait? At $13 for lunch and $17 for dinner? That's hard to recommend—that'll buy a lot of fresh shrimp in this town.

Debi's, 10 W. State St., 912/236-3516 (menu line), is where the locals go for a modest meat-and-three or vegetable plate for under $5, and guests are in and out of there in an hour. It's open weekdays only for breakfast and lunch, Mon.–Fri. 7 A.M.–2:45 P.M.

⚡ Savannah

Casual Dinners

You can make dinner out of appetizer plates of seafood and cold beers at a dozen places on River Street. Many restaurants also feature live entertainment most evenings. Some of the best choices for visitors are the places with a view, such as **Huey's,** 115 E. River St., for steamed oysters, or the grittier **Bayou Café,** up the Abercorn ramp. **Kevin Barry's,** 117 W. River St., serves Irish potato soup and corned beef on rye in addition to other pub grub in their lively two-story tavern with a nice waterfront view.

Moon River, 21 W. Bay St., 912/447-0943, offers burgers and bratwurst to wash down with their signature brews in a crowd-pleasing, brew-pub atmosphere.

At City Market, **Vinnie Van Go Go's,** 912/233-6394, offers a nice perch overlooking Franklin Square. It's good for people-watching over decent cheap pizza and tumblers of house red.

The aromatic **Saigon,** 4 W. Broughton St., 912/232-5288, offers a whole new take on such local favorites as grouper, flounder, and shrimp, from tom yum shrimp seasoned with lemongrass and lime to fish filets grilled with sweet chili and ginger sauce. Lunch specials run $7; most dinner entrées are under $10. They serve lunch on weekdays only and are open for dinner every night at 5 P.M.

MODERATE

Low Country Cuisine

In City Market, **Belford's,** 315 W. St. Julian St., 912/233-2626, anchors the western end of the complex with two floors and a wide patio overlooking Franklin Square. Their signature shrimp-and-grits is served over wilted collards ($24 for dinner and $15 for lunch); they also offer grouper, crab cakes, and she-crab stew, along with steaks and pasta. You can get a $10 "buffalo-style" (spicy) oyster po-boy sandwich at lunch. They serve a $6 breakfast buffet (along with menu items) 8–11 A.M., lunch 11:30 A.M.–3:30 P.M., dinner 5:30–10 P.M., and Sunday brunch 11:30 A.M.–3 P.M. The dress is casual.

At City Market, **Bistro Savannah,** 309 W. Congress St., 912/233-6266, is the city's most venerable bistro, serving creative twists on Southern coastal cuisine in a comfortably appointed storefront. Entrées (starting at $18) include flounder topped with an apricot-shallot glaze. They're open Sun.–Thurs. 6–10:30 P.M. and Fri.–Sat. 6 P.M.–midnight.

Alligator Soul, 114 Barnard St., 912/232-7899, serves specialties from across the South, from an excellent North Carolina rainbow trout to Crescent City fried rabbit gumbo. Their Tybee Island anise-tinged shrimp boat comes served in a carved-out eggplant. Desserts are equally exotic, such as fresh peach bread pudding with bourbon sauce and chocolate-and-port fondue served with pound cake and strawberries. They're squirreled away in an underground lair off Broughton Street—a funny choice in as scenic and temperate a place as Savannah (at night, at least)—but it's cozy. It's open for lunch on Fri. and Sat.; dinner is served Mon.–Sat. starting at 5 P.M.

Italian

At City Market, **Garibaldi's,** 315 W. Congress St., 912/232-7118, is a Northern Italian bistro featuring such daily blackboard specials as veal *murat* with a great wine selection. Dinner for two with a modest wine might run $80 or more, and prime-time reservations are recommended. It's housed in a welcoming, wood-paneled, dimly lit storefront—a nice date spot. Dinner is served Sun.–Thurs. 6–10:30 P.M. and Fri.–Sat. 6 P.M.–midnight. Along with Bistro Savannah, it's an old favorite at City Market.

Il Pasticcio, 2 E. Broughton St. at Bull St., 912/231-8888, offers gourmet Italian cuisine—including seafood fettuccine, risotto, and meat and fish dishes—starting at $18. Or you might put together a dinner from several appetizers (most under $10), such as ricotta-stuffed eggplant, pesto gnocchi, baked calamari, and lobster ravioli. It's a stylized modern affair, with white-draped tables and tile floors in a glass-walled corner storefront—good for people-watching, inside and out. It's open for dinner nightly starting at 5:30 P.M. The nightclub **Après** is upstairs.

Contemporary American

Around City Market, **Sapphire Grill,** 110 W. Congress St., 912/443-9962, is a little slice of Atlanta in the Coastal Empire. In a stylized interior of chrome and brick, they offer such trendy selections as tuna mignon, shrimp brochette, and bass-and-grits, along with steaks and vegetarian specials (starting at around $17). They have an extensive list of French and Californian wines; and their wine bar is open late. Dinner is served Sun.–Thurs. 6–10:30 P.M. and Fri.–Sat. 5:30–11:30 P.M.

The minimalist **A Vida,** 113 W. Broughton St., 912/232-8432, is popular with students for its wine bar; they also serve inventive specials such as sugar-glazed pork chops with red-cabbage marmalade and duck breast with a fig-and-port sauce (starting at $18). It's open nightly for dinner starting at 5 P.M.

FINE DINING

Savannah is known for its fine restaurants in historic settings. While some meals may not cost much more than moderately priced restaurants above, the style is more formal, the service more starched, the atmosphere more genteel. Dress is evening resort wear—men wear jackets—and reservations are recommended. Accessibility may be an issue; call to confirm.

Within the landmark pink 18th-century mansion on Reynolds Square, the ⛰ **Olde Pink House,** 23 Abercorn St., 912/232-4286, offers elegant Southern dining in historically appointed dining rooms upstairs, complete with powdered-wig portraits in gilt frames. The menu is more contemporary than the setting would lead you to believe, and it serves as a delicious introduction to low country cuisine: blue crab–stuffed black grouper with hoppin' John, lobster rubini with stone-ground grits, pork tenderloin with collards and yams, and so on (most entrées are above $20). Downstairs, you can order off the same menu (and come as you are) at the subterranean **Planters Tavern,** a dark pub with a long convivial bar, couches, and a roaring fire. Or look no further than the appetizers—say, the delicious fried salmon with

© CORY BURGAMY

Olde Pink House

honey and walnut glaze. A small plate, cocktails, and vocalist Gail Thurmond on the piano may be all you need. The restaurant and tavern are open nightly.

In the Victorian district, ⛰ **Elizabeth on 37th,** 105 E. 37th St., 912/236-5547, set in a handsome turn-of-the-20th-century mansion, is a short cab ride from the historic district. Nationally recognized namesake chef Elizabeth Terry was among the originators of "gourmet Southern" cuisine, using fresh local ingredients and reinterpreting the classics in sophisticated contemporary ways. Some favorites among the daily specials include an curry-laced black-eyed-pea cake over greens as an appetizer, an entrée of broiled flounder in a cream, crab, and sherry sauce, followed by a pecan-almond tart topped with praline ice cream and Gentleman Jack caramel sauce. ("Some of the best food I've ever eaten in America" was what one well-traveled Swiss businessman had to say; for another diner, the setting evoked colonial Malaya.) Dinner for two runs around $100, not including selections from the extensive wine list. Elizabeth's serves dinner Mon.–Sat. 6–9:30 P.M.

Savannah

Several of Savannah's historic inns are also known—or are becoming known—for their on-site restaurants. Within a luxurious historic inn, **17 Hundred 90,** 307 E. President St., 912/236-7122, serves continental cuisine, seafood, steaks, and the house specialty, rack of lamb Dijon. It's open for lunch weekdays only, dinners nightly starting at 6 P.M. At the Marshall House, **45 Bistro,** 123 E. Broughton St., 912/644-7896, serves French and American bistro classics Mon.–Sat. The mansion at Forsyth Park promises to offer exceptional dining as well in its **700 Drayton** restaurant, which comes complete with its own cooking school.

In the same range as those above, **45 South,** 20 E. Broad St., 912/233-1881, presents tuna carpaccio and crab-cake appetizers among its local seafood specialties. Dinners are served Mon.–Sat. starting at 6 P.M.

BEYOND DOWNTOWN

If you want a change from the historic district, several restaurants out east make good destinations. Also try Tybee Island.

Three miles east of downtown, **Johnny Harris,** 1651 E. Victory Dr., 912/354-7810, "the fanciest barbecue restaurant in Georgia," has been serving 'cue since 1924. The local institution has a main dining area and a more casual bar out back (it's also the smoking section). There's BBQ salmon, shrimp, and lamb, in addition to the traditional mustard-laced pork and ribs (plates start at $13); they also have steaks and chicken (smoked or fried). Dinner for two would run around $50 or so. It's a big, family-friendly place with easy parking. It's open Mon.–Thurs. 11:30 A.M.–10:30 P.M. and Fri.–Sat. until midnight.

Getting There and Around

BY AIR
Savannah International Airport
The nicely designed, modern and efficient Savannah International Airport, 912/964-0514, 16 miles west of downtown (off I-95 north of I-16), is served by several major airlines, including Delta, Continental, United, and USAir, along with several smaller carriers. Shuttle flights make the 45-minute run between Atlanta and Savannah. There's a small visitors center and a SCAD art gallery in the terminal.

A taxi ride downtown runs around $20 for one passenger and $5 for each additional passenger.

BY TRAIN
Amtrak
Amtrak passenger trains make six stops daily at Savannah's terminal, with direct service to cities up and down the Atlantic seaboard, including New York City, Baltimore, Washington, Richmond, Charleston, Jacksonville, and Miami. Savannah is one of Amtrak's package-tour destinations (one reduced price for combined train fare and lodging); call 800/USA-RAIL

(800/872-7245) for more information about rates and schedules.

The terminal is four miles west of downtown, 2611 Seaboard Coastline Dr., 912/234-2611, an isolated but staffed outpost. Taxis charge about $5 for one person to downtown.

BY BUS
Greyhound/Trailways
Savannah's Greyhound bus depot, 610 W. Oglethorpe Ave., 912/233-2135, is conveniently located at the western boundary of the historic district, within walking distance of the Savannah Visitors Center, historical attractions, restaurants, and B&Bs; it's also convenient to city shuttles that loop through the district. From here passengers can make connections to most cities in the region and beyond. Five buses run daily between Savannah and Atlanta's Hartsfield International Airport (about $100 round-trip). Several charter companies also run this heavily traveled route.

Next door, the Econolodge appears halfway decent; the Thunderbird, across the street from the depot, is best avoided.

Savannah

BY BOAT
Thunderbolt Marina
The Intracoastal Waterway weaves through Savannah's marshlands and down the Georgia coast, connecting Savannah to cities on the Eastern Seaboard. The Thunderbolt Marina, 912/352-4931, is a popular stop. See *Vicinity of Savannah* for information.

In cooperation with CAT, the **Savannah Belles Ferry,** 912/447-4000, provides shuttle service across the Savannah River from the historic River Street area to Hutchinson Island, home to the International Trade and Convention Center and the Westin Savannah Harbor Hotel. The ride takes two minutes shore-to-shore. The fare is $1 (when they collect it), and it's a cheap scenic tour. It makes the crossing around every 20 minutes daily 7 A.M.–11 P.M. You can pick up the ferry from the *Waving Girl* statue down by the Marriott Hotel or at the Hyatt Hotel dock at the foot of Bull Street, behind city hall. Check schedules for the last boat over; at certain times, it may be 10:30 P.M. (miss it, and you're in for a 15-minute cab ride).

BY CAR
Interstate Highway Routes
I-95, coastal Georgia's major north-south artery, connects Savannah with the rest of the Eastern Seaboard. I-16 heads west out of Savannah to Macon, where it meets I-75 for the run into Atlanta. Savannah's historic district lies 10 miles east of the intersection of I-95 and I-16.

The distance from Savannah to Atlanta is 250 miles; to the Golden Isles resorts, it's 90 miles; to Charleston, South Carolina, it's 110 miles; to Jacksonville, Florida, it's 140 miles.

Rentals, Cabs, and Driving Tips
Visitors staying downtown don't need a car, but major car rental agencies are well represented in town and at the airport, including Avis, 912/964-1781; Budget, 912/964-4600; Hertz, 912/964-9595; National, 912/964-1771; and Thrifty, 912/966-2277.

Taxi fare within the downtown area runs around $2–3 (10 cents per every one-twelfth of a mile). Try **Savannah Cab Company,** 912/236-2424, or **Yellow Cab,** 912/236-1133. Or for a more exotic mode of transit within the historic district, call **Savannah Pedicab,** 200 W. Congress St., 912/232-7900, for a modified rickshaw ride (you can also hail empty pedicabs on the street; they're often found around City Market.)

To park downtown, purchase a ticket from automated kiosks to park in the street, and display the ticket on your dashboard. Meters (if operable) are designed to accept credit cards as well as cash.

When navigating around the squares, use standard roundabout protocol: Yield to vehicles already in the square; they have the right of way. Making a left turn from a divided street is permissible. The same rules apply as a right turn on red—you're permitted to turn after coming to a complete stop, unless signs tell you otherwise.

By Bus or Van
Chatham Area Transit (CAT), 912/233-5767, runs municipal bus service as well as frequent *free* shuttle service around the historic district aboard motorized trolley cars. The free shuttle is designed to offer convenient service from downtown hotels, inns, and the Savannah Visitors Center to local historic sights, squares, River Street, and other attractions. The trolleys are wheelchair accessible. Bus fare is 75 cents for anyone taller than the fare box.

INFORMATION AND SERVICES
Visitor Information
The central **Savannah Visitors Center,** 301 Martin Luther King Jr. Blvd., 912/944-0455, is open year-round Mon.–Fri. 8:30 A.M.–5 P.M. and weekends and holidays 9 A.M.–5 P.M. A knowledgeable staff, maps and brochures, and a film orient the visitor to the historic district. Many city tours also leave from here. There are satellite centers at the airport and a hospitality center at 1 River Street; a nearby public elevator transports visitors up and down the bluff.

Interstate drivers will find a **Georgia State Welcome Center** near the South Carolina border off I-95. Go there for statewide information, as well as information and maps for Savannah and the Coastal Empire.

The **Savannah Convention and Visitors Bureau,** P.O. Box 1628, Savannah, GA 31402-1628, 912/944-0456 or 877/728-2662, is headquartered at 101 E. Bay St. at the corner of Drayton, where they have racks of brochures to leaf through during business hours (open Mon.–Fri. 8:30 A.M.–5 P.M.). Contact them via email at info@savcvb.com; or see savannahvisit.com.

The 161-year-old **Georgia Historical Society,** the oldest such organization in the Southeast, is housed in 1874 Hidgson Hall, 912/651-2125, at the southwest corner of Gaston and Whitaker Streets. The organization is the source of most of the historical research done in Savannah, and it hosts a monthly lecture series and occasional special events.

Consulates and Currency Exchange

Consulate offices in Savannah include Brazil, Denmark, Germany, Italy, Norway, and Sweden.

Exchange international currency at **American Express** and **Nationsbank,** each of which has a number of branches in the historic district and throughout the city.

Practicalities

Automatic teller machines for several financial institutions are found around **Banker's Square** (officially named Johnson Square), downtown's stately financial center at the head of Bull Street. The **UPS Store,** 22 W. Bryan St., 912/233-7807, offers packaging, shipping, fax, and photocopying services.

Internet access is available in several coffee shops downtown, including Gallery Espresso (see *Coffeehouses*). Complete office services, such as wi-fi Internet access, fax, photocopying, and shipping, is available 24 hours a day at **Kinko's,** 7929 Abercorn St., 912/927-8119, five miles south of the historic district, between Montgomery Cross and White Bluff Roads.

In the historic district, the 24-hour **Gregory M. Parker Market,** 222 Drayton St., 912/231-1001, is a very handy round-the-clock resource for major newspapers and periodicals (including the *New York Times* and the *Irish Times*), as well as for gourmet groceries, deli items, picnic supplies, and reasonably priced wine and beer. They also pump gas out front (another gas station is located at the corner of Bay Street and Martin Luther King Jr. Boulevard).

Department stores are found in Southside shopping malls, 5–10 miles south of the historic district along the commercial corridor of Abercorn Street (Hwy. 204): the **Savannah Mall,** at the Ogeechee River (near I-95), anchored by the regional Parisian department store, and the older **Oglethorpe Mall,** 7804 Abercorn St. at Mall Blvd. An **outlet mall,** 11 Gateway Blvd. at I-95, discounts name-brand clothing and merchandise.

The most unusual assortment of treasures can be found at **Keller's Flea Market,** 5901 Ogeechee Rd., 912/927-4848, which calls itself "the largest flea market in the Coastal Empire." It's one mile east of I-95 (around nine miles south of the historic district). Hours are Fri.–Sun. 8 A.M.–6 P.M. year-round.

Important Telephone Numbers

In **emergencies,** dial 911. The Savannah **police** (nonemergencies) can be reached at 912/232-4141. **Candler General Hospital** is located at 5353 Reynolds St., 912/354-9211.

Vicinity of Savannah

As hard as it may be to pull yourself away from historic Savannah, it would be a shame to come to town and not sample the surrounding low country. Within minutes of downtown, you can find yourself in wild wetlands of salty tidal creeks, abandoned rice fields, and silvery oyster beds—as well as the inviting sands of Georgia's Atlantic beachfront. The most popular attractions are to the east, including Bonaventure Cemetery, Fort Pulaski, and Tybee Island, 18 miles east of Savannah.

North of Savannah is the Savannah National Wildlife Refuge, as well as South Carolina's popular resort island of Hilton Head (38 miles north of Savannah). South of Savannah are the marsh islands, including Skidaway Island State Park.

NORTH OF SAVANNAH
Savannah National Wildlife Refuge

Ten miles north of Savannah via Hwy. 17, the Savannah National Wildlife Refuge, 912/653-4415, straddles the border of Georgia and South Carolina on either side of the Savannah River. Here the abandoned rice fields of 18th-century plantations have been restored to wetlands. Now only wild rice grows in the fields between the raised levees, attracting more than a hundred species of native and migratory birds. Alligators, bobcats, and deer are among many other wildlife species sheltered in the refuge. Visitors can walk along levees and trails.

The **Tupelo Swamp Walk** is a favorite of birders and photographers. The shorter **Cistern Trail** also reveals waterfront wildlife. The five-mile **Laurel Hill Nature Drive** allows drivers to get a glimpse of the landscape from the seat of a car.

From Savannah, take Hwy. 17A eight miles to where Highways 17 and 17A meet. Remain on Hwy. 17 by turning left, and go two miles to Laurel Hill Wildlife Drive. Find trail guides here at the shelter. Note that the refuge closes during hunting seasons and sensitive waterfowl periods.

Hilton Head Island, South Carolina

Thirty-eight miles north of Savannah (about an hour and fifteen minutes), Hilton Head Island is a fully developed upscale beach resort. The island was named after English sea captain William Hilton, who explored the island in 1664. Sea Island cotton, rice, and indigo plantations thrived here before the Civil War. Here, a "plantation" now refers to one of the many exclusive gated vacation-home communities or resorts on the island.

To reach Hilton Head from Savannah, take Hwy. 17 north eight miles from downtown, then veer right onto Hwy. 170 Alt. Take a right turn onto Hwy. 170 north, another right turn onto Hwy. 46 east, then another right turn onto Hwy. 278 east onto the island. (Though it sounds complicated, it's a well-traveled path, just stay to the right and follow the Lexuses and SUVs.)

New Ebenezer

For an offbeat excursion, travel to a remote corner of the state around 30 miles northwest of Savannah, where the remains of New Ebenezer recall a once thriving colonial town. The town was originally founded in 1734 by Salzburg Lutherans escaping religious persecution in Europe. New Ebenezer houses the oldest public building still standing in Georgia: the 1769 **Jerusalem Lutheran Church** (Sunday services are held at 11 A.M.) A small heritage museum is open Wed., Sat. and Sun. 3–5 P.M. A short nature walk leads visitors around the colonial ruins. From I-95, take Hwy. 21 past Rincon; then take Hwy. 275 north to the river.

SOUTH OF SAVANNAH
Wormsloe Historic Site on the Isle of Hope

The Isle of Hope shelters many old estates, one of which dates from the colonial era. The state-operated **Wormsloe Historic Site**, 7601 Skidaway Rd., 912/353-3023, retains the tabby ruins of the 1739 estate of Noble Jones, one of Savannah's

Savannah

first settlers and prominent early leaders. All that remains of the once expansive estate are the stately entrance archway and an arcade of live oaks leading to the softly eroding outlines of the villa's tabby foundation. (The fountain that was once part of the estate now graces Columbia Square downtown.)

The visitors center exhibits artifacts excavated at the site; a slide show covers the establishment of the 13th and final American colony. Living-history programs throughout the year feature colonial costumes and early American crafts demonstrations; the most notable event being the Colonial Faire and Muster, in February. Wormsloe is open Tues.–Sat. 9 A.M.–5 P.M. and Sun. 2–5:30 P.M. Adult admission is $2.50; it's $1.50 for children.

For a scenic approach from Savannah's historic district, drive east on Victory Drive to Skidaway Road, turn right, and continue south to LaRoche Avenue, then turn left and follow LaRoche to the river, where the riverfront is lined with antebellum mansions. Follow the main street south to Wormsloe.

SKIDAWAY ISLAND

Twenty-five minutes from downtown Savannah, Skidaway Island holds near-wild corners where visitors can see the surrounding marshland habitat close-up. The area makes a nice excursion from Savannah and provides a peaceful briny-scented respite from the urban environment. To reach Skidaway from Savannah's historic district, take Abercorn Street (Hwy. 204) south to Mall Boulevard, turn left, then in short order turn right on Hodgson Memorial Drive, left on Montgomery Crossroads, then right on Whitefield Avenue east to the Diamond Causeway.

On this Hwy. 204 spur over the Diamond Causeway, you pass over the **Moon River** of Johnny Mercer fame, one bridge west of Skidaway Narrows. At this juncture, the famed river is nowhere near "wider than a mile," as the song says, but there's a small highway sign that identifies the river; it makes a good photo opportunity (watch out for speeding traffic).

On the western shore of the island, **Priests Landing** provides a put-in point for boating excursions, including a sea-kayak trail to Wassaw Island. To reach the landing, follow the Diamond Causeway over to Skidaway Island, pass the state park, and head north on McWhorter Road. Turn right at Priest Landing Road and continue northwest to the harbor.

Skidaway Island State Park

Situated amid the live oaks, draped Spanish moss, and sandy pines of the maritime forest, Skidaway Island State Park, 912/598-2300, makes an scenic getaway close to the city (about a half-hour drive to the historic district). The parking fee is $2 per car.

The park has a 588 acres of marsh island habitats. Observation towers provide a scenic overlook. The mile-long ADA-accessible **Sandpiper Nature Trail** loops through the marshlands of Skidaway Narrows; there's also a three-mile **Big Ferry Trail.** The park also has a pool that costs a dollar or so for day use.

Skidaway's 88-site **campground,** 912/598-2300, is scenically set at the edge of the marsh. It features a pool, water and electric hook-ups, drive-throughs, a disposal station, hot showers, and laundry facilities among its well-maintained amenities. Campsites run $22–24; for reservations, call 800/864-PARK (800/864-7275), www.gastateparks.org. There's a small shopping center less than a mile away with a well-stocked convenience store.

University of Georgia Marine Education Center and Aquarium

At the northern tip of Skidaway Island, UGA's aquarium, "fish line," 912/598-3474, houses an up-close collection of sea turtles, sharks, and beautiful tropically colored fish and sea creatures representing coastal Georgia habitats—more than 200 animals in all. Native American historical exhibits trace the coast's history back thousands of years with pottery, tools, and ample explanation. It's a charming, low-key introduction to coastal history, ecology, and marine life. A nature trail and picnic area makes the most of the view of the Wilmington River.

The aquarium is open Mon.–Fri. 9 A.M.–4 P.M. and Sat. noon–5 P.M. Admission is $2 for adults and $1 children.

WASSAW ISLAND

One of the least developed islands on the east coast, Wassaw Island preserves the natural subtropical environment of the barrier islands in pristine shape. Now a **national wildlife refuge** and the highlight of a string of federally protected Savannah coastal refuges, Wassaw Island is accessible only by boat and open to the public for day-use only.

Owned by the Parsons family (originally from Maine) as a family retreat since the 1850s, Wassaw was never heavily farmed, logged, or cleared for cropland, as were most of the other barrier islands in the low country. In the mid-1960s, Parsons heirs contacted the Nature Conservancy, who found an anonymous donor to buy the island and transfer the title to the U.S. Fish and Wildlife Service to create a wildlife refuge. The Parsons family still maintains a 180-acre "home parcel" in the center of the island (and they request that visitors respect their privacy).

With seven miles of deserted sands and dolphins swimming in warm waters offshore, **Wassaw Beach** attracts visitors for beachcombing, swimming, and hiking. At the northern end, **Boneyard Beach** gets its name from the skeleton-like driftwood—bleached a ghostly white by the sun, sand, and salt. Offshore ruins of an 1898 **Spanish-American War fort** testify to the constantly shifting shorelines of the barrier islands; the fort was once hundreds of feet from shore and is today partially covered by each high tide.

Twenty miles of trails—old Jeep roads, shell roads, and footpaths—weave through an old-growth maritime forest dominated by live oak, palmetto, and slash pine and traverse freshwater sloughs. Hikers can take loop trips of various lengths; the island is 10 miles tip-to-tip. (Bring insect repellent to hike interior trails in warm months.) The island has 2,500 upland acres and 10,050 acres with marsh.

To reach the island, you'll need to either charter a boat or sail out yourself. Lists of marinas and charter-boat services are available at the Savannah Visitors Center, or call **Savannah Coastal Refuges,** 912/652-4415.

Paddlers can follow a **sea kayak trail** that leads through the Wilmington River from Skidaway Island's eastern shore to the northern tip of Wassaw Island, putting in at Priests Landing; see *Skidaway Island* for directions. Small-craft sailors follow the Intracoastal Waterway to the U.S. Fish and Wildlife Service dock at the southern end of the island.

EAST OF SAVANNAH

Highway 80 stretches east of town 18 miles to the Atlantic coast. On the way, drivers pass through small fishing villages and over the high arched bridges spanning the Intracoastal Waterway to the popular beach resort at Tybee Island. Detour often in order to discover the quiet appeal of the low country—a haunting cemetery here, an egret rookery there, and a creek-side crab-shack dinner to top it all off.

Fort Jackson

On the Savannah River two miles east of downtown, off the President Street extension, Fort Jackson, 912/232-3945, dates from the War of 1812 and served as headquarters for the Confederate defense of the Savannah River during the Civil War. Its brick batteries face the water, with a view of the port to the west and the wild marsh to the east. The fort's 32-pound cannon, one of the largest black-powder cannons still operational in the United States, is still fired for occasional special events.

The fort is open daily 9 A.M.–5 P.M. (admission is $3.50 for adults and $2.50 for children). Each May, the fort hosts the annual **Scottish Games and Highland Gathering,** a traditional plaid-and-bagpipe affair held midmonth.

Scuba divers take note: A sunken ironclad rests at the bottom of the channel out from the fort by marker 82A (the water's often too murky to see much; check with Tybee Island dive shops for conditions). One decent dive shop is **Atlantic Fishing and Diving,** 1712 Butler Ave., 912/786-7865.

Savannah

Ⓜ Bonaventure Cemetery

"One of the most impressive assemblages of animal and plant creatures I have ever met," was what naturalist John Muir had to say about this riverside haunt. "Never since I was allowed to walk the woods have I found so impressive a company of trees as the tillandsia-draped oaks of Bonaventure." Muir spent several days in the historic cemetery in 1867, camping out and waiting for the funds to continue his travels.

Today Bonaventure is just as captivating, with folks strolling among the statues and dusty lanes, glancing at Hebrew inscriptions on the graves of Savannah's Jewish founding families, and searching for the memorials of such celebrities as lyricist Johnny Mercer and Pulitzer prize–winning poet Conrad Aiken, with its transcendent inscription "Cosmos Mariner—Destination Unknown." Stones and pennies are among the offerings most commonly left by visitors.

The cemetery figures prominently in the *Midnight in the Garden of Good and Evil* story. The statuette image that graced the cover of "The Book" was originally located here; it can now be seen at the Telfair Academy of Arts and Sciences in downtown Savannah.

Turn left off Hwy. 80 onto Mechanics Avenue, turn left again onto Bonaventure Road, turn right at the stop sign, and enter the cemetery through the gate.

Oatland Island Education Center

At the Oatland Island Education Center, 711 Sandtown Rd., 912/898-3980, 175 acres of different coastal habitats—salt marsh, maritime forest, tidal creeks, and freshwater ponds—shelter such native residents as wolves, Florida panthers, deer, black bears, bobcats, and alligators in natural habitats. Sheep, geese, and mules roam the grounds. Self-guided trails lead visitors across the marsh boardwalk to an observation tower overlooking a bluff of sawtooth palmettos for an overview of the local environment.

Operated by the local school board, Oatland Island is a sparsely developed attraction that provides a close look at the area's ecology and wildlife.

Sometimes too close—when no school groups are around, the grounds can be deserted, and you walk the trail alone, hearing only the shells crush below your feet, when around a bend in the trail, surrounded by nothing but forest, you find yourself eye-to-eye with a natural-born predator. It's a little surreal, a little scary, and very exciting.

At the center's heritage home site, 19th-century cabins serve as stage for a **Folklife Festival,** which draws more than 200 artisans demonstrating and selling traditional arts and crafts each November.

The center and grounds are open Mon.–Fri. 8:30 A.M.–5 P.M. and Sat. 10 A.M.–5 P.M. Admission is $3 for ages four and up. To get there from downtown, take the President Street Extension toward Tybee, cross the Wilmington River, and watch for small signs to your right.

Ⓜ Fort Pulaski National Monument

The perfectly preserved brick behemoth of Fort Pulaski, 15 miles east of Savannah via Hwy. 80, 912/786-5787, sits placidly behind a moat along green tidal marshlands like a medieval fortress. The irregular pentagon occupies a site at the mouth of the Savannah River that has held forts since 1761. The current structure was painstakingly built over an 18-year period beginning in 1829; earlier ones succumbed to the Revolution or hurricanes. With the advent of rifled cannons in the Civil War—capable of bursting through even Pulaski's eight-foot-thick walls—the era of masonry forts was gone.

Even before Georgia officially seceded in 1861, the state's governor, Joseph E. Brown, defied the Union by expelling Federal troops from Fort Pulaski. When the Civil War began, the Yankees promptly took it back. Here Union troops blockaded the Savannah River and waited out the war until Sherman arrived in 1864. Today, the annual **Labor Day Encampment** recaptures garrison life with costumed living-history programs, right down to the ball games that were a popular Yankee pastime during the two-year occupation.

The fort is open daily 8:30 A.M.–6:45 P.M. Memorial Day–Labor Day; till 5:15 P.M. during the rest of the year. Admission to the fort is $2 per person or $4 maximum charge per vehicle. Set on Cockspur Island in the lush marshlands, the fort makes a scenic side trip from Savannah. Picnic grounds and self-guided trails are also available at the site.

Old Savannah-Tybee Railroad Trail

From the late 19th century until 1933, the Savannah-Tybee Railroad transported passengers between the city and the beach. Today 6.5 miles of the gravel railroad bed has been made into a trail serving walkers, joggers, and bicyclists. The trail is lined with trees and provides scenic views of the river and local wildlife. Find the entrance off Hwy. 80 across from Fort Pulaski.

Tybee Island

Once called Savannah Beach, Tybee Island attracts summer vacationers to its sandy shores, while a year-round community of 3,000 mainland expatriates populate the "Republic of Tybee." Ten years ago, the island held a funky Coney Island–style appeal, with corn dogs, cheap efficiencies, and rickety-tik amusement park, but with the influx of city people drawn to new upscale hotels and condominium complexes, Tybee now qualifies as a full-blown modern beach resort. Yet it retains its traditional appeal and laid-back haunts, like a down-home breakfast joint, a soda fountain, and baskets of shrimp served at the back river.

Tybee's beach is 18 miles east of downtown Savannah via Hwy. 80. The highway dead-ends into beach parking areas. Commercial development is centered at Tybrisa Ave. and along the main Butler Avenue drag. The **Tybee Island Visitors Center,** 209 Butler Ave., 912/786-5444, is on Hwy. 80 as you approach town. Here you can pick up maps, calendars, and other information. Also see tybeevisit.com.

A TYBEE-STYLE WEEKEND

Nowadays, you could go to Tybee and stay at an oversized condo, get a facial, and eat at George's, but true Tybee style means traveling far more close to the ground. Here's an itinerary to capture that good old-time Tybee flavor.

Friday Night

Stop at North Beach on your way in and head to the sand, where the North Beach Grill serves up conch fritters and popcorn crawfish in a Caribbean-flavored beachfront shack with a reggae soundtrack—a welcome introduction to island living. Settle in at the 17th Street Inn or under the pines and palmettos at River's End campground.

Saturday Morning

Walk up or down the beach to the pier and pavilion at 15th Street. Head in one block to the Breakfast Club for the Grill Cleaner's Special, and introduce yourself to your countermates. Pick up sunscreen, airbrushed T-shirts, and other indispensable provisions at T.S. Chu's (the island's oldest general store, on the main drag of Tybrisa Street), and station yourself on the Strand with an umbrella and a towel for a day at the shore.

Saturday Afternoon

Once you've had enough sun, head up to the Sugar Shack for burgers and Georgia peach milkshakes, and head west. You could see Fort Pulaski or walk the Savannah-Tybee Railroad Trail, 6.5 miles of old crushed-stone rail bed through the marsh—a great place to spot egrets, herons, and other wildlife. For a sure thing, visit the Oatland Island Education Center, where such indigenous Georgia species as Florida panthers, wolves, bobcats, and alligators can be seen on a 2-mile trail through salt-marsh and maritime-forest habitats.

Saturday Night

In the late afternoon, head to the Sentient Bean at the foot of Forsyth Park in downtown Savannah. The locals and SCAD students there will know the best bet for the night's entertainment—gallery openings, who's playing where—or the café itself could be featuring a local songwriter or politically

Savannah

charged reading. Before heading out, buy picnic supplies at the natural grocery next door. After a night on the town, on your return to Tybee, stop by Doc's Bar to see if the band's still playing.

Sunday Morning

For an easy adventure, take a boat over with your picnic sack from Tybee's back-river marina to Little Tybee Island, a wilderness marsh with a deserted shoreline. For a more ambitious undertaking, kayak from Wilmington Island to Wassaw Island, a lush barrier island that's now a national wildlife refuge. On your route, look for the ruins offshore of a fort originally built on the island for the Spanish-American War, evidence of the constantly shifting sands.

Sunday Afternoon

Wind up back at Tybee's marina around sunset for fresh shrimp and cold beer at A.J.'s Dockside, and settle in to watch the show.

SIGHTS

With its wide shore and low dunes anchored by sea oats and pampus grass, Tybee's 4.7-mile white-sand beach is the island's primary attraction. Most of the action is at the south shore, called the Strand, while North Beach offers a quieter corner of shoreline for sunbathing, swimming, and beachcombing. Quieter still is Little Tybee, a wilderness island across the inlet accessible only by boat.

The Strand

Tybee's grand **Pavilion and Pier** at 15th Street heads up the Strand, the island's most popular stretch of beach. The pier offers a scenic promenade out over the beach and ocean, and is appealing to strolling families and couples all day and late into the evening. Many beach concerts and

festivals are held at the pavilion. Snack bars and restrooms are located around the pavilion; showers are nearby. At the inlet at the southern tip of the island, the beach narrows, and the shoreline drops into deeper swimming holes (with strong currents); you might see dolphins nearby.

Public parking lots charge $7 for all-day use; there are also metered spots (bring quarters).

North Beach

At the island's northern tip, North Beach offers a

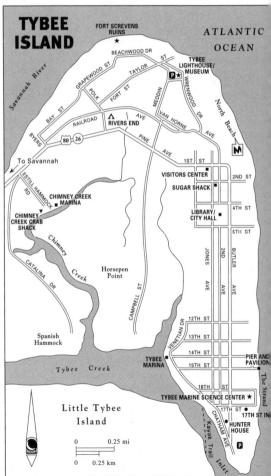

quieter corner of shoreline and is home to Tybee Lighthouse, the island's main attraction. An official stop on the Coastal Birding Trail, North Beach is also reportedly the best place in Georgia to find purple sandpipers. Find the **North Beach Birding Trail** near the museum. Park for $7 all day or at metered spots to access all North Beach attractions.

Tybee Lighthouse and Museum

Georgia's oldest and tallest active lighthouse, 154-foot Tybee Lighthouse, 30 Meddin Dr., 912/786-5801, was built in the late 19th century on a site that has held a lighthouse since 1736. The adjacent museum, housed in an 1898 artillery battery, tells Tybee's history from colonial days through World War II. You can climb to the top of the recently restored lighthouse and enjoy a view of the entire island. At the lighthouse are the ruins of **Fort Screven** embattlements, headquarters of Savannah's coastal defense from the late 1800s through 1924.

Operated by the Tybee Island Historical Society, the lighthouse and museum are open Wed.–Mon. 9 A.M.–5:30 P.M. One admission ticket ($4 for adults and $3 for children) covers both attractions.

Tybee Island Marine Science Center

The Marine Science Center, 1510 Strand, 912/786-5917, houses an aquarium of native species, a touch tank, and other marine life exhibits—a good rainy-day or sunburned activity. The center hosts a summer sea camp for children, and nature walks year-round, including evening beach walks that cover bioluminescence and constellations. Their Tuesday-evening lecture series highlights topics of local history and wildlife.

Find the center off the 14th Street parking lot, just steps from the beach. It's open daily but closes Tuesdays at noon. Admission is $1 for everyone age three and up.

Little Tybee Island

A wilderness marsh island, Little Tybee is an uninhabited nature preserve (600 upland acres; 6,500 acres with marsh) accessible only by boat at the southern tip of Tybee Island. From back-river marinas on Tybee's west side, you can rent boats or find someone to take you over to its 4.5 miles of empty beach. Camping is permitted. It's also a favorite birding spot: osprey and bald eagles nest on the island, and they say a roseate spoonbill and reddish egret have also been sighted.

RECREATION
Boating and Fishing

Few visitors venture west to the "Backriver," a neighborhood of year-round residences and summer cottages on the marsh side of the island. Here at the **Tybee Marina,** 1315 Chatham Ave., 912/786-7508, you might find someone to shuttle you across the small inlet to Little Tybee Island, or you can dart over on your own in a canoe or sea kayak—it's a pretty straightforward run, but be mindful of the tides and currents just the same. Beginners ought to go out with a rising tide; check tide tables in local papers or at the marina.

Two other marinas on the island are on Lazaretto Creek, 912/786-5848, home of the shrimp fleet (dolphin tours also leave from here), and at Chimney Creek, 40 Estill Hammock Rd., 912/786-9857, next door to the famed crab shack, for freshwater or offshore fishing charters, hoists, bait, tackle, gas, ice, and overnight dockage.

 Guided Sea Kayaking Excursions
Call **Sea Kayak Georgia,** 1102 Hwy. 80, 912/786-8732, seakayakgeorgia.com, for guided kayak trips and instruction. Their three-hour barrier-island tour takes paddlers through the marsh and tidal coastal habitats. It's a great way to get out into the still and quiet of the marsh, surrounded by the tall cordgrass, and to see coastal ecology up close. The cost runs around $55 per person.

ENTERTAINMENT
Festivals

Tybee's favorite event is the annual **Beach Bum Parade,** on the Friday before Labor Day, when islanders come armed with water guns of every description and soak anyone who comes within range of Butler Avenue. It's the "world's biggest water fight," they say. A tradition since 1987, the parade starts around 6:30 P.M. in the North Beach parking lot and continues down the island to the parking lot at South Beach.

The other big events include the **Fourth of July** celebration, which culminates with a huge fireworks display from around the pier at "dark thirty" (around 9:15 P.M.) and the two-day **Seafood and Music Festival,** in late August. Another homey event is the annual boat parade at Christmastime, when islanders compete for trophies for the most highly decorated vessel.

Nightlife

Live music can be heard at Tybrisa Street bars, headed up by **Doc's Bar,** 10 Tybrisa St., 912/786-5505, for live blues and jazz. Right at the sand, **Fannie's on the Beach,** near 17th St., 912/786-6109, features live music the likes of the Backriver Ramblers and has two floors of decks overlooking the ocean. On the back river, **A.J.'s Dockside,** 1315 Chatham Ave., is the best place to be at sunset, though the music doesn't get started until after dark. A few beachfront bars also feature live music, and concerts are often held at the pavilion on the 15th Street pier.

Shopping

The island's oldest store and a local landmark, **T.S. Chu's,** 6 Tybrisa St., 912/786-4561, appears stocked with its original dusty inventory, as well as such practical everyday provisions as fishing tackle, hardware, and beach towels—"if it's something you use, you'll find it at Chu's."

ACCOMMODATIONS

Unlike the large deluxe resort hotels on Hilton Head, a few islands to the north, lodging on Tybee is a mix of old and new motels, economy chains, a few multistory beachfront hotels, and several new condominium developments (with more on the way), along with B&Bs and many old-fashioned clapboard beach bungalows.

Oceanfront rooms are of course the most desirable, in addition to places right on the Strand, and then anything on the east side of Butler Avenue. Staying on the west side of Butler Avenue means having to cross four lanes of Hwy. 80 traffic to get to the beach.

Summer is the high season, and rates are typically cut nearly half in winter.

B&Bs

At North Beach, the **Lighthouse Inn,** 16 Meddin Dr., 912/786-0901, offers three rooms in a comfortable clapboard house in a historic residential district. It was originally built to house officers of Fort Screven nearby (they say this was the bandmaster's residence). The cheerful yellow house with rockers on the wide front porch is set in a bend of the lane around 50 yards from the entrance to the lighthouse and museum, a five-minute walk to the sand and birding trail (doubles cost around $100).

Down by the Strand, the **⚊ 17th Street Inn,** 12 17th St, 912/786-0607, converts an old two-story beach house a half-block from the beach into eight minisuites, each with private entrance. The retro interiors—an era of linoleum, built-in drainboards, mosaic-tiled shower stalls, and the like—have been scrubbed but not overhauled, capturing that well-worn Tybee verve. The front rooms are larger and have full (but tiny) kitchens and porches overlooking the street (rooms cost $120–170).

Nearby, **Hunter House,** 1701 Butler Ave., 912/786-7515, occupies a 1910 clapboard with a wide veranda overlooking the ocean. It's only a couple of blocks from all the action, but at night, from a rocking chair on the wide 2nd-story veranda, it feels peacefully above the fray (rooms cost around $100). The Hunter House is also noted for its restaurant.

Hotels, Motels, and Condos

With 210 rooms, the **Ocean Plaza Beach Resort,** off 15th St. at the oceanfront, 912/786-8400 or 800/215-6370, is the largest motel on Tybee and is in the center of the action (summer doubles cost $150). The relatively new 60-room **Super 8,** 16 Tybrisa St., 912/786-8806 or

800/800-8000, is next door, just 400 feet from the pier (summer doubles cost $100).

Several new three-story condominiums are right on the Strand, with wide verandas overlooking the ocean. Ideal for large families or groups, a three-bedroom, two-bath, full-kitchen condo rents in summer for around $250 daily or $1,500 weekly. Condos are typically furnished by individual owners, so the style and decor vary considerably, though each has all the necessities. **Tybee Beach Vacation Rentals,** 912/786-8805 or 800/755-8562, manages two such condo complexes, along with dozens of other properties all over the island.

Camping

Camp under live oaks and Spanish moss at the **River's End Campground and RV Park,** 915 Polk St., 912/786-5518 or 800/786-1016. Rates start at $25 per night and cover two people, one camping unit, and one vehicle (more for hookups, extra people, or extra cars). The campground is dominated by RVs, but tent campers could stake out shady corners and make themselves comfortable as well. Cabins are also available, starting at $100 per night. The 10-acre grounds have a pool, dump station, and small store. It's in the residential district of North Beach, a short walk east to the lighthouse and sand, and a short walk south to convenient roadside businesses along Hwy. 80.

FOOD AND DRINK

Casual

Start at the **M Breakfast Club,** 1500 Butler Ave., 912/786-5984, for hefty portions served in a comfortably casual hash-house atmosphere 6 A.M.–1 P.M. Go early or sit at the counter to avoid the line for tables. Try the Grill Cleaner's Special: diced potatoes, Polish sausage, green peppers, and onions, scrambled with eggs and topped with two cheeses. To get there, follow the crowds.

The **Sugar Shack,** 201 1st St., 912/786-4482, is another old-time Tybee favorite. It's been whipping up fresh Georgia peach or Oreo milkshakes ($3) and basic American lunch fare for breakfast, lunch, and dinner for more than 25 years. It's open daily 7 A.M.–10 P.M. and can be found at the bend of Butler Avenue.

"In the shadow of Tybee's lighthouse," the beachfront **M North Beach Grill,** 41A Meddin Dr., 912/786-9003, is a Caribbean-colorful, screened-in shack for popcorn crawfish or conch fritters, along with poached salmon and shrimp Creole dinners (entrées start at $16). Eat inside at small round tables, at the long bar, or beside the palms on the patio to the island rhythms of reggae music. It's open daily in season for lunch 11:30 A.M.–4 P.M., and for dinner starting at 6 P.M.

At the **Chimney Creek Crab Shack,** off Estill Hammock Rd., 912/786-9857, clattering platters of crab, shrimp, oysters and other fresh seafood are served along with frothy pitchers of beer under the Christmas lights strung between the palms at the creek-side deck of its waterfront cabin. Order boiled shellfish by the pound—shrimp, blue crab, rock crab, or the low country boil (a spicy mix of sausage, shrimp-in-the-shell, potatoes, and corn-on-the-cob). It's open 11:30 A.M.–10 P.M., till 11 P.M. Fri.–Sat. It's a great spot at any time, but particularly at dusk. A landmark on both the AAA and Georgia DOT maps, the Crab Shack is hardly undiscovered (it even has its own gift shop), but it's evocative nonetheless.

At the Tybee marina, **A.J.'s Dockside,** 1315 Chatham Ave., 912/786-9857, offers a low-key back-river alternative on Tybee's southwestern side for plates of shellfish and ice cold beer, with a patio out over the water. It's open Tues.–Sun. 5–10 P.M.

Upscale

Hunter House, 1701 Butler Ave., 912/786-7515, serves shrimp, seafood, and steak specialties daily, starting at $17, in their inn by the south shore. The cocktail lounge makes a nice rendezvous; you can take your drinks out to porch rockers overlooking the ocean. Dinner is served nightly 6–9 P.M., till 9:30 P.M. Fri.–Sat.

The "new" Tybee is perhaps best represented by **Tango,** 1106 Hwy. 80, 912/786-8264, a splashy, two-story cabana with colorful seating and island decor. A tiny patio overlooks the marsh. You might not need more than the Tango Pu-Pu Platter, an appetizer sampler of conch fritters, calamari, empanadas, spring rolls, and chicken satay on your own hibachi ($20 for two). Also, there's jerk chicken, Rasta Pasta, gado-gado, and a dozen tropical drinks served in wacky-tacky glasses. Dinner is served Wed.–Mon. 6–10 P.M.; the bar is open till midnight. Reservations are recommended.

George's of Tybee, 1105 E. Hwy. 80, 912/786-9730, is the most upscale newcomer to the emerging Tybee restaurant scene, offering an "eclectic American" menu of seafood and steaks in a ranch-style cabin right off the main highway into town. It's open Tues.–Sun. 6–10 P.M.

The Coast

Not one but two radically different coasts make up Georgia's Atlantic seaboard. The mainland coast seeps into tidal marshlands—a miles-wide expanse of tall green reeds. Within sight of the mainland, but a world away, the outer coast is made up of a string of remote barrier islands, where high dunes and white-sand beaches meet the gentle ocean, and the calls of gulls squawk over the distant hum of a trawler's engine. Together the two coasts make up the "low country," a beautiful province with a distinct history and culture shaped by the land.

Only one-tenth of Georgia's 100-mile outer seashore is developed beachfront, attracting vacationers to barefoot cafés, historic lighthouses,

and regal island resorts. The rest is largely wild and uninhabited, unless you count feral horses, boar, deer, sea turtles, and shorebirds (historians say the islands have fewer human residents now than at any other time in the last 4,000 years). As Audubon fancifully remarked about St. Simons Island in the 1850s: "I was fain to think I had landed on some of those fairy islands said to have existed in the Golden Age."

The unspoiled marshlands have a different appeal. Struggling to define their compelling nature, Pat Conroy wrote in *The Prince of Tides,* "I would have to take you to the marsh on a spring day, flush the great blue heron from its silent occupation, scatter marsh hens as we sink to

Must-Sees

Look for **M** to find the sights and activities you can't miss and **N** for the best dining and lodging.

M Old Atlantic Coast Highway: A quiet, scenic route through the bygone days of the first transcontinental highways (page 283).

M Fish Shacks: On a remote stretch of coast, a fishing village offers "fleet fresh" seafood out of well-worn shacks (page 286).

M Route 99 Loop: An excellent bicycling touring route through a remote corner of the coast, past local shrimp fleets, the Ridge of old homes, and an island visitor center (page 287).

M Altamaha River Canoe Trail: Take a paddling excursion down the mighty Altamaha, what the Nature Conservancy calls "One of the Last 75 Great Places" (page 291).

Jekyll Island Club Hotel

M Hog Hammock: Members of a rare cultural community offer lodging on remote Sapelo Island for a getaway with a close-up look at a remarkable history and ecology (page 293).

M The Village at St. Simons Island: A nice patch of urbanity on the coast, a busy jumble of shops, cafés, clubs, and attractions right at the beach (page 306).

M Little St. Simons Island: "Summer camp for adults" is the appeal of this ecosensitive, exclusive but not fussy private island resort (page 311).

M Jekyll Island National Historic Landmark District: Oversee the dominion of 20th-century industrial barons from a breezy table at the raw bar on the pier across from the landmark Jekyll Island Club Hotel (page 312).

M Sea Camp: Spend the night in sheltered coves on the Cumberland Island national seashore with wild horses and lush subtropical flora (page 323).

our knees in mud, open you an oyster with a pocketknife and feed it to you from the shell and say 'There. That taste.'"

The subtropical coast is dotted with evidence of its human history. Ancient shell middens on outlying islands attest to the Native Americans who thrived here on the same diet of shellfish that today's residents enjoy. The orchards of Spanish friars have taken root and grace island wilderness with orderly stands of fruit trees. The perpendicular levees of abandoned rice plantations where thousands labored in tidal fields now shelter acres of wild rice as a feast for the birds who now inhabit the wetlands. The ruins of forts built of tabby—a combination of shell, lime, and sand (abundantly available local materials)—erode softly to a sort of colonial middens of rounded foundations. Seven different nations have left traces of their claim to this land.

The contemporary human history is just as compelling. The natural isolation of the islands enabled a tightly knit African community to hold on to its beliefs and traditions, and the distinct Gullah dialect, folklore, cuisine, and music is still in evidence today. One island became a retreat for Northern industrialists until it was thought that to concentrate so much wealth and power onto one small island might make the country vulnerable; their mammoth "cottages" and clubhouse are now open to everyone for stays. On another island, a family envisioned a pencil empire, but the island's trees proved too gnarly; and the private preserve of the Carnegies is now open to paying guests.

Even the bygone days of the Atlantic Coast Highway have Gothic stories to tell—of old-time political bosses, roadside swindles, drug smuggling, and a near-feudal life enduring into the 1970s.

From Savannah, you can hop on I-95 south and blast clear over the Florida border in little more than an hour. Detour once, however, and you'll find yourself drawn into an unfolding Southern landscape of strangely silent marshlands, historical oddities, and people who every day walk out their front doors into centuries of their ancestors' footsteps—a history as thick and palpable as the humidity on a summer's day.

PLANNING YOUR TIME

A nicely varied trip to the coast could include part lazy road trip, part outback adventure, a river trip, a visit to a remote island, and a visit to a play island. You don't need to do much planning (except for river trips and remote-island visits) unless you're arriving on a summer weekend. Even river trips can be catch-as-catch-can if you're willing to ride the next boat out, but if you're looking for, say, a women-only overnight paddling trip down a blackwater river, you'll need to work around an outfitter's dates of departure—unless you want to pay custom rates. You'd likely be able to charter a boat at a marina to go out that day or the next, but island ferries require more advance planning.

To visit Cumberland Island, make ferry reservations your first call. For Sapelo Island, decide between a daytrip or overnight trip, and then reserve a room or a tour; proprietors then make ferry reservations in your name.

Pack for the sport: cycling, tennis, golf, and swimming gear; Tevas or an old pair of sneakers for paddling; clothes that cover limbs for hiking; binoculars and brimmed hats for birding. Take (or buy locally) insect repellant, such as Avon's Skin So Soft for gnats in spring and fall and Deep Woods Off with deet for ticks in late spring and summer; also bring bite cream or aloe vera.

Casual dress is perfectly fine for the mainland, though adhering to rural rules of modesty (nothing too revealing or sloppy) would earn you a warmer welcome. On the islands, vacationers dress resort-casual, though slightly fancier for dinner (collared shirts and khakis for men, sundresses and sandals for women); shorts and flip-flops work most other places.

THE NATURAL ENVIRONMENT

Georgia was among the first states to enact legislation permanently protecting tidal marshlands, and many islands are either federal wildlife sanctuaries or restricted parkland. As a result, coastal ecology has been impressively preserved in its near-wild state along most of the coast—a sharp contrast to neighbors to the north and south, South Carolina and Florida.

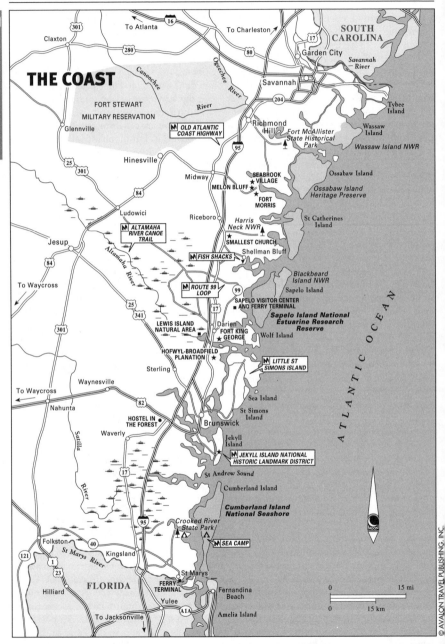

THE COAST

SOUTH CAROLINA

To Atlanta
To Charleston
Garden City
Savannah River
Savannah
Claxton
Tybee Island
Canoochee River
Ogeechee River
Wassaw Island
FORT STEWART
MILITARY RESERVATION
Richmond Hill
Fort McAllister State Historical Park
Wassaw Island NWR
Glennville
M OLD ATLANTIC COAST HIGHWAY
Hinesville
Ossabaw Island
Midway
SEABROOK VILLAGE ★
Ossabaw Island Heritage Preserve
MELON BLUFF ★
FORT MORRIS ★
Ludowici
Riceboro
St Catherines Island
Harris Neck NWR
M ALTAMAHA RIVER CANOE TRAIL
SMALLEST CHURCH ★
Jesup
Shellman Bluff
M FISH SHACKS
Blackbeard Island NWR
M ROUTE 99 LOOP
Sapelo Island
To Waycross
SAPELO VISITOR CENTER AND FERRY TERMINAL ■
Sapelo Island National Estuarine Research Reserve
LEWIS ISLAND NATURAL AREA
Darien
FORT KING GEORGE ■
Wolf Island
HOFWYL-BROADFIELD PLANATION ★
M LITTLE ST SIMONS ISLAND
Sterling
Sea Island
Waynesville
To Waycross
St Simons Island
Nahunta
HOSTEL IN THE FOREST ●
Brunswick
Waverly
Jekyll Island
M JEKYLL ISLAND NATIONAL HISTORIC LANDMARK DISTRICT
Satilla River
St Andrew Sound
Cumberland Island
Cumberland Island National Seashore
Folkston
Crooked River State Park
Kingsland
M SEA CAMP
St Marys River
FLORIDA
St Marys
Hilliard
FERRY TERMINAL
Fernandina Beach
Yulee
To Jacksonville
Amelia Island

ATLANTIC OCEAN

0   15 mi
0   15 km

© AVALON TRAVEL PUBLISHING, INC.

Barrier Islands

The barrier islands are long (north to south) and narrow (east to west), with white sand beaches at eastern shores, tidal marshlands at western shores, and dense vegetation in between. They were formed when the polar ice cap melted, flooding the lowlands to the west and isolating the high sand dunes to the east. Vegetation stabilized the dunes, allowing the eventual growth of thick forests.

As strong offshore winds constantly shift sand from here to there, this island-building process continues. The **transitional maritime forest** starts with wispy **sea oats,** the first plant to set roots in the sand. (Because of their importance to local ecology, it's illegal to pick or trample sea oats in Georgia.) These begin to collect the shifting sands and attract varied vegetation, such as **yuccas, panic grass,** and **prickly pear cactus.** As the ecosystem matures, **live oaks** predominate. Though they weather the salty sea breeze better than most trees, the live oaks are nevertheless shaped by the corrosive spray, which gnarls the limbs into strangely twisted shapes and warps the canopy into a dense slanted crown. Shielded in the delicate substory below are floating strands of **Spanish moss,** vines of wild **muscadine** grapes, fan-shaped **palmettos,** and several varieties of **pines.** Coastal **mulberry** trees fueled early English visions of establishing a silk industry in the new Georgia colony. As you head away from the sea, island woodlands give way to open savannas, old rice and cotton fields, and freshwater ponds, until the land reaches the western tidal marshlands.

The islands shelter wildlife common to the coastal plain. Mammals such as **white-tailed deer, armadillos, opossums, raccoons,** and **squirrels** now run wild with once-domestic species brought to the islands long ago, such as the **feral hogs** and **donkeys** on Ossabaw Island, or the **wild horses** on Cumberland Island (said to descend from the stables of early Spanish missionaries). Little St. Simons harbors a population of **fallow deer,** a European species brought to the island in the 1920s; they're smaller than the **white-tailed** variety common to the rest of the islands. The once-populous **bobcat** is being reintroduced to the islands, starting with Cumberland. St. Catherines Island sponsors a captive breeding program

for the New York Zoological Society; **zebras, antelope, gazelles,** and other rare and endangered species are found there.

Made up largely of protected refuges and lying right along the Atlantic Flyway, the islands attract more than 200 species of songbirds, shorebirds, and wading birds. One commonly sees—and hears—**Carolina chickadees, bluebirds, northern cardinals, mockingbirds, owls,** dozens of **warblers,** and **wild turkeys.** Of course, the beach attracts **brown pelicans, gulls,** and many varieties of shorebirds. The state's Department of Natural Resources—a big player in coastal management—sponsors a **bald eagle** "hacking" program on the coast, releasing eaglets hatched in captivity.

With no predators besides man, the **eastern diamondback rattlesnake** thrives on the islands but is usually cautious, well fed, and inactive in hot temperatures. Other venomous snakes on the islands are **canebrake rattlers** and **cottonmouths.** All visitors and hikers would be wise to stay on trails, watch where you put hands and feet, and stay off dunes (to protect fragile vegetation as well as to avoid sunning snakes).

On the beaches, visitors will find **ghost crabs, horseshoe crabs, sponges,** and such beachcombing trophies as **sand dollars, whelks** (look inside their rattling cases to find miniature whelks), and spit-shined **olive shells.** Delicate corallike twigs, in varying shades of white, orange, and purple, are called **sea whips.** Collectors should be sure to remove only uninhabited shells, and only a handful at that, and only in areas where such collecting is permitted.

Dolphins and **manatees** swim close to shore and throughout marshland waterways. The rare **right whale,** of which only 325 are estimated to exist worldwide, calves solely off the Georgia coast.

Tidal Marshlands

A scenic maze of cordgrass-lined tidal creeks, rivers, and estuaries, Georgia's marshlands stretch from 5 to 10 miles between the mainland and barrier islands. At 250,000 acres in all, they're the most extensive on the east coast. Marshlands produce more biomass per acre than any other ecosystem.

NEITHER LAND NOR SEA

The concave Southern Atlantic coastline, known as the Georgia Bight, creates the exceptionally high tides that shape coastal ecology. Tidewaters accumulate toward the middle of the curve, so Georgia tides can vary as much as 10 feet between high and low tide, compared with three feet at the top or bottom of the bight (see map).

Along the Atlantic Seaboard, only Maine has a greater tide differential. At high tide, seawater penetrates as much as 40 miles up some coastal rivers—supporting Georgia's extensive salt marshes (5–10 miles wide) and the estuaries farther upriver where freshwater and saltwater meet.

This creates a large area neither completely land nor sea, but one or the other, depending on the time of the tide. It also means a greater risk to boaters unfamiliar with local tide patterns, who may find themselves stranded or lost on unrecognizably swollen or shallow waterways.

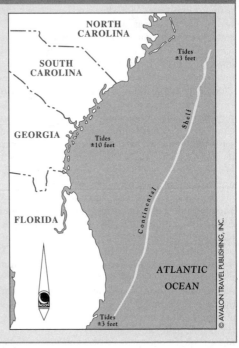

Spartina alterflora defines the marsh; solid acres of this smooth **cordgrass,** vividly green most of the year, turn golden in the fall. Besides the **great blue heron** and **marsh hen** Conroy wrote of, many other bird species inhabit the marshes: the **snowy egret,** the rare **least tern** and **osprey,** and dozens of varieties of **ducks** and **geese.** Marshlands are the natural habitat for many varieties of shellfish, supporting the **oysters, mussels, clams, blue crabs,** and **shrimp** that fuel the local commercial seafood industry. **Alligators** inhabit shallow waters.

Mainland

The mainland edgewater once produced the greatest wealth for colonial Georgia; here grand rice plantations thrived as early as the 1740s. Today, only **wild rice** flourishes in the shallow ponds between the levees, attracting **ducks** and other marshland birds. Tall **pine** forests—long the mainstay of the state's lumbering, turpentine, and paper and pulpwood industries—stand alongside groves of coastal palms and palmettos.

In 1774, the coastal travels of naturalist William Bartram moved him to file this extravagantly romantic report: "the beautiful woods presented a view of magnificence inexpressibly charming and animated." Today you can retrace his steps on the Bartram Trail, following routes established by early Native Americans or colonists.

Climate

Coastal Georgia's climate is subtropical. Summers are hot and humid, with afternoon thundershowers. Temperatures climb above 90°F about 55 days in summertime, mostly in July and August. Fall stretches warm summer days into October; the short, mild winters rarely experience freezing temperatures. Spring is warm and occasionally wet. Though spring and fall are the most temperate, summer is the high season for coast visitors; winter holidays run a close second (though daytime temperatures may not rise above the 50s some days). For saltwater fishing, crabbing, and shrimping, late summer and fall are best.

Along the southeastern coast of the United States, June through October is hurricane season, yet tropical cyclones rarely hit the Georgia coast—at least not with the frequency and severity of neighboring states north and south. Yet even storms that stay offshore can bring torrential rains or severe thunderstorms (sailors take warning). Weather radio equipment is a valuable precaution for boaters.

HISTORY

To appreciate the history of the southeastern coast, you need to know a little something about oyster shells. As the refuse of every coastal population dependent upon the flourishing food source, oyster shells mark the passage of time. Pre-Columbian shell rings, called middens, resulted from the natives' practice of discarding shells behind a central campfire. The resulting glistening white heaps created an alkaline environment so hostile to plant life that only the resistant cedar took root—today, stands of tall cedars indicate the location of middens.

The Spanish used the shells to make an adobelike material called tabby, from which they constructed forts and missions along the Georgia coast in the mid-16th century. Subsequent inhabitants followed suit, and today you can find tabby ruins left by every nation that has claimed the coast—from French Huguenots and the colonial British, to the fledgling United States, the Confederacy, and even a short-lived Black Republic in 1865. Tabby is still used as a construction material today, and crushed oyster shells serve as gravel for shell roads and paths.

Colonial Times

Little evidence remains of the French and Spanish, or of the pirates common to that age (though the hidden treasure of famous brigand Edward Teal, for whom Blackbeard Island is named, supposedly lies off the Georgia coast). The British influence, in contrast, is still keenly felt in Savannah, the original settlement of the Georgia colony and the southernmost outpost of the British in America. From Savannah, the British faced off against the Spanish, who also claimed the "Debatable Land" of the Georgia coast.

After founding the city in 1733, British General James Oglethorpe ventured south to establish Fort Frederica on the Spanish-named San Simeone, provoking the Spanish into venturing north from their stronghold in Florida. At the Battle of Bloody Marsh in 1742, they waged one of the most decisive battles in the history of the world. Though little more than a skirmish, it decided the fate of the new continent. After being routed in the St. Simons ambush, the retreating Spanish abandoned the goal of continental domination.

The colonial town of New Inverness, settled by Scottish Highlanders in 1736, remains today as Darien, but most other coastal colonial towns fell victim to severe Revolutionary War fighting or changing fortunes. Only an occasional old fort or church stands today in such ghost towns as Ebenezer, Midway, and Sunbury.

The early American coastal economy grew on rice, indigo, and a strain of high-quality but temperamental cotton that flourished only on the islands, earning it the name Sea Island cotton. Huge plantations with hundreds of slaves supported these industries under subtropical conditions so harsh that most planter families lived elsewhere half the year (facts which came to define the character of the low country).

Civil War

At the outbreak of the Civil War, Georgia Governor Joseph Brown ousted Federal troops from Fort Pulaski near Savannah, and after war broke out at Fort Sumter, the Federals took Fort Pulaski back, blockading Savannah and waiting the length of the war for the action to catch up to them.

When Sherman arrived in Savannah in December 1864 after his march through Georgia, the city surrendered without a fuss, and from headquarters in the Green-Meldrim House, Sherman sent a telegram to President Lincoln, delivering him the city of Savannah as a "Christmas present."

PRAYING FOR SHEETROCK

History. . . is what Darien has the way other communities have rich topsoil, or a wealth of hidden talent, or fine high-school athletics. Coastal people understand history personally, the way religious people do, the way ancient people did. They own history in a way lost to most Americans except in a generic, national sort of way, because the rest of us move around so much, intermarry, adopt new local loyalties, and blur the simple narrative line.

Melissa Fay Greene

"The Book" of the central coast is *Praying for Sheetrock*, the 1991 story of the tribulations McIntosh County faced in joining the 20th century, as told by *Temple Bombing* author Melissa Fay Greene. Like *Midnight in the Garden of Good and Evil*, in simply recounting the improbable history of this quiet backwater—a land of "prehistoric Indians, Spanish missionaries, Blackbeard the pirate, French and English explorers, Sir Francis Drake, slaveholders and slaves, Confederates and Yankees, the victorious General Sherman, freed slaves, and unreconstructed Rebels"—Greene's report reads like fiction.

Her tale centers on Atlantic Coast Highway days, when vacationers and interstate commerce up and down the Eastern Seaboard would of necessity pass through tiny downtown Darien. "The heyday of Darien and U.S. 17 lasted from the 1930s through the mid-1970s," Greene writes, "an era during which a multitude—a plague—of locally owned two-bit tourist businesses thrived along the route. About two-thirds of them were legal, too."

Ruling over this land in a near-feudal way was the local sheriff, who oversaw the vice scene and found ways to reward his loyal subjects by bestowing upon them trifles of its rewards. Meanwhile, the rest of the country was moving into the 21st century, and the local African American community would no longer settle for occasional handouts. How the community found its voice, and at what price, is what makes the story so compelling.

Traveling through Darien today looks remarkably similar to how Greene described it looking more than 30 years ago: "All-U-Can-Eat catfish restaurants, the county courthouse, a library, some hardware stores, and 18th-century British fort, a car wash, and a wide, hot main street—U.S. 17." But it's quieter now that traffic has moved out on the interstate.

Sherman's next task was providing for the thousands of liberated slaves his army had attracted on their March to the Sea. After conferring with local black leaders (members of Savannah's 3,000-member free black community), Sherman issued his famous Field Order No. 15, granting the islands and riverside plantations to newly freed slaves—the "40 acres and a mule" that forms the basis for calls for reparations to this day. The coastal African American community established a low-country republic in 1865, naming St. Catherines Island its capital. Yet the agreement proved to be short-lived—during Reconstruction, the land was taken back by the government and returned to former landowners.

From Plantations to Resorts

The collapse of the plantation system left many estates abandoned; today many plantation houses can be seen in either restorations or ruins. Some estates and islands were occupied by new Northern owners, who sought out the low country as a winter retreat. The most famous of these getaway spots was Jekyll Island, where such early American industrialists as Rockefeller, Goodyear, and Vanderbilt established an exclusive enclave centered on the regal Jekyll Island Club (which is still one of the East Coast's most distinguished hotels).

With the construction of bridges to the mainland, four of Georgia's islands became popular resort destinations, and today their local economies depend on tourism as well as an extensive seafood industry. The remaining islands are nearly all protected as natural refuges, and much of the marshland coast—once holding busy colonial seaports and crowded plantations—has reverted to its original natural state, save for a shrimp fleet here and there.

North Coast

Before the interstate freeways, beachbound vacationers from the entire length of the Eastern Seaboard drove the Atlantic Coast Highway south into Florida. Carved out of the pines and bridged across the river and marshlands, Georgia's stretch of the route was sprinkled with road motels, truck stops, and souvenir stands selling peaches and shell ornaments. After I-95 was completed in the 1970s, the lucrative caravans instantly disappeared—and along with it, a way of life, leaving the forest and marsh to reclaim much of the land, save a few hulking mid-century ruins.

Old Atlantic Coast Highway Route (Hwy. 17)

Today the old Atlantic Coast Highway (Hwy. 17) makes a great route for exploring the region, which remains out of time with the efficient streams of I-95 traffic to the west. The appeal is likewise out of time—detours disintegrate into boat ramps at the water's edge, with only a set of ruins, an old cemetery, or an overgrown entryway arcade of majestic oaks to suggest all that had passed here before.

The following guide to coastal attractions along and around Hwy. 17 starts at Hwy. 204, at the southern boundary of the city of Savannah, and includes reference points for the I-95 thoroughfare. Interstate drivers might note that I-95 exits are numbered to correspond with the distance from the Florida border, thus Darien's exit 49 is 49 miles north of Florida, Richmond Hill's exit is 90, and so on.

Birders might note that Fort McAllister, Fort Morris, Melon Bluff, and Harris Neck are all official stops on the **Coastal Birding Trail**. Find songbirds and wading birds in all seasons and waterfowl in winter. Harris Neck in particular is one of the best places to view nesting wading birds, such as wood storks, great egrets, snowy egrets, and anhingas in May and June.

OGEECHEE RIVER

The 245-mile Ogeechee River courses from Georgia's Piedmont, through Fort Stewart outside

Savannah (the home of the 24th Infantry Division), and to blackwater cypress swamps before emptying into Ossabaw Sound, 15 miles south of Savannah. The suburban sprawl of the metro region stretches just across the Ogeechee to Richmond Hill (so far, at least—signs demanding "No Condos on the Ogeechee" testify to pressures for increased development).

Here Hwy. 17 is a busy four-lane route, congested with traffic and construction at last visit. Bicyclists might want to start the route further south, when the last of the metro traffic turns off to Hinesville.

Savannah-Ogeechee Barge Canal

Off Hwy. 204 northwest of I-95, the **S & O Barge Canal Nature Center**, 681 Argyle Rd., 912/748-8068, reopens a corridor of a canal system built in 1831 to haul barges between the Savannah and Ogeechee (S & O) Rivers. When the 16-mile waterway first opened, it served a vital role in the economy of South Georgia, transporting lumber, cotton, rice, bricks, guano, naval stores, peaches, and other goods. Use of the canal began to decline as railroads were built, and, coupled with a yellow fever epidemic and serious flood damage, the canal was closed in the 1860s.

The Ogeechee River terminus of the canal was restored and reopened in 2000 as a multipurpose linear park that offers a taste of history along with a sampling of the distinct tidal river swamp habitat environment of the Ogeechee. A half-mile walk along heel or towpaths is a good way to enjoy the area and see the old locks. A museum relates the details of canal history and maintains exhibits on local flora and fauna. It's a good place to watch for songbirds, birds of prey, and wading birds in all seasons and is an official stop on the **Coastal Birding Trail**, designated on a state brochure available at the museum.

The canal center is open daily 9 A.M.–5 P.M. Admission is $2 for adults and $1 for children. The center is 15 miles southwest of downtown Savannah. From the intersection of I-95 and

Hwy. 204, go west on Hwy. 204 (Argyle Road) for 2.3 miles; the turnoff is to the left.

Bamboo Farm and Coastal Gardens

Under a mile southeast of I-95, the Bamboo Farm, 2 Canebrake Rd., 912/921-5460, affords the unusual opportunity to wander through a maze of several varieties of towering bamboo, listening to the hollow rustle of the canes as they catch the breeze and watching the light filtering through the delicate leaves. Operated by the University of Georgia College of Agriculture, the farm is one of the largest bamboo groves in the U.S., with stands up to 75 feet.

Keller's Flea Market

An unusual assortment of treasures can be found at Keller's Flea Market, along Hwy. 17 at 5901 Ogeechee Rd., 912/927-4848, "the largest flea market in the Coastal Empire," one mile east of I-95. Hours are Fri.–Sun. 8 A.M.–6 P.M. year-round.

RICHMOND HILL
Fort McAllister State Historic Park

On the far side of the Ogeechee River south of Richmond Hill, the best-preserved earthwork fortifications of the Confederacy can be found in a quiet, shady corner of Georgia's coast. Set on an inviting low bluff overlooking the estuary, the historic site provides easy access to the pine-and-palmetto forest and serene coastal marshlands—a nice respite to the urbanity across the river, and a scenic stop for through-travelers.

The sand and mud earthworks at the 1,725-acre historic park, 3894 Fort McAllister Rd., 912/727-2339, were attacked seven times by Union ironclads but did not fall until captured in 1864 by General William T. Sherman. The fort's military history unfolds at a new **Civil War museum,** open daily 8 A.M.–5 P.M. Admission is $2.50 for adults and $1.50 for children. The fort features living-history programs that reenact the fort's "Baptism by Fire" in July, the Labor Day Encampment, and December's "Winter Muster." There are also 4.3 miles of hiking trails; bicycle, canoe, and kayak rentals; and a boat ramp and dock. Gates are open daily 7 A.M.–10 P.M. The

parking fee is $2. The park is 10 miles east of I-95 on GA Spur 144 (off I-95 exit 90).

Camping and lodging: The state park's 65-site campground is nestled among live oaks up against the salt marsh. Developed campsites cost $17–19; primitive campsites are $3. There are also two-bedroom cabins ($110). For reservations, call 800/864-7275 or visit gastateparks.org.

MIDWAY

Around five miles north of Midway, Hwy. 17 drops to a quiet two-lane corridor through tall stands of Georgia pine. Along the route, an ancient truck stop, **Ida Mae and Joe's,** 912/884-3388, no longer pumps gas but remains a convivial local roadhouse, outliving both Ida Mae and Joe (open 6 A.M.–8 P.M.). When we were last by, they were serving a plate lunch of smoked sausage and red rice, rutabaga, speckled butter beans, and fried squash for around $6.

Midway Church and Museum

Downtown Midway reveals a faint shadow of its distinguished past at the 1792 Midway

Ida Mae and Joe's

Church and Midway Museum, on Hwy. 17, 912/884-5837. Settled by Massachusetts Puritans in 1754, the town was outraged when colonial Georgia failed to send representatives to the first Continental Congress. So the ex–New Englanders sent one of their own, Lyman Hall, who, along with neighbor Button Gwinnett, became two of Georgia's three signers of the Declaration of Independence. The small museum, set in a raised cottage-style house typical of 19th-century coastal architecture, tells more about the town's revolutionary history. Hours are Tues.–Sat. 10 A.M.–4 P.M. and Sun. 2–4 P.M.; closed Mon. and holidays. Admission is $2.

The church and museum are west of I-95 exit 76, around 30 miles south of Savannah.

OFF HWY. 84

A detour along Hwy. 84 several miles east from either Hwy. 17 or I-95 exit 76 leads past several quiet historical and ecological sites to the ghost town of Sunbury, now marked by a state historic site.

Seabrook Village

Exhibits at Seabrook Village, 660 Trade Hill Rd., 912/884-7008, are intended to portray Gullah community life from 1865 to 1930 with a schoolhouse, cottages, and outbuildings, while gardens and farmyards illustrate lessons in self-sufficiency. You can wander the secluded 104-acre site on your own, or you might find someone in the office Tues.–Sat. 10 A.M.–4 P.M. willing to show you around.

Melon Bluff

In an effort to turn the tide of coastal development, a local family has opened 3,000 acres of their land at Melon Bluff as a private nature preserve, and they offer kayaking trips and overnight lodging in a reconverted plantation barn built in the 1930s (doubles cost around $100); call 912/884-5779.

Fort Morris State Historic Site

Fort Morris once defended Georgia's second-busiest port at Sunbury. The earthworks are all that remain of that time, but the small museum tells of the busy town and the Revolutionary War battles fought there against the British. Rebuilt for the War of 1812, the fort is now a 70-acre state historic site, 912/884-5999.

The museum is open Tues.–Sat. 9 A.M.–5 P.M., Sun. 2–5:30 P.M., and on most Monday holidays. Admission is $1.50–2.50. There's also a mile-long nature trail.

SOUTH NEWPORT
Harris Neck

Part of Sherman's Reservation, granted by the Union General's Field Order No. 15 issued in Savannah in 1865, the Harris Neck peninsula was also deeded to the formerly enslaved by the will of Margret Ann Harris, who operated a rice plantation here up to the Civil War. For 50 years, around 75 African American families thrived here in a self-sufficient community, until in 1942 the federal government claimed eminent domain and ordered residents off the land, citing national security.

According to the McIntosh Sustainable Environment and Economic Development association (which leads tours of the area; call SEED at 912/437-7821), the community was promised the land back after the war, but instead, houses were bulldozed and the land was transferred first to McIntosh County hands, then back to the federal government, which established the national wildlife refuge in 1962. Descendants' efforts to regain the promised land continue to this day.

The **Harris Neck National Wildlife Refuge,** 912/652-4415, contains 3,000 acres of saltwater marsh, deciduous woods, croplands, and grasslands. The refuge shelters deer, geese, possums, armadillos, and raccoons; its wetlands harbor more than 225 species of birds. An arcade of live oaks draped with Spanish moss leads to a loop road through the maritime forest and past a ghostly World War II airstrip. Fifteen miles of paved roads and trails are open to hikers and bicyclists. To reach the refuge, take I-95 exit 67, go south on Hwy. 17 for one mile, then drive east on Hwy. 131 for seven miles.

At the end of the highway, boaters enter refuge tidewaters or head out to Blackbeard Island from a public boat ramp.

Smallest Church in America

The "Smallest Church in America" (or at least in all of Georgia) is a 12-seat whitewashed concrete block cabin endowed by the inheritance of local grocer Mrs. Agnes Harper and deeded to Jesus Christ. The 10- by 15-foot sanctuary with imported stained-glass windows was built in 1949 so that travelers passing through could stop for interdenominational worship and meditation. Local ministers lead services here on the third Sunday of the month; it can be reserved for such special events as weddings through the McIntosh Chamber of Commerce, which maintains the site (the dress code for the betrothed should include thoroughly covered skin or a *lot* of mosquito repellant).

It's open round the clock for a nice solitary retreat (but as they say in these parts, "You're never alone if the Lord's with you"). Kindly switch down the lights as you leave.

the "Smallest Church in America" in South Newport

© CORY BURGAMY

SHELLMAN BLUFF

This small backwoods fishing village on the Julienton River offers two of the best home-style seafood restaurants in the state and two marinas where you can charter boats to remote barrier islands. Sailors drifting off the Intracoastal Waterway follow their noses to the bluff-side restaurants, bringing occasional New England Topsider-types to this isolated corner of coastal Georgia. (Also a little coastal trivia: One of the largest seizures of smuggled marijuana ever nailed by U.S. Customs agents—12 tons—occurred here in 1975.)

To reach Shellman Bluff, take Hwy. 17 south of South Newport's small church; look for the next turnoff to the left, named Minton Road (signs say Shellman Bluff). Follow the paved road east to its end, where roadside signs direct you to restaurants and marinas to the left; at the next fork, turn right to the small village. First-timers may want to head back to main routes before dark to most easily retrace their steps.

Fish Shacks

At **Hunter's Cafe,** 912/832-5848, let the screen door bang behind you and order great crab stew, broiled stuffed flounder, or one of many other local seafood specialties served with a bluff-side view of the salt marsh. The café is open Tues.–Sun. for lunch and dinner (closed Mon.), but call to confirm before detouring. They also have a fabulously dark and tiny bar.

Or follow signs to **Speed's Kitchen,** down past the Baptist Church, for the best fried seafood on the coast (dinners only, open Thurs.–Sat. 5–10 P.M. and Sun. noon–9:30 P.M., 912/832-4743).

Boat Charters

Fisherman's Lodge, 912/832-4671, and **Kip's Fish Camp,** 912/832-5162, can arrange charters to ferry adventurers out to remote barrier islands for hiking or fishing (or, in season, hunting). You can reach the Blackbeard Island National Wildlife Refuge and Wilderness Area and Sapelo Island's northern shore from here.

⋈ ROUTE 99 LOOP

Route 99 (a loop turnoff from Hwy. 17 or I-95's exit 58) takes drivers on a backcountry adventure through the heart of the old coast. North to south from Eulonia to Darien, old fishing villages, nests of summer cottages overlooking the delta, and knots of trailers and shacks with swept yards remain unchanged over generations.

The route makes a great bicycling excursion—a small ridge adds variety to the flat coastal plain, and many intriguing side trips can yield discoveries along the way. The local speed limit is 40 mph, and while some drivers may exceed that, others are happy to meander along the scenic route.

East of Hwy. 17, 3.5 miles to **Crescent,** a road swings off the highway a mile and a half to the river, where the **Pelican Point Restaurant and Bar,** 912/832-4295, perches over a scenic panorama of Sapelo Sound. The moderately priced restaurant features "fleet fresh" seafood and live entertainment most weekends. It's open Mon.–Fri. starting around 5 P.M., Sat. from 4 P.M., and Sun. noon–10ish.

Four miles farther south of Crescent off Hwy. 99, **Meridian** is the home of the Sapelo Island Visitor Center and the jumping-off point for Sapelo Island tours.

A couple of miles below Meridian, a historic marker points down a half-mile dirt road to the **Thicket,** where tabby ruins of an 1816 sugar mill and rum distillery remain standing near the marsh.

Ridgeville, locally called "the Ridge," marks the high elevation on the route. Historically, elite families were drawn to this area as an escape from the hotter summer temperatures at the

water's edge, and many 19th-century homes and estates remain visible.

The route winds up at Darien, where Fort King George is well worth seeing. The town also has several restaurants to refresh after your detour—see Darien and the Altamaha River section.

Sapelo Island Visitor Center

At the mainland ferry dock in Meridien, the Sapelo Island Visitor Center, 912/437-3224, gastateparks.org, is operated by Georgia State Parks as part of the Sapelo Island National Estuarine Research Reserve. Exhibits cover the University of Georgia Marine Institute and Hog Hammock community on Sapelo, island habitats, and the Gray's Reef National Marine Sanctuary offshore. The center is located off Route 99 eight miles northeast of Darien. Nature trails lead from the center through the maritime forest and marsh and salt pans around the facility.

The center arranges half-day and daylong public tours of the island, offered year-round on Wed. 8:30 A.M.–12:30 P.M. and Sat. 9 A.M.–1 P.M. From June through Labor Day, an additional tour is offered on Fri. 8:30 A.M.–12:30 P.M. From March to October, an extended tour is offered on the last Tues. of the month 8:30 A.M.–3 P.M. Tours cost $10 for adults and $6 for children under age 18, including ferry fare, and reservations are required.

The visitors center is open Tues.–Fri. 7:30 A.M.–5:30 P.M., Sat. 8 A.M.–5:30 P.M., and Sun. 1:30–5 P.M. The center is closed Mon. (Note that at last visit gate hours posted at the entrance bridge were outdated.)

Darien and the Altamaha River

To casual visitors, the sleepy town of Darien at mouth of the Altamaha River appears little more than a tidal backwater to speed through on the way to beach resorts farther south—the town's biggest annual event is the blessing of the local shrimp fleet each April—yet scratch below the surface, and Darien reveals a gold mine of historical riches and intrigue.

HISTORY

Darien sits at the mouth of the great Altamaha River, and every nation ever to lay claim to this coast has left its mark here. In the 16th century, the Spanish established a presidio, populating it with missionaries whose aim it was to convert the coastal Native Americans to Christianity. It wasn't long before the native peoples rebelled, and as a warning to Europeans who might follow, they killed the Spanish and impaled the heads of the priests on tall poles facing the river.

At that time, the Altamaha marked the frontier of what was known as the "Debatable Land" claimed by both England and Spain. In 1721 (12 years before Savannah was settled), the British established **Fort King George** on the site, making Darien the first British outpost in what would become the Georgia colony. James Oglethorpe, the general responsible for founding the Georgia colony, specifically recruited Scottish Highlanders to populate and defend this frontier, because the Scots were renowned for their military might.

The first of the McIntosh clan arrived in 1736 and named the town New Inverness; another boatload arrived six years later. Many residents in Darien today trace their lineage back to these original settlers (descendants of the later embarkation are still jibed as "newcomers").

Antebellum Plantations and Seaport

Under the new name of Darien, the town developed into an important seaport, exporting lumber that was cut in the interior and floated downriver to port. Rice and cotton cultivation gave rise to huge antebellum plantations, each

of which required hundreds of slaves forced to work under grueling conditions. One of these, the Hofwyl-Broadfield Plantation, is now a state historic site that illuminates the details of rice cultivation.

One plantation owner, Pierce Butler, brought to Darien in 1838 his British wife—an actress named Fanny Kemble. Kemble was appalled to witness first-hand the hardships of slavery, and the record she kept of her observations was published in England as the *Journal of a Residence on a Georgia Plantation.* Kemble's fierce indictment of slavery was considered largely responsible for turning British popular opinion against the South during the Civil War.

Across the bridge from Darien, along the southern shore of the Altamaha River, a brick 75-foot rice-mill chimney marks the old **Butler Island** rice plantation, where Kemble wrote her famous journal.

Civil War

Though the Georgia coast was only lightly touched by the Civil War compared to the interior, here again Darien made history. The town was burnt to the ground by none other than the famous all-black regiment, the 54th Massachusetts. Offended that his troops be asked to perform such tasks as town-sacking instead of fighting battles, their commander Colonel Robert Shaw demanded that they next be sent to the front lines. His wish was granted, and their next assignment, an assault on South Carolina's Fort Wagner, led to the death of the commander along with nearly his entire regiment (a story recounted in the film *Glory.*) After her son's death, Sarah Shaw raised funds to rebuild Darien's St. Andrews Church, which was burned to the ground on Shaw's regrettable order.

The town and lumber industry were rebuilt and regained prosperity; later, the seafood industry was introduced, and it continues to this day.

Atlantic Coast Highway Heyday

In the late 1950s and 1960s—the free-wheeling

days of the early transcontinental highways that predated the interstate highway system—Darien was back on the map.

The meandering two-lane through town became part of the Atlantic Coast Highway and was soon congested with truck commerce and Florida-bound travelers. As the saying goes, the locals soon discovered that "a Yankee was worth two bales of cotton, and was a lot easier to pick." Many ways were devised to exploit this new resource, and the town gained notoriety for shady dealing. Admittedly, this was an unsavory time in many parts of the South, and Darien might have slipped through it unnoticed if another historical expose hadn't hit the market in 1991. Melissa Fay Greene tells the story in *Praying for Sheetrock,* as a compelling allegory of the struggle for civil rights in the South.

Darien bears its historical infamy with pride. Read up before you go to get the most out of your visit.

SIGHTS

The **McIntosh County Welcome Center,** on Hwy. 17 at the bridge, 912/437-4192, mcintoshcounty.com, distributes brochures on local attractions and maps for self-guided historical walking and driving tours of the area. You can also inquire here about Sapelo Island tours, river trips, and boat charters. It's open Mon.–Sat. 9 A.M.–5 P.M.

Riverfront Park

From behind the visitors center, Riverfront Park stretches along the northern shore of the wide Altamaha River, creating a scenic promenade and public boardwalk that passes the local shrimp fleet and the tabby ruins of cotton warehouses and naval stores up on the bluff, a short walk to the west. Here too is the waterfront restaurant Skipper's and a condominium development under construction. To the east, the park connects to a **bike path** that leads to Fort King George.

Fort King George

Fort King George served as the southern outpost for the British empire in North America from 1721 until it was abandoned in 1736, after which

General James Oglethorpe brought Scottish Highlanders to the site. Today at the state historic site off Fort King George Dr., 912/437-4770, a reconstructed cypress blockhouse, Native American exhibits, and a self-guided tour illustrate the remote spot's turbulent history. Remains of three sawmills and tabby ruins can also be seen.

Costumed guides deck themselves out in full British regalia for historical reenactments in spring and fall, and July 4th brings Cannons Across the Marsh. Every now and again, boat tours are available.

It's open Tues.–Sat. 9 A.M.–5 P.M., Sun. 2–5:30 P.M., and most Mon. holidays. Admission is $2–3. It's three miles east of I-95 exit 49.

Hofwyl-Broadfield Plantation

The Hofwyl-Broadfield Plantation, five miles south of Darien on Hwy. 17, 912/264-7333, makes an intriguing stop. The state-operated historical site commemorates Georgia's unusual rice culture, and a modest antebellum house recalls plantation history.

Start at the visitors center, where a slide show and exhibits relate stories of the rice fields, then follow a half-mile walk through the quiet maritime forest of live oak and pine to the house and farmyard (the site once served as a dairy farm). Guided tours allow visitors to see the home as kept by Ophelia Dent, the last heir, who left the plantation to the state of Georgia in 1973. One outbuilding was hastily converted to a payroll shed after the Civil War abolished slavery.

Nature-lovers will want to detour off the paths to see the rice levees, which are now thriving wetlands for native and migratory birds. (Also note the observation towers off Hwy. 17 just north of the historic site.)

The historic site is open Tues.–Sat. 9 A.M.–5 P.M., Sun. 2–5:30 P.M., and most Mon. holidays. The last house tour is at 4:15 P.M. Admission is $1.50–3.50.

ACCOMMODATIONS

The most predictable accommodations are at the interstate gulch around I-95 exit 49: the 63-room **Hampton Inn,** 610 Hwy. 251, 912/437-5558 or 800/HAMPTON (800/426-7866), and, across the street, the 65-room **Comfort Inn,** 912/437-4200 or 800/228-5150. Rates at both start around $80, including continental breakfast.

On Vernon Square in downtown Darien, **Open Gates Bed & Breakfast**, 301 Franklin St., 912/437-6985, opengatesbnb.com, is operated by a young couple who bought the property after the first proprietor, Carolyn Hodges, passed on a few years back. The house was rumored to have a ghost before, and now you can be sure it has at least two, so attentive was the spirit of the original innkeeper.

The house was built in 1876 by a wealthy timber baron and offers five guest rooms comfortably appointed, including two with shared bath and one studio above the carriage house. There's also a pool. Rates are $90–120 and include full breakfast. Hosts Kelly and Jeff Spratt are professional biologists who are happy to arrange guided tours of the Altamaha River by motorboat, canoe, or kayak.

It's a block from Riverfront Park and short bike ride to Fort King George. The inn is the closest lodging to the Sapelo Island dock in Meridien, eight miles northeast (about a 20-minute drive).

FOOD AND PROVISIONS

Atop the interstate exit (I-95 exit 49), Hwy. 251—on either side of the overpass—offers several easy choices of places to eat or get takeout for island excursions.

Smokey Joe's BBQ, 912/437-2555, has decent plates of BBQ pork, ribs, and chicken, or a rack-o-ribs to go ($14.50). They're open daily 10 A.M.–10 P.M.

Across the street, **Kentucky Fried Chicken,** like many KFCs in the South, serves a lunch buffet in addition to standard buckets. The factory outlet mall has a food court that includes **Subway**.

None of these will be open for an early morning tour, however. The **Huddle House** east of I-95 is open 24 hours, and a couple of gas-station minimarts at the overpass are also open long hours for provisions, or go to Archie's.

Archie's Seafood

The most venerable restaurant in town is **Archie's Seafood,** 912/437-4363, a 60-year-old whitewashed concrete block building on Hwy. 17 downtown, for such traditional plates as all-you-can-eat fried shrimp specials ($6 at lunch buffet), or whole fried river catfish with sides of tater logs and slaw, all washed down with quarts of sweet tea. It's open daily 7 A.M.–10 P.M. for a very local crowd.

The newest restaurant in town, **Skippers' Fish Camp**, 85 Screvan St., 912/437-FISH (912/437-3474), serves more modern fare in a scenic waterfront setting right at the docks alongside the shrimp fleet. There's a great view from the main dining room and also from the oyster bar, a cozy screened-in tree-hut across the expansive patio. You might start with a half-pound of steamed Sweet Georgia shrimp and move on to their signature whole crispy flounder ($18) before peach cobbler or pecan pie. They also have steak, BBQ ribs, and salads topped with fried oysters or shrimp. A full bar includes Guinness and Corona, inexpensive California wines, and a martini menu ($8 apiece). It's open daily, 11 A.M.–10 P.M. It's a

© CORY BURGAMY

nice spot anytime, but particularly at sunset. We spotted a baby alligator in the marsh outside.

ALTAMAHA RIVER

The mighty Altamaha River starts around Lumber City at the confluence of the Oconee and Ocmulgee Rivers, and flows 137 miles through hardwood forests, cypress swamps, and tidal marsh south of Darien. Named "one of the last great places" by the Nature Conservancy, the Altamaha is one of the most biologically diverse river systems in the southeast, supporting abundant plant and animal life, including 120 rare species. Unbridled by dams, more freshwater flows into the Atlantic from the Altamaha than from any other river in the southeastern U.S.

At the mouth of the river, the 21,000-acre **Altamaha State Waterfowl Management Area** is among the most important stopover and resting spots for migratory birds on the Georgia coast. Observation platforms overlook the area; look for trailheads off Hwy. 17 just south of the Darien bridge.

Altamaha River Canoe Trail

The river's entire length makes up the Altamaha River Canoe Trail. East of Hwy. 84, a 300-foot-wide **scenic buffer** along each bank of stretches for 25 miles to inside the McIntosh County line. The swamps and upland hammocks offer good picnicking, camping, and fishing spots. Access is available from boat ramps in Wayne, Long, Glynn, and McIntosh Counties.

Just upriver from Darien, the river passes through the 6,000-acre **Lewis Island Natural Area,** which harbors the largest known grove of ancient bald cypress in Georgia—believed to be over 1,000 years old. The island is not accessible during high water.

The coast's premier outfitter, **South East Adventures,** 912/638-6732, southeastadventure.com, runs daylong ($80) and multiday Altamaha River kayaking and camping trips (three-day trips cost $325 and include meals and gear).

Sapelo Island and Outlying Islands

Adventurers often travel to far corners of the globe to discover an isolated subtropical island with a culture, language, and history all its own—but few would guess that they could find all that on Sapelo Island, U.S.A.

Sapelo is graced with the beauty of all the Sea Islands—powdery shell paths through pine-and-palmetto forests, startled herons gliding across abandoned rice fields—yet beyond that, Sapelo is home to a Geechee community largely descended from a single slave. The only other residents are the biologists who inhabit the marine research institute there.

Access to the island is restricted to protect island ecology, but a daily ferry runs for islanders and guests by advance reservation. Tourists interested in a day-trip can sign up for a guided island tour sponsored by the county, or make arrangements with island residents, who also offer tours.

The 30-minute ferry ride to the island is reason enough to travel to Sapelo. The *Anne Marie* gracefully weaves through still blue-green marshlands, past oyster beds, and alongside schools of dolphins into wide Doboy Sound; the mysterious island looms on the horizon. Then there's the island itself—far removed from civilization, overgrown with thick forests, and with a wide untrammeled beach studded with whelks, sea whips, and olive shells.

As remote as Sapelo Island is, outlying islands beyond Sapelo are even less accessible. To reach the other barrier islands on the north coast—Ossabaw, St. Catherines, Blackbeard, Wolf, and Egg—visitors need to arrange independent boat charters. Try either of two marinas in the small fishing village of Shellman Bluff, a detour off Hwy. 17 from South Newport.

HISTORY

One of the few Sea Islands that retains its Native American name, Sapelo was called Zapala by the

SEA ISLANDERS

The land, climate, isolation, and history of Georgia's coast have shaped a character unique to the coastal low country. Visitors emerging from the pine barrens of Georgia's southeastern interior will quickly sense a seaward expansiveness, a Creole flavor, and the distinct drawling coastal accent. But most unusual by far is the fascinating African American culture created by the peculiar regional history.

Enslaved people on the coast had a different experience from enslaved people on the mainland. Because slave ships unloaded their human cargo directly at the coast, enslaved Africans avoided the culturally destructive assimilation common to those dispersed throughout the interior. Rice planters sought slaves from rice-growing regions of West Africa, who would already be skilled in the grain's cultivation. Large coastal plantations enslaved hundreds of workers, keeping these communities intact, and planters fled to cooler highlands for almost half of each year, allowing Africans to continue cultural practices that were banned. They were thus able to hang on to a group identity and hand down cultural traditions from generation to generation. Over the years, this African heritage melded with American experiences to create the rich amalgamated cultural heritage of the Sea Islanders.

In Georgia, the Sea Islanders are called Geechee, after the local Ogeechee River. Like the term Cajun, the term has historically been used derisively. The broader term for this folk culture and language throughout the low country (which includes the southern South Carolina coast) is Gullah. The Gullah dialect, spoken today by an estimated 250,000 people, combines African syntax and occasional African words with Southernisms and folk language, producing a unique lexicon with a sound all its own. As an example, the Bible in the Gullah dialect translates the Gospel according to Luke as "De Good Nyews Bout Jedus Christ Wa Luke Write."

Julie Dash's 1992 film *Daughters of the Dust* is a poetic portrayal of a Sea Islander family at the turn of the 20th century. Some Gullah practices are also recounted in John Berendt's best-seller, *Midnight in the Garden of Good and Evil.*

Today, while the inevitable forces of modern life and popular mainland culture conspire to erode traditional folkways, recent revivals to preserve Gullah culture help to ensure its viability.

Folklore and Beliefs

One story tells of a captured Igbo (Ebo) leader who, upon debarkation from a slave ship, led

---

Creek, who hunted and fished here when Europeans arrived. But its native history dates back thousands of years—some of the earliest pottery found in North America was unearthed here. Of the **shell middens** on Sapelo, the largest measures 12 feet high and 300 feet in diameter.

In the 16th century, the Spanish established a mission named **San Jose de Zapala** on the north end of the island. Later a small colony of refugees from the French Revolution founded a community nearby called La Chatelet, which has been Anglicized to **Chocolate.**

But the greatest change to the island was brought by Thomas Spaulding, who bought the island in 1802 and built a large cotton and sugarcane plantation at the island's south end. The tabby remains of the sugar mill still stand. When the Civil War came, the Spauldings abandoned

the island, and their rambling **South End** house, made of tabby walls three feet thick, fell to ruins under the occupation of Federal troops.

Former slaves of the Spaulding plantation remained on the island and established their own self-sufficient and self-regulated communities. They lived in such isolation through the generations that they retained many of the West African beliefs and traditions that mainland African Americans had lost through assimilation and repression.

In 1936, tobacco magnate R. J. Reynolds bought the island and later established the marine institute and wildlife refuge here. The state now owns most of the island and maintains the institute, refuge, the national estuarine sanctuary offshore. Georgia State Parks operates a group campsite and the Reynolds mansion as a dormi-

his 17 fellow tribesmen into the water instead of submitting to slavery. The Geechee elevated this story to the mythological tale of the people who "walked back to Africa." Though the historical episode happened on Dunbar Creek on St. Simons Island, every sea island has adopted its own Ebo Landing, where the spirits of the dead Africans remain.

Spiritual healers ("conjure doctors") were important members of the community, able to placate the spirits of the dead that vexed the living and upset the balance of life. Such beliefs sprang from West African Vodun ("voodoo" or "hoodoo" in its Haitian form; Haiti was a way station for many slave ships) mixed with elements of Islam and Afro-Christianity to create the folk mythology of the Geechee.

Low Country Cuisine
After plantation owners abandoned the barrier islands, the formerly enslaved inhabitants of necessity developed self-sustaining communities dependent on local seafood, vegetables, and rice. Low country cuisine incorporated shellfish into okra soup (okra seeds were brought by slaves from Africa), she-crab soup, and many other dishes seasoned with West Indian spices. Also brought from Africa, benne seeds now accent popular benne wafers.

Performing Arts and Crafts
Traditional Sea Island music is a rich blend of spirituals, gospel, blues, sea chanties, and work chants that trace their rhythms back to African roots. The Georgia Sea Island Singers, performing traditional musics and dances on the coast and around the globe for more than 25 years, are perhaps the best-known practitioners of this unique style. Says Singer Frankie Quimby, "I'm a firm believer that you can't know where you're going until you realize where you've come from."

The Geechee also carry on the African tradition of coiled-grass basketry, perfected by none better than Allen Green of Sapelo Island. Seine-net weaving was an important practical craft for islanders.

The Sea Island Festival, held in Neptune Park on St. Simons Island in mid-August, brings together folksingers, storytellers, and artisans to celebrate this heritage. Sapelo Island, home to the Geechee community of Hog Hammock, also hosts festivals and homecomings for mainlanders and islanders alike.

tory and conference center—all under the rubric of the **Sapelo Island Natural Estuarine Research Reserve.**

Hog Hammock
In the 434-acre private parcel of Hog Hammock, descendants of Spaulding slaves (many descended from a single slave, a West African Muslim named Bailli) carry on their unique Geechee heritage. The community today numbers around 70—including several families whose children ferry over to mainland schools each day—but the majority of the residents are of advanced age, as the youth are drawn to wider educational and economic opportunities on the mainland. The future is uncertain for this cultural enclave unless the islanders can solidify an economic base to hang on to its next generation. Over the past decade, the establishment of several businesses bringing tourists to the island has contributed to the community's prospects.

For more information about these efforts, contact the **Sapelo Island Cultural and Revitalization Society** (SICRS), devoted to historic preservation, economic development, and land retention, at P.O. Box 1, Sapelo Island, GA 31327, 912/485-2179. Their offices occupy a cottage in Hog Hammock (between the Tabby Cottage eatery and The Wallow).

GUIDED TOURS
McIntosh County-Sponsored Tours
For the official tour, contact the **Sapelo Island Visitor Center,** 912/437-3224, on the

mainland at the dock in Meridian (eight miles northeast of Darien), to make reservations for island bus tours. Pick up tickets here before boarding the ferry. Only people whose names are already on the ferry roster will be permitted to board. The visitors center is closed on Mon.

Tours are offered year-round on Wed. 8:30 A.M.–12:30 P.M. and Sat. 9 A.M.–1 P.M. From June through Labor Day, an additional tour is offered on Fri. 8:30 A.M.–12:30 P.M.

From March to October, an extended tour is offered on the last Tuesday of the month, 8:30 A.M.–3 P.M. Tours cost $10 for adults and $6 for children under age 18, including ferry fare, and reservations are required.

On the half-day tour, guides take sightseers around the southern and central parts of the island while explaining local history and ecology. The full-day tour includes North End sights.

The combination of the peculiar history, heat, isolation, and such random sights as the entangled landscapes, armadillo roadkill, pickled animal parts at the marine institute, and the lilting Geechee dialects makes for an exotic American adventure. (Not for everyone—tourists with more mainstream interests are better off sticking to the resort areas farther south, and young children could be miserably uncomfortable on a tour with such uncommon appeal.)

Islander Tours

Several Hog Hammock residents also guide visitors around the island, in either a bus, a van, or mule train. Contact **Stanley Walker,** 912/485-2206, or **Maurice Bailey,** 912/485-2206. You can pick your own itinerary or leave it to the natives, but all tour arrangements must be made in advance. Costs start around $40.

Paddling Tours

Paddling excursions to Sapelo and from Sapelo over to Blackbeard Island are organized by the St. Simons–based outfitter **SouthEast Adventure Outfitters,** 912/638-6732, southeastadventure.com; call for dates and rates for kayak and canoe trips and overnight camping excursions.

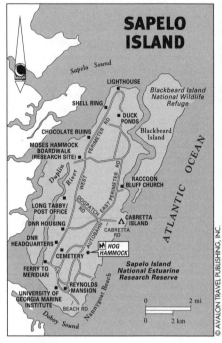

© AVALON TRAVEL PUBLISHING, INC.

SIGHTS
Central Sapelo

A church, eatery, two hostelries, and a community center constitute downtown Hog Hammock, the island's only privately owned parcel, surrounded by houses, trailers, and a cemetery. To the east, the state group campground at **Cabretta Beach** has a bathhouse and platform shelters.

On the island's back-river side just north of the state ferry dock, ruins of a small **sugar mill** dating back to 1803 can be seen next to the Long Tabby building, which houses the post office (Sapelo is one of the few places in the country where the U.S. Postal Service boats in the mail).

South End

At South End, the **Reynolds Mansion** is the island's Big House, a palatial villa constructed of tabby walls three feet thick, surrounded by statuary and shaded by moss-draped live oaks. Built by cotton magnate Thomas Spaulding and later occupied by Howard Coffin (the founder of the

GRAY'S REEF

East of Sapelo Island by 17.5 nautical miles, in ocean waters 50–80 feet deep, lies America's northernmost coral reef. **Gray's Reef National Marine Sanctuary,** one of 10 federally protected marine sanctuaries nationwide, is named for Milton B. Gray, the biologist credited with discovery of the reef in 1981. Here, a 17-square-mile area of concentrated limestone outcroppings rise above an otherwise barren seafloor to heights of eight feet, attracting an abundant and colorful collection of unique sea life (not to mention scuba divers and fishing boats).

Tropical atolls of hard corals cover the outcroppings. Soft corals (called octocorals because of their eight tentacles) wave hypnotically, earning such names as sea whips, deadmans fingers, knobby candelabra, and sea feathers. The coral-reef community attracts and shelters anemones, sponges, jellies, worms, mollusks, crabs, lobsters, shrimp, and many temperate and tropical varieties of fish. Schools of barracuda, amberjack, scad, and spadefish move through underwater currents warmed by the Gulf Stream, along with threatened and endangered varieties of sea turtles. The waters surrounding Gray's Reef also contain the only known calving grounds for the most highly endangered of all great whales— the North Atlantic right whale *(Eubalaena glacialis)*—only an estimated 325 individuals exist.

Gray's Reef is one of the most popular recreational dive sites off the Georgia coast, and it's the best-known destination for offshore sport-fishing.

For more information, see Georgia Department of Natural Resources, gadnr.org, Coastal Resources Division.

Cloister Hotel on Sea Island), the house was lastly the residence of R. J. Reynolds before the property was turned over to the state. The interior is open only to groups by advance reservation and some county-led tours.

On the back river just south of the state ferry dock is the **University of Georgia Marine Institute,** housed in a former dairy set around a central fountain topped with a statue of a wild turkey. County-led tours enter the labs to view display jars full of mysterious biological substances.

At the southern tip of the island, **Nannygoat Beach** offers a boardwalk over the dunes, a picnic shelter, and restrooms. Within a mile up the road, a boardwalk leads out to the marsh, and a trail leads into the forest for a close-up look at coastal habitats.

North End

At the north end of the island, the 1820 **Sapelo Lighthouse** was deactivated in 1905 and lay in disrepair for most of the century until the bright red-and-white-striped beacon was restored in 1998, bringing it back in business. The century-old **First African Baptist Church** of Raccoon Bluff, once the center of a thriving community, was restored in 2000 with help from the historic preservation department of the Savannah College of Art and Design.

On the back river side are the ruins of the French community called **Chocolate** and ancient **shell middens,** the largest of which measures 12 feet high and 300 feet in diameter. **Blackbeard Island** can be reached by boating across Blackbeard Creek at the northeastern side of Sapelo.

SPECIAL EVENTS

The island hosts an annual **Sapelo Island Cultural Day Festival** in October, featuring Gullah and Native American arts and crafts, storytelling, gospel music, Sea Island music, low country cuisine, and more. Call 912/485-2197 for prices and more information.

ACCOMMODATIONS AND CAMPING

The Wallow

The Wallow in Hog Hammock, 912/485-2206, operated by Cornelia and Julius Bailey, occupies a newly constructed raised wooden cabin in the center of a rural compound of houses, trailers, and outbuildings set among shrubs, plantings, and the rare shade tree. A wide front porch extends the length of the cabin, lined with colorful rocking chairs.

Inside, a large communal kitchen and parlor with TV are divided by a ten-person table, and a hall leads to six modestly decorated and comfortable bedrooms, some with twin beds, each with tiny baths (shower stalls and accordian-door closures). There's plenty of air-conditioning.

Rates start at $65 and include transportation to and from the dock, but guests need to bring all their own food and drink. (There is one eatery on the island, but don't be caught short.) The kitchen is furnished with a coffeemaker and microwave, as well as a stove, oven, and refrigerator for guests' use. (Such basics as cooking oil, salt, and pepper seem to be on hand, but you couldn't necessarily count on it.)

Inquire about bicycle rental, storytelling, island history, camping, and the watering hole and craft shop next door. The family is also opening a studio cabin up the road about a mile.

The Weekender

The Weekender, in Hog Hammock, 912/485-2277, operated by Nancy and Caesar Banks, offers a decade-old low tabby cabin with three comfortable bedrooms; it's minimally but comfortably outfitted with chenille spreads, each with private bath and shared kitchens. Linens and cooking utensils are provided, but guests need to bring food and drink.

The lounge—where old Chevy bench seats constitute the booths, and fawning fan letters and photographs adorn the walls—best reflects an island sense of thrifty reuse and Geechee generosity of spirit. Rates start at $60 and include transportation to and from the dock. Inquire about bicycle use and camping.

The Banks also operate the island's only eatery, which opened in the last few years—see *Food and Drink*. It's best to confirm hours of operation when making reservations.

State of Georgia Facilities

The state authorities now open the 13-bedroom South End **Reynolds Mansion** to groups of 16–29 by advance reservation; call 912/485-2299 or visit gastateparks.org. The rooms are furnished and decorated by the state, many with twin beds in dormitory style, within what was once a glamorous plantation villa that hosted three presidents. As a result, there's a strangely Soviet aura to the place, and you're not quite sure whether to be happy or sad that the fountains are dry and the basement bowling alley is silent. Nevertheless, it's a great venue for an overnight 50th birthday party for 25 of your closest friends, which was what was going on there when we were last by.

Camping: Also for groups, the state maintains the primitive beachfront Cabretta Island campground with platforms for freestanding tents and a bathhouse with hot showers. Call 912/485-2299 for more information.

FOOD AND DRINK

The Banks family serves authentic Gullah cuisine in the **Tabby Cottage,** in Hog Hammock, 912/485-2199, the island's only eatery. It's open Tues.–Thurs. 8 A.M.–1 P.M. and Fri.–Sat. 8 A.M.–5 P.M. Advance reservations are required. Note that it is closed Sun.–Mon., but they say that arrangements can possibly be made for Monday by advance reservation.

George and Lulu Walker may also be able to provide meal service; call them at 912/485-2270.

If **B. J.'s Confectionery** is not bolted shut (with a broomstick through the door handles), Viola might be out front weaving baskets. Her handcrafted creations hang from empty cabinets around the old café that looks like it served its last meal in the Johnson administration. The store part—a box of instant rice, a bottle of bleach, several individually wrapped rolls of toilet tissue—resembles a store in Nicaragua at the height of the U.S. embargo, but Viola stocks cold drinks (usually offbeat brands: Mr. Pibb, Bubble-Up), some candy, and hot dogs.

If worse comes to worst and you need to eat, the Senior Center might be able to spare a plate for $5 or so after serving the island's elderly population. There's also a big potluck after (three-hour) church services in Hog Hammock.

GETTING THERE AND AROUND

The Department of Natural Resources operates daily ferry service for residents and guests from the dock in Meridian, 10 miles north of Darien on Route 99. The only visitors allowed on the ferry are those listed on the official tour, overnight guests, or guests at state facilities by advance reservations. The resident/guest rate is $1; your hosts meet you at the dock.

Bicycles are not allowed on the ferry; neither are canoes, lawn chairs, oversize coolers, fuel, or "anything the captain deems too large or dangerous." Most local proprietors make bicycles available for guests.

At the dock, a waiting room provides restrooms and a vending machine that dispenses water and soda. At last visit, the snack vending machine was empty and perhaps inoperable.

Also at last visit, the sign at the gate to the dock listing operating hours was outdated. If you have reservations on a ferry, rest assured the gates will be opened in plenty of time for passengers to park, walk the short distance to the dock, and embark before departure.

OSSABAW ISLAND

Ossabaw Island was protected in 1976 as Georgia's first Heritage Preserve, and today it's operated by a public–private partnership. Shelters on the island are open only to selected educational or artistic nonprofit groups.

Rare wild hogs (introduced to the island 400 years ago) and donkeys (introduced earlier this century) roam at will around Ossabaw, another island that retains its Native American name. A few tabby buildings date from slavery days, and a hunting lodge and helicopter wreck stand as relics of more recent eras.

For more information, contact the Department of Natural Resources island manager, P.O. Box 14565, Savannah, GA 31416, 912/485-2251.

ST. CATHERINES ISLAND

Named capital of nearly every nation and enterprise that ever claimed the Sea Islands, St. Catherines Island has the most fascinating history of all. In the 16th century, Spanish missionaries established their domain on Georgia's Sea Islands,

© CORY BURGAMY

on the deck of the *Anne Marie*

TURTLE CROSSING

© KAP STANN

Five endangered sea turtle species swim in coastal waters. One of these, the loggerhead sea turtle, nests on Georgia's barrier islands. Weighing an average of 150 pounds (though individuals of the species have been known to reach 300 pounds), a female loggerhead digs a nest onshore, then deposits about 100 eggs the size of Ping-Pong balls.

When hatching, baby sea turtles are instinctively drawn to the brightest spot around (nature designed it to be the moon's reflection off the water, so that they safely find their way to water). With development encroaching on their nesting grounds, the turtles may head inland, toward artificial lights instead. Many coastal communities have launched "Lights Out" campaigns to urge beachfront dwellers to turn their lights down or off at night during nesting season to avoid this confusion. Once adults, only females return to land; males spend their entire lives at sea.

constructing a string of presidio-missions designed to convert natives to Christianity. The capital of these island settlements was **Santa Catalina de Guale;** its ruins here still attract archaeologists studying the Spanish mission system. As for the origins of the word "Guale" commonly seen in connection to coastal history, the name is conjectured to be a Spanish corruption of the Muskegon word *wahali,* meaning "south."

The British settled Savannah in 1773 and soon pressed the Creek for additional land. As the British progressively overstepped original territorial agreements made with Creek Chief Tomochichi, a half-Creek princess named Mary Musgrove Bosomworth took up the cause of her people. She successfully negotiated with the British to retain at least St. Catherines Island as Creek territory.

After her death, a famed local American Revolutionary came into the picture. Button Gwinnett, one of Georgia's three signers of the Declaration of Independence, bought the island and moved here with his wife and daughter. Legend has it that after Gwinnett was killed in a duel on the mainland in 1777,

his spirit returned to inhabit his island home and is seen most often sailing stormy waters in the sound.

The island passed down to a planter, who established a flourishing cotton plantation here before the Civil War, which was abandoned when war broke out. The historic plantation house, cottages, and tabby slave cabins remain in use.

In 1864, General Sherman allocated the Sea Islands (and much of the coastal low country) as the exclusive domain of the newly freed. The entrepreneurial Tunis Campbell quickly declared himself governor of this new Black Republic, from headquarters here on St. Catherines Island. When Congress repealed Sherman's directive during Reconstruction, returning ownership to the planters, Campbell was removed by Federal troops.

Eventually, after changing hands from heir to heir, the island came under the control of a private foundation. This foundation established the **Rare Animal Survival Center,** of the New York Zoological Society, on the island in 1974. Because of its captive breeding program, St. Catherines is off-limits to the general public. In 2004, the society announced plans to discontinue the program.

For more information, contact the **Georgia Conservancy,** 912/897-6462.

BLACKBEARD ISLAND

Named for Edward Teach, the famous "Blackbeard" of swashbuckling fame (legend says his hidden treasure may remain buried off Tybee Island), Blackbeard Island is separated from northeastern Sapelo Island by a thin creek. Originally bought by the U.S. Navy in 1800 as a source of live-oak timber for shipbuilding, in 1940 the Interior Department took it over and designated it a national wildlife refuge. In 1975, half of its 5,618 acres were set aside as a national wilderness area.

Hikers use several miles of trails, roadways, and beaches for wildlife (especially birdlife) viewing. From March 15 to October 25, fishing is allowed on two large freshwater ponds; saltwater creeks are open to fishing throughout the year, except during managed hunts in the fall and winter.

For more information, call the coastal refuges office, 912/944-4415.

WOLF ISLANDS

Actually, three islands—Wolf, Egg, and Little Egg—make up the Wolf Island National Wildlife Refuge, a low-lying preserve of 4,000 acres of tidal marshlands with only 135 acres of forests. Limited recreational opportunities appeal mostly to anglers and bird-watchers.

For more information, call the coastal refuges office at 912/944-4415.

Brunswick, Golden Isles Gateway

The islands of St. Simons, Jekyll, Sea Island, and Little St. Simons, first called the Golden Isles by the Spanish (a term happily revived by local promoters), offer visitors easily accessible beach playgrounds with plenty of things to see and do and accommodations that range from moss-draped campgrounds to the world's most exclusive resorts. The largest, St. Simons and Jekyll Islands, are bridged to the mainland at Brunswick. Sea Island is bridged to St. Simons Island, and Little St. Simons Island is accessible by boat from a dock on St. Simons.

Located 75 miles south of Savannah and 290 miles southeast of Atlanta, the port city of Brunswick is the jumping-off point for vacationers headed to the Golden Isles. Most people rush through Brunswick on their way to the beach—to judge by the dingy Hwy. 17 corridor, you might guess why. Yet the marsh is beautiful—poetically celebrated in Sidney Lanier's *Marshes of Glynn*—and the town has historic highlights they're eager to show visitors.

But its greatest appeal might just be that there's little that'a resortlike about it. As the islands grow increasingly rarefied, Brunswick can offer a welcome flip side—a working shrimp fleet, a tree-house hostel, and killer barbecue, to name a few highlights.

The **Brunswick Visitors Center,** 4 Glynn Ave., 912/265-0620 or 800/933-2627, can be found on Hwy. 17 just south of the entrance to the Torras causeway over to St. Simons. They offer maps, events calendars, and lodging, dining, and recreation brochures in six languages. The center is open daily except holidays 9 A.M.–5 P.M. Inquire here about the new Georgia Heritage Theme Park planned to open in the area in 2005.

SIGHTS

Historic Districts

Historic downtown Brunswick is centered at the intersection of Newcastle and Gloucester Streets, the traditional commercial corridors of the city. It's a bit forlorn, with several empty storefronts, but a few popular restaurants, cafés, and shops are leading the way towards a revival. The restored **Ritz Theater,** built in 1898 as a grand opera palace, provides a new performing arts venue and a gallery in the lobby.

The residential **Old Town** district, off London Street several blocks east of Union, holds

Sidney Lanier Bridge

many impressive Victorian houses and buildings shaded by venerable oaks, none more treasured than the 900-year-old **Lover's Oak,** at Prince and Albany Streets.

Waterfront

A block from the downtown Newcastle Street strip, Brunswick's working waterfront is anchored by the **Mary Ross Waterfront Park,** on Bay at Gloucester Street. Here a plaza green is the venue for several city festivals, and the pavilion holds a **farmers market** on Tuesdays, Thursdays, and Saturdays.

A Liberty Ship model now stands in the park to represent the 99 ships of this type produced by Brunswick's shipyards in WWII (a new park planned for the foot of the gleaming Sidney Lanier Bridge in 2005 will honor local shipworkers).

The shrimp fleet can be seen here along the East River docks.

Brunswick History Museum

The local history museum, 1327 Union St., 912/265-4032, occupies the 1907 Lissner House and contains archaeological exhibits, historical photographs, and displays that tell the town's story, from its commemoration of the hometown of King George (Brunswick is named after Braunsweig, Germany) to the development of local industry. It also serves as a downtown information center. The museum is open 10 A.M.–5 P.M. daily.

Marshes of Glynn Overlook Park

Off the Hwy. 17 strip through town, a small turnout park provides a scenic overlook of the tidal marshlands poetically rendered by Georgia poet Sidney Lanier as "A league and a league of marsh-grass, waist-high, broad in the blade/Green, and all of a height, and unfrocked with a light or a shade/Stretch leisurely off, in a pleasant plain. . ." (But the better overlook might be from the patio at Spanky's with a cool beverage in hand.)

RECREATION AND ENTERTAINMENT
Georgia Department of Natural Resources

A useful resource in Brunswick is the coastal headquarters of the Georgia Department of Natural Resources (D.N.R.), off Hwy. 17 South,

© CORY BURGAMY

912/264-7218, under the Sidney Lanier Bridge over to Jekyll Island. The D.N.R. provides maps, hunting and fishing licenses, seasonal guides and directories of recreational resources, precautionary information, and the most accurate information on coastal flora, fauna, and habitats—all free or low-cost.

It's open Mon.–Fri. 8 A.M.–4:30 P.M. A nature trail outside weaves through marsh and woodland areas.

Paddling Excursions

Two-hour kayaking expeditions through the Marshes of Glynn here are led by the St. Simons–based **SouthEast Adventure Outfitters,** arranged through their St. Simons office, 912/638-6732, southeastadventure.com ($30 day trips; $35 full-moon trips). Tours depart from their Brunswick store on Hwy. 17 next to Spanky's restaurant, where they sell and rent kayaks and other recreational equipment.

Festivals

The **Blessing of the Fleet and Seafood Festival** are celebrated together on Mother's Day weekend in May. The **Brunswick Stewbilee,** in October, honors the city's namesake Georgia barbecue staple, Brunswick stew, and also features downhome Southern blues.

ACCOMMODATIONS AND CAMPING

Motels

Brunswick motels are less expensive than staying on the islands, yet without the amenities of sand, surf, or scenery. Arriving to the islands on peak-season weekends without reservations, you might need to resort to them. Newer chains are found out by the interstate (making them convenient for I-95 through-travelers) clustered around exits 38 and 36. Among the dozen chain motels off exit 38, the **Jameson Inn,** 912/267-0800, offers a nice regional chain alternative. Among another dozen at exit 36, find **Hampton Inn,** 912/261-0002; **Best Western Brunswick Inn,** 912/264-0144; and **Motel 6,** 912/264-8582. Older, cheaper, more run-down properties are

strung along Hwy. 17 north of the causeway to St. Simons.

Hostel in the Forest

Some of the most distinctive bargain lodging in all of Georgia is found outside of town at the **Hostel in the Forest,** 912/264-9738, foresthostel.org, a wooded hideaway down a bumpy dirt road, where peacocks roam the grounds and guests stay in screened-in geodesic-dome dormitories or tiny picture-window tree houses. The $20 charge includes a $5 lifetime membership fee and a communal supper. There are also laundry facilities and the occasional sweat lodge.

Look for the hostel symbol sign on Hwy. 82 (southwest of Brunswick, a mile west of Hwy. 17, 1.5 miles west of I-95), turn left, and follow the rugged dirt driveway a half mile down.

Blythe Island Regional Park

The 40-site campground at **Blythe Island Regional Park,** 6616 Blythe Island Hwy., 912/261-3814, is geared to fisherfolk who use the park's marina for easy access to tidewater and offshore fishing. They have ice, bait, gas, showers, laundry facilities, a 200-berth dock, and a small lakefront swimming beach. Sites are in an exposed treeless field right off the highway, most suitable for RVs (starting at $19 with full hookups).

FOOD AND DRINK

A few old Brunswick classics are hidden among the dozens of fast-food outlets and national chain restaurants in town. A mandatory stop on the Georgia Barbecue Landmarks Trail, the **Georgia Pig,** on Hwy. 17 a quarter mile east of I-95 exit 29, 912/264-6664, offers brick-pit barbecue pork, beef, sausage, and ribs in a log cabin with picnic-table seating inside and out. An excellent plate of ribs with two sides costs $8.50, or buy a slab ($17) and pints of slaw to take back to camp. It's open daily 11 A.M.–7 P.M., sometimes later; credit cards are accepted.

Another culinary landmark is **Willie's Wee-Nee Wagon,** 3599 Altama Ave., 912/264-1146 ("We relish your bun"), which offers a $2,000 reward "if you can find a better fried porkchop sandwich in Glynn County." It's open Mon.–Sat. 10 A.M.–10 P.M. It's across from the college.

Downtown, the **Cargo Portside Grill,** 1423 Newcastle St., 912/267-7330, offers grazing dishes like fried green tomatoes and signature crab cakes, and entrées (starting at $19) of sesame catfish, beef tenderloin, and chalkboard specials. It's open for dinner only starting at 5:30 P.M. Tues.–Sat.

Spanky's, 1200 Glynn Ave. on the water off Hwy. 17, 912/267-6100, is a perky local hangout for okay buffalo fingers and beach music, but the best thing is the view: watch kayakers come in as a storm rises over the marsh. It's open daily, from 11 A.M. to at least 9:30 P.M.

Pam's, 4344 Hwy. 17N, 912/267-7267, outside the Federal Law Enforcement Training Center, bills itself without contest as "the largest law enforcement dinner club in the world." Inside, the shoulder patches of thousands of the nation's police forces line the walls, brass plate partner memorials cover the bar, and autographed glossies of the likes of George Wallace and Lester Maddox are among the treasured memorabilia. Pam's serves a selection of meat-and-potato platters (even Kiddie Copper specials) and frequently schedules Free Beer customer-appreciation nights. Look for the decommissioned black-and-white outside, marked "Pam's."

St. Simons Island, Little St. Simons, & Sea Island

As you cross the high span of the Torras causeway, everything suddenly changes. You leave mainland reality behind and enter the pristine realm of the jungly islands, with their slow tropical pace, white sands, and serene blue-green marshlands. The low-key resort town on the island is lively but not raucous, a convivial mix of vacationers and islanders, with a relaxed pace that leaves mainland worries far behind. For Californians it may evoke a resemblance to Avalon, on Catalina Island.

The world-class Cloister resort—site of the G-8 summit in 2004—is on Sea Island, bridged to St. Simons. Guests bound for the private Little St. Simons Island resort depart from a dock at the north end of St. Simons.

HISTORY

Originally the hunting grounds of the native Creek, the islands were fought over by major European powers: the French, Spanish, and English. This contest was ultimately decided here on St. Simons Island, where the skirmish called the Battle of Bloody Marsh marked the Spaniards' last attempt to expand their continental dominion north of Florida.

British General James Oglethorpe, founder of the Georgia colony, established Fort Frederica here on the back-river side of St. Simons, both to secure his new settlement at Savannah and also to provoke the Spanish by claiming the "Debatable Land" south of the Altamaha River. From here he led troops to the marsh battle in 1736.

In the plantation era, the land grew Sea Island cotton (a few tabby ruins remain from that time), and, like the rest of the islands, became home to a Geechee community when the islands were occupied by Federal troops in the Civil War. The mythologized Geechee folktale of the slaves who "walked back to Africa" has its origins here on St. Simons: upon debarking from a slave ship, a captured Igbo leader from Nigeria led his tribesmen into the ocean rather than submit to slavery. Though the original Ebo's Landing is on St. Simons (on private property up Dunbar Creek), in Geechee folktales each island has its own, inhabited by the spirits of the Africans.

The popularity of St. Simons' turn-of-the-20th-century resorts increased dramatically after the bridge was built in the 1920s, and it has steadily increased ever since. In addition to its tourist attractions, the island also houses a year-round residential community, making it the most "well-rounded" of the Golden Isles.

SIGHTS

Much of the action is at the southern tip of the island. Follow Kings Way south of the causeway (veer right) to Mallory Street to find the central

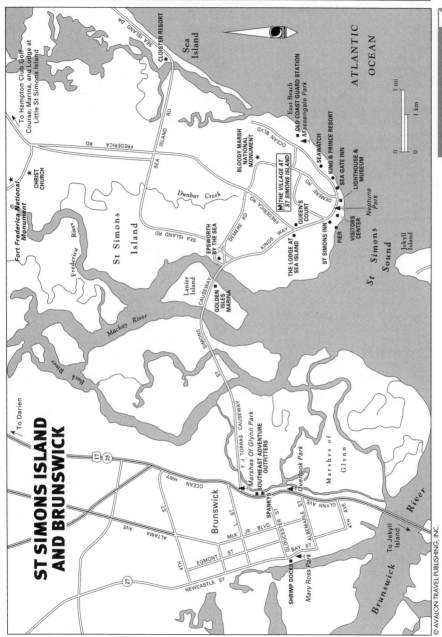

GEORGIA'S BARRIER ISLANDS

Only three of Georgia's 13 major barrier islands are bridged to the mainland; the rest are defined by their inaccessibility. Travelers willing to put a little effort into planning will be rewarded by rare wilderness and abundant wildlife encounters.

By Georgia law, all beaches are public property up to the high water mark. Beyond this, the private islands are accessible by invitation only, but refuges offer the chance to explore all island habitats.

Use the index of this book to navigate to more information on these islands.

Tybee Island

"Savannah Beach," accessible by car 18 miles east of town, is Georgia's most developed barrier island, with a popular pier and pavilion at the Strand, as well as a campground and many motels and inns.

Little Tybee Island

Uninhabited Little Tybee is accessible only by boat, a short motorboat ride from Tybee's back-river marina to four miles of deserted beach. Primitive camping is permitted.

Wassaw Island

A federally owned wildlife refuge accessible only by boat, Wassaw is one of the least-spoiled barrier islands on the east coast. Charter a boat from a local marina or follow a paddling route from Skidaway Island.

Ossabaw Island

State-owned and operated in cooperation with a private organization, Ossabaw Island is accessible only by boat and is open only to educational or artistic groups.

St. Catherines Island

The New York Zoological Society has operated a captive breeding program for endangered animals on the island and has discouraged visitation. It's accessible by boat only.

Blackbeard Island

A federally owned and operated national wildlife refuge, Blackbeard is accessible only by boat, either from mainland marinas or via excursions from Sapelo Island.

Sapelo Island

Largely state owned and operated as a marine research center and refuge, Sapelo has daily ferry service; passage is restricted to public tours or overnight guests by advance reservation.

Wolf Island

A federally owned and operated national wildlife preserve, Wolf Island is accessible only by boat; it lacks the varied habitats of larger barrier islands.

Little St. Simons Island

Privately owned and operated as an exclusive (but rustic) resort, Little St. Simons is accessible only for guests by boat from St. Simons Island.

Sea Island

Accessible by car from St. Simons Island, Sea Island is home to the deluxe Cloister Hotel and tiny residential community.

St. Simons Island

Bridged to the mainland and developed since 1736,

St. Simons is accessible by car from Brunswick for vacationers interested in its rich history, scenic beauty, fun village, plenty of recreation and upscale beach resorts.

Jekyll Island

Once the exclusive preserve of wealthy tycoons, state-owned Jekyll Island is accessible by car from Brunswick; visitors are drawn to its attractive historic district and affordable family resorts and campground.

Cumberland Island

A national seashore maintained by the NPS, Cumberland is accessible by daily ferry service from St. Marys. Camping is permitted at a developed campground or at backcountry sites; exclusive private lodging is also available.

Little Cumberland Island

At the north tip of Cumberland Island, Little Cumberland is privately owned and accessible by ferry from Jekyll Island only for residents.

Subtropical Precautions

On remote islands, transportation is by foot only, so wear comfortable walking shoes (in summer, choose light hiking shoes; for marsh exploration, bring old sneakers). Bring all food and plenty of water.

Overexposure is the number one medical emergency on the islands, so avoid the hottest times of day and confine strenuous outdoor activity to early morning or late afternoon. Wear sunscreen, sunglasses, and a hat (for the most protection, dress in lightweight, long-limbed clothing).

Carry insect repellent (locals favor Avon's Skin So Soft, available in local stores). Sand gnats act up in spring and fall and can be a nuisance on still days; if you can't choose a breezy day, see the beach early and retreat to the forest midday. Mosquitoes are most noticeable at dusk in the summer, in heavily wooded areas, or a week after heavy rains.

Avoid chiggers and ticks (found in high grass or thick woods) by dousing bare ankles and legs with repellent or tucking long pants into socks. Perform a thorough "tick check" after a wilderness hike; chiggers are harder to detect (if a red spot itches a few hours later, cover the area with clear nail polish to suffocate them).

Encounters with venomous snakes are rare; snakes are nocturnal, naturally cautious, and inactive in cold or hot weather. To be most cautious, stay on cleared trails, and watch where you place hands and feet—especially in woods, tall grass, or at the edge of low wet areas. If you plan on serious backcountry travel, you might consider a snakebite kit.

For the flip side, don't let caution overshadow the opportunity to see the wilder coast; spontaneous day-trippers armed with only a pair of shorts, a fanny pack of trail mix, and a sense of adventure might wonder what all the fuss was about. Determine your own measure of safety and margin for error, but remember that there's no backup if you've misjudged. Conserve emergency-rescue resources by being adequately prepared.

(Note: During winter hunting seasons, remote island preserves may be open to hunters only.)

village, Neptune Park, and lighthouse museum at the Atlantic shore. The historic district is on the west side of the island on the Frederica River, a drive up the commercial corridor of Frederica Road (veer left coming in off the causeway).

M The Village at St. Simons Island

The lively central village at Mallory Street and Kings Way consists of several blocks of attractive Victorian and modern storefronts that mix practical neighborhood shops with souvenir stands, gourmet restaurants, and margaritaville saloons. Mallory Street dead-ends into a public parking lot and public pier at Neptune Park.

Neptune Park

Within the compact bluff-side park, a Spanish-style civic center holds a small **visitors center,** a **library** (used paperbacks for sale, cheap), and the **Casino Theatre,** which hosts local theater productions, 912/638-3031. The Casino's public pool is open June–Aug. Tues.–Sat., 912/638-4722. Town festivals are often held in the park, including three days of Independence Day festivities leading up to fireworks on July 4th.

From Neptune Park you can board a **trolley tour,** 912/638-8954, to survey the island.

St. Simons Lighthouse Museum

Within Neptune Park, the historic St. Simons lighthouse and museum, 101 12th St., 912/638-4666, overlooks the village and coastline; climb the 129 steps for a panoramic view. The museum contains exhibits and presents slide shows on coastal history. They're open Mon.–Sat. 10 A.M.–5 P.M. and Sun. 1:30–5 P.M.; admission is $3 for adults and $1 for children.

South Point and East Beach

A short drive up Ocean Boulevard and east off Arnold Drive, **Massengale Park** provides beach access, parking, showers, and shady picnic sites in a wooded area adjacent to a wide stretch of beach.

East Beach, further north on Ocean Blvd. off 1st St., anchored by the old Coast Guard Station, provides a large exposed parking lot and boardwalk to a lifeguard-staffed beach. Next

St. Simons Lighthouse at Neptune Park

© KAP STANN

door, **Driftwood Nature Center,** 912/635-5032, offers educational programs and exhibits.

Bloody Marsh National Monument

Looking nearly as it must have when the British pummeled the Spanish in 1742, the Bloody Marsh Battle Site is as anticlimactic as the skirmish itself, impressive in its humility considering that the outcome decided control of the American continent. The National Park Service opens the gates 8 A.M.–4 P.M. daily (no charge), and there are no other services besides parking.

Fort Frederica National Monument

At a quiet, scenic bend in the Frederica River on the west side of the island, Fort Frederica National Monument, at the terminus of Frederica Rd., 912/638-3639, nps.gov/fofr, attests to the former glory of the fortified village established here by General James Oglethorpe in 1736. By the 1740s, Frederica was a thriving village of 500.

After the 1742 Battle of Bloody Marsh, however, the military threat from the Spanish declined, and the fort's regiment was soon disbanded.

With only the tabby outlines of the fortifications, barracks, and houses still visible, the site resembles a subtropical "Dogville." The museum contains artifacts found at the site, shows a film, and rents self-guided audio tours. Living-history programs are scheduled in the summer.

The gates open daily 8 A.M.–5 P.M.; the museum opens at 9 A.M. Admission to the site costs $5 per vehicle or $3 per person not arriving by car. Take Frederica Road (or the parallel bike path) a few miles north from the causeway to its conclusion.

Christ Church

In 1736, Methodism's founders John and Charles Wesley led services under the oak trees at the site of the present church. The congregation was officially formed in 1776, and the first church built here was largely destroyed by occupying Union troops during the Civil War. The current sanctuary, a stately, Gothic structure still set among the oaks in the scenic field, dates from 1886. The adjacent cemetery contains the graves of early settlers, marked with marble statues and stone grave markers shrouded by Spanish moss.

Christ Church is open daily 2–5 P.M. There's no charge, but donations are welcome. Find it off Frederica Road a half mile from Fort Frederica. Across the street, a short nature trail loops through a pretty patch of forest.

RECREATION

Water Sports

The premier outfitter on the Georgia coast, **SouthEast Adventure Outfitters,** 313 Mallory St., 912/638-6732, southeastadventure.com , is based in the village. They organize guided sea kayak and canoe trips, from two-hour outings to multiday excursions up and down the coast. Among their most popular local excursions is a three-hour guided sea kayak tour that samples a great variety of coastal ecology as it loops through the marsh and onto a remote beach (starting at $49, child discount, minimum 120

lbs. to ride independently, tandems also available for ages 6–12). The store stocks a great selection of outdoor gear and supplies, along with maps and guides that are hard to find elsewhere. It's open daily 10 A.M.–6 P.M.

The **Golden Isles Marina,** 206 Marina Dr. at the causeway, 912/634-1128, gimarina.com, is a major stop on the Intracoastal Waterway along the Eastern Seaboard, offering dockage and other services for visiting sailors. It's also the center for all kinds of water sports, including fishing charters, sailboat charters, parasailing rides, dolphin tours, and personal watercraft rentals. Several marine supply shops stock all matter of navigational resources and marine supplies, and a few popular restaurants and taverns at the marina are nice places to unwind after a day on the water, particularly at sunset.

The **Island Dive Center,** 912/638-6590, at the Golden Isles Marina, organizes scuba-diving trips to Gray's Reef and other submerged sites (inquire about the hidden treasure recently retrieved from a wreck three miles offshore). There are also personal watercraft rentals.

For a low-key motorboat rental and bait, try the small creek-side marina on the northeastern end of St. Simons Island at **Village Creek Landing,** 526 S. Harrington Rd., 912/634-9054; they have a no-frills restaurant there if you come back in empty-handed.

Inquire at the visitors center at the mainland side of the Torras causeway or at Georgia D.N.R. at the foot of the Sidney Lanier Bridge in Brunswick for helpful recreation guides listing local charter captains and other services and resources.

Golf

The island boasts several exclusive golf courses: **Sea Island Golf Club,** 912/638-5118 or 800/732-4752, where ruins of an old slave hospital remain visible; **Sea Palms Golf and Tennis Resort,** 912/638-3351 or 800/841-6268; and the King and Prince Resort's **Hampton Club,** 912/634-0255, which even has an island green. (Thrifty golfers find scenic courses on Jekyll Island for half the price as on St. Simons.) Many island hotels offer golf or tennis vacation packages with unlimited play.

Bicycling

The island's flat terrain and slow pace make it ideal for bicycling. A scenic, shady bike path runs from the village and beaches and follows Frederica Road north. Maps are available from the many bike rental outlets, such as **Benjy's Bike Shop,** 1300 Retreat Place, 912/638-6766, in front of the Winn-Dixie shopping center. Detour on shell roads to find secluded interior marshlands, Geechee communities, and old fish camps.

ENTERTAINMENT

The **Island Players,** 912/638-3031, a local theatrical group, presents productions of musicals and drama in the Casino Theatre in Neptune Park during their season from fall through spring.

Nightlife is centered along two blocks of Mallory Street downtown, a busy, lively scene where several saloons offer live music most summer nights—beach music and classic rock is most popular; there's also a karaoke place and blues.

Murphy's Tavern, on Mallory Street a half block north of Kings Way, is the best local watering hole and pool hall (closed Sun.), though the new **Village Pub** across the street is attracting locals to a more upscale setting.

On the north end, **Ziggy Mahoney's,** 5514 Frederica Rd., 912/634-0999, a corner club next to Bennie's Red Barn, comes to life at 8 P.M. with live music (favorite oldies, beach music, and sometimes audience participation skits) and a wide dance floor for a casually dressed-up older crowd. It's open Wed.–Sat.

There's a seven-screen **cinema multiplex,** 912/634-9100, at the Sea Island Shops mall at the intersection of Sea Island Road and Frederica Road.

Festivals

In March, there's a Fort Frederica Festival. In summer, Jazz in the Park stretches out from May to September. In July, St. Simon's celebrates Independence Day with festivities and fireworks at Neptune Park on July 4th. The Georgia Sea Island Festival is held in Neptune Park in mid-August.

ACCOMMODATIONS

St. Simons has a nice range of lodging choices from good to luxurious—you can't go wrong if you aim for the village or along the beachfront. A number of chain motels and hotels are located along Frederica Road, but there's no point in staying on the island and still having to drive to the beach (but you may end up there if you've arrived on a summer weekend without a reservation); these include a Days Inn, 912/634-0660, and Hampton Inn, 912/634-2204.

Note that summer rates may be twice as high as October to March off-season rates, weekday rates are generally lower than weekends and holidays, and ocean-view rooms may cost a third more than rooms facing inland.

$50–100

The United Methodist Church retreat center, **Epworth by the Sea,** 100 Arthur Moore Dr., 912/634-0642, welcomes all vacationers to its quiet compound overlooking the serene backriver marsh (a drive to the beach). Tidy guest rooms in an older motel complex (expansion is

© KAP STANN

hunting lodge at Little St. Simons Island

under way) are inexpensive (around $65 in season) and they have a pool, pier, tennis courts, and a good, inexpensive cafeteria. Alcohol is prohibited on site. Also on site are a church and two restored tabby cabins that once held enslaved families.

The best economical choice is the 23-room **Ⲙ Queens Court,** 437 Kings Way at Mallory, 912/638-8459, a nicely shaded two-story original court motel right in the center of the action and a busy block away from the beach (rates start at $65; more for efficiencies and suites). There is no pool.

The modern 34-room **St. Simons Inn by the Lighthouse,** 609 Beachview Dr., 912/638-1101, is a 34-room newer motel built atop its garage (rooms with microwaves and refrigerators start at $80 with continental breakfast). It has a pool, some kitchens, and is conveniently set across from Neptune Park at a slightly less hectic corner than Queens Court.

$100–150

The 48-room beachfront **Ⲙ Sea Gate Inn,** 1014 Ocean Blvd., 912/638-8661 or 800/562-8812, is a quiet, older, two-story oceanfront motel under a half-mile from the village. From the exterior, it doesn't make much of an impression, but inside, a bright, spacious lobby opens out to a nice V-shaped layout of two wings set around a pool and landscaped grassy courtyard, separated from the beach by high shrubs that provide privacy (rooms with kitchens start at $100).

The 28-room **Ⲙ Village Inn,** 500 Mallory St., 912/634-6056 or 888/635-5111, is a nice new choice, though you may not know it to look at the courtyard 1930s design already lushly overgrown (they won an environmental-design award for building around the live oaks on site). Right downtown, the contemporary inn is set around an old beach cottage that now serves as a pub and breakfast room. They have a pool, and most rooms have small ironwork balconies (rates start at $140 with deluxe continental breakfast). They're across from the Dairy Queen and Murphy's Tavern.

Over $150

For more than 65 years, the **Ⲙ King and Prince Beach and Golf Resort,** 201 Arnold Rd., 912/638-3631 or 800/342-0212, has presided over a wide stretch of beach under a mile east from the village. The sprawling three-story Mediterranean-style oceanfront hotel features an elegant dining room, a casual bar-and-grill, cafés (including a Starbucks), tennis courts, and five pools indoors and out. It offers all the typical resort amenities without the customary isolation; you can walk to town or to local restaurants. Room rates start at $180; new two- and three-bedroom villas are also available (a more attractive alternative than the island's boxy condominium developments further up the sand). Inquire about package golf plans at their Hampton Club course.

Several new four-story condominium developments at East Beach may resemble beach houses on steroids; nevertheless, they're right at the sand and big enough for families vacationing together. For two- and three-bedroom units at **Beach Club,** 1140 Ocean Blvd.; **North Breakers,** 1470 Wood Ave.; or **Shipwatch,** 1524 Wood Ave., call 912/638-5450 or 888/787-4666.

FOOD AND DRINK

Typical island style is to have breakfast at your hotel, lunch at popular cafés in the village, and dinner at one of the venerated island restaurants that generations of loyal vacationers look forward to returning to every summer.

Breakfast and Lunch

Frannie's Place, 318 Mallory St., 912/638-1001, offers breakfast all day, signature crab cakes, and award-winning Brunswick stew, along with salads and vegetarian entrées (under $10) in a homey yellow cottage in the center of downtown. It's open for breakfast and lunch Wed.–Sat.

Fourth of May Cafe, 444 Ocean Blvd. at Mallory St., 912/638-5444, offers full griddle breakfast daily 7 A.M.–1 P.M. and lunch/supper 11 A.M.–9 P.M. in their workaday corner café. Daily Southern meat-and-two specials (pot roast, jambalaya, baked chicken) with cornbread and two sides run $7.50; they also make deli sandwiches for there or to go, along with a handy selection of beer and wine.

More Southern specials are on the menu at **Barbara Jean's,** 214 Mallory St., 912/634-6500, such as crab cakes, catfish, and vegetable plates (entrées start at $8). There are also meal-size salads topped with grilled salmon or chicken. It's open daily 11 A.M.–10 P.M.

Mullet Bay, 512 Ocean Blvd., with its wrap-around veranda and giant palms, makes a nice spot for a cool afternoon tea (or piña colada), but the food is less distinctive than the setting.

Bargain hunters will enjoy the cafeteria at **Epworth by the Sea,** 100 Arthur Moore Dr., 912/634-0642, which serves three good hearty meals a day at low prices at the Methodist retreat center along the scenic back river.

Pick up fresh seafood to go at **Gisco,** 2020 Demere Rd. at Frederica Rd., 912/638-7546, by the airport traffic light—the place offers low country boil (shrimp, sausage, cob corn and red potatoes), steamed shrimp by the pound, crab soup, seafood gumbo, and dips and spreads by the pint. It's open Tues.–Sat. 9 A.M.–6 P.M. A convenient package store next door sells beer and wine.

Seafood and Steak Dinners

On Ocean Boulevard near East Beach are two side-by-side seafood restaurants, **Crabdaddy's Seafood Grill,** 1217 Ocean Blvd., 912/634-1120, and the **Crab Trap,** 1209 Ocean Blvd., 912/638-3552. They're both lively, popular spots for oysters, rock shrimp, and other seafood served fried, blackened, or grilled (entrées start at $15). At the Crab Trap, wear the bib or not, and toss your shells in the hole in the center of the table when you're done; Crabdaddy's sautées things in merlot. They attract the resort set from the King and Prince just down the way, but they're casual and welcome all comers. The party crowd in the parking lot drinking wine as they wait for tables is a scene in itself. Both restaurants are open for dinner at 5 P.M. nightly in season.

A couple of miles from the village, **Bennie's Red Barn,** 5514 Frederica Rd., 912/638-2844, at South Harrington Road, is a 50-year tradition on the north end—it's a little clubby, but it's a big place with a wide choice of well-prepared, generous plates of seafood, wood-fired steaks (including a 24oz. T-bone), salads, a children's menu,

and great cheesecake (though they're known for pecan pie and key lime pie). Entrées start at $14. It's open for dinner at 6 P.M. nightly in season. Live music (mostly boomer oldies) is featured next door Wed.–Sat.

A very casual alternative is **Village Creek Landing,** 526 S. Harrington Rd., 912/634-9054. In an isolated corner of the island, the Landing serves no-frills steamed or fried shrimp, crab, oysters, and combination platters accompanied by cold pitchers of beer in a two-story wooden cabin overlooking the marsh. Dinner is served Thurs.–Sun. starting at 6 P.M. (closed in winter). It's a beautiful spot to watch a panoramic sunset. Their small creek-side marina sells bait and rents boats.

INFORMATION AND SERVICES

A small **visitors center** at Neptune Park distributes information on area sights and lodging 9 A.M.–5 P.M. daily. The small commercial center in the village contains a coin-operated laundry, minimart, and used bookstore.

Out Frederica Road near the airport you'll find the central business activity: supermarkets, shopping malls, banks, office centers, and gas stations.

The closest full-service medical facility is on the mainland; call the **Southeast Georgia Regional Medical Center,** 3100 Kemble Ave., Brunswick, 912/264-7000.

SEA ISLAND

Separated from St. Simons Island by a small stream, Sea Island protects a tony enclave of imposing residential estates and the preeminent Cloister Hotel. To reach the island, take Sea Island Road across St. Simons Island, and cross the bridge over the marshlands. The island is open to residents and hotel guests only.

Cloister Hotel

The world-class Cloister Hotel, Sea Island Dr., 912/638-3611, 800/SEA-ISLAND (800/732-4752), seaisland.com., occupies 57 acres at the southern end of Sea Island, from the marsh beach to miles of ocean sands. Sprawling Spanish-style buildings are surrounded by immaculately landscaped lawns, gardens, ponds, and live oak trees. This exclusive resort hosted the G-8 summit in 2004.

Here blue-blooded families find a familiarly formal style, impeccable service, and deluxe amenities. Two pools, four lounges, four restaurants, and a full-service spa serve guests in 269 rooms. A social, busy activities staff maintains a full schedule of kayaking, snorkeling, bicycling, food festivals, boat rides, ghost stories, children's programs, big band dancing. . . the works.

The **Sea Island Golf Club,** 912/638-5118, offers 54 holes open to guests only. The **Cloister Racquet Club** maintains 17 clay courts ("rested and groomed twice every 24 hours"). The **Sea Island Stables** provide horses for beach rides or instruction.

High-season rates at the hotel include three meals a day and start at around $400 a night for two people, including three meals daily; golf or tennis package rates include unlimited play.

LITTLE ST. SIMONS ISLAND

Now here's a real jewel. Little St. Simons Island, privately owned by the same family for generations, offers an exclusive retreat for the rich and rustic. The pristine 10,000-acre island harbors a compact combination of habitats: marsh, ocean, woodland, ponds, and a savannah that looks out of Africa. This diversity attracts more than 200 species of birds; experts say it's among the best bird-watching sites on the East Coast. Fallow deer (a European breed, smaller than the common white-tailed deer), old rice levees, shell middens, and seven miles of hard-packed sands are among the island's many other sights.

The island's rice plantation was owned by Pierce Butler, whose famous wife, British actress Fanny Kemble, chronicled antebellum life in her *Journal of a Residence on a Georgia Plantation,* an influential treatise against slavery.

At the turn of the 20th century, the island was sold to a pencil manufacturer who intended to farm the island's cedars. But the cedar turned

out to be too twisted to use, and the owner retained the island as a private retreat—the last family-owned barrier island in Georgia. In 1976, island housing was converted to an inn.

The Lodge on Little St. Simons Island

The innkeeper of the Lodge on Little St. Simons Island can be reached via post at P.O. Box 21078, St. Simons Island, GA 31522-0578, 912/638-7472 or 888/733-5774, fax 912/634-1811, littlestsimonsisland.com.

Overnight guests choose from two lodge rooms with two twin beds in each, a two-bedroom honeymoon cottage, or two modern four-bedroom cabins, all centrally located near a small shaded pool and dock. Guests may book individual rooms in the lodge or houses, whole cabins, or the whole island. Rooms are air-conditioned; no TVs or telephones are provided.

Hearty, healthy meals are served family-style in the hunting lodge (brook trout stuffed with wild rice was on the menu at a recent visit). A genteel cocktail hour before dinner also encourages socializing. The lodge comes fully stocked with board games, taxidermy, old family photos, and a library of books on local history and ecology.

Rates include all meals, recreation, and transportation to and from the dock at St. Simons, starting at $500 double for a two-twin lodge room in high season ($375 low season Jan. and Sept.). A double in Michael Cottage costs $550/$425 high/low season. To rent the whole island (sleeps 30) costs $6,500 in high season. Discounts for single occupancy, child occupancy, and weekly rates are available.

Staff naturalists and guides maintain a full slate of daily recreational activities: canoe trips, horseback riding, fly-fishing, birding, and interpretive programs. The bike barn is always open for leisurely rides along shell-and-sand roads to the beach and remote corners of the island.

The island's captain shuttles guests between Little St. Simons and the Hampton Club Marina, at the northern tip of St. Simons Island. Day trips may be available by prior arrangement—definitely a worthwhile prospect to experience a small slice of island life (call for schedule and fees).

Jekyll Island

State-owned Jekyll Island, a self-contained resort, is a playground of beach, bike paths, boat rides, golf courses, tennis courts, and a giant water park—all in a beautiful natural and historical setting with affordable accommodations and one of the best car-camping spots on the coast. Trade in the car as quickly as possible for bikes, in-line skates, golf carts, or flippers.

The island's premier hotel, the Jekyll Island Club Hotel, once served as the exclusive getaway of America's richest tycoons. In 1904, Jekyll Island was considered "the richest, most exclusive, most inaccessible club in the world." Today, it's among the most "democratic" subtropical islands in the world, as its operators act with near-missionary zeal to bring the former elite preserve "to the people."

It's very easy to visit Jekyll Island: you pay a $3 parking fee at the entrance gate and receive a map of every road, historic site, commercial enterprise, and special event venue. Amazingly, for such well-charted territory, there are still secluded corners—from deserted "boneyard" beaches and woods full of deer, to haunting tabby ruins strewn with languid Spanish moss, and serene marshlands inhabited only by egrets, herons, and fiddler crabs.

For maps and guides stop at the Jekyll Island Welcome Center, 912/635-3636 or 877/4JEKYLL (877/453-5955), jekyllisland.com, on the long causeway out to Jekyll.

HISTORY

Named for Sir Joseph Jekyll by General Oglethorpe, Jekyll Island was established as a Sea Island cotton plantation by French nobility escaping the French Revolution during the antebellum era. After the Civil War, a member of the remaining du Bignon family conceived of the idea of selling the island to a club of wealthy men—which seemed less far fetched after Thomas Carnegie, brother of Andrew Carnegie, bought property on Cumberland Island to the south.

Founding members included such famous names as Morgan, Rockefeller, Vanderbilt, and Pulitzer. Building the majestic Jekyll Island Club, club members also constructed individual family "cottages" the size of mansions around the club for their own use. From 1886 to 1942, they engaged in an opulent lifestyle of lawn parties, croquet, and elaborate feasts.

As the Depression took its toll and the tycoon era waned, so did Jekyll. When World War II brought threatening German submarines to coastal waters, it was considered incautious to concentrate so much wealth and power on one vulnerable island—it was estimated that winter residents controlled one-sixth of the world's wealth—and the club disbanded as families moved on to more modern resorts.

In 1946 the state went looking for a coastal island for a public park and found owners receptive. The island came under state control and was in turn leased to Jekyll Island Authority in 1950, a public-private partnership created in 1950, to operate as a resort. The clubhouse hotel closed in the early 1970s and sat vacant for more than a decade before historic preservation of "Millionaires' Village" became a priority and was recognized as a way to attract visitors. The strains of development versus environmental concerns led to legislation in the late 1990s limiting development to no more than 35 percent of upland acreage.

SIGHTS

Along the Atlantic shore, Jekyll offers 10 miles of wide white-sand beach for sunbathing, swimming, and beachcombing. The convention center is at the central dunes at the primary public beach; here too is a small commercial district. Much of the beach to either side is lined with motels. Golf courses are in the center of the island.

Jekyll Island National Historic Landmark District

Along the Jekyll River, the rambling four-story Queen Anne–style **Jekyll Island Club,** built in 1887, elegantly dominates Jekyll's 200-acre historic landmark district (with all those gazebos and turrets, it could fit as well into Nantucket). Surrounding it are 33 original 19th- and 20th-century buildings, including several restored millionaire cottages open to guided tours. The clubhouse and three cottages now constitute the Jekyll Island Club Hotel. Many of the outbuildings have been turned into shops.

For an historical overview, start at the stables. Here the **Island History Center,** on Stable Rd., 912/635-4036, offers an audio-visual presentation and historical photographs outlining the island's unusual history. It's open daily 9 A.M.–5 P.M.

From here **tram tours** depart several times during the day in season. Guides relate tales of the rich and famous with a zesty mix of awe and comeuppance. Tours range 45–90 minutes, including cottage interiors or not, and one tour focuses on historic preservation by taking guests into a house under restoration. Rates are $10–17.50 adults.

Of cottages open to drop-in visitors, **Goodyear Cottage,** on Riverview Dr., houses the Jekyll Island Arts Association, which displays different exhibits monthly. It's open Mon.–Fri. noon–4 P.M. and Sat.–Sun. 10 A.M.–4 P.M. Next door, **Mistletoe Cottage** showcases the work of Jekyll Island sculptor Rosario Flores; exhibit hours are 2–4 P.M. daily.

Faith Chapel, on Old Schoolhouse Lane, 912/635-3400, is open each afternoon 2–4 P.M. Built in 1904, the picturesque wooden chapel is ornamented by stained-glass windows designed by Louis Comfort Tiffany.

Horse-drawn **carriage rides** can be a nice way to view the historic district; they're available during the day from the Island History Center and around dusk at the bell stand of the Jekyll Island Club Hotel.

North End

North of the historic district along the back river, glistening tabby ruins are all that remain of colonial-era **Horton's Brewery** and the 1742 **Horton House** across the street, along with a small cemetery. Further up the route is the **Clam Creek Picnic Area** and the back river fishing pier, the campground, and **Driftwood Beach,** at the north tip.

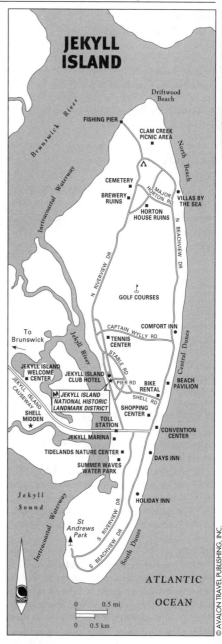

South End

Historically, the south end was where the island's African American community lived. Today, the south side is largely wild and dominated by the gigantic **Summer Waves Water Park** and **Tidelands Nature Center** next door, near the Jekyll Harbor Marina. Down at the southern tip, **St. Andrews Park** features a picnic area that overlooks St. Andrews Sound.

RECREATION

Water Sports

The **Summer Waves Water Park,** on Riverview Dr., 912/635-2074, summerwaves.com, provides 11 acres of rides and a million gallons of water in its wave pool, lazy river, and Pirates Passage—a completely enclosed speed flume in total darkness. Its three-story water slides can be seen popping out of the forest canopy from the mainland. There are kiddie rides for those under 48 inches tall, snack bars, and lockers. General admission is $17, $15 for those under 48 inches, age 3 and under free, and age 60 and over $10. Discounted admission after 4 P.M. is $9. It's open daily mid-May–mid-Aug. and weekends at the fringes. High-season hours are Sun.–Thurs. 10 A.M.–6 P.M., Fri–Sat. 10 A.M.–8 P.M.

Jekyll Island Marina, on the Intracoastal Waterway just south of the Jekyll River bridge, 912/635-3137, provides docking and services (such as showers and a pool) for visiting sailors, along with charter fishing trips and scenic boat tours.

In the historic district, **Jekyll Wharf,** 912/635-3152, also provides some charters and tours, and offers water taxi service to St. Simons Island.

For canoe rentals or guided kayak excursions, call the **Tidelands Nature Center,** 912/635-5032.

Fishing

A public pier at the north end of the island is popular for fishing and crabbing; there's also St. Andrews Park on the south end. Two freshwater lakes permit fishing; one of these is behind the outdoor amphitheater at the historic district, and the other is across from Villas by the Sea. Surf fishing is also permitted. A shop on the island rents rods; bait and tackle are available at several locations. Licenses can be obtained at the campground.

Golf

The first golf course was established on Jekyll Island in 1898. Today Jekyll is Georgia's largest public golf resort, with 63 holes on three 18-hole courses—Pine Lakes, Oleander, and Indian Mound, and the historic Great Dunes 9-hole course. Opened in 2002, Pine Lake includes "family tees" for beginners. Green fees for 18 holes are $40, or $57 with a cart. Call 912/635-2368 or email golf@jekyllisland.com up to six months in advance to reserve tee times.

Tennis

The **Jekyll Island Tennis Center,** just north of the historic district, 912/635-2074, features 13 clay courts, seven of which are lighted. Tournaments are held throughout the year, and tennis camps are available in summer.

Bicycling

The best way to get around is by bicycle; 20 miles of bike trails wind around the island. Rent bikes behind the miniature golf course across from the central dunes gazebo, or at hotels, or at the campground. The charge is around $10 per day. Tandems, kiddie seats, trailers, even surreys are widely available.

Horseback Riding

Victoria's Carriages, 912/635-9500, sponsors trail rides that depart from the Clam Creek picnic area at the northwestern end of the island Mon.–Sat., weather permitting. Reservations are required, call or inquire at the Island History Center, on Stable Road.

Birding

The **Coastal Birding Trail** identifies three spots around Jekyll particularly good for birding: on the causeway (watch for trail signs off Hwy. 520), at north end beach, and at south end beach.

Nature Walks

Tidelands Nature Center, next to Summer

Waves, 912/635-5032, conducts walking tours on local ecology and natural history, including nighttime turtle walks in nesting season from June through mid-August. Daytime walks generally start at 9 A.M. and cost $5 for adults and $3 for children.

ENTERTAINMENT

Performing Arts

Local theater troupes present performances at the amphitheater at the historic district, including the Jekyll Island Musical Theatre Festival, from late May through July.

Festivals

The island is known for its long-standing **Jekyll Island Bluegrass Festival,** now approaching its 30th year, held in January at the convention center. In late May, the season kicks off with a gigantic beach party, with sand-castle contests, kites, and concerts on the sand. Independence

© KAP STANN

Rah Bar at historic Jekyll Wharf

Day brings fireworks and festivities on July 4th. In December, historic homes are draped in Christmas decor for holiday tours.

Nightlife

You can hear live music on the historic Jekyll Wharf in summer. The Jekyll Island Club Hotel hosts a range of events in summer, from dinner dances to magic acts. Villas by the Sea has a karaoke bar. People in search of nightlife typically head to St. Simons to hear live music in the village.

ACCOMMODATIONS AND CAMPING

Jekyll has a diverse selection of good-value lodging at its premier hotel, condos, or motels and offers one of the best campgrounds on the coast.

Expect higher room rates in summer, weekend, and holiday periods; weekdays or the October-to-March off-season are lower. And ocean views command a premium. Prices quoted are for standard rooms in spring and summer. Most places offer package deals for golfers or tennis players.

The heart of the historic district, **M Jekyll Island Club Hotel,** 371 Riverview Dr., 912/635-2600 or 800/535-9547, jekyllclub.com, remains one of the landmark hotels on the Eastern Seaboard. Facing the scenic back-river marsh, the rambling four-story Victorian clubhouse features flagged turrets, balconies, verandas, and all modern conveniences, along with an outdoor pool, indoor tennis courts, and the only tournament-level croquet greensward within a 125-mile radius.

Inside, a refined decor has been restored to 19th-century elegance, with Grecian columns, arched doorways, leaded glass, and mahogany furnishings. Guest rooms are located within the clubhouse, the adjacent annex, the detached Sans Souci building of the same vintage, or within historic 1917 Crane Cottage and 1904 Cherokee Cottage, a stone's throw behind. In the clubhouse, they have a fine dining restaurant, a casual café, and a basement pub; in Crane Cottage, there's a Napa-style bistro. The hotel hosts a full calendar of recreation and entertainment, including children's programs, lectures on historical and ecological topics, tours, high tea, and a cooking school.

High-season rates start at $160 for a standard double; higher for cottage rooms, deluxe rooms, or suites. There are plenty of package rates—romantic getaway weekends and the like. Transit is available from surrounding airports, including Savannah and Jacksonville, as well as from the Amtrak station in Jesup.

Motels

Half a dozen oceanfront motels are strung along Beachview Drive, including such chains as the 84-room **Days Inn,** 912/635-9800 or 888/635-3003, close to the action on the beach; the 198-room **Holiday Inn,** 912/635-3311 or 800/7JEKYLL (800/753-5955), on the beach but further south somewhat isolated from the action; and **Quality Inn,** 912/635-2202 or 800/281-4446, in the center of the action but across the street from the beach (fine for golf- and tennis-prone adults, but not for surfbound kids crossing the main drag, as there's no light). The independent 38-unit **Beachview Club,** 912/635-2256 or 800/299-2228, is right on the beach, with two floors of efficiencies and suites nicely laid out around a palm-shaded courtyard pool.

All properties are well maintained and offer nice amenities, with fairly comparable rates starting at $100 double in the high summer season (slightly more for Beachview; slightly less for the Quality Inn; also note the Holiday Inn cuts its rates nearly in half after Labor Day).

Condos and Cottages

At the secluded north end, **N Villas by the Sea,** 912/635-2521 or 800/841-6262, rents one- to three- bedroom townhouses on 17 beautifully wooded acres right at the beach. Spacious two-story condos have all the comforts of home (they may be bigger than home), including complete kitchens with dishwashers and coffeemakers, two bathrooms, TVs in the living room and each bedroom, ceiling fans, and balconies. The complex has a shaded pool, restaurant, karaoke bar, and coin-operated laundry. A two-person minivilla starts at $120; a four-person two-bedroom starts at $160.

Vacation homes on the island are rented out by **Jekyll Realty,** 912/635-3301; or **Parker-Kaufman Realtors,** 912/635-2512.

Camping

One of the best car-camping spots on the coast is under the live oaks and Spanish moss at the 206-site **N Jekyll Island Campground,** 912/635-3021 or 866/658-3021, on 18 wooded acres at the north end of the island across from the backriver fishing pier. Only the periphery sites have much privacy, but all are nicely set under the canopy. Tent sites are $19 a night, or $28 for full hookups (including cable; a disposal station is also available). There's a 14-day limit in the high season. A small store open long hours sells food, ice, bait, propane, and other supplies, and rents bikes—it also serves as a neighborhood gathering place, with porch rockers out front to encourage conversation.

FOOD AND DRINK

Historic District

At the Jekyll Island Club Hotel, within the expansive Victorian room overlooking Jekyll River, the **Grand Dining Room,** 912/635-2600, is open daily for three meals during the week and lavish brunches on Sunday ($25 adults). The dinner menu reflects classic low country cuisine with such specialties as Georgia white shrimp and fresh crab, along with continental lamb and steak entrées. With entrées starting at $20 (and early bird specials 6–6:45 P.M. for $22), prices are reasonable, considering the refined setting and service. Breakfast and lunch are casual, but dinner is formal; men wear jackets, and some women wear long skirts. A **Victorian tea** is served daily 4–5:30 P.M. in the Riverview Lounge off the dining room.

Courtyard at Crane, within the center courtyard and loggia of the hotel's Italian Renaissance villa, serves Napa-style specials the likes of lobster-salad croissant sandwiches and Mediterranean platters of grilled vegetables and fresh mozzarella. Alfresco lunches are served daily; dinner is served Sun.–Thurs. starting at 5:30 P.M.

For breakfast and light lunches, **Cafe Solterra**

starts with sticky buns and Danishes and moves into healthy soups, salads, and sandwiches, and tasty snacks (there's also beer and wine). The hotel also has a pool bar for alfresco dining and a small basement pub that serves bar food.

Across from the hotel on the wharf, **Latitude 31,** 912/635-3800, offers an indoor air-conditioned restaurant overlooking the river and marsh for a dinner clientele largely drawn from the hotel, but if you head to the back you'll find the more casual **M Rah Bar** for you-peel-'em shrimp or low country boil ($19 single, $33 double) inside at the six-stool bar or outside at patio tables at the edge of the wharf (lunch or dinner). They're both closed on Mondays.

Outside the Historic District

At the Jekyll Harbor Marina just south of the bridge, **SeaJay's Waterfront Cafe,** 912/635-3200, serves buffet-style low country boil (crab and shrimp served with corn, sausage, and red potatoes) and local-favorite Brunswick stew, indoors or out in a friendly pub atmosphere. Beyond that, you're down to family restaurants in motels or the golf clubhouse. Note that the Huddle House is open 24 hours.

SERVICES

A small strip shopping center where the main road dead-ends at the ocean features a pharmacy, 912/635-2246; post office, 912/635-2625; a hardware store that sells fishing licenses and rents rods and reels; coin-operated laundry; a bank with a 24-hour ATM; clothing and souvenir shops; a market that sells produce and groceries and rents videos and VCRs; and a Flash Foods minimart open long hours. The nearest full-service supermarket is in Brunswick.

Within the historic district, upscale shops sell gifts, clothing, jewelry, and Christmas ornaments. **Jekyll Books and Antiques,** 912/635-3077, sells old and rare books from within historic Furness Cottage. The **Commissary,** 912/635-2878, sells gourmet coffee and tea and other specialty food items; the **Island Sweet Shoppe,** 912/635-3135, offers fudge, chocolates, and ice cream. There's also a flower shop and gift shop within the hotel.

St. Marys, Gateway to Cumberland Island

The premier attraction of the southern Atlantic coast is Cumberland Island, a pristine barrier island protected and managed by the national park system. Overlooking the looming wilderness of Cumberland across the marsh, the city of St. Marys is home to the NPS dock that ferries passengers and campers over to the island. The small downtown at the waterfront is a pleasant place to start off or wind up a day on the island, with several restaurants and cafés and a few places to stay within walking distance of the dock.

Inexpensive modern motels can be found around I-95 in St. Marys and neighboring Kingsland—be sure to leave in plenty of time to drive the few miles to the water; traffic police are prepared to cite drivers speeding to catch the ferry. Crooked River State Park makes a nice rustic base of operations (the same caution applies).

Getting There

Southbound drivers can continue along Hwy. 17 south of the Golden Isles for a back-road route to St. Marys, but frankly, this stretch west of I-95 doesn't hold as strong and appeal, so drivers may prefer just to hop on I-95 and exit at Hwy. 40 to reach St. Marys.

St. Marys is 20 miles north of Jacksonville International Airport in Jacksonville, Florida.

HISTORY

St. Marys has three oddly juxtaposed major industries: not only is it the point of departure for one of the Atlantic Seaboard's most pristine ecological marvels, but it is also home to the Kings Bay Naval Submarine Base (where nuclear-powered subs are made) and the site of a huge odoriferous paper and pulpwood mill. (You can usually identify at a

The Coast

glance which of these three concerns draws people to town.)

The town started out as a Timucuan Indian village, visited by French Huguenots in 1562 and settled by the Spanish a few years later. The Spanish occupation lasted about a hundred years, until the British forced their retreat into Florida.

In the mid-18th century, a band of exiled Acadians ended up settling here after they were denied refuge in Savannah (the British there feared the Catholic Cajuns would act as spies for the marauding French or Spanish). Before long, the Cajuns picked up and moved again, this time to the French colony of Santa Domingo (Haiti). The slave rebellion there displaced them once more, and some of those families returned to St. Marys. You can still make out the French names on grave markers in historic Oak Grove Cemetery.

SIGHTS

Downtown Waterfront

The center of the action is where the main Osborne Street drag meets St. Marys Street along the waterfront. Several blocks of commercial development line both streets either side of this intersection. The *Cumberland Queen* ferry dock is on St. Marys Street a block south of Osborne.

Next door to the dock, the city's **Waterfront Park,** with its fountain, flowers, and porch swings, makes a lovely place to linger while waiting to board. A walk further down St. Marys Street leads to a marsh boardwalk and Oak Grove Cemetery.

Orange Hall

Along Osborne Street, the three-story Greek Revival mansion called **Orange Hall,** 912/576-3644, at the corner of Conyers, is now an antebellum house museum. It's open for tours ($3) Mon.–Sat. 9 A.M.–5 P.M. and Sun. 1–5 P.M.

Orange Hall also houses the **St. Marys Welcome Center** on the ground level (same hours). The Historic Register house heads up a couple of blocks of attractive 19th- and early 20th-century homes, churches, and commercial buildings (descriptive historic markers at the sidewalk include Braille translations).

Cumberland Island National Seashore Museum

The NPS Seashore Museum, 201 Osborne at Bryant St., 912/882-4336, contains artifacts ranging from Native American basketry to ornate silver settings, illustrating the island's diverse history. It's open 1–4 P.M. daily; no charge.

Submarine Museum

The Submarine Museum, 102 W. St. Marys St., 912/882-ASUB (912/882-2782), occupies a converted movie house on the waterfront. It contains a periscope, torpedo models, deep-sea diving suit, subs from World War I to the Trident, and a display dedicated to the eight submariners who received Medals of Honor. Admission is $2 for adults and $1 for children. It's open Tues.–Sat. "1000–1600" and Sun. "1300–1700."

RECREATION

Paddling Excursions

Up the Creek, 111 Osborne St., 912/882-0911, offers kayaking instruction and local tours; also inquire about bike rentals.

The St. Simons–based **SouthEast Adventure Outfitters,** 912/638-6732, southeastadventure.com, runs kayaking excursions from the mainland to the less-traveled northern end of Cumberland Island, dodging manatees and submarines. A three-day trip including boats, guides, food, and gear runs around $325 per person.

Many trips start at Crooked River State Park (see that section), which also offers fishing and hiking.

Festivals

St. Marys celebrates St. Patrick's Day on March 17; hosts a Mardi Gras parade the Saturday before Mardi Gras; has fireworks on July 4th; and hosts a Rock Shrimp Festival the first Saturday in October.

Neighboring Kingland's Catfish Festival, on Labor Day weekend (catfishfestival.org), is a major regional event, drawing folks from up and down the coast for two days of live entertainment, bike rides, a 5K run, a parade led by Cecil the Catfish, and of course, plenty of fried catfish and other regional culinary specialties.

© KAP STANN

Cumberland Island

ACCOMMODATIONS

Downtown Waterfront

The **N Riverview Hotel,** 105 Osborne St., 912/882-3242 or 888/882-1807, has anchored the waterfront commercial district since 1916. With its checkerboard linoleum foyer, worn wooden check-in counter, and flocked wallpaper, it's a vintage throwback to boardinghouse days. Eighteen simple guest rooms on the 2nd floor, each with private bath, open up to a wraparound veranda with a view of the docks and Cumberland Island. A bar and restaurant occupy the ground floor. Rooms run around $65 and include a continental breakfast.

Two bed and breakfast inns down the block are set in two-story clapboard houses with wide verandas and period-furnished guest rooms (starting around $90, including a full breakfast): the **Goodbread House,** 209 Osborne St., 912/882-7490, and **Spencer House Inn,** 101 E. Bryant St., 912/882-1872.

Motels

The **Cumberland Kings Bay Lodges,** 603 Sand Bar Dr., 912/882-8900 or 800/831-6664, is con-

veniently located off Hwy. 40, four miles from the ferry dock. The modern motel has efficiencies, a nice pool, and a grassy lawn topped with a gazebo (rooms start at $39).

A dozen chain motels can be found on Hwy. 40 around I-95 exit 1 in Kingsland, including **Best Western,** 912/729-7666; **EconoLodge,** 912/673-7336; **Hampton Inn,** 912/729-1900; **Super 8,** 912/729-9600; and **Jameson Inn,** 912/729-9600.

FOOD AND DRINK

Downtown Waterfront

Arrive nice and early for your ferry and have breakfast across from the ferry dock at the **Riverside Café,** 106 W. St. Marys St., 912/882-3466. It's open daily 7 A.M.–9 P.M. year-round for breakfast, lunch, and dinner. A well-turned breakfast plate of eggs, grits, and toast is $3.

Seagle's Waterfront Cafe, 912/882-4187, within the Riverview Hotel at the corner of Osborne and St. Marys Streets, serves rock shrimp along with other seafood and steaks for lunch and dinner in a corner place at the riverfront (closed Sun.). You can order from the same menu across the lobby at **Seagle's Saloon,** a colorful joint for watching sports, hearing live music on weekend nights, or just conversing with the locals at the bar or at tables inside and out (open nightly).

M Lang's Seafood Restaurant, 307 St. Marys St., 912/882-4432, offers steaks and seafood straight off the boat from their marina down the block. The marsh-front restaurant commands a beautiful view of the water, and it's a nice walk down from the ferry dock (a park on one side, a marsh boardwalk on the other). Lunch and dinner are served Thurs.–Sat.

Across from the ferry dock, **Trolley's Bar and Grill,** 104 W. St. Marys St., 912/882-1525, is a cheery pub for peel-and-eat shrimp, burgers, and kid food. **Greek Mediterranean Grill,** 112 Osborne St., 912/576-2000, offers traditional Greek specialties such as moussaka and dolmas, along with American dishes.

INFORMATION AND SERVICES

Within Orange Hall, on the corner of Osborne and Conyers Streets downtown, the **St. Marys Welcome Center,** 912/882-4000 or 800/868-8687, stmaryswelcome.com, distributes information on attractions, lodging and dining. It's three blocks from the waterfront.

Two large shopping centers on Hwy. 40, on either side of the intersection with Charlie Smith Sr. Hwy., are anchored by major supermarket chains. A few small shops downtown stock sunscreen, insect repellent, and other necessities.

CROOKED RIVER STATE PARK

Crooked River State Park, 6222 Charlie Smith Sr. Hwy., 912/882-5256, gastateparks.org, sits on a low secluded bluff overlooking the beautiful sound and marshlands. The 500-acre park lies on a seven-mile dead end of Spur 40, so stock up before you arrive. The parking fee is $2 per car.

The park's features includes a pool, a boat launch popular with anglers, and 1.5-mile nature trail that winds through the maritime forest and salt marsh. On the way to the park, in the thick woods across from the nuclear submarine base, you can see the tabby ruins of the 1825 McIntosh Sugar Works.

Cottages and Camping

The park has 11 fully equipped cottages with screened-in porches, nicely set overlooking the marsh ($85–110 a night for two bedrooms).

A campground has 62 sites surrounded by woods; they're perhaps better for RVs, but tents are OK too. It's best at the periphery ($20–22 per night).

For lodging or camping reservations, call 800/864-7275 or see gastateparks.org.

SATILLA RIVER

The blackwater Satilla River rises in the middle of South Georgia and courses through a winding route lined with cypress trees and white sandbars into St. Andrews Sound east of Woodbine. The Satilla offers mellow paddling, fishing, and camping adventures—ideal for families.

St. Simons–based **SouthEast Adventure Outfitters,** 912/638-6732, southeastadventure.com, runs kayaking excursions down the river. Day trips run $80 with lunch. Overnight trips may include a stay in a private riverfront lodge; see satillalodge.com.

Cumberland Island

The premier attraction of the southern Atlantic coast is Cumberland Island, a pristine barrier island protected and managed by the national park system. To preserve the natural environment and wilderness experience, only a limited number of visitors are allowed over to the national seashore each day. You can camp and backpack, or explore the trails, beach, and history of Georgia's largest and southernmost barrier islands.

HISTORY

The Timucuan inhabited Cumberland Island for more than 3,000 years. A tribe distinct from the Creek of the northern islands, the Timucuan lived similarly, depending on oysters as a primary food source and discarding the shells in huge mounds (middens), which are now typically found near cedar groves. (Cedar is one of the few plants able to root in the high alkaline soil produced by eroding shells; look for cedars at the marsh fringes of Cumberland's forests to find middens.)

In the late 16th century, Spanish soldiers and priests built forts and missions on the islands, though the only remnants of their hundred-year occupation are the wild horses on the island—believed to have descended from Spanish herds. Native rebellions, pirates, and threats from the hovering French and English finally persuaded the missionaries to abandon attempts to convert the Timucuan to Christianity, and the island returned to Timucuan control.

Oglethorpe Establishes First Dungeness

In 1736, General James Oglethorpe, extending his domain south after founding the new Georgia colony at Savannah, built two forts on the island and a hunting lodge he called Dungeness at its southern end.

Skirmishes were fought with the Spanish, but the island remained essentially uninhabited until Revolutionary War General Nathaniel Greene bought the island, logged the live oaks for the Navy's sailing ships, and built a house he called Dungeness as well. Fire destroyed the house a hundred years later, and his heirs abandoned the island.

Carnegie Era

In 1881, Thomas Carnegie (brother of Andrew Carnegie) bought much of the island and built yet another house at the former Greene homesite. Carnegie's mansion burned down in 1959, but the ruins are still visible today, surrounded by the old stables, carriage houses, and other outbuildings.

Carnegie's widow, Lucy, built homes on the island for each of her children, and of these, **Plum Orchard** is overdue for restoration and is occasionally open to tours. Another, **Greyfield,** is operated as an exclusive lodge by Carnegie heirs, and two other homes remain in use on pockets of private property.

© KAP STANN

"boneyard" beach

At the northern tip of the island, a small freeman's community dating back to the 1890s remains at the Settlement, centered around First African Baptist Church. This tiny white sanctuary built in the 1930s was where the late John F. Kennedy, Jr. and Carolyn Bessette were married.

National Seashore Established

The park service bought most of the island in 1972 to establish the Cumberland Island National Seashore, and in 1982, the northern part of the island was designated a wilderness area.

SIGHTS

On a day trip, a good strategy is to get off at the Dungeness (first) stop, see the historic sites, head out to the beach and go north along the sand, then loop back across the dunes at the campground to catch the ferry back from the Sea Camp dock. Watch for dune crossing markers, and leave ample time to get back to the dock; if you miss the ferry, you'll have to charter a boat back.

There's also a marsh trail at the southern tip of the island (disembark at Dungeness, walk out to the beach, and turn right), which leads to boardwalks over the marsh and dunes, and the trails through the forest between the two docks (the River Trail or Nightingale Trail).

Rangers offer guided history walks, nature walks, seine netting workshops, and short videos or movies among their daily programs.

Dungeness Historic Sites

The first ferry stop docks near the Dungeness historical site. Here a small museum (the old icehouse) tells the story of the Native American islanders, European exploration and settlement, Sea Island cotton, and of the families who lived here in the high-style plantation era.

The ruins of Dungeness, the 1884 home built by the Carnegies atop the ruins of the original Dungeness house of Nathanael Greene's widow, can be seen along the short walk between the west-side dock and the east-side beach.

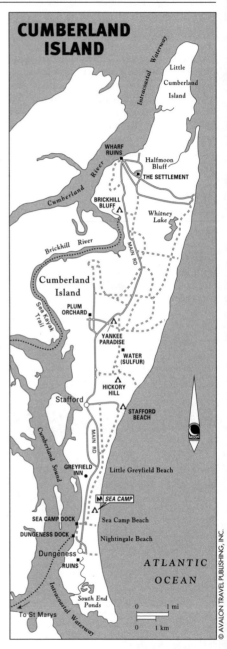

Plum Orchard

Considered by the World Monuments Fund to be one of the world's top 100 endangered historic sites, Plum Orchard is an 1898 Greek Revival mansion built by the Carnegies and donated to the National Park Foundation by family members on 1971. Rangers occasionally lead tours of the vacant site, which is overdue for restoration. Inquire at the visitors center.

ACCOMMODATIONS AND CAMPING

The Greyfield Inn, 904/261-6408 or 800/292-6480, greyfieldinn.com, operates out of a four-story mansion built in 1901, once a winter retreat for the Carnegie family. Still in family hands, the beautiful period-furnished house (right down to the original family china) sits on a 1,300-acre private compound in the midst of the national parklands. The house's library, porch swings, honor bar, bicycles, marsh shore, and easy access to the beach complement 11 guest rooms in the main house (three with private baths). The place evokes "the slightly down-at-the-heels retro elegance of faded aristocracy," as described by the *New York Times,* along with all the quirkiness of a century-old house sitting on a salt marsh island—delicate plumbing and the like. One of the last holdouts to 20th-century modernity, innkeepers finally relented and installed air-conditioning a few years back.

Rates start at $350 a night for one or two people and include a private ferry to and from the island, breakfast, picnic lunches, and elegant formal dinners of poached salmon and the like—jackets are required for men. (The innkeeper tells the story of a sparky camping couple who made dinner reservations, hauled a white dinner jacket and heels along with their camping gear, and enjoyed an elegant dinner around the table with the inn guests before heading back to camp!) Bicycle use and naturalist-led tours are also included.

Greyfield's ferry runs from Fernandina Beach, Florida, where the inn's administrative office is located. Jacksonville International Airport is 29 miles away; local limousine services provide transportation from the airport to the dock for around $40.

Sea Camp

Visitors may camp overnight at the Sea Camp campground ($4 a night) or at primitive backcountry sites ($2) for a maximum of seven nights; advance reservations are required. Upon arrival, campers disembark at the second island stop (Sea Camp), where sites are assigned. It's a short quarter-mile walk to the campground. Some wooden "pony" carts are available to haul gear, but these can be awkward unless you're a pony. If you can rig something with a strong-wheeled luggage carrier that'll transport a packed ice chest over a bumpy shell road, so much the better.

The Sea Camp campground, sheltered by a 15-foot-high dune and a thick canopy of stunted oaks, is carved out of the dense palmetto substory. Well-secluded sites round out like little private nests, each with a picnic table, a small latched food locker (string up or secure the rest of your food), and ample space to set up one or more tents. Two group camps accommodate 12 people maximum at each site. The bathhouse has toilets and cold-water showers.

Backpacking: Backpackers must register at the visitors center after disembarking to obtain backcountry permits and sign up for one of four primitive camping areas. Each has a well nearby, but you must treat the water before drinking.

GETTING THERE

A private concessionaire operates a public passenger ferry (no cars, bikes, or pets) from St. Marys to Cumberland Island. Though not required, reservations are highly recommended and are accepted up to six months in advance. Cumberland allows only 300 people a day, a limit quickly reached on certain days in popular seasons. The island is closed to visitors during five annual deer hunts in winter.

Once you have reservations, arrive at the St. Marys dock 30 minutes before departure with adequate food, water, and supplies for a day's outing; a tiny concession on the boat sells sodas and some packaged snacks. Passengers receive a trail map and ranger orientation before departure. The ferry does not transport bicycles or pets.

Day-trippers can choose to get off at either at the Dungeness or Sea Camp dock. All overnighters disembark at Sea Camp. Drinking water and restrooms are available at both docks, with more in the campground and historical area.

Private boats may dock at Sea Camp, near the ranger station, for day-use only—first-come, first-served. Call ahead and let them know of your arrival. Beware if approaching from the north—according to rangers, St. Andrews Sound is the third most dangerous inlet on the East Coast.

LITTLE CUMBERLAND ISLAND

Off the northern tip of Cumberland Island, Little Cumberland Island holds a privately owned community accessible by members of the home-owners association only; a ferry operates from Jekyll Island for residents. Also, according to the Georgia Department of Natural Resources, the island is also home to one of the oldest logger-head sea turtle research projects in the world.

AMELIA ISLAND, FLORIDA

Around 25 miles south of the Georgia line via I-95 or the two-lane Hwy. 17 to Hwy. A1A east, Amelia Island is a developed resort island, the northern-most barrier island in Florida. In fact, resort development here is quite a contentious subject—see John Sayles's 2002 film *Sunshine State,* which addresses development pressures on Amelia Island.

The historic downtown is centered at Atlantic Avenue and Centre Street, home to antique and vintage flea-market shops, several B&Bs, restaurants, and cafés. Here the **N Florida House Inn,** 20 S. 3rd St., 904/261-3300, offers all-you-can-eat Southern boardinghouse meals for lunch and dinner as they have since 1857. The menu varies daily, but typically includes such entrées as fried chicken, fish fillets, broccoli casserole, cheese grits, coleslaw, biscuits, and cornbread. The fixed price, around $12 per person (child discounts), includes dessert and iced tea. Lunch is served Tues.–Sat. 11:30 A.M.–2:30 P.M.; dinner is served

5:30–9 P.M.; Sun. brunch 10:30 A.M.–2 P.M. They also offer lodging upstairs in 14 air-conditioned bedrooms and one suite, starting at $120 for doubles, including a full Southern breakfast.

Nearby, **Fort Clinch State Park,** 904/277-7274, preserves an 1847 fort occupied by Confederate forces during the Civil War and reactivated during the Spanish-American War in 1898. The park also offers beach access, fishing in the ocean or Cumberland Sound, and a nature trail through a coastal hammock.

Around the rest of the island, you'll find older motels along the northern portion of the beach-front road. Further south, the beachfront is dominated by the **Amelia Island Plantation Resort,** 800/874-6878, and other exclusive resort developments.

CUMBERLAND ISLAND FERRY SERVICE

Spring, Summer, and Fall Schedule: From Mar. 1–Nov. 30; ferries depart daily. Ferry departs St. Marys: 9 A.M., 11:45 A.M.
Ferry departs Cumberland Island: 10:15 A.M., 4:45 P.M. daily, also 2:45 P.M. Wed.–Sat.

Winter Schedule: From Dec. 1–Feb. 28; ferries depart Thurs.–Mon. (No ferry service is available Tues.–Wed. in winter).
Ferry departs St. Marys: 9 A.M., 11:45 A.M.
Ferry departs Cumberland Island: 10:15 A.M., 4:45 P.M.

Fares: Adults $12, seniors $9, children 12 years and under $7, plus a day-use fee of $4 per person per day.

Directions: Ferry boats depart from the NPS dock on St. Marys Street, in downtown St. Marys. From I-95 exit 3, follow Hwy. 40 east to waterfront. Arrive 30 minutes before departure (standby tickets can be available if there are no-shows). The boat ride takes 45 minutes.

Reservations and Information: Call 912/882-4335 or 888/817-3421 for reservations Mon.–Fri. 10 A.M.–4 P.M. Also see nps.gov/cuis.

Know
Georgia

The Land

From the air, Georgia resembles a giant green apron, with a ring of mountains at its neck and a waistband dividing the upper plateau from the wide skirt of the coastal plain. Two mighty Appalachian rivers string along its sides and define the state's territory; the Savannah River forms the border with South Carolina to the east, and the Chattahoochee River separates Georgia from Alabama to the west. In the north, Georgia shares a mountainous border with Tennessee and North Carolina; to the south lies Florida. To the southeast, a cool hundred miles of Atlantic coastline is fringed with islands as wild now as before the days of states and borders.

The 59,265-square-mile state blossoms to the surface with the lush seasonal landscapes the Southeast is famous for: colorful mountain forests and meadows, acres of cotton fields and peach orchards, and evergreen stands of Georgia pine. With this classic southeastern country, it's no wonder the region produced a culture so deeply rooted to the land. And Georgia, the largest state east of the Mississippi, has more of that land than anybody.

GEOGRAPHY

Appalachian Mountains

Georgia's rugged northern terrain comprises a compact set of three geological subregions, all part of the Appalachian mountain range: the **Blue Ridge Province** in the east, the steep **Cumberland Plateau** in the west, and the **Ridge-and-Valley** region in between.

The crashing together of continental plates some 300 million years ago sent these southern Appalachians towering as high as the Rockies, but since then, their once bare jagged peaks have eroded to well-worn mountaintops covered with forest. The softer central region eroded even further, creating the V-shaped Great Valley between the two rounded ranges.

This high valley cut a natural route both for the railroad tracks that put Atlanta on the map in 1843, and for the invading Union army of William Tecumseh Sherman that burnt it to the ground 21 years later. Now the modern trail of I-75 slices through it, bisecting the state and carrying winter-weary Midwesterners to warm southern beaches.

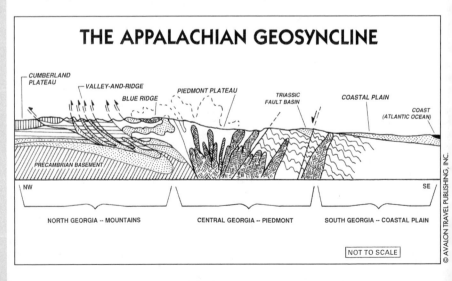

THE APPALACHIAN GEOSYNCLINE

CUMBERLAND PLATEAU · VALLEY-AND-RIDGE · BLUE RIDGE · PIEDMONT PLATEAU · TRIASSIC FAULT BASIN · COASTAL PLAIN · COAST (ATLANTIC OCEAN)

PRECAMBRIAN BASEMENT

NW · SE

NORTH GEORGIA -- MOUNTAINS · CENTRAL GEORGIA -- PIEDMONT · SOUTH GEORGIA -- COASTAL PLAIN

NOT TO SCALE

© AVALON TRAVEL PUBLISHING, INC.

West of the valley, the long, linear mesas of the dry Cumberland Plateau sit on a bed of sandstone, shale, and limestone at the intersection of three states—Georgia, Alabama, and Tennessee. Isolated until relatively recently by its stark geography (the northwest tip of the state for many years was accessible only from neighboring states), the area attracts adventurers for hang gliding, spelunking (Ellison's Cave is the deepest east of the Mississippi), and wandering through fantastic boulder formations (follow the directive of signs on barns throughout the mountains and see Rock City!).

East of the valley lies the Blue Ridge Province. Here the famous Blue Ridge Mountains and the Cohuttas (a continuation of the Smoky mountain range) create a landscape of knobby peaks, narrow gaps, and streaming waterfalls in moist coves. The state's highest point is here: 4,784-foot **Mount Enotah,** which is better known by its nickname, Brasstown Bald, because of its grassy crest surrounded by tall forest. A Cherokee story rivaling that of Noah's Ark ascribes mythological status to the mountain. It was here, the story goes, that the People's giant canoe came to rest after the Great Flood. Such "balds" can be found throughout the Blue Ridge, and botanists are at a loss to explain what caused them. Some speculate that they occurred due to lightning-set fires, localized insect infestations, or prehistoric tribes clearing the grounds.

The discovery of a gold belt that runs from the Carolinas through North Georgia started the nation's first gold rush in Dahlonega ("precious yellow color" in Cherokee), sending thousands of prospectors to Georgia's Blue Ridge in search of fortune. After the boom went bust, spent miners turned back to farming and logging. Today, abandoned mines, pioneer cabins, gristmills, and covered bridges recall that earlier era. You'll still see an occasional horse-drawn or mule-driven plow, but most land that was once farmed, logged, or strip-mined has since returned to second-growth wilderness, now protected as a national forest. (Virgin forest was rare even when colonists arrived—Native Americans customarily cleared land for hunting grounds.)

From along the divide of Georgia's Blue Ridge, waters rush to either the Atlantic Ocean (via the Savannah River) or the Gulf of Mexico (via the Chattahoochee or Tennessee Rivers farther north). River runners are drawn to the region's challenging white water, in particular the "Wild and Scenic" Chattooga River. The awesome Tallulah Gorge, placid high-country lakes, many panoramic waterfalls, and trout streams by the dozens add to the region's allure.

But trekkers know North Georgia best as the foot of the 2,144-mile **Appalachian Trail.** Claimed to be the oldest and longest continually marked footpath in the world, the A.T. crosses through 14 states and eight national parks between Springer Mountain, Georgia, and Mount Katahdin, Maine. Georgia's 83-mile stretch is less congested, and often more rugged, than the trail farther north.

Piedmont Plateau

The high shelf of rolling foothills and broad valleys that lies between the steep Appalachians and the flat coastal plain is the Piedmont Plateau. From the Italian word meaning "foot of the mountain," the Piedmont was so named by European settlers who noted the region's resemblance to southern Europe. Comprising 31 percent of the state's area, this region also holds nearly all of Georgia's major cities, including Macon, Augusta, Columbus, Athens, and the capital city of Atlanta.

With only one natural boundary (at the banks of the Chattahoochee River), Atlanta expands outward, not upward, so while skyscrapers fill downtown, the rest of town spreads out through thick woods. This sprawl, the lack of natural landmarks visible over the trees, and long, winding routes can make metro Atlanta a challenge for newcomers to navigate without a good map.

Stone Mountain is a dramatic vantage point overlooking the city. This 1,683-foot-tall dome east of town—the largest piece of exposed granite in the eastern United States—rises in stark contrast to the forested hills all around. Table-flat exfoliated slabs, some as big as a house, lie at its base like huge shingles, and the dense, dry surface harbors an enclave of desert plant species. The rare geological and botanical outcropping is matched by an equally unusual relief carving on its face; three Confederate leaders on horseback represent the South's version of Mount Rushmore. Smaller granite outcroppings sprinkled around the Piedmont are less celebrated locally as geological wonders than as the source of swimming holes in abandoned quarries.

As you move south, the cooler, rolling uplands around Atlanta and Athens begin to heat up and smooth out. **Pine Mountain,** north of Columbus, is the southernmost contour on the widening lowland plateau.

The Fall Line

The narrow band where the Piedmont meets the coastal plain marks the "fall line," the coastline of an earlier geological era. Along this line, Appalachian rivers spill from upland to lowland in a long run of waterfalls and rapids, below which smooth waters flow to the sea. Recognizing the potential for water power and transportation, early Europeans ventured upriver from the Atlantic coast and settled wherever rivers crossed the fall line. Augusta was founded on the Savannah River in 1735, Macon on the Ocmulgee River in 1825, and Columbus on the Chattahoochee in 1828. Likewise, you can map the fall line along the eastern seaboard by simply connecting the dots of major inland cities, from Columbus, Georgia, clear north through Washington, D.C.

Coastal Plain

Though Georgia is the seventh-fastest-growing state in the nation, you wouldn't know it by looking at the rural coastal plain region covering the entire southern half of the state. Since colonial times, this pastoral plantation country has been Georgia's prime agricultural region. Today's top five cash crops—peanuts (Georgia is the number one peanut-growing state in the nation), tobacco, corn, cotton, and soybeans—thrive here, along with the state's signature crops of peaches and pecans.

Two significant subregions create contrasting terrain. Antebellum plantations flourished here in the **Black Belt,** a fertile crescent of rich, dark soil running through the middle of the state and dipping into its southwestern corner. The sandier soils of the southeastern interior hold the **pine barrens** that support the state's logging, paper, and pulp industries (more than half the state is owned by lumber and pulpwood companies).

Rivers stained red from iron-rich clay drain the region. The Ocmulgee and Oconee Rivers meet near Lumber City to form the oceanbound Altamaha River; the Chattahoochee and Flint Rivers meet at Lake Seminole. With all the respective forks and tributaries of each, no wonder the original residents of these plains were dubbed Creeks.

Several naturalist nuggets are hidden within this vast interior. **Providence Canyon** (south of Columbus), affectionately considered the Little Grand Canyon, features dramatically striped red-to-white walls that drop without warning from its flat, forested rim. **Sand dunes** along the Flint River (south of Albany) attest to the region's origins as an ancient seabed—you can still find prehistoric sharks' teeth among the dunes. Along the wild banks of the isolated Ocmulgee, densely packed 18-foot-high **canebrakes** resemble a forest of fishing poles. Wilder still are the region's scattered **swamps,** placid refuges for distinct varieties of plants and animals.

Okefenokee Swamp

Named from the Seminole term *ecunnau finocau,* meaning "earth trembling," the Okefenokee Swamp, in Georgia's southeast pocket, is the largest wildlife refuge in the eastern United States. According to Seminole legend, the swamp was created after a dispute between the beavers and the People; the angry beavers broke their dams to flood the area and then abandoned the newly created swamp. (Interestingly, beavers have never been among the many species that thrive here, such as alligators, otters, wild turkeys, wild hogs, and many types of birds, including waterfowl.)

Scientists tell it a different way. They say a sudden uplifting in the eastern ridge isolated coastal waters, creating a new inland sea. Vegetation eventually filled these waters, turning them into a vast peat bog. Swamp "ground" is actually no more than twisted roots covered with sand

and a few feet of leaf mold. The famous Suwannee River (as in "Way Down upon the. . . ") and the crooked St. Marys River both spring from headwaters in the swamp.

The primeval nature of the Okefenokee—its black waters stained with tannic acid and strewn with reptiles and amphibians, its dark knob-kneed cypresses draped with Spanish moss—encourages folktales of swamp haunts and foreboding. But "far from being a place of mystery, danger and menace," wrote early swamp naturalist John Hopkins, the Okefenokee is rather "a haven of peace and a refuge from the greater hazards of the outside world."

Atlantic Coast

Georgia's Atlantic coast is actually made up of three separate coasts: the sandy seaward beaches of the dozen or so **barrier islands** farthest east, the **mainland coast** to the west, and the wide **tidal marshlands** that flow between them. From Savannah in the north to St. Marys at the Florida border, 100 miles of semitropical shore is largely preserved in its natural state.

Georgia's marshlands, measuring 5–10 miles across, are the most extensive and productive on the eastern seaboard. Where a visitor sees largely a serene panorama of soft grasses, shrimp boats, and oyster beds, under water the marsh busily churns out more food and energy per square mile than any other ecosystem.

Of the barrier islands, which buffer the marsh and mainland from harsh coastal storms, only four are bridged and developed as resorts (Tybee, St. Simons, Sea Island, and Jekyll). The rest are permanently protected sanctuaries accessible only by boat to a limited number of visitors. Shell middens (circular mounds of discarded oyster shells), ruins of Sea Island cotton plantations, and wild horses descended from those left by the Spanish in the 17th century attest to the long and varied history of these beautiful palmetto islands.

About 17 miles east of Sapelo Island, in waters 50–70 feet deep, lies **Gray's Reef,** a national marine sanctuary and one of the largest "live-bottom" reefs off the southeastern coast. Its limestone

outcroppings attract a wide variety of plant and animal life, not to mention divers and anglers.

CLIMATE

The only thing dry about Georgia is a county that doesn't sell liquor; the rest of the state is well watered and downright lush. Road shoulders soften with saturation; hydrants occasionally explode to release pressure from too much water. But unlike other wet places, where it's always raining (Seattle comes to mind), southeastern skies are mostly clear. The land just has a way of hanging on to moisture. Of course, the region has drier spells too, but what Georgians consider land ravaged by drought would look like a rainforest out west.

Rainfall averages 50 inches a year, varying from 70 inches in the extreme northeast mountain region to 45 inches around the fall line. In summer, daily afternoon thundershowers typically douse the day's heat for a few minutes, until the sun returns and turns the water to steam. In winter, snow falls in North Georgia's mountains—7–10 inches worth supports the East's southernmost ski run in Sky Valley—and sometimes as far south as Atlanta.

The southeastern United States averages mild, comfortable temperatures in the 60–70°F range most of the year, without the harsh winters and freezing temperatures that are typical farther north. Summers, however, are decidedly subtropical, with high humidity and temperatures that can reach uncomfortable highs in the 90s most days in July and August.

Temperatures year-round stay cooler in the mountains and warmer at the coast, so predictably, people seek refuge by the coast in winter and in the mountains in summer. City folk complain how much more insufferable South Georgia feels in comparison to the Piedmont uplands, but the difference may appear slight to sweltering visitors.

Travel Seasons

If you have to choose just one season, either spring or fall would be a good choice. Seasonal colors—whether spring flowers or autumn leaves—are spectacular, and the climate is at its most comfortable.

Early spring (mid-March–mid-April) brings rain, and temperatures can fluctuate from the 50s to 80s. Many flowering trees and wildflowers bloom during March and April. Late spring (mid-April–May) turns summery, with consistently warm and dry days.

Subtropical southeastern summers are often maligned for their heat and humidity, but where else can you experience those hot summer nights? And summer's what those verandas, porch swings, and mint juleps are all about. It starts heating up in June, and July and August are scorching. Flatlanders flee to cooler temperatures in North Georgia. Early September can be just as hot, but somehow, with the summer crowds gone, it just feels cooler.

From mid-September to mid-October, Georgia experiences delightfully warm and clear Indian summer. By the third week in October, temperatures begin to drop; fall colors generally peak around this time too. Temperatures fall faster in November. Then the winter chill sets in, reaching its frostiest between December and February and usually continuing through to early March. Because many flatlanders are apprehensive about driving in unfamiliarly icy conditions, visitors have the scenic snowy mountains to themselves in winter. Of course, many travelers aim for warm southern beaches in winter.

FLORA

A spectacular abundance of plants covers the South with lush green growth. Each of more than 1,400 species of trees, shrubs, wildflowers, and herbs has its own story to tell, woven into the natural and cultural history of the Southeast. The brief summary that follows outlines broad features and has just a few specifics; for more details, ask any Southerner. The South's rural heritage has produced a culture finely tuned to the natural environment; most residents can describe in detail the particular characteristics and uses of area plants as though they were members of the family.

KUDZU

Any interstate traveler is bound to notice the unstoppable vine that seems to shroud whole forests along Georgia's highways like a hexed storybook kingdom. The devilish weed is kudzu (KUD-zoo), a vine of the genus *Pueraria*. Imported from Japan to the South earlier this century for erosion control, it has overstepped its boundaries. With no natural predators, kudzu thrives like a scourge, often overpowering the naturally varied landscape. It inspired James Dickey to devote a poem to the "green, mindless, unkillable ghosts" of kudzu, in which he writes "In Georgia, the legend says/That you must close your windows/At night to keep it out of the house."

The Japanese turn the plant's hardiness to their advantage. Some pull root fibers to weave into valued cloth, or reduce the roots to powder as a thickener and a botanical medicine for digestive disorders. Others simply grab a handful and throw

© SCOTT TEEPLE

it into a pot, steaming fresh kudzu shoots, deep-frying kudzu leaves (in tempura batter), or pickling kudzu greens and flowers (served seasoned with soy sauce, miso, or salt).

Trees

Georgia is trees: hardwoods and softwoods, deciduous and coniferous, flowering varieties, and species used for industry, agriculture, and art. The prevalent **pine, cedar, oak, elm, sycamore,** and **poplar** appear, along with **red maple, willow, hickory, gum,** and **tulip** trees. The most famous of many flowering trees is the **magnolia,** which, along with the common **dogwood** (pink or white), blooms in March and April. **Chinaberry** and **crape myrtle** trees also add flowers to the landscape.

The Appalachian Mountains beat all for the number and variety of trees; here, more tree types than in all of Europe (130 compared with 85) thrive in dense protected forests. Undisturbed "Great Appalachian Forest" patches shelter some of the largest hardwoods in the eastern United States, including **red spruce, sugar maples, beeches,** and **buckeyes**—trees more common to New England or Canada than to the American South.

The coastal plain is dominated by **longleaf and slash pine,** which once fueled a tremendous turpentine business and still support a lumber, pulp, and paper industry. **Live oaks** here and on the coast support the misnamed **Spanish moss;** neither moss nor Spanish, this epiphyte—a plant that gets all its nutrients from the air—is a distant relative of the pineapple. The short, fat **saw palmetto** covers the coast with its large, fan-shaped fronds. **Bald cypress** looms over the swamps with branchless trunks below a thick canopy, and its knobby "knees" of roots protrude above the water's surface.

Forests reveal the regional history as clearly as rings in a tree. You can accurately date the evolution of a long-abandoned farm or clearcut by observing a predictable second-growth succession. In a year, broom sedge and short pines begin to mask manmade marks; after 30 years, such broadleaf varieties as oaks and hickories have returned. The Southeast has a very forgiving nature—ample moisture, ample space, and ample time heal most everything.

Flowers

One of the South's most magnificent traits is an abundance of lusciously flowering plants. About 1,500 varieties of trees, shrubs, herbs, and wildflowers ensure blooms in all but the coldest months. From when the first white **serviceberry** blooms in early March till the last yellow **witch hazel** petal falls in December, the southeastern woods bloom naturally into a wild garden.

Besides towering magnolias and the delicate dogwood trees so closely associated with the South, two common flowering shrubs grow into flowering thickets as high as trees: **mountain laurel** and **rhododendron** reach heights of 30 feet, surrounding visitors with their delicate white blossoms. Miles of fruit orchards bloom in spring in the state's fruit-producing midsection, including the unusual Southern **pawpaw** and famous Georgia **peaches** (whose pink blooms peak in late March). Homey flower gardens are often decorated with such old-fashioned favorites as **snapdragons, sweet peas, candy tuft, larkspur, love-in-a-mist,** and **azaleas.**

The most compelling feature of a Southern garden, however, is not its beauty but its fragrance. Sweet **honeysuckle,** hot **gardenia,** and whispery scents of draped **wisteria** are among hundreds of languorous scents that grace Georgia's air; gardeners design "fragrance gardens" especially to tickle the olfactory nerves.

Grasses

Regional ecology (and even regional culture) can be defined by a single distinctive grass. South Georgia's **Wiregrass** region takes its name from the wiry stalks that inhabit the pine barrens, and locals embrace the name to describe the particular folk heritage of the region. Out on the coast, the productive estuarine ecology—and economy—revolves around the marshland's smooth **cordgrass** *(Spartina alterniflora)* that shelters the complex food chain. The beaches, meanwhile, are stabilized by **sea oats** *(Uniola paniculata),* a grass so critical to the local environment that it's protected by law.

FAUNA

Mammals

The **white-tailed deer,** the favorite game of south-eastern Native Americans, is now Georgia's most abundant large mammal. **Black bears, wild hogs, feral horses** (thought to be descended from those left by the departing Spanish in the 17th century), and an occasional endangered **Florida panther** (also called puma, or cougar) round out the larger resident animals. **Otters, minks, bobcats, coyotes, foxes,** and **beavers** can also be found. Many homeowners encourage **bats** to move into specially constructed bat boxes as a natural alternative to electric bug-zappers—one bat may eat thousands of mosquitoes in a single night. But what you see the most around the state are **opossums, raccoons, rabbits, squirrels** (the gray variety, that is; humans rarely see Georgia's flying squirrels), and **armadillos.** The armadillos in particular are so abundant that locals consider them "weed wildlife." The common sight of their lifeless shells along roadways has led to the Southern joke: "Why did the chicken cross the road?—To show the armadillo it could be done."

As for marine mammals, the extremely rare **right whale,** of which only about 350 are known to exist in the world, calves only off the Georgia coast. The endangered **West Indian manatee,** a slow-moving seal-shaped sea mammal, lives in shallow coastal waters and feeds off the smooth cordgrass of the salt marshes. Beachgoers readily see **dolphins** swimming close to shore.

Reptiles and Amphibians

American alligators—the largest, oldest, and most famous of Georgia's reptiles—can grow to a length of nearly 20 feet and inhabit rivers, swamps, and marshes in South Georgia. Once on the brink of extinction, alligators are now strictly protected; campgrounds around their favorite habitat, the Okefenokee Swamp, close at dusk to prevent poaching. Thirteen species of **lizards** live in Georgia, as does a rare amphibian; the **lungless salamander** is not only lungless but blind as well, inhabiting the pitch-black depths of Appalachian caves.

Freshwater turtles (locally called snappers, cooters, or tappins) include 150-pound alligator snapping turtles, soft-shell varieties, and box turtles. Of the five species of **sea turtles** found in Georgia (all threatened or endangered), the **loggerhead** is most common, nesting on all barrier islands. Georgia's **Caretta Project** uses volunteers to monitor nesting grounds to protect the eggs from predators. The critically endangered **Kemp's ridley sea turtles,** as well as the **green, leatherback,** and **hawksbill** varieties, swim in Georgia waters but nest elsewhere.

Of 42 types of **snakes** found in Georgia, six are venomous: the **copperhead, cottonmouth, coral snake,** and three **rattlesnake** varieties, including the **eastern diamondback.** Diamondbacks reach lengths of eight feet, making them the largest and most dangerous snakes in the region. They inhabit the southern coastal plain, and though diurnal (active during the day), they avoid going out in temperatures over 85°F and remain relatively inactive through the winter. Pit vipers (the subfamily of snakes to which rattlers belong) are potent symbols in Southern culture, as their abundance in the Bible Belt might lead you to presume. Periodic "rattlesnake roundups" inspire local festivals, and the Primitive Baptist sect demonstrates its faith with snake handling.

The largest of Georgia's nonvenomous snakes (which include water, coachwhip, corn, rat, and pine snakes) is the farmer's favorite, the **king snake.** It'll grow longer than a man is tall and feeds on rodents and other small animals.

Birds

Georgia is a birder's paradise. It's in a transition zone between northern and southern bird habitats, and its statewide wetlands shelter migratory species along the eastern migratory flyway. Birders can spot more than 350 species of birds at different seasons. Around the state you'll see—or hear—the **mockingbird, brown thrasher, towhee, cardinal, blue jay, catbird, robin, crow, ruby-throated hummingbird,** and several species of **wren, thrush, warbler,** and **woodpecker** (most notably the endangered red-cock-aded variety of Woody Woodpecker fame).

Purple martins adopt "martins' gourd" bird-houses (carved from large gourds), which are hung throughout the Southeast to entice the insect-eating birds to roost. Scavenger **buzzards** feast on roadkill and barely budge for cars; predatory **owls** and **hawks** compete with snakes for rodents. Hunters track **wild turkey, dove,** and **quail**—whole resorts in southwestern Georgia are devoted to quail hunting.

A spectacular variety of birds appear in dramatic settings in the Okefenokee Swamp; look for **ospreys, egrets, herons,** endangered **woodstorks,** plenty of **waterfowl,** and the occasional **bald eagle** (the state's nesting program should eventually boost eagle sightings).

Fish

Though North Georgia may be famous for its mountain **trout,** plenty of other freshwater varieties breed here, such as **bream, pike, sunfish,** and **black bass.** In Middle Georgia, add **catfish** and **carp;** farther south still you'll find **redfish, bass, mullet, drum, shad,** and **mackerel** in the rivers of the coastal plain.

In estuarine marshlands, shellfish such as **shrimp, blue crabs,** and tidewater **oysters** support a commercial fishery valued at $20 million a year. Saltwater species inhabiting Georgia's Atlantic coast include **spotted sea trout, flounder, Southern stingray,** and various species of **shark.** Beachcombers can discover **sponges, corals,** and colorful purple and tangerine **sea whips,** alongside **clams, horseshoe crabs, sea cucumbers,** and **sand dollars.**

ENVIRONMENTAL ISSUES

Many natural habitats such as woodlands and wetlands, mountain coves, wild swamps, and shifting islands are vanishing throughout the Southeast. But in Georgia, many of the most pristine examples of these strange and wondrous ecosystems are steadfastly protected, accessible only to limited numbers of adventurers.

Georgia was among the first states in the nation to pass legislation protecting its tidal marshlands, which are the most extensive and productive of any on the East Coast. And North Georgia's Appalachian woodlands fall largely under the protection of the 727,000-acre Chattahoochee National Forest—though local environmentalists keep a close eye on federal foresters. Similarly, the exotic Okefenokee Swamp shelters one of the largest wildlife refuges in the nation, and only 300 visitors a day are allowed onto majestic Cumberland Island. Overall, the state's environmental record surpasses that of many Southern states, yet Georgia confronts many of the same challenges as its neighbors.

Some say the worst environmental carnage happened a century ago. In the early 20th century, the land was so overworked with cotton, it plumb wore out. Rampant logging ravaged the forests, and strip-mining for gold brought down the hills. Gradually, persistent second-growth and conscientious preservation restored much of the land, but nevertheless the landscape has been forever changed by dammed rivers, drained swamps, and clear-cut logging. Luckily, the southeastern environment has a very forgiving nature—it has to.

Today, a major industrial threat to Georgia's environment comes from pulp and paper manufacturing. Yet the industry is such a critical part of the state's economy that many legislators are tempted to look the other way when influential pulp and paper companies flagrantly exceed Environmental Protection Agency standards for dioxin emissions. Besides the noxious odors and emissions from paper mills, warm wastewater entering rivers and estuaries attracts marine animals, exposing them to pollution and the lethal propeller blades of boats they would otherwise avoid.

Military bases (particularly the nuclear-powered Trident submarine base near Cumberland Island, of all places) and nuclear-energy plants (the most notorious offender is on the South Carolina side of the Savannah River) contribute to making Georgia a big producer of hazardous wastes, which is unfortunately not ameliorated by state spending on waste management. Elsewhere around the state, reckless development in fragile areas creates additional ecological danger zones.

As is true nationwide and particularly insidious in the South, environmental hazards disproportionately hit impoverished minority communities, whose dissent often goes unheard. Fortunately, many national and local environmental advocacy organizations are active in Georgia. The Georgia Conservancy, founded in 1967, deserves credit for strengthening the protection of the state's most pristine, fragile, and otherwise indispensable natural areas. Environmental activists work closely with the Georgia Department of Natural Resources, the state agency that administers preservation efforts and endangered species–restoration programs, in addition to maintaining state parks, historic sites, and wildlife management areas.

But perhaps the biggest friend to Georgia's environment is a Southern sense of stewardship and a citizenry predisposed to be naturally suspicious of ardent developers, moneymen, or commercial zeal of any kind. Whether this spirit can predominate over the competing tradition of patronage that has allowed key industries to have their way with the land is yet to be determined. Beloved bonds to the land and a way of life hang in the balance.

History

Near the intersection of two busy country highways in North Georgia sits an unusual rectangular mound in a fenced field. What's most unusual is not the mound itself (though such mounds throughout the state are the cause of much curiosity and speculation), but the fact that this ancient aboriginal earthwork is topped like a cake with a lacy white latticework gazebo. Together these two cultural symbols span the entire human history of the state.

FIRST INHABITANTS

Georgia's aboriginal mounds are so integrated into the character of the Southeast that it's hard not to see them as natural miniature mesas dotting the landscape. Yet they were constructed with extraordinary human effort; basketful by basketful, heaps of earth were shaped into high mounds up to three stories tall by communities that flourished in this region 2,000 years ago. For these ancient civilizations, such earthworks—hundreds of which remain visible throughout Georgia today—served as ceremonial grounds, tombs, or residence platforms for high-status individuals.

Many historians assert that three of the four most interesting archaeological sites east of the Rocky Mountains are in Georgia. All three are aboriginal earthworks: Ocmulgee Mounds near Macon, Kolomoki Mounds in southwest Georgia, and Etowah Mounds in northwest Georgia (the latter is considered to be among the most important finds in all of North America).

Excavations reveal artifacts dating back 10,000 years. You'll hear the term **Paleo-Indian** to describe these earliest relics, preserved from when nomadic hunters—descendants of Asian groups that migrated across the Bering Straits to North America 50,000 years ago—stalked woolly mammoths and giant sloths. Hunter–gatherers of the subsequent **Archaic** period (9000–1000 B.C.) left the first traces of crop cultivation, traded with far-off tribes, and created the earliest pottery in North America at Stallings Island in the Savannah River, near Augusta, and on coastal islands.

The **Woodland** period (1000 B.C.–A.D. 900) saw fully realized villages and croplands, accompanied by an increasingly sophisticated civilization. Pottery was graced with decoratively stamped designs. An impressive trade network stretched from the gulf and ocean to the Great Lakes. Amazingly elaborate religious ceremonies also came into being, and the first mounds were built. The earliest mounds were cone-shaped gravesites—tribal leaders were buried with sacrificed relatives or attendants and accompanied by such "grave goods" as pottery, jewelry, and decorated sheets of mica. Yet Georgia's most astounding earthworks from this period do not fit that pattern. At Kolomoki Mounds, near Blakely, the 56-foot-high mound is rectangular and resembles an Aztec temple; it was valued primarily as a ceremonial platform. And the Rock Eagle effigy mound, near Eatonton, takes the shape (when viewed from above) of a bird of prey—probably an eagle, which held a high place in Native American mythology—constructed from heaped rocks, not earth.

The **Mississippian** period, beginning about A.D. 900, brought the highest cultural achievements in the Southeast (or, some argue, in all of North America). About this time, Mississippians migrated east, displaced the Woodland peoples, and developed centralized chiefdoms. They built large villages around a central plaza, thatched huts that served as dwellings, and earthlodges that hosted community meetings. Competitions were held on ball fields in the plaza; spectators sat on raised earthen bleachers. The flat-topped earthen mounds served as sacred grounds; elaborate temple rites accompanied an increasingly complex set of religious beliefs. Artifacts also reveal Mesoamerican influences, likely borrowed from traveling Aztec traders.

The Mississippians farmed extensively, primarily "the three sisters"—corn, beans, and squash—which remain staples of Southern cooking to this day (and also have ancient ties to Mesoamerica). Hunting and gathering of abundant natural food sources continued to supplement agriculture.

Ocmulgee Mounds, preserved as a national monument, allows visitors to enter a restored earth lodge and view huge mounds from this period. Etowah's sacred grounds near Cartersville (an hour and some north of Atlanta) display impressive ceremonial mounds and some of the finest examples of early (and Mesoamerican-influenced) Southeastern art.

After 300 years, this mound-building culture disappeared. Surrounding populations adopted the sites and some traits of the Mississippians, creating an amalgamated culture (called Lamar) that flourished up until the Europeans arrived in the 17th century. Of the subsequent subgroups that survived widespread annihilation from European-borne diseases, the Cherokee

and Creek Confederacy dominated the region that became Georgia. Chickasaw and Choctaw groups were also present, and later, the Seminoles broke off from the Creek.

While each aboriginal tradition distinguished itself in many significant ways, all shared certain common characteristics, particularly those that sprang naturally from adaptation to the climate, the land, and its resources—a heritage that continues to differentiate the American South from the rest of the country today.

EUROPEAN EXPLORATION AND SETTLEMENT

In 1540, Spanish explorer Hernando de Soto marched through Georgia with 600 horses and an army of 900 soldiers, in search of gold to rival that of the Inca empire. His hapless pursuit led him through every region in Georgia—an invader's package tour. De Soto encountered (brutally, in most cases) the Timucuan in South Georgia, the Guale (pronounced Wallie) on the coast, the Creek and remaining Lamar moundbuilders in the central Piedmont, and finally the Cherokee in North Georgia. Here gold was indeed underfoot—in a rich vein that would go unexploited for three more centuries—yet de Soto passed it by. Though his golden dream never materialized, he left an indelible mark on history, exposing Native American populations to European diseases against which they had no natural immunity. Whole tribes were wiped out; up to three-quarters of the estimated southeastern Native American population died of influenza and smallpox.

Battling for Domination

Georgia's coastal islands staged the competition for European domination of North America: French, Spanish, and British forces battled for control of Georgia's coast for hundreds of years. French Huguenots first came ashore in 1562, but within a few years, the Spanish pushed out the temporary shelters of French traders and constructed a string of forts ("presidios") up the coast. Missionaries followed in the wake of the armies, setting up farming villages and attempting to convert the Native Americans to Christianity. These presidios endured for more than a century, despite the ever-threatening presence of the English and French, rebellious Creeks, and pirates of every stripe. The missionaries finally abandoned the islands in 1686, leaving groves of orange, lemon, fig, and olive trees that still grace the islands. Some say the wild horses on Cumberland Island descended from the stables of the early missions.

The 13th and Final Colony

In 1733, British General James Oglethorpe arrived on the bluffs of the Savannah River to found the southernmost English colony there. He named it after King George II, who sanctioned the effort as a buffer community between the British settlement of "Charles Towne" to the north and Spanish strongholds to the south. This 13th and last of the British colonies was first envisioned as a utopian enterprise, a socially philanthropic experiment in which Oglethorpe offered those jailed for excessive debt a chance for a new life if they would come and populate the new colony (and relieve England of the burdens of a cripplingly harsh social policy). European Protestants and other persecuted religious refugees soon expanded the scope of this mission, and some adventurers also tagged along.

Oglethorpe mapped out the new town of Savannah—to exacting 18th-century British specifications still evident today—with the cooperation of local Yamasee chief Tomo-chi-chi. The close relationship between Oglethorpe and Tomo-chi-chi (aided by Mary Musgrove, a mixed-race interpreter and negotiator) culminated in a trip together back to England, where the British royal court doted on the befeathered "American savage."

The original Georgia Trustees (the investors who oversaw the colony) dreamed of creating a silk industry in Savannah, yet silk never took hold the way cotton did. They also hoped to impose a strict set of moral and commercial rules on the colonists, but these fared no better and soon proved impossible to maintain. The prohibition of alcohol and restrictions on land sales were the first to go. Lastly went their prohibition of slavery.

Oglethorpe believed that slavery contradicted the colony's purpose to "relieve the distressed," and asserted: "Give in, and we shall occasion the misery of thousands in Africa." More critical historians claim that his humanitarian sentiments were likely of secondary importance to considerations of pure military necessity; as his frontier position demanded a strong defense, he wanted only settlers who could also be soldiers (and armed slaves could rebel). Economic pressures from slaveholding neighbors in South Carolina led to the repeal of the prohibition against slavery 16 years after the founding of the colony.

To secure Georgia's position against the Spanish, Oglethorpe established forts along the 100-mile coast of "Debatable Land" between Savannah and Spain's northernmost outpost, St. Augustine, which is now in northern Florida. Skirmishes between the two powers shifted advantages back and forth for years until an ambush in 1742 in a remote island marsh decided which European power would control American shores.

In the Battle of Bloody Marsh, on St. Simons Island, the British ambushed and repelled the invading Spanish. Though a relatively minor engagement, it unnerved the retreating Spanish enough to finally abandon their ambitions for expansion north, and ultimately to relinquish their final hold on North America. Thus this skirmish, fought in a sandy marsh on one of Georgia's remote Sea Islands, became one of the most decisive battles in the history of the world.

The American Revolution

As the newest colony and one begun by British philanthropy, Georgia remained steadfastly loyalist and was the only colony not represented in the first Continental Congress. Yet in 1776, Georgia joined the rest in declaring independence. Two years later, British forces attacked the coast and captured Savannah, and by the end of 1779, every important town in Georgia had fallen under British control. With British occupation supported by many local Tories, the fighting took on a civil character. England's eventual withdrawal from Georgia brought about widespread confusion and disorganization in government, as well as many disputes over contested private property. (Later generations, remembering their grandparents' vivid accounts of the local turbulence, resolved to staunchly defend the land during the Civil War.)

ANTEBELLUM GEORGIA
King Cotton
Once Eli Whitney invented the cotton gin in Georgia in 1793 (dissenters say Catherine Greene did the inventing, yet named her farm mechanic Whitney as a more credible male inventor), cotton production soared. Georgia's annual cotton production rocketed from 1,000 bales in about 1790 to 20,000 bales 10 years later, doubling in the next decade, and peaking at 701,000 bales by the advent of the Civil War. Slavery, a dying institution before the cotton gin, was revived as a cheap labor source to fuel this increased production. The plantation system arose, as one historian put it, as a "kind of agribusiness whose machines were human beings."

Slaveholding planters established their dominion. Sufficient free time enabled the planter class to advance its education and engage in a complex social and political life. Even at the height of the plantation system, the members of this oligarchy exercised power out of all proportion to their number. In 1860, the overwhelming majority of farms in the state—31,000—consisted of no more than 100 acres, most all of which functioned without slave labor. By contrast, there were fewer than 1,000 "plantation-size" farms of more than a thousand acres—where the money, power, and slaves were concentrated. Which is to say—contrary to what *Gone with the Wind* may lead people to believe—the overwhelming majority of the cotton-producing population was steadfastly middle class, with interests far removed from those at the top of the plantation hierarchy. Widening class divisions ultimately shaped Southern politics for many generations.

Only certain geographical regions supported large-scale slaveholding plantations. On the coast, large plantations flourished with rice crops as well as a high-quality strand of cotton known as Sea Island cotton. The remainder of the large cotton-producing plantations were in a fertile crescent across the middle of the state and down into southwest Georgia. Called the Black Belt for its rich, dark soil, the region's name could also describe its demographics. Despite the revolutionary changes that swept through the South in the intervening century, the legacy of slavery continues to influence population patterns. Historically slaveless regions, such as northern Georgia, have fewer African American residents to this day.

Yet not all blacks in the South before the Civil War were enslaved. From colonial times on, slaves who bought their freedom, escaped, or were manumitted (released from slavery) joined African immigrants (many of whom were former slaves from Haiti) in free black communities in Georgia's cities. Though small in number (in 1860, Savannah's free black population of 3,000 was the largest in the state), such settlements were highly significant. Though their liberties were restricted, free blacks enjoyed basic rights denied to slaves, such as the ability to forge family bonds, operate businesses, exercise leadership in public life, and carry on traditions lost in the African diaspora. A few managed to amass wealth and hand down their enhanced social position through generations. Of this quiet black elite, a few even owned slaves. Well-off or not, free man or slave, many Southern blacks (and whites) fought for the abolition of slavery and risked their lives and livelihoods to escape slavery or to help others escape.

Expansionism
In the early 19th century, the federal government blew the lid off the Yazoo Land Frauds, a scandal in which corrupt politicians and speculators conspired to sell 50 million acres of Georgia territory for their personal gain (and 'twasn't theirs to sell anyhow). As part of the bargain struck with the federal government to extricate the state from the mess, Georgia lost its vaguely mapped western territory to what became Alabama and Mississippi. The new boundary was

set at the eastern bank of the Chattahoochee River. Yet the misappropriation would ultimately unleash a series of events with unforeseen consequences far more dire.

The Georgia legislature agreed to cede the fraudulently sold territories back to the U.S. government, *but only if* federal troops would remove Native Americans from what remained of the territory Georgia claimed as its own. Well, Georgia ceded the land but the feds declared that as a sovereign power, the Native Americans could not be evicted. Georgia perceived this turn of events as an encroachment on the original agreement, and the ensuing wrangling over where states' rights ended and federal jurisdiction began in this economically motivated and racially charged debate was to foreshadow the coming of civil war. On this earlier score, however, Georgia emerged victorious.

While various treaties (at best questionable, if not outright fraudulent) slipped lands out from under the Creeks, the highly organized Cherokee resisted any bullying to move them from their ancestral homelands. To bolster their defense, they officially established the Cherokee Nation, centered in North Georgia. In 1827, the Cherokee chartered a constitution of representative government based on the U.S. Constitution and declared New Echota as their capital. One of their most extraordinary cultural achievements around this time was the creation of a syllabary (phonetic alphabet) of the Cherokee language; the printing press that produced a bilingual newspaper in English and Cherokee is among many artifacts on display in New Echota today.

Gold Rush

What sealed the fate of the Cherokee was the discovery of gold. In 1829, a white man hunting on Cherokee territory spied on the ground what looked to him "like the yellow of an egg." It turned out to be part of a rich gold belt that signaled the first major gold rush in U.S. history, sending thousands of prospectors into North Georgia. The center of the gold boom was Dahlonega (named for the Cherokee word for yellow metal), the largest of several North Georgia towns that retain their gold-rush character.

In 1838, President Andrew Jackson sent troops to evict the Cherokee from the newly exposed gold country. Pulled from their homes and rounded up into jails, the Cherokee (along with dozens of other Native American groups from throughout the Southeast) were exiled to Oklahoma on a torturous forced march that became known as the Trail of Tears.

CIVIL WAR

The Civil War was the single most defining historical event in the South, or, as many historians assert, in the whole nation. Much of that history was written across the face of Georgia: the Atlanta Campaign, battle and blaze, Sherman's March to the Sea—these and other events that decided the fate of the Confederacy have been memorialized in landmarks across the state and were implanted into the American imagination by Margaret Mitchell's classic Civil War novel *Gone with the Wind.* Though more than a century has passed, the Civil War lives on in the regional collective memory as if fought in this lifetime. Even the term "Civil War" can generate debate, as it describes the Union position—that of a single nation torn apart, rather than two separate opponents. To the South it was the "War Between the States," a term still heard occasionally today.

From Secession to Bloodshed

The Southern states, dependent on an agricultural slave economy, developed social and political systems dramatically different from those in the industrialized (but still slaveholding) states of the north. The escalating national debate over the legal status of slavery in western territories highlighted these differences, fueling an animosity that sparked secession. Starting in 1860, 11 southern states voted to form their own Confederate States of America.

Yet the South was never monolithic. Many Georgians opposed secession, and others supported it only reluctantly. Views on slavery ran a similar gamut. Foremost in the minds of many

PAST AS PRESENT

In 1886, Atlanta journalist Henry Grady traveled to New York to deliver a dinner speech on the "New South." When asked what he intended to say, Grady responded: "I have thought of a thousand things to say; five hundred of which if I say they will murder me when I get back home, and the other five hundred of which will get me murdered at the banquet." His predicament is one with which even contemporary writers of Southern history can sympathize.

No other part of America lives so intimately with its past as the South, nor is a sense of personal and regional history as acute in any American as in a Southerner. The region's history, and its retelling, best exemplifies how history is more a matter of selective interpretation than the mere recitation of facts. And in the South, interpretations vary. *Widely.*

The South claims at least three histories: the most familiar one, the textbook kind written by Northerners, is different from white Southern history, which in turn is distinct from a history of the black experience in the South. For the traveler, these complex realities mix with one's own observations to fascinate even the historically impaired. Few places in the United States can engage you like the South in red-hot debate on events that happened 150 years ago.

Confederate victory fields, African American heritage sites, and Native American historical sites make some of the South's most interesting stops because they tell stories often omitted from the mainstream history books. Read the spin on federal brochures about Southern historic sites for a sense of the fine line writers must walk to please Northern editors without offending local sensibilities.

This guide attempts to address a few major points and relate some of the untold stories (for further reading, see Suggested Reading). Yet travelers to the South should keep in mind what one 88-year-old former slave said:"I know folks think the books tell the truth, but they shore don't." Discover for yourself.

nonslaveholding Southerners—from whose ranks the majority of soldiers rose—was the notion of states' rights: the idea that the United States was a federation, rather than a republic, and that states could withdraw their membership if the Union no longer served their needs. Georgia Governor Joseph E. Brown, in fact, so opposed centralized government that in the midst of the war, he threatened to secede from the Confederacy!

While slavery served as the initial point of contention, early on, President Abraham Lincoln focused exclusively on preserving the Union and insisted abolition was not at issue. Yet no matter what the politicians and armies proclaimed as their purpose, slaves recognized the war as heralding the long-awaited end of bondage. As Union General William T. Sherman described in one encounter with a slave, "He said he'd been looking for 'the Angel of the Lord' ever since he was knee-high, and though we professed to be fighting for the Union, he sup-

posed that slavery was the cause, and that our success was to be his freedom."

Early in the war, the only action in Georgia was on the coast. Georgia's governor seized Savannah's coastal Fort Pulaski even before Georgia officially seceded. One of the first Union moves was to take the fort back. Here the Union troops, besides monitoring a blockade of the Savannah River (none too effectively, according to accounts of successful blockade runners), waited out most of the war until the action caught up to them. To hear a Southerner tell the story, the languid troops often passed the time playing baseball; to this day locals host period-costumed ball games at the fort annually in honor of the ball-playing Yankees. Federal troops also occupied the Sea Islands, making the isolated refuges a sanctuary for escaping slaves.

Farther down the coast, the port city of Darien was burnt to the ground by the famous all-black regiment, the 54th Massachusetts (scenes recounted in the film *Glory*), despite the objections of the troop commander. Upon later insisting that his men be considered for real warfare rather than such punitive actions, the regiment received and accepted an assignment so challenging it resulted in the death of the commander and most of the regiment.

Elsewhere in Georgia, as yet untouched by war, Georgia's munitions plants in Augusta, Macon, Columbus, and Athens churned out Confederate army supplies, which were then transported through Atlanta's railroad network. Naturally enough, Atlanta soon became the Union's major target.

The Atlanta Campaign

Sherman rightly theorized that a crushing blow to Atlanta would cripple the entire Confederacy. With that plan in mind, Union troops headed south from Chattanooga, Tennessee, in the fall of 1863, only to be stopped at Chickamauga Creek. A Confederate victory at high cost, the Battle of Chickamauga was remembered as the two bloodiest days of the war, with 35,000 casualties. A national park now commemorates the site.

Union General William Tecumseh Sherman coined the phrase "War is Hell."

The next spring, Sherman's troops plowed through northwest Georgia, following the railroad lines and engaging the Confederate army three times before being repelled outside of Atlanta at Kennesaw Mountain on June 27, 1864. Surrounding the city, Sherman fought four more battles for its control. Atlanta finally surrendered on September 2, 1864. Sherman ordered the city burned, and the resulting fire destroyed 90 percent of Atlanta's 4,000 buildings, leaving only smoldering chimneys, nicknamed Sherman's Sentinels.

Sherman's March to the Sea

After torching Atlanta, Sherman led an army of 60,000 on a march designed to "make Georgia howl." His army cut a 60-mile-wide swath through the Georgia countryside—burning houses, crops, and whole towns in his path—a routing which by Sherman's own estimation caused more than a million dollars in damages. At Georgia's Confederate capital, Milledgeville, Sherman's officers paused to stage a mock session of the Georgia legislature and lit boxes of Confederate money to fuel fires to boil coffee. As it happened, a few emaciated Union soldiers who had escaped the POW camp at Andersonville (now a national cemetery) straggled into the encampment. When Sherman learned of the horrible conditions there, he swept through the rest of Georgia with an increased vengeance.

Upon reaching Savannah on December 22, 1864, Sherman was reportedly so impressed by the beauty of the town that he spared it and offered it to President Lincoln as a Christmas gift. "I beg to present you," he wrote, "the city of Savannah, with 150 heavy guns and plenty of ammunition; also about 25,000 bales of cotton." Still reeling from Sherman, Georgia surrendered its armies to Union General Wilson after his army charged through Columbus in April 1865.

Sherman's March, unprecedented for destroying nonmilitary targets (private property largely occupied by women, children, and slaves, as most all white men had left to fight), left a legacy of animosity among landowners. For blacks, Sherman represented liberation, and tens of thousands of freed slaves picked up to follow

© AVALON TRAVEL PUBLISHING, INC.

the army. Once he reached Savannah, Sherman sought to rid the army of responsibility for these masses and conferred with local leaders of the free black community before issuing his famous Field Order No. 15.

This order set aside the barrier islands and the coastal mainland "low country" of Georgia and South Carolina exclusively for former slaves. On this new homeland, Sherman decreed, each freed man would be apportioned to newly freed slaves (the "40 acres and a mule" that remains the foundation of calls for reparations to this day). Yet the promptly proclaimed Black Republic on "Sherman's Reservation" was short-lived; federal legislation during Reconstruction rescinded Sherman's decree and returned property to former landowners. The liberated slaves were left with "nothing but freedom"—landless, powerless, and impoverished.

The most scrutinized, mythologized, and controversial event in U.S. history, the Civil War took the sacrifice of 620,000 lives to transform the founding principle of U.S. democracy—that "all men are created equal"—from abstract theory to a practical reality. Unfortunately, for many, that promise remains unfulfilled. As contemporary historian Barbara Fields asserts, "If some citizens live in houses and others live on the streets, the Civil War is not over—and regrettably, it can still be lost."

RECONSTRUCTION AND THE "NEW SOUTH"

After the war, Georgia's economic, political, and social systems lay in shambles: the smoldering ruins of Sherman's March stood as a visual symbol of widespread demoralization, confusion, and grief over shattered families, the dead, the missing, and the maimed. Farms lay fallow, with an agrarian depression on the way. Into this scene marched victorious Yankee troops to impose a mandatory "reconstructed" system of society, labor, and government. Though Georgia moved through this tumultuous time with less strife than in neighboring states (Georgia's higher proportion of white unionists smoothed the transition), its effect was like a second colonization, this time by the North.

Many Southern whites considered Reconstruction the worst of evils, characterized by opportunists bent on exploiting the defeated South. Northerners who arrived by the trainload with tapestry duffels were derided as "carpetbaggers" and their local collaborators as "scalawags." To blacks, Reconstruction transformed slaves to free citizens, guaranteeing the right to vote, hold office, and otherwise engage in an unprecedented interracial democracy. In any case, Reconstruction didn't last long: after five or six frustrating years, the federal government opted out of the region's internecine struggles, leaving the door open for the return of white supremacy in Georgia in 1871. Reconstruction's libertarian goals didn't meaningfully resurface until the modern civil-rights movement.

In the decades that followed, entrenched patterns and new realities confronted each other like opposing continental plates—sometimes realignment was painstakingly slow and deliberate, at other times so violent that deep dark fissures cracked the unstable surface. Throughout the South, segregation was institutionalized by Jim Crow laws, originally instigated by disputes over passenger seating on the very railroads that brought modernization to the South. "White" and "Colored" signs led to separate—not equal—train cars, waiting rooms, bathrooms, and water fountains. Schools, restaurants, and neighborhoods needed no signs to announce their exclusivity. Voting restrictions effectively denied voting rights to blacks. Worst of all, the outrageous Ku Klux Klan (said to be named after the sound of a gun being loaded) waged horrifying violence

DIXIE FLAG FLAP

While the Confederate flag may symbolize only Southern pride and independence to many Southern whites, it is a symbol inextricably linked with slavery and white supremacy. The debate over using features of the Confederate flag on many state flags throughout the American South has been argued for the past decade. In 1992, civil-rights advocates first persuaded then-governor Zell Miller to propose replacing the state's "stars and bars" state flag, which was adopted in 1956 as a protest over court-ordered racial integration. After an uphill battle from traditionalists in both the legislature and electorate, a new state flag was approved eight years later. The redesign includes miniature versions of all former state flags.

the 1956 state flag

the redesigned state flag

against blacks while the entire judicial system—local, state, and federal—turned the other way, strengthening the emerging apartheid.

The Atlanta Compromise

Atlanta, however, began to distinguish itself as the socially and racially progressive capital of the New South. The International Cotton States Exposition, held in Atlanta in 1895, provided an early platform for enlightened voices. At that forum, local journalist Henry Grady promoted the New South as eager to compete on the national economic scene, and black educator Booker T. Washington shared the stage. Though many considered Washington's conciliatory message too undemanding (local civil-rights leader and cofounder of the National Association for the Advancement of Colored People [NAACP] W. E. B. DuBois dubbed it the "Atlanta Compromise"), it nevertheless initiated a vital dialogue between blacks and the white power structure.

Throughout the state, expanding rail networks, manufacturing, and industry replaced the plantation economy, and the old agricultural system was replaced by sharecropping, in which tenant farmers worked the land for a share of the crop. Post–Civil War changes in the social order raised the voice of the yeomanry, the class of peasant farmers who ushered in the Populist movement of the 1890s. Although Populism constituted the largest agrarian political revolt in American history and was a force to be reckoned with, Populists never assumed control in Georgia.

Georgia's small, pioneering farm communities of the late 19th and early 20th centuries—often nostalgically recalled in Georgia's cultural history—were happily self-sufficient until the arrival of the boll weevil in 1914. This insect infestation wiped out the cotton crop that the South had grown singularly dependent upon, sending many poor farming families north in search of jobs. Blacks in particular left in such numbers that the period is remembered by African Americans as the Great Migration. After this devastating blow, the region was hit harder still by the nationwide economic collapse of the Great Depression in 1929.

Recovery was slow; the regional economy remained stagnant for decades. Yet despite the hardships of the early 20th century, Southern culture made tremendous strides forward during this period, propelling dramatic new literary and musical movements.

World War II brought economic opportunity to the struggling region. Georgia's major military bases were commissioned, and many Southerners—black and white—enlisted in the armed forces. Military service offered "more than a job" to African American soldiers in particular. Since the Civil War, when the 54th Massachusetts regiment refused pay until its wages were made equal with those of white soldiers, the military found itself strangely ahead of the times—often less discriminatory than the civilian society (North or South). After World War II, Southern soldiers carried back to the South broadened visions of a more equal society, ushering in the following era of revolutionary change.

Civil Rights

Explosive strife and violence characterized the civil-rights era of the 1960s in the South, yet once more Georgia was spared the greatest wrath of the times—thanks again to Atlanta's favored position in the vanguard of white-and-black alliance and progressive social justice. Martin Luther King Jr. was born in Atlanta in 1929 and was raised in the city's comfortable black middle class. Here he preached at his family's Ebenezer Baptist Church and later founded the Southern Christian Leadership Conference in the church basement.

In 1963, Atlanta mayor Ivan Allen Jr. testified in Washington in support of federal civil-rights legislation, the only Southern mayor to do so. And early on, pragmatic white business leaders—such as Coca-Cola magnate Robert Woodruff and *Atlanta Constitution* editor Ralph McGill—aligned with the African American elite and political advocates such as Dr. King, ensuring a relatively progressive slate of city leaders who brought their influence to bear on statewide politics.

Elsewhere around the state, one of the hardest-fought civil-rights battles centered on the reform of Georgia's educational system. In Albany, the first attempt to integrate the schools brought a violent mob scene that Dr. King attempted to reconcile peaceably. In January 1961, Charlayne Hunter (now Hunter-Gault, a one-time *MacNeil–Lehrer News Hour* reporter) walked into the University of Georgia in Athens, becoming the first African American to integrate the state institution.

Another battle was waged in the courts in an effort to overturn the state's unjust voting laws. Before the historic Supreme Court decision in *Baker vs. Carr* mandated "one man, one vote," a county unit system accorded nearly equal electoral weight to all counties, regardless of population, offsetting more numerous liberal, black, and urban votes in favor of rural conservatives. The 1962 decision marked the turning point for post-Reconstruction Southern politics by dissolving the county unit system.

In 1964, Jimmy Carter won the governorship, replacing race-baiting Lester Maddox. As governor, Carter established a reputation for his humanitarian ideals—a reputation that would help catapult the peanut farmer from Plains into national politics in 1976, when he was elected 39th president of the United States.

In 1973, Atlanta elected Maynard Jackson as mayor—the first black mayor of a major Southern city. Jackson set and enforced strict quotas for minority contracts and representation (though the term "minority" doesn't fit for a city that's two-thirds African American), widening professional opportunities and prompting a retro-migration of African Americans, who were leaving shrinking economic opportunities in the urban North. After serving the maximum mayoral term, Jackson was succeeded by former United Nations ambassador Andy Young, who brought an international perspective to Atlanta's City Hall. Young was in turn succeeded by Jackson again, who continued as before to preside over Atlanta's burgeoning economy. In 2001, the mayor's race was a tight battle between three African American candidates, with the victorious Shirley Franklin becoming the city's first woman mayor.

The South Rises Again

The opportunity to host the 1996 Summer Games represented a global affirmation of everything the state's promoters have been putting forward for years. Won on Atlanta's reputation for racial harmony (a message hand-carried by the globally respected Andy Young), this modern platform has served to redefine the state for the century to come.

Government and Economy

Georgia's 56 senators and 180 representatives comprise the state legislature, which meets in the state capitol each January to begin a 40-day legislative session. Since its founding as the 13th British colony, Georgia's capital has shifted several times—from its original location in Savannah to Augusta, Louisville, Milledgeville, and finally Atlanta in 1877. The state's governors are elected to four year terms; a maximum of two terms may be served consecutively.

Georgia has the largest number of counties (159) of any state besides Texas—a significant statistic in local politics, history, and culture. Georgians identify themselves more often by county than by city or region (and often identify destinations the same way, which can confuse travelers who tend not to navigate by county lines).

The state has historically voted so solidly Democratic that party nomination has often been tantamount to general election, creating a tradition of hotly contested primaries and anticlimactic elections (by state law, voting in a party primary is not limited to members of that party). Though more than half of Georgia's voters remain registered Democrats today, conservative "Dixiecrats" are now an endangered species.

The 1998 election brought significant biracial trends to the political arena. A powerful turnout of African American voters delivered Democratic victories in Georgia's gubernatorial election and throughout the South. Roy E. Barnes was elected governor despite falling short of the 40 percent of the white vote usually considered necessary for a Democratic victory, which analysts predict will spell a heightened sensitivity to the concerns of blacks within the party.

In Georgia's second Congressional district, a significant crossover of whites voting for an African American candidate was considered responsible for the reelection of Representative Sanford Bishop Jr., whose rural constituents appeared particularly grateful for his fight to preserve federal price supports for peanuts in 1996. As Camilla farmer James Lee Adams Jr. told the *New York Times,* "I think most of us have gotten beyond the white and black issue; we prefer to focus on the green." Yet Bishop's victory is sure to be used as artillery by foes of racial majority redistricting policies built on the premise that whites are unwilling to vote for black candidates.

Economy

Service industries comprise nearly three-fourths of Georgia's gross state product, but manufacturing is the single most important activity and the largest employer, accounting for 20 percent of the gross state product. Georgia is the nation's leading textile producer; agribusiness and mining also contribute to Georgia's economic base, and in 2000, tourism brought in $16 billion.

Georgia leads the nation as the largest producer of peanuts and pecans; it ranks second in poultry sales and third in peaches. In order, the

THE MAN FROM PLAINS

From peanut farmer in Plains, to governor of Georgia, to 39th president of the United States, Jimmy Carter rose from humble South Georgia roots to take over the nation's highest office in 1977. While his Southern manner was much caricatured by the national press (the brown cardigan of his fireside chats, Brother Billy, the Playboy "lust in my heart" interview), Carter was one of the country's most sincere humanitarian presidents, as evidenced by the successful Camp David accords, Panama Canal treaties, and his human-rights and energy policies.

Since 1980, when his reelection bid failed, Carter has continued his commitment to civil rights and humanitarian causes by monitoring free elections worldwide, mediating overseas disputes, and constructing low-income housing with the Georgia-based organization Habitat for Humanity. It's been said, without exaggeration, that Carter is the only man ever to use the U.S. presidency as the steppingstone to greater public service.

Among the books Carter has written are *Sources of Strength, An Hour Before Daylight, The Virtues of Aging, The Blood of Abraham, Always a Reckoning, Talking Peace, Living Faith, Keeping Faith, Christmas in Plains,* and *An Hour Before Dawn.*

© RICK DIAMOND/JIMMY CARTER CENTER

The Carter Library in Atlanta displays testaments to his administration's successes—including the original brown cardigan. Through the adjacent Carter Center, the Atlanta Project tackles local social justice campaigns. Carter resides in Plains, where Carter's birth home and high school are open to public tours.

state's biggest cash crops are peanuts, tobacco, corn, cotton, and soybeans.

Atlanta—the undisputed commercial, transportation, and financial capital of the state and region—is home to such global concerns as Coca-Cola, Delta Air Lines, Lockheed, United Parcel Service, Georgia-Pacific, and Cable News Network (CNN). Redefining its historical position as a transportation hub, Atlanta operates Hartsfield-Jackson International

Airport, the largest passenger terminal complex in the world.

The city's business reputation brought in half a million new jobs during the 1980s, and convention business in the capital doubled between 1985 and 1995. Expansion of convention-center facilities in 2004 promises to continue that upward trend. The number of hotel rooms in Atlanta is likewise projected to have doubled between 1995 and 2005.

The People

Georgia is the ninth-largest state in the nation, with a population of just under 8.7 million. Georgia was the only state east of the Mississippi to grow more than 25 percent during the 1990s. Atlanta fueled two-thirds of that growth: the metro Atlanta region was ranked number four among fastest-growing metropolitan regions in the United States. Atlanta dominates the state's urban centers with a metro population of 4.1 million, followed by Augusta, Macon, Savannah, and Columbus as the state's largest cities.

The state has also grown in diversity, particularly in Atlanta. The hispanic population in the urban area grew a whopping 362 percent during the 1990s, and now, latinos make up 6.5 percent of the city's population. The Asian population was up 167 percent in the 1990s, and now Asians make up 3.3 percent of the population. The remaining population remains around three-fourths Caucasian and one-quarter African American, but even here, there were interesting shifts. Whites were found to be moving back into central city areas, and for the first time, suburban DeKalb county now has a black majority.

All that being said, here's the real information: Georgians are what make a trip to Georgia so memorable. Southern hospitality, a strong sense of place, an oral-history tradition, and the leisurely pace of a semitropical region all combine in friendly residents who greatly enrich the most casual encounter. And of all the Southern states, Georgia is the most accessible, by virtue of its gateway capital. Scenes on a bus, a question asked

of a ranger, an inquiry about local history made at a roadside stand—such moments may wind up as the best stories of your trip. So given that a trip begins with its people, here's a brief look at where those people came from, and how they all ended up being the Georgians of today.

ABORIGINAL HERITAGE

Long before the Civil War defined the geocultural region known as the South, aboriginal nations developed a regionally distinctive culture in the American Southeast. Today's Southerners hold similarities with these ancient traditions as a natural consequence of shared land-use patterns, climate, and natural resources, but also directly from practices passed down from Native Americans to European settlers. In turn, settlers passed on European traditions to Native Americans, prompting colonists to dub the five major Southeastern nations—the Creek, Cherokee, Seminole, Chickasaw, and Choctaw—the Five Civilized Tribes. All of these groups were present in Georgia at the time of European settlement, as were other tribes who were wiped out by European-borne diseases. Yet the region was overwhelmingly dominated by the Creek Confederacy and, in the mountain region, the Cherokee. As well as can be approximated, the state's Native American population before colonization numbered about 10,000.

Local historian Sam Lawton likes to point out how similar the customs of the Native American southeasterners were to our own. "They'd start the day with a cup of a strong black caffeinated beverage," he explained, "then the town council would meet to discuss the affairs of the day." Their principal crops of corn, squash, and beans—all staples of Southern cooking today—as well as techniques for their cultivation and preparation, were handed down to Europeans. Their main meal consisted of *sofkee,* now served throughout the Southeast as hominy grits. They engaged in serious sports competitions and enthusiastically celebrated the harvest. The use of native plants as sources of food and medicine also became woven into the fiber of Southern culture, as did a rich folklore.

Yet much was unique to aboriginal traditions. Their matrilineal society organized marriage, child-raising customs, and other social structures around women. (Early women's suffrage advocates pointed to the freedoms and rights accorded Cherokee women to advance their cause.) And the European practice of land ownership was entirely foreign to Native Americans, who lived on more communal terms.

Their belief structure centered on three worlds: the Earth, the Sky Vault, and the Under World. The native southeasterners believed that the Earth was an island resting on a large sea. Above the Sky Vault was the Upper World, which represented perfection; there, earth creatures lived, but in greater sizes than on Earth. The Under World below represented chaos and disorder; its features were inverted from the Earth. For example, when it was summer on Earth, it was winter below, and vice versa—springs that felt cold in summer and warm in winter affirmed this belief. (See "The Cherokee Story of Creation.")

The Creek Confederacy, a dozen distinctive groups sharing the same Muskogean linguistic roots and similar characteristics, came together in a centralized government based in Ocmulgee, at the site of the ancient temple mounds. The Upper Creeks lived centrally on the Piedmont;

Know Georgia

THE CHEROKEE STORY OF CREATION

In the beginning, when people and animals shared a common language, all living things dwelled above the sky. But after a while the creatures became so crowded, someone wondered if they might find more room in the ocean below. The little water beetle went down to investigate. Finding no firm place to land, he dove into the water and brought up mud. The mud grew and spread into the circular island of earth (which was later fastened to the sky with four giant ropes at each cardinal direction).

The great buzzard flew all over the earth to see if the land was yet dry enough to live on. When he reached Cherokee Country he was very tired, and his giant wings flapped against the ground. Wherever his wings struck the earth a valley appeared, and mountains formed whenever his wings turned back up again. The heart of Cherokee Country is full of mountains to this day.

The Cherokee believe in another world below the earth; high mountain streams form the trails to this underworld, and the doorways are mountaintop springs. The world below experiences seasons opposite from those on earth, evidenced by the fact that springwaters are always cooler than the mountain summer air and warmer than winter's air.

When the animals and plants were first made, the Great One instructed them to stay awake for seven nights, and while they all tried, as time went on many dropped off to sleep. On the seventh night only the owl and panther and one or two others remained awake. To these animals the Great One gave the power to see at night and prey on those that had fallen asleep, which thereafter always will sleep after the sun goes down. Of the trees, only the cedar, pine, spruce, holly, and laurel were awake to the end, and to them it was given that they always stay green while the others shall lose their leaves every winter.

See Cherokee Publications in the Suggested Reading for more Cherokee myths.

the Lower Creeks, in South Georgia. The Europeans named them for their riverine culture along Georgia's many waterways.

The Yamacraw, who first negotiated with the British to permit Georgia's first European settlement in Savannah, were an "outlawed" tribe of the Creek. Similarly, the Seminoles broke away from the Creeks ("Seminole" means "runaway" in the Creek language), some say over disputes about slavery. Seminoles particularly welcomed escaping slaves, leading to the Seminole Wars of 1816 and 1825, when federal troops fought to take back escaped slaves. The majority of Seminoles were pushed south into Florida, and their descendants and culture reflect African influences to this day.

The Cherokee, distinguished by their Iroquoian language and highland culture, lived in the Appalachian mountains of Georgia, Tennessee, and North Carolina and established the capital of the Cherokee Nation in Georgia's New Echota in 1828. Their advanced culture and government, which included a written Cherokee language and a representative government and constitution modeled on that of the United States, did not protect them from a forced removal once gold was discovered within their territory. The Five Civilized Tribes were exiled to designated Indian territory in Oklahoma in 1838 along the tragic Trail of Tears; of 16,000 forced migrants, 4,000 died. Their banishment effectively ended their land-based southeastern traditions and forced them to adapt to new conditions out west. Southeastern reservations are home to small groups whose ancestors managed to escape the removal. Other individuals and families remain scattered throughout the population or have assimilated into Anglo culture. Many Georgians claim to have Indian blood, primarily those in former Cherokee territory. And a glance at a state map reveals many names of Native American origin, such as Chattahoochee, Dahlonega, Oconee, and Ossabaw. Native American cultural events, including powwows, crafts demonstrations, and the like, are held at aboriginal historic sites throughout the state.

EUROPEAN HERITAGE

The Georgia colony was originally settled by the British and Protestants fleeing religious persecution in continental Europe, notably Germans and Moravians. A Jewish community led by German Jews consisted mostly of Sephardic families originally from Spain and Portugal who had escaped the Inquisition. Soon Highland Scots and Irish Catholics joined this mix (as well as religious minorities; see the *Religion* section, later), yet the dominant influence continued to be from Anglo-Saxon Protestants, Scotch, and Irish.

Today, Anglo-Saxon traditions have been most keenly retained by Appalachian mountaineers. In acknowledgment of Scotch and Irish heritage, Scottish Highland Games continue to be celebrated throughout the state (Atlanta and Savannah hold the largest games), and Savannah celebrates St. Patrick's Day for a full week.

Southern Highlanders

As heirs of one of the oldest and most culturally rich folk cultures of the United States, the Appalachian Southern Highlanders carry on 19th-century traditions in the mountains of North Georgia and neighboring states. In fact, North Georgians hold more in common with fellow mountaineers three states removed than with flatlanders in their own state. Always known for being a breed apart, the mountaineers have cultivated a reputation for fierce independence—a characteristic that may stretch back more than three centuries. Many Southern Highlanders descend from groups in disputed borderlands between Scotland and England, where constant feuding that lasted for generations forced residents to develop adaptive resilience and self-sufficiency. America's Southern Appalachian frontier, populated by the Cherokee when the first immigrants arrived to settle the wilderness in the 1750s, re-created familiar strife.

The isolation of mountain communities meant that old folkways that had long died out elsewhere were carried on over time, and many continue today. Though the old-timers who depended on traditional skills and crafts to survive are the last of a breed, younger generations have picked up many of these traditions to preserve their cultural heritage. A national revival of interest in Appalachian folkways has also contributed to the effort to celebrate this distinctive culture.

Unique arts and crafts, music, and a rich set of folk beliefs are among the highlights of Appalachian culture. Pottery from Georgia clay, basketry from native vines, and whittled carvings from Appalachian hardwoods are local specialties, along with weavings and quilts in traditional patterns. Each craft has its own cultural significance and history.

Bluegrass music emanates from the Appalachians, and foot-stompin' festivals, dance halls, and concerts in North Georgia continue this tradition. Old-time mountain music evokes Elizabethan influences, and old ballads passed down through generations are often accompanied by dulcimer. Language also reveals this heritage; the term *reckon* was used by Chaucer before it became a term synonymous with the Southern Highlands.

AFRICAN HERITAGE

The gruesome slave trade that brought captured Africans to North America (95 percent were taken to the Caribbean or Latin America) operated mainly from Africa's west coast in a region stretching from Senegal to Angola, principally the central Gold Coast region (now Ghana, Togo, Benin, and Nigeria). In Georgia, Africans from the Gambia River and Sierra Leone's rice-cultivation areas were valued workers for coastal rice plantations, bringing the specific traditions of the Wolof and Mandinka nations to the low country.

Many former Haitian slaves resettled in Savannah around the time Santo Domingo slaves rebelled in 1804, lending the coast a distinctive Creole nature. This influence may date back even further, to the time of the Revolutionary War, when the French brought an all-Haitian unit to fight the British in Savannah—historians speculate that some wounded soldiers stayed and were assimilated.

Communities of "Free Men of Color" had existed in Georgia's cities from colonial times on. The communities were composed of some African immigrants and many former slaves who either bought their freedom or were released from slavery (manumitted). Escaping slaves sought refuge in backcountry swamps, caves, or in the islands. Many escaped to Native American villages—the Seminoles were particularly welcoming, and Seminole culture reflects the African influences of these "Black Indians" to this day.

Vestiges of African culture managed to survive, despite the slavery system's determination to repress it. African-influenced traditions are now considered inextricably Southern—including the commonplace "swept lawns" (sweeping a dirt apron around humble homes as practiced in West Africa) and the indispensable okra (an African vegetable transported to America by slaves). The folklore of trickster Br'er Rabbit and other such slave tales (first recorded by Georgia's Joel Chandler Harris) have become emblematic of Southern storytelling. And the wedding ritual of "jumping the broom" (in which the bride and groom hold hands and jump backward over a broom) has distinct American roots—the ritual got started in slavery time to sanctify a slave marriage not legally recognized by white overseers.

Today's African American Georgians celebrate their ethnic heritage in many ways. Martin Luther King Day in January, Black History Month throughout February, Juneteenth (the June 15 abolition anniversary), and Kwanzaa (December's seven-day Afrocentric fest of thanksgiving) are American-born celebrations that bring out African, Afro-Haitian, Caribbean, and distinctly Southern traditions.

Sea Islanders

A rich slice of African culture endures on the Sea Islands off the Georgia and Carolina coast. These remote islands harbor a fascinating history. Once they served as sanctuaries for escaping slaves; later they were left to slaves when plantation owners fled during the Civil War; and at war's end they became part of a black republic after Union General William T. Sherman reserved the islands for newly freed slaves. Here self-sufficient communities have lived for generations, largely outside the traffic of mainland society and commerce. In their isolation they have managed to meld old African traditions and beliefs with their American experience. Islanders developed a distinct dialect called Gullah (short for Angola, from where many African were thought to originate), a combination of American, West Indian, English, and African languages; it's still commonly heard on the coast today.

Gullah communities at the mouth of Georgia's Ogeechee River led to the local name, Geechee, to describe the people and their dialect. As in the Appalachian folk culture, the true practitioners of this heritage are of such advanced age that the culture is in decline. The fact that younger generations are called to the mainland for education, jobs, or other opportunities, combined with inevitable 20th-century intrusion and exposure, leave to question the future of these largely self-governed communities.

The Gullah historically practiced folk religion that combined threads of Islam, Afro-Christianity, and voodoo influences from the Caribbean (also called hoodoo). In this tradition, conjure doctors use magic and "conjure bags" of plant roots believed to possess special powers, or mojos (charms), to protect or malign.

Geechee folklore tells stories of haunts (spirits of the dead, pronounced haints), hags (disembodied spirits of living witches), and plat-eyes (evil, shape-shifting spirits, commonly with one big eye hanging out in front). When such forces troubled the lives of the living, root doctors or conjure doctors were called in to subdue the spirits. Other island legends are rooted in American history: one tale tells of groups of Africans in chains walking back to Africa—a mythological ending for slaves who chose drowning over bondage.

SOUTHERN CULTURE TODAY
A Patchwork Quilt
Today's Southern culture borrows from all these beginnings to create a patchwork quilt of Southern traditions. A scrap from the Cherokee, an-

other from the Yoruba, and yet another from the Spanish Inquisition or the Irish Sea—all were laced together with a common history and compelling natural environment to produce the rich cultural fabric of the region today. Here, oral traditions, social manners, customs, beliefs, and folklore impress visitors with the importance of values of family, church, and community.

Americans tend to overstate differences between the races, and many outlanders commonly consider that gap wider in the South. Yet Southerners of any color can also be thought to share as much in common with one another as with racial counterparts in other regions.

Besides, it's a misperception to believe that white is white, black is black, and red is red. Though many exceptionally stable families in the South can trace consistent bloodlines back for centuries, for many others, the color line was substantially blurred by intermarriage or by exploitation of slaves by masters. The late Alex Haley, who traced his Southern lineage back to Africa in *Roots*, writes in his final work of his grandmother, the product of an elective biracial relationship, to make the point that if you look back far enough, we're all, in the most real sense, brothers and sisters.

Religion
"The South is by a long way the most simply and sincerely religious country I ever was in," said Victorian rationalist Sir William Archer. "It is not, like Ireland, a priest-ridden country; it is not, like England, a country in which the strength of religion lies in its social prestige; it is not, like Scotland, a country steeped in theology. But it is a country in which religion is a very large factor in life, and God is very real and personal."

Today religion continues to make up an important facet of Southern culture. People who recall the Carter administration remember how the new Southern president astonished Washington with casual references to his strong religious beliefs and by constantly offering blessings and prayers at public occasions. In this way, Jimmy Carter represented many Southerners, whose lives are filled with church picnics, re-

SCRIPTURE CAKE

4-1/2 cups I Kings 4:22 (flour)
1 cup Judges 5:25 (butter)
2 cups Jeremiah 6:20 (sugar)
2 cups Samuel 30:12 (raisins)
2 cups Nahum 3:12 (figs)
2 cups Numbers 17:8 (almonds)
2 tablespoon I Samuel 14:25 (honey)
1 pinch Leviticus 2:13 (salt)
6 Jeremiah 17:11 (eggs)
1/2 cup Judges 4:19 (milk)
2 tablespoon Amos 4:5 (leaven)

Season to taste with II Chronicles 9:9 (spices); mix like a fruitcake, and bake at 350°F.
(Thanks to Jenny Rogers of Southside Baptist Church, Columbus.)

vivals, homecomings, Sunday clothes, Sunday dinners, fire and brimstone, and Vacation Bible School. The literature and moral code of Southerners are woven with Biblical quotes and themes of faith and grace, damnation, and redemption. Though overwhelmingly Protestant—and predominantly Southern Baptist at that—Georgia's religious tradition draws from spiritual roots as deep and varied as its people.

The first nonindigenous religion practiced on Georgia's shores was Catholicism, brought to coastal Georgia by Spanish missionaries in 1566. For more than a century, Jesuit and Franciscan priests worked to convert the Native Americans to Christianity until finally abandoning the effort along with the missions.

Groups fleeing religious persecution were among Georgia's original settlers in Savannah in the early 18th century. European Protestants, Jews, Quakers, and Puritans all found religious freedom here. Yet this freedom was selective: Roman Catholics were originally banned from the colony when it was founded in 1733, for fear they'd act as spies for the encroaching Spanish or French. The fears subsided (but not before a group of Cajuns were made so unwelcome that they continued south to St. Marys to settle),

and by 1792 Savannah had its own Catholic chapel. A major religion was founded in the new colony: John Wesley established the Methodist church in 1738 and also taught the world's first Sunday school here.

Savannah's early Jewish community, though led by German Jews, descended largely from Spanish or Portuguese families who had escaped the Inquisition. In 1735, Savannah Jews established Temple Mikvah Israel, now the third-oldest Jewish congregation in North America. Threatened by occasional Spanish successes at coastal battles, many of these original families moved north, yet those that remained (or returned after British victory) formed a strong Jewish community that continues today. In Atlanta, a Jewish museum tells the story of the capital's Jewish community. Elsewhere in Georgia, "circuit rabbis" administer to scattered Jewish populations, holding monthly or bimonthly services in the venerable rural tradition of Southern "circuit preachers."

When slavery was introduced in Georgia, slaves often attended Christian church services segregated in the upper "slave gallery." As exceptions to this, several early churches organized expressly for Africans are now honored as landmarks in the African American community: the congregation of Augusta's Springfield Baptist Church dates from 1733, and Savannah's First African Baptist Church dates from 1788. After emancipation, former slaves formed many churches, predominately Baptist, but the two strongest black churches up north, the African Methodist Episcopal (AME) and African Methodist Episcopal Zion also gained a strong following in the New South. Not simply places of worship, these churches provided a critical social structure for communities cut off from full participation in the social, political, and economic life of the broader society.

The 1960s civil-rights movement inspired many African Americans to rediscover African religious traditions, notably Islam. Malcolm X's mentor, Nation of Islam leader Elijah Mohammed, was born Robert Poole in Georgia's Washington County. Today traditional Islamic customs are practiced in homes and mosques in Atlanta and elsewhere by Muslims of many races.

At the fringes of the dominant Protestant sects, the Primitive Baptists continue to prove their devotion by handling poisonous snakes. Foot washing is also among the ritual practices of these "Hardshell" Baptists, who are most often found in isolated mountain communities.

Visitors are welcome at the restaurant and craft shop operated by a traditional Mennonite community in Montezuma (southeast of Macon), where the Plain People continue Amishlike customs (though, unlike the Amish, they do not forsake such modern conveniences as electricity and automobiles).

Language

The Southern dialect enlivens the speech of Georgians, from the barely perceptible Atlanta "y'all" to the lengthening lyricism of a coastal drawl. Even in a short time, a visitor traveling through different regions can perceive local variations in speech patterns.

Regional vocabulary, idioms, and manners of speech also spice up the local language. Mountain valleys, summits, and waterfalls become "coves," "knobs," and "cataracts." If you're "fixin' to" buy liquor, find a "package store"; if you want it to go, ask for a "go cup." Folks don't die, they "pass."

Formal addresses of "sir" and "ma'am" are in constant use. Southerners appreciate when visitors adopt such conventions, though non-Southerners aren't expected to be as polite as locals. Also abiding by more conservative rules of address, it's generally considered polite not to address people by their first names unless specifically invited to. As with titles, names tend to be long and inclusive; for example, a building named for a popular politician in Atlanta uses his entire name and nickname—The James H. ("Sloppy") Floyd Building. You'll find the mark of politeness in local newspapers, where second references to names are preceded by a title (Mr. This or Mrs. That instead of simply This or That), and readers are requested to "*please* turn to page X."

In matters of usage, possessive apostrophes have been somehow dispensed with—take for example the coastal place names St. Catherines, St. Simons, and St. Marys. If you used the apostrophe, you'd be regarded as another punctuation-crazy outlander.

Transportation

GETTING THERE

By Air

Most people come to Georgia through Atlanta's Hartsfield-Jackson International Airport (ATL), world's largest airport. ATL-based Delta Air Lines is among the 32 passenger airlines with domestic and direct international flights to and from Atlanta. From an airport terminal station, modern light-rail trains whisk passengers downtown in 10 minutes.

By Car

A web of interstate freeways connects Georgia with the Eastern Seaboard (I-95) and the Midwest (I-75), as well as with other parts of the South (I-20, I-85). **Georgia Welcome Centers,** run by the state tourist board, are situated at each interstate freeway entrance to Georgia. There are also two inland, in Macon and Plains, for maps and information on local lodging, attractions, and services.

By Bus

Greyhound-Trailways operates a bus network linking major American cities with cities throughout Georgia. For information and fares, call 800/231-2222.

By Train

Amtrak operates two lines through Georgia. The **Crescent** connects New York and Washington, D.C. with Atlanta, Birmingham, and New Orleans. It also stops in Gainesville, the jumping-off point for the Appalachian Trail. The **Silver Meteor** runs the length of the Atlantic seaboard from Boston to Miami, stopping in Savannah—where Amtrak offers package deals (train fare and lodging)—and Jacksonville, Florida, the closest city to Georgia's Okefenokee Swamp and Cumberland Island.

Though generally more expensive than regularly discounted air travel, riding the trains is a leisurely and civilized way to travel, and occasional special excursion fares make rates more competitive. For fares and schedule, call 800/USA-RAIL (800/872-7245).

By Boat

If you have a boat, a scenic way to come to Georgia is via the **Intracoastal Waterway,** a marsh-lined corridor largely sheltered between the mainland and barrier islands. The passage takes sailors past Georgia's port cities of Savannah and Brunswick. Marinas in Thunderbolt (outside Savannah) and at St. Simons Island make the most popular stops along Georgia's 100-mile coast.

GETTING AROUND
Driving

The most practical way to get around the state is by car, and it's the best way to get a flavor for the back-roads rural heritage of the South. You can rent a car at the airport or in any big city; all major car-rental agencies are well represented, and most have toll-free 800 numbers and websites to begin your inquiry. Daily rates are discounted for weekly or monthly rentals, and watch for special weekend rates.

The maximum speed limit in Georgia is 65 mph on interstates through rural stretches, 55 mph near urban areas. Georgia requires drivers to turn on their headlights whenever they use their windshield wipers—which makes common sense once you've seen a typically dark Georgia thundercloud advance on the horizon. You're permitted to turn right at a red light after coming to a complete stop, unless signs tell you otherwise.

Interstate freeways offer the quickest routes to and fro, but they can also be the least inter-

esting. Before the interstates opened, the early transcontinental highways handled the load, giving rise to hundreds of road motels, roadside stands, and dinky small-town attractions designed to entice travelers en route. Since tourist business moved out to the interstates, many have fallen by the wayside into a sort of modern ruins, and those that have survived have mellowed into Route 66–like Americana classics. Georgia's Old Atlantic Coast Highway or the Old Dixie Highway, from Chattanooga to Atlanta, best illustrate this past heyday.

Through some curious loophole in constitutional law, Georgia Highway Patrol sets up occasional drug checkpoints on the side of the road. Police may wave select cars over and unleash a drug-sniffing dog to search out contraband. At the first sign of "Drug Check Ahead," you'll see drivers pull cars over to the shoulder and dart

Mountain honey and Appalachian crafts are among the pleasures of country roadside stands.

into the forest before continuing down to the checkpoint.

Trailers and RV owners are easily accommodated with wide passing lanes on country highways; plentiful campgrounds offer pull-though sites, hookups, disposal stations, and other services. Hitchhiking may well result in pleasurable encounters with hospitable locals who treat you to cheap colorful tours, but no one with any conscience could unreservedly recommend it, particularly for women.

Buses and Van Shuttles

Greyhound-Trailways, 800/231-2222, runs regularly scheduled bus networks throughout the state. Charter bus companies also compete for passengers on the popular route from Atlanta to Savannah. **Groome Transportation,** groometrans.com, provides frequent van service from the Atlanta airport to several cities, including Athens, Macon, and Columbus.

Trains

Considering how vital the railroads were to the development of the South, it's a shame you can't get around Georgia on a train more easily. Amtrak does stop in other Georgia towns besides Atlanta, Savannah, and the above-mentioned Gainesville, but not at times that are convenient for most tourist travel. Georgia offers two excursion train rides, however: one in North Georgia's Blue Ridge and the other in South Georgia's city of Cordele.

Intrastate Flights

The busiest intrastate flight is the hourlong run between Atlanta and Savannah; call Delta Air Lines for a schedule. It is possible to take commuter flights between Georgia's cities, but considering that most major cities are concentrated on the Piedmont, surface shuttles (see *Buses and Van Shuttles,* above) are most often used instead.

Bicycling

Georgia's different topographic regions present increasingly easier terrain from north to south. North Georgia's mountainous country highways offer the greatest challenge, yet even at their most undulating, the shoulders are wide and the pavement smooth. The same excellent road conditions are maintained all through the state, across the rolling hills of the Piedmont and the long, flat expanses of the coastal plain. The scenery throughout—the outstanding natural environment, antebellum architecture, quaint town squares, orchards, and roadside produce stands—and the leisurely Southern pace make bicycling a wonderful way to see Georgia.

As for specific routes, it would take an exceptional biker to tackle metro Atlanta's byways, with their fast-paced traffic, winding narrow routes, and sprawling urban development—but it's been done, and work is under way to complete off-road thoroughfares.

Rewarding long-distance routes include the coastal highway, a nice touring route in McLemore Valley in northwest Georgia, the stretch from Athens to Macon in central Georgia, and the areas around Plains, Thomasville, or along the Chattahoochee River in South Georgia. For a copy of state-designated bike routes throughout Georgia (emphasizing useful connections to the state parks), contact the Georgia Department of Industry, Trade, and Tourism, P.O. Box 1776, Atlanta, GA 30301-1776, 404/656-3590.

Tips for Travelers

CONDUCT AND DRESS

In Atlanta, for the most part anything goes for casual dress, but if you're doing business, visiting churches, or attending social dinners, more formal rules apply (jackets and ties for men, commensurate formality for women). In the rest of the state, visitors may draw unwelcome negative attention by appearing too casual (cut-off shorts, overpatched jeans, or anything sloppy or revealing). A posted dress code at one military museum, for example, forbids sleeveless shirts, rubber thongs, too-short skirts and shorts. Clean and tidy are strong social-class indicators and are held in high esteem. Outward manifestations of neatness extend to keeping cars clean and trimming lawns to stubble (homeowners may be ticketed and fined for even lightly overgrown lawns).

Unfamiliar cultural traits may frustrate visitors unless they can likewise adapt. As in every near-tropical climate, time moves more slowly (except perhaps in bustling Atlanta); vacationers would be wise to adopt the local pace, or at least be patient with it. Also be aware that many well-meaning Southerners hate to say no (it's considered impolite to be too direct or to contradict), so to be hospitable, they may appear to agree when they might not.

As an endearing example, Philip Kurland, of the Plains Trading Post in Jimmy Carter's hometown, had so many visitors asking him "where the peanut trees were" that he told a reporter "For a while, I tried explaining where peanuts come from, but I found out it's better to say, 'I don't know.'"

Photo etiquette also demands a certain cultural sensitivity. Many photographers will no doubt be attracted to the kind of dramatic back-country scenes you can see only in the South—lean-to shacks, ancient country stores with homemade signs, and grizzled portraits—yet visitors need to exercise standard rules of courtesy. Always ask before taking pictures of people,

Time moves slowly in Georgia; have a seat.

© KAP STANN

particularly in run-down areas, and don't always expect a positive response. Locals are extremely sensitive about how the national press tends to portray Southerners as hillbillies or hicks and see nothing scenic in perpetuating stereotypes.

Georgia-born writer Roy Blount Jr. spoke for many Southerners when he observed during Bill Clinton's first presidential campaign "New York columnists toss around the term 'cracker' pretty loosely, and now 'Bubba' is taking over as an ethnic term. There's no other ethnic group you could use such a slur about so loosely."

Twelve years later, little seems to have changed. The *New York Times* covered a book review of Jimmy Carter's 2003 Revolutionary War novel with the headline "Founding Bubbas" (the newspaper later printed the letters of offended readers).

VOLUNTEER AND STUDY OPPORTUNITIES

Habitat for Humanity

Volunteering can mean a "working vacation" and a great cultural foray into local communities. One of the most worthwhile local endeavors is volunteering at the international headquarters of **Habitat for Humanity,** 121 Habitat St., Americus, GA 31709, 912/924-6935 or 800/HABITAT (800/422-4828), habitat.org. Housing can be arranged for visiting volunteers.

Koinonia

Habitat for Humanity originated in a neighboring farming commune called Koinonia (Greek for "fellowship"). Koinonia attracts volunteers to its ecumenical Christian community to plant, harvest, build, and repair in exchange for room, board, and a small living allowance. For more information, write to Koinonia Partners, 1324 Dawson Rd., Americus, GA 31709, koinoniapartners.org.

Campground Hosts

Campground hosts can stay free in state parks and in Georgia's national forests in exchange for acting as a resource to other campers. Retired folks with well-equipped trailers typically fill these positions. For more information, contact the volunteer coordinator at Georgia's State Parks Division, 404/656-6539, or the state's U.S. Forest Service office, 404/536-0541. A directory of outdoor volunteer jobs nationwide occasionally lists positions in Georgia (most jobs include housing and a small stipend); call the American Hiking Society, 703/385-3252.

Artists-in-Residence

Artists can apply to the Georgia Department of Natural Resources, the authority that oversees the state parks and lands, to stay for two weeks in retreat communities on Georgia's Sapelo Island. The Artist-in-Residence program furnishes an apartment; artists needs to provide their own linens, meals, and transportation. For more information, click on Artist-in-Residence Program at gastateparks.org, or write the Georgia Department of Natural Resources, 2 Martin Luther King Jr. Dr. S.E., Ste. 1352, Atlanta, GA 30334.

ACCESS FOR DISABLED TRAVELERS

Atlanta prides itself on its ultramodern infrastructure and architecture, which means mostly barrier-free buildings and public transportation. Hartsfield-Jackson International Airport is one of the most accessible in the country; several car rental agencies offer lift-equipped vans; specially equipped tour companies offer guided city tours; and "all-access" nature trails are designed to accommodate wheelchairs and other mobility aids. For more information, contact the city's **Disability Coordinator** at 404/330-6026.

One small historic town in southwest Georgia has evolved into a monument of sorts to the challenge of physical disability. It's **Warm Springs,** where natural mineral springs attracted polio-stricken President Franklin D. Roosevelt for soothing hydrotherapy. FDR's Georgia cabin, dubbed the Little White House, is now a state historic site that emphasizes the man's triumph over disability. His specially adapted cars, wheelchairs, and cane collection are on display, and the site provides wheelchairs and guides to visitors by reservation. The new FDR Museum is designed for universal access. The nearby historic village is likewise extraordinarily sensitive to people with physical challenges. The Warm Springs hospital administers physical-therapy treatment, and restoration of the original mineral baths was completed in 1997.

Similarly in Macon, the **Georgia Academy for the Blind** has sensitized the community to the special interests of people with disabilities, and one can find aural, tactile, and fragrant exhibits around town. Elsewhere around the state, special-needs travelers can find all-access boardwalks, piers, and trails, and popular fragrance gardens.

TRAVELING WITH CHILDREN

The family-oriented, multigenerational Southern culture ensures that children's activities abound in Georgia. The greatest hits are **Zoo Atlanta, Imagine It! Children's Museum, Six Flags over Georgia** and **White Water** in and around Atlanta. But there are also living-history and natural-science museums, as well as festivals, parades, and such regionally specific events as battle reenactments and storytelling marathons.

North Georgia's diverse recreational opportunities are largely open to children; rafting excursions or strenuous group hikes may have minimum-age requirements, and gold-panning and exploring old mines are some mountain favorites.

State parks and many private campgrounds design special children's activities and entertainment during popular seasons; throughout the state, families don't need to look far to find amusements, arcades, water slides, batting cages, skating rinks, miniature golf, and swimming pools.

Author's daughter's favorite? Floating down the cool, shallow shoals of the Chattahoochee River on an inner tube on a hot summer day through the ersatz-Bavarian town of Helen (lots of German chocolate too).

WOMEN TRAVELING ALONE

Georgia's cities are about the same as other American cities as far as a woman's safety is concerned; standard precautions apply (avoid walking alone late at night, no flashy jewelry, etc.). Traditional Southern chivalry has its charms, and can add to a woman's safety factor, but this can also backfire if you're perceived as a "loose" outlander.

Women will find Atlanta's feminist bookstore **Charis Books and More** in Little Five Points to be a good local resource for women's events and support (see the *Atlanta* chapter).

GAY AND LESBIAN TRAVELERS

Atlanta has one of the nation's largest gay populations, and the community has grown into a vocal political force. The free weekly newspaper *Southern Voice* carries news and events of particular interest to the gay community.

Atlanta's Midtown district is the center of the city's gay community, with its venerable **Out-Write** bookstore and many bars and clubs both in Midtown and beyond. Cosmopolitan Savannah also has a large gay population and is a popular stop on the itinerary of gay travelers.

Yet Atlanta and Savannah can be very different from the rest of Georgia. While most places welcome all business, be aware that some conservative family operations may be less tolerant of alternative anything (which includes revealing dress, rowdiness, and drinking alcohol, as well as same-sex couples). Resorts and hotels throughout the state that cater mostly to city folk will be most welcoming to gay travelers.

The recommendations of places to stay in this guide have been made with the comfort of a wide variety of travelers foremost in mind.

Information and Services

HEALTH AND SAFETY

Tropical Precautions

One of the most pleasurable aspects of traveling in the Southeast is its generally mild and seasonal climate. During the summer, however, visitors unfamiliar with subtropical weather can find the extreme heat and humidity oppressive. Heed all cautions. Wear loose, light, long-limbed clothing and hats, sunglasses, and sunscreen (Photoplex or Shade UVAGUARD blocks both UVA and UVB rays). Drink and eat often, stay out of the sun, and avoid exertion during the midday heat. Travelers who presume their cool-climate stamina will remain unchanged may suffer heatstroke. Heat exhaustion is the number one medical emergency in the summer—scale down your ambitions.

Also in summer, insects are most active—again, by taking precautions, you can reduce this bother to a minimum. Mosquitoes usually appear only around dusk, or around stagnant water. Use insect repellent—*Consumer Reports* rates a product called Ultra Muskol the highest, though locals use Avon's Skin So Soft hand lotion for everyday repelling—and carry an insect-bite cream such as Benadryl. Wear long-limbed clothing and tuck pants into socks for the greatest protection against ticks, and perform a thorough tick check after a wilderness walk. Red rashlike patches are the sign of chiggers; get rid of them by covering the area with clear nail polish. Coastal residents claim no-see-ums (gnats too small to see) and sand fleas are most bothersome on windless afternoons; try to pick a breezy day for beachgoing, or retreat indoors midday.

Hypothermia

Hypothermia—the inability to maintain sufficient body heat—presents another danger, and not just in cold weather. Overexertion, coupled with coldness, wetness, and wind, may bring on symptoms such as shivering and poor coordination, even in mild temperatures. Avoid it by keeping clothing warm and dry, staying in motion, and, of course, seeking shelter. Always pack for emergencies: spare clothing, extra food and water, matches, a flashlight, a compass, and a stocked first-aid kit. Three toots on a whistle or three smoky fires set in a triangle signal distress. Wilderness adventurers should leave detailed itineraries with someone at home and at the appropriate ranger station.

Crime

Urban hazards are of a different nature. As in most American cities, you must stay alert, be aware of your surroundings, and exercise reasonable caution—for example, leave fancy jewelry home. That said, Atlanta is no worse than comparably sized American cities, and security in tourist areas is high.

On the other side of the fence, you'll also want to avoid any needless encounters with local law enforcement, particularly in more rural regions. Obey speed limits to avoid speed traps common around small towns, and be aware that things "untidy"—such as a beat-up old foreign car, poor grooming, or sloppy or revealing dress—will often attract negative attention from backcountry police.

MONEY

Generally, prices in Georgia are lower than the United States average, making it an excellent travel bargain. Compared to other states, for example, gasoline in Georgia is less expensive, and food is cheap. Labor prices are dramatically lower than in other regions, and consequently, travelers will find exceptional guides and staffed services to enhance their trip without tremendous additional costs. For example, for little more than it costs to rent canoe equipment in California, in Georgia you can not only rent the equipment, but also obtain the expert services of an experienced local guide.

As with the rest of the United States, most establishments geared toward travelers accept major credit cards and traveler's checks. Banks are generally open from about 9 or 10 A.M. until about 4 or 5 P.M.; some have reduced hours on Saturday. Plentiful 24-hour automatic teller machines link up to interstate banking networks. Georgia sales tax is six percent; hotel tax varies depending on city but is 14 percent in Atlanta.

Discounts for admissions, tickets, restaurant meals, etc., are widely available to youths, people over 65, AAA members, and members of the U.S. military (sometimes restricted to active military, or military in uniform). Student discounts are less widespread, but it can't hurt to ask. Some restaurants also offer discounts to clergy on Sundays.

Tipping: For taxi drivers, tip 10 percent plus $1 per bag; restaurant servers 15 percent; at buffets and counters, leave 10 percent, a little less for table clearers at cafeterias; hotel doormen services $1.

COMMUNICATIONS
Telephones and Emergency Numbers
Be forewarned: the explosive population and popularity of cell phones have necessitated three statewide shifts in area codes within eight years. Folks barely had enough time to reprint stationery and adapt to the boundary shift of area codes in 1992, when another shift in late 1995 and again in 2001 created a challenge for those trying to nail down a correct number.

Atlanta has had to adapt to two 10-digit dialing zones: 404 or 678 in the central city; 770 or 678 in the surrounding metro region. The 706 area code continues to wrap around the mountains and the eastern Piedmont, with a disjunctive pocket around the city of Columbus. A wide area around Macon carries the 478 area code. Southwestern Georgia is now 229. The coast and southeastern region is the only region that remains unchanged, with 912.

Dial 1 before dialing a number with a different area code. For directory assistance, dial 411. Many businesses have toll-free (no charge) long distance numbers, which carry an 800, 877, or 888 prefix in place of an area code. Some of these toll-free numbers, which should also be preceded with a 1, only operate within the state.

In emergencies, dial 911. For traveler's aid, call 404/527-7400. To receive tourist information, call 404/656-3590, and for up-to-the-minute weather reports, call 404/455-7141.

Business Hours
Business office hours are now fairly standardized to weekdays (Mon.–Fri.) from 8 or 9 A.M. to 5 or 6 P.M. Most stores open later—about 10 A.M.—on weekdays and Saturdays, and stay open to early evening (often later in heavily trafficked urban areas and malls). Outside metro Atlanta, many businesses shut down on Sundays (except for the restaurants that do a big trade in traditional midday dinners).

U.S. Postal Service hours generally run 8:30 A.M.–5:30 P.M. on weekdays; some are open until noon on Saturdays. Private mailing companies (e.g., Mail Boxes Etc.) stay open longer hours and offer additional services such as wrapping, packaging, photocopying, and facsimile transmission.

Media
The morning *Atlanta Constitution* carries the major news of the city and region, as well as of the state and the South. Atlanta's free alternative newsweekly *Creative Loafing* carries entertainment listings, as well as news for the metro area and Athens. The other daily newspapers throughout the state are painfully unnotable. South Georgia hotels tend to distribute *USA Today* before a local or Atlanta paper.

As for television, the **Cable News Network (CNN)** broadcasts out of Atlanta. **Peach State Public Radio** syndicates an innovative slate of programs throughout the state.

Internet
Public Internet access is readily available in metro Atlanta and other cities, but less so rural regions. Besides hit-or-miss Internet cafés, one reliable source of Internet access is the photocopy shop **Kinko's,** 800/2KINKOS (254-5667), kinkos.com,

which offers online computer access among its services. Many branches are open 24 hours.

Maps and Information

Georgia's Department of Transportation sends out free state road maps depicting all state parks and historic sites; call 404/656-5336. An eager state Department of Industry, Trade, and Tourism produces many publications; its statewide directory includes a road map and list of state park services, and its semiannual events calendar covers standard Georgia travel. To request information, call or write the Georgia Department of Industry, Trade, and Tourism, P.O. Box 1776, Atlanta, GA, 30301-1776, 404/656-3590.

Eleven state welcome centers at interstate freeway borders, local tourist offices or welcome centers, and convention and visitor bureaus (CVBs) distribute useful maps, including walking-tour and driving-tour maps, along with other information.

INTERNATIONAL SERVICES

Language Assistance

Multilingual Visitor Services Representatives, sponsored by the city and federal tourist boards, meet all arriving international flights to Atlanta's Hartsfield-Jackson International Airport to assist inbound and connecting passengers with translation and other needs. Also in the international terminal is an international Calling Assistance Center, a computerized telephone system that displays information in six languages.

Foreign Consulates

Foreign consulates and government representatives in Atlanta include Austria, 404/264-9858; Belgium, 404/659-2150; Canada, 404/532-2000; Denmark, 404/876-5511; Finland, 404/815-3582; France, 404/495-1660; Germany, 404/659-4760; Greece, 404/261-3313; Israel, 404/487-6500; Italy, 404/303-0503; Japan, 404/240-4300; Korea, 404/522-1611; Latin American countries, 404/638-1800; Mexico, 404/266-2233; Nigeria, 770/394-6261; Switzerland, 404/870-2000; and United Kingdom, 404/954-7700.

MISCELLANEOUS

Voltage

Electrical power outlets in the United States run only on a 117-volt AC system, which means that only appliances of that approximate voltage will run as manufactured. You'll need a transformer to run a 200- or 220-volt appliance. You can find transformers and adapter plugs to fit American appliances at department stores, electronics supply stores, specialty travel stores, or department stores.

Time Zone

Georgia follows eastern standard time (EST), five hours earlier than Greenwich Mean Time. From the first Sunday in April until the last Sunday in October, Georgia, like most of the United States, goes on daylight saving time, which advances the clock one hour across all American time zones. Though Georgia's border with Alabama constitutes an official change in time zones, some border cities in Alabama maintain Georgia time (such as Phenix City, across the Chattahoochee River from Columbus).

Index

Kids' Stuff

American Adventures: 76
Babyland General Hospital (Cabbage Patch Kids doll adoption store): 114
Cecil B. Day Butterfly Center: 175
Center for Puppetry Arts: 47
Coca-Cola Space Science Center: 181
Flat Rock Park natural rock slide: 182
Imagine It! The Children's Museum of Atlanta: 46–47
National Science Center's Fort Discovery: 149

Okefenokee Swamp Park: 215
Six Flags Over Georgia: 73
Splash Island Water Park: 206
Summer Waves Water Park: 314
tips for traveling with children: 357
Tybee Island Marine Science Center: 271
Uncle Remus stories at the Wren's Nest: 47
University of Georgia Marine Education Center and Aquarium: 266–267
White Water Park: 76

Nightclubs

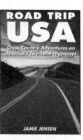

U.S.~Metric Conversion

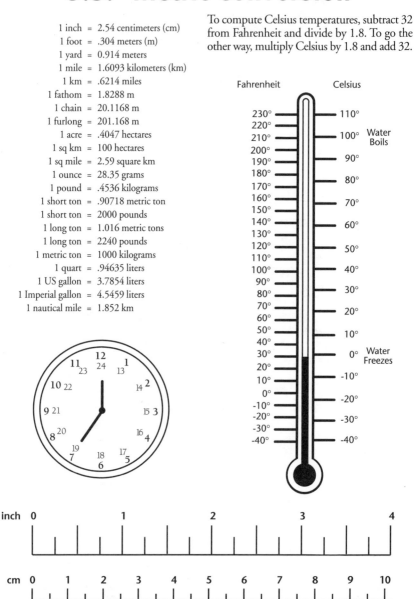

1 inch = 2.54 centimeters (cm)
1 foot = .304 meters (m)
1 yard = 0.914 meters
1 mile = 1.6093 kilometers (km)
1 km = .6214 miles
1 fathom = 1.8288 m
1 chain = 20.1168 m
1 furlong = 201.168 m
1 acre = .4047 hectares
1 sq km = 100 hectares
1 sq mile = 2.59 square km
1 ounce = 28.35 grams
1 pound = .4536 kilograms
1 short ton = .90718 metric ton
1 short ton = 2000 pounds
1 long ton = 1.016 metric tons
1 long ton = 2240 pounds
1 metric ton = 1000 kilograms
1 quart = .94635 liters
1 US gallon = 3.7854 liters
1 Imperial gallon = 4.5459 liters
1 nautical mile = 1.852 km

To compute Celsius temperatures, subtract 32 from Fahrenheit and divide by 1.8. To go the other way, multiply Celsius by 1.8 and add 32.

Fahrenheit   Celsius

230°   110°
220°
210°   100°   Water Boils
200°
190°   90°
180°
170°   80°
160°   70°
150°
140°   60°
130°
120°   50°
110°
100°   40°
90°
80°   30°
70°
60°   20°
50°
40°   10°
30°
20°   0°   Water Freezes
10°
0°   -10°
-10°   -20°
-20°
-30°   -30°
-40°   -40°

12
11 24 1
23   13
10 22   14 2
9 21   15 3
8 20   16 4
19   17
7   18 6 5

inch 0   1   2   3   4

cm 0 1 2 3 4 5 6 7 8 9 10

Keeping Current

Although we strive to produce the most up-to-date guidebook humanly possible, change is unavoidable. Between the time this book goes to print and the moment you read it, a handful of the businesses noted in these pages will undoubtedly change prices, move, or even close their doors forever. Other worthy attractions will open for the first time. If you have a favorite gem you'd like to see included in the next edition, or see anything that needs updating, clarification, or correction, please drop us a line. Send your comments via email to atpfeedback@avalonpub.com, or use the address below.

Moon Handbooks Georgia
Avalon Travel Publishing
1400 65th Street, Suite 250
Emeryville, CA 94608, USA
www.moon.com

Editor: Christopher Jones
Series Manager: Kevin McLain
Acquisitions Editor: Rebecca K. Browning
Copy Editor: Wendy Taylor
Graphics Coordinator: Justin Marler
Production Coordinators: Justin Marler,
  Domini Dragoone
Cover Designer: Kari Gim
Interior Designers: Amber Pirker, Alvaro
  Villanueva, Kelly Pendragon
Map Editor: Kat Smith
Cartographers: Kat Kalamaras, Mike Morgenfeld
Indexer: Valerie Blanton

ISBN: 1-56691-702-6
ISSN: 1078-7267

Printing History
1st Edition—1995
5th Edition—May 2005
5 4 3 2 1

Avalon Travel Publishing is an Imprint of
AVALON Avalon Publishing Group, Inc.
publishing group incorporated

Some photos and illustrations are used by permission and are the property of the original copyright owners.

Front cover photo: © J. G. Nash

Printed in USA by Worzalla